DENNIS BRAIN
A Life in Music

STEPHEN GAMBLE
WILLIAM C. LYNCH

Number 7 in the North Texas Lives of Musicians Series

University of North Texas Press
Denton, Texas

Printed in the United States of America.

10 9 8 7 6 5 4 3 2 1

Permissions:
University of North Texas Press
1155 Union Circle #311336
Denton, TX 76203-5017

The paper used in this book meets the minimum requirements of the American National Standard for Permanence of Paper for Printed Library Materials, z39.48.1984. Binding materials have been chosen for durability.

Library of Congress Cataloging-in-Publication Data
Gamble, Stephen, 1963–
Dennis Brain : a life in music / Stephen Gamble, William C. Lynch.—1st ed.
p. cm.—(Number 7 in the North Texas lives of musicians series)
Includes bibliographical references.
ISBN 978-1-57441-307-6 (cloth : alk. paper)
1. Brain, Dennis, 1921–1957. 2. Horn players—England—Biography. I. Lynch, William C., 1943– II. Title. III. Series: North Texas lives of musicians series; no. 7.
ML419.B72G36 2011
788.9'4092—dc22
[B]

2011002967

Dennis Brain: A Life in Music is Number 7 in the North Texas Lives of Musicians Series

Contents

Foreword

In November 2004, my memories of Dennis Brain were suddenly revived when I received an email from a Stephen Gamble. It read in part:

> I am very interested to read that you received lessons from Dennis Brain at the Guildhall School of Music and Drama in 1946, when Dennis was still in the RAF. I am co-writing [with William Lynch] a large biography of the Brain family with a focus on Dennis Brain in particular. . . .

That was the beginning of almost six years of observing and sometimes taking part in the progress of this book, which I believe strongly needed to be written.

In early January 1946, I, a nineteen-year-old American soldier, arrived at the Guildhall School of Music and Drama in London. As WWII ended in Europe, I was transferred to the Army's 1st Division band, after having served as an artilleryman in Germany. To keep us busy while we were waiting to be sent home, the Army had developed an extensive education program, ranging from instruction at the company level to studying at European universities and schools. I had been chosen for the latter—I was being sent to England to study horn.

At my first lesson, I presented myself to my new teacher. I had heard his name, but the significance hadn't registered. He introduced himself and didn't seem at all perturbed that I failed to recognize that I was talking to the most famous hornist in England—possibly in the world. Dennis Brain greeted me in a quiet, friendly manner with an easy smile. Before I began playing for him, we chatted about our instruments. He looked at my horn which, I believe, was an Army-issued Conn 6D. I looked at his—it was his Raoux single F horn with piston valves. We tried each other's horns and commented on the difficulties we had playing the other's instrument.

At the end of the term, with my study concluded, I returned to my Army unit in Germany. A few months later, I returned home to Boston, carrying with me a copy of Brain's recording of Britten's Serenade for Tenor,

Horn, and Strings with Peter Pears. How that fragile shellac recording made it home safely on the long trip in a crowded troop ship, I have no idea. I played the album for some of the hornists I knew. The reaction was generally astonishment at Dennis's technique and artistry. One of these hornists was Willem Valkenier, then principal horn of the Boston Symphony Orchestra. After he listened to the recording, he told me that he wouldn't attempt to play the Serenade. Whether he really meant that, I don't know, but I think it illustrates the impact of Brain's virtuosity on at least one of the finest hornists of that era.

In the fall of 1946, I began my studies at Boston University, working toward a degree in music performance. As the years passed, my correspondence with Dennis became more infrequent. One highlight, however, occurred in October 1950 when he appeared at Symphony Hall in Boston with the Royal Philharmonic Orchestra, under the direction of Sir Thomas Beecham. He invited me backstage before the rehearsal and I had a few moments to reminisce about my days in London. That proved to be one of my last contacts with him—and then came the awful news of his fatal accident on September 1, 1957.

After the shock wore off, the memories of my time with Dennis gradually began to fade. Even before he died, it had become clear to me that I would never achieve the level of horn playing that I would need as a professional, and I began an almost fifty-year career as a university professor of radio and television.

Although my memories of Dennis were fading, his life certainly did not go unnoticed. In 1976, Stephen J. Pettitt published Brain's definitive biography, *Dennis Brain: A Biography*; a second edition, updating the original, was published in 1989.

Like many biographies, however, a time comes when new information creates the need for a new biography.

I believe that authors Stephen Gamble and William Lynch, with new biographical sources, hitherto unknown recordings, both commercial and private, and a renewed perspective from the passage of time, have fulfilled this need. *Dennis Brain: A Life in Music* is a painstakingly researched and well-written history of Brain's life, his influence on the world of music making, and a source of countless examples of his artistry. The result is a testament to the authors' tenacity, their love of the horn, and their admiration for one of the world's greatest hornists, Dennis Brain.

—*Edwin L. Glick*
Denton, Texas
September 2010

Preface

At the age of thirteen I was lucky enough to meet and have a number of lessons from Dennis Brain (my parents lived quite close to where he and his wife lived in London). At that age I was quite simply in awe of his technique, being unaware of the subtleties that make the difference between great and inspirational performers. As a young person, slow music was more boring than fast music, and also I assumed that all horn players played as he did! It was only later in life, having listened to many performers, that I came to realize that he had a unique talent for expressing and enhancing the underlying possibilities of a phrase, whether it be in a concerto or just two or three solo notes in a complex orchestral composition.

Although Mozart made a well-known exception to this, most music consists of black symbols on a white page, and it is the performer's task to add aural shading, color, and nuance to the composer's instructions. The player can also, subtly, alter the dynamics of a phrase, its articulation, and the way in which it is projected. A single note can be played accurately but in an ungainly style or transformed into a surprisingly beautiful sound from its beginning to its end, and the same is true of a phrase or a complete composition. One only has to listen to different people reading the same text passage aloud to appreciate the variety of interpretations that can be achieved in the performance of music.

Most of us are likely to be able to recognize speech that holds our attention and gives us the anticipatory delight to hear more. In music, it should be just the same, but in many instances we get only a technically excellent performance of the notes on the page. Without exception, Dennis Brain gave us the former, always playing with exceptional sensitivity, linking phrases together so that the whole sentence or movement flowed as a cohesive statement whilst, at the same time, producing little subtleties of inflection, rubato, and tone color that never cease to amaze and delight the experienced listener.

As with all the arts, fashions come and go, the more successful returning time and time again. In Dennis's case, some might say that his sound is too lightweight compared with most of today's players with their larger bore instruments but, as with all "progress," there is a downside. At strong volumes, the modern horns can have a tendency to swamp or cloud over other instruments rather than blending with and adding extra color to the ensemble. At quieter dynamics, the old narrower bore instruments had a more focused sound, the character of which could be appreciated from the furthest seat in the concert hall. Dennis's sound had these characteristics on his single B-flat horn and possibly even more so on his Raoux.

Apart from his huge, natural technical skill, Dennis's outstanding talent was the innate ability to charm, surprise, make one smile, and make one wish for more. Very much like the person himself. He surely ranks with the finest players on any instrument at any time.

—James Diack, ARCM, Hon. ARAM
October 2010

Introduction

Dennis Brain was one of the most celebrated musicians of the twentieth century. The number of websites paying tribute to Dennis Brain is a testament to his legacy. Tributes from colleagues demonstrate that his appeal was not just to horn players. And although people all over the world today who listen to classical music have never heard of him, others have not only heard of Brain's name but have seen him live and heard him in recitals, on radio, and on commercial recordings.

More than two decades have passed since Stephen Pettitt produced a second edition of *Dennis Brain: A Biography*,[1] now out of print. This new biography presents a detailed account of his career and is illustrated with previously unpublished photographs. We discuss recordings and film media not previously listed in the published literature. It is not a personal biography, except in so far as the authors have been able to discover his letters, or to quote recollections by colleagues, friends, and family members.

Brain's importance as a musician and champion of the horn as a solo instrument cannot be overestimated. The solo horn repertoire expanded considerably because of his example. Composers needed little encouragement to write for him. Some of these works are still performed today, notably the Jacob Concerto, Bowen Concerto, Sir Malcolm Arnold's Concerto No.2, Seiber's *Notturno*, Britten's Serenade, and Searles's *Aubade*. A selection of the works written for Brain are discussed and analyzed, with reference to radio archives, off-the-air private recordings, and commercial recordings.

Brain was not merely a soloist at the top of his profession. He was also a consummate musician in chamber groups as well as playing his part in orchestral works. We discuss his Quintet, formed in 1946, and chronicle the works written for them, as well as their broadcasts and concerts. In chapters focusing on his work in orchestras, the reader can follow Brain on tours to the United States with the RAF Symphony Orchestra (1944–45), the Royal Philharmonic Orchestra (1950), and the Philharmonia (1955), with newspaper criticisms and photographs.

Brain's influence on his colleagues and on subsequent generations of horn players continues to be significant. Part of this influence has been through commercially released recordings, supplemented by issues of radio broadcasts. The discography of Brain's recordings has expanded since 1989, and part of the purpose of this book is to recognize these recordings.

Brain taught only occasionally, and this aspect of his career has received little attention, so the authors have gathered descriptions and anecdotes about his approach. We have also reproduced Brain's articles about the horn, which give interesting insights into his musical tastes as well as information about what he advocated as some key principles of the horn player's art. These and other documents, including a reconstruction of his "Early Horn" lecture-recital of July 1955, are brought together for the first time. The chapter on Brain's instruments and mouthpiece, with considerable technical detail, will be of interest to horn players, although perhaps not to general readers.

Towards the end of his life, Brain expressed the desire to be a conductor-soloist, and he started a chamber orchestra that gave a handful of concerts before his untimely death in a car crash at the age of thirty-six. The final chapter concerns the new directions Brain's career was taking in the last decade—leading his trio for violin, horn, and piano and conducting his chamber orchestra. It concludes with the many tributes to Brain that began after his death and which continue through commemorative concerts that show the admiration accorded him by a new generation of musicians in the twenty-first century.

We have attempted to add life, color, and humor to a fuller portrait of Brain through interviews with a wide circle of his family, friends, former students, and colleagues, whose accounts and fond anecdotes still abound. Fortunately for future generations, his musical legacy is assured in the recordings that already exist and by those that continue to be released.

—Stephen Gamble and William C. Lynch

Octave Designations

Octaves are designated throughout the text as in the *Harvard Dictionary of Music* and *The Horn Call.*

C, C c c' c'' c''' c''''

CHAPTER 1

The Early Years (1921–1939)

Dennis Brain was born into a musical family and was expected to become a musician. He studied horn with his father at home and as a student at the Royal Academy of Music. Information on Brain's childhood and student days is scarce; however, we know that he showed early promise and that by the end of his studies at the Academy, he was performing and recording professionally.

Family

The Brain family name is synonymous with the horn—his father, Aubrey Brain (1893–1955) uncle Alfred Brain (1885–1966) and grandfather A. E. Brain (1860–1929) were all distinguished horn players.

Brain's mother, Marion Brain (1887–1954), was a contralto (*Pls. 1–3*) and under her maiden name, Beeley, sang in Wagner's *Ring* at the Royal Opera House, Covent Garden until the late 1920s. Before World War I, Sir Edward Elgar had written "Hail, Immemorial Ind!" in his opera *The Crown of India* especially for her. Judging from the few recordings available, she possessed a voice of great warmth and power. She had superb breath control and could sustain a long phrase without taking any unmusical breaths, a characteristic that was later to be one of the key attributes of her son's horn playing.

Brain's parents met during the Denhof Opera Company's tour of 1913, and they were married in 1914. Dennis's brother, Leonard, who became an oboist, was born in 1915. Dennis was born in London on May 17, 1921. At that time, his father was third horn in the London Symphony and Royal Philharmonic Orchestras.[1]

One of the earliest photos of Brain, taken about 1924, is a charming picture that could not possibly show what a great musician he would be (*Pl. 4*). Next to him is Grandpa Basil Beeley, his mother's father, of whom we know only that his family included engineers who manufactured boilers at Stalybridge, Cheshire. Photographs from the 1920s show Brain on the beach with his family or in the shallows at Viking Bay, Broadstairs, Kent, a favorite holiday destination.[2] (*Pl. 5*)

Roy Plomley, interviewing Brain in 1956, asked whether it was expected he would be a musician, to which Brain replied:

> Yes, it seemed to be accepted in my family that, at a suitable age, I would take up the horn perhaps and become a horn player . . . I started [piano] when I was about seven or eight; my mother was wise enough not to teach me the piano herself but sent me to the local piano teacher who was very good, and when I was about fourteen, my father thought, I suppose, that perhaps it was about time that I did something with the instrument and he tactfully came up to me one day and said, "I've found another instrument—would you like to see what you can do on it?" So I did and I've been going ever since.[3]

Although a family anecdote tells of him picking up his father's horn and blowing a perfect note at the age of three, he didn't start playing the instrument seriously until (as he said) he was about fourteen. Aubrey believed that the horn should not be played until the permanent teeth had developed. As a treat, he allowed his son to blow his horn every Saturday morning so the boy's interest in the instrument would be sustained.[4]

Early Education

From the age of seven, Brain received his education at Richmond Hill Preparatory School, where he also played the bugle in the school cadet band.[5]

Violinist Sir Vivian Dunn, a colleague of Aubrey Brain in the BBC Symphony Orchestra who rode to rehearsals with him, recalled that, in about 1930, Aubrey would take his son to the rehearsals, which took place at a factory underneath old Waterloo Bridge. Dennis would have seen some of the world's greatest conductors with one of the world's most outstanding orchestras rehearsing the standard orchestral repertoire as well as many new works receiving first performances. What excellent training this must have been for him, observing his father leading the horn section![6]

After Richmond Hill, Brain attended St. Paul's School, London. He sang treble in the school choir (not as soloist) and took part in school concerts. His piano lessons were continued with the school's Director of Music, Henry

Wilson, who also encouraged him to take up the organ. At one of the school's Music Society concerts on December 19, 1935, he performed the first movement of Beethoven's Pianoforte Sonata in G. Also at St. Paul's he became friends with his contemporary and later a composer, Peter Racine Fricker. The two maintained a long musical association throughout their careers. A photograph (*Pl. 6*) from his years at St. Paul's School shows Brain with his first horn in about 1936.[7]

In the summer of 1936, after only three years at St. Paul's, Brain left the school and continued lessons with his father at home. He returned to St. Paul's for "old boy" concerts with his brother. For example, on December 21, 1937, with pianist Norman Tucker, Leonard and Dennis performed a trio for oboe, horn, and piano by Paul Rogers. On December 20, 1938, he visited again, but this time as an orchestral player in works by Boccherini, Bach, and Mozart. The second horn in the concert was Denis Mason, who was later to play third horn in the Royal Philharmonic Orchestra.[8]

Royal Academy of Music

Brain studied at the Royal Academy of Music, where his father taught horn, from 1936 to 1939. In September 1936 he won a Stokes scholarship and began his studies in horn, piano, harmony, organ, composition, and conducting.

His piano studies were under the guidance of Max Pirani and harmony under Montague Phillips. Another student in 1936 was Douglas Moore, who had had the honor of playing the opening phrase of Strauss's *Till Eulenspiegel* for the composer at the Royal Academy, shortly before Moore went to the BBC Symphony Orchestra as seventh horn. Aubrey told Moore, "I hope Dennis doesn't follow me into the BBC." He wanted his sons "distributed in other orchestras."[9]

Brain played principal horn in 1937 in the Ernest Read Symphony Orchestra (not an Academy orchestra), conducted by Ernest Read, a champion of music-making among young people. Clarinetist Jack Brymer recalled his first meeting with Brain during the interval of one of their evening concerts. Leonard Brain introduced them:

> As we entered the band room, the fresh-faced lad with the shock of hair falling over his brow was amusing his friends by playing the first Strauss Horn Concerto finale at double speed. It was perfectly obvious that there was nothing he couldn't do with the horn, and that here was the world's greatest player of the next generation. He joined the orchestra the next week, and it was as if he had done it all before, so perfectly did he master the quite complicated works he had to sight-read.[10]

King George VI was crowned in 1937. On May 21, the Academy's First Orchestra performed a special "Coronation Concert" at Queen's Hall. The personnel included the professors, leading their respective sections. The horn section comprised Aubrey and Dennis Brain, William Grant, James Kirby, and Douglas Moore.[11]

Lessons with Aubrey Brain

At the Academy, Aubrey (*Pl. 7*) was determined to treat his son the same as other students. Flutist Gareth Morris later recalled Brain waiting for his regular lesson:

> I should tell you that when Dennis was a student in the Academy, his father was his own professor, you see, and this was a very serious thing. Aubrey Brain considered his son to be just one of the students and that was it. He behaved as toughly as he would to anybody else. Not that it was necessary with Dennis because he wanted to play the horn more than anything. I remember often sitting with Dennis perhaps in the canteen and he'd keep looking at his watch, "It's my lesson, I mustn't be late." "Oh, must go." Up he'd go to his lesson.[12]

Brain's actual horn lessons with his father during the Academy years may have taken place at home. Brain told Edwin Glick that his lessons at school consisted primarily of taking tea since his father gave him his lessons at home.[13]

The precise details of these lessons are not known, although we can gather from the way Aubrey taught other students at the Academy that they would almost certainly have followed the same pattern. He used Oscar Franz's treatise, *Grosse theoretisch-praktische Waldhorn-Schule* (1880), which Douglas Moore remembered preparing from cover to cover. Aubrey also demonstrated horn technique, phrasing, and so on, in lessons. One student, Aileen Hunter (née Way), remembered that he would demonstrate the Mozart concertos and Strauss Concerto No. 1. In the Franz treatise, he was fond of the Gallay study on page 62, which, Aileen recalls, he played *pianissimo* and straight through in one breath—his breath control was legendary.[14]

Moore recalled that Aubrey had a fantastic ability to demonstrate a piece. He would then listen to the student perform the work, such as the Strauss Concerto No. 1, all the way through without interruption. Finally, he would ask the student to play it again and comment on phrasing, intonation, and so on.[15]

Donald Froud, a student in Aubrey's later years, recalled how Aubrey fought to preserve the "English" style of horn playing and inspired his pupils to prefer it to the prevalent "German" sound that was gaining popularity in British orchestras. Aubrey was more of a coach than a teacher, as he explained:

> If you took some piece into a lesson, you came out of that lesson playing it better. He never attempted to teach technique. He used to say, "If you know in your head how you want this to sound and you strive to play it that way, the technique will follow, but you can practise technique all day long and yet never become a musician."[16]

Aubrey's Academy students included many of the distinguished horn players who emerged as soloists or orchestral players in later years. Their success is testimony to the quality of his teaching. Froud remembered some of Aubrey's dictums, such as "You are the only person in the world who hears every note you play, so therefore you must be your own sternest critic." Going through the score of the Strauss Concerto No. 1 with Froud, Aubrey asked, "What is the most important note in this piece?" Donald pointed to the first high b-flat." Aubrey shook his head, "No—the most important note is always the one you are about to play next!"[17]

Another student, Christopher Hortin, found Aubrey's teaching at the Academy inspiring and related the following account:

> In lessons with Aubrey, I was always in such awe of him. . . . To get me to play phrases he would make up little ditties to the music, something that I found very useful when in course of time I had pupils of my own. He would sing the opening fanfare of the Strauss First Concerto to "Hark to me, I'm the horn. . . ." He often said, "Look after the little notes, the big ones can look after themselves."[18]

John Burden, another horn student, looked back on his Academy days and meeting Dennis Brain. They soon became friends, and Burden later recalled one particular weekend when Brain visited Tiverton in Devon, where Burden's father was vicar of one of the local parish churches. "It was good fun," he recalled, "but I shall never forget the interminable long notes!" Morris remembered Brain mentioning this visit while they were students at the Academy. Brain had found the atmosphere there with prayers at mealtimes austere. Although Burden's father wanted his son to be a clergyman, he recognized his talent for the horn and arranged for him to see the leading professor at that time, Aubrey Brain. Burden remembered playing Mendelssohn's Nocturne from *A Midsummer Night's Dream* at his first meeting with Aubrey at the Academy.[19] He was accepted. Burden recalled Dennis's swift progress on the horn there:

> He had only started playing for about one year so initially we were on the same level, but he soon shot ahead, though we did share the first horn seat at rehearsals and concerts. Sir Henry Wood [known as Timber] was the orchestral conductor and trainer. Dennis and I both did the conductor's course where Timber was the chief instructor with Ernest Read doing most of the course.[20]

Other Academy Classes and Ensembles

Brain took the conductor's class with Ernest Read in December 1938. In addition to lessons with his father and (from September 1938) organ with G. D. Cunningham, Brain participated in chamber music with various combinations of other students. Concerts of chamber music at the Academy were under the supervision of Herbert Withers and, in addition to the traditional repertoire, students could perform their own compositions. One by Douglas Moore, *Adagio* in C minor for three horns and piano (manuscript lost) was given its first performance on May 3, 1937, and was mentioned briefly in *Musical Times*. Moore (*Pl. 8*) recalled many years later that when he suggested Brain play first horn, he replied "No, it's your composition!" William Grant played second and Brain played third—he was quite happy not to take the limelight.[21]

The Academy had several student orchestras, including the First Orchestra, with various conductors, including Sir Henry Wood. Brain was usually the principal. The professors, including Aubrey Brain, watched the concerts and sometimes joined the students. Concerts took place in Duke's Hall or Queen's Hall. [22]

The Academy staged an opera each year. In 1938, it was *The Marriage of Figaro* with Brain on first horn and Burden on second. Meanwhile, Burden had decided to develop his own conducting skills by forming a small chamber orchestra, the Burden Chamber Orchestra, mainly from students at the Academy. It started with only strings, but soon wind players were added to perform all twenty movements of Handel's *Water Music* and Bach's Suite in B minor. Brain was the organ soloist in one of Handel's concertos. Burden recalls that the orchestra personnel included Brain, principal horn, Burden, second, and Andrew McGavin, third. Leonard Brain was principal oboe, Gareth Morris principal flute, and Marjorie Lavers led the violin section.[23] At the end of 1938, Brain had several musical awards to his credit, including the E. F. James Prize and the Ross Scholarship for wind players.[24]

A flutist who was to become one of Brain's closest friends and colleagues, Gareth Morris, enrolled as a student in September 1938. Morris remembers

Brain being pointed out to him in the student canteen and his being impressed to hear that this person was the son of the famous horn player. Morris had heard Brain's father in broadcasts of wind quintet music.

Dennis and Morris met when they played in a rehearsal of the Grieg Piano Concerto with Sir Henry Wood conducting the Academy's First Orchestra. A charming little flute solo in the concerto is echoed by the horn; a little later this exchange is repeated. The first time he played it, Morris was surprised to hear the horn imitate every nuance of his phrasing precisely. Intrigued, he subtly changed his phrasing of the solo on its next appearance. Again, the horn's mimicry was perfect. After the rehearsal, Morris went up to the platform where Brain was sitting with the horn players and said, "Hello! I think we've made friends!" Brain replied with a smile, "Yes, I think we have!" They were close friends from that day onwards.[25]

Morris remembered Aubrey's character at this time, "I found him charming, a little shy, and not nearly as much fun as Dennis." He recalled the first days and weeks at the Academy, with a dictation teacher who played the rhythms incorrectly and thought his students incompetent when they wrote precisely what he played:

> It was like a university—you made what you chose to make of it. I remember an amusing aural training class. Dennis and I were in it together. There was an old chap who did the aural classes and we had to write the dictation. He would say, "Now you boys, I am going to play this and you write it down. Now then, come along!" So Dennis and I wrote absolutely accurately, triple dots, and he said "Now then you boys are never going to get on if you don't learn to do things properly!"[26]

Asked how he would characterize Brain's qualities as a horn player and musician, Morris commented:

> There is something supremely beautiful about his playing—touching and also an aristocratic style which most of the others lack—if not all. I don't think he said, "I will play in this style." He chose an instrument upon which he could do his way of playing.[27]

Brain's public debut with the Busch Chamber Players took place on October 6, 1938, at Queen's Hall. Brain's father had been asked to find a suitable second horn (*Pl. 9*) because his usual second, Francis Bradley, was not available. Aubrey took the risk of engaging his son. Lady Barbirolli, then Evelyn Rothwell, played the principal oboe part in the Bach Brandenburg Concerto No. 1 and vividly recalled that concert. The Busch Chamber Players were "like a family," she said. Dennis played impeccably as second horn, as did Aubrey on first. Burden, who was in the audience, recalled, "It was great stuff!" *The Daily Telegraph* critic wrote:

> In the F major concerto Aubrey Brain was in his accustomed place as first horn but he had a new partner, his 17-year old son, Dennis, whose first appearance this was—a Queen's Hall event of no little interest. The famous family keeps up its traditions in the representative of the new generation. Son seconded father with a smoothness and certainty worthy of his name.[28]

Quintets

Chamber music was an important part of Brain's Academy experience. He and his friends read quintets on Monday evenings in a practice room. The flute professor at the Academy, Charles Stainer, although he did not coach the students, lent them music.[29] Morris recalled one rare occasion of a private concert:

> The Principal, Sir Stanley Marchant, was going to give a lecture on wind instruments—at the Royal Institute in Albemarle Street. I was summoned to the Principal—to his room—and he told me that I was to play in this thing and it was Leonard, Dennis, Alwyn Kell (probably), and I suppose it would be James Richens (bassoon). The point was that he said, "Now you must not wear your dinner jackets—white ties and tails." I hadn't got white tie and tails. So he said, "You've got to wear that." I thought, "This is a great honour. It's my first year."
>
> So I telephoned home quickly and told my parents this tale. They always wanted the best for their boys and would say, "It doesn't matter if we're overdrawn!" I had to go to Austin Reed. He (Principal) had telephoned Austin Reed and got a man he knew there to see to me. I got the whole equipment—waistcoat and everything. Meanwhile, Dennis had told his father, who said, "What rubbish! Absolute nonsense!" So I had tails and none of the others had and we went back to dinner jackets.
>
> The point is that that is the only wind quintet thing I remember doing at the Academy and that was at the Royal Institute in Albemarle Street. I don't know what we played except I do remember *Air and Variations* of Rossini. It shows off all the instruments—each instrument has a variation.[30]

Morris recalled his early quintet playing as a student:

> When we were students at the Academy, we immediately started to play wind quintets. Our wind quintet playing went on after student days

> and after the war and developed into the Dennis Brain Wind Quintet and Dennis Brain Wind Ensemble. The original members were the two Brain brothers, me, and two other players [Alwyn Kell and James Richens]. We did change the bassoon and we did change the clarinet. . . . We grew up together, as it were, and learned our wind quintets together.[31]

Recordings and Other Performances

Brain made his first recording on February 16, 1939, playing second horn to his father in Mozart's Divertimento K.334 for two horns and strings with the Léner Quartet. This was a Columbia recording on five 12-inch 78 rpm discs that was eventually issued on CD by EMI in 1991. Father and son play with precision, demonstrating powerful air supply and an elegant, aristocratic style. Stately, mesmerizing, refined, and perfectly synchronized, they make the most of what is not Mozart's most charming horn writing. Aubrey and Dennis had performed this divertimento earlier in the winter with the Laurence Turner Quartet at Queen's Hall; it was broadcast on March 2, 1939, and then performed again for the London Music Festival at Queen's Hall on April 25, 1939.[32]

The London Schubert Society performed a concert of Schubert's music in Duke's Hall on February 21, a few days after the recording of K.334. Brain, the Menges Quartet, Alwyn Kell (clarinet), James Richens (bassoon), and Victor Watson (double bass) performed the Octet D803. The *Daily Telegraph* critic drew attention to the names of Brain and Kell, and he commented on the "poetic effect" of the horn playing, which showed the inheritability of wind playing in families.[33]

The combined orchestras of the Royal Academy and Royal College of Music, conducted by Sir Henry Wood, gave a "Handel Festival" concert at Alexandra Palace on June 3, 1939. (*Pl. 10 & detail Pl. 11*) Morris, who played in the concert, remembered that the music was excerpts of Handel's *Messiah* (not the *Water Music* or *Music for the Royal Fireworks*), and Isobel Baillie was the soprano soloist. Brain was also there and is seen from the rear, with the bell of his horn visible at the end of the horn section, as pointed out by Morris. The photographer curiously took the picture looking out from behind the orchestra towards Sir Henry Wood and the large audience behind him.[34]

The Brain brothers, David Sandeman (flute), Margaret Jacob (clarinet), and Mary Hunt (bassoon) performed Denis Matthews's *Partita* for wind quintet, written for his friends, at the Academy on June 7, 1939.

Last Academy Term

At the end of the term in 1939, Brain was awarded a silver medal for harmony, bronze medals in composition and organ, and certificates in horn and aural training.[35]

Continuing his BBC broadcasts of chamber music, Brain performed "with staggering technique and style" a movement from a Mozart concerto with the BBC Symphony Orchestra in a program entitled "Monday Night at Seven" as recalled by flutist Gerald Jackson. Then on June 21, 1939, on the Regional Service, Brain gave a complete performance of Mozart's Concerto in E-flat Major K.447 with the BBC Empire Orchestra. He was beginning to spread his wings as a soloist.[36]

Above: ***Plate 1*** Marion Beeley, ca. 1910.
Collection, Brain family. With permission from Audrey Brain.

Right: ***Plate 2*** Marion Beeley, ca. 1915.
Gamble collection. With permission from Audrey Brain.

Plate 3 Marion Brain, Christmas, 1914.
Gamble collection. With permission from Audrey Brain.

Above left: ***Plate 4*** Dennis Brain with Grandpa Basil Beeley, ca. 1924. *Gamble collection. With permission from Audrey Brain.*

Above right: ***Plate 5*** Dennis Brain with Leonard Brain, Aubrey Brain, and two unidentified children, in the water at Viking Bay, Broadstairs, Kent, England, ca. 1927. *Gamble collection. With permission from Audrey Brain.*

Right: ***Plate 6*** Dennis Brain in his St Paul's School years, ca. 1936, holding his first instrument. *Gamble collection. With permission from Audrey Brain.*

Above left: ***Plate 7*** Aubrey Brain, ca. 1930. *Brain family collection. With permission from Audrey Brain.*

Above right: ***Plate 8*** Douglas Moore (1918–2006), June 30, 2005, at his home in Haslemere, Surrey. *Photograph by Stephen Gamble.*

Plate 9 Aubrey and Dennis Brain, ca. 1938. *From John Burden's scrap book. With permission from John Burden.*

Plates 10–11 Handel Festival Concert, June 3, 1939, Alexandra Palace. With the combined student orchestras of the Royal Academy of Music and the Royal College of Music, conducted by Sir Henry J. Wood. Isobel Baillie, soprano soloist in excerpts from Handel's *Messiah*. Plate 11 (detail) shows Gareth Morris (top right) and Dennis Brain (bottom left) seen from the back. *With permission from Gareth Morris and Patricia Morris.*

CHAPTER

2

The RAF Years (1939–1946)

Brain was in the Royal Air Force (RAF) during World War II and a year afterwards. He continued studies at the Royal Academy of Music during the war and augmented playing in the RAF Symphony Orchestra with musical engagements in London and the provinces.

RAF duties took Brain to RAF bases at home and abroad and to some extent restricted outside engagements. Sometimes he had to turn down offers of work owing to schedule conflicts and to his increasing demand as a soloist. His concerts as well as broadcasts in solo repertoire increased from 1941 onwards on home and overseas transmissions. This was in addition to many chamber music recitals and broadcasts with strings and other combinations. He was not restricted to classical music but ventured into the sphere of dance bands, light music, and music for the film industry. With so many musicians away in the services abroad, he was much in demand for film soundtracks as well as in the many ensembles and orchestras being established in and around London during the war years. It was a short train journey from Uxbridge, Middlesex, and he was usually free of duties from mid-day onwards.

Joining Up

The outbreak of war in September 1939 temporarily interrupted studies. On September 26, the Brain brothers enlisted in the RAF (*Pls. 1–2*). They signed up for seven years and were not discharged until September 26, 1946. Gareth Morris, their flutist friend from the Academy, returned from a holiday and found the brothers in uniform. Soon he joined them. After basic training, they became members of the RAF Central Band at Uxbridge, where their commanding officer, Wing Commander O'Donnell, was busy planning the formation of a large symphony orchestra, with Air Ministry approval.[1]

Morris recalled the warm welcome they received at Uxbridge: "The regular bandsmen there (it was their profession and their life) gave us the warmest of welcomes. Of course, they adored Dennis. There were horn players there, regular bandsmen and here comes the greatest virtuoso in the world. They absolutely loved him and he loved them too. They all welcomed us with delightful open arms."[2]

Meanwhile, the Royal Academy experienced a shortage of musicians. The Brain brothers were invited to return for the spring and summer terms in 1940. Their father was in Bristol with the BBC Symphony Orchestra, which had been evacuated in September 1939, so Brain continued his studies with the organ and carried on his horn playing unsupervised.[3]

Norman Del Mar, a horn student of Frank Probyn at the Royal College of Music, joined the RAF Symphony Orchestra as second horn. Del Mar remembered those days: "Probyn got me into the RAF Band (Probyn was my horn teacher at the College, a very distinguished gentleman) and he got me of his own initiative into the RAF Band because he said it would be very good for me to 'be with the Brain boys' as he put it. Leonard, of course, was with Dennis in the RAF Band. I met Dennis first actually in barracks."[4]

Brain and Del Mar soon became firm friends, embellishing and improvising on the standard repertoire, all made more enjoyable because their conductors rarely noticed. Del Mar remembered Brain at this time:

> If he was game for anything, this was his motto—anything that turned up, we'd have a go at. That would be the fun of it and when we used to sit in the RAF, the whole point of everything was to try and catch the conductors out, as much as one could, by exaggerating every musical point to its utmost. Every phrase had to be precisely so and you'd look out of the corner of your eye to see if they noticed. If they did, it was one up to them, if they didn't, it was one up to us. Dennis always—and between us we concocted all kinds of horn *obbligatos* for the most ridiculous pieces![5]

Sir Henry Walford Davies's *RAF March Past* became a horn cadenza for Brain, "much to the fury of the regular first horn," as Del Mar recalled, and he and Brain used to "add scales and flourishes."[6]

John Burden, who had been a student with Brain at the Academy, joined the RAF Orchestra at Uxbridge briefly. He recalled:

> I had applied to the RAF Central Band and soon I was to join Dennis, Norman Del Mar and various members of famous string quartets who made up the RAF Orchestra which was formed in addition to the band: Griller, Hirsch, Martin, Grinke, etc . . . I did not stay long at Uxbridge

> but long enough to take part in the famous National Gallery lunchtime concerts with Myra Hess who used the RAF Orchestra.[7]

Del Mar hated the routine at the barracks and managed to get a job as driver to the commanding officer. The routine consisted of roll call at 8:45 a.m., followed by three hours of "rehearsal." The rehearsal was rather a joke because there weren't any practice rooms and all the musicians practicing at once created a great cacophony of sound. The rehearsal time was punctuated by a break of tea and "wads." This consisted of thick slices of bread and dripping, which Brain consumed in large quantities.

After rehearsal, a favorite gathering place was Pam's Pantry with its comfortable alcoves where Brain sat with his friends. He always enjoyed a healthy appetite and would have second helpings of the first course as well as two puddings (desserts). A telephone behind the counter would ring often during meals for one or other of the musicians and Beryl, the waitress, would call them to the telephone where they would secure an engagement. One of the concert agencies that telephoned was ENSA. Walter Legge was the artists' manager, and it was his contacts with the RAF players that began Legge's plans to form an orchestra after the war.[8]

Del Mar, Brain, and Morris got on well together and were often in each other's company in and out of barracks. One of their friends, Irene Grainger, who married John Burden, made a cartoon of them (*Pl. 3*). She also made a watercolor painting of Brain (*Pl. 4*) showing that she was an accomplished painter as well as a talented caricaturist.[9]

Outside Work

Brain had many opportunities to play outside the RAF. He wrote short missives in reply to letters from the BBC, accepting or regretfully turning down engagements when he was unable to get away from his duties or other musical commitments. He adopted a polite and succinct style of letter writing for the BBC that usually stated that either he would be happy to accept the engagement offered, "subject to the exigencies of the Service" or that, with regret, he must decline the engagement because of other commitments. The impression one gets from reading them is that he was very organized and that he enjoyed the stimulus of being constantly busy.[10]

During the War, Brain auditioned with the Scottish Orchestra, as recalled by Morris: "He gave an audition with the Scottish Orchestra one season and the conductor was George Szell who said, 'Come again when you've had some experience.' The next time they met, Dennis was the First Horn of the Philharmonia Orchestra!"[11]

The occasion when Szell conducted the Philharmonia during Brain's tenure may be the same one that is related by a violinist in the orchestra, Donald Weeks:

> On one occasion when George Szell was conducting the Philharmonia in the early 1950s, as a one-time horn player himself he interested himself in taking a look at the instruments used by the horn section. When he reached Dennis Brain's place he said to him, referring to his Raoux piston-valve horn with a B-flat crook, "Mr. Brain, on this instrument it isn't possible!"[12]

In addition to film music, engagements were available at late night broadcasts on the North American, Latin American, Afrikaans, French, and Eastern services. Dame Myra Hess founded regular lunchtime concerts at the National Gallery; admission was a shilling and all the musicians received a flat rate fee. The RAF Symphony Orchestra also gave concerts there, and Brain was soloist with them, for example, in Mozart's Horn Concerto No. 4 on April 6, 1942.[13]

Morris remembered that Hess had told O'Donnell, "It would be my dream to play with the RAF Symphony Orchestra." He recalled the film with Hess and the RAF Orchestra, playing Mozart's Piano Concerto No. 17 in G. Brain cannot be seen in this, but he would have been there. His brother is seen in close-up playing the oboe.[14]

One of the works performed at the National Gallery was Roy Douglas's *Six Dance Caricatures* for wind quintet. In addition to Brain, the players for the first performance were John Francis (flute), Natalie James (oboe), Richard Walthew (clarinet), and Cecil James (bassoon). Douglas recalled that, during the war when he was the pianist for propaganda films at Denham Studios, the two horn players were Brain and Del Mar, who arrived for sessions in uniform. Denham Studios was close to RAF Uxbridge, so they were the obvious choice of horn players for films made there during wartime.[15]

The London Wind Players

The National Gallery concerts featured several new chamber ensembles—notably, Harry Blech's London Wind Players and Karl Haas's London Baroque Ensemble. Brain was the original principal horn of both of these ensembles. Blech (1910–1999) was a British violinist and conductor who specialized in Haydn and Mozart; during the war, he played in the RAF and drew on its personnel for the London Wind Players. Karl Haas (1900–1970) escaped from Germany in 1939, specialized in Baroque music, and played the viola d'amore.

Dame Myra Hess had approached Blech with the proposal that he form a group of wind players to take part in all the Beethoven and Mozart works for winds. One concert was recalled by Audrey Brain, who was in the audience (before she met Dennis or Leonard; she later married Leonard). She remembered Brain leading the horns (Vivian Grey, Norman Del Mar, and Livia Gollancz) in Mozart's *Gran Partita* for thirteen wind instruments K.361, which they performed at the National Gallery on August 19, 1942.

A concert on May 26, 1943, included the Mozart Serenade No. 12 in C minor K.388 and the Quintet for piano and winds in E-flat K.452 with pianist Angus Morrison. For the Serenade, the players were (in addition to Brain and Del Mar) Natalie James and Peter Newbury (oboes), Pauline Juler and Richard Walthew (clarinets), Cecil James and William Smith (bassoons).[16]

Brain made twenty-six solo appearances at the National Gallery during and after the war. Works that he performed several times there include the Brahms Trio and the Mozart Quintet K.407.[17]

The London Baroque Ensemble

Karl Haas's London Baroque Ensemble, formed in 1941, was in fact a chamber orchestra that could be sub-divided, as required, for smaller groups of chamber music. With wind instrumentalists added to his original string players, the ensemble gave a concert at the National Gallery on June 26, 1945, that included two works for winds: Haydn's F major Divertimento and Mozart's Sextet in B-flat, K.270. Brain and Del Mar were the hornists.[18]

Composer Sir Malcolm Arnold, a colleague in the London Baroque Ensemble in its early days, presented Brain with a souvenir book of the National Gallery concerts during wartime (listing concerts by the London Baroque Ensemble, the London Wind Players, the New London Orchestra, the RAF Symphony Orchestra, and others). The title page is inscribed, "Dennis Brain from Arnold. London Oct. 14th 1944—here's hoping this isn't 'Bitterer & Higher'" What he meant by the remark isn't clear. Opposite the inscription is a photograph of the public waiting to be admitted to the concert at 12:23 p.m., in their hats and coats (*Pl. 5*), with St. Martin-in-the-Fields church in the background.[19]

An American in England and Benjamin Britten

Through a series of six live early morning broadcasts to America, *An American in England*, Brain met the composer of the incidental music, Benjamin Britten. Britten was so impressed with Brain's virtuosity that he began to write especially difficult horn solos for these programs. During this series, Britten began a new solo work especially for Brain and tenor Peter Pears—the Serenade Op. 31 for tenor, horn, and strings. This is one of the greatest solo works for horn written in the twentieth century and remains a favorite among horn players as well as the public. Chapter 10 describes the work and Brain's performances of it.

Britten used breaks during the RAF rehearsals for the broadcasts to America to go over the finer points in the score with Brain and to make any adjustments. The Serenade makes full use of the horn's range, from *pianissimo* top c'''s to pedal notes, off-stage, and hand-stopping.[20]

The first performance of the Serenade took place on October 15, 1943, at Wigmore Hall, with Pears and the Boyd Neel Orchestra, conducted by Walter Goehr. Decca recorded the work with these soloists on May 25, 1944, with the Boyd Neel Orchestra, conducted by the composer.[21]

Unpublished takes by Decca have been preserved by the British Library Sound Archive and show a variety of tempi that were considered. The commercially issued sides were well-received by the critics. *The Gramophone* commented on Brain's "ravishingly beautiful" tone, especially in the Epilogue and Prologue.[22] Curiously, in spite of its popularity, this first recording was not reissued in the LP era until the 1970s; since then, other LPs and CDs have been issued.

Burden recalled his early performances of this challenging piece. One was a concert in Leeds with Pears, conducted by Josef Krips. After the concert, a critic made the gaffe that "Dennis Brain played with his usual elf-like ease." At the Leeds concert, Burden decided to play the Epilogue and Prologue without the natural harmonics because, as he explained, "I don't personally disapprove of the out of tune natural harmonics, it is most effective. It is just that programme notes should explain to the audience what it is all about."[23]

Wartime Recordings

Brain made Decca recordings before the Serenade that helped to establish his reputation and to pave the way for that work. The year 1943 was particularly busy, and he took part in recordings of Ferguson's Octet for winds and strings and Brahms's Four Songs Op. 17 for female chorus, two horns, and harp. These had been performed at the National Gallery: the Ferguson on February 17 and the Brahms on December 30, the same day as the recording. *The Times* critic wrote favorably of the Ferguson Octet performance at the National Gallery:

> Howard Ferguson's Octet, a compact work in four movements, claimed only the last twenty minutes of the hour. . . . The scoring is exceedingly effective; the ideas are serious and diversely disposed if not entirely free of reminiscence, but why should not music occasionally remind one of former pleasures? Ferguson does not rely on precedents; his thought is his own, his aim is beauty, and his pursuit of it is spontaneous.[24]

On June 21 that year, Brain also recorded (for Columbia) Mozart's Concerto No. 4 with the Hallé Orchestra, conducted by Laurence Turner and Sir Malcolm Sargent. Sargent was late and so the second movement was recorded first with Turner conducting and then Sir Malcolm arrived in time to conduct the rest. Del Mar had written the long cadenza in the first movement.[25]

Brain and pianist Denis Matthews made a recording of Beethoven's Sonata Op. 17 for Columbia at EMI's Abbey Road Studios on February 21, 1944. *The Gramophone* commented:

> The performance of this charming work could not be bettered. You feel that there are here two real musicians thoroughly enjoying themselves and communicating that enjoyment. Dennis Brain's tone is most beautiful, ravishing indeed in the frequently recurring C (above middle C). The whole of the other-worldliness of the French horn seems to be contained in that note . . . The recording, too, is extraordinarily good. This may be small Beethoven but it falls on the ear like an April shower on the parched earth.[26]

Towards the end of the same year, Decca recorded Mozart's Quintet K.407 with Dennis accompanied by three members of the Griller Quartet and Max Gilbert on second viola. The *Musical Times* critic did not care much for the piece but praised Brain who, particularly in the last movement, made his instrument "dance like a clarinet." Brain plays the entire piece with dexterity, accuracy, and gracefulness, one of the most beguiling of Mozart's chamber works.[27]

Decca recorded the Bach Brandenburg Concertos over several days in June and October 1945. Although the players couldn't be named for contractual reasons, Brain and Del Mar played first and second horn in the first concerto. In 2005, Dutton re-issued this set on CD.[28]

Opportunities to broadcast were plentiful during the war, but Brain's name often does not appear because players in chamber music were not always named. He would have played anonymously on numerous occasions for broadcasting in various orchestras. Sometimes a colleague has been able to give information not otherwise documented. For example, Neill Sanders (*Pl. 6*), Brain's colleague in the Philharmonia (and also in the London Baroque Ensemble), remembered taking part with Brain in some French propaganda broadcasts during wartime:

> Our real connection started about 1942 when we started doing a series of broadcasts together with the BBC. It was in fact after Dunkirk and the fall of France. They were really French propaganda broadcasts with news and music. The music was composed and conducted by a French composer, Francis Chagrin, of a string quartet and two horns—Dennis and myself.

> The news was interspersed with code messages for the Resistance in France. You might get a message like "Marcel the cock will crow three times at midnight!" That might mean they were dropping supplies or they were pulling an agent out or dropping an agent in and the music was quite exciting too. I can still recall doing a version of *Don Quixote* for string quartet and two horns which kept Dennis and me very much on our toes. I can still remember the times—2:15 to 5:15 on Wednesday afternoon at Maida Vale Studios.[29]

Solo and Chamber Music

Brain broadcast increasingly from 1941 onwards as soloist as well as in chamber music and with various orchestras.

For the BBC Home Service, he performed in Brahms's Horn Trio on November 9, 1941, with Frederick Grinke (violin) and John Pauer (piano). He was soloist in Mozart's Concerto No. 4 on September 17, 1942, with the BBC Symphony Orchestra, conducted by Sir Adrian Boult. He took part in Mozart's Quintet K.407 with the Silverman Trio and Keith Cummings (second viola) on October 24, 1942. Although numbered among works for the chamber repertoire, Brain considered it as being one of the more soloistic pieces and in 1956 campaigned for a higher fee commensurate with performance of solo works. On that occasion, he was unsuccessful in obtaining a solo fee for what the BBC continued to classify as chamber music.

For the European Service, broadcasting to Germany on November 20, 1942, he performed the Beethoven Sonata with Matthews. This was pre-recorded the same day. His fee was £7.7s.0d "to include one mechanical reproduction in each of the transmissions forming the Overseas Service." Brain agreed to the contract and signed it.[30]

For the Empire Service, Purple Network, broadcasting to South Africa on May 3, 1943, he played the first movement of Mozart's Concerto No. 4 in an arrangement for horn and piano by Francis Sanders. The pianist was John Wills, who occasionally accompanied Brain for broadcasts during and after the war. Brain performed Mozart's Quintet K.407 again on Sunday, May 16, 1943, with members of the Blech Quartet and Watson Forbes (second viola). His fee was still £7.7s.0d.[31]

The Brahms Horn Trio, which Brain broadcast many times from the 1940s onwards, was performed at the National Gallery on April 26, 1943, with Blech and Matthews. The same three broadcast it again on July 29, 1943. The BBC had written "We shall be glad of your assurance that you have obtained permission from your Commanding Officer to fulfil this engagement at the fee offered." The fee remained the same.[32]

For the Latin American Service, Brain played Haydn's (attributed) Horn Concerto No. 2 in D major in a horn and piano reduction by Breitkopf, accompanied by B. Mason, on August 9, 1944. This was also pre-recorded on August 2 at Aldenham. Brain rarely performed it in the full orchestral version, and this appears to have been the only occasion he played it in this Breitkopf edition. Brain found the leaps between high notes and the pedal notes awkward because he had to shift his mouthpiece position for low notes, a problem he shared with his uncle Alfred, who recorded it six years later for Capitol.[33] Another soloistic work in the chamber repertoire, Beethoven's Sextet Op. 81b for two horns and strings, was broadcast on the Home Service with Del Mar and the Blech Quartet on August 1, 1945.[34]

Brain performed a new and challenging work, Seiber's *Notturno* for horn and strings, with the Boyd Neel Orchestra, conducted by Seiber, at Wigmore Hall on December 3, 1945. *The Times* critic did not care for Seiber's music and gave a negative review of the concert and the *Notturno*.[35]

Although the war was over, the Brain brothers were still in the RAF, and outside engagements continued to be restricted. Brain performed Beethoven's Sonata with John Wills for the Eastern Service, broadcasting to India, Burma, and Indonesia on May 31, 1946. He gave a rare solo recital with an unnamed pianist for the Home Service on August 11, 1946. The program included Dukas's *Villanelle*, Glazunov's *Reverie*, and Senaillé's *Allegro Spiritoso*.[36]

Light, Popular, and Classical Orchestral Repertoire

London musical life also offered Brain and his colleagues opportunities to play music outside the classical repertoire. Brain and Del Mar joined Geraldo and his Orchestra when he required extra wind players. The repertoire was light popular vocal and instrumental music with some jazz, including an arrangement of "Where in the World" that Brain later remembered performing.[37]

During wartime, several orchestras were formed, including a "session" orchestra called the National Symphony Orchestra (NSO), which included, when they were available, some of the finest musicians that any orchestra could wish for—with Brain and Del Mar were Arthur Gleghorn and Gareth Morris (flutes), Leon Goossens (oboe), Reginald Kell and Bernard Walton (clarinets), John Alexandra and Cecil James (bassoons). The fluid nature of the pool of players in London at that time meant that musicians moved about from one orchestra to another so that a session orchestra like the NSO could not expect to have the same complement of players from one concert or recording session to the next.

The Phoenix Theatre was the NSO's regular venue for Sunday afternoon concerts starting in October 1942. One of the concerts on November 29, 1942, included Prokofiev's "Classical" Symphony, Beethoven's *Rondino* for wind instruments (Op.Posth.), Beethoven's Symphony No. 8, and Mozart's Piano Concerto No. 27, K.595. The pianist was Clifford Curzon and the conductor, Charles Hambourg. The personnel list for that concert shows Dennis Brain, Alwyn Hart, Norman Del Mar, and Leonard Fleming in the horn section. They are seen together in a photograph of about this date (*Pl. 7*).[38]

Morris recalled that both he and Brain played in concerts with the Walter Goehr Orchestra, which gave some important first performances of modern repertoire at Wigmore Hall. Among the concerts Gareth Morris remembered was one on January 30, 1943, in which Stravinsky's *Dumbarton Oaks* was played. The critic of *Musical Times* commented:

> Musical Culture Ltd. have been giving concerts at Wigmore Hall with an orchestra under Walter Goehr. Programmes included (January 16) Mozart's Serenade in E-flat K.375, Fauré's Ballade for piano and orchestra (Olona Kabos), Bliss's Serenade for baritone and orchestra (Roy Henderson); (January 30) Bach's six-part Ricercare, Mozart's Divertimento K.334, Britten's *Les Illuminations* (Peter Pears) and Stravinsky's *Dumbarton Oaks* Concerto. This series has also included French concerts of chamber music (January 24) Faure and Chausson; February 7, Baudelaire music; February 14, Rameau, Debussy, Couperin and Ravel.[39]

The Times newspaper mentioned Morris as the flute soloist at the concert on January 16. The works at that concert clearly required horns (K.375 and K.334), so it is more than likely that Brain was also playing.[40]

For light music, the orchestra broadcast under the name Orchestre Raymonde conducted by George Walter, which was Goehr's pseudonym. They played light classical arrangements of works by Johann Strauss II, Joseph Lanner, Haydn Wood, and others. A broadcast for the Home Service on January 3, 1943, included *Marche Militaire* (Schubert, arranged by Leo Wurmser), *Danse lente* and *Dolce lamente* (Cesar Frank arranged by George Walter), Suite, *The House that Jack Built* (John Greenwood), *Waltz Aquarellen* (Josef Strauss), Polka: *Tick-Tock* and *Czardas* (Johann Strauss). Brain was also soloist with them on occasions, for example, playing Mozart's Concerto No. 4 on April 8, 1942.[41]

In October 1940, the Brain brothers looked for accommodation outside the RAF barracks and discovered 16, the Greenway, Uxbridge, which soon became a favorite meeting place for their friends. It remained Brain's address until he was bombed out in 1944. Fortunately, he was not injured.

Leonard had left the previous year to get married. Brain's new address was Elsworthy Terrace, Swiss Cottage, where he shared lodgings with violinist Thomas Carter. About this time, he also met his future wife, Yvonne Coles, who was then a student of the professor of piano at the Royal Academy, Harold Craxton.[42]

Another orchestra where Brain was principal horn was Alec Sherman's New London Orchestra. They performed all Mozart's piano concertos with Dame Myra Hess at the National Gallery between 1943 and 1945, although the RAF tour of 1944–45 (see below) took Brain away for a few months. Morris recalled being present at a concert in which Brain was the soloist (no date but wartime) with the New London Orchestra at Golders Green. Morris was in the audience, sitting next to Aubrey Brain:

> The concert was at the Dome, Golders Green; a concert by the New London Orchestra. His father came to listen to it. I was not playing because, of course, there are no flutes in the Mozart horn concertos. So, I was sitting listening next to Aubrey. Dennis was playing wonderfully, and easily, when his father said to me, quite seriously, "I hope that it's not too easy for him."
>
> His father thought that, if it was going to be so easy for him, he would just play it through and miss all sorts of shadowy subtleties. But, of course, that was not the case at all. It was not as easy as all that for Dennis to play the horn. He practised his long notes and scales daily. His standards were colossal. I know what it meant to him and how he would not do certain things that would perhaps make him too tired to play. But I know what his father meant. It was not so easy for Aubrey and there was possibly a tiny bit of jealousy. Perhaps though it genuinely worried him to think that Dennis could play the Mozart with more ease, with the danger that it could sound too slick.[43]

United States Tour

In late 1944, the RAF Symphony Orchestra prepared for a long tour of the United States in an exchange with the US Air Force Band. The tour would visit twenty-eight states and cover 12,000 miles. On November 30, 1944, 104 musicians left Euston Station and traveled via Morcombe to Gourock, Firth of Clyde, where they boarded the grand ocean liner *Queen Elizabeth*. They arrived in New York on December 8. A photograph from the RAF scrapbook of the tour shows the arrival (*Pl. 8*), with Morris, center, carrying his flute case, Brain partly obscured, and Del Mar behind him.[44]

Their first stop was Camp Kilmer, New Brunswick, where Morris recalled that the RAF Orchestra's laundry had been sent away, and when it returned all the clothing had shrunk a quarter of the size! Fortunately he decided not to send his laundry in! They stayed two nights there. The Symphony Orchestra rehearsed for a first concert (*Pl. 9*) in Washington at Constitution Hall on December 18. The elegant proscenium with its decorations was a fine backdrop to the orchestra. The program included Lance Corporal Matthews's arrangement of Bach's D minor *Toccata and Fugue* played by the combined forces of the Symphony Orchestra and Central Band, and works by Sullivan, Coates, Elgar, Tchaikovsky, and Smetana. After the concert, the NBC radio broadcast the RAF Symphony Orchestra in seven more works, including Tchaikovsky's *Swan Lake*. The concert was repeated the following day and enthusiastically received by the audience.[45]

Brain had no solo engagements on this tour, except performing in Mozart's Quintet K.407 (first movement only) with members of the Griller Quartet at the British Officers' Club in Washington.[46] A photograph shows the RAF Symphony Orchestra outside the Alamo in San Antonio, Texas (*Pl. 10*). The photo also has the words the "San Antonio Aviation Cadet Center," bottom right, presumably where the RAF Orchestra was based at the time. Brain, on the end, is looking is looking through his camera view finder. Had he noticed the photographer's cue to look straight ahead like the rest? Next to him, Morris looks ahead with impassive gaze and behind him is Del Mar, smiling broadly. Brain was a keen photographer and he had an eye for a good picture. He used a Contessa camera. Another photograph during the tour shows him taking a snapshot of some puppies sitting in a wooden bucket (*Pl. 11*).[47]

During the tour, they had time to enjoy the resorts of Miami, Nassau, and others, and they were welcomed everywhere by their American hosts. From Miami to Nassau, the RAF Symphony performed in a flat-bottomed boat that caused them all to be seasick! One by one, they left and the last two playing were Morris and Matthews! Morris remembered how Brain was sick fairly early on and at the end he thought, "Whatever happens, I must win this competition!" In fact, it was Matthews who finally lasted the longest.[48]

Los Angeles

The tour arrived in Los Angeles on January 26, 1945, for a four-day visit. Their schedule included a dance at the Miramar Hotel, a concert at Santa Monica on the twenty-sixth, another at Santa Ana Air Base, and visits to the film studios of MGM and Twentieth-Century Fox. The Brain brothers spent most of the four days with Uncle Alfred, his second wife Straussie, and family. Al and Straussie took them, with some friends and family, to The Tropics, a local restaurant in Los Angeles. Here they naturally discussed horns and mouthpieces. Alfred gave his nephew one of his small conical mouthpieces which Dennis found very suitable and used for the rest of his career. It was very small, with such a tiny rim that a dime or a British silver three-penny piece would not quite sit inside the cup.[49]

The next day, Alfred took his nephews around the chicken farm and as a generous gift gave them the day's takings—$100—to spend in Los Angeles (*Pl. 12*). In the evening, the Brain brothers and Morris were invited to a party at Al and Straussie's home at Gardena. Morris recalled Alfred at this time. "A very colourful character. I don't think he was as elegant a player as Aubrey. He was a bit of a joker." Morris remembered large quantities of alcohol were consumed. Leonard Brain described it more colorfully as "a sea of alcohol." As the guests approached the house, they found Alfred sitting on the roof, playing his horn. The party started at 6:00 in the evening and didn't finish until 6:00 the following morning. At about midnight, Brain's Raoux was produced, and the American players tried one by one to get a note on it but failed. He was persuaded to play some fugues by Bach, a rendition of a passage from the *Flight of the Bumble-Bee*, and Kreisler's *Schön Rosmarin*. The Los Angeles Philharmonic horn section and other horn players from LA were also present, including James Decker.[50]

Alfred Brain (*Pls. 13–14*) had emigrated to the States in late 1922. For many years, he had enjoyed great success as a studio horn player in Hollywood and also earned a reputation for fine solo as well as orchestral playing in various orchestras, notably the Los Angeles Philharmonic and the Janssen Symphony Orchestra. He was also famous as a host and frequently catered for large parties, cooking all the food himself.[51]

For Dennis and the other players in the RAF Symphony (*Pl. 15*), Los Angeles was the highlight of the whole tour. While in California, they also visited San Francisco on January 31 for a concert in the Civic Auditorium. The works performed included Dvorak's *Carnival Overture*, Bach's *Toccata and Fugue in D minor*, two movements from Coates's Suite *London Every Day* ("Westminster" and "Knightsbridge"), Alford's *Cavalry of the Clouds*, Walton's *Crown Imperial,* and Sousa's "Stars and Stripes Forever."[52]

Returning Home

The orchestra made their long journey back to Washington over land via Denver and Omaha. John Hollingsworth conducted them in some of the concerts after O'Donnell sustained a leg injury. O'Donnell was well enough to conduct them on February 26 at Constitution Hall in Washington. Morris remembered a relaxing evening off with Brain on February 27 in New York:

> We were walking down the street and spotted the 400 Club with the sign in red lights, "Tommy Dorsey and his Band." We went in and paid for one

> night's membership. Tommy Dorsey was thrilling to hear. He spoke to us in the break. We were in our uniforms. In the US, the Americans thought we were real heroes—fighter pilots—they didn't want to believe we were only musicians! Dennis mentioned his father was a leading horn player in England. Dorsey hadn't heard of Aubrey Brain. We went out of the club with Dorsey to have a drink a little further up the street in a bar. He was very courteous. . . .[53]

Returning to London from the RAF tour, Brain found Dame Myra Hess at the National Gallery still giving her series of Mozart's piano concertos. About a month later, he was resuming concerts and broadcasts. He performed Mozart's Divertimento in F, K.247 with Del Mar and the Blech Quartet on the Home Service on June 24, 1945.[54]

The following year was also busy with concerts at the National Gallery. The London Baroque Ensemble gave a concert on March 25, 1946, with some unusual combinations of instruments, including Haydn's Divertimento *a tré* in E-flat for horn, violin, and violoncello (composed 1767), in which Dennis was joined by David Martin and William Pleeth. Also on that concert were C. P. E. Bach's four (of six) sonatas Wq 184, for two flutes, two clarinets, two horns, and bassoon, Haydn's marches for the Derbyshire Volunteer Cavalry for two clarinets, two horns, trumpet, three bassoons, and side drum (1794), and Haydn's *March for the Prince of Wales* (1792). The performers in these works included (with Brain and Del Mar) Gareth Morris and Edith Schragenheim (flutes); Bernard Walton and J. Fell (clarinets); Cecil James, Ronald Waller, and Vernon Elliot (bassoons); and Harold Jackson (trumpet). In the audience was one of Brain's students at the Guildhall School of Music and Drama, Edwin Glick.[55]

Dennis accompanied the RAF Symphony Orchestra on April 1, 1946, to Germany where they toured British military camps. He was away for a month. When he returned to London, he still had a few months of RAF duty, but he formed his chamber ensemble before leaving the RAF. He also continued his association with the London Wind Players and the London Baroque Ensemble after leaving the RAF.[56]

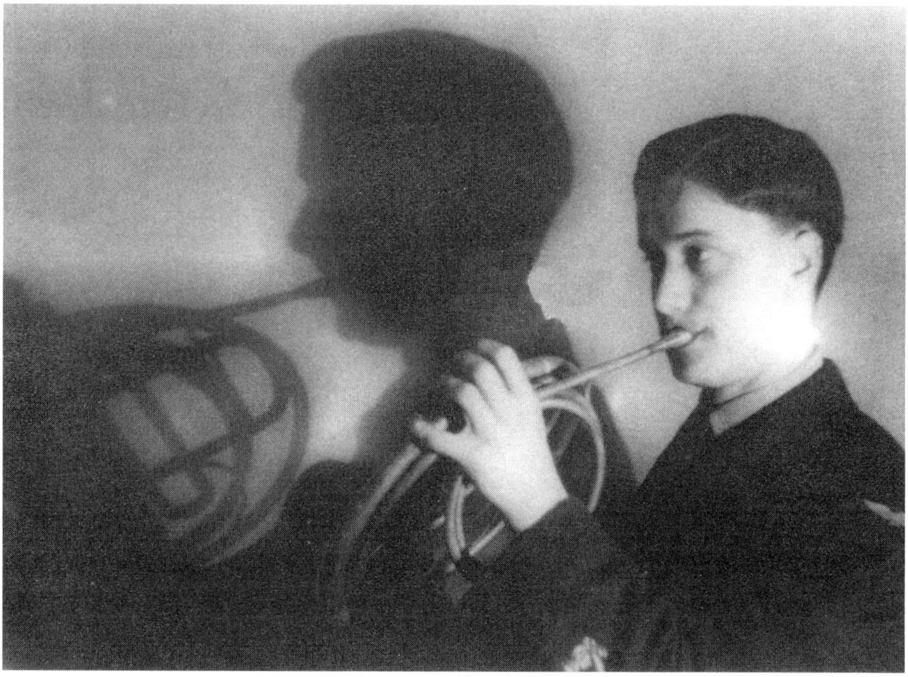

Plate 1 Dennis Brain playing his Raoux Millereau horn, about 1940. *Gamble collection. With permission from Audrey Brain.*

Left: ***Plate 2*** Leonard Brain and a dog, ca. 1940. *Brain family collection. With permission from Audrey Brain.*

Below: ***Plate 3*** Cartoon of Dennis Brain, Norman Del Mar, and Gareth Morris by Irene Grainger. *Morris family collection. With permission of Gareth and Patricia Morris.*

Plate 4 Dennis Brain playing his Raoux Millereau ca. 1940. Watercolor by Irene Grainger. *Private collection, with permission of the owner.*

Left: ***Plate 5*** National Gallery, London before a concert at 12.23 p.m. Reproduced from *National Gallery Concerts 10th October 1939–10th October 1944* by Dame Myra Hess, DBE, and other contributors. The book is inscribed from Arnold to Dennis Brain. *Gamble collection.*

Above right: ***Plate 6*** Neill Sanders. *With permission from Ann Meade Sanders.*

Plate 7 Horn section of the National Symphony Orchestra: Dennis Brain, Alwyn Hart, Norman Del Mar, and Leonard Fleming, 1942. *With permission from Stephen Pettitt.*

Plate 8 Royal Air Force Symphony Orchestra, arriving in the United States at the start of their tour, 1944–1945. Reproduced from the RAF tour's scrapbook, "Tour of Royal Air Force Central Band in the United States 1944–1945." *Collection, Wing Commander Gilbert Singleton MCGI, FRSA.*

Plate 9 Washington D.C. First Concert. *RAF tour scrapbook.*

Plate 10 RAF Symphony Orchestra at The Alamo, San Antonio, Texas. Dennis Brain is seen pointing his camera away from the photographer at the viewer's far left. *RAF scrapbook.*

Plate 11 Dennis Brain, photographing some puppies in a wooden bucket. *RAF scrapbook.*

Plate 12 Dennis Brain, Alfred Brain, Leonard Brain, Los Angeles, January 1945. Inscribed by Al Brain "Always to remember the wonderful evening with you January 27th 1945. Uncle Al and Aunt Straussie." *Gamble collection. With permission from Audrey Brain.*

Left: ***Plate 13*** Robert Wittenberg, Olga Wittenberg (Alfred Brain's daughter by his first marriage), Straussie, and Alfred Brain, ca. 1940. *Gamble collection. With permission from Audrey Brain.*

Above right: ***Plate 14*** Alfred Brain in profile, ca. 1940. Detail of the original photograph. *Gamble collection. With permission from Audrey Brain.*

Plate 15 RAF Symphony Orchestra, Denis Matthews (piano) and Wing Commander R. P. O'Donnell during the United States tour. *Gamble collection. With permission from Audrey Brain.*

CHAPTER

3

The Brain Quintet and Ensemble

Brain formed the Dennis Brain Wind Quintet in 1946, while still in the RAF. It later expanded and was named the Dennis Brain Wind Ensemble.

Wind Quintet

Brain's participation in new chamber music ensembles created during wartime may have given him the idea of starting his own ensemble before he was released from RAF duties. Still in uniform, he established the Dennis Brain Wind Quintet, which after demobilization in September 1946 became very busy, giving concerts in the British Isles and occasionally for broadcast.

Brain returned from his month's tour with the RAF Symphony Orchestra in Germany at the beginning of May 1946. He was too late to take part in the Quintet's first concert at the Chelsea Town Hall on April 30, 1946, with Denis Matthews at the piano. As his horn colleague Norman Del Mar remembered, he played in Brain's place and flutist Gareth Morris (*Pl. 1*) also took part. Morris's diary usually indicated "Q" for Quintet engagements, which invariably included works for other combinations. The diary is the source of many details of the Quintet's schedule.[1]

The Quintet gave their first broadcast on September 26, 1946, playing Hindemith's *Kleine Kammermusik*, Op. 24, No. 2. Brain wrote to the BBC on September 1 to confirm availability but pointing out that two of the members were on holiday. At this stage of program building, he did not know what they would be expected to play. The BBC was dictating to the musicians. Later, with Brain's increasing fame and experience, the letters show that they listened to suggestions from him concerning suitable works for broadcasting.[2]

While Brain was in Germany, Heinrich Jacoby (1909–1990), a pupil of Paul Hindemith (from 1927–1930), wrote his Quintet Op. 19 for flute, oboe, clarinet in B-flat, horn in F, and bassoon. The original score and parts give the date of composition as "20 April to 1 May 1946." Although there is no evidence that the Quintet performed this work, it is certainly a piece that was intended to be played by them and is part of a collection of manuscript and published music scores that they used for their engagements.[3]

The winter of 1946–47 was busy with concerts across the country. In addition to Brain, the original personnel (*Pl. 2*) were Morris, Leonard Brain, clarinetist Stephen Waters, and bassoonist Thomas Wightman. In this early photograph, the group is augmented by George Malcolm on the piano. Wightman emigrated to Australia in May 1950 and was for a time replaced by John Alexandra. Alexandra continued to substitute for a number of years, but eventually their regular bassoonist became Cecil James, who was also principal bassoon with both the London Baroque Ensemble and later the Philharmonia Orchestra.[4]

The following list of repertoire (1947) for the "Brain Ensemble" is from a letter dated February 2, 1947, addressed to E Lockspeiser, Esq from their first agent, Joan Ingpen (Ingpen & Williams). In the letter, the personnel noted (in addition to Brain) are Morris, Leonard Brain, Stephen Waters, Tom Wightman, with pianists Denis Matthews and Kathleen Long.

Mozart: Quintet for piano and winds in E-flat major K.452

Beethoven: Quintet for piano and winds in E-flat major Op. 16

Poulenc: Sextet for piano and winds

Roussel: *Divertissement* for flute, oboe, clarinet, bassoon, horn, and piano Op. 6

Janáček: *Mládi* (Youth) Suite

Hindemith: *Kleine Kammermusik*, Op. 24, No. 2

Ibert: *Trois Pièces Brèves*

Matthews: Quintet (Partita) for flute, oboe, clarinet, bassoon, and horn

Nielsen: Quintet for flute, oboe, clarinet, bassoon, and horn, Op. 43

Arrangements of Mozart and Haydn for wind quintet[5]

The ensemble repertoire was extended to include many more works, some especially written for them. One not listed above was Malcolm Arnold's lost quintet, which was rediscovered by Jonathan Wortley, executor for Stephen Waters, the Quintet's regular clarinetist. The manuscript was missing the horn part. In his article about the lost Arnold Quintet, Paul Harris describes its history and surmises that Brain had taken his part. The quintet was written for the wind principals of the London Philharmonic Orchestra: Richard Adeney (flute), Michael Dobson (oboe), Stephen Waters (clarinet), John Alexandra (bassoon), and Charles Gregory (horn). The manuscript is dated December 20, 1942. Waters was the link between the LPO wind principals and Brain's Quintet. After it was first broadcast with these players, it was lent to Brain and then it disappeared. Paul Harris retrieved the parts and reassembled the score. Members of the music faculty of the University of North Texas performed the quintet's US premiere on March 3, 2003, from parts newly published by Spartan Press.[6]

The Quintet gave a Wigmore Hall recital on March 4, 1947, including the Roberto Gerhard Quintet—a new and difficult work which had been written for them. Morris recalled this work and the circumstances of its composition:

> Roberto Gerhard's Quintet was written for the Dennis Brain Wind Quintet. It had been commissioned through Mrs. Hackforth who ran concerts at Cambridge at the Guildhall. She and her husband, a professor with a chair in medieval history at Cambridge, had a house in Selwyn Gardens . . . I was invited to stay the night there on one or two occasions for concerts.
>
> Gerhard was an exile from Spain who had settled in Cambridge. He also wrote a beautiful flute piece for me. Gerhard's music was Schoenbergian and also Catalan in influence. He was very busy there, giving concerts twice in a season.[7]

The winter of 1946–1947 was severe—one of the worst on record. Leonard Brain remembered the Wigmore Hall concert on March 4, 1947, when they first performed the Gerhard Quintet described above by Gareth Morris:

> You may remember in those days all the electricity was turned off except for perhaps an hour in the afternoon when we were allowed to rehearse in the hall; there was no heat, we were freezing cold, and we played the Poulenc Sextet with Poulenc himself. He sat at the piano and played very loudly, and then took all the applause. We also played the Wind Quintet by Roberto Gerhard. This, when we got to know it thoroughly, is a marvelous work, but then we'd hardly skimmed the surface of it and my wife who came to the concert said she'd never seen five such worried men—all counting like mad.[8]

This was not the first British performance of Poulenc's Sextet. It was first broadcast on the Third Programme on December 3, 1946, with the London Wind Quintet, Charles Gregory, horn. Normally the Brain Quintet rehearsed very little, but they did for new, difficult, and unfamiliar works, such as the

Gerhard. According to a concert bill, the pianist was Natasha Litvin, so Poulenc as pianist must have been a last-minute change.[9]

The authors have the parts for Poulenc's Sextet, except the piano part (Pl. 3). The only occasion Poulenc accompanied them in this piece was the Wigmore Hall concert, and each part bears Poulenc's and Brain's signatures. Various pencil annotations throughout indicate where each player takes the lead for a particular phrase. Poulenc's mood on the occasion of the Wigmore Hall concert was not good. Morris recalled that he "thumped and banged" through the Sextet and it wasn't a very enjoyable experience for any of the players. Perhaps his fingers were chilled? After the performance, Poulenc expected the Quintet members to all bow as he passed by![10]

Almost exactly a year after their first broadcast, the Quintet gave a pre-recorded recital on the Eastern Service on September 24, 1947. This included Ibert's *Trois Pièces Brèves*, the Allegretto from Matthews's *Partita* for wind quintet, and three movements from Mozart's Divertimento in B-flat, K.270.[11]

Morris, later recalling their concerts, said, "In our Wind Quintet, it was very much Dennis's ensemble and he would lead—with a look—but it was masterly. Not that anyone really leads—you talk to each other." Considering how busy they were, very little was recorded commercially. In fact, they only recorded Mozart's Quintet K.452, and Mozart's Divertimento K.289, with different players from their regular quintet. Fortunately, many BBC broadcast recordings have been preserved and recently issued on the BBC Legends label. These testify to the excellence of the Quintet's playing.[12]

An important first broadcast performance was the Gerhard Quintet on November 26, 1947, and for that occasion, Brain requested a new set of parts. He returned the BBC's contract because he found the joint fee unsatisfactory for a work of such difficulty, requiring a lot of rehearsal. It appears the BBC was prepared to give five men only forty guineas for this extremely difficult piece.[13]

Brain sometimes returned contracts querying the fees (see Chapter 6). Performing works of unique difficulty and rarity, he was certainly in a position to object to fees that invariably were fixed according to whether a work was considered to be "chamber music" or in the "solo" class. His request for ten more guineas seems fair. The broadcast on the Third Programme included other performers in works by Gerhard and Wellesz. The members of the Quintet were the same as for the first broadcast on September 26, 1946. Gerhard was asked what he would tell an audience before a performance, to which he answered that he would request that they "lend a willing ear." David Drew, who wrote the program notes for a performance given on March 3, 1952, briefly states that it was "constructed according to serial principles, and the basic seven-note series is announced by the bassoon at the beginning of the work."[14]

Not long after the Quintet was formed, Leonard Brain's wife, Audrey, remembered a bad night with a thick fog. The Quintet had not returned from an engagement. Audrey and Dennis's wife, Yvonne, were kept waiting up into the very early hours.

> It would have been Wales or England. I ought to know where they were but it was when we got terrible—fogs—really thick ones and after this particular wind quintet engagement, they should have been back about eleven. It got to about three in the morning and my sister-in-law rang me and said, "Have they come home yet?" They would travel in two cars—Leonard's car and possibly not Dennis's but somebody else's. Leonard took Wilf Parry. I said to Yvonne, "No, no sign!" Eventually at three, Leonard arrived, having got Wilf home. They had met this fog—they couldn't see a thing. Instead of going on the road, they'd gone down a track which they thought was a road and it took them right into a farm yard! So they had to extricate themselves from that and get back and find the road again. It was very difficult. Usually one car followed the other, so of course they all went down the track—might have been three cars . . . They were very worrying times because we did get awful fogs in those days.[15]

Throughout its existence, the Quintet worked with a pianist, enabling them to play works that might extend the number of five to six players for sextets or for works without flute such as the Mozart K.452 and Beethoven Op. 16. Pianists included, at the outset, Denis Matthews and Kathleen Long, and later George Malcolm (See far right in *Pl. 2*) and Wilfrid Parry. Rosalyn Tureck also played with them during the *Bienniale di Venezia Internationale di Musica Contemporanea* on September 12, 1956. That appears to have been a unique occasion. Another pianist who played with them was Lamar Crowson.[16]

Audrey Brain recalled that Malcolm fell out of a window, breaking his wrists. He fell on his hands and the wrists were broken cleanly so that eventually he was able to play without any loss of power, but it temporarily made him unable to perform with the Quintet. Parry became the next regular pianist, and his association continued with them for many years. He had already taken part in concerts with Brain since 1948.[17]

One of the first occasions when Brain performed with the Quintet, augmented with other players, was a European Service broadcast on February 18, 1948, of Janáček's *Mládi* suite for wind sextet, with Wilfred Hambleton (bass clarinet). Also on the broadcast was Roussel's *Divertissement* for winds and piano Op. 6, with Ernest Lush.[18]

A popular choice of quintet was Fricker's Op. 5, which was first broadcast on January 3, 1949. This piece received its first concert performance at a South Place Concert, Conway Hall, London on February 27 with the same players. *The Times* critic gave the following review, March 1, 1949:

> The Brain Wind Ensemble played at Conway Hall on Sunday night in the South Place concert series, and again last night in one of the Boyd Neel Monday night concerts at Chelsea Town Hall.
>
> Sunday's programme included the first performance of the Wind Quintet by Peter Racine Fricker, which in 1947 won the prize in memory of Alfred J Clements, the founder of the South Place Sunday concerts. There was evidence of serious thought behind all its four movements, with some skilful counterpoint in the canonic variations of the third, and some imaginative instrumentation in the scherzo-like Badinerie and Musette preceding it. . . .
>
> Of the two classical works, Beethoven's Quintet (Op. 16) for oboe, clarinet, bassoon, horn, and piano was the more earnest. But like Milhaud, Mozart, in his Divertimento (K.270) for two oboes, bassoon, and horn (which Anthony Baines had slightly rearranged for Mr. Brain's consort of flute, oboe, clarinet, bassoon and horn), showed that the works for wind ensemble are more digestible when short-winded and light. The players, Messrs Gareth Morris, Leonard Brain, Stephen Waters, Thomas Wightman, and Dennis Brain, were joined by Mr. George Malcolm when piano was required; each is individually reliable, and together they have achieved a most satisfactory ensemble.[19]

The Quintet, again with George Malcolm, gave an interesting broadcast on the French Service on April 6, 1949, playing Roy Douglas's *Six Dance Caricatures*, the Gerhard Quintet, and Beethoven's Quintet Op. 16. Morris noted in his diary "listen to WQ European." In this instance, he was listening to a pre-recorded program.[20]

Among the Quintet's broadcasts, a curious one occurred on September 7, 1950. The players were Morris, Sidney Sutcliffe (deputizing on this occasion for Leonard Brain), Waters, and Alexandra. The other performers were Marie Korchinska (harp), the Aeolian String Quartet (Alfred Cave and Leonard Dight, violins, Watson Forbes, viola, and John Moore, cello) with Roy Watson (double bass.) Clearly the Quintet is augmented but the name "Ensemble" is not given. The name change came later, as the BBC letters indicate. The works performed included a Rossini Quartet, Bax's Nonet for wind instruments, harp, string quartet, and double bass, and Hindemith's *Kleine Kammermusik,* Op. 24, No. 2.[21]

Morris remembered with amusement that there were occasions for the unexpected, such as the time when they were performing at Saffron Walden in 1956 and the plaster from the ceiling collapsed on top of the piano and the chair where Brain had been sitting. The work being performed at the time was Fauré's Fantasy for flute and piano, with Parry, and they carried on playing! Morris remembered, "At the end of the piece, Wilfred got up calmly to investigate the damage!"[22]

On another occasion, Morris recalled that they had finished an engagement at Sherborne in Dorset. It was about 9:30 in the evening and they had returned to the hotel for a meal. They were told, "Sorry, the dining room is closed and no meals are being served." This did not go down well—they were tired and hungry. Brain said helpfully, "I saw a fish and chip van in the square outside!" This wasn't quite the sort of cuisine they had in mind, but there was nothing else, so off they went to queue for fish and chips, which they bought in newspapers and ate in their white ties and tails in the hotel lounge![23]

Although Leonard Brain was the oboist from the outset, there were occasions when he was not available, owing to his work in the Royal Philharmonic Orchestra. Sutcliffe recalled that on such occasions, he (Sutcliffe) would "enjoy the privilege of deputising with the Wind Quintet which was always a thrilling experience." He remembered a particular occasion:

> I remember finishing recording with the Philharmonia 10–1, 2.30–5.30, at Kingsway Hall, and then climbing into Dennis's Citroen and driving some hundred miles or so to a distant music club. The concert was at 8 p.m. and I saw Dennis look at his watch whilst driving. He suggested it might be as well if I changed into tails. Whilst struggling to do this I reflected that it seemed an uncomfortable waste of time as I'd only have to wait for Dennis to change on our arrival. On reaching the hall, however, I found myself propelled on to the platform to sight read the Ibert trio, while Dennis got ready. He then came on to the platform and played superbly as always!
>
> That was an emergency, of course, but I have known Dennis to calmly wade through an excellent dinner and five minutes later play the Dukas horn piece with a panache that suggested he'd spent the whole day preparing for the event![24]

In addition to performance of concert favorites, the Quintet encouraged new compositions. The repertoire broadened and included, besides standard works, more taxing and modern compositions such as quintets by Gerhard,

Schoenberg, or Fricker and even an unpublished quintet by Dinu Lipatti, a virtuoso pianist, who had written it especially for them.[25]

The Quintet gave a concert at Wigmore Hall on January 28, 1952; *The Times* critic gave a detailed account:

> On Saturday the Dennis Brain Wind Ensemble . . . provided a programme that skilfully avoided the monotony that so easily besets the wind ensemble. It was all modern, and the five works divided themselves into three main categories, those of which the inspiration came from the instruments, those in which the music merely happened to avail itself of the possibilities of the medium and one which the backbone was some sort of programme. This last was a suite by Milhaud with the various and not easily identifiable title of *The Chimney of King René*. This was at once charming and entertaining stuff which had in some of its movements that peculiarly gallic wistfulness to be found for instance in Ravel's "Infante defunte" and occasionally in Poulenc.
>
> Fricker's and Hindemith's quintets had the most musical substance, though neither went on too long for the comfort of the ear, which is the chief danger in treating a wind ensemble as though it was a consort of strings. Ibert's Three Short Pieces (a suite, in fact) had a delicious Christmassy, nursery atmosphere, and Janáček was equally happy in evoking the village band (of superior skill, of course) in the sextet, *Mládi* (the additional instrument being the bass clarinet). The players showed their musicianship—their skill can be taken for granted—in the manipulation of blend and balance, the adjustment of solo line, accompanying figuration, block harmony in the flux of tone.[26]

The Milhaud was later recorded with the Quintet by BBC Transcription Service at an Aldeburgh Festival recital on June 22, 1955. This has been issued most recently on the BBC Legends CD label. Ibert would surely have been horrified to read the critic's comments about his music being "Christmassy" and having "nursery atmosphere." Ibert's piece is witty, light-hearted, and delightfully rhythmical in a way that is clearly intended to entertain. There is nothing of Christmas or the nursery about it. The horn plays gently in the background, unobtrusively, and occasionally leads, but for the most part it is the flute that leads, as normally is the case with a quintet. Ingpen, their first agent, commented that *Mládi* was a particular favorite of Brain's.[27]

The Quintet gave the first English broadcast of Schoenberg's Quintet Op. 26 on March 9, 1952. This transmission took place a few days after they had played the piece at a "Society for Twentieth-Century Music" concert at Hampstead Town Hall in North London on March 3. It was the second work to be composed in Schoenberg's new twelve-tone system but had been neglected in performance for many years. Brain's Quintet had, therefore, given it a rare airing.[28]

Brain wrote to the BBC on February 27, 1952, requesting an extra rehearsal, which was agreed. Audrey Brain explained that the Quintet rarely spent much time rehearsing unless a piece was especially difficult. She remembered that the Roberto Gerhard Quintet was one such piece and was also on this concert. Leonard remembered that in the two performances of the Schoenberg Quintet that they gave, his brother conducted "every bar of that music either with his eyebrow or with the bell of his horn or his little finger. . . ."[29]

Other works performed over the years included quintets by Francis Chagrin, Egon Wellesz, Franz Reizenstein, and Kenneth Essex. Fricker's Quintet was a favorite and is a delightful piece with a declamatory horn solo in the Canonic Variations. Morris recalled the circumstances leading to the composition: "It's got a terrific badinerie in it. I used to play the Badinerie of Bach [the final movement of the B minor suite for flute and strings, BWV 1067] an awful lot. He said to me, 'Would you like another badinerie for the Wind Quintet?' I said, 'That would be nice, yes.' Some badinerie, isn't it? A good piece. We played it quite often."[30]

It does indeed have a fine badinerie with virtuosic playing required especially for the flutist. Pettitt relates how Fricker's Quintet first came to the public's notice:

> Peter Racine Fricker, one of Dennis's old schoolfriends at St Paul's, completed a Wind Quintet in June 1947 and sent a score of it to Dennis, more for his comments than anything else. To his surprise, he opened the *Radio Times* one day to find the work scheduled for a broadcast that week, in January 1949, the first work of his ever to be presented by the BBC. Dennis's kindness to an old schoolfriend did more than give the Quintet a wider public than it might otherwise have had. It won Fricker the Clements Memorial Prize and thus launched him on a successful composing career. Dennis's Quintet played the new work numerous times from then on, both in England and in Europe.[31]

The Quintet went abroad for the West Berlin Festival in September 1951 to record for Radio in the American Sector. In Berlin, they were joined by Conrad Hansen for Mozart's Quintet K.452 and also played the quintets of Fricker, Ibert, and Milhaud. Leonard remembered the occasion:

> In 1951, we played in the West Berlin Festival, and we went along to record the Mozart Quintet in what had been Siemens' private concert hall in the back of his house. It was one of those September days when the temperature

dropped right down. Now in Germany the pianos are tuned to 445 and we're used to playing at 440; we couldn't get up to the pitch. The piano-tuner was standing by—a little man who looked rather like Giapetto—he came along with his bag of tuning forks and he said, "Please choose the one!" We chose the one, and he said "Go away." We came back in half an hour, and there was the piano, beautifully in tune at the pitch we could play at.[32]

Wind Ensemble

With the augmentation of the Dennis Brain Quintet for the broadcasting of a wider repertoire of works came the suggestion that the name should be changed to Dennis Brain Wind Ensemble. The earliest indication of this name change is in a letter from Brain to the BBC on June 19, 1951:

> Thank you so much for your copy of our programme on July 12th.
>
> I have one or two suggestions as to the presentation of it, as you will see from the enclosed sheet; namely that Mr Fuller & Mr Cockrill should be placed first & followed by the members of the Ensemble playing in the hall & then the "extras."
>
> I would, on thinking it over, prefer the title left in unless you think it is going to be too much, in which case perhaps it would be better to include the names in the order which I have numbered them.
>
> The reason for the title "Ensemble" rather than "Quintet" is that the personnel can then fluctuate, according to the programme, & not be tied down.[33]

The "extras" mentioned in the letter were Gervase de Peyer, Peter Parry, and Aubrey Brain as second to his son, in a rare appearance with them. The works performed were also not standard repertoire but new works, including Phyllis Tate's *Songs of Sundry Natures* and Seiber's Serenade Op. 2 for two clarinets, two horns, and two bassoons.[34]

Brain sent a letter to Denis Stevens of the BBC in November 1951 with a list of works for wind instruments that he had gleaned from his own music library. Stevens had suggested to Brain that he make such a list. This provides a rare glimpse of the contents of Brain's library, which after his death remained for many years in obscurity before it was sold at Sotheby's in 1996. The bulk of the collection of approximately six hundred and seventy-five items, including original autographed scores of works written for him or for his father, is now again in private hands. The works for wind that Brain mentions in the following letter to Stevens on November 3, 1951, are listed in Appendix A.

> You may remember, a short time ago, your suggestion to me, to send a note to you of various works for wind combinations.
>
> At last I have searched through my music, and the results of my findings are in the enclosed list, with appropriate timings.
>
> I hope you will find them of some use. [35]

Stevens replied with some interesting suggestions, but what came of these plans for future broadcasts is not known.

Members of the Quintet, without flute, took part in a broadcast on April 3, 1953, of works by Mozart, Schubert, and Tomasi. The pieces included part of the Schubert Octet, a trio by Tomasi for oboe, clarinet, and bassoon (*Concert Champêtre*), and Mozart's Serenade in C minor K.388.[36]

The deliberation over the changing of the name continued for several years. Here is another letter from Brain to Carrell at the BBC on the subject:

> I have much pleasure in confirming my recent conversation with Mr Middlemiss, that my group should, from now, be called the "Dennis Brain Wind Ensemble," thereby making it possible to augment or diminish as necessary, that either George Malcolm or Wilfrid Parry should be included in the group when required, i.e. for the Mozart or Beethoven Piano and Wind Quintets, etc., and that for our first broadcast in their new form one extra rehearsal will be allowed, to be arranged with Mrs. Wallis at a time mutually convenient.
>
> My object in this is to be in a position to play music for any wind combination, and piano, should the occasion arise.[37]

The Quintet broadcast on September 22, 1953, for the Third Programme another work that they rarely played: Nielsen's Wind Quintet Op. 48. This is a delightful, lyrical, and energetic piece which sadly Brain and his Ensemble never recorded.[38]

Always keen to promote new works for the repertoire, Brain wrote to the BBC in support of Kenneth Essex's Quintet, which had been first broadcast by them on August 22, 1949. The first we hear of this piece is in a letter dated July 2, 1946, from Essex to the Reading Panel of the BBC, enclosing a private recording of it performed by (in addition to Brain) Lionel Solomon (flute), Florence Wolf (oboe), Bernard Walton (clarinet), and Paul Draper (bassoon). We do not know the present whereabouts of this recording, if it has survived.[39]

The Gerhard Quintet received another airing on March 24, 1954, but it appears from his diary that Morris was unable to play. The program was recorded and broadcast again on December 20, 1954.[40]

The Ensemble's first and only appearance at the York Festival on June 26, 1954, at the York City Art Gallery ended with the Fricker Quintet. The same program was played the next day at Kenwood Orangery, Hampstead. The concert of varied pieces, not simply quintets but also for horn and piano and other combinations, was well received. The critic of the *York Evening Press* commented that the City Art Gallery was packed to capacity and the audience listened appreciatively to "wonderful playing." The players listed included Sutcliffe, who was deputizing for Leonard Brain. Otherwise, they were the usual team, joined by Parry. The critic of the *Northern Echo* commented that "Mr. Dennis Brain has grouped around him a quintet of extremely fine artists, and the Ensemble were delightful to hear."[41]

The Ensemble performed the Fricker Quintet again, with the first performance of Fricker's Sonata for horn and piano, at Conway Hall, Red Lion Square, Holborn, on March 20, 1955. They also performed an arrangement for wind quintet by Anthony Baines, made especially for them, of Mozart's Divertimento in B-flat K.270, and Mozart's Quintet for piano and winds K.452.[42]

Brain was a regular artist at Aldeburgh's Festival, and on June 22, 1955, in Aldeburgh Parish Church, his Ensemble performed a variety of works by Mozart (K.270 arranged by Baines), Beethoven (Quintet Op. 16), and Milhaud (*La Cheminée du roi Renée*) in a recital with Peter Pears and Benjamin Britten. Brain wrote to the BBC concerning the order of the works to perform and reminded them of their change of bassoonist: Cecil James, who had been playing with them for a number of years.[43]

Not satisfied with modern works written for them, they also explored rare and little performed works, for example, an unusual program of unpublished wind quintets by Johann Christian Bach and trios by Handel (manuscript) and Mozart (K.229, Boosey & Hawkes) on July 13 and 14, 1955. In addition to Brain, the players were Stephen Waters and Archibald Jacob, Neill Sanders, and Cecil James. The first program comprised the Quintet No. 1 in E-flat, Trio in D for two clarinets and horn by Handel, and J. C. Bach's Quintet No. 2 in E-flat. The second program, on July 14, comprised J. C. Bach's Quintet No. 3 in B-flat, Divertimento No. 2 in B-flat K.229 by Mozart, and J. C. Bach's Quintet No. 4 in E-flat. Both programs were recorded. Stanley Sadie, who discovered these quintets in the library of the Royal Irish Academy of Music in Dublin, later gave a full account of their history and discovery.[44]

The Ensemble was busy in 1956 with concerts and broadcasts, including a concert at Farnham in Kent in January, Brighton in March, a brief tour of Ireland in January, and a broadcast of wind octets by Alfred Uhl and Mozart

(Serenade K.388) in February. Brain, writing to the BBC on August 15, 1955, mentions the wind octet by Uhl "for the same instruments as those of Mozart" and as a possible partner to one of the Mozart works.[45]

The Ensemble made its first tour of Italy in 1956, arranged with Mrs. Erede in Turin. It was a short tour, from March 26 to April 11. They visited Milan (March 26), Palermo (April 3), Messina (April 4), Florence (April 7), L'Aquila (April 8), Rome (April 9), and Turin (April 11). In Messina, a woman in the audience wore a black shiny dress that crackled every time she moved, and it was jokingly suggested that she was concealing a packet of crisps (potato chips)! Parry went with the group as their pianist in the Beethoven and Mozart Quintets.

As Morris recalled, no radio or television broadcasts were made of the tour. At the Piccola Scala Theatre, Milan, on March 26, Morris was the soloist in Mozart's Flute Concerto in G major K.313. Four of the winds also performed Mozart's Sinfonia Concertante K.297b conducted by Nino Signanoni. The program was repeated the next day at the same theatre. Morris recalled, "We may have taken the Fricker but I don't think the Italians would have appreciated it!"[46]

They suffered badly with dry or sore throats during the tour and discovered that an Italian brandy called "Stock" was the perfect cure. Parry recalled:

> Driving back one day (incidentally it was his [Brain's] car and my car—we got a wind quintet between us, myself and my wife), driving from Naples to Rome and we had arranged to stop at a little place on the West coast of Italy called Terracina, for tea. I suddenly spotted Dennis through my driving mirror and this brought out all my sporting instincts. I thought, "now whatever happens, he mustn't overtake me." Well, luckily I did get into the place first—the car park—and Dennis came in about five seconds later, got out of his car, came across to me and said, "Congratulations, Stirling!" For those of you who don't know (I'm sure most of you do), of course he was referring to [race car driver] Stirling Moss.[47]

Back in England later in the month, four members of the Ensemble broadcast on the Home Service on April 26, 1956. It was part of a series of nine weekly concerts of chamber music to celebrate the bicentenary of Mozart's birth. The work was Mozart's Quintet in E-flat K.452 before an invited audience at Broadcasting House. Lamar Crowson was the pianist. The day before, at Goldsmiths' Hall, London, they had played the same work with Kathleen Long.[48]

It was 1956, their tenth anniversary. The occasion was celebrated with a concert at Wigmore Hall on April 30 that included a new work written for them—Gordon Jacob's Sextet for piano and winds, in memory of Brain's father, who had died in September of the previous year. Proceeds from the concert went towards the Aubrey Brain Memorial Trust to promote a wind scholarship, as stated on a concert bill. Unreserved tickets were three shillings and reserved were six and nine shillings.[49]

The quintets in the concert included Denis Matthews's *Partita* in F major and Brain's own arrangement of Mozart's Fantasia in F minor and major K.594, originally for mechanical organ. A work written for Aubrey Brain in 1938, York Bowen's Sonata for horn and piano Op. 101, was also included, with Bowen at the piano. The following review appeared in *The Times* on May 1, 1956:

> The concert given by the Dennis Brain Wind Ensemble (Messrs. Gareth Morris, Leonard Brain, Stephen Waters, Dennis Brain, and Cecil James) at Wigmore Hall last night was not only a celebration marking the tenth birthday of this highly skilled group but was also designed to raise funds for the projected Aubrey Brain Memorial Scholarship for wind players.
>
> Of outstanding interest in the programme was the new sextet for piano and wind, which Dr. Gordon Jacob had written for the occasion. Dedicated to the memory of Aubrey Brain (Mr. Dennis Brain's father), the work (or much of it) grows from the opening theme ABEBA, derived from the musical letters in his name, and has a strong elegiac feeling in its prelude and epilogue, as also in the central cortège of the five movements. But Dr. Jacob has rightly also found a place for vivacity, grace, and wit in the music, so that, with brilliantly effective scoring in its favour as well, the sextet is assured of a place in the repertory.
>
> Equally welcome on this occasion was the sonata for horn and piano, Op. 101, written by York Bowen in 1938 for Aubrey Brain. Its warmly felt romantic idiom may indicate an accepting rather than an exploratory state of mind; nevertheless the music is immediately pleasing to the ear, and is extraordinarily well disposed for both horn and piano. The sonata was played with generous imaginative response and superb control by Mr. Dennis Brain and the composer at the piano.
>
> Sentiment crept into the programme again with the inclusion of a partita in F major for wind quintet by Denis Matthews, a close friend of the group who appeared in their first concert 10 years ago. Though only a student work, several times paying overt tribute to French models, it leaves no doubt what the composer Mr. Matthews could have been had the piano not claimed him.
>
> There were also a fluent neo-classical concerto for flute, oboe, clarinet, bassoon, and piano by the contemporary Italian composer Ghedini,

> and a wind quintet arrangement of Mozart's fine first fantasia in F minor for mechanical organ. Both Mr. Wilfrid Parry and Mr. George Malcolm appeared as assisting pianists, as well as Mr. York Bowen. The performances throughout the evening were all of birthday excellence.[50]

The Ensemble played Brain's quintet arrangement of Mozart's Fantasia K.594 for mechanical organ several times. Leonard Brain sent the parts to Oxford University Press with a view to their publication in 1975, but although a signed and dated Memorandum of Agreement has survived, nothing appears to have come of the venture.[51]

The group also returned to Italy (Venice) that year for a concert on September 12 to play at the Ca' Giustinian-Sala Delle Colonne. This was the 19th Festival *Bienniale di Venezia Internationale di Musica Contemporanea*. The concert the ensemble gave there, with pianist Rosalyn Tureck, included Wallingford Riegger's Concerto for piano and winds, Fricker's Sonata for horn and piano, and his Quintet.[52]

A new work, *Dialogue No. 4* for winds by Venetian composer Gian-Francesco Malipiero, had been written for them to play at the Festival. This was later recalled by bassoonist Cecil James:

> I well remember taking part in the performances of this work by this very distinguished Italian composer. It's a shortish work in one movement but very effectively written, of course, for the winds and we gave the first performance in Italy. In fact it was in Venice, in the composer's home town and he actually was in the audience and later we gave the first performance over here which was at the Edinburgh Festival.[53]

Morris recalled an incident at the rehearsal for this concert. The Ensemble was rehearsing and had reached a pause. Pianist Harriet Cohen came down center aisle, mounted the stage where they were seated and addressed them, "Wonderful to see you all!" Turning to Brain she said, "What? No kiss?" Her face was white with make-up and she bent down and kissed him on the cheek and then walked off. Brain was speechless but Morris imagined that if he had said anything it would have been, "Oh dear!"[54]

Their concert received the following review in *Strad*:

> In a concert which did not come up to expectations, the Brain Wind Quintet presented a new work by Gian-Francesco Malipiero. Following a rather dull piece by Peter Racine Fricker, Malipiero's quintet started out with promise and a feeling of gaiety, but it wore itself out en route. An interesting concerto for piano and wind quintet by Wallingford Riegger was given a surprisingly pedestrian interpretation.[55]

Clearly, the critics were not all in agreement about the quality of Brain's Ensemble. This criticism of Fricker's Quintet is not a fair one, in our opinion. A pity that this appears to be the only review of that concert, so we do not know if it was merely personal bias or reflected the playing that day.

Back again in England, the Ensemble gave a recital at the Plaza Theatre, Newbury, on November 29, 1956, that included, according to the concert program, "Divertimento No. 4 An Oubradous" by Mozart for oboe, clarinet, and bassoon. The printer had misread Brain's handwriting which actually read, "Arr. Oubradous." Also in the program were Beethoven's Sonata (with Parry), Poulenc's Trio for oboe, bassoon, and piano, *Villanelle* by Dukas, and Mozart's Quintet K.452. The signatures of the artists on the concert program (Pl. 4) are Brain, Parry, Waters, Sutcliffe, and Alexandra. A sudden change of personnel had occurred after the program was printed. Leonard Brain's name is printed. It's curious to find Alexandra playing with them at a time when James was their regular bassoonist. Perhaps he also had a conflicting engagement. The program also refers to the group with the unusual title, "Brain Wind Quartet and Pianoforte."[56]

From time to time, Brain wrote to the BBC with suggestions and lists concerning what repertoire to broadcast for his Ensemble. As mentioned above, two works written for them were the Gordon Jacob Sextet, in memory of Aubrey Brain, and Malipiero's *Dialogue No. 4* for wind quintet. In the following letter to Gould on November 28, 1956, Brain adds other works for quintet in their repertoire:

> I have pleasure, at Mr Cook's suggestion, in sending details of two works "peculiar" to my ensemble which I hope may be of interest to you.
>
> The Gordon Jacob Sextet was written for the ensemble's 10th anniversary as a tribute to my father, and the Malipiero, for the concert which we gave this year at the Venice Festival.
>
> We have also in our repertoire, the Quintet of Franz Reizenstein and Divertimento of Francis Chagrin.
>
> **Gordon Jacob Sextet for Piano & Wind Quintet.** 25 minutes
>
> In Memoriam Aubrey Brain
>
> 1. Elegiac Prelude
> 2. Scherzo
> 3. Cortege
> 4. Minuet & Trio
> 5. Rondo with Epilogue

G. F. Malipiero. 8 minutes
Dialogue, for Wind Quintet
In one movement

Franz Reizenstein Wind Quintet. 15 minutes app

1. Andante con moto
2. Molto vivace
3. Intermezzo. Andantino
4. Allegretto moderato

Francis Chagrin Divertimento Wind Quintet. App 10 minutes

1. Allegro molto vivace
2. Andantino
3. Allegretto scherzando[57]

The Ensemble appeared at the Salzburg Festival on July 30, 1957. Karajan, then Director of the Festival, was in the audience at the Mozarteum. A recording of this concert was discovered by Lynch during the course of researching this book; it is preserved in the Austrian Radio Archives. The concert included some old favorites: Mozart's Divertimento in B-flat K.270 and Quintet K.452, Hindemith's *Kleine Kammermusik*, Op. 24, No. 2, and the Poulenc Sextet. Parry was the pianist in the Mozart K.452 and Poulenc.[58]

The same program was performed at the Edinburgh Festival on August 22, 1957, at Usher Hall. It was not recorded, but their second and final concert of that year was recorded and was broadcast by the BBC on the Home Service on August 24. The concert included the new work written for them by Malipiero, *Dialogue No. 4*, Beethoven's Quintet, Dukas's *Villanelle*, Marais's *Le Basque*, and finally, Fricker's Quintet. The whole recital has been preserved in the BBC archives and demonstrates that the ensemble maintained high standards in live performance. The Fricker Quintet performance in this recital was issued by the BBC on their Legends label in 2006. The music critic of *The Times* was at the concert and gave the following favorable review:

> The Dennis Brain Wind Ensemble has also given a couple of concerts, one in the Usher Hall on Thursday evening and one in the Freemasons' Hall yesterday morning. Their basic constitution is a sextet of woodwind, horn and piano. They played three quintets, Beethoven's without flute and with piano, Fricker's and Malipiero's with flute and without piano. Wind music aims less at conveying ideas and emotions than at constructing patterns.

> Fricker's ingenious work in four short movements therefore seemed more positive than Malipiero's discursive single-movement Dialogue. That the fluent expertise of Mr. Brain and his colleagues in executing these exercises is note-spinning is a source of musical pleasure.[59]

Christopher Grier, music critic of *The Scotsman*, reporting on the last concerts, noted a preference for the acoustics of Freemasons' Hall over Usher Hall for the Ensemble's concert on August 24.

> The second of the Dennis Brain Wind Ensemble's concerts was given in the Freemasons' Hall on Saturday morning, a change of site which was all to the good—especially when the piano was involved as in Beethoven's early Quintet in E-flat. The resulting blend was undoubtedly superior to that of the Mozart Quintet in the Usher Hall a few days ago.
>
> A felicitous performance of the Beethoven Quintet, with its heart easing slow movement, was only a prelude to the much sterner pleasures that lay ahead. Malipiero's 4th Dialogue that came next was one of a series of seven works dedicated to the memory of Manuel de Falla. It is a piece of musical dialectic in which each instrumental speaker is almost self-consciously aware of its own identity though prepared, for the sake of artistic unity, to allow for some mutual concessions. The arguments are pungently and lucidly expressed, and combine to make an attractive example of well reasoned disputation. It was having its first performance in this country by the same ensemble who gave its premiere in Venice last year.[60]

Leonard Brain arranged with BBC Transcription Service for the last Edinburgh Festival broadcast to be preserved on record and used for future broadcasts. A set of three discs survive in their original yellow BBC Transcription Service covers. On the last record, which has the Fricker Quintet as the final item of the Edinburgh Festival recital, Leonard has written in pencil on the cover, "last grooves."[61]

Left: ***Plate 1*** Dennis Brain with Gareth Morris, ca.1950. *With permission from Gareth Morris and Patricia Morris.*

Plate 2 Dennis Brain Wind Quintet, with George Malcolm (piano). No date. *Reproduced with permission from* The Herald, *Gareth Morris, and Patricia Morris. Copyright* The Herald, *114 West Street Farnham, Kent, England.*

Plate 3 Poulenc Sextet. Detail of the horn part, showing the signatures of Dennis Brain and Francis Poulenc. *Collection of the authors.*

NEWBURY & DISTRICT ARTS SOCIETY

CONCERT

Brain Wind Quartet
and Pianoforte

LEONARD BRAIN	Oboe
STEPHEN WATERS	Clarinet
JOHN ALEXANDER	Bassoon
DENNIS BRAIN	Horn
WILFRID PARRY	Piano

PLAZA THEATRE

Thursday, November 29th

7 p.m.

G. W. SIMPSON & SON, LTD., PRINTERS, NEWBURY.

Plate 4 Concert program, Plaza Theatre, Newbury, Berkshire, England, November 29, 1956. Signed by the players. Leonard Brain's name was printed in the program but the oboist was Sidney Sutcliffe, who occasionally substituted. *Collection of Tony Catterick.*

CHAPTER

4

Royal Philharmonic Orchestra

Brain was principal horn in the Royal Philharmonic Orchestra starting with its founding in 1946. His participation declined because of other obligations, particularly to the Philharmonia Orchestra, and in his last years was only sporadic.

Formation of the Royal Philharmonic

Brain had already been principal horn of the Philharmonia Orchestra for about eleven months before Sir Thomas Beecham (*Pl. 1*) formed the Royal Philharmonic Orchestra. Brain continued his commitments to the Philharmonia and by very skilful scheduling was able to maintain steady solo and orchestral activities in both for some years. He played at the RPO's first concert at the Davis Theatre, Croydon, on September 15, 1946 (*Pl. 2*). The horn section at the outset was Norman Del Mar, Roy White, and Frank Probyn in addition to Brain. The music critic of the *Monthly Musical Record* gave the following enthusiastic account of the first two concerts:

> Sir Thomas Beecham, having parted company with the London Philharmonic, has organized a new orchestra, The Royal Philharmonic by name, which was launched at a concert given in the enormous Davis Theatre at Croydon. This is a scene too large for ideal music-making, but our age is one, it seems, in which nothing less than an audience of 4,000 can pay for an orchestral concert. With Sir Thomas exerting all his charm, the first two concerts of the season were magnificent. John Pennington led the orchestra, which boasts admirable players in all departments.

> On the first afternoon Delius's *Over the Hills* was given an outstanding performance, and on the second, *Sibelius's Tapiola.*[1]

It is possible to imagine how beautiful the horn solos in particular must have sounded in that first concert in Delius's *Over the Hills and Far Away* because it was recorded a few years later when Brain still led the horns. It is a piece particularly rich in solos.[2]

Brain remained principal until he found the commitments for both orchestras too much and he had to choose between them. He chose the Philharmonia, but continued, when engagements permitted, to take part in a few of the RPO concerts until the end of 1956. Many now celebrated gramophone recordings were made with Beecham and the RPO, and until about December 1953 (with the exception of 1949), Brain is heard in the horn solos of works by Berlioz, Delius, Dvorak, Haydn, Mendelssohn, Mozart, Paisiello, Sibelius, Wagner, and others.[3]

Brain's colleagues in the RPO included clarinetist Basil Tschaikov, known as Nick. Tschaikov recalled:

> Dennis was one of Beecham's favourite players and I remember that as Tommy walked onto the platform at the beginning of a rehearsal his eyes would swivel round to glance as to whether Dennis was there that day. If he was, Tommy would smile to himself, obviously pleased.
>
> Even so, I remember that on one occasion Dennis had told the orchestral manager he would not be available for a concert when *Ein Heldenleben*, which has a very important part for the principal horn, was on the programme because he had already accepted an engagement to play one of the Mozart horn concertos with another orchestra. When Beecham was informed, he said, "Please tell Mr Brain that he either makes himself available for our concert, or he will not play with the orchestra again."
>
> Dennis did not do the concert and though he was one of Sir Thomas's favourite players, he did not play in the orchestra again for a year or more. Beecham would rather let him go than have his authority challenged.[4]

This took place in December 1948 when Beecham and the RPO returned to London from a tour of Bradford, Leeds, Manchester, Hanley, and Wolverhampton. *Heldenleben* was in the program during this short tour, and the London concert that marked the end of the tour was at Royal Albert Hall on December 15. Brain's engagements clashed and for a year in 1949, when White assumed the post of principal, Brain had to leave the RPO and was back again in 1950 for only a few concerts until his commitments elsewhere became less demanding.[5]

Brain made a recording with Beecham of *Ein Heldenleben*, which the authors believe has one of Brain's loveliest recorded orchestral solos in the coda. Tschaikov remembered the special talents that Brain showed in orchestral music:

> During the 60 years I have now been in and around music, especially the orchestral world, he stands out as one of the very greatest players on any wind instrument. I continue to listen to recordings we made when he was in the orchestra and his playing if only of a few notes still gives me enormous delight. In the 1947 recording of *Ein Heldenleben*, by Richard Strauss, there are some wonderful examples of this talent. In particular towards the end of that work where there is a lovely duet between the violin and the horn that is of breath-taking loveliness. On this recording this passage is played with great sensitivity by the then Leader, Oscar Lampe, and the late, great Dennis Brain. It was taking part in performances like that, when Beecham combined masculine tenderness, subtle rubato, sensitive phrasing and dynamic outbursts of energy, that made working with him something very special indeed.[6]

Beecham chose works, such as this *Ein Heldenleben* or the fairly obscure Goldmark's *Rustic Wedding Symphony*, that nobody else recorded at that time. He also worked with the best players who could be found and, as his principal clarinetist Jack Brymer remarked, made them play "better than their best."[7]

Beecham laid plans in 1946 for a Delius Festival. Six concerts with the Royal Philharmonic and a seventh with the BBC Symphony Orchestra were to begin on October 26 at Royal Albert Hall, marking the London debut of the RPO. First performances of works by Delius included *Sur les Cimes*, Prelude to Act 3 of *Folkeraadet*, Act 3 of *Koanga*, and Act 3 of *A Village Romeo and Juliet*.[8]

An interesting concert took place at the People's Palace on February 22, 1947. It included Paisiello's Overture to *Nina o la pazza d'amore*, with its brief but heroic horn solo, and Strauss's *Bourgeois Gentilhomme* (suite) which has ample soloistic opportunities. Both these works were recorded during a session the next day and at later sessions. Brain is heard in both works. Although it is not known for certain if he was playing at that concert, he most probably was. On January 21, 1947, he wrote a letter to Miss Nisbett of the BBC, stating that he was "already engaged on February 22nd and unable to accept an engagement in the Schubert Octet."[9]

The RPO and Beecham gave concerts in the spring of 1947 at the Drury Lane Theatre that included Mozart's Divertimento K.131, which they soon recorded for HMV in November. As part of a year marking the centenary of

Mendelssohn's death, on November 2 among other works Beecham conducted the incidental music to *A Midsummer Night's Dream*. In the Nocturne, Brain attracted the attention of the *Daily Telegraph* critic who wrote, "Mr Brain sounded notes of rare and lovely mellowness." The critic of *The Times* commented on "some consummate hornplaying" in the Nocturne from *A Midsummer Night's Dream*.[10] Curiously, Brain never recorded the Nocturne with Beecham, but he later made two recordings of it with the Philharmonia.[11]

Richard Strauss was present for rehearsals and concerts at the Strauss Festival, Drury Lane, in October 1947. The critic of the *Monthly Musical Record* gave an account:

> At Drury Lane, Sir Thomas Beecham launched a series of Sunday concerts with two Strauss programmes (October 5th and 12th), at which the venerable composer was present. No building in London makes a more satisfactory concert hall, and the Royal Philharmonic Orchestra, now in its second year, must on the strength of the concerts be allowed very high place among metropolitan orchestras. *Don Quixote* and *Ein Heldenleben* were superbly played, and perhaps with a finer delicacy than the conductor used to obtain in his fiery youth . . . The programmes were noteworthy for leaving the beaten track. From Sir Thomas we were given the *Bourgeois Gentilhomme* suite, the last scene from *Ariadne* and an extract from *Intermezzo*. . . .[12]

A private off-the-air recording of the Intermezzo from the concert on the October 12 broadcast by the BBC exists. Brain's tone is heard in the orchestra.[13]

In the same year, Beecham and the RPO gave broadcasts in June and July of Berlioz's *The Trojans*, and the BBC recorded the second part of the opera from a Third Programme broadcast on July 4. Brymer joined the orchestra as its first clarinet for the first studio broadcast of this epic piece and described it as his "baptism of fire." A private recording on acetates preserves parts of the broadcast performances. Brain played superbly in the *Royal Hunt and Storm* as did the whole orchestra, spurred on and inspired by electrifying conducting from Sir Thomas. Dennis's brother thought that the final bars of that horn solo "were one of the most beautiful examples of horn-playing he had ever heard." Brain, playing *pianissimo*, was expected to play ever quieter by Beecham until the sound was almost inaudible, yet he managed to keep the last note constant, slowly dying away.[14]

The RPO went from strength to strength, with some changes in the woodwind personnel. The orchestra first appeared at Glyndebourne with Beecham in July 1948 for four Mozart concerts. Dennis could not be present for all four, but he played with Terence MacDonagh, Brymer, and Gwydion Brooke in Mozart's Sinfonia Concertante K.297b on July 14. He performed

Mozart's Concerto No. 4 with the Municipal Philharmonic in Guildford on July 15 and returned to Glyndebourne on July 16 as soloist in Mozart's Concerto No. 2.[15]

Sir Thomas invited Brain back to his old job in early 1950, and Brain agreed to return for concerts and gramophone recording sessions, but he could not commit himself fully, so his position was shared with Alan Hyde and Charles Gregory. White, who had occupied the principal chair for 1949, returned to Australia. This year was also the start of a new Glyndebourne series of Mozart operas (*Cosi fan tutte* and *Don Giovanni*) conducted by Fritz Busch. Excerpts of *Cosi* were commercially recorded by HMV in the weeks following Glyndebourne and in one of these, Brain is heard in the taxing obbligato of *Per Pietà*, sung by Sena Jurinac.[16]

Brymer remembered touring with Brain while they were both in the RPO. The following reminiscence suggests how frenetic their concert schedule could be:

> The travel on these tours was tedious and uncomfortable, in badly sprung and draughty motor-coaches. As a result, several of us made our own arrangements, and managed to sleep at home, if only briefly. Dennis Brain and I were together in this all the time. I left my car at his Hillingdon home, after which we would proceed at great speed in his to Leicester, Nottingham and Birmingham in turn, coming home each night at about 2 a.m. and leaving the next afternoon . . . Dennis was such a superb driver and such relaxed company that I always found it possible to sleep on the return run with him, simply leaving him to the occupation he enjoyed almost as much as his playing—tearing through the night in a fast car.[17]

Brain's commitments to the Philharmonia increased, and at times his absence from the RPO was keenly felt. In Usher Hall at the Edinburgh Festival on August 27, 1950, Beecham conducted a performance of the Haydn Symphony No. 40, which has a very taxing obbligato for the two horns in the minuet and trio. Sir Thomas looked over at the first desk of the horns to find that Brain wasn't there. Rather than risk a missed note, he left out the whole of the movement![18] Beecham had made an excellent recording of the Haydn Symphony No. 40 for EMI in 1948. *Gramophone* critic Edward Sackville-West thought it "among the very best of the Haydn recordings." It is very fine, and the horn-playing by Brain and Ian Beers in the minuet and trio could not be bettered.[19]

Another successful recording that especially highlighted his skillful and beautiful playing was Rossini's *Cambiale di Matrimonio* Overture. He plays the fast repeated solos slightly differently each time, no doubt paying particular attention to any markings by Sir Thomas on his part. Lionel Salter wrote the first review for *Gramophone*: "The performance here is full of clarity and vivacity, the horn solos (which almost certainly owe their origin to the fact that Rossini's father was a horn-player) are admirable, and the recording is fresh and realistic."[20] Of all the recordings that feature Brain's artistry in the orchestra, this one shines as one of the most outstanding. He never recorded this work again.

United States Tour, 1950

In the autumn of 1950, Beecham finished preparations for a tour of the United States with the RPO. It had been his dream for a long time to take an orchestra that he had formed on such a tour. He planned fifty-two concerts in forty-five cities in sixty-four days. It was a huge success. The orchestra had been booked on the luxury passenger liner *Queen Mary*. Brain was keen to go on the trip, and his wife went with him. In addition to Brain, the horn section during the tour comprised Ian Beers (second), Denis Mason (third), Frank Probyn (fourth), Sydney Coulston (fifth), and James Brown (sixth).[21]

The tour received some publicity from Brymer in an article in which he described the types of instruments used by the woodwinds and the brass that helped to give the RPO its distinctive sound. He described Brain's instrument:

> For solo work he invariably uses the French instrument—a fine old Raoux . . . and modified only last year to play in B-flat, with a cut-out valve which raises the pitch to C natural. He does not now use the F horn at all, although he was trained on the instrument and used it until 1948. He also, however, uses a German system horn with apparent unconcern, and prefers it in some works wherein he feels its own particular sound is called for.[22]

A souvenir booklet of the tour (*Pl. 3*) gives the concert itinerary, starting on October 13 in Hartford, Connecticut, and finishing on December 15 in Bethlehem, Pennsylvania. The list of works performed during the tour indicates that not only Brain performed concertos, but also Beecham's wife, Betty Humby Beecham (piano) and some of the other principals: David McCallum (violin), Gerald Jackson (flute), Terence MacDonagh (oboe), Brymer (clarinet), Gwydion Brooke (bassoon), and Anthony Pini (cello). Brymer remembered how the public expected to see the top players with such a prestigious orchestra:

> The soloists within the orchestra were not difficult to find—with such names as Dennis Brain, Anthony Pini, David McCallum, Terence MacDonagh,

> Gerald Jackson and Gwydion Brooke, this was hardly surprising. Most of them played more than one concerto on the tour, which in itself wasn't surprising in three months of programmes. What would now be considered as amazing was the fact that they always played after a long day of bus travel, and invariably played the rest of the programme as well as their concerto. They were the principals, and if you paid to hear the RPO, you paid to hear them.[23]

Aware of the wider-bore "German" horn used by American orchestras, Brain decided to take both his Raoux horn and the Alexander B-flat single that he had bought earlier that year. The Orchestra left Southampton on October 7. In addition to solo concertos—the Mozart Concerto No. 2 K.417 and the Sinfonia Concertante K.297b—the orchestral repertoire chosen for the tour provided ample opportunities for Brain to shine. For example, Berlioz's "Royal Hunt" and "Storm" from *The Trojans*, music by Delius, including *Over the Hills and Far Away*, Mozart's Symphony No. 40 and Rossini's *Cambiale di Matrimonio* Overture, recorded only shortly before the tour.[24]

The first concert of the tour was at Bushnell Auditorium, Hartford, Connecticut, which inspired the music critic of the *Hartford Times* to praise Brain as well as other "first-desk men" in their performance of the Beethoven Symphony No. 8. The rehearsal for that first concert had been a difficult one for the hungry and exhausted players who had only eaten bacon and eggs at a roadside diner on the bus journey! Instruments were found that had not been seen since before they left London—and they had to get back into playing condition for the first concert! On the boat, there had been little time for rehearsal.[25]

Not all the newspaper reviews were kind to the players, as the RPO's principal flute, Gerald Jackson recalled:

> We felt we were under intense scrutiny at Boston, where the acoustics gave one the added sense of being under a microscope. The platform suggested a stage set to a Victorian play, but our eventual public reception was possibly the most tumultuous of all. But Boston is also renowned for her hard critics, and the *Christian Science Monitor* was the only paper not to offer us fulsome praise. It made us smile after lavish encomiums elsewhere to learn that our woodwind section, our "Royal Family," had suddenly become "pedestrian."[26]

Brain's first solo engagement of the tour was at the Lyric Theatre, Baltimore, on October 20, with MacDonagh, Brymer, and Brooke in Mozart's Sinfonia Concertante. The horn part, which is not technically difficult, nonetheless calls for dexterity and gracefulness in a rapid ascending scale. Dennis and his colleagues repeated the same work at New Brunswick on October 30. The RPO gave two concerts at Carnegie Hall in New York on October 27 and 29. The first contained orchestral works with plenty of horns but no solos. The second featured Rossini's Overture *La Cambiale di Matrimonio*.[27]

Brain performed as soloist on November 26 in Mozart's Concerto No. 2 at Orchestral Hall in Chicago. That night was recalled by Chicago horn player Philip Farkas at the International Horn Society's symposium at the University of North Texas on May 17, 1991:

> I first met Dennis Brain when the Royal Philharmonic came to America with Sir Thomas Beecham, and I went to the concert in which Dennis Brain played the Mozart No. 2. During it he scratched one little note and afterwards some of the players in his orchestra told me "We don't know what happened to Dennis. This is the seventh performance he's played in America and he never did that before!" So, this was a pretty good start—seven without a scratch![28]

Owing to Betty Humby Beecham's frequent indisposition as piano soloist during the US tour, Brain sometimes stepped in to play the Mozart second. The first occasion was on November 12 at the Municipal Auditorium in New Orleans. The morning rehearsal was recalled by Brymer: "Next morning we were rehearsing at ten o'clock, but it didn't help very much, because most of us had been out all night, and Beecham, knowing this, just played a few bars of Dennis Brain's Mozart Concerto, a line of Sibelius's *Tapiola* and left the rest to the inspiration of the evening. He was very wise. It was a magnificent concert."[29]

The concert of that day was reviewed by Ed Brookes in the *Times-Picayune*:

> Lady Beecham was scheduled to appear as soloist in Delius' Concerto for Piano and Orchestra, but illness prevented her from coming to New Orleans and a pleasant substitution was made, Mozart's Concerto for Horn and Orchestra with young Dennis Brain as soloist.
>
> Mozart's music is a field in which Sir Thomas has long shown special aptitude and this was no disappointment. The score required mostly strings and they appeared to excellent advantage. Sir Thomas seemed to revel in its light-hearted air. Brain is a very accomplished instrumentalist who played surely with a pure, mellow tone through the Mozartean intricacies.[30]

A candid photograph with Beecham (*Pl. 4*), was taken during a concert interval at Memphis, Tennessee, on November 14. It shows how genial and relaxed Beecham could be with his players.

In Lexington, Kentucky, on November 18, the music critic of the *Kentucky Kernel*, Ed Coffman, found Brain and Brymer backstage:

> Both musicians were impressed by the Coliseum. Brain, who looked very young, commented, "It is so vast." Brymer said that the acoustics were fine for such a large place; however, they were a little too loud.
>
> Both liked America very much. Brain: "It is such a large country." Brymer: "All of the cities are different." . . . Brain wanted to see a baseball game. He said that he was a cricket fan and wanted to see how the two games compared. He saw the North Dakota-Kentucky football game. His comment was: "I really enjoyed your football game, but it is so different from our game of football." At this time another orchestra member joined in commenting on the game. "You go for the man instead of the ball."
>
> Brain and Brymer were enthusiastic about Sir Thomas. They agreed that he was "the nicest conductor. All of us in the orchestra go for him in a big way. He is very much of an intellectual. He draws the music out rather than driving you to playing. He is a stimulant rather than an irritant. He is a very musical conductor."[31]

In Illinois, the orchestra members were given a warm welcome at the university where concerts took place on November 21 and 29. At the first concert, Betty Humby Beecham had been scheduled to play the Delius Piano Concerto but owing to illness, the concerto highlight was MacDonagh playing Handel's Oboe Concerto. Hugh Hough of the *The Illini* reported: "Beecham pulled out all the musical stops in recreating Nature's blackest moments in 'Chasse Royale et Orage' from Berlioz' *Les Troyens* and the closing scene from Strauss' *Feuersnot* was no less spectacular."[32] For the second concert in Chicago on November 26, Brain again played the Mozart Concerto No. 2, as scheduled. The house was packed to the rafters and the concert was well received. Claudia Cassidy, critic of the *Chicago Tribune*, was impressed by Brain's performance of the Mozart Concerto K.417 and described his playing as "matchless."[33]

His narrow-bore Raoux attracted a lot of curiosity from the Chicago horn players, who amusingly referred to it as the "gas pipe." He took the joke well. Perhaps unknown to the Americans, he was already considering abandoning the use of the narrow-bore "French" type of instrument in favor of the wider-bore "German" Alexander that he had also brought with him on the tour. After the concert on November 25, the Chicago players came around and one by one attempted to get a note out of the Raoux but without success![34]

Milan Yancich, then a Chicago horn player, remembered Brain's impact:

> The main attraction for all the horn players in Chicago was the presence and appearance of Dennis Brain as soloist with the Royal Philharmonic.

> He had become a major musical personality as a horn soloist on the world stage.
>
> I had an absorbing and delightful visit with Dennis Brain at Geyer's workshop. He was a man of simple charm and blessed with an attractive and winning personality. I played on his Raoux horn which had been rebuilt from a single F horn into a double horn with a C alto attachment. (For the uninitiated, the modern double horn is usually built in F and B-flat keys). It was originally a single F horn and it was on this horn that he had performed the Benjamin Britten Serenade for Tenor, Horn and Strings.
>
> Unlike the modern day French horn with rotary valve action, his horn had piston valves like the trumpet. It responded and had the feel of a mellophone. When I first held his horn in my hands it was of feather weight compared to my own Geyer horn. The horn was very easy to play, it responded quickly and the high register was superb in its response. When Brain played on my Geyer, he struggled to attain the high C. He had an embouchure where he set his mouthpiece into the lip (*einsetzen* embouchure) rather than the customary on the lip setting (*ansetzen* embouchure). The rim of his mouthpiece was quite thin. He stated that the placement and setting of his embouchure was almost the exact opposite of his father's, and that when he articulated it was different from the customary technique of most horn players.[35]

Phillip Farkas, principal horn in the Chicago Symphony Orchestra, gave a party for the Brains on the evening of the second concert in Chicago. Brymer and his wife, Joan, were also invited. At the party, candles had been lit on the buffet table and Yvonne remarked how lovely it was to see them because, owing to rationing since the war, they were in short supply in the UK. Aluminum foil (which the Brains had not seen before) was also a novelty, and after the party they were delighted to receive rolls of foil and a large supply of candles![36]

The RPO tour continued in Illinois, Wisconsin, Indiana, and Michigan. Brain performed the Mozart Concerto No. 2 again in Madison, Wisconsin, on November 27 and in Fort Wayne, Indiana, on December 2. A candid photograph of Brain with Ian and Dorothy Beers (*Pl. 5*) shows the three taking refreshment at a roadside diner.[37]

The other work featuring the horn, Mozart's Sinfonia Concertante, was performed again at Lafayette, Indiana. A third Carnegie Hall concert in the evening of December 13 included a New York premiere of Vaughan Williams's *In the Fen Country* with Joseph Laderoute (tenor) and the Schola Cantorum of New York. Berlioz's "Royal Hunt" and "Storm" from *The Trojans* was also in the program. The next work after Berlioz also has a brief horn solo near the beginning: Wagner's *Der Fliegende Holländer* Overture. The final work, Berlioz's *Te Deum* Op. 22 also has a lot of horn writing in it, but the horns do not receive a mention from critic Olin Downes, writing in the *New York Times* on December14. The concert hall was packed.[38]

So ended one of the greatest orchestral tours of any British orchestra. Bags were packed and the orchestra installed again on the *Queen Mary* for the return journey, which passed without incident. The ship reached Southampton on December 21.[39]

Festival of Britain 1951

The Festival of Britain 1951, the centenary of the first Great Exhibition, ran for five months, from May through September, and showcased science, invention, industry, and culture throughout the British Isles. The Festival contributed to making 1951 a busy year for the RPO. Although some concerts were in London, most were in the provinces, and Leopold Stokowski assisted Sir Thomas with the conducting. Brain was soloist with his wind colleagues in another performance of Mozart's Sinfonia Concertante at Royal Albert Hall on March 28, conducted by Beecham. The critic of the *Monthly Musical Record* commented that the wind soloists played with "the utmost finesse." *The Times* critic wrote: "As though to show that monumental Mozart is not Sir Thomas Beecham's exclusive view, this performance reproduced a chamber atmosphere, with its reduced orchestra and restrained dynamics, which brought forward the suave blend and elegant phrasing of Messrs. MacDonagh, Brymer, Brooke, and Brain."[40]

The Brain brothers with Brymer travelled by car on May 10 to the Sheldonian Theatre, Oxford, for a concert preceded by a rehearsal. They were late setting off. When they arrived, they discovered Sir Thomas had arrived early for rehearsal of Sibelius's First Symphony, which required an approximately two-and-a-half minute clarinet solo at the beginning. Brymer had not even reached his seat before Sir Thomas started the drum roll that immediately preceded his long clarinet solo. Fortunately, a clarinet in his hand, he proceeded to walk towards the platform, playing "pied-piper" fashion! Sir Thomas conducted his solo with great enthusiasm, without a baton.[41]

Brain was again soloist with the RPO at the Davis Theatre, Croydon, on May 30, in yet another performance of Mozart's Sinfonia Concertante. The soloists were the usual wind principals.[42] Then came another Glyndebourne Festival, conducted by Fritz Busch in Mozart's *Cosi fan Tutte* on July 24. At the dress rehearsal, so pleased was Busch with Sena Jurinac's singing and Brain's playing in *Per Pietà* that he asked the soprano to sing the aria again! The evening concert on the same day was a great success—Brain even surpassing his playing at the dress rehearsal. Testament has published a CD of another rehearsal (in July 1950) of *Cosi fan tutte*—with the same orchestra, soloists, and conductor.[43]

Increasing Solo Engagements (1952–1953)

Brain's increasing commitments outside the RPO led to the appointment of Alan Civil as co-principal horn from 1952. Civil remembered Sir Thomas's reaction to hearing Brain execute the horn solos:

> During this time in the RPO it was always a delight to watch the expression on Sir Thomas Beecham's face when Dennis had a solo to play. The many Delius works that we performed so often with "TB" were great favourites with him, and the lengthy phrases that have always tested the horn player's endurance and control created no problems for Dennis. The end of *La Calinda* with its 11-bar solo I am certain Sir Thomas conducted deliberately more slowly on each successive performance just to catch Dennis out and make him break the phrase (needless to say, unsuccessfully!).[44]

The Delius works in which Brain can be heard include *Brigg Fair*, *Over the Hills and Far Away*, *Appalachia*, and *A Mass of Life*. *Gramophone* critic Alec Robertson singled out for special praise the Prelude, "On the Mountains," in the complete opera recording made in 1952 and 1953:

> The orchestral playing, needless to say, is of the finest quality throughout and the engineers are to be warmly congratulated on the superb recording of it they have achieved. . . . Most splendid of all is the section called "On the Mountains" (side 2), in which the recording catches so much of the thrilling and exhilarating spirit of the music and also of the poetical picture painted by the orchestra (with the horns prominent) before the great cry with which the chorus enter.[45]

Another of these Delius works to feature the solo horn is *Appalachia*, and Alec Robertson described as a high point in the piece: "After the first brief entry of the chorus there is a piece of recording so perfect in tone and balance that it should become a *locus classicus*. The scoring is: horn solo, string accompaniment (violins divided) and interjections by clarinet, cor anglais, oboe, and flute (letter R, page 77 in the miniature score.)"[46]

Brain appeared as soloist with conductors other than Beecham. For example, there was a concert at the Royal Festival Hall on March 2, 1952, conducted by Eugene Goossens, reviewed in *Musical Times*:

> Mozart's horn concerto no. 2 (K. 417) brought Dennis Brain from his seat in the orchestra to give his usual, wonderfully accomplished account of the solo. Mr Brain must feel, however, as with several other solo works for his instrument, that the intrinsic musical interest is here secondary to the technical virtuosity required: he might well commission a work to challenge his interpretative as well as his technical skill.[47]

Of course, by this date he had inspired Hindemith, Britten, Jacob, Lutyens, Seiber, and a good many others to write works for him that did just that! Strange for the critic to overlook these works—especially Seiber's *Notturno* and Britten's Serenade, both requiring a master to play them. The concert was also reviewed in *The Times*: "Mr Dennis Brain's playing of Mozart's second horn concerto was of that subtlety and polish that we have learned to expect of him. No matter here for strong personal declarations of feeling either: the manner is everything and Mr. Brain gave it its air of breeding."[48] A performance from Brain that did not evince "strong personal declarations of feeling" would be hard to find in the recorded evidence of his art. This performance was not recorded.

Brain also appeared as soloist in 1952 with members of the regular RPO in a slightly different guise—The Royal Philharmonic Chamber Orchestra—in its first appearance at Edinburgh under the baton of John Pritchard. The work was Mozart's Concerto No. 4, rehearsed on August 24. On the day of the rehearsal, he took part in Act 1 of Berlioz's *L'Enfance du Christ* with the RPO but had to leave after the interval to drive back to London. The next day, he was soloist in Mozart's Concerto No. 2 with the London Symphony Orchestra, conducted by Stanford Robinson. This is another example of how taxing his performance schedule could be. Then he had to return to Edinburgh to play Mozart's Concerto No. 4 with the RPO Chamber Orchestra, on August 26, at Freemasons' Hall. This was reviewed in *The Scotsman*:

> How Dennis Brain achieves such a seemingly effortless and relaxed performance is a secret known only to himself. This quality is not necessarily found in all great artists and one would not, for instance, associate it with Szigeti, but when it is present the listener sits back complacently knowing that there is not the remotest possibility of unease. That it might be taken for granted is the only danger. There was no fear of this yesterday when Dennis Brain played Mozart's Horn Concerto in E-flat major, K.495; no one could fail to appreciate the soloist's feeling for melodic line; the elegance

> of the phrasing and the unhurried subtlety with which he brought out every little nuance of his part.[49]

W. R. Anderson briefly mentions Brain's "superb performance" of the Mozart Concerto in *Musical Times*. The Third Programme also organized a studio broadcast from Edinburgh with the Royal Philharmonic Chamber Orchestra on August 28th; Brain was again soloist in Mozart's Concerto No. 4.[50]

Irving Rosenthal, writing in New York's *Woodwind Magazine*, mentioned Brain as one of the personnel for a performance at the 1952 Edinburgh Festival of Strauss's *Ein Heldenleben*:

> The Royal Philharmonic under Sir Thomas Beecham also elicited much well deserved praise for their performance of *Ein Heldenleben*. . . . Mr Dennis Brain, well known horn soloist and leader of the horn section, cannot fail to be mentioned as being one of the most outstanding artists of our time. His technical achievement, while quite dazzling, was matched by a high musical intelligence and a warm, full tone.[51]

He appeared again as soloist in Strauss's Horn Concerto No. 2 at the Royal Festival Hall on April 11, 1953, Beecham conducting. *Musical Times* critic "A. J." wrote:

> The concerto soloists, Dennis Brain and John Kennedy (son of Lauri Kennedy), are the leaders of their respective sections in the orchestra. If occasionally in the Strauss the soloist's attack on the individual notes was not so clear as one had expected, this is only to compare Brain one day with Brain another. The work itself, extremely difficult to the soloist and with plenty of those modulations which sometimes annoyingly suggest false-naivety, is not one of the better products of Strauss's final back-to-Mozart stage.[52]

Solo engagements now had priority over orchestral ones outside the Philharmonia; however, exceptions included a performance (*Pl. 6*) of Strauss's *Symphonia Domestica* conducted by Eugene Goossens at Royal Festival Hall on February 10, 1954. The concert program lists the horn section as Alan Civil, Ian Beers, Andrew Woodburn, Frank Probyn, Aubrey Thonger, Paul Dudding and Walter Worsley in addition to Brain. Brain was again soloist with the RPO at Royal Festival Hall on April 22, 1954, this time conducted by Anthony Bernard, in Britten's Serenade with Richard Lewis, tenor. *The Times* critic was not very happy with the concert but Brain was praised:

> Mr Richard Lewis sang Britten's Serenade in a careful, attentive sort of way that yet missed the savour of the word: it was not a matter of articulation but of "framing his line to the life of the words," in Byrd's phrase, or of catching their "energy," as was said of Purcell. The figuration of Britten's

string accompaniment needs the tension of a bow-string whether it is soft or loud, this was limp.

Mr Dennis Brain's horn playing alone equalled in distinction the imaginative quality of the song-cycle.[53]

Leaving the RPO

In a sense, Brain left the RPO several times—and came back again—owing to increasing commitments outside. Such was the demand for him as a player, and the flexible arrangement with Walter Legge (founder and manager of the Philharmonia), that Beecham used him for as long as was practicable. If he were available, Beecham would make sure to engage him for concerts, if not for recording sessions. Brain's increasing solo and orchestral commitments outside the RPO came to a head in 1953.

Several authorities give conflicting dates when he actually left; for example, Pettitt gives April 7, 1954. All of these dates do not help matters when the evidence of personnel lists in concert programs, as well as recollections by his colleagues, show that he was present with them in their concerts, when he was free, until about December 1956.[54]

Beecham, recently returned from America, presented a program at Royal Festival Hall on March 27, 1954. The concert program lists Brain as the principal. The rest of the horn section was Civil, Beers, Woodburn, and Probyn. *The Times* reviewed the concert but made no mention of Brain. The piece that particularly showed off the horns was Méhul's *Le Jeune Henri* Overture, which the critic described with rather mixed feelings as "a characteristic piece without good tunes, but full of effective moments, and a full measure of horn calls."[55]

RPO gave a concert at Royal Festival Hall, conducted by Beecham, on April 7, 1954, the date Pettitt gives as Brain's last with the RPO. The work most requiring the horns was Rossini's *Semiramide* Overture. *The Times* critic made no reference to Brain.[56]

Apparently Brain played after this date with the RPO. The next concert he played, as an orchestral player, was on November 8, 1956, at the Royal Festival Hall, conducted by Beecham. It included Delius's *In a Summer Garden*, which has an especially beautiful solo for the principal horn. Brain received special praise in *The Times:*

It contained three Beecham favourites, Haydn's Symphony No. 93, Delius's *In a Summer Garden*, and a suite from Bizet's Music for *L'Arlesienne*. He has played them to us before, and he still loves them; the Royal Philharmonic Orchestra, whose horn department was once again led to glory by

> Mr. Dennis Brain, sparkled in Haydn, melted in Delius, and blazed in Bizet's Farandole.[57]

Brain led the horns again for a Wagner night at Royal Festival Hall on December 6, 1956, Beecham conducting. Although *The Times* critic had handsome compliments to make of the playing generally of the orchestra, no mention is made of Brain.

The long gap in appearances with the RPO may explain why April 7, 1954, and May 3, 1954, are given as leaving dates. He came back from time to time for concerts, but his participation in recordings probably ended with the December 1953 sessions for Philips, as the following letter of October 8, 1968, from Civil to Martin Prowse, suggests.[58]

> Thank you for your letter and enquiries. I will attempt to cast my mind back to the "good old days."
>
> Dennis was given a slight remonstrative talk from Sir Thomas in the early months of 1953 to the effect that it was either R.P.O. exclusively or out; out meaning the tempting offer from Walter Legge boss of the Philharmonia of eleven guineas per session or concert not to play with the R.P.O. When one considers that E.M.I employed the Philharmonia for as many as 300 sessions each year and the talented conductors of the day, von Karajan, Cantelli & Furtwängler, all Legge men, it was understandable that Dennis should go over to the orchestra where above all he had many opportunities to play concertos at International Festivals, Lucerne, Aix, and others.
>
> At this time, the horns in the R.P.O. were Dennis, Ian Beers, myself, Frank Probyn, Andrew Woodburn and occasionally Alan Hyde. In the Legge band, Dennis, Neill Sanders, [Edmund] Chapman, [Alfred] Cursue, Thonger and Denis Mason were pretty regular although the interchange between players still continued and several discs could have at least three first horns on them. I played top horn for at least 80% of the time in the R.P.O. in 1953 doing Glyndebourne, Edinburgh, etc. There were occasions when I would rehearse a programme as 1st and play 3rd for the performance which entailed a sliding system of the section; very frustrating. . . . Certainly by 1954, Dennis was installed in the Philharmonia and the horn sections of both orchestras seemed static.
>
> Now for the different works you queried: *Appalachia* contained three first horns, Dennis, Hyde and myself with Woodburn mainly third player. *The Marriage Contract*, I played the later recording. The "Pastoral" must have been Dennis and the Goldmark a mixture but mostly Dennis top and somehow but I cannot reason why I think Eddie Chapman was on third. The Méhul was recorded at Walthamstow Town Hall with Dennis, Beers

> and myself off-stage and the tutti hunting section had eight players. *Siegfried* if you mean the Philips version was Dennis, myself as third and John Burden first Wagner tuba.[59]

The following paragraph in the letter concerns horn personnel in the Philharmonia Orchestra's section and recordings. Some explanation is required for the composers named in the above letter. The "Méhul" he refers to is the recording made for Philips in December 1953 of Méhul's *Le Jeune Henri* Overture. In his article, "The Unfamiliar Dennis Brain," Prowse aptly described the horn section "in full cry." Beecham appears to have increased the number of horns required to boost the exhilarating sound of the section playing together. The same article describes other RPO recordings featuring Brain. Delius's *Appalachia* is considered in relation to two other works recorded by the Philharmonia, Bruckner's Fourth and Sibelius's Fifth Symphony: "In each case the call by the first horn, slow, expressive and romantic, contains the essence of Dennis Brain's magic, distilled in a few notes. Swelling from nowhere the notes evoke space and calm."[60]

The "Goldmark" in the quotation above refers to Goldmark's *Rustic Wedding Symphony*, recorded in May 1952. The "Siegfried" is a little more difficult to work out because Wagner's opera *Siegfried* was not recorded by Beecham. In December 1953, "Siegfried's Funeral Music" (*Götterdämmerung*) was recorded for Philips at Walthamstow Town Hall and at the same venue on April 20, 1954, also from *Götterdämmerung*, "Siegfried's Rhine Journey." As Civil states in his letter that by 1954, Brain had left, it may be assumed that the 1953 recording is the one he must be referring to and not the 1954 recording, with its clear exposed solo, most likely played by Civil. The "Pastoral" refers to Beecham's recording of Beethoven's Symphony No. 6, recorded in December 1951 and May 1952. Civil's letter is a rare document giving an insight into who played first horn on these recordings.[61]

One wonders who is playing the horn solo at the start of another April 1954 recording: Wagner's *Flying Dutchman Overture*, recorded at the same venue, Walthamstow Town Hall, a few days before "Siegfried's Rhine Journey," on April 16, 1954. It is probably Civil performing the solos in both those Wagner recordings.[62]

Brymer described a concert at the Royal Festival Hall (no date given) in which they came to grief in the "Danse générale" of Ravel's *Daphnis and Chloë*. They played all the *Daphnis and Chloë*—not just the Suite No. 2. He recalled:

> There were times when things went wrong. . . . There was *Daphnis and Chloe* at the Festival Hall which was the greatest disaster I have ever heard in a concert platform but at the same time, not complete. Now what happened

> was this, the E-flat clarinet came in a bar early in the pantomime and Sir Thomas couldn't catch his eye to get rid of him so that the result was that half the orchestra thought "We know this!" and they jumped a bar ahead and the others said, "No, no!" These two vehicles were going towards this corner and you could tell that when they got to the corner (which was the change of time) it was going to happen—and it did. The whole thing fell apart. Terrible noise! There was one great moment when Ernie Clifford Seville on the bass flute was making a sort of wooo noise on his own. All you could hear. Then the choir came in and it all dissolved into perfect harmony again. But as he came off, Sir Thomas looked at Norman Miller, who was the manager of the orchestra and said, "All your fault—you wanted to put the damn thing on!" So he wasn't terribly upset. People who were there said "This, although it was a disaster, was nonetheless only thirty seconds in fifty-eight minutes . . . of the greatest Ravel you could hear anywhere."[63]

What is not revealed in this anecdote is that Brymer and Brain were holding the piece together, as described by Alan Jefferson in his book, *Sir Thomas Beecham: A Centenary Tribute*:

> After some persuasion, he agreed to play the Suite again at the Royal Festival Hall . . . he did it from memory and came to grief in the huge climax in the *Danse générale*. Dennis Brain and Jack Brymer held it together over the ostinato side-drum beats until Frederick Riddle came in with his signpost on the viola, thus taking Beecham and the whole orchestra safely home. And that was the last time that he included anything by Ravel in his programmes.[64]

Another principal who played for the RPO, flutist Gerald Jackson, also mentioned Brain playing with the RPO until very late: "But although Dennis left the R.P.O. in 1952, he frequently came in again afterwards for our gramophone sessions—that is, until he died in his motor-car."[65]

This presents yet another leaving date of 1952 to further confuse and complicate the actual date when Brain left the RPO. Perhaps Jackson had in mind the presence of Civil as co-principal from 1952. His comment about the gramophone sessions, however, is hard to believe when listening to the RPO recordings after about December 1953. By the spring of 1954, Brain was devoting most of his orchestral work to the Philharmonia, as Civil's letter makes clear.

Left: ***Plate 1*** Sir Thomas Beecham Bart., C. H. *With permission from Shirley Lady Beecham.*

Below: ***Plate 2*** Royal Philharmonic Orchestra, first concert, Davis Theater, Croydon, Surrey, England, September 15, 1946. *Photograph, Croydon Advertiser.*

Plate 3 Cover of Royal Philharmonic Orchestra United States tour book, 1950. *Gamble collection.*

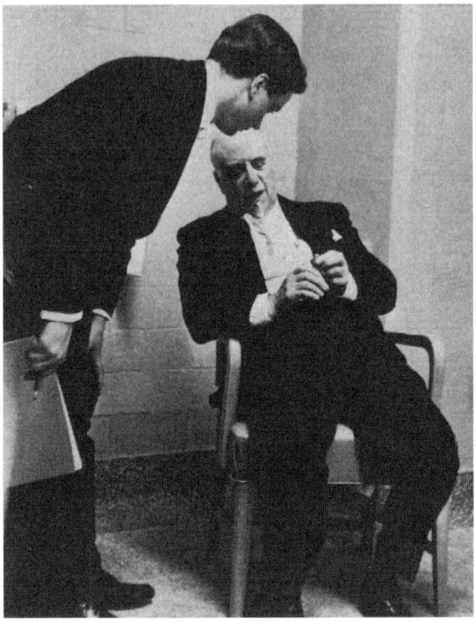

Plate 4 Sir Thomas Beecham, talking to Dennis Brain. RPO United States tour, Memphis, November 14, 1950. *With permission from Shirley Lady Beecham.*

Plate 5 Ian and Dorothy Beers with Dennis Brain at a roadside diner, during the United States tour of 1950. *With permission from Dorothy Beers and Tony Catterick. Catterick collection.*

THE
ROYAL PHILHARMONIC ORCHESTRA
Administrator: Norman K. Millar
12b St. George Street, London, W.1

First Violins
David McCallum (*Leader*)
A. Leavins (*Sub-Leader*)
A. Hepton
A. Brudagary
J. Soutter
A. Davis
S. Robins
N. Rouse
D. Rael
L. Stone
I. Aarons
A. English
G. Lauland
E. Eaden
G. Briscoe
R. Bossart

Second Violins
Oscar Rosen (*Principal*)
H. Ball
F. Maybank
A. Pievsky
A. Ross
A. Letch
L. Salzedo
A. Bryan
M. Farren
N. Lederman
I. Lester
S. Caplan
T. Fowler
A. Ives

Violas
Frederick Riddle (*Principal*)
K. Essex
A. Newnham
V. Howard
H. Legge
R. Allen
A. Stanley
R. Conway
P. Long
R. Patten
M. Claymans
B. Owe

'Cellos
John Kennedy (*Principal*)
H. Rogerson
H. Robinson
S. Mant
D. Vigay
C. Sharpe
H. Wilkinson
C. Pruvenees
J. Marchant
W. Hanesworth

Basses
Jack Silvester (*Principal*)
F. Chesterman
W. Colborne
E. Ineson
C. Cheeseman
D. Vaughan
A. Walton
C. Payne

Flutes
Robert Hanlon (*Principal*)
G. Markham
G. P. Goody

Piccolo
Clifford Seville

Oboes
Terence MacDonagh (*Principal*)
J. Black

Cor Anglais
Peter Graeme

Oboe D'Amore
Leonard Brain

Clarinets
Jack Brymer (*Principal*)
B. N. Tschaikov
C. Chapman
F. Hughes

Bass Clarinet
Stephen Trier

Bassoons
Gwydion Brooke (*Principal*)
E. Wilson
J. Castaldini
A. Waters

Contra Bassoon
Cuthbert W. Harding

Horns
Dennis Brain (*Principal*)
A. Civil
I. Beers
A. Woodburn
F. Probyn
A. Thonger
P. Dudding
W. Worsley

Trumpets
Richard Walton (*Principal*)
H. Barker
P. Jones
H. Barr

Trombones
Sidney Langston (*Principal*)
J. Whelan

Bass Trombone
Harry Spain

Tuba
Francis F. White

Timpani
Lewis Pocock

Percussion
Stephen Whittaker (*Principal*)
F. Bradshaw
F. Kennings

Harps
Tina Bonifacio (*Principal*)
M. Davidson

Orchestral Manager
George Orrell

Librarian
George Brownfoot

Plate 6 Royal Philharmonic Orchestra personnel for Royal Festival Hall concert, February 12, 1954, conducted by Sir Eugene Goossens. *Tony Catterick collection.*

CHAPTER

5

Philharmonia Orchestra

Formation of the Philharmonia

Brain was the original principal horn of the Philharmonia Orchestra when Walter Legge formed the orchestra in 1945. It was to be an orchestra with "style" but not any particular style, comprising a body of hand-picked players of the highest caliber, and many distinguished conductors rather than one conductor molding the sound. This ensured that, under Legge's direction, the Philharmonia boasted a wide repertoire with a variety of different readings of standard works—such as the symphonies of Beethoven, Brahms, Sibelius, and Tchaikovsky—as well as readings of lesser-known works.

The new orchestra's reputation was soon established as one of the world's top ensembles, and conductors as well as players competed for the privilege of taking part in its concerts and recordings. Legge made it clear from the outset that he would tolerate no passengers in the orchestra. Everyone was constantly on their toes, not knowing if they would be hired or fired the next week.[1]

Joan Ingpen, the Philharmonia's agent, remembered how Legge started the Philharmonia by engaging players from the RAF Symphony Orchestra at the end of the war:

> Spring 1945, they were all just being demobbed from the Air Force Orchestra and Legge said to [cellist] Jimmy Whitehead, if he would collect a good ensemble of chamber orchestra-sized strings, he, Legge would give it a lot of recording because he didn't feel that what existed at that time was as good as he wanted. Jimmy said he would. He asked me to manage it and put it

> together. Of course, he himself in no time at all approached various wind players and it became a small symphony orchestra at its very first concert.[2]

Not all the Philharmonia's players were discharged from the armed forces in 1945. The Brain brothers had to wait until their period of service ended in September of the next year. They were with the RAF Symphony Orchestra for concerts at the Potsdam Conference in Germany on July 20, 23, and 24, 1945. The concert venues were the British Delegation, the Prime Minister's house, and the New Palace of Sans Souci. On his return to London, Brain found Legge organizing more concerts to take place in the autumn at Kingsway Hall. The first, on October 27, was the Philharmonia's début under Sir Thomas Beecham (*Pl. 1*).[3]

Brain, meanwhile, took advantage of the gap between the Potsdam concerts and the Philharmonia's début to prepare for his wedding on September 8 at Petersfield parish church in Hampshire. The wedding photographs show him in his RAF uniform, together with his wife (Yvonne), best man (Gareth Morris), and bridesmaids (*Pls. 2–3*). Brain's parents didn't attend. The photographs show that it was a cheerful occasion.[4]

After the honeymoon, the couple moved into their first house, a bungalow in Hayes, Middlesex, with a large garden. It was near Uxbridge and therefore convenient for Brain to continue his RAF duties.[5]

The Philharmonia's début concert was an all-Mozart program: Symphony No. 40 in G minor, the Clarinet Concerto K. 622 (with Reginald Kell), Overture to *Don Giovanni*, the Divertimento in D major K.131, and German Dances 1, 2, 3, and 5 from K.600 and No. 3 from K.605. The audience was delighted and so was Beecham, who remarked, "The privilege of directing this magnificent concert of artists is such that my pleasure would be diminished if I accepted a fee. I would, however, gladly accept a cigar." The players assembled for that first concert included concertmaster Leonard Hirsch and principals Arthur Gleghorn (flute), Alec Whittaker (oboe), Reginald Kell (clarinet), John Alexandra (bassoon), Harold Mortimer (trumpet), and James Bradshaw (tympani). In addition to Brain and Del Mar, the horn section included Alan Hyde and Frank Probyn.[6]

The first orchestral recordings of the Philharmonia included Tchaikovsky's Piano Concerto No. 1 with Benno Moiseiwitsch, one of Brain's favorite pianists. It was recorded at the Friends' Meeting House, Euston Road on August 30 and 31, 1945. They recorded Sibelius's Violin Concerto with Ginette Neveu, conducted by Walter Susskind, at Abbey Road on November 21, 1945. Butterworth's *Banks of Green Willow*, conducted by Maurice Miles for a recording on February 19, 1946, has a horn part that drew the attention of the *Gramophone* critic:

> It is an idyll scored for small orchestra: woodwind, horns, trumpet, harp and strings. It is built upon two folk tunes: the first, that named in its title, the second, *Green Bushes*, of which there are many versions, English and Irish. . . . The first side works up No. 1. There are two subsidiary phrases, one in octave horns, the other a syncopated violin lilt. A simple piece; sadness must enter as we listen: the life cut short, the whole life of the land and the folk, seen through the modal melancholy of Green Bushes . . .[7]

Weber's *Der Freischütz* Overture was recorded at Abbey Road on March 12, 1946, conducted by Walter Susskind. It was an early triumph, and the horns especially shine. *Gramophone* critic Alec Robertson commented:

> This recording . . . gave me a very great deal of pleasure. Here is playing of real quality and an interpretation by a conductor, Walter Susskind, who is an excellent musician and has a genuine dramatic instinct.
>
> We get at the start some lovely playing by the horns with a perfectly balanced string accompaniment: and the *tremolandi* that follow create a really eerie effect. The brass blaze out finely and there is a real thrill in the swirling up of the strings near the close.[8]

Other orchestral recordings in 1946 included Elgar's *Sea Pictures* with contralto Gladys Ripley, conducted by George Weldon and recorded at Abbey Road on May 28, 1946. It has some pleasing horn playing, especially No. 4, *Where Corals Lie*, which *Gramophone* reviewed in July 1946.

In early 1946, Brain was also soloist in two Kingsway Hall orchestral concerts, Sir John Barbirolli conducting. Brain was featured on February 9 in Mendelssohn's Nocturne from *A Midsummer Night's Dream*. He performed Mozart's Horn Concerto K.447, conducted by Susskind, on March 23. *The Times* critic wrote:

> Mozart's horn concerto in E-flat, played by Dennis Brain with his unfailing accomplishment, completed the eclectic scheme. Wind instruments make somewhat impassive soloists, so that concertos for them must be short. This one is short and uneventful till the finale when Mozart takes, what is rare with him, a leaf out of Haydn's book and plays unexpected tricks with a tally-ho rondo.[9]

The star players on wind instruments were especially numerous in England at this time, and none could be described as "impassive" players, least of all Brain. Not long after this performance, on March 27, 1946, he recorded Mozart's Concerto No. 2 with the same conductor and orchestra. The record company, Columbia, offered him the choice of a lump sum or royalties on the sale of the record. He chose the fee, which was about £10, but the record sold well, so Brain could have made substantially more if he had chosen to take the royalties. At this time, the horn was still struggling to be accepted as a solo instrument. The *Gramophone* critic wrote favorably of the recording: "Beautifully recorded and played beyond expectation… Nowadays a player may make light of much of it, but it is still a remarkable feat, to my mind, to play it as Mr. Brain does, with so much variety of tone and volume."[10]

For the first concert of the Philharmonia's 1946–47 season, September 19, 1946, Brain appeared as soloist in Mozart's Concerto No. 3 with Susskind conducting. He played it from memory for the first time. The performance was reviewed by the *Daily Telegraph* the following day: "Dennis Brain played one of Mozart's horn concertos with a truly wonderful beauty of tone and technical assurance and one asked 'was anything like such horn-playing known a generation ago?'"[11] This was praise indeed, considering the great reputation that his father had had with the public and the critics in the years prior to the war. The success of the Mozart Concerto No. 2 recording was followed by another for Columbia: the Strauss Concerto No. 1, with Alceo Galliera conducting. Brain considered that this best represented his playing. He commented, "It makes a welcome change from the Mozarts and it really is the greatest fun to play." In the Galliera recording, the final movement is played at breathtaking speed. He entered into the spirit of the music and played brilliantly.[12]

The success of the Philharmonia's orchestral recordings continued, and Brain had an opportunity to shine in *Per Pietà* from Mozart's *Cosi fan tutte*, sung in English by soprano Joan Cross, and recorded at Abbey Road on January 2, 1947. *Gramophone* critic Alec Robertson, after devoting a paragraph of praise for the singer, wrote of the obbligato horn parts:

> I am glad to say that the lovely orchestral accompaniment, which contains an obbligato for two horns "that almost amounts to a little concerto," is recorded with due regard to its importance. Altogether, this record has done much to restore my faith, sadly shaken recently, in opera in English, and the engineering department of HMV![13]

Herbert von Karajan gave his public début with the Philharmonia on April 11, 1948, at Royal Albert Hall. The two previous days had been Karajan's first recording sessions with them, at Abbey Road. Dinu Lipatti, piano soloist in the concert début, recorded Schumann's Piano Concerto. The concert included Beethoven's Fifth Symphony and Strauss's *Don Juan*. The players warmed to Karajan, who wasted no time in rehearsal. For the final rehearsal of the Beethoven, he spent only eight minutes and asked the players to "play the symphony's climax with as much volume as they could muster consistent with a balanced and fully rounded tone."[14]

In spite of great success, the Philharmonia remained without a government subsidy and experienced financial difficulties in the first three years. Help came unexpectedly from the Maharajah of Mysore, India, who saw the Philharmonia as the ideal vehicle for the promotion of his favorite composer—Nicholas Medtner, a Russian exile living in London—and in 1948, gave a financial guarantee to help the orchestra if they would agree to promote and record Medtner's works. The arrangement was terminated in 1951 because of difficulty transferring funds from India, but by then the Philharmonia was on a secure financial footing.[15]

At this time, Gareth Morris, who had resisted invitations from Legge to become principal flute, finally agreed to join the orchestra. At that time, as Morris recalled, the players played for fees, not contracts. Before he joined, he had been principal in six chamber orchestras in London and was kept busy with concerts, recordings, and broadcasts. Work in these other chamber orchestras continued for the present, and both Morris and Brain could be found performing for Anthony Bernard and his London Chamber Orchestra, Alec Sherman and his New London Orchestra, and Harry Blech and his London Mozart Players.[16]

Further successful recordings with Karajan in November 1949 included Balakirev's Symphony No. 1 and Roussel's Symphony No. 4. No recordings were made with Karajan during 1950, Legge adhering to his intention not to have one conductor mold the sound of the orchestra. Yet Karajan's partnership with the Philharmonia was a very satisfying one, and perhaps the most prominent, and it could not be long before he returned. Ian Beers, the Philharmonia's second horn, left in May 1950 to work for the RPO. Aubrey Brain played second temporarily until the last week in May, when Neill Sanders was appointed to the position.

The Philharmonia performed the premiere of Strauss's *Vier letzte Lieder*, a historic concert, with Kirsten Flagstad and Wilhelm Furtwängler. The work contains some magical moments for the horn, most notably "September." The *Musical Quarterly* reported that Brain's solo was "as fine as anyone will ever hear." Aubrey, who played second in that concert, thereafter played fifth horn until he moved to Sadler's Wells in the winter of 1950 as second to Livia Gollancz. Aubrey Thonger joined the Philharmonia as fifth horn (to replace Brain's father) in 1949.[17]

Furtwängler conducted the orchestra again on November 13 and December 11, 1950, in two Mysore concerts. Hans Keller, critic of the *Music Survey*, wrote:

> As was to be expected, the most overpowering interpretations in the Philharmonia Orchestra's first two concerts under the greatest developer and deepest experiences among living conductors were those of the symphonic

> and evolving works: above all the 5th Beethoven, but also the 5th Tchaikovsky, Brahms's Haydn-Variations, and "The Hebrides" . . . The Tchaikovsky became not only a great, but even an immeasurable work: does then its weakness simply consist in its occasionally hiding its strength, which it needs a Furtwängler to uncover?[18]

Furtwängler returned for the 1951 season to conduct on February 22 at Royal Albert Hall in Weber's Overture *Der Freischütz*, Bruckner's Seventh Symphony, and Beethoven's Fifth Piano Concerto with Edwin Fischer. Brain was soloist again in Hindemith's Horn Concerto, a first London performance, at Kingsway Hall on April 16, conducted by Del Mar. He also performed Britten's Serenade with Pears at that concert.[19]

Karajan continued his association with the orchestra in June 1951 with recordings of piano concertos by Grieg, Beethoven (4th and 5th), Mozart (No. 23), and Franck's *Symphonic Variations* with Walter Gieseking. Then November and December sessions produced Bartok's *Concerto for Orchestra*, the first session of Handel-Harty's *Water Music*, Sibelius's Symphony No. 5, Strauss's *Till Eulenspiegel* and *Don Juan*.[20]

A young conductor, Guido Cantelli, was being tested in the winter of 1951. He conducted four concerts in Royal Festival Hall. Brain could not play the first one but did perform in the other three. The repertoire during these four concerts featured Brain in some of the famous orchestral solos, particularly Wagner's *Siegfried Idyll* and Brahms's Symphony No. 3, both of which they soon recorded with Cantelli. The Wagner was issued by Testament on CD a number of years ago.[21]

Furtwängler again conducted on October 25, 1951, in Brahms's Symphony No. 1 with its sublime, soaring solos in the Finale from the first flute (Morris), and the first horn (Brain). In the same concert, Dame Myra Hess was soloist in Beethoven's Fourth Piano Concerto. Furtwängler returned again to conduct a final concert with the Philharmonia on April 24, 1952. Flagstad sang Wagner's *Wesendonck Lieder* and the closing scene from *Götterdämmerung*.

Brain could not be available for every Philharmonia concert or recording session due to his many other commitments, although Legge had first call on his services. A concert program, for example, from 1951 gives the horn personnel as Edmund Chapman, Neill Sanders, Aubrey Thonger, and Alfred Cursue.[22]

Karajan recorded, from April to July 1952, three works and finished a fourth that feature Brain: the Divertimento No. 15 K.287 for two horns and strings, Brahms's First and Tchaikovsky's Fifth Symphonies, and the Handel-Harty *Water Music*, which had been started in November 1951. It is no coincidence that he chose these and other works he had so successfully recorded, to showcase his Philharmonia partnership on their first European tour in May. Three weeks and sixteen concerts commenced in Paris on May 12 and included Berne, Zürich, Milan, and Vienna.

Legge continued to plan for concerts back in London and hoped that Toscanini would conduct. As an inducement to the maestro, Legge arranged for him to hear a broadcast of the Philharmonia's second Milan concert of May 20. Elisabeth Schwarzkopf had bought a second-hand Hudson automobile and knowing Brain's enthusiasm for cars, she gave him opportunities to drive the car around Milan. After the concert on May 20, Legge received a telephone call from Toscanini's daughter, asking if Legge could come to Toscanini's house to discuss conducting the Philharmonia in London later that year. Legge, of course, was delighted and shared the driving with Brain. Schwarzkopf and Morris were passengers and some snapshots (*Pls. 4–7*) of their journey capture the tension as well as the thrill of driving in some of the most spectacular as well as the most hazardous alpine scenery to be seen anywhere. They encountered severe snow drifts and black ice conditions at the entrance to the St. Gothard Pass, which they had to cross. It was closed to traffic.

Morris recalled that they waited until early morning for the ice to melt before they could proceed safely. Three of the snapshots show Morris, Legge, and Brain standing on the road near the Hudson, or investigating the entrance of St. Gothard, while the ice thawed and the morning dawned. Another (See *Pl. 4*) taken some distance on the journey to Zürich, shows Legge and Morris standing by the side of the Hudson saloon. Brain behind the wheel appears to have sunglasses or goggles on. Schwarzkopf probably took the photos. Brain was always a careful driver and would not have risked taking himself or any passengers over roads covered in black ice with sheer drops down steep precipices!

In Vienna, they all celebrated the success of engaging Toscanini with a meal at one of the top restaurants. After a three-course meal of the finest Viennese cuisine, when discussing what they would have for desert, Brain said with a straight face, "I don't suppose they have bread-and-butter pudding?"[23]

Like Brain, Karajan was a keen motor enthusiast. Douglas Moore related an occasion where Karajan noticed Brain was reading a motor magazine during a Philharmonia rehearsal. "Karajan put his baton down and said, 'Mr. Brain, why when I give you a cue each time, you're not ready to play?' He said, 'Herr Karajan, I've found you a suitable car!' Karajan replied, 'Oh yes? Come and show me!' It might have been a Ferrari or an Aston Martin—one of those pop cars!"[24]

The above exchange may have been a little tongue-in-cheek because normally Karajan would address Brain by his first name. Their shared motoring enthusiasm found expression during the Philharmonia's second European tour in 1954 when Brain was passenger next to Karajan in the maestro's fabulous new sports car: a gull-wing Mercedes. A detailed and amusing account of this is given in Alexander Kok's autobiography.[25]

One of the most historic series of concerts given by the Philharmonia featured the Brahms Symphonies, Haydn Variations, and Tragic Overture, conducted by Toscanini in the Royal Festival Hall. The concerts were broadcast live and also recorded. The concerts on September 29 and October 1, 1952, have been issued on LP and CD several times, most recently on the Testament label.[26]

After the concerts, Toscanini invited a few of the players backstage to his dressing-room. Brain was among them and so was Morris; both were struck by how unexpectedly kind and approachable he was. Neville Cardus, the *Manchester Guardian* critic, described Brain's playing in the Finale of Symphony no.1 as "beautifully intoned" and thought his solo in the first movement of Symphony no.2 was the highlight of the evening. [27]

A photograph of about this date shows Guido Cantelli, arms linked with Toscanini, and with Brain, Sanders, Manoug Parikian (leader), and other players standing with them. Cantelli was soon to conduct a successful series of concerts with them at the Royal Festival Hall, starting on October 5. *The Times* critic reviewed the first concert: "Daphnis was prefaced by the Pavane for a Dead Infanta; it was treated with apt nostalgia and was chiefly notable for Mr. Dennis Brain's glorious playing of the horn solo."[28] Karajan made further recordings in November and December of 1952 featuring Brain: Beethoven's "Eroica" Symphony and the *Quoniam* in Bach's B Minor Mass. In the *Quoniam*, Brain's beautiful articulation of his part is the centerpiece of that recording.

The Philharmonia, with its glittering array of conductors and soloists, continued to produce some of the most groundbreaking performances on record, notably the *Vier letzte Lieder* of Strauss with Schwarzkopf, conducted by Otto Ackermann. These were recorded in Watford Town Hall on September 25, 1953.[29]

Brain's father had been the first member of the BBC Symphony Orchestra to be drawn from its ranks to perform a concerto when he recorded Mozart's Concerto No. 3 in 1940. It's a very aristocratic reading of the concerto and played impeccably throughout by both soloist and orchestra. Brain was enormously proud of his father's achievements and always thought that he could never sound as good; however, when he recorded all four Mozart concertos with the Philharmonia and Karajan in November 1953, here was a horn player with all his father's superb qualities but with greater depth, subtlety, and flexibility.

The record was an instant success, remains one of EMI's top best-sellers in its Classical catalogue, and has never been deleted. The recording sessions went smoothly, and it has often been claimed that Brain didn't have the scores up on the stand but was reading motoring magazines. Del Mar once remarked that Brain would not have needed a note up on his stand because he would have played the Mozart concertos in his sleep. Be that as it may, he most probably did have the scores on the stand but for rests or any other spare time available during sessions, he would have brought a motoring magazine or two to read. He would never have read them while he was playing.[30]

Brain and his wind colleagues performed the Mozart Sinfonia Concertante, with Karajan conducting, at the Royal Festival Hall on June 24, 1954. *The Times* critic wrote: "Mr. Karajan rightly allowed that young Mozart's Adagios are like the old man's Andantes. The four soloists, unidentified in the programme, as were their colleagues in the orchestra, but recognizable as Messers Sutcliffe, Walton, James, and Brain, D., brought ravishing tone to this movement, and excelled in the brilliant variations of the finale."[31] Karajan's Philharmonia recordings in 1954 included Strauss's *Ariadne auf Naxos* and Mozart's *Cosi fan tutte*, both of which featured Brain in solos. Also recorded in 1954 were some operatic intermezzi, which featured Brain unexpectedly playing the organ part to Mascagni's *Cavalleria Rusticana*.

A few days later, the Philharmonia was on tour again in Europe. Karajan went with them, conducting concerts at Aix-en-Provence Festival on July 28 and 30, and two of the nine concerts, during three weeks, at the Lucerne Festival. Brain had bought a movie camera and was trying it out on his colleagues in the more relaxed moments at Aix. The conducting at Lucerne was shared with Rafael Kubelik, Ferenc Fricsay, Edwin Fischer, André Cluytens, and Wilhelm Furtwängler. The Philharmonia and soloists, conducted by Furtwängler, made a live recording of the concert on August 22 of Beethoven's "Choral" Symphony with the Lucerne Festival Chorus. The soloists were Elisabeth Schwarzkopf, Elsa Cavelti, Ernst Häfliger, and Otto Edelmann. Brain played the fourth horn solo. At Lucerne, Legge arranged for a photograph (Pl. 8), which shows (left to right) Manoug Parikian, Gareth Morris, Walter Legge, Jane Withers (the Orchestra's Managing Director), and Brain. Behind them is a picturesque view of Lake Lucerne. Brain was not able to take much vacation during his career, but he made a holiday out of this tour, travelling with his wife and their young son, Anthony, then two years old.[32]

Karajan recorded Beethoven's *Abscheulicher* from *Fidelio* in September 1954 with Schwarzkopf singing at her best and supported by the Philharmonia with the horns led by Brain. When the recording was first issued on Columbia long-playing record, it was coupled with a fine performance of Beethoven's Fifth Symphony; the recording date remains a mystery.[33]

Preparing for a tour to the United States made 1955 a busy year. Karajan recorded Sibelius Symphonies No. 6 and 7 in July and later the same month Beethoven's "Choral" Symphony with the Vienna Singverein and soloists Elisabeth Schwarzkopf, Marga Höffgen, Ernst Häfliger, and Otto Edelmann. Brain was with them, as related by C. B. Rees, who talked to Brain on July 29 before his performance of the Mátyás Seiber *Notturno* with the London Symphony Orchestra, conducted by Basil Cameron:

> He told me that he had just flown back from Vienna where he had been with the Philharmonia Orchestra to record Beethoven's Choral Symphony with the Choral Singverein of Vienna Gesellschaft der Musikfreunde, under Herbert von Karajan. This was one of the first records to be made by the new Stereosonic system by which two sound tracks are put on one tape, and together they give a more spatial effect to the music.[34]

Touring America with Karajan

Karajan and the Philharmonia toured the East Coast of America in 1955. When the orchestra arrived at their home during the tour, the Hotel Annapolis in Washington DC, Brain was reported by the *Washington Evening Star* as saying that he looked forward to enjoying the "biggest steak in town."[35]

As with the earlier tour with the RAF Symphony Orchestra, Brain was not called upon to play solo works. None of the other orchestra's principals played solo works either. The horns, in addition to Brain, were Neill Sanders (second), Alan Civil (third), Alfred Cursue (fourth), Aubrey Thonger (fifth) and Andrew McGavin (sixth). The orchestral pieces they took with them did feature the horns as in Mozart's Divertimento K.287 and the Hamilton Harty arrangement of Handel's *Water Music*. Both were also recorded with Karajan, and the American public was now familiar with a large repertoire of orchestral works produced for EMI's American company, Angel.

Although Brain did not appear as soloist, the American newspaper critics did not neglect to mention him as the "celestial horn player" (*Chicago Tribune*, November 7, 1955), the "wonderful horn player" (*Philadelphia Sunday Bulletin*, November 12, 1955) or "the peerless, dependable Dennis Brain" (*Philadelphia Inquirer*, November 16, 1955). R. A. Patton, critic of the *Kalamazoo Gazette* (November 9, 1955) reporting on the concert at Central High School auditorium, Kalamazoo, on November 8, described Brain's tone as "rich and perfect beyond criticism." The works performed at the concert included Mozart's Symphony No. 39, Ravel's *Rhapsodie Espagnole*, Beethoven's "Pastoral" Symphony, and Verdi's Overture to *La Forza del Destino*. The critic of the *Saturday Review* on November 12 gave some of the most enthusiastic accounts of the horn playing during the tour. Writing of the Divertimento of Mozart:

> Written for a quartet of strings and two horns, the Divertimento was played by perhaps thirty strings and, still, two horns. This is a perilous procedure unless the conductor is discreet, the concertmaster (who has the equivalent of a concerto to play in the middle movement) expert. Karajan and his superior string master, Manoug Parikian, qualified unequivocally.
>
> The horn players who contributed so much to the success of this introductory venture were "merely" the admirable Dennis Brain, heard here previously when he toured with the Royal Philharmonic under Beecham, and his able associate, Neill Sanders. Brain's strength is as the strength of ten, especially when he is playing softly. Together they wound their sound in and around that of the strings with a definition and purity that delighted the ear. Bolstered by other members of the section, the playing of the horn quartet was a spectacular feature on another program, of Harty's arrangement of the Handel *Water Music*. Few vocalists to be heard in the months to come will produce so secure a trill and turn as Brain and mates provided for the closing bars of the "Air." It was barely audible, but audibly perfect.[36]

The critic of the *New Yorker* singled out Brain for special praise:

> The wind instruments in the Philharmonia are played with exceptional precision and elegance of style, and here the work of certain individual artists attracts special attention. The most arresting of these is unquestionably the first horn player, Mr. Dennis Brain. An incomparable master of his difficult instrument, he plays his notes not only with faultless accuracy but with an aristocratic sense of musical phraseology that might be the envy of many a concert violinist or pianist.[37]

The critic of the *New York Nation* also mentioned Brain: "The visiting Philharmonia Orchestra of London opened its first concert in Carnegie Hall with a performance of four movements of Mozart's Divertimento K.287—a small-scale performance using a reduced group of strings that had the suavity and finish of von Karajan's style with Mozart, and that exhibited the beautiful playing of the orchestra's strings and its great solo horn, Dennis Brain."[38]

The critic of the *New York Times*, commenting on October 26 on the Philharmonia's first appearance at Carnegie Hall, described Brain as "the ablest in the trade" and drew attention to his former principal position in the Royal Philharmonic. Another critic, Hugh Thomson of the *Toronto Daily Star*, on November 12 described his solos as "veritable threads of gold running through the score." He was referring to Brain's playing at the concert of the previous evening in Toronto's Massey Hall. The program included Beethoven's "Pastoral" Symphony, Debussy's *La Mer*, and Verdi's Overture to *La Forza del Destino*. At the concert the previous night in Masonic Auditorium, Detroit, the works included the Handel-Harty *Water Music*, Brahms's *Variations on a Theme by Haydn* and Tchaikovsky's Symphony No. 4. The critic of the *Detroit Free Press*, J. Dorsey Callaghan, noticed on November 11 the "miraculous French horn section headed by the famed Dennis Brain. . . ." Other works performed during the tour that featured the horns included Sibelius's Fifth Symphony, which elicited the following praise from the critic of the *Michigan Daily:* "Sibelius's Fifth Symphony was the high point of the evening. From the beautifully executed Horn introduction to the gigantic climax of the persistent disjunct theme of the brasses that ends the composition, Von Karajan brought new meaning to this work."[39]

He was reporting on the concert the previous night at Hill Auditorium, Ann Arbor, Michigan, which also included Mozart's Symphony No. 39 and Brahms's *Variations on a Theme by Haydn*. The final concert of the tour, at Symphony Hall in Boston on November 19, drew the following praise from Rudolph Elie of the *Boston Sunday Herald*, speaking of the Divertimento K. 287:

> The Mozart, however, in which Mr. Von Karajan used a reduced string body, was exquisitely done beyond words to tell. Here the real distinction, the unanimity of artistic advancement of the players, the high virtuosity of each musician (not to mention the superb attainment of Dennis Brain, perhaps the greatest living horn player) gave this incomparably lovely work a radiance and a warmth and indeed a humanity it hardly ever has a chance to reveal.[40]

Harold Rogers, critic of the *Christian Science Monitor* was another who found Brain's playing in the Divertimento especially delightful: "Mr. von Karajan opened his program with a lucid reading of the Mozart Divertimento in B-flat, K.287. With a gentle baton and a caressing left hand he gave us Mozart in his sheerest beauty of sound—restrained, graceful, elegant, and scintillating. Dennis Brain's French horn was a joy to the ear and a lift to the heart."[41]

Brain made time on October 26 to appear on NBC television in the *Today Show*. The NBC Studio Archives have the following description of the broadcast: "Oct. 26, 1955–Wednesday (cont'd) 'B': "Dennis Brain, one of the foremost French horn players in the world, currently a soloist with the Philharmonia Orchestra of London—he speaks of his visit to New York, speaks of the French horn as a musical instrument and difficulties in playing it, history of the instrument, etc. (The Philharmonia Orchestra of London—which is different from the London Philharmonic Orchestra—was giving series [*sic*] of concerts in US at this time.)"[42]

Andrew McGavin, sixth horn in the Philharmonia section for the tour, remembered that Brain had appeared on television but not that he ever did anything to show off. Brain was a keen promoter of his instrument—he didn't promote himself.[43]

The following are extracts from the American press that especially highlight the horn playing during the tour. Their first concert in Constitution Hall in Washington DC received the following praise from Paul Hume in the *Washington Post* for Mozart's Divertimento K. 287: "The brightness of the slender-bored horns favored by the discerning Englishman matches the perfect sheen of the strings, who played the most dazzling passages, scales, arpeggios, and melting songful adagios."[44]

Another critic, from the *Washington Evening Star*, wrote with enthusiasm for the performance of this work, especially Manoug Parikian's solo playing and the "high horn parts" which "were a joy." They played a shortened version, possibly because the concert lasted two hours and fifteen minutes. The critic of the *Washington Daily News* also praised the horns who "alone would certainly lift a lesser orchestra into first rank."[45]

At Carnegie Hall, the Mozart Divertimento elicited the following praise from the critic of *New York Herald Tribune*:

> Within the first ten measures of the Mozart "Divertimento" (K.287) it was clear beyond the slightest doubt that the London Philharmonia is in the champion class . . . The two horns must come from another planet; their octaves and fifths, velvety and clear, blended with the strings like homogenized milk . . . Mr von Karajan molded this little masterpiece with solicitous care and well-nigh infallible musicianship that filled everyone with admiration.[46]

The critic of the *New Haven Register* commented on the many empty seats in Woolsey Hall for the concert on October 27, which he apparently enjoyed, especially the woodwinds and the horns in the Handel-Harty *Water Music*.

> The opening work last evening, the Handel-Harty "Water Music" suite emphasized the silken sonorities of the strings and the beautiful precision playing of woodwinds and horns. The ensemble playing, both in balance and texture, was notable for the sheer beauty and pure quality of the sounds. The solo work of the winds was like so many tonal jewels whose lustre shone over opulently molded backgrounds. This performance also brought forth some of the most masterful horn playing that it has ever been my pleasure to hear.[47]

Evans Clinchy of the *Hartford Times* (October 28) also admired the horn playing in the Handel-Harty piece.[48]

The critic of the *Grand Rapids Press* gave special credit to Karajan for the Philharmonia's playing at their concert in the Civic Auditorium in Grand Rapids, Michigan, on Monday November 7: "Certain qualities of the orchestra on this occasion are to be credited to von Karajan. One is the extraordinary clarity with which the inner voices are constantly in evidence. Each little counter-melody is to be heard weaving in and out of the music's fabric; whispering woodwinds are heard distinctly beneath massed strings; muted French horns cut through the densest orchestration."[49]

The works performed at the concert were the Handel-Harty *Water Music*, Beethoven's "Pastoral" Symphony, and Debussy's *La Mer*. It's interesting how the critic describes the horns. At this time, Brain had long since changed to the wider bore German instrument, and yet he managed to play in the same focused, penetrating way that he did on the narrower bore instrument of the previous decade. The critic of the *Springfield Union*, reporting on the concert the previous day (November 16) at the University of Massachusetts, Amherst, was also impressed by the carrying power of the horns through the orchestra:

> Mr. von Karajan seems to be satisfied with a performance within a relatively small framework, providing every detail is completely clear. He has some marvellous players, including the famous Dennis Brain heading the horn section. The playing of the horn quartet in the Aria of the "Water Music" was spectacular as it emerged through the orchestral pattern. There was much to admire in the clever contrasts and sustaining interest in the various episodes of the "Water Music," a work which in less able hands, could become monotonous.[50]

Several of the newspaper critics noted the difference in the sound but not always with the same impartiality. The orchestra returned to Constitution Hall on October 29, and the program comprised the Handel-Harty *Water Music*, Beethoven "Pastoral" Symphony, and the Bartok Concerto for Orchestra. The *Washington Post* critic praised the horns in the Handel: "The horns in the orchestra, proud in Handel's might, were dexterous and distant all at once, when the music suddenly came as though from far away."[51]

Karajan had recorded all these works in 1952 and 1953 with the Philharmonia. Indeed, many of the works performed by the Orchestra during the tour had been recorded commercially. The tour must have considerably boosted the sale of these records.

The tour's last rehearsal and concert in Boston has received a full account by several writers, so it is not necessary to repeat the story except to say that Karajan's close relationship with the Philharmonia was soon to end. It was not merely a matter of tempers flaring at the end of an exhausting tour; it concerned his new appointments. During the tour, Karajan had received news that he was to succeed Furtwängler as conductor of the Berlin Philharmonic, and his engagements with the Philharmonia and other commitments had to be tailored accordingly. Karajan did tour Europe with the Philharmonia in early 1956. Back in London, a concert at the Royal Festival Hall on June 20 was reviewed in *The Times.* Strauss's *Vier letzte Lieder* was performed with its incomparable soloist, Schwarzkopf.[52]

Neill Sanders, who was for seven years second horn with Brain in the Philharmonia, in 1991 remembered that 1956 concert. In 1990, EMI had made it available commercially for the first time on CD. Sanders remembered that Karajan changed the order of the songs. They finished with "September": "The net result was that we had the horn solo coming last and what we heard from Dennis was something so incredibly beautiful, the whole place was just spell-bound. The scalp on my neck started tickling and my hair started standing up and I had never heard anything so beautiful before or ever since. It was just incredible."[53] *The Times* critic complained about "September" being placed last. Brain had recorded the songs with Schwarzkopf, conducted by Otto Ackermann, but perhaps it was in live performance that this piece is heard best.[54]

Other Conductors and the Philharmonia

The Philharmonia's conductors were so numerous that to do justice to the subject would require more than a chapter. As this subject has been well-documented by Pettitt and Hunt, to name just two, we consider only a few solo concert appearances of Brain and two orchestral concerts: *Vier Letzte Lieder* with Jurinac, conducted by Rankl, and *Das Lied von der Erde*, with Dermota and Fischer-Dieskau, conducted by Klemperer.

An important concert was the first public performance in England of Hindemith's Horn Concerto, on April 16, 1951, Del Mar conducting. Also in the same program was Britten's Serenade, with Pears. *The Times* critic was not greatly impressed with the piece but praised the conductor, soloist, and orchestra:

> Hindemith's music, of which we have heard little of late, is always well made and generally rather drab. The new concerto runs true to form, and its most interesting movement is its last, in which a cadenza for the soloist carries by the implication of its phrasing a verbal message about the transfiguration of the present into the past. Thus an instrument comes one degree nearer to becoming articulate than in Beethoven's instrumental recitatives.
>
> Mr. Brain gave what shape and colour the short movements would take, and in this final movement achieved some sort of eloquence. He later joined Mr. Peter Pears in a finely wrought performance of Britten's Serenade, in which there is no drabness at all but only gleams of silver.
>
> Mr. Norman Del Mar, having a first-class professional orchestra instead of his lusty enthusiasts down in Chelsea, proved himself a conductor with a sensitive touch.[55]

Modern works written for Brain rarely elicited words of praise from music critics. Performances of the Serenade with Brain did not attract uniform praise, although the piece was generally liked.

Following the successful first European tour with Karajan in May 1952, the orchestra's first broadcast concert was not with Karajan but with Karl Rankl on July 12, 1952. The chief work was Strauss's *Vier letzte Lieder*, sung by Sena Jurinac. By a chance, it was partly recorded off-the-air. Brain is heard very clearly in "September."[56]

Del Mar returned to conduct on one of his rare appearances with them, at the Royal Festival Hall on February 24, 1954. *The Times* critic wrote appreciatively:

> Mr. Dennis Brain took a rest from Mozart horn concertos, and gave us the second, and less familiar, of Richard Strauss's two horn concertos in E-flat, a late work imbued with all the ebullience of *Till Eulenspiegel* and all the nostalgia of the *Four Last Songs*, one whose most devilish difficulties Mr. Brain dispatches as though he had had 25 years to get them under his control.[57]

Brain continued to play concertos, but most of his time in the Philharmonia was spent making recordings of the orchestral repertoire. His orchestral playing did not escape the notice of the concert-goers and critics. Music critic Alan Blyth recalled the last Edinburgh Festival of 1957 in which Brain played the first horn part in Mahler's *Das Lied von der Erde* at Usher Hall on August 29. The Philharmonia was conducted by Otto Klemperer and the soloists were Anton Dermota and Dietrich Fischer-Dieskau:

> I do recall him playing wonderfully in *Das Lied*. . . . It was more than anything the strength and beauty of his playing, allied to his almost casual

> insouciance as though it were the easiest thing in the world to play the horn that made him so remarkable. He was, of course, incomparable in the Mozart concertos and those by Richard Strauss, his recordings of which are, to my ear, still unsurpassed.[58]

Recollections by Philharmonia Colleagues

Brain had already made a reputation as a brilliant young soloist before he joined the Philharmonia. The players soon found that his musicianship set new standards not only for brass and wind playing but also for all other musicians, irrespective of their instruments. Arthur Wilson, who joined the Philharmonia in 1951 and in 1963 became principal trombonist, which he remained for many years, remembered one occasion:

> When Flagstad was doing one of her many farewell performances, *Siegfried* has the Horn Call in it, and he [Dennis] stood in this studio and I have never heard it played so loud! It was phenomenal—with shockingly high notes! And it was a most exciting build up! How to do it with such confidence is quite remarkable. He was a wonderful player, no doubt.[59]

Joan Ingpen, Philharmonia's agent until 1950, recalled an episode of Brain's busy life playing the horn solos in film music: "He was impeccable. What can you say about Dennis? You never had to do a re-take. It just seemed to flow out of him naturally."[60]

Ingpen also recalled an occasion after a long film recording session when the conductor, Ernest Irving, congratulated Brain for not making a false note the whole day. Another colleague in the Philharmonia, Hugh Bean, summed up his qualities, which continued to leave their mark in recordings many years later:

> He had so mastered technical problems that they were totally put in the background. What Dennis Brain's playing to me still has, is a lightness of touch, a charm and one might almost say an insolence in his mastery. He didn't just play a fast passage immaculately, he was thumbing his nose at the same time. With that came an exhilaration in listening to Dennis that for me and plenty of my colleagues is as fresh today as when Dennis was playing.[61]

Morris, who joined the Philharmonia in 1948, remembered the special seating arrangement that Brain adopted for the Philharmonia horn section. Like his father in the BBC Symphony, Brain sat on the far right end of the section:

> Usually the first horn sits next to the first trombone. Dennis Brain reversed—he sat on the end there. Conductors said, "Very interesting,

> Mr. Brain prefers to sit there. He obviously feels that if he's apart a little from it all he can blend with everybody because he can hear the whole ensemble, probably." But in fact, Dennis insisted on sitting there so he could get to the coffee more easily at the interval![62]

On occasion, however, he did not sit at the right end of the section. He is known to have been seated second place in from the right at Khachaturian's recording sessions with the Philharmonia in November and December 1954 with the section of Thonger, Brain, Sanders, Chapman, and Cursue.[63]

Basil Tschaikov, a clarinetist colleague of Brain's in both the Royal Philharmonic (from 1947) and the Philharmonia, and also from time to time in the London Baroque Ensemble, remembered Brain's Raoux horn, which, to his ears, sounded more refined than the later German instrument. For example, he remembered a performance of the Wagner *Siegfried Idyll* with Beers (second horn), especially the little interjecting octaves, which he thought were "magical." Beers was Brain's second in the RPO from 1947 to 1948 and second in the Philharmonia from 1949 to 1950. Tschaikov summed up Brain's qualities: "He always had the audience in the palm of his hand. His playing was so effortless, refined and though sensual never smaltzy. He was one of those players who in some magical way made it easy for anyone to play with him."[64]

Hugh Bean drew attention to the complete recording made with Karajan of *Der Rosenkavalier* in 1956. It was recorded over many sessions in December, and the part of the work that particularly impressed Bean was the Introduction, as he recalled:

> He [Dennis] also had the property of being able to mould the section. I would urge you to hear the opening of the 1956 *Rosenkavalier* with the Philharmonia. That is a horn section setting the world on fire! Dennis is at the end. It wasn't anything obvious or tangible that he did but just his presence there made four, five, six, seven—whatever number of horn players were there—a tightly moulded unit and to hear our section catch fire like the beginning of that Karajan *Rosenkavalier* of 1956 is still I think a great thrill.[65]

Examples of Brain's special qualities in recorded orchestral repertoire, as well as in his concert appearances, recorded or unrecorded, has highlighted some of the key moments in his career with the Philharmonia—a virtuoso orchestra with conductors of international repute. Brain's artistry as a soloist with the Philharmonia was not confined to appearances in front of the orchestra, but included many opportunities to shine as one of them.

KINGSWAY HALL
KINGSWAY, W.C.2

PHILHARMONIA
CONCERT SOCIETY
(Walter Legge and Victor Schuster)
AUTUMN, 1945

PHILHARMONIA
ORCHESTRA
(Leader: Leonard Hirsch)

Sir THOMAS BEECHAM
Bart.

REGINALD KELL

Mozart Concert

1945
Saturday October 27, at 3 p.m.

Programme 6d.

IBBS & TILLETT,
124, Wigmore Street, W.1

Plate 1 Philharmonia Orchestra's first public concert, conducted by Sir Thomas Beecham, October 27, 1945, Kingsway Hall, London.
Gamble collection.

Plate 2 Dennis and Yvonne Brain's wedding, Petersfield, Hampshire, September 8, 1945.
With permission from Yvonne Brain.

Plate 3 Dennis and Yvonne Brain's wedding, with Gareth Morris and bridesmaids.
With permission from Yvonne Brain.

Plate 4 Gareth Morris, Walter Legge, and Dennis Brain (behind the steering wheel) on their way to see Toscanini at Zurich via St. Gothard Pass. See plates 5–7 for the same journey. *With permission from Gareth Morris and Patricia Morris.*

Plate 5 Dennis Brain and Hudson saloon, entrance of St. Gothard Pass. *With permission from Gareth Morris and Patricia Morris.*

Plate 6 Gareth Morris, walking at the entrance to the St. Gothard Pass. *With permission from Gareth Morris and Patricia Morris.*

Plate 7 Entrance to the St. Gothard Pass, black ice melting at daybreak. Walter Legge, Dennis Brain, and Gareth Morris (Elisabeth Schwarzkopf taking the photograph). *With permission from Gareth Morris and Patricia Morris.*

Plate 8 Manoug Parikian, Gareth Morris, Jane Withers, Walter Legge, and Dennis Brain. Lucerne, 1954. *With permission from Gareth Morris and Patricia Morris.*

CHAPTER 6

A Horn Virtuoso's Letters

In his now famous *Desert Island Discs* appearance on the Home Service, August 13, 1956, Brain mentions that he is a bad correspondent and that he would choose to take a typewriter with him to his desert island to remind him every time he wakes up that he does not have to write a letter! Yet all his correspondence was handwritten. Some of his correspondence, perhaps, will never come to light—letters he wrote to the general public, to concert agents, friends, colleagues, composers, and family.

Those letters that remain reveal much about what kind of man he was, music apart. They show that he was polite, modest, generous, with a good sense of humor. The letters also suggest that he was excellent at time-keeping and organization of his musical schedule. The time-keeping was something he also did as a challenge; when, for example, traveling from Dieppe to Nice, he would look at a notebook he kept of the times for journeys to work out his previous records for the distance traveled by car and how he could beat his own record.[1]

In his letters to the BBC, it is clear he has a sense of his own worth and is persistent in fighting for higher fees for solo and chamber music engagements. No doubt, in pressing for the right fee, he was not thinking of himself first and foremost, but as a provider for his family. One is reminded, however, of the business-like approach of his uncle Alfred, who by insisting on double the fees, helped not only himself but other horn players working at the time in Los Angeles.[2]

Sometimes Brain's letters give a glimpse of the private person, such as his ambitions to be a conductor, or occasionally they reveal his musical taste. Never do we hear a bad word about anybody. He is not a gossiper. He does not crack jokes at other people's expense.

It may be true that Brain did not enjoy writing letters, but he certainly had a busy correspondence with the BBC. Most of these letters are straightforward acceptances or refusals to take part in a broadcast. Sometimes if a subject especially interested him, he would write at length.

Postcard to Ernest Tomlinson

While in Düsseldorf on January 28, 1957, Brain wrote to British composer Ernest Tomlinson concerning the new work Tomlinson was writing, *Rhapsody and Rondo* for horn and orchestra. This was later given a first performance at the Royal Festival Hall on June 22, 1957, and also broadcast live on the BBC for the Light Programme Music Festival that year.

> As you see I am away but have time to catch up on various things. I think your idea for a horn theme is fine, providing one doesn't jump about outside an octave. The phrase at the bottom of the manuscript is difficult at speed because it is over an octave for each jump. Otherwise I look forward to a new work & will ring when I return.[3]

Letter to Walter Legge

In the winter of 1957, Brain was scheduled to record the Haydn Concertos for EMI. This letter of April 19, 1956, to Walter Legge shows how much advanced planning could be required for important projects.

> Thank you so much for your suggestion that I should record the Haydn Concerti.
>
> Nothing would give me greater pleasure, except perhaps that Elisabeth and you would find a way to come to my concert on April 27th—to lend invaluable encouragement.
>
> You have been so helpful so far, in helping me to avoid clashes, that I think it only fair that you should hear something of the result, and I personally would value very much your opinion.
>
> I find the first Haydn much better than the second, which is apparently doubtful, and have a Photostat score of it, which is quite interesting. It has in the second movement writing which is much more adventurous than Mozart, a finale which is not $^6/_8$!
>
> I was sorry to hear of Mr Ackermann's indisposition, and hope he will soon be well.[4]

The invitation was for the third concert of the Dennis Brain Chamber Orchestra at Wigmore Hall.

Letter to Gerard Hoffnung

Brain's musical interests encompassed the light-hearted and humorous, such as the first Hoffnung Festival Concert, November 13, 1956, at the Royal Festival Hall. Over three thousand people were in the audience, and the concert was also broadcast on television. Many people were involved in the creation of this concert, which had been inspired by Hoffnung's little book of cartoons, entitled *Hoffnung Music Festival.*

Not surprisingly, Hoffnung was the central figure in the concert, excerpts of which were issued commercially by EMI. Mrs. Hoffnung recently told the authors that the recording had remained in the EMI catalogue until 2010. Brain played the hosepipe in a movement from an alphorn concerto by Leopold Mozart, accompanied by the strings of the Morley College Symphony Orchestra conducted by Norman Del Mar. Brain also played the organ part in the *Grand, Grand Overture* written for the concert by Malcolm Arnold.

> After the concert, Brain, with characteristic modesty, returned the check for his fee to Hoffnung with the note:
>
> Thank you so much for your letters and cheque, which I am returning as I think we arranged in the end that I should receive only expenses.
>
> These expenses, incidentally, amount to about half a dozen connections, to join together the various experimental pieces of hosepipe now lying somewhat festooned about the garden! And are more than balanced by being allowed to play the first instrument in the Royal Festival Hall that I have not had to practise—the organ in the Grand Overture. My wife and I enjoyed the concert immensely, and look forward to the next![5]

Letters to the BBC

Aside from routine acceptances or refusals for broadcasts, Brain occasionally makes efforts to promote a new concerto or other work for the horn, including chamber music. Such works promoted in broadcasts include concertos by Gordon Bryan and Kenneth Essex. Brain often sent letters querying the amount of the fee for solo or chamber music. They reveal his sense of humor and clear business sense. He could have made substantially more in fees if he had gone to America and made a career there, so money per se clearly did not attract him, but the correct fee certainly did. Usually, the BBC gave him what he requested, no doubt aware that they could not risk losing someone so irreplaceable. Some BBC internal letters concerning Brain's broadcast engagements indicate how much they valued him.

This letter from July 6, 1942, is an early example of proposing a solo broadcast. Brain is deferential in his letter, partly perhaps because of admiration for his father. In the letter, he is clearly not backward in promoting himself by mentioning some professional solo engagements.

> My father suggested I should write to you concerning the possibility of playing a Mozart horn concerto with the BBC Symphony Orchestra.
>
> If this would be possible I should like to play No 4 in E-flat K.495, which I have broadcast with Walter Goehr & also played at the National Gallery with Wing Commander O'Donnell and the Air Force orchestra of which I am a member.
>
> I have always wanted to play one with the BBC Orchestra & so hope you will be able to arrange it.

The broadcast of the Fourth Concerto was on April 8, 1942, with the Orchèstre Raymonde, conducted by Goehr. Brain wrote on March 19, 1942, to confirm his availability for that broadcast, "subject, of course to the exigencies of the Service" which he sometimes added as a standard phrase. The above letter refers to the broadcast of the same concerto on September 17, 1942, with the BBC Symphony Orchestra. He wrote again on August 17 to confirm the timing of Mozart's Concerto No. 4 for that broadcast.[6]

This letter of July 15, 1944, shows that music went on, in spite of the inconvenience of bombs.

> I shall be free to broadcast the Mozart Quintet on Aug 8th with the Dorian Quartet.
>
> If there is any doubt of it not going out because of these bombs would it be possible to pre-record it.
>
> As you see I have changed address & have a telephone at last, the reason being that I was bombed out though not hurt.[7]

He was increasingly in demand during the war, in spite of his commitments to the RAF. One letter mentions two engagements: a transmission on the Afrikaans service on May 3, 1943, and Ferguson's Octet for winds and strings on April 19, 1943.[8]

His admiration for other distinguished musicians on various instruments is known, but he does not often appear to have expressed opinions about them. This letter of August 17, 1947, is rare, for it contains his personal opinion of a soprano, Victoria de Los Angeles. If he did have anything to say, he was always positive and encouraging.

> Further to our chat the other day, I have pleasure in sending you some "literature" about Victoria de Los Angeles and about our musical activities in

> Barcelona. The Spanish criticisms of this singer are rather over-lauded with "exuberancia" but they do I think point to a unanimous opinion of her worth.
>
> I should be grateful if you would ask your secretary if she could send me two seats for all or any of the proms beginning August 22 to Friday Aug. 29th? And for Sept. 9th to 10th?
>
> Also 6 copies of Prom programme for Sunday to interested Spanish musicians?
>
> I have written to Alec Robertson mentioning your name with many thanks & kind regards, . . .[9]

Letters Querying Fees

Brain often returned BBC contracts requesting higher fees, either for himself alone or in chamber music that was difficult for all the players. He was not representing only himself in asking for more money. From wartime onward, his solo engagements increased, and with the demand for his services, he naturally expected to receive higher fees commensurate with what he received outside the BBC. In fact, the BBC usually paid less than his outside fees and gave all sorts of reasons for not giving him what he asked for.

One of the earliest requests for more money was a letter on May 18, 1946. Brain was to give a recital on the Eastern Service on May 31. The "program as broadcast" file tells us that he was broadcasting on the Green Network to India, Burma, and Indonesia at 17:30 (5:30 p.m.), accompanied by pianist John Wills, in the Beethoven Sonata. Brain states in his letter that he is returning the contract for the Eastern Service broadcast, asking for a fee of fifteen guineas.[10]

He wrote again on July 27, 1946, returning another contract, requesting fifteen guineas. In this instance, he apparently won the argument because a BBC note on the letter indicates that the contract is to be reissued:

> I'm sure you will remember the last time I gave a solo recital, on an overseas service, I received fifteen guineas.
>
> I feel, & I'm sure you will agree, as this recital is on the Home Service it is of greater importance than the previous one, particularly as it includes a work very seldom done if not before Villanelle of Paul Dukas. Therefore, I think it is worth the same as before if not more & so I am sending the contract back for revision relying on your usual generosity.
>
> [in pencil, bottom "reissue at 15 gns card"][11]

In this letter of November 24, 1946, a few months later, he makes a strong claim for a fee of twenty guineas for the performance of a concerto on

December 6, 1946—the Strauss Concerto No. 1, presumably, although the letter does not indicate. These demands for more money must be viewed in the context of his increasing reputation as a soloist.

> I have just received your contract for the Strauss Concerto on Dec. 6th.
>
> As one's fee, I feel, should be graduated according to the nature of the work, difficulty & importance, etc., ten guineas chamber music, fifteen solo recital & I think I should receive twenty guineas for a concerto which is my usual outside fee.
>
> I know you'll agree. I have sent this contract back in anticipation of that event.[12]

One of the interesting aspects of these demands for more money was the re-evaluation of the importance of works for the horn in the chamber music repertoire. The BBC graduated fees according to which class they fell into, so in some cases a chamber work like the Brahms Trio or the Mozart Quintet K.407, requiring as much, if not more work for the horn player than a concerto, received the same standard chamber music fee. Brain did his best to change that and to press for higher fees. This letter of November 29, 1947, is an example:

> I am so sorry to send another contract back but I do feel that with a work such as the Brahms Horn Trio, the master piece of the very small horn repertoire, one should receive a little more than for an ordinary chamber music broadcast.
>
> I think fifteen guineas would be more appropriate don't you? [13]

In this instance, he succeeded in obtaining the higher fee.

Brain was less successful with other similarly soloistic works of the chamber repertoire. Sometimes there were disputes as to whether a piece was in the concerto or the chamber music class. For example, Vinter's *Hunter's Moon* for horn and orchestra, written for John Burden during the war, Brain classed as a concerto. He wrote to Carrell on April 9, 1949, returning an unacceptable contract for performance of this piece with the Variety Orchestra. Carrell's reply on April 27 clearly considered the piece to be chamber music, for which Brain's BBC fee was £15.15 and requested he return the contract with his acceptance at the earliest opportunity. The argument continued into May 1949 with another letter from Brain stating his case as forcibly as he could:

> Thank you for your letter concerning my engagement with the Variety Orchestra on Tuesday, 26th April.

> I think you must have been misled as to the nature of the work I was performing on that day, as it does fall into the concerto class, even though it may not be named as such.
>
> I feel that any work in which I have to perform in front of an orchestra with their accompaniment must be classed as a concerto, regardless of length, & as this engagement was exactly similar to my previous one with Mr. Jenkins on Feb. 1st, I naturally assume that it will be paid at the same rate & am therefore returning this contract for your amendment.[14]

This does not appear to have had a happy conclusion, and no evidence has surfaced that the BBC amended the contract fee. Brain later wrote to inform them that his concert agents, Ibbs & Tillett, had raised his concerto fee to twenty-five guineas and requested that the BBC amend a contract he was returning to them, to show consistency in what he received for outside solo engagements. The BBC was polite as ever in their response but made it clear that as they dealt directly with him by letter and not through his agents, the fee would remain the same.

> [In pen, top centre: "to pay 25 gns" and in pencil "I & T [Ibbs & Tillett] do not arrange his broadcasts"]
>
> My agents, Messrs Ibbs & Tillett have decided from the next season onwards to raise my concerto fee to Thirty guineas where possible. [In pencil: "25 or 30"]
>
> As I am sure you will agree that all my concerto engagements should be paid at the same fee, I am returning this contract for suitable amendment & would appreciate your views on the matter.[15]

According to the BBC's annotations of the above letter, it appears they agreed to meet him half-way and pay twenty-five guineas. He was more successful in getting a full concerto fee for performing in Mozart's *Sinfonia Concertante* K.297b, although the horn is only one of four soloists. One of the BBC staff has penciled a note on Brain's letter of August 29, 1950, "I'm afraid he's right!"

> Whilst agreeing that the Wind Concertante of Mozart is not for solo performers, I do feel that it is in the nature of a concerto, & is, incidentally, more difficult than most solo works, & as such should receive the full concert fee.
>
> I am therefore returning the contract for your consideration.[16]

His humor is expressed in the next polite refusal on August 21, 1952, to agree to the fee stated in a contract sent to him by the BBC for a concert broadcast:

> Thank you for your contract dated 15th August which I am returning, as I feel sure you will agree, that each separate performance of a concerto should be paid at the full rate. After all, I am not expected to give a "special ¾ performance" and inevitably, the second time is more difficult than the first.
>
> Stamped "22 Aug 52"; in pencil, bottom left corner and inscribed, "Tell him of the agreement with ISM"[17]

The note inscribed by a member of staff at the BBC refers to the BBC's agreement with the ISM (Incorporated Society of Musicians) that allowed for 25 percent of the fee to be payment for the rehearsal and the remaining 75 percent for the performance itself. The BBC replied to Brain's letter on August 25, explaining these new rules that had been adopted since the previous Christmas.[18]

A surprising offer from the BBC to Brain came in 1949. They were considering who should replace Aubrey Thonger as principal horn of the BBC Symphony Orchestra that year. In the event, the position went to Douglas Moore. Brain's reply on December 7, 1949, shows how much in demand he was at this time in other orchestras and as a soloist. It also shows what deference he had to his father, who had been principal horn of that orchestra from its foundation until his early retirement at the end of the promenade season of 1945.

> Thank you so much for your letter & its proposal regarding the position of Principal Horn of the Symphony Orchestra, a seat which my Father held with such distinction for so many years.
>
> It is, of course, a part of tradition which I should like to maintain in the family, but my commitments take me well into the autumn of next year, & at present I do not see any arrangement to which we could come.
>
> I feel, therefore, that it would be rather pointless, at the moment, to talk anything over, though I most certainly appreciate your consideration of me for the responsible position of First Horn.[19]

The BBC replied trying to change his mind, and his second reply gives another reason why he chooses to turn down the offer.

> I have thought over most carefully the question of the position of Principal Horn of the BBC Symphony Orchestra, & feel that, at the moment, I am too young to accept a permanent contract.
>
> I appreciate the honour that you should approach me for such a position, and regret that I am unable to accept at the present time.[20]

This reason—"I am too young"— is not convincing. Had he not been the original principal horn of both the Philharmonia Orchestra since 1945 (aged twenty-four), and Royal Philharmonic Orchestra since 1946 (aged twenty-five)? At this time, his father was still alive, was the Horn Professor at the Royal Academy, and continued to play in London's orchestras (second horn, Sadler's Wells, from 1950, occasionally in the Philharmonia until 1950, etc.) but not for the BBC Symphony (except for a year as fifth horn in 1951), and that his declining health had been the cause of his early retirement. It must have been embarrassing for Brain to be offered the position. Although Brain was not one to refuse a golden opportunity if it came along, here we see that he cares very much for his father's feelings, and it is understandable why he should write this letter.

Brain's restlessness with his role as soloist has been remarked on by several of his colleagues. Whether it was restlessness or not, or something more positive (i.e., exploring additional avenues to express his musical talents), the following letter to Maurice Johnstone on November 14, 1951, concerning the post of conductor of the BBC Northern Orchestra, is interesting. The date is also surprisingly early, several years before he had established his Chamber Orchestra.

> No doubt Mr. Coulston has informed you of our talk together, a few weeks ago, regarding the position of Conductor of the BBC Northern Orchestra, during which he advised me, should I be serious, writing to the BBC in London. On giving the matter further thought, I felt that I should let you know that my interest in the position is no idle whim.
>
> Naturally, I have no desire, for obvious reasons, to give up the Horn. Mr. Coulston, in fact, suggesting that it would be possible to do both, as my solo playing takes up only a small part of my time, but feel that I should like to take a more directive part in music than is at present possible, which prompts this letter with the query as to the course I should pursue.
>
> I realize, of course, that the post may have been filled by now. Nevertheless, I would appreciate being considered as a candidate, if not now, then perhaps in the future.[21]

Johnstone, head of North Regional Music and one of the most important people in broadcasting, replied on November 21, expressing his complete astonishment that Brain should choose a career that was already well-supplied with excellent conductors. The BBC's duty, he said, was to promote professional conductors. He drew attention to the fact that Brain was "a supreme master" of the horn. He recommended that if Brain were indeed serious about his ambition to conduct, he should consult Herbert Murrell who would, no doubt, advise him that he ought to pursue the career outside of the BBC.[22]

Another aspect of Brain's career was his promotion of new works for the horn, which was enthusiastic, and he certainly helped many new composers establish their careers. He was keen to bring forward new solo works for the instrument, and one concerto that he liked performing was that of Gordon Bryan. He recommends it to the BBC in this letter of March 20, 1950:

> I shall be quite free to play a concerto at the Promenade Concert on Thursday, August 17th.
>
> Might I suggest, that, as the No. 4 Concerto of Mozart has been played rather more frequently than the others, I play instead, either No. 2 or 3, or, the new work of Gordon Bryan on theme of Scarlatti for Horn & String Orchestra, which had such a success at Bournemouth on December 1st last.[23]

The performance of the Gordon Bryan Concerto at Bournemouth Winter Gardens on December 1, 1949, with the Bournemouth Municipal Orchestra conducted by Rudolf Schwarz was broadcast on the BBC Home Service. He followed up the letter above with another promoting the idea of the Bryan Concerto:

> Many thanks for your letter regarding the choice of Concerto for the Promenade Concert on August 17th.
>
> I should like, very much, to play the Mozart Concerto in Eb, No. 3, K.447, which is approximately 14 minutes in length.
>
> May I mention a new concerto for Horn & Strings which was very well received at its first performance on Dec. 15th 1949, in Bournemouth with Rudolf Schwarz. It is by Gordon Bryan, on themes of Scarlatti and is a very charming work, duration 16 minutes.
>
> As I shall be performing it in Bromley on April 22nd no doubt Sir Adrian, who is conducting on that occasion, will give you a separate opinion on it. [24]

Apart from promoting new works for the horn, Brain also was keen to explore existing repertoire. He wrote the following letter to Leonard Isaacs on December 4, 1953, recommending Kurt Atterberg's Concerto Op. 28 (composed 1926):

> I saw Walter Goehr a few days ago and suggested that I play on April 12 the second concerto of Mozart, K.417, as it is less frequently done than the others. It is about 13 minutes in length.
>
> May I ask you of the possibility of broadcasting the Hindemith again—also the Kurt Atterberg which I believe has not yet been performed, though I may be wrong there.[25]

Brain also performed existing repertoire by established composers rediscovered in modern times. For example, Haydn's *Divertimento a tré* (1767), at the National Gallery in 1946 (see Chapter 2), Haydn's Concert Trio, *Pietà de Mé*, composed in 1791 (BBC, 1956) and Vivaldi's Concerto for two horns, RV538, for his lecture-recital, *The Early Horn* (BBC, 1955). With other soloists, he gave the first modern performance of Haydn's *Concert Trio* for the Third Programme on December 16, 1956, which was broadcast the next day. He wrote to ask for the part to be sent to him, adding "Obbligati can be treacherous things!" For the actual performance, the music was transposed from the original key of E-flat major to D major, but even in transposition, it proved to be difficult.[26]

The following list that Brain sent to Leonard Isaacs is taken from his own private music library in 1951. This contains not only works for quintet (mentioned in his letter to Denis Stevens of the same date and listed in Appendix A) but also concertos that are hardly heard of nowadays, including those by Atterberg and Gillmann. Brain has systematically divided the list into categories. His handwriting is rather difficult to make out at times.

> It occurred to me that you might care to have a note of some lesser known works for Horn & so am enclosing a list of such pieces, with approximate timings, in the hope that they may be of some use to you.
>
> I am sending also, at his request, a list of wind chamber music to Mr. Stevens.
>
> **Concertos for Horn**
>
> Strauss. No. 2 in Eb Normal Orchestra. Up to 2 horns, 2 trumpets, 2 tympani. 18'
>
> Hindemith. in F, as above, no trumpets. 15'
>
> Scarlatti, Arr. Gordon Bryan. Strings. 15'
>
> Gordon Jacob. Strings. 18'
>
> Weber. Concertino. 15'
>
> Chabrier. Larghetto. 10'
>
> Kenneth Essex. Concerto. 20'
>
> Kurt Gillmann Concerto. 20'
>
> Seiber: Notturno Strings. 10'
>
> Hugo Cole. Concerto. Strings, Flute, 2 Oboes. 20'
>
> Driessler. Concerto. Strings. 18'
>
> Atterberg. Concerto. Strings & Percussion. 20'

Horn & Piano

Hindemith. Sonata. 15'

Samuel H Adler. Sonata. 15'

Schumann. Adagio & Allegro. 10'

Ecklebe. Sonata [hole punched in letter where timing was written!]

H. Ranch. Two Little Suites. 15'

G. F. Linstead. Sonata. 15'

Koechlin. Sonata. 15'

Reuchsel. Reverie & Villanelle. 5'

Dukas. Villanelle. 5'

Tcherepnin. Melodie d'Amore 4'

[Tcherepnin] Enchantment. 4'

Busser. Cantecor 10'

Nielsen. Canto Serioso. 5'

Soussemire. Fantasie. 5'

Leon Stekke. Poème Sylvestre. 15'

With Orchestra & Piano

Tomasi. Chant Corse. 5'

Paul Vidal. Pièce de Concert. 8'

[Wind Quintet]

Florent Schmitt. Lied & Scherzo. 15'

Horn & Double Wind Quintet 15'

[Horn Quartet]

Tcherepnin. Suite for Horn Quartet. 15'

Brain's handwriting is difficult at times to make out and such names as "Ecklebe" and "H Ranch" may not be accurately deciphered.

Some of the above pieces have been published. For example, Samuel H. Adler's Sonata for Horn and Piano, published in 1951, was written in 1948. We contacted the composer, in case Brain had met him or corresponded. Adler was surprised to learn that Brain possessed his piece and also delighted, but he had had no contact with him. Paul Vidal (1863–1931) wrote *Pièce de Concert* for the entrance exam to the Paris Conservatoire in 1924. It was published by Masters Music Publications, in Boca Raton, in 2001.[27]

Isaacs replied to Brain on November 12, 1951, thanking him for the list and reminding him of a forthcoming broadcast of the Schoenberg Quintet on March 9, 1952. For more information on this broadcast, and a list of repertoire from Brain's library that he sent to Isaacs, see Chapter 3 and Appendix A.[28]

Letters to Fans

Not much is known about Brain's fan mail. He must have received countless letters from fans, but whether he would have had the time to respond is doubtful. Here is one that he wrote to a young amateur horn player, Martin Prowse, in December 1953:

> The answer to your letter concerning my forthcoming engagements. I shall be playing Mozart No. 2 Concerto on January 6 in the Wigmore Hall, live. Concerts in Derby on January 13 and with the Philharmonia Orchestra on January 10. Otherwise I shall be recording where, of course visitors are not allowed.
>
> Should you be able to come to any of the concerts, do come round and make yourself known.[29]

CHAPTER

7

Teacher and Lecturer

Teacher

Brain was too busy performing to have much time to teach or to demonstrate and perform for lecture-recitals. Very early on, he had possibly his first experience of teaching when, as a student at the Royal Academy of Music, he gave horn lessons to the future founder of the National Youth Orchestra, Dame Ruth Railton. We do not know any details of these lessons. Many years later, in her autobiography, Dame Ruth remembered, "Dennis taught me to play the horn and I did his harmony papers for him. He was a true friend and a fine musician, with a simple style, his own beautiful sound, and personal qualities still remembered years after his tragic death."[1] During the 1950s, Brain's involvement with the NYO was an interesting extension of his teaching by demonstration. This could not, however, be a regular activity owing to his many other commitments.

Like his father, he taught by demonstration, although, unlike his father, he does not appear to have made much use of horn treatises or study pieces for his students to practice. By contrast, his uncle Alfred did not teach by demonstration. Alfred would have the student play and would make observations and suggestions. Brain later acknowledged his debt to Uncle Alfred, who had been a great inspiration during his brief stay in Los Angeles in early 1945. Dennis's letter to his uncle is quoted in Chapter 11.[2]

How to convey in words precisely all that is required to produce a sound is not easy. It appears, from the accounts of lessons, that Brain was not always able to explain in words exactly what he was demonstrating. His demonstrations, especially for younger pupils with little experience of playing, could be daunting. Morris, speaking about one horn lesson, reveals something of this difficulty:

> We were going to play somewhere out of town. I very often went with Dennis in his car and went round to his house to meet him there. We had a little chat when I got there. I was sitting in an adjoining room. I think the man arrived while I was there. Dennis said, "I'm awfully sorry, I've got a chap coming to have a lesson." So I said, "That's fine, I'll read the paper." The lesson started and I heard the most colossal horn playing! Absolutely tremendous! It wasn't a very long lesson and as the chap departed, there was just time to say goodbye. Dennis came in. "Lesson's over." I said, "Do you know Dennis, I am amazed that you'd be bothered to teach somebody as bad as that! Obviously hopeless! I didn't think you could accept pupils like that—why have him?" Dennis said, "Oh—it was me!" I said, "Well, try and do better next time!" He was rattling off *Till Eulenspiegel*! It wouldn't be showing off. It would be just, "This goes like this." Quite innocent.[3]

His teaching sometimes had the effect of causing pupils to feel that they could not hope to achieve the same brilliance. Brain demonstrated but could not explain how he had arrived at, for example, a certain method of tonguing.

Brain did not impose his way of doing things on pupils. As James Diack recalled, "His approach was very much less formal than was usual for the time. In no way did he ever attempt to influence his students to play in his style." If students played something differently, he would accept that their way was also valid. This could be considered a fault—to be so accommodating to students that he allowed them to do something that he would not do himself. The way he taught suggests he was not concerned with establishing a school of horn playing. Yet in his articles on the horn, he clearly is trying to promote his kind of sound in preference to others. His articles are reproduced in Appendix D.[4]

Accounts by a few students give a picture of Brain as a teacher. The most detailed are of Kaoru Chiba's lessons. Chiba was at that time already a professional horn player and had been offered work by Karajan in Germany, so he was not a typical pupil. Edwin Glick and Cyril Taylor at the Guildhall School of Music and Drama are more typical, and James Diack was only a teenager when he studied with Brain. Other students (about whose lessons no accounts survive) included Sten Engström (second horn of the Stockholm Royal Philharmonic at the time of his lessons in the 1950s), and Joe Henderson, an American wartime student.[5]

Kaoru Chiba (1928–2008)

Kaoru Chiba was known to his friends and colleagues as "Bachi." His parents were graduates of Tokyo Conservatory of Music. Chiba also studied the horn there from April 1945 to April 1949, and while studying, he was invited by Dr. Daigoro Arima, the first Dean of Kunitachi University, to join the NHK Symphony Orchestra as an apprentice. Arima was Vice-Secretary General of the Orchestra. Chiba was first horn of the NHK Symphony Orchestra for thirty-six years, until retirement in 1983. So outstanding was his playing that two years prior to his lessons with Brain, Chiba received an invitation from Karajan to play in Berlin, which he declined. This was in 1954, around the time of Karajan's Japan tour in April that year. The invitation to be first horn of the Berlin Philharmonic was offered again in 1966, during Karajan and the Berlin Philharmonic's three-week tour of Japan in April but again declined for the reason that Chiba could not obtain "fresh and delicious sashimi" in Berlin. Chiba was a renowned gourmet, entertaining musicians from many great orchestras worldwide. He later returned to his alma mater as a professor and was also professor at several other universities.[6]

Several published accounts about Chiba's lessons with Brain have appeared in Japanese and offer insights about the lessons and observations of Brain as a performer in concert and at recording sessions. The fullest account of Chiba's lessons is the earliest that was published. It is in the form of an interview between Genri Nakagawa and Chiba in 1973.[7] Another important source of information is an interview with Chiba by Akashi-Minami High School students, October 4, 2004. Chiba recalled that, having telephoned Brain on his arrival in London, he first met him in December 1956 during a lunch break, half an hour before the start of a recording session of Strauss's *Der Rosenkavalier*, conducted by Karajan. Brain was surprised to see that Karajan and Chiba were already well acquainted. Karajan was also surprised to see Chiba there and said, "What on earth are you doing here? Why didn't you come to Berlin? So you are going to have lessons with Dennis? That's a jolly good idea!" Brain said to Chiba, "So, you are already a fine player!"[8]

According to yet another account, published in 1989, with Karajan's permission, Chiba was allowed to sit behind Brain and the horn section so he could study the way his future teacher played. This was during the sessions recording and rehearsing *Der Rosenkavalier*.[9]

During one of these sessions, Chiba arrived as usual but he discovered that Brain was away for a one-and-a-half hour lunch break (customary at that time in the Philharmonia). Someone joked that he was probably at the BBC broadcasting a recital. He returned very punctually just five minutes before the start of the afternoon's take.[10]

Chiba remarked that when he first met Brain, he seemed an ordinary and very modest person. He later discovered that his first impression was a true one. Nakagawa asked Chiba to describe the lessons that took place in those four months. They were private lessons starting at 10:00 a.m., one-and-a-half hours long, one lesson per week. Chiba came to the house in Frognal and on the first occasion, he was five minutes early. Brain suddenly appeared with shopping bags and wondered if he was late for the lesson, but Chiba reassured him that he (Chiba) had arrived early.

From the outset, Brain was concerned to know what his pupil's difficulties were. Chiba said that he could not play the high or low tones or "give fast tonguing." Brain replied, "As I have also suffered troubles in playing high tones, I might be able to help you to some extent." The implication was that they could both learn together, although Brain's modesty and kindness to his distinguished pupil probably prompted Brain's self-effacing response.

Brain's security in the high register is attested by the recording, for example, of the Haydn Symphony No. 40 with Beecham and the Royal Philharmonic. This was recorded on Brain's old Raoux horn, not the Alexander B-flat single horn, which would have given greater security in the higher range. Another fine example of this security in the high register is the incomplete recording made of the Haydn Symphony No. 31 "Hornsignal" with an orchestra conducted by Jack Westrup. By that date (1952), Brain had changed to the B-flat Alexander, but he had also recorded Borodin's *Prince Igor* Overture with the Philharmonia conducted by Issay Dobrowen in 1949 when he was still playing his Raoux, albeit with a B-flat crook.

It is interesting, however, to find Brain making this comment about his own high notes at this time. Very close to this date, on December 16, 1956, he had a rare difficulty with high notes, playing the exceedingly taxing obbligato solo of Haydn's Concert Trio *Pietà di Mé*, in the first "live" modern performance, which was broadcast on the Third Programme the next day. The piece was transposed down to D major from the original key of E-flat major.[11]

As reported by other students, Brain was not able to explain how to play the horn. He would ask his second horn in the Philharmonia how he produced rapid tonguing and received a similar sort of response, "You always do it like this . . . but it is better to do it like this in general. . . ." While his pupil was deep in thought, Brain told Chiba something very curious: "You may be running forwards in the opposite direction to where you should be going." The lessons were much enjoyed, in spite of learning trials and errors together. Chiba mentioned a few works that were played during these lessons: "Dennis asked me to play whatever I liked at first, so I played Mozart's Third Concerto.

After my performance Dennis suggested, 'You are making good progress at present. You have nothing to worry about. How about Hindemith's Sonata or another piece?' He made me play some scales and arpeggios for practice. He never taught me a printed étude."[12]

In another account of the lessons, given in an interview with Satoshi Kuwahara for the "Seiron" magazine (*Sankei Shimbun News*) in 1999, Chiba remembered another curious piece of advice that Brain offered in playing works by Mozart: "You must play Mozart as if you are passing through a narrow straight corridor whose walls have been freshly painted. Don't stop. Don't incline to the right or to the left!" Kuwahara asked what Brain meant—was he speaking of the horn concertos or works generally by Mozart? Chiba replied, "It's about the composer—it may be a warning not to interpret the music too severely."[13]

It is interesting to find that Brain did not use printed exercises—perhaps because his student was already a seasoned professional and any "étude" would have been superfluous. Nakagawa asked Chiba if he achieved good results from Brain's teaching during these four months. Chiba replied:

> His scales and arpeggios are my treasures. They are very substantial practice. As you know, the horn has an F crook or a B-flat crook. However, he treated the horn chromatically. In a manner of speaking, he tried to get rid of the white and black keys. He made me play two octaves in the B major scale. It took one month to complete. To play B major scale on a B-flat horn was just like trying to play C major on the piano in C sharp minor. Although the fingering was complicated, he never avoided it. He advised, "You are not a child. It is a lifelong problem so you should practice it at any time."
>
> Arpeggios were two octaves. Some notes were given by using keys, and the others were by lip control without keys . . . Two months later, he advised me to play trills to extend the compass. As I said, I had a complex of high tones so he made me play trills. In my case, the practice was right. I became able to play the high tones easily. With regard to works, I learned Hindemith's Sonata and Berkeley's Trio from Dennis.[14]

Chiba gave further glimpses of these lessons in conversation with Akashi-Minami High School students in 2004. In answer to the question, "What kind of concrete lessons did you have with Dennis Brain?" he replied, "Musical interpretation. Even when I had a slightly different idea musically, he respected it, saying, 'Well, I wouldn't play that way, but yours is also valid.' However, he was very strict and accurate in teaching how to interpret music."[15]

They differed in the way a certain passage might be played, but Chiba found that Brain was "never dogmatic." He made no attempt to imitate Brain's technique and was very much in awe of him. Brain did not explain how he played fast notes, fast tonguing, or extremely high notes. These came to him naturally, but to explain how was not possible for him. Chiba tried to ask some questions and Brain replied, "Give me one week. I will ask Alan Civil."

The Akashi-Minami students asked the question "What was the most characteristic thing about Dennis Brain's playing?" Chiba replied:

> Nothing excessive. No profusion, no withering. Always just "right," faithful to what was written there. Others might try and claim to "empathize" with the composer in some other means, but Dennis Brain was firmly in the opinion that one should treat music itself as the sole means to interpret. "You just read the music," he often said. He always avoided any sort of overtly self-conscious interpretation.[16]

Chiba described Brain's appearance as a performer. It was formal, like one delivering a valediction at a graduation:

> He came out carrying his horn under his right arm, stopped at the centre of the stage and bowed straightly. He stood to attention without turning. He placed his horn abruptly two bars before the end of an introduction. After the performance his returning action was quite the same as the entrance.
>
> Of all the pieces I heard him play, the Haydn Horn Concerto (No. 1) still sticks in my head and ears. His intonation was exact and his tone spread softly. . . . I experienced the illusion that only Haydn's music was on the stage, although Dennis was playing it. All of Dennis Brain's solo pieces are available now on records but his superb Haydn (No. 1) has never been published. The recording machines at that time (especially the microphone and its setting) must have been incapable of capturing his warm tone, spreading all over the hall.
>
> Whenever Dennis appeared in Philharmonia concerts, I took my seat just behind the horn section where the chorus usually sat. I am sure that Dennis recommended me to sit there to let me know how to carry the sound towards the front seats (the bell of the instrument turns backwards) rather than because of the cheapness of the ticket![17]

Chiba's description of the way in which Brain caused the sound to carry forward is consistent with his teacher's way of holding the horn. He played his instrument with the bell raised to shoulder height, the bell facing backwards and the sound bouncing off the wall and carrying forward. It is likely that this, combined with the focused sound that he produced, caused the sound to carry well through the orchestra so it could be heard clearly in the soloistic passages. When Chiba returned to Japan after Brain's death, one of his friends, Chiyo Matsubara, observed how Chiba had changed the way he held his horn:

> Bachi came back from London and Germany after Dennis Brain's unexpected car accident. Before studying with Dennis Brain, Bachi was fascinated with Godfried von Freiberg's (Vienna Philharmonic) sound and musicianship. At that time Bachi preferred to play a single F horn with the bell on his leg. But when I saw him in Osaka, he played an Alexander B-flat horn with the bell lifted high.[18]

The observation by Matsubara concerning Chiba's way of resting the bell on the leg prior to his lessons with Brain also recalls the following passage from an article that Brain published in *The Conductor*, in 1954: "the Italians who rest the horn on their knees and produce a woolly, tubby sound. . . ." This is not so clearly a criticism as the following, which Brain wrote about two years later: "The horn should never be rested on the knee. In this position the sound goes straight into the body, resulting in a muffled noise with no carrying power."[19]

James Diack (b. 1938)

James Diack received a number of lessons in the last three years of Brain's life, when Diack was still a teenager, although not an absolute beginner. Dennis's approach was informal, unlike that of his father, Aubrey. Diack remembered the lessons:

> During the years I was at Stowe School I had three or four lessons a year during the three years prior to his tragic death.
>
> At that age I didn't really appreciate how special he was, but he was very special to me as he could play all the notes and not make any mistakes!
>
> It is possible that he got bored with my repeated heroic attempts to master what was to him a simple technique. Talking about cars, in which we were both interested, was presumably an excellent way of changing the subject!
>
> He would play a few fast scale passages from a Mozart Concerto demonstrating tonguing, and I would say, "I can't possibly play as fast as that—was that double tonguing?" And he would say, "No, single tonguing!"
>
> I now know, especially after some thirty years teaching the Horn at the Royal Academy of Music, that I was tonguing backward and forwards

> in my mouth rather than flicking my tongue up and down behind my teeth. Later I learned how to double tongue so that I could nearly match his speeds. Nearly![20]

His way of teaching a student was to demonstrate by playing, not analyzing a piece step by step and then putting it back together again. An aspect of these lessons concerned how Brain might play a piece for public performance in a variety of ways, as Diack explained:

> An interesting thing that I do remember is that he would mention he had to play a particular work and would demonstrate to me a passage and say, "I wonder whether I might play it differently. What do you think of it this way?" It seemed amazing to me, that he should be interested in my opinion! Then he'd play it slightly differently. In retrospect, what he was probably doing was using a little bit of rubato, slowing down, then speeding up gradually and then slowing down again on the final note, in order to alter the momentum of the music. All probably too subtle for me at the time, but in hindsight quite magical and totally uncontrived.[21]

The many recordings that survive of Brain's artistry show that he was very adaptable in his interpretations of the same pieces (allowing, of course, for the wishes of the conductors), and his sensitivity to a musical phrase is apparent in these. To convey this aspect in teaching could only be done by demonstration and much depended, no doubt, on the age, sensitivity to musical sounds, and experience of the pupil being appropriate to appreciate these nuances. Diack concluded:

> Dennis's method of teaching by demonstration was effective but I was not of an age to appreciate what it was all about. He didn't give advice about breathing, phrasing or embouchure. By today's standards, he had a pretty unusual embouchure. I was in awe of his playing and thought I could never play as well as that, even if I practiced for months. I now know how to practice but he never taught me.[22]

What Brain was teaching him, or trying to teach him, was only fully appreciated retrospectively after Diack had entered the horn profession, as he recalled:

> I was definitely too young to appreciate his teaching but I actually benefited enormously ten or fifteen years later in retrospect. When I left education, I was First Horn of the Bournemouth Symphony Orchestra for a while and then the BBC Welsh Orchestra. I had also worked in France and played for French radio. Then I free-lanced a lot in London with all the big London

> orchestras, including the London Mozart Players. When I started, it was very cheeky of me to even think of playing a concerto when I had heard Dennis Brain. I found that when I was practicing or playing a phrase in the orchestra, I would be wondering what Dennis might have done with that phrase, had he played it. This started a lot of experimenting with phrasing.[23]

Edwin Glick (b. 1926)

Edwin Glick was a student for a few months in 1946 at the Guildhall School of Music and Drama. He had been sent there by the US Army's First Division Band in Germany. Brain was still in uniform. His instrument was the Raoux Millereau on which he had established his reputation during the war. Glick's horn was a double rotary valve instrument, possibly a Conn 6D. Brain tried out his pupil's horn and found it difficult, no doubt owing to his unfamiliarity with the rotary valves as well as the different placement of the harmonics on the B-flat side. Likewise, Glick tried out his teacher's Raoux and had difficulty with the piston-action keys. He recalled the time he was with Brain:

> Although I certainly played a lot during my lessons, I only remember a few things about them. One was that Dennis got me away from using the B-flat part of the double horn and to play exclusively on the F side. . . . At the time I studied with him, Dennis played a "peashooter" (I believe it was a piston valve Raoux single horn). . . . He told me that when his uncle Alfred moved to the US, he had to change from that style horn to the rotary valve "German" horn that was then in use throughout the world, and that he had had some severe difficulties in converting. Of course, Alfred later became one of the most successful musicians in Hollywood. Dennis said that he was somewhat concerned about having to switch horn types if he went to the US, but evidently soon after that, gave up the peashooter for a more conventional rotary-type, wider-bore instrument from Alexander.
>
> I also remember asking him how he could hit a high E-flat above high C so convincingly and so confidently (as he did in a Haydn chamber work—Divertimento for violin, cello and horn.) His matter-of-fact answer is indicative of the man. He said simply, that if he had to play as high as that, he would simply practice up to a high G. He knew then that if he could hit this ultra high note in practice, he could certainly hit the lower one in performance. And he said this without a trace of bragging. It was simply his way of solving the problem.[24]

In retrospect, Glick thought he was not ready to be studying with Brain. He needed someone who could improve his playing. Brain, he said, was a naturally gifted player who was usually not able to analyze particular difficulties of students. With more time, Glick believes, he might have learned to play more musically, if not with greater technical skill.

Cyril Taylor (b. 1927)

Another student at the Guildhall School of Music and Drama in 1946, one who had been awarded a scholarship, was Cyril Taylor. His type of instrument at this time was an old Boosey & Hawkes piston-valve single horn in F. According to Taylor:

> My lessons with Dennis, who was still wearing his R.A.F. uniform by the way, not yet having been demobilized from his war service, were graced by him being a very ordinary man who was brilliant. He taught by demonstrating a great deal, afterwards saying that this might be the way that one should play a passage. He said you should breathe like an opera singer, which he had learned from his mother, and that one should never clip off notes using your tongue.
>
> Horn playing was a matter of confidence with courage and correct breathing. He was very keen on long notes and my lessons, always given in the Green Room incidentally, often used to last for an hour and a half. He let one progress at one's own speed, in an easy going manner. He was kind, considerate, helpful and yet was a "man's man." I couldn't fault him in the way I was treated, looked after and taught.[25]

Lecturer

Brain was a keen promoter of the horn as a solo instrument. He gave lecture-recitals on the horn during the 1950s, including one at the Scottish Orchestra Club (date not known, about 1950) and at the Royal Festival Hall on February 1, 1955. The BBC broadcast "The Early Horn" for the BBC Third Programme in 1955 and "No. 7, The Horn" in a series *Talking About the Instrument* for the General Overseas Service, in 1956. Brain also gave other talks on radio that reveal something of his personal tastes in music, such as a program entitled, *On a Personal Note,* on the Home Service on July 23, 1956. His contract for that program states that he was to "present a programme of horn music on gramophone records" for a fee of twenty-five guineas, including the writing of his own script and "presentation at the microphone." Plans for the broadcast of "The Early Horn" went on for several years, an indication of how difficult it was to arrange for him to do a broadcast talk when he had such a hectic schedule. The following letter from Brain to John Harris concerns plans for a broadcast talk with the Far Eastern Service in the series *I Speak for Myself* that did not take place. The first mention of the program in the surviving correspondence is a fragment of a letter from 1950.

> Thank you very much for your letter, suggesting I give a talk in your series, "I speak for myself."
>
> As this is something I have not attempted before, I should need more time to prepare, both the talk & myself, than I have free up till the end of the year. I have to go abroad—i.e. in September & then I go to America with the Royal Philharmonic Orchestra in October.
>
> Perhaps, should the series still be running, we could discuss the matter further when I return at the beginning of the New Year.[26]

L. M. Stapley, producer of *I Speak for Myself*, replied on August 9, 1950, regretting that Brain could not take part in the series but hoping he would be able to give a talk in the following year, if the series was still running.[27]

This letter in 1951 to Alec Robertson apologizes for mislaying a letter concerning the idea for a broadcast talk that became "The Early Horn."

> On receiving your letter I put it in the bureau to be attended to later, and, as time went by, I must have been under the delusion that I had replied to it, as it went out of my mind until one day last week, when my wife came across it during her tidying of my papers; and so I really must apologise for my apparent lack of haste in not replying before now, and hope that you will forgive me.
>
> Should it still be possible to record a talk similar to that given to the Scottish Orchestra Club, would late Autumn or the New Year be suitable? If so, on what lines, length of programme & of talking? Playing &c, would you like it to take.
>
> I am so glad you like the Hindemith, it is a most interesting & musical work instead of the more usual virtuoso piece.[28]

Robertson had written to Brain on April 24, 1951, congratulating him on a recent performance of the Hindemith Concerto conducted by Del Mar for a Mysore concert with the Philharmonia. Robertson's reply to Brain's late response made suggestions that were adopted for "The Early Horn" broadcasts four years later, although the details of the broadcast at this stage are not discussed. Robertson states, "I think listeners will be glad in your case to hear something about the technique of horn playing, both in orchestral and chamber music works. We will record the illustrations separately from the talk and it would be very interesting if you could play some passages which will be heard after in their proper context as records you have made. But please plan the programme as you like!" Robertson again wrote on the subject in October, suggesting Brain record his talk in November of that year and asking him to suggest two free days when the recording could be made.[29]

Another letter, from Brain to Roger Fiske, dated June 4, 1955, gives further information closer to the broadcast:

> I am happy to let you know that I am hard at work on the speech of our programme on The Early Horn, having seen Mr. Morley-Pegge who, in addition to showing me some hunting calls, will have been by now to the British Museum to further his research.
>
> I find, as I was once told, that it is not what to put in, but what to leave out which is the difficulty. However when I return, next Wednesday, I will send to you everything that I have written for your approval, censorship etc.![30]

Brain was away when he wrote the following letter to Fiske in May concerning what to include in the program. Although, with the exception of the Mozart K.412, the suggestions were not included in the broadcast, the letter shows that he was keen to explore and extend the boundaries of what the public was used to listening to.

> I am sorry not having written before now, but as I am away at the moment I am at last catching up on my correspondence.
>
> However I think it would be best if I telephone you on my return, perhaps Monday, and meanwhile here are some answers and suggestions.
>
> I have recorded K.412 and it is published by Goodwin & Tabb.
>
> On June 1st I go to Germany to perform a concerto by Franz Danzi 1763–1826, and the last movement might be interesting to play as it is in $^2/_4$ not $^6/_8$! And shows what contemporaries of Mozart were doing & lasts, I imagine, about 3 minutes and is quite charming. Otherwise I can only suggest Mozart's Horn duets, and if one could find them, one of Punto's Concertos which would then tie up with Punto as the first performer of Beethoven's Sonata.
>
> I am afraid that I have not any bright ideas at the moment.[31]

Fiske wrote a long and detailed letter to Brain on May 31, 1955, concerning the content of the broadcast and indicating that they could take their time putting it together because it was being recorded. Most of the broadcast has survived as fragments made by private enthusiasts. The BBC did not preserve the broadcast.[32]

Critic C. B. Rees remembered being in the audience at an earlier lecture-recital in 1955, given at the Royal Festival Hall. As for the later "Early Horn" lecture, he recalled Brain performing on the hose-pipe:

> Earlier this year he gave a fascinating lecture-recital on the instrument at the Royal Festival Hall. He traced its development from the crooked hand-horn to today's "plumber's nightmare." His skill in illustrating his points was such that you felt he could draw music from a gas-pipe, and indeed he actually produced a snatch of "Oberon" with a mouthpiece which was inserted into a length of rubber tubing.
>
> His control is phenomenal. . . . Those of us who never even managed a penny whistle can only gape in amazement.[33]

Brain also visited schools to give occasional lecture-recitals or concerts, such as the one he gave at George Watson School, Edinburgh, in February 1956 with Wilfrid Parry (piano) and at Portora Royal School, Northern Ireland, in March that year. A former pupil of Aubrey Brain's, Christopher Hortin, remembers Brain coming to his school, High Wycombe Royal Grammar School, in 1946, together with a small ensemble that included Leonard Brain, oboe, and Richard Newton, bassoon. On that occasion, Brain played the rondo from Mozart's Horn Concerto No. 4 as well as taking part in chamber pieces with the other players.[34]

The Early Horn

See Appendix B for a transcript of Brain's lecture/demonstration "The Early Horn."

Talking About the Instrument: No. 7, The Horn

See Appendix C for a description of Brain's illustrated talk in the BBC radio series *Talking About the Instrument.*

Articles

Brain wrote articles for brass journals (see Appendix D):

> "French Horn Playing," *The Conductor*, October 1954, pp. 3, 8.
>
> "About the French Horn," *Brass Today*, London: Besson & Co., 1957, pp. 60–63.
>
> "The French Horn," a variant of the 1957 article, in *Brass Today*, London: Besson & Co., 1961, pp. 19–20.

Lecture-Recital

Brain gave a lecture-recital at the Portora Royal School in Northern Ireland in 1956. The school magazine reported on the event (see Appendix D).

CHAPTER

8

Reminiscences by Colleagues

The memories of colleagues and friends abound with engaging and amusing anecdotes that help to compensate for the lack of personal letters (Chapter 6). One of the most striking aspects of these reminiscences is how vivid they are and how they help to paint something of a character sketch of Brain.

The word "colleague" in this chapter includes musicians other than horn players in orchestras throughout the British Isles and in other countries. Horn players provide their reminiscences in Chapter 9.

In a career of nineteen years from 1938 to 1957, Brain worked with many of the finest musicians in the British Isles and abroad. The Discography mentions only a few of the enormous number of musicians with whom he performed. Without a personal diary and with such a busy schedule, it is impossible to determine precisely where he was all the time.

It would be impossible to mention all the musicians who remember Brain and recall the music they made together, but this chapter includes some of the more prominent.

Brain was a private person, so it is difficult to find much information about what sort of person he was. Nice people are not always very interesting to describe—one can sum up their personal characteristics in a few words—and he was certainly a very pleasant person who was liked by many in the music profession and, it appears, anybody with whom he came in contact.

Among famous musicians, Brain particularly admired jazz trombonist Tommy Dorsey, pianist Benno Moiseiwitsch, violinist Jascha Heifetz, Philharmonia principal trumpet Harold Jackson, and clarinetist Reginald Kell.

Gareth Morris (1920–2007)

Of all the colleagues with whom he played over the years, flutist Gareth Morris was perhaps the one with whom Brain had the closest friendship. He had been best man at Brain's wedding, and they worked together regularly from 1938 until the last concert at Edinburgh. Morris broadcast several tributes over the years. The following is an extract from a BBC tribute on May 17, 1996:

> Lots of people didn't understand Dennis . . . but they imagined from his apparent simplicity that perhaps all he could do was play the horn and he wasn't terribly bright. In fact, Dennis was extremely intelligent—very bright indeed. No fool, was Dennis! But I think that I should emphasize how really good he was. I don't like trying to find things that are bad in people but with Dennis I wouldn't think of trying to find anything about him that I didn't like . . . I've often thought, was there anything about Dennis that irritated me? . . . Selfish? No!
>
> Well, is it selfish do you think, when he drove me all over the continent so very often, trying to beat his own record from, shall we say, Dieppe to Nice? He'd have in his diary how long it took him last time he did it, you see. So when we started, he'd open his little diary and off we'd go. This sort of conversation could take place, "Dennis we are just passing the most ancient walled city in France. Within those walls is the most magnificent Romanesque Cathedral." [Dennis:] "Oh good!" "Are we going to stop and look at this amazing monument to civilization?" [Dennis:] "Perhaps when we come back." Then on we'd go and I'd say, "Almost floating in the sky, Dennis, is the magnificent Cathedral of Bayeaux." [Dennis:] "Oh good, I've seen a picture of it!" Then one day I said to him, "Dennis, can we stop and have some coffee?" [Dennis:] "Let's wait until we get there." So I thought, I know, I'll say something else, so I said, "Dennis, can we stop I want to go to the lavatory!" [Dennis:] "I think we're nearly there!" So I said, "Dennis, it is now getting urgent that I visit the lavatory!" I'd think to myself for a split second, "Was that selfish of Dennis?" No! Of course it wasn't! The whole thing was a joke and he did want to beat his own record, didn't he? No, I can't say Dennis was selfish. So I have come to the conclusion that there isn't anything I can find about Dennis that I didn't absolutely love. And he was clever too. To hear him play the great solos in the orchestra was triumphant.[1]

BBC *Music Magazine* broadcast a tribute by Morris on May 21, 1961. He remembered his friend's great admiration for Aubrey Brain and played some of Aubrey's finest orchestral recordings with the BBC Symphony Orchestra, including Strauss's *Till Eulenspiegel*, conducted by Fritz Busch in a recording from 1933.

Morris described his friendship:

> We knew each other well; I was best man at his wedding, and he played the organ at mine, so I know that the endearingly modest artist the public saw on the concert platform was exactly what he really was. All his tremendous success had left him entirely unspoiled and everybody loved him. Very many a nervous concert-goer, venturing behind the scenes to ask for Dennis Brain's autograph had been entranced to find a disarmingly natural young man, putting his horn back into its case, and agreeing with the sweetest of smiles that he'd enjoyed the concert too. His fabulous virtuosity was a legend almost before he had had an opportunity of displaying it. I have heard him play the *Flight of the Bumble Bee* as perfectly as any flautist could possibly hope to. . . .[2]

He recalled that Brain admired many other outstanding musicians and was generous with his praise of other horn players. Morris described his key attributes as a musician:

> In spite of all the wonderful things he could do on his horn, I think the outstanding quality of Dennis Brain's playing was the magic with which he could invest the simplest phrase. Somehow his own guileless personality shone through his noble sound. . . .
>
> Dennis Brain made friends quickly and easily, and the many distinguished composers who produced works specially for him not only did so for his playing but also because they liked him so much. His quaint humour was difficult to describe; his jokes were "family ones" as it were; but how he enjoyed them! And nobody who knew him will ever forget how his laugh rang round the room as he delightedly relished somebody else's *bon mot.*
>
> Hindemith was quick to enjoy Dennis Brain and his playing; and as an amateur of the horn, sent him a photograph of himself inscribed, "From one great horn-player to another"—but not before he had composed a concerto for him. . . . It displays so well Brain's marvellous facility not to speak of his masterly musicianship. I can still see him tossing it off with such delightedly apparent ease in the recording studio.[3]

Morris recalled that the whole profession had a high regard for Brain:

> There wasn't any jealousy of any kind in the horn profession. Nobody ever said anything against him or against his playing. There could be, couldn't there? Somebody who would say, "He's very good of course, his father was famous, it was easy for him to get into the profession." They could say that, couldn't they? They didn't. So I regard him as a very remarkable character. When I listen to him playing now, he invests those phrases with such sweet beauty and then . . . he touches you with a little phrase he turns a corner on. A remarkable artist.[4]

Regarding Hindemith, Morris recalled his humor and his special affection for Brain:

> Do you know, Hindemith had a great sense of humour? Everybody thinks he was a cold academic! He was very musical. We were recording (including the Horn Concerto) in the Kingsway Hall, a lot of works in 1956. Hindemith came for a week. *Symphonia Serena*, Symphony for Concert Band. Lovely music. Clarinet Concerto, too, with the Frenchman, Cahuzac.[5]

Hindemith had stepped in at the last minute to fill a gap in recording sessions caused by Klemperer having to return to Germany because his wife had died. When asked if Brain was playing the orchestral horn solos in these works recorded with Hindemith, Morris replied, "It was Dennis, of course."[6]

Brain was strict about practicing long notes and advised the same in his articles on the horn (Appendix D). Morris remembered this dedication to long tones:

> He always did his daily stint . . . whenever we were on tour abroad. I mean, of course, long after RAF days. I'm thinking of orchestral tours I did with him and wind quintet tours. If we had a day off, Dennis always did his long notes every morning, first thing. . . . His standards were absolutely the very highest. He was never satisfied. An example to everybody, to all wind players and I would say all players on *any* instrument.[7]

Alan Rawsthorne wrote *Concertante Pastorale* for Morris and Brain. Morris described how much they looked forward to it, but then it was advertised before they had even received their parts:

> It's a very good piece. The *Concertante Pastorale* for flute, horn and strings. One movement. You can hire the parts and Oxford University Press have published the score. Rawsthorne had come to me and said he wanted to write a piece for both Dennis and myself to play together. At that time, Rawsthorne's wife, Jessy Hinchcliffe, played the violin in the Philharmonia. Rawsthorne was taking rather long to produce the work. I asked Jessy, "How's Alan getting on with our *Concertante*?" "Oh, he's doing it!" she replied.
>
> Later, Dennis had discovered that the concert premiere had been advertised at Hampton Court Orangery with Alec Sherman and the New London Orchestra. He said, "I've seen the advertisement." We had not even received our parts! I got annoyed and said to Jessy, "Is Alan doing that concerto?" Alan replied through Jessy, "Tell Gareth to shut up. Ask him what his favourite note is!" I said, "Low C." When it came to the performance, it ends on 13 bars of low C's for the flute![8]

Jack Brymer (1915–2003)

Clarinetist Jack Brymer gave a BBC Radio 3 tribute to his friend and colleague in 1979. He emphasized Brain's uniqueness as a musician as well as a horn player, illustrating his tribute with extracts from celebrated recordings. For example, he played the third movement from Brain's recording of Strauss's Concerto No. 2 with Wolfgang Sawallisch, and he related the following about an unexpected performance:

> Dennis went to Cardiff to play Strauss's First concerto with the BBC Welsh Orchestra and Rae Jenkins, without a part, of course. To his astonishment he found that, somehow or other, they had rehearsed the brand new unrehearsed Second concerto and with two hours to go they had no chance of getting the orchestral parts of No. 1 so Dennis just played No. 2, as he did everything else which was ever put in front of him. Probably not at sight but certainly without any preparation. But of course, he knew No. 1 from boyhood.[9]

Brymer, as his next recording, played Blake's Elegy from Brain's second 1953 recording of the Britten Serenade with the New Symphony Orchestra of London, conducted by Eugene Goossens. To frame it, he added a personal reminiscence of Brain playing this piece at an Edinburgh Festival:

> One occasion when he performed this Serenade startled me with his incredible ability to switch off completely when he wasn't concentrating on his art. We were in the wings at Freemasons' Hall during the Edinburgh Festival one morning and he was discussing the journey home with Leonard, his brother. "If we leave right away we can get to Newark for dinner tonight," he said, "I know a good place there—steaks!" He then strolled on and gave one of his very finest performances of the Britten Serenade. Quite an ovation. When it was over, he wandered over to us, "No," he said "Not Newark—Stamford. It's a better restaurant." He had taken up just where he'd left off.[10]

Brain performed the Britten Serenade several times at the Edinburgh Festival, and it is not possible to say which one this anecdote refers to. He performed it at his first appearance at the Festival in September 1948 with Scottish tenor John Tainsh and the Boyd Neel Orchestra. Another Edinburgh performance was on January 21, 1955, with Peter Pears and the Scottish National Orchestra conducted by Karl Rankl in Usher Hall.[11]

Brymer, continuing his tribute, turned to the outstanding stereo recording made late in 1956 of the Hindemith Horn Concerto—a work that nearly didn't get recorded commercially.

> Another composer to write especially for Dennis was Paul Hindemith, who composed a concerto for him in 1949. I once saw a marvellous photo of Dennis, trying to show Hindemith how to get the sound out of his ancient horn. At the time, it was an old priceless French Raoux with patches soldered all over it. . . . Dennis gave the first performance of the Hindemith Concerto in Baden Baden the next year. The composer gave him a copy of the score and wrote on it, "To the unsurpassed original performer of this piece from a grateful composer." It's in Hindemith's usual dryly witty style. Two short opening movements, followed by a much longer one in which the horn has a declamatory passage over tremolando strings.[12]

William Waterhouse (1931–2007)

William Waterhouse, fourth bassoonist in the Philharmonia and later bassoonist in the Melos Ensemble, sent the following reminiscence:

> I still have the clearest memories of Dennis Brain after all these years. But unfortunately my personal contact was restricted to the work I did with the Philharmonia between the Spring of 1952 and July 1953. During this time whenever four bassoons were required, either by the orchestration or for doubling, I was the regular 4th bassoon (I still possess most of the programs). I was lucky enough to do the amazing May '52 tour of Europe with Karajan: Tchaikovsky 5th was played many times, and in particular I'll never forget how Dennis Brain used to phrase the opening of the slow movement. . . .[13]

Basil Tschaikov (b. 1925)

Clarinetist Basil Tschaikov described Brain the person and musician:

> My main recollection of Dennis was as a superb musician who whenever I heard him play gave immense pleasure. He was a very quiet man and unlike other outstanding horn players did not throw his weight about, or argue and try to put down conductors. As you will probably have been told many times, at rehearsals he had the ability to be reading a motor magazine until a few beats before an important entry and come in perfectly.[14]

One of the concerts of historic interest with the London Baroque Ensemble that Tschaikov recalls was the first British performance of Strauss's posthumous *Symphony for Winds* (*Fröliche Werkstatt*) at Royal Festival Hall on January 23, 1953. This life-affirming and vigorous piece, written at the end of Strauss's life, was broadcast with the same players a few days later on January 28. It was not recorded by the BBC but, by chance, an off-the-air recording was made of most of it, and this is preserved at the British Library Sound Archive.[15]

Tschaikov remembered that the Handel Trio Overture in C major for two clarinets and horn (recorded with Fred "Jack" Thurston, Gervase de Peyer, and Brain in December 1949) had been performed with Brain earlier at Chelsea Town Hall. The clarinets on the earlier occasion were Jack Brymer and Basil Tschaikov.[16]

Tschaikov remembered the first time he heard the Britten Serenade performed with Brain in 1943. He recalled that the Epilogue and Prologue were considered remarkable for the out of tune notes (natural harmonics), when they were first heard.[17]

Lady Evelyn Barbirolli (1911–2008)

Woodwind players, as well as brass players in particular, benefited from Brain's example, but tributes came from all sections of the orchestra, indicating that his qualities were appreciated by the whole profession. Another wind player *par excellence*, oboist Evelyn Rothwell (Lady Barbirolli), remembered occasions when she and Brain took part in chamber music broadcasts for the BBC at Manchester and elsewhere. The Hummel Septet was a favorite, and she broadcast this in several performances with Brain (it had also been recorded by the BBC at least once) during the 1940s and 1950s.

One particular occasion was fixed in her memory. It was a rehearsal prior to a broadcast of the *Music in Miniature* program, and the work was a movement from Mozart's Quintet K.452:

> Dennis was the horn player. I was the oboe player . . . I think we were interviewed slightly in the programme as far as I remember—just introducing pieces, more or less. We'd all played it several times and Dennis particularly wasn't too keen on rehearsing so we had a last-minute rehearsal because it was difficult to find the tempi for that particular work. We got there early to have a final go and Dennis was late. He came in, all beaming smiles and we were asking where he was and he showed us a very beautiful horn with a painted bell and he said, "I was busy buying this!" Somebody else asked him, "Dennis, you're not going to use that are you?" He said, "Yes, of course, why not?" So we played the broadcast and Dennis played on this horn with the painted bell![18]

No broadcast has yet been found in *Radio Times* that exactly matches the information Lady Barbirolli described. A few nearly match it, and the work was popular. They played together in several *Music in Miniature* broadcasts in the 1940s and 1950s. It was a popular program that was broadcast regularly on the Light and Home Services during the evenings, and Brain was one of the regular musicians. The identity of the horn with a painted bell is not known. Lady Barbirolli added, "Yes, I do remember vividly. We were all so impressed he had this lovely instrument and he played just as he always did!" In the 1940s, he bought a hand-horn with detachable valves from Farquharson Cousins, made by Raoux in 1818, with a floral pattern on the bell. This horn is discussed in Chapter 11.

Of Brain's engagements as soloist with Sir John Barbirolli, Lady Barbirolli recalled that Sir John was "always fascinated by any natural, gifted talent" and said that Brain "was the personification of that." She remembered an occasion at Edinburgh, prior to a concert:

> I remember once that it was at the Edinburgh Festival and I was trying to do some practice. John was rehearsing and Dennis came into the artists' room and I said, "Do you want to practice?" He was doing a concerto that night. He said, "Yes, if I don't practice for one day, nobody notices, if I don't practice for two everybody notices and it's three now or four so I think it's time I did a bit of practice!" So I got out of the room and left him to it![19]

Denis Wick (b. 1931)

Denis Wick, a British trombonist for whom Gordon Jacob wrote his Trombone Concerto in 1955, remembers meeting Brain when he occasionally appeared as soloist with the City of Birmingham Symphony Orchestra where Wick was first trombone from 1952 to 1957. Wick remembers him as the outstanding brass player of his time. He gave the following reminiscence in an article for *The Horn Player*:

> My brass-playing idol since boyhood had been Dennis Brain. I had always tried to model my own trombone playing on him. He had perfect everything; production, range, brilliant flexibility. Of course, for me he was only to be heard on those wonderful (78 rpm) records. Then he actually played with the CBSO as a soloist, and I could hear him in the flesh. I took every opportunity to do so, and even plucked up courage to ask his advice. He was so kind—he took a great interest, answered my questions thoughtfully and asked me if I had ever considered working in London. Chance would have been a fine thing!

He recalled that on several occasions, he went to see Brain to ask his advice. On one occasion, Wick asked, "Do you find it hard to find time to practice?" He replied: "With great difficulty. The best exercise you can do is loud lip trills—plenty of them!" Some time after this, Brain spoke again with Wick and asked him "How are the trills going?" Wick had recently played the premiere of the Jacob Trombone Concerto. This had been broadcast from the Birmingham Town Hall on the Home Service some time after the concert premiere of November 15, 1955. The premiere was at Derby Baths, and Brain got to hear about it. He asked, "What's it like?" Wick replied "It's very hard work." Brain said, "Like the Horn Concerto."[20]

Arthur Wilson (1927–2010)

Arthur Wilson, principal trombone in the Philharmonia Orchestra for twenty-seven years (from 1963), remembered the impact Brain made on the brass section of the Philharmonia from the time Wilson joined in 1951 as second trombone:

> I was stumped. For the first three years there, I didn't hear a blemish from Dennis Brain and that's saying something for a brass player. Harold Jackson, the Trumpet, was a giant of a player as well who was there at the time but with Dennis—I was lost for words. I thought, "If it goes on like this, it's not for me!" I was used to more human errors!
>
> He played on a French horn with a piston action, which is a smaller bore than the ones used today. I think that I may safely say that the ones used today are a more German design. Americans are even bigger. Beautiful for Mozart recordings—Horn Concertos—which he recorded with Karajan. . . . There was no doubt, for example—a musical point—the narrow bore instrument was wonderful for nimble things like Mozart and the Siegfried Horn Call but there is a big *sostenuto* tune at the end of Brahms Symphony No. 1 (in the last movement) and the sound broke up a bit—Dennis couldn't hold it. So he did change. I didn't notice any difference—it was just as wonderful as ever. . . .
>
> It was accepted that you heard one or two cracks in a concert in a horn section. One had to learn to live with that. Of course, when someone like Dennis came along, it became a thing of the past. I did hear just one and it was spectacular (as you might imagine). . . . He used to play the solo in Ravel's *Pavane pour une infante défunte* magnificently.[21]

Roger Lord (b. 1924)

Roger Lord was one of the oboists engaged by Karl Haas for recordings and concerts of the London Baroque Ensemble when Brain was the principal horn:

> I was first introduced to Dennis Brain by Gilbert Vinter who directed the BBC Midland Light Orchestra in Birmingham, where I became oboe/cor anglais (it was then a theatre-sized band) in 1947, and Dennis turned up as a soloist. On one of these occasional appearances, I remember he played *Hunters' Moon*. . . . In the broadcast, Dennis somehow cracked one note, and I remember our second horn, Ted Primmer, afterwards telling us that that was a serious matter for someone like Dennis, with *his* reputation.
>
> I would see Dennis around at various film or recording sessions and also when I was asked to play for Karl Haas occasionally. . . . It has just come back to me that I think I was playing for the Philharmonia when Karajan was recording a Concerto with Dennis at Abbey Road. Karajan wandered over to where Dennis was playing, to make a point, and when he looked at the music stand, to see the solo part, he found that there was a copy of "Motorsport" magazine in place of the music.[22]

The film sessions to which Lord refers were not solo appearances. Like many other instrumental musicians who also worked in orchestras, they augmented their incomes with film sessions for orchestral music. They never knew who would turn up for a session.[23]

Felix Aprahamian (1914–2005)

Music critic Felix Aprahamian first met Brain during the war. He went with Norman Del Mar to hear Brain perform Del Mar's organ sonata, especially written for Brain, at the Alexandra Palace, which had a magnificent organ until a bomb destroyed it. Aprahamian also worked for the BBC and, no doubt, encountered Brain as one of the many artists engaged for broadcasting. In 1979, he remembered Brain's horn playing:

> I'd say that by example, his influence was paramount and after his death, standards of horn playing certainly improved. I remember him as the prince of horn players. The true French horn he played when I first heard him was jokingly referred to as a peashooter by those who use the wider bore German instrument but when it came to attacking notes crisply and cleanly, he left others standing. In comparison with his, their attack often sounded like the squeezing of toothpaste out of a tube. Yet in nuances and sheer expressiveness, Dennis was also second to none.[24]

Colin Horsley (b. 1920)

Pianist Colin Horsley, OBE, remembered Brain as a colleague in performances of both the Brahms and the Berkeley Horn Trios. He remembered the first performance of the Berkeley Trio for the Chamber Music Society at the Victoria and Albert Museum, South Kensington. Cartoons after Raphael's designs, commissioned by Charles I, were a conspicuous backdrop. Manoug Parikian was the violinist:

> What a natural artist he was! . . . Yes, I enjoyed playing the Brahms Horn Trio with Dennis so much that I thought of asking Lennox [Berkeley] to write one for us—so I commissioned it. With Manoug, we played it with the Brahms at the Aix-en-Provence Festival in the Courtyard of the Archbishop's Palace which had been turned into an Opera theatre with red-plush seats but it was open to the sky. They guaranteed that in July there would be no rain! However the wind got up and we had to use clothes-pegs to keep the music on the stands. . . .
>
> We were all invited to stay at Sir John Heathcote-Amory's lovely home (Knightshayes, Tiverton) but Dennis drove down for the concert and immediately afterwards, back to London. It was a great concert—Dennis as usual, on superb form. His playing was effortless and a glorious sound. He just sat and played and seemed imperturbable. He was very nice to work with but he rehearsed the bare minimum—after all he played everything, apart from the Berkeley, since his cradle days. He took care of his lips. The Berkeley, he just played through and then made some adjustments (tonal balance) with the violin, for instance.
>
> I remember him first as a student at the RAM when I was a student at the RCM. Even then, he was considered sensational.[25]

Wolfgang Sawallisch (b. 1923)

Wolfgang Sawallisch, the distinguished German conductor, worked with the Philharmonia, producing some of the finest ever recordings of the works of Richard Strauss and also of Karl Orff and Wagner. In Orff and Strauss orchestral works, Sawallisch remembered Brain playing the horn solos, and in the following extract from a letter, he also described the sessions recording the two Strauss concertos:

> What I can say is done in two or three words. First of all, Dennis Brain was and is the best Horn player I ever heard and with whom I worked in an orchestra. Everybody agrees.

I will never forget the recordings of the Horn Concertos by Richard Strauss. During all sessions for both, I cannot remember that he (technically) played one wrong note. After many repeats and recording more and more of the same bars, he was never tired or unwilling to do it. For instance, the last movement of the Second Concerto, which is extremely difficult for the orchestra, he never played without emotion or only as a technical exercise. I remember the orchestra was nervous because it happened that we always had something to record again. Dennis performed the breaks ten times and always more perfect—it was simply incredible! He was never angry, always polite and extremely patient.

You listed on the reverse of your letter, the recordings of orchestral pieces I recorded with the Philharmonia and Dennis Brain. You can hear it! This sound was Dennis—both of Orff's small operas!

He was indeed THE ideal master of the instrument.[26]

CHAPTER

9

The Legacy—Horn Players Look Back

Horn players who have either known Brain or have been influenced by his example have offered tributes and recollections of him. Their words describe Brain's many-faceted talents as a musician as well as a horn player. Over fifty years after his death, Brain has continued to influence new generations of horn players around the world,. In his lifetime, he was an international figure in the world of classical music, and today that status is magnified rather than diminished.

Brain had a captivatingly beautiful tone. So did his father, who some critics are willing to say had an even more attractive tone than his son.[1] Both father and son possessed a bright and penetrating, compact sound that is rarely heard in other players.

Brain's horn sound was like pure gold, the result of many years of hard, practical exertions. His phrasing was subtler, more elegant, and more musical than that of any other horn player, which, combined with his beautiful tone and brilliant technique, made him the greatest of the great.

For generations that have not had the opportunity to hear him in person, an increasing number of CD releases are available to inspire any aspiring player. In 2009, Beulah issued *The World of Dennis Brain* which, in addition to some rare recordings of the 78-rpm era, contains the premier release of Edward Williams's incidental music for winds made for British Transport Films' *Open House* (1951). In 2008, EMI issued a four-CD set, *Dennis Brain the Horn Player*, which collects some of the more famous recordings that he made for EMI from 1944 to 1956.

The horn players represented in this chapter have been inspired by his concert performances, broadcasts, and the recordings made during his lifetime and those that have appeared subsequently.[2]

James Decker (b. 1921)

James Decker met Brain at the famous party described in Chapter 2 at Gardena, Los Angeles. Like the other horn players, he listened to Brain playing at that party on a battered old Raoux horn, from which Brain coaxed the most beautiful sounds. Decker was a colleague of Dennis's uncle, Alfred Brain, Jr., in the Los Angeles Philharmonic and the Hollywood film studios. Dennis remained a seminal influence on him, as indeed so too did Alfred. Decker was a founding member of the Los Angeles Horn Club, whose first president was Alfred.

Alfred had a different horn sound from that of his nephew, but they both shared qualities such as clean articulation, musical sensitivity to the nuances of a phrase, and a sound that had great carrying power.

Here is Decker's tribute to Brain, published in the British Horn Society's journal, *Horn Player*, in 2007 to commemorate the fiftieth anniversary of Brain's death.[3]

> Dennis was extremely well thought of by all the Hollywood musicians. His musicianship, which was outstanding in quality, is what impressed us most. We all had a different concept of sound, but his fitted perfectly. None of us would be able to duplicate the facility he possessed with the sound we established for film sound tracks.
>
> I think it was in '45 when I first met him in Los Angeles. Al Brain had a party at his home and he invited some of the film studio horn players in the area to meet his nephew Dennis who was on a tour in America with the RAF Orchestra and Band. During the evening, Jack Cave (1st horn at MGM) asked Dennis to play something for us on his old piston horn Dennis was using at that time. He laughed and got his horn out and played a violin solo piece—I can't remember the name of it—perhaps it was *The Flight of the Bumble Bee.* It was like what Raphael Mendez (famed Hollywood trumpet soloist and composer) did on the trumpet; we just hadn't heard anything like that done on a horn before! I couldn't stay but a half-hour so that's about all I remember.
>
> The Horn Club of Los Angeles came into being in 1951 "To promote activities for the benefit and enjoyment of players of the horn, to stimulate interest in the horn, and to extend its literature." It consisted of some of America's finest players at the time. . . .
>
> Because so many Dennis Brain horn recordings were being sold at the time, suggesting a market interest in the horn, Capitol Records (EMI) expressed interest in having the LA Horn Club record a multiple-horn ensemble with works from some of the Hollywood composers. The

> reasoning was that if one horn (Dennis) could sell so many records, maybe more horns would be even better. Little did they know! The LA Horn Club responded and member George Hyde composed *Color Contrasts* (Seraphim S-60095)—a piece for eight horns, which he conducted during the recording session.
>
> We felt very stunned when word arrived about Dennis's tragic accident. He truly was an inspiration to all of us. In talking to horn students of today, particularly to those who, for one reason or another, haven't heard of Dennis Brain, it becomes clear that such a student isn't worth spending time to teach. There are players today who play extremely well; however, we here all still feel that Dennis holds the "KING" position.[4]

Alan Civil (1929–1989)

Alan Civil knew Brain from when Civil was a pupil of Aubrey Brain during the war. Their close association, however, began when Civil joined the Royal Philharmonic Orchestra in 1952 and the Philharmonia Orchestra from 1955 to 1957. Civil was first introduced to Brain during the war at Bedford, where the BBC Symphony Orchestra had been evacuated. Brain was on leave from the RAF at the time. Civil wrote in 1966:

> He asked me what make of instrument I played on and, being rather ashamed of my old French model that had collected so many dents over the years, I was reluctant to show it to him, whereupon he produced his Raoux-Millereau, the condition of which made mine look in comparison like a new instrument straight from the workbench. Not only did it have the worst dents I have ever seen on a brass instrument but most of the stays were bound round with sticking plaster and black insulating tape.
>
> From this moment we discussed openly our problems—or rather, in retrospect, it seemed to be only my problems that we spoke of. For instance, I said that my "F" natural was a bad note, whereupon Dennis took out the first valve slide of my horn and, breaking a matchstick in half, proceeded to insert the small piece of wood crossways into the neck of the tubing.
>
> "Now try your F," he said.
>
> With some apprehension at this "do it yourself" adjustment, I cautiously sounded the note, knowing full well what a treacherous one it had always been, but now a beautiful precise round F emerged. Dennis chuckled and said, "Have you any more bad ones that we can fix?"
>
> This, my first meeting with such a great artist, remains so vivid in my memory, and, from the moment I joined the RPO and played next to him, the matchstick episode provided a constant source of amusement. . . .

Civil remembered Brain's love of cars and good food and how a plate of spaghetti, consumed quickly between two halves of a recording session, had no adverse effect on his embouchure or his beautiful playing, whereas a simple cheese roll caused problems for the other horn players who joined him for these breaks. At the recording sessions, Brain would arrive with several copies of motor magazines to read in the rests.[5]

Norman Del Mar (1919–1994)

Hornist and conductor Norman Del Mar's friendship and professional association with Brain is documented in Chapter 2. The following tribute, given shortly after Brain's death, is all the more poignant for being so emotionally charged with the recent loss.

> Dennis and I met for the first time in the barracks of the RAF at Uxbridge in the autumn of 1939. We were both in effect still students, though the war had broken into our last years at the Academy and College respectively. Neither of us had embarked on our professional careers as yet. . . .
>
> We sat together day after day in the Central Band playing our endless paddings and chuck-chucks (military band horn parts are notoriously dull) in 1001 different ways to amuse ourselves and each other. I cannot remember any more how it happened that we became so close so quickly but I do know that within these three months we were inseparable and if one of us was sent on a short tour with the band without the other the post fairly hummed with our letters. Dennis came to my parents' house in Chalfont regularly and we consumed enormous helpings of what we perhaps rather greedily referred to as T. T. or T. P.—that is, treacle tart and treacle pudding, which my mother soon learnt were his favourites.
>
> Our conduct in the band was proverbial as together we discovered points of interest and delight in the wide range of music we covered. Sometimes it was the over emphasis of dynamic markings in, for example, the New World Symphony, Dennis growing purple in the face as he laughed and blew simultaneously. The selection from Kreisler's "A King Stepped Out" sprouted a most interesting horn obbligato over the years, while the William Tell overture was never without its descant of "Turkey in the Straw," the two fitting together perfectly as Walt Disney discovered. As for the horn parts of the Air Force March, they were practically a Concerto in themselves by the time we had done with them. We were essentially the naughty boys in the corner, but I think our highly respected C. O.—Wing Commander O'Donnell—sensed that there was no malice in our giggling and foolery for we got away with murder. . . .

The two stayed together in the RAF Symphony Orchestra, and often had other engagements together.

> Before long, the RAF Orchestra was formed and we either toured or remained at Uxbridge together, meeting so many important figures in English Music who were gradually absorbed into that remarkable organisation. Naturally enough Dennis was courted by every orchestra or group which sprang up or had managed to survive during these war years. We had got so used to playing together that I was fortunate enough to be automatically engaged with Dennis whenever a second horn was required.
>
> We made a recording of the first Brandenburg Concerto with Boyd Neel, playing not off the conventional printed parts which were edited in a way we hated but from a book of studies which quoted the relevant movements practically intact in the form adapted by Bach for two Cantatas! Dennis had transformed the pages we needed and this Heath Robinson double part tickled our fancy so that instead of a virtuoso piece of exceptional difficulty it turned into a field day in which every moment was the greatest fun.
>
> As can be imagined Dennis's fame spread like wildfire and with it his self-confidence—not conceit; it is important to stress that one of the fantastic things about Dennis was his absolute lack of any kind of self-importance. He was right up to the end like a school boy who just happened to be able to do something better than anybody else and thought it the hugest fun. Thus, although we all pulled his leg like mad, there really was nothing offensive in the slightest in his way of going up to every composer he met and asking if he would write him a concerto. The composers mostly obliged and Dennis's cupboard is full of more concertos than the average listener has ever heard of. But the climax to this activity was when the RAF Orchestra was engaged to transmit a series of programmes to America once a week in the middle of the night.

The meeting of Brain and Britten is well-known, but Del Mar's recollection adds another perspective.

> The composer of the Incidental Music for these important broadcasts was Benjamin Britten. Needless to say Dennis made a bee-line for him. Britten was fascinated and week by week in that studio at three a.m. of a Sunday night would pick Dennis's brains on points of horn technique and his own personal style. The result is now world famous and one of Britten's finest works. Not a Concerto at all—but the Serenade for Tenor voice, Horn and Strings. "You mean to say," Ben asked once, "that you can pitch a top C at will in safety?" "Sure," said Dennis gaily, obliging on the spot, and throwing in an illustration on the possibilities of hand stopping for good measure.

> Down it all went into the Elegy, one of the most hair-raisingly difficult but inspired passages of the work; and so far as I know, in all the hundreds of times he played it, Dennis never missed it once.

Brain and Del Mar also enjoyed playing light music.

> Dennis's motto was always "Game for anything" and again this was no boast, but a genuine thirst for adventure. As a result we found ourselves on assignments of every conceivable kind including dance or light music, and together with the circle of musicians known as the "session boys." We were always proud to be able to claim the friendship of Geraldo's band with whom we played so often, and with Dennis's versatile and fluent artistry he was always easily persuaded to be experimented upon as soloist in some popular or jazz arrangement.

They stayed together after the war.

> When the war came to an end and we were released from the RAF, our casual professional work was at last enabled to become permanent. The Philharmonia and the Royal Philharmonic Orchestras were formed and for a time we played in both. . . .
>
> I had by this time formed a student orchestra which gave concerts at the Chelsea Town Hall. The proof sheets of the posters for this came through at one of Sir Thomas's rehearsals. Dennis was to play the Strauss 1st Horn Concerto and I had put in a section from the second act of Siegfried to enable him to play the whole of the famous horn call as well. We couldn't resist showing Sir Thomas the leaflets and, nudging each other, we advanced towards the great man immediately the rehearsal was over. To our incredulous delight he announced that he would come. And came he did, arriving just as Dennis embarked enthusiastically on the ringing solo which begins the Strauss Concerto. Dennis became especially fond of this concerto; "after all," as he said, "it makes a change from the Mozarts, and it really is the greatest fun to play!"

Brain was branching out, and Del Mar speculates on where these ventures might have taken him.

> The solo repertoire at his disposal was unquestionably too small for such an intelligent and finished artist, and I feel sure that I am doing his memory no disservice by saying that we, his friends, had all become conscious of a growing restlessness beneath his natural manner and bonhomie. To prevent himself from growing stale he launched several new schemes of increasing enterprise. The first of these was his Wind Quintet which even in a comparatively short time became famous both in this country and on the continent.

> But the venture, which was becoming increasingly close to his heart, was his new group of some 20 picked players from amongst his friends in the orchestral profession. With these he had started giving concerts in which he both played and conducted. The debut of this ensemble took place with considerable éclat at the Wigmore Hall in April last year, and during the summer it spread its wings at the Aldeburgh and Edinburgh Festivals. . . .
>
> Dennis had no pretensions as an assertive conductor and always behaved at his own concerts exactly as he had always behaved—as a natural and unself-conscious musician enjoying himself with his friends and colleagues. But these concerts provided exactly the outlet he needed and he was full of elaborate plans and ideas which we used to discuss at length during our regular get-togethers at each other's houses. What the project might have turned into; where it might have led him; these are unanswerable questions. . . . We can at any rate say that in his instinctive and faultless artistry as a horn-player he had virtually accomplished all there was to accomplish and in that sense his life was complete. It is we who loved him who in that love suffer now from his loss; it is not a question of one horn player as compared with another. Dennis was Dennis and there can never be anyone again like Dennis.[6]

Until he took up conducting as a full-time career in 1947, Del Mar was frequently second horn with Brain in various orchestras for concerts and recordings. In those years from 1939 to 1947, he could observe Brain leading the horn section: "I reckon he was an absolutely splendid leader of a horn quartet. Supposing a work like the Handel Harty Water Music—the way in which the four horns would come in. He would lead us in so firmly and so surely that none of us had any time to think about it. One didn't get nervous or anything like that."[7]

Del Mar wasn't present for the recording of the Mozart concertos with Karajan, but he repeated a much-circulated anecdote of Brain reading motor magazines during the recording sessions:

> In the Mozart Horn Concertos, for instance, he wouldn't want to have the scores up, he would have played them in his sleep. I wasn't there—I always wish I had been there when he recorded them with Karajan. He had up the scores on the stand and Karajan went over to him to point out a particular phrasing he wanted to change and of course there wasn't a note of music on the stand—all those scores were copies of the *Autocar*![8]

Del Mar had opportunities to conduct concerts in which Brain was the soloist, and notably these included the first British performance of the Hindemith Horn Concerto with the Philharmonia Orchestra, described in Chapters 5 and 10.

Neill Sanders (1923–1992)

Horn player Neill Sanders worked with Brain from wartime onwards and was with him right up to the last concert. At the 1991 horn symposium, Sanders recounted the years he worked with Brain.

> He was an extraordinarily busy man, of course, and you might be amused by a recollection of one day of Dennis's life told me by a trumpet player. I did spend many days with Dennis but this one is quite amusing because he started off in the morning at Shepperton Film studios (about 30 miles west of London). The composer had written specially difficult parts for Dennis, who of course wrote all those off and then a trumpet player who was also called Denis—Denis Clift—drove to Cambridge sixty miles north of London where they rehearsed (with the London Mozart Players) the Overture and then they rehearsed the Symphony. Then on walked Dennis and he rehearsed this concerto. In the evening, of course, they played the Overture, Dennis did this concerto and off he went. Denis Clift stayed on and finished the Symphony and probably had a couple of drinks and then he drove back and decided to switch the radio on. There was Dennis Brain playing the Brahms Horn Trio live on the air![9]

Sanders did not claim any special relationship, and the same has been said by others of his colleagues. With such a busy schedule as he had, there must have been precious little time for much socializing outside of concerts, tours, and the world of music generally—particularly after he was married and with two children. Like many others, Sanders's relationship professionally with Brain was a happy one, lasting about fifteen years.

After the war, Sanders was in a hospital with tuberculosis, and after he recovered, he was offered two key posts, taking both: first horn of Melos Ensemble and second horn of the Philharmonia Orchestra.

> I can remember three cracked notes in fifteen years with Dennis. It really was extraordinary accuracy. His embouchure was interesting. As you can see it was an inset embouchure but it led eventually to certain—not problems—things he had to get over because he had a lump of gristle on his bottom lip where he rested the mouthpiece so that when he went down to the bottom he literally had to change position.
>
> Dennis was safe as houses up to the E-flat. Beyond E-flat he had to worry about getting his bottom lip up of course which is very difficult with a lump of gristle but he overcame that. He also had swollen lips occasionally—he had rather puffy lips like mine and you might be amazed to know that in fact he recorded Strauss 1 with a swollen lip!

We used to work 10–1, 6–9 every day and so he started off the first movement and really was in trouble but this was not apparent. The afternoon he spent mowing the lawns—came back a little bit better at night and the next day he shifted onto Strauss 2 and with further results they always sound marvelous.

We also did the Brandenburg together when he had a swollen lip—he just put his feet round the edge of the chair and gripped like mad! It was just tremendous. A remarkable man to work with.

Sanders describes Brain as a colleague.

He was very courteous, always—it was just natural with him. Whenever we finished a concert, he'd turn round to the section and thank them. Or if we'd done a series of recordings, he always said thanks to the rest of us. I never heard him say a nasty word about anyone. If he couldn't say anything nice, he just kept quiet. You could tell when he was very quiet! But he said nothing and he was very easy to play with.

His tutti playing was just as immaculate as his solo playing. His concentration was tremendous—he didn't fool around on the job. The nearest I heard him fooling around was our opening concert at the Carnegie Hall (1955) when we did an encore which was the Force of Destiny Overture. He played the violin part—which was quite remarkable!

Brain had a quiet influence on those around him.

His influence on his colleagues was absolutely enormous. He was very modest and he could out-play everyone and so people couldn't really be obstreperous when Dennis was anywhere within sight because there was this modest man sitting at the back of the orchestra. His influence was so remarkable and it was very noticeable after his death by the difference in people's egos that suddenly started coming out.

He sat the wrong way round, as his father did. He was on the right hand side of the section. You need a lot of big ear as second horn but you got used to it quite well and strange to say it was very useful to me after I left the Philharmonia. I went as First Horn to the London Philharmonic. The section they'd got was at sixes and sevens and they wanted me to try and get it organized. I didn't want to go in and say, "You do this and do that," so I thought the best thing to say was that I had been playing the wrong way round for seven years, would they mind if I played that way. Well, of course, they couldn't so they had to grant me something (they didn't like it)—so they sat the wrong way round for about a month and we had a very nice horn section without hurting anybody's feelings! That was thanks to Dennis.

Sanders had discussed future plans with Brain shortly before his death.

> Three weeks before his death I had a word with Dennis and said I was thinking of leaving the Orchestra. I had been there seven years and I was very busy with Melos. I was also working with the English Opera and I thought it would be a little easier if I went back to being a First Horn again. To my surprise, Dennis said, "Well, I'm thinking of leaving too!" He had just started his Chamber Orchestra—we had in fact done two or three concerts and had got a tour booked (I think) in Scotland and he had enough solo work where he could be independent of the Orchestra. However great you are, coming to do Beethoven 2 is more difficult than playing Mozart 2 at times—it really is! I can remember we used to start all our tours off with the high Mozart—the divertimento K. 287—with Karajan and then Cantelli started doing it. It's quite a tough piece to do on tour for an opening concert. Dennis said, "I think enough's enough—that's the last time we do this!" That's the last time we played that divertimento.
>
> The problem for Dennis was that his contract was owned by Walter Legge. In fact Walter Legge was a very crafty man and all the great artists were not in fact signed up by EMI or HMV. They were all signed up by Legge who had all their contracts in his pocket. Dennis faced the problem of trying to get out of the Philharmonia where he was Legge's prize jewel and still keep a recording contract and record his concertos.
>
> That's what was causing his worry but in fact his life (if you want to question how his life would have gone on) would have gone on very well, I think, with his conducting with his little orchestra. He'd played two concertos with them and conducted things like *Dumbarton Oaks* (Stravinsky) very well. I think it would have been a very great future for him but eventually he would probably have given up the horn and just run his orchestra . . .[10]

Andrew McGavin (b. 1922)

Horn player Andrew McGavin was in the Philharmonia Orchestra for several years, including the 1955 US tour with Karajan. He was "bumper" (assistant) to Brain and wrote the following reminiscences.

> I am very proud to have known and played with Dennis and of course I cannot possibly speak highly enough of him as a player and a person. . . . I first played with him on several occasions during the war when on leave from the army. He was in the RAF, and I was with the Grenadier Guards Band.

After the war we met on freelance engagements and then when I left the LSO after seven years I was invited to join the Philharmonia on their tour of America. That was in 1955 and was a great success for the orchestra. Dennis was hailed as a star who attracted very much admiration especially among horn players. They arranged parties everywhere for our horn section but actually Dennis did not always attend. Although very popular and a very desirable companion he did make sure of his sleep and rest.

He very rarely showed off his virtuosity just for the sake of doing so. He certainly would if asked to and one of those occasions occurred on a TV show with Eric Robinson in the fifties. In the show, Eric introduced Dennis by saying: "This wonderful player can play fiddle parts on the French horn"—his words, and asked Dennis to demonstrate. Dennis simply put the instrument to his lips and played *Humoresque* beautifully just as a violinist would have. He really made it sound so easy.

Dennis had what I can only describe as "Magic." He could do exactly as he wanted with any phrase required of him and I never heard him play anything that was not quite perfect and very beautiful. I found him so very modest and unassuming. He would arrive at an engagement, play magnificently and then go on his way.

He was very knowledgeable on any aspect of motoring and was a highly skilled driver which makes his death so hard to understand.

One very true description of him was made at his funeral. The word which summed up this brilliant man was "serene." He was able to rise above anything that was unpleasant among his colleagues and was never unkind about anyone. Certainly a superb example of "serenity."[11]

James Diack (b. 1938)

James Diack's lessons with Brain are discussed in Chapter 7. He remembered Brain's performance of some key works written for him—Seiber's *Notturno* for horn and strings and the Hindemith Horn Concerto. These and other pieces are discussed in Chapter 10.

Considering the quality of works written for Dennis, apart from the Britten Serenade, one stands out for me above others. It is a work which I have performed once and that is the Mátyás Seiber *Notturno*. A difficult and atmospheric piece. It contains a lot of big slurs, and requires much stamina. I have not come across any musician on any instrument who doesn't like the Britten Serenade. The Hindemith Concerto is, in many ways, unlike Hindemith. It's very humorous and sometimes magical. . . . The Schoeck Horn Concerto (not written for Dennis but first performed by him) is another interesting piece, especially the slow movement.[12]

Diack mentioned that Brain was often described as "imperturbable" or fearless when playing either a solo passage in an orchestral composition, or a solo in a concerto. Rarely did he appear to have difficulties. Diack observed:

> His accuracy in concert and "live" recording was, at that time, truly exceptional but some of the most hazardous entries for the horn occur in orchestral pieces. A good example might be in the slow movement of Beethoven's Fourth Symphony. A very quiet high Bb on the Horn is preceded by a similar phrase on the clarinets who are able to play petrifyingly pianissimo. In this sort of situation one might possibly have heard Dennis, back stage before the concert, deliberately, quietly, splitting that note just to make sure of its "centre" on that day.[13]

Diack related a conversation with flutist Gareth Morris, describing Brain's sound and how he responded to the requirements of the recording studio: "Gareth Morris, speaking of the quality of sound [of Dennis's playing] commented on its astringency which he thought was lovely and the fact that Dennis was so good with recording balance of everything. When you listen to them they all played to one mike, and that they played very well together as a group."[14]

Among Brain's favorite performers a surprising choice was Frank Sinatra, a singer whose studied and ostentatious style, for all its technical brilliance and musicianship, bears few of the qualities one associates with Brain's playing. Yet his appreciation of Sinatra's singing might perhaps tell us something about what he thought about phrasing. Diack thought they were not dissimilar in their handling of the nuances of a musical phrase: "Like Dennis, Frank Sinatra, I think, calculated every breath mark and every nuance of every statement or phrase. You can tell that. Dennis did exactly the same thing without thinking about it quite so much."[15]

Diack discussed what it was that made Brain different from other players:

> A lot of horn players now can possibly play faster, higher, lower, louder and more quietly than Dennis Brain. So what is the difference? It is normally difficult at a young age, or with limited listening experience, to realize the subtleties in great performances, whether in the Arts or any other activity. One needs the experience of the inferior, the boring, the amateur or the just competent, to appreciate the exceptional.[16]

Diack considers that few horn players of today have the "natural imagination" that Brain had in his phrasing. Often they do not think further than playing notes successfully and with faithful observance of the written notation. Also, composers are not always the best judges of the most effective way to perform their pieces. Brain's phrasing of slower passages, rather than fast ones, Diack thought, exemplifies his "magic." The opening phrase of Schubert's *Auf dem Strom*, is a good example.

> Very few people now would play it as interestingly or sympathetically as that. When he was playing within an ensemble, he was exceptionally sympathetic to what was going on around him. If he suddenly had to produce a diminuendo on a note because something else was more important, he would do that at the end of a lung-full of air and that is difficult! To shut down from mezzo piano to pianissimo, you need a vast control and preferably a full diaphragm of air.
>
> Consider, for example, Othmar Schoeck's Horn Concerto—the slow movement. Listen to the way the high notes appear. Also, to the ending of that slow movement. It's absolutely mind-blowing that these notes come out of nothing, as if there was no effort. There must have been huge effort behind it. I don't think that anybody even now, however good, would be capable of that degree of imagination and sensitivity. Of course, this is slightly implying that there is only one good way of playing a piece or only one magic way but there are of course a hundred ways. Maybe he did his thinking unconsciously.
>
> It's very easy now to criticize sound—in other words his was, shall we say, thinner or lighter by today's standards. We now have players who can play louder (in the fatter sense of the word) and faster and lower and higher but few can approach his sublime, imaginative and artistic skill in transporting the audience to an unawareness of technical difficulties. There are moments of sublime pleasure, even for the inexperienced ear. He could take the audience into an ethereal world.[17]

Brain was master of the silences as well as the sounds. Like a comedian who knows when to deliver his punch line to greatest effect, he played his solos, whether in the solo, chamber, or orchestral class, with timing that always sounded just right. He was always aware of the music-making around him and interacted so well with other players musically, whatever the size of the ensemble. Perhaps he found more music within him to express because he enjoyed hearing a fine piece of playing from his fellow musicians.

Speaking of a private recording of Brain in Vivaldi's Concerto for two horns, RV538, Diack observed his response to a potentially tedious repeat: "I listened to something Dennis did—a little double concerto for two horns. There is a little phrase in there where the two horns have to repeat the section. Dennis adds a touch of humour at the end of the second repeat by producing the notes in a more staccato fashion which makes it sound even cheekier. You wouldn't find a modern player doing that!"[18]

Barry Tuckwell (b. 1931)

Barry Tuckwell was, apart from Brain, arguably the most distinguished horn soloist of the twentieth century. Like Brain, he inspired many composers to write for the instrument. Thea Musgrave, Don Banks, Oliver Knussen, and Robin Holloway wrote concertos for him. In 1968, at age thirty-seven, he had moved out of the orchestra to concentrate on his solo engagements and conducting. Tuckwell was interviewed several times for BBC radio in the 1980s and 1990s, and invariably Brain was discussed. The following are extracts from the BBC's *Mining the Archive* seventy-fifth birthday tribute to Brain on May 17, 1996:

> The horn two hundred years ago was one of the most popular solo instruments. It declined in popularity in the 19th century and came back in the 20th century, first with Aubrey and then Dennis and then it was like an explosion. Suddenly the horn was a wonderful solo instrument. Everybody saw it as an instrument worth listening to but that was always, I think, definitely because of Dennis.
>
> I don't think it's just a question of technique because there were horn players before him with extraordinary techniques and there are horn players now with a really exceptional command and dexterity on the instrument. No, Dennis had something more than that. There are certain musicians who will walk onto the stage and as soon as they come something is happening and they haven't even started to play. Dennis had that, as well as technique but he also had a way of playing the horn which I don't think you can copy because that was him which made it very exciting.[19]

Tuckwell had first met Brain after a concert with the London Mozart Players at Chelsea Town Hall in about 1950. Brain had performed the Haydn Concerto No. 1 and the Mozart Sinfonia Concertante.

> I was absolutely knocked out by this. I was still a wild, colonial yokel and I went round to say hello, wondering what sort of reception I'd get. He had just had some new valve stuck on his horn. He said, "Look," handing me the horn to try. I thought, "What?" He was a very nice person, without a side [assumption of superiority] and although he had this projection as a superstar, he was just a very nice person who you'd be very happy to sit down with and have a cup of tea with.[20]

Anthony Halstead (b. 1945)

Anthony Halstead never knew Brain, but he was inspired by his fabulous playing. Halstead is an outstanding horn virtuoso, especially of the natural horn, who has successfully combined a career as soloist and conductor. He was interviewed for BBC radio in 1994; here is an excerpt:

> Brain was tremendously influential in putting the horn on the map—the modern horn—as a solo instrument. The way that he could turn a phrase in the Mozart Concertos. . . . If authenticity means to move the spirit to deliver the composer's intentions in the most wonderfully moving way, then his recording of the Mozart concertos must be one of the supreme achievements of the gramophone. But Brain played for most of his recording career on a horn which was not as mechanical, not as machine-like as the modern orchestral horn, and many of his early recordings were made on a very narrow-bore instrument which had an extra length of tubing as well which gave it that characteristic singing tone quality. . . .
>
> I remember hearing his recording of the Britten Serenade. I think it was the second one that sticks in my mind. I think he'd actually just moved over onto the modern German instrument but he had a special one made with a narrow mouth pipe (like one of the crooks for the natural horn) and a small French bell on it.[21]

Halstead described the technical obstacles of the Prologue to Britten's Serenade, referring to Brain's second recording of it with Eugene Goossens conducting the New Symphony Orchestra of London:

> Nobody has played that rising 6th quite with that intensity and that searing, searching quality up to that written top A, which Britten notates as an A. In fact, the reason why a lot of horn players don't get that right (including myself many times) is because really the note in the harmonic series which is nearest to what Britten wanted was actually the written B-flat for the horn, not the written A. If you try and play the A, you sure as anything won't get it—you'll get an A-flat. So you have to set your lips somewhere approaching a B-flat and it's all on the lips, of course, and the breath.[22]

Michael Thompson (b. 1954)

Michael Thompson is another British virtuoso who has found Brain's example an inspiration. Thompson has taken an active part in keeping Brain's memory alive for modern concert-goers and music-lovers in general. Like Brain, he was principal horn of the Philharmonia Orchestra and has also made many outstanding recordings of the solo repertoire as well as chamber music. In 2000, he wrote a tribute article from which the following is an extract:

> My school had a record library and I found in it an LP of someone called Dennis Brain playing some concertos by Mozart. I took it home and

listened to it. It is tempting to say that this first hearing was a revelation, a crossroads in my musical life, but it wasn't like that. I had nothing with which to compare these performances and assumed that this was just the way the horn was played. In a way I was right, and it was then and remains now probably the most important lesson I ever learned.

There was nothing flashy or ostentatious about Dennis Brain's playing. It took time and a broadening musical awareness to appreciate just how close to perfection these Mozart recordings are. For many horn players, myself included, they are still the benchmark by which all others are measured. It's hard to say exactly what makes them so special but words like "elegance," "wit" and "honesty" spring to mind.

By the time I joined the Philharmonia, I had listened to all available Brain recordings: the Britten Serenade (1944), with Dennis at his most light-footed in the Hymn, the Nocturne from Mendelssohn's *Midsummer Night's Dream* with his exquisitely long phrasing, the sheer beauty of his sound in the Hindemith Concerto and so many more.

But Dennis Brain's greatness was so much more than mere accuracy, important though that is. His legacy is enormous. He inspired composers to write for the horn and in his performances and recordings demonstrated a profound respect for the music. His phenomenal technical ability never intruded, so that the listener could ignore the degree of difficulty and focus on the musical message. He showed generations of horn players to come that it is possible to rise above the notorious difficulties of the instrument. Dennis Brain was first and foremost a great musical artist; the horn was simply his voice.

Since Dennis Brain's death, subsequent generations of British horn players have found their own different ways of trying to take his legacy onward. The debt we owe him as a source of inspiration simply cannot be overstated. Although he did hardly any teaching, he led by example. Imitation may be the sincerest form of flattery but in the case of Dennis Brain it can also be the best way to learn. I sometimes say to students that all you need to play the horn is a fingering chart and Dennis Brain's recordings.[23]

In the following extract from a BBC Radio 3 broadcast, Thompson remembers Richard Strauss and Brain's connection with that composer:

The Second Concerto, written in the 1940s, was first performed by the principal horn of the Vienna Philharmonic, at the time, who was Gottfried von Freiberg, a very great exponent of the Vienna horn. Other than that, in this country, Strauss did actually conduct the Philharmonia orchestra in its very early days so Dennis Brain would also have played for him. In fact, Dennis gave, I believe, the second performance of the Second Concerto. Speaking of Dennis Brain, there's a wonderful recording of the *Four Last*

> *Songs* with Elizabeth Schwarzkopf and the Philharmonia Orchestra which was recorded in 1954 and Dennis is playing the hauntingly beautiful horn solo in "September" and this is a wonderful moment, I think, for horn players because this is actually perhaps the last orchestral horn solo that Strauss ever wrote.[24]

Donald Froud (b. 1932)

Donald Froud was a postwar pupil of Aubrey Brain's from 1948 and has had a distinguished career as professional horn player. He remembers Brain as a person and musician:

> He was perhaps the most courteous man that I ever met. When I was still a student, if I met him in the street he would say, "Hello, Donald, how are you getting on?" And he would listen to the answer. He was never too busy to talk to and encourage amateurs. I recall an occasion when he asked Arthur Davison, conductor of the Royal Amateur Orchestra, if he could play a concerto with them, as he had never played a horn concerto in the Duke's Hall. I was Arthur's fixer at that time and I used to play for his concerts including the final rehearsals. Dennis insisted on rehearsing with the orchestra before the day and, when I arrived at the school in Marylebone, I found no less than ten horn players had turned up from somewhere.
>
> So I sat down to listen and Dennis ran through the Strauss Concerto. He thanked all the orchestra profusely and then came over to me. "Donald," he said, "I don't think I've met any of these horn players. Could you introduce them to me?" Well, I had no idea who they were either, but they all introduced themselves and he had a look at their instruments, blew a few notes on one or two and wished them all well. Then he said, "I'm sorry but I have to go now because I've got to broadcast in Maida Vale Studios at 10.15." He left us at one minute past ten o'clock and presumably he got there in time. What I do know is that he gave immeasurable pleasure to ten amateur horn players.[25]

Tony Fairley (b. 1937)

Tony Fairley, one of Ifor James's first pupils and now a semi-professional horn player from Newcastle, remembered fondly an occasion when he met Brain after a concert. It was an evening meeting of the Newcastle Chamber Music Society on February 17, 1955, a concert with the Brain-Pougnet-Parry Trio. The works included the Brahms Horn Trio and the Beethoven Horn Sonata. Fairley recalled that the concert was "absolutely brilliant, a revelation to me."

At the end, he was invited backstage to meet the great man himself and they chatted for a few minutes about how Fairley came to play the horn, about lessons and what sort of grade he was up to. Fairley then introduced his three friends, Eric Stevenson, Tom Johnston, and Geoff Versleys, who were hovering in the background. The conversation turned to fast cars and some other areas of music generally. After about twenty minutes they bade farewell and were all struck with Brain's friendliness and general lack of any "side"—he really appeared to be interested in four total strangers who had this common bond.[26]

Christopher Hortin (b. 1934)

Christopher Hortin, another pupil of Aubrey Brain's, remembered occasions when Aubrey's son was soloist:

> I went to see the Jacques Choir and Orchestra doing the Bach B minor mass in High Wycombe town hall about 1950. Dennis played the "Quoniam" brilliantly. A local musician told me, "Dennis always replies to the offer of a date for so much money, 'Just double it!'" I was in the London Senior Orchestra under Ernest Read when Dennis played the K.447 Concerto in the Davis Theatre, Croydon, for a children's audience in 1956, I think. Then I was the fourth horn for the Hoffnung Festival at the Royal Festival Hall. After playing hosepipe, and a bit of organ, Dennis (and Norman Del Mar) joined our horn section for a straight performance of Respighi's *Roman Festivals*.[27]

Mark Biondolillo (b. 1960)

Mark Biondolillo is a professional horn player who lives in Hampton, Virginia. He studied horn with Karen Thornton, a Fulbright scholar and former pupil of Alan Civil's, at Jacksonville University. He has lectured at Virginia Commonwealth University on the influence of Brain on horn playing. Biondolillo plays a single B-flat/A Alexander built by George McCracken to the specifications of Brain's B-flat/A Alexander single horn. He described what he considered Brain's greatest secret:

> More and more I am convinced of one thing, one of the greatest secrets of horn playing is the powerful air-column one must have. When this air usage is right, things just seem to fall in place. Dennis had this. Just listen to the Schumann *Adagio and Allegro*, for instance. Beautiful, liquid slurs, especially the E-flat arpeggio up to G after the low section of the Adagio. Who can replicate that? It comes from rock-solid diaphragm support, lifting those muscles up slightly as one progresses higher in the register. Some things we have to find out through trial and error![28]

Richard Kittrell (b. 1944)

American hornist Richard Kittrell, a pupil of Toscanini's NBC Symphony principal horn Arthur Berv, and a long-retired professional who still plays regularly, remembered Brain's qualities on records and radio broadcasts:

> For me, Dennis's playing in the Mozart concerti and Hindemith concerto, e.g., are unsurpassable, both musically and technically (hardly a unique opinion). Of course, my only source for judgment is the recordings. Those who, in person, heard him perform would have been better qualified to assess the player under real conditions, free of multiple takes or the editor's splicing blade. But the recorded performances are of such high caliber that they stand as irrefutable evidence of his superiority as a hornist and a musician.
>
> More recently, we have benefited from the release of many of Dennis's live concert performances; they reveal that, yes, he is human and therefore fallible, but they are mostly consistent with the stellar level of playing evinced on his recordings. In retrospect, now, with an abundance of contemporary hornists of high quality, it could be reasonably argued that there are a very few who have since equaled him, and no-one can argue against the merits of the putative pre-eminent hornist since Dennis Brain, Barry Tuckwell, who recorded and performed, at the highest level, virtually everything of value in the horn literature.
>
> And after the eras of Brain and Tuckwell, we might ask the question: will there ever be another singularly transcendent hornist to dominate the musical world as have they? Putting the very subjective qualities of tone-concept and musical taste aside (*de gustibus non est disputandum*), there are yet none who have surpassed Dennis Brain, and as long as the horn remains "the horn," it's difficult to imagine that anyone ever will.[29]

Martin Prowse (b. 1939)

Martin J. Prowse, a British amateur horn player who is an exponent of the Vienna horn and for many years a collector of Brain's recordings (donated in 2007 to the Royal Academy of Music for study purposes), described Brain's special qualities:

> It would be impossible to enumerate all those instances of a rapid staccato passage, a glacially smooth slur, a confident legato phrase or even a long held note that appears from nowhere and merges again with the surrounding orchestral texture. Yet these are features which betray Dennis Brain's instinctive awareness of the role of the horn in relation to the other sections of

> the orchestra. In his hands a solo like that in the Andante of Tchaikovsky's Fifth Symphony would emerge, grow, develop and discreetly withdraw again, showing the sensitiveness of the artist in placing a musical phrase in context, not demanding undivided attention by brash self-advertisement. Listen, too, to the way the horn follows the clarinet at the beginning of the "Shepherd's Hymn" in Beethoven's Pastoral Symphony. Here the octave interval is so controlled as to make the change almost imperceptible. To talk of a "leap" or "jump" in this case would be to misunderstand Dennis Brain's ability to treat a phrase as an organic growth, where the concept of vertical intervals is replaced by that of horizontal development.[30]

Franklin Zimmerman (b. 1923)

Franklin B. Zimmerman is an American musicologist and conductor who specializes in Baroque music. His catalog of Henry Purcell's works is considered one of the most crucial contributions to Purcell research; the Z catalog numbers derive from his surname.

> Dennis Brain's wife, Yvonne, had been a class-mate of a young lady I knew at the University of Southern California. Receiving a Fulbright scholarship to Oxford, and armed with a letter of introduction to Dennis Brain, I voyaged to England in September of 1952.
>
> No sooner had I arrived in London, I began to track down Dennis, hoping that he might take me on as a pupil. First I attended a Saturday morning Children's concert at the Royal Festival Hall, where he was featured as a soloist in a Mozart Concerto. When I hurried back at intermission, hoping to meet him, I discovered that he had already left for a rehearsal at Yalding House. Missing him there as well, and also at a nearby restaurant where, as I was told, he had gone for a quick lunch, I followed him back to the Royal Festival Hall, where he was scheduled to appear as soloist in another concert. Once again, he was gone—this time to an unknown destination—before I could catch up with him at interval time. Finally, I met with him shortly before midnight at Yalding House, where he had just finished broadcasting the Dvorak Serenade.
>
> When I recounted the day's adventures, he commiserated, then invited me to a party he was throwing at his home near Hampstead Heath later that week. Of course, I accepted, gladly, but postponed popping the question as to whether or not he would take me on as a pupil.
>
> Later that week, I arrived at his door at the appointed time, and he and his wife greeted me warmly. Then, as the party was winding down, he said he felt like taking a spin in his ancient Citroen, and wondered if I would

like a ride back to Edgeware, where I was temporarily staying. Of course, I accepted, and used that time to pop the question at last. "No," he answered, "my schedule is so crowded I scarcely have time to keep up. But I can recommend you to my Father, Aubrey, who will surely take you on." I took down the telephone number, promising to call as soon as I got to Oxford, where I was scheduled to matriculate the next day. I did call, and soon was signed on as a student of Aubrey Brain.

In the following summer, I was accepted into the National Youth Orchestra, where I was so fortunate to engage in nightly chamber sessions with colleagues of Dennis Brain from the RPO, Philharmonia, and other orchestras.

It was after one of these post-concert sessions that Dennis came to me and asked if I would drive back to London with him that very night. Apparently he drove back in that manner to be with his family quite often. Unfortunately, I had made arrangements with a young Scottish lady for the evening, and could not go, whereupon he drove down to London alone. Nothing went wrong on that occasion, but only a few years later, under similar conditions, he met with his fatal accident. By then I was seeing Aubrey Brain's widow quite often and he [Dennis] quite frequently, for she played viola in the London Senior Orchestra and in Ernest Read's Children's Concerts where I had been accepted as Associate Conductor. We shared the sorrow of Dennis's tragic death. [31]

Bob Gibson (b. 1936)

Los Angeles horn player Bob Gibson received his first lessons at age twelve on a B-flat horn from Alfred Brain, Jr. in 1948. Gibson remembered that Alfred never took his horn out of the case, but buzzed his mouthpiece and gave instructions for breathing and embouchure. Gibson went on to be a student of Sinclair Lott. He joined the US Air Force Band after eleventh grade. He was stationed at Parks Air Force Base in 1953, then in France for three years, and finally a year in Wiesbaden, Germany.

I met Dennis Brain at his home in Hampstead, North London, when I was eighteen and stationed with the US Air Force Band in France. I knew Dennis was over in England and we (The US Air Force Band) were getting ready to go to Bushey Park, just outside London. We were going to combine with the Air Force Band there and then go to Edinburgh with them for the Military Tattoo. This was about 1954 or 1955.

I got Dennis's address and wrote asking when he was going to record the Strauss Horn Concertos, and it just so happened that he was in the process of recording them. We corresponded a couple of times, and he said that if I was ever in the area to look him up. Sure enough, I gave him a call and found out how to get there, and that afternoon he wasn't doing anything so I went on over.

I had my 8D horn with me because Dennis had said, "Bring your horn." He played on it and he still sounded like Dennis Brain! I told him that I had taken lessons from his uncle, and I think that's why he wanted to find out what I was doing. We played a few of the Mozart Duets. It was really quite an experience. We played those pieces and then he went through them in transposition. He'd take one and he could play it in all the different transposed keys, which got very interesting.

Then I had to get back and thanked him very much. He let me know when the recordings came out, and he sent me an autographed picture which the Los Angeles Horn Club has now.

To conclude, what can I say about this incomparable artist, except that Dennis Brain was a very fine player and a very nice person.[32]

Walter Hecht (b. 1946)

Walter Hecht, who during the 1960s and 1970s played for the Hollywood studios in Los Angeles, recalls his lifelong "obsession" with Brain:

My first horn teacher, Richard Ballou, first introduced me to the magical sound of Brain in the first recording he made of Britten's Serenade. Ballou had recommended I buy the recording, and his parting comment at my first lesson was that this was the "best possible example of horn virtuosity that can be heard."

I bought the recording—and for some months did not go further than to play the Prologue over and over again, which to my untutored ears sounded like the most beautiful and astounding virtuoso playing humanly possible. I would try to copy the notes as best I could. Can you imagine my surprise when I first played the recording all the way through? I became an avid collector of his recordings from that moment on.

Brain's rare film appearances fired my imagination even more. With live film footage, one cannot make the repeats and cuts that one does in recordings. This made film media far more inspirational to me. My junior high school bandmaster, Wallace Umber, deepened my interest in Brain by showing me, and his other students, rare (and now unobtainable) footage of Brain's appearance on NBC's Today Show (October 26, 1955), hosted by Dave Garroway, a copy of which could be loaned at that time to teachers from the Smith-Holst Library in Los Angeles.

In this television appearance, Brain played an excerpt from the Britten Serenade featuring his "woodpecker-like tonguing." Umber also showed a film from the British Information Service of "Instruments of the Orchestra" which had five-seconds of Dennis playing an arpeggio (apparently inserted during editing as he did not play with the orchestra in the film).

Some years later, I learned that these films had been labeled "obsolete" and destroyed. For decades, I have been searching for surviving copies of the two films with no success. As far as I know, both are gone now, according to the original sources.

I was able to purchase my own new copy of the Beethoven Horn Sonata as a 16mm film from the film's director, Ken Cameron. For several years I lectured on Brain and showed this film at the universities and colleges in the Los Angeles area. Twenty-five years later, it was put into public release in at least two formats.

I sincerely hope that the "missing" films can be located and released to the public, like the Beethoven. I will continue to look whenever a possible source is uncovered. My obsession continues![33]

CHAPTER

10

Selected Performances

No other wind player of modern times has received the recognition and acknowledgement for his proficiency and musical prowess in the form of dedicated compositions as has Brain.

The earliest work composed for Brain (at his request) is Benjamin Britten's Serenade. It is considered by many to be the greatest contribution to contemporary horn repertoire and continues to attract attention through performances by new generations of horn players.

The last work dedicated to Brain, immediately following his death, was Francis Poulenc's *Elégie* for Horn and Piano, which premiered one year after his death. The work expressively relates to Brain's life as described by Wilfrid Mellers: "The enigmatic structure of this piece must surely have some allegorical, if not some explicitly programmatic, intention. The ferocious *agitato* snarls like Death himself, who destroyed Dennis Brain in a car accident. . . ."[1]

The following discussions are of a selection from among the many works written to recognize Brain. Commemoratory acknowledgments are either a dedication by the composer or a premiere performance by Brain. The Poulenc Sextet is included even though it does not fit these categories because of its prominence in Brain's performing life. When possible, the work recorded by Brain is reviewed with respect to the score; however, in some instances, either the score or a recording were not available.

Benjamin Britten

Serenade for Tenor, Horn and Strings (Op. 31)

Score: Hawkes & Sons (London), Ltd, Winthrop Rogers Edition, Horn in F

Benjamin Britten (1913–1976) composed his Serenade, which he dedicated to Brain and tenor Peter Pears, in March–April 1943 at the request of Brain, who was in the RAF Central Band, for which Britten was writing incidental music for a series of wartime radio documentaries (see Chapter 2).

Britten wrote about the passing of Brain: "It has robbed us of an artist with the unique combination of superb technical command of his instrument, great musicianship, a lively and intelligent interest in music of all sorts, and a fine performing temperament, coupled with charming personality. It has robbed us of a man of rare generosity, simplicity and charm. . . ."

And about their collaboration on the Serenade:

> His help was invaluable in writing the work; but he was always most cautious in advising any alterations. Passages which seemed impossible even for his prodigious gifts were practiced over and over again before any modifications were suggested, such was his respect for a composer's ideas. . . . Some of my happiest musical experiences were conducting this work for him and Peter Pears—a succession of wonderful performances progressing from the youthful exuberances and brilliance of the early days to the maturity and deep understanding of the last few years.[2]

The Serenade consists of eight settings, as described by composer and writer Lloyd Moore.

> The Serenade opens with a Prologue for solo horn played on the instrument's natural harmonics (causing some notes to sound deliberately out-of-tune), evoking an atmosphere of "natural," primeval innocence. This mood is sustained in the twilit landscape of Cotton's Pastoral with its gently descending arpeggio figures in the voice and horn, and the more vigorous setting of Tennyson's Nocturne, notable for its cadenza-like fanfare passages ("Blow, bugle, blow") with their highly characteristic chains of thirds.
>
> The relatively uncomplicated nature of these first two settings makes the contrast with the third, Blake's Elegy, all the more effective: this is one of Britten's most overt and explicit representations of, as [the work's dedicatee] Edward Sackville-West put it, "the sense of sin in the heart of man." The quietly heaving syncopations in the strings and plodding double bass arpeggios are straight-forwardly diatonic but are disturbed by the chromatically

meandering horn line which proceeds by way of falling semi-tones, often effecting a flattening from major to minor, intensified in the closing bars by the eerie use of hand-stopped glissandi.

The following Dirge maintains the dark tone, the tenor's obsessively repeated ground oblivious to the developing fugue in the strings which begins pianissimo, gradually building to a powerful climax (marked by the horn's dramatic entry with the fugue subject), before retreating back into the shadows. The tension is dispelled by the following fleet-footed setting of Ben Jonson's Hymn to Diana in which the strings play pizzicato throughout.

The final song, Keats's Sonnet, in which the horn is silent, is an *Adagio* of rare beauty which gains its highly distinctive sound from the juxtaposition of unrelated triads, a prime example of Britten's genius for discovering fresh uses for the most basic musical elements. Finally the horn closes the cycle with the Epilogue, an exact repeat of the Prologue with which it began the work, but this time played offstage, the innocence of the opening now left far behind.[3]

Marshall lists three recordings of the Serenade with Brain.[4]

Conductor	Soloist	Dates	Label
Britten	Pears	May 25 & Oct 8, 1944	London CD (426 996-2)
Hollingsworth	Pears	July 30, 1953	BBC Live
Goossens	Pears	Nov. 25–27, 1953	London, LL 994

The first performance by Brain, not recorded, was on October 15, 1943, at Wigmore Hall, London with Peter Pears, conducted by Walter Goehr. Brain would have played his Raoux narrow-bore horn for this and the 1944 recording. Although we cannot be certain, he most likely used a B-flat crook except in the Prologue and Epilogue, for which he likely used an F crook. He performed the Serenade again on a BBC Third Program broadcast on September 10, 1950, with Richard Lewis, tenor. Soon after this, in 1951, he changed to the Alexander B-flat/A horn and subsequent performances would be on this Alexander horn. We cannot determine unequivocally which horn Brain used in the 1953 recordings, but it was likely the B-flat Alexander with an F extension.

The performance conducted by John Hollingsworth was a Promenade concert at the Royal Albert Hall. Brain also performed the work on November 18, 1954, at Edinburgh with the Reid Orchestra. Other performances include the First Edinburgh Festival in 1948 with John Tainsh and the Boyd Neel Orchestra conducted by Boyd Neel, and on March 12, 1950, with the London Chamber Players and Peter Pears, conducted by Anthony Bernard.[5]

Brain also performed the Serenade with Anthony Bernard conducting the Royal Philharmonic Orchestra at Royal Festival Hall in London with Richard Lewis on February 22, 1954, for the 1953–1954 Concert Season. (*Pl.1*)

In the solo horn Prologue and Epilogue, Britten instructs the performer to use only the (F) horn's natural harmonics, causing several harmonics to sound out of tune to the ear that is more accustomed to a tempered scale. The partials (natural open harmonics) on the horn double every octave about the fundaments (C_1 below the bass clef for written F horn), resulting in eight partials in the highest octave (c'' to c''') as seen in *Plate 2*. The thirteenth and fourteenth partials are a" and b-flat" respectively. The thirteenth partial is called for in the third from the last measure. Brain plays the fourteenth partial in the 1944 recording with the Boyd Neel Orchestra. That he missed the thirteenth partial and played the fourteenth partial in error, as reported by several critics of the day, is unlikely. The final song (Sonnet) does not include the horn, allowing the horn player to move off-stage for the Epilogue.

As with so many of his recordings, Brain's performance of the Britten Serenade will undoubtedly remain as the standard by which others will be measured. So successful was the Serenade that ten years later Britten wrote a second work for Brain with tenor voice and piano accompaniment. This is the elegiac Canticle III: *Still Falls the Rain* (Op. 55), written to a tragic poem by Edith Sitwell. Brain established the standard for its performance with his playing, of the "dark opening, slithering chromatic scales, and thunderous low notes."[6]

Following Brain's death in 1957, Britten initiated a new work in Brain's memory. Although Britten never finished the work, English composer Colin Mathews (b. 1946), who had worked with Britten, completed it in 2005. The work, titled *In Memoriam Dennis Brain* for four horns and strings, received its London Premiere on September 1, 2007, at the Proms, Cadogan Hall, exactly fifty years after Brain's death. A performance with Richard Watkins, Michael Thompson, Peter Francomb, and Chris Griffiths with the Northern Sinfonia, Thomas Zehetmair, conducting, can be heard on the CD *Unknown Britten*.[7]

Malcolm Arnold

Concerto No.1 for Horn and Orchestra (Op. 11)
Concerto No.2 for Horn and Orchestra (Op. 58)

No recorded performance by Brain

Malcolm Arnold (1921–2006) took up the trumpet at the age of twelve and five years later obtained a scholarship to the Royal College of Music in London, where he studied composition with Gordon Jacob and trumpet with Ernest Hall. He joined the London Philharmonic Orchestra in 1941 as second trumpet, becoming principal trumpet in 1943 and a full-time composer in 1948. (*Pl. 3*) Arnold's most significant works are generally considered to be his nine symphonies. He also wrote a number of concertos, including two for horn: No. 1 in 1945 and No. 2 in 1956.

Arnold participated in a brass concert at St. Peter's Church, Eaton Square, in London in 1943. For the event, he arranged several pieces of fourteenth-century music for brass trio, including Guillaume de Machaut's *Double Hoquet*. In Arnold's arrangement, the bumpy rhythms implied by the title became even more pronounced, but were taken in their stride by the trio, which included Brain. This encounter was the start of a friendship that lasted until Brain's death fourteen years later.[8]

Concerto No. 1, Op. 11

Arnold's first horn concerto was written for Charles Gregory, first horn and Chairman of the London Philharmonic Orchestra, who premiered it on December 8, 1946, with Ernest Ansermet conducting. It is the longest and most expansive of all Arnold's concertos. Brain gave the first broadcast performance with the BBC Midland Light Orchestra conducted by Gilbert Vinter on May 18, 1951, on a Home Service broadcast from Birmingham.[9]

Hugo Cole provides a review in his book on Arnold.[10]

> The first movement ($\frac{4}{4}$ *Allegro comodo*) opens with a bold and expansive theme which could easily have been written for the old open horn. In the atmospheric second movement ($\frac{3}{4}$ *Andante con moto*) the horn ruminates, elaborating on short melodic phrases, often over static harmony or persistent tonic-dominant ostinatos.
>
> The orchestra introduces both the main themes of the last movement ($\frac{6}{8}$ *Allegro con brio*) in its opening tutti. The horn takes up the first of these quietly and in legato, making magic out of the slurred rising octave c–c', ideally placed in the best part of the register. The movement ends peacefully,

> the horn meditating on the legato theme as the pace slackens and orchestra quietly affirms the home key of F major.

We have not determined if the May 1951 broadcast performance was recorded by the BBC. If a recording of either concerto exists, it is likely of this broadcast.

Concerto No. 2, Op. 58

Brain gave the premiere of the second concerto with the Hallé Orchestra on July 17, 1957, at the Cheltenham Festival, only a few weeks before his death. *Musical Times* states: "A Horn Concerto with string orchestra by Malcolm Arnold, which the composer conducted on the previous evening, is an altogether slighter work, mainly designed to exhibit the extraordinary virtuosity of the soloist, Dennis Brain."[11]Arnold wrote his second horn concerto for Brain intending to test the limits of endurance and technique of the horn player. Reportedly, Arnold re-wrote portions of the horn score after being told by Brain that parts of the horn score were beyond the technical means of any performer.

Cole also provides an overview of this concerto: "Though there is much brilliant and taxing music in the Concerto, Arnold here pays tribute to the musician as much as to the virtuoso. Many song-like tunes are perfectly adapted to display Brain's artistry in shaping cantabile phrases, the warmth and purity of his tone, and his clarinet-like fluency."[12]

> The concerto consists of three movements: I. Con energico (4/4), II. Andantino grazioso (3/4), III. Vivace (3/4). Because no recordings of Malcolm's composition by Brain are known to exist, an evaluation of Brain's interpretation of the work cannot be performed. Sadly, the BBC did not broadcast or record the July 17 performance of this concerto. Unless some unknown patron recorded it, this historic performance has been lost to history. Brain performed the concerto only this once.

Peter Racine Fricker

Wind Quintet Op. 5

Score: Composer's Horn Manuscript in Five Parts with Alternative Finale

Peter Fricker (1920–1990) quickly gained fame within the musical community for his work, not only because of his prize-winning compositions but also because of his early association with Brain. They also shared an interest in the organ. Fricker's career appeared promising as one of Britain's youngest post-war composers. He was Professor of Composition at the Royal College of Music in London, then in 1952 became Director of Music at Morley College, succeeding Michael Tippett. In 1964 he assumed a position as visiting Professor of Music at the University of California, Santa Barbara. Six years later, he immigrated to the United States and became Chairman of the Music Department at UCSB.

Fricker composed the Wind Quintet for Brain in 1947. The Dennis Brain Wind Ensemble gave the first performance on February 27, 1949, at Conway Hall in the South Place Concert Series. (*Pl. 4*) Brain and members of the Boyd Neel Orchestra performed it the following night at Chelsea Town Hall. Brain's Ensemble performed it in London at Wigmore Hall in January 1952 as part of a concert of wind music. The quintet received acclamation as a delightful work performed by skilled players who demonstrated their musicianship. The Ensemble also performed it at the York City Art Gallery during the York Festival on June 26, 1954, repeated the next day in Hampstead, North London, again in Holborn on March 20, 1955, and finally, as described in Chapter 3, in Venice at the *Biennale di Venezia XIX Festival Internazionale di Musica Contemporanea* in the Ca' Giustinian, Sala delle Colonne on September 12, 1956.[13]

Brain's last performance of the Fricker Quintet was on August 24, 1957, only one week before his death, at the Edinburgh Festival in Freemasons Hall. The performance was broadcast live on the BBC Home Service and recorded, and is now available on a BBC label.[14]

Fricker's Quintet is in four movements:

- I Moderato
- II Badinerie Vivace-Musette. Moderato e sostenuto
- III Canonic Variations: Tema. Poco allegro-Canon I (at 4th); Adagio-Canon II (at 5th); Poco andante-Cannon III (at 2nd)-Canon IV (at 6th); Vivo-Adagio-Canon V (at 7th); Adagio
- IV Finale: Vivo

The first movement, in two parts, begins in $\frac{4}{4}$ then changes to $\frac{3}{4}$ at measure twenty. The principal theme is introduced by the horn in the first measure, with variations later. At rehearsal number 9, measures 1–3 (in $\frac{3}{4}$), it calls for a tied low A, pianissimo, over three measures and into the fourth; however, Brain plays only the first measure.

The second movement is in two parts, beginning in $\frac{12}{8}$ for the Badinerie Vivace, then to $\frac{3}{4}$ ($\frac{6}{8}$) for the Musette. The Badinerie's main theme is introduced by the flute, followed by several repeats. A short but impressive horn solo appears at rehearsal number 14, measures 8–10, in a staccato figure that Brain articulates especially well.

Movement three begins in $^{6}/_{8}$ with a horn solo in triplets lasting eleven measures. Although measures 12–13 call for stopped horn, Brain performs this section pianissimo, but not stopped.

The Finale is in $^{12}/_{8}$ ($^{3}/_{8}$, $^{3}/_{4}$, $^{3}/_{8}$) with some $^{4}/_{4}$. The horn is introduced at rehearsal number 22 with four measures of descending whole notes, followed by a horn solo that is tightly woven into the wind texture but with the horn noticeably in command. A less pronounced solo with the horn in a lower register appears later. At the end, the horn speaks authoritatively at Subito vivo and is joined by the full ensemble to close the work.

Kenneth Essex

Concerto for Horn and Orchestra

Score: Unavailable

Although only limited data on composer Kenneth Essex (1915–1955) and his Concerto exists, the authors have been able to establish an approximate date for this composition and discover details of the process leading to its first performance through his correspondence with the BBC. Essex suffered a massive stroke on May 7, 1955, at the age of forty, shortly after the first broadcast performance of the concerto on April 20 by Brain and the BBC Scottish Orchestra conducted by Gerald Gentry.[15]

Essex wrote music for Pathé News and was a composer of incidental music, for which he often wrote under pseudonyms such as "Rufus Isaacs." The first performance of the concerto on the BBC is available from the National Sound Archives and includes a voice narrative. We know of no commercial issues of this performance.[16]

The date of composition (originally for horn and piano) is documented in BBC correspondence with Essex beginning on March 10, 1953, in which Essex submits his score for consideration.[17]

> I enclose herewith my Horn Concerto with recording of the same for your consideration.
>
> I would like to point out however that this recording is made with piano instead of full orchestra.
>
> Perhaps you will let me hear from you about this work in due course.

Essex writes again about the score and parts:

> I am so pleased to hear the view on my Horn Concerto.
>
> I'm afraid there are none done of the parts but will put them in hand when I get the score back from your programme builders say 6.6.4.4.3 or what do you suggest?

> I will collect the records when in Town.
>
> Please forgive this shocking writing but had a stroke last New Year's Eve.

Essex in another note to the BBC advises that the parts are now complete:

> I am glad to say that the parts of my Concerto for Horn and Orchestra are now complete and consist of 2 flutes (second doubling piccolo); 2 oboes (second doubling cor anglais); 2 B-flat clarinets (second doubling bass clarinet); 2 bassoons; 4 horns; 3 trumpets; 2 tenor trombones; 1 bass trombone; 1 tuba; 3 timps (1 player); percussion (3 players), harp and the string parts I have 9 firsts; 7 seconds; 5 violas; 5 cellos; and 4 basses; as well as soloist's Horn part.
>
> I thought I would let you know the details of the orchestra required in the hope that you will soon be able to fit this work into your programmes.

An endorsement from Brain is documented in his correspondence to the BBC on July 24, 1953:

> Mr. Kenneth Essex suggested I write you concerning his Wind Quintet and Horn Concerto.
>
> As I believe it was my Wind Ensemble which gave the first and many subsequent performances of this work, I wondered if it would be possible to broadcast it again, as it is some considerable time since the last broadcast, which may have been overseas.
>
> Should the occasion arise, I should be delighted to perform his Horn Concerto.[18]

The correspondence suggests that the score (with piano only) existed as early as 1953 and the parts to the score were completed later that year. However, a letter dated January 24, 1949, from Philip York Bowen (son of composer York Bowen) on behalf of De Wolfe Music Publishers and Printers suggests the score had been in existence as early as 1949.

> Mr Dennis Brain in a letter to Mr. Kenneth Essex (from which I have his permission to take an extract) says: "I should very much like to play your Horn Concerto but it is always difficult for a professional to get a performance of a new work. . . . the BBC are about the only people who would perform a contemporary concerto but I think all unpublished works have to go through their reading panel."
>
> I have looked carefully at this work and it seems to me that in view of Mr. Brain's liking for it and the fact that it is not over-long (16 minutes), it would be a suitable item for broadcasting subject to its acceptance by the Panel. Will you therefore be good enough to submit the full score which I am now sending you to the Panel for its consideration?[19]

Essex wrote to the BBC on February 25, 1955, regarding the 1954–1955 Promenade Concerts season and mentioning the BBC broadcast on the Third Program in April. Maurice Johnstone, Head of Music, Programs (Sound) replied, but was not encouraging, and a letter from his secretary in March states, "if, at a later date, the Prom. Committee should wish to see the score, or to hear the recording which you mention, he will, of course, contact you immediately."[20]

In correspondence from 1955, Essex attempts to promote interest in his works by extending invitations to select BBC staff to the first performance of his concerto. These efforts also were apparently unsuccessful. Essex apparently did not compose his concerto for a specific performer.[21]

The following description of the Essex concerto is from a April 20, 1955, broadcast by Brain with Gerald Gentry conducting the BBC Scottish Orchestra. The concerto is in three movements. As noted in Essex's correspondence, the scoring is for a large orchestra.

Movement I is relatively unstructured. The orchestra has a big sound. The horn entrance is bold and stately but less dramatic than the Strauss Horn Concerto No. 1.

Movement II is slow. The strings begin with a light reed background transitioning to a bass reed later followed by the entrance of the horn. The horn theme is echoed by the strings and later reclaimed by the horn. The horn re-enters with a serene but non-melodic theme that exploits the instrument's range. The theme is eventually taken over by a full orchestra, and the movement is resolved by the horn and the strings.

Movement III opens with a brief horn fanfare of four notes, which is taken over by the strings and at times is reminiscent of dramatic film music. The horn work includes large intervals over a wide range and is accompanied by magnificent orchestration. The work is well suited to Brain's style of playing, and he makes it sound easy. The movement concludes with the horn suspended on a high single note while the orchestra races to resolve the harmony.

This is an outstanding horn composition, differing from most others in its orchestration. Efforts should be made to locate the manuscript and publish it.[22]

Paul Hindemith

Concerto for Horn and Orchestra, Op. 119

Score: B. Schott's Söhne, Mainz, 1983

Paul Hindemith (1895–1963) was born in Hanau, Germany. He studied at the University of Music and Performing Arts (originally "Dr. Hoch's Conservatory") in Frankfurt, Germany, and gained a reputation as Germany's leading young composer at the age of twenty-five. He left Germany in 1937, settling in America, where he taught at several major universities, eventually becoming Professor of Music at Yale University, in New Haven, Connecticut. He became an American citizen in 1946.

Willie Ruff, author, hornist, and a former student of Hindemith when at Yale, wrote in *The Horn Call*:

> Hindemith had a life-long love affair with the sound of the horn. The quality of the instrument's ancient and majestic clarion spoke directly to his inner man. . . . In 1949 Hindemith was in Europe enjoying a leave from Yale. While there, he was invited to conduct a special orchestral concert. His anticipation was immense, for he was to have as his soloist the great horn virtuoso Dennis Brain. For weeks, it is said, he spoke of nothing else.
>
> He would be hearing Dennis Brain in person for the first time, but the Mozart horn concerto they were to perform together was an old friend. Predictably, even as they rehearsed with the orchestra, Brain's artistry and elegant tone fanned Hindemith's old flame.

This stimulated Hindemith's desire to compose his horn concerto in April 1949 as a spontaneous tribute to Brain. Ruff continues, "Just as predictably, all else went to the back burner, even a handsome commission from Columbia University for an orchestra piece. Hindemith began sketching and orchestrating fragments for the horn."

Luther Noss, Dean Emeritus of the Yale Music School and curator of the Hindemith Collection at Yale, told Ruff: "His [i.e., Hindemith's] wife, Gertrude, assuming that he was laboring at the Columbia University commission, wrote friends that 'Paul is extremely busy writing a horn concerto for Columbia University.' All thanks to the power of Dennis Brain."[23]

The premiere performance of Hindemith's concerto took place during his third European tour in Baden-Baden on June 8, 1950, with Brain and the Southwest German Orchestra conducted by Hindemith. After the performance, the composer gave Brain a copy of the printed score inscribed "To the unsurpassed original performer of this piece from a grateful composer."[24]

Brain gave a second performance of the work, the first to be recorded, on West German Radio, January 22, 1951, with the Cologne Orchestra conducted by Joseph Keilberth, in Cologne, Germany. This was followed by a third performance on April 19, also in Germany. Brain's second recorded performance was in London on November 19, 1956, with Hindemith conducting the Philharmonia Orchestra for EMI.[25]

Other known performances and broadcasts of the Concerto with Brain include:

March 3, 1951, Third Program, Orchestral Concert, with the London Philharmonic Orchestra conducted by Norman Del Mar. First performance in England.[26]

April 16, 1951, Kingsway Hall, with the Philharmonia Orchestra conducted by Norman Del Mar.[27]

September 1, 1954, Edinburgh Festival, Usher Hall, with the Hamburg Radio Orchestra conducted by Hans Schmidt-Isserstedt.

The concerto was first commercially recorded by Franz Koch (horn) and the Vienna Symphony Orchestra on the Nixa label and was reviewed for the first time by Lionel Salter in *Gramophone*.[28]

Brain's friend, flutist Gareth Morris, related the following to the authors regarding a performance of the Hindemith work while in Germany:

> Dennis told me that (I didn't know the piece—nobody did) there is a flute bit in that that the flute players in Germany never got right. So I said, "Oh, where is it?" Dennis replied, "I won't tell you!" So we did it and afterwards I said, "Did I get that bit right?" Dennis said, "Yes." [I said,] "Oh, where was it?" He said, "I'm not going to tell you." I don't know now! He never told me. That's one of his quaint little jokey things.[29]

Several less than flattering encounters of conductor Otto Klemperer with Brain regarding a planned recording of the Hindemith Horn Concerto on October 7, 1954, were reported upon by several sources. In her book *On and Off the Record*, Elisabeth Schwarzkopf reports a discussion between Walter Legge and Brain who approached Legge during the interval of the recording session. "Guv-nor, I can't risk it with that old man; he's got no rhythm and he can't or won't accompany me."[30]

Klemperer's style and tempo was too slow for Brain's manner of playing. Brain feared the work would never be published and refused to attend the evening recording session. Legge, sensing that the orchestra sided with Brain, substituted the Hindemith concerto with another Hindemith work which appeased Klemperer and retired the situation at hand. Peter Heyworth confirms this anecdote in his book[31] and Pettitt relates a similar accounting.[32]

Hindemith wrote the Horn Concerto for an English performer, knowing that the premiere and early performances would take place in Germany. Thus, both English and German terms appear, with preference given to English (titles, tempo markings, instrumentation, and special directions in English only).[33]

The concerto is in three movements:

I Moderately fast

II Very fast

III Very slow

The scoring is flute and piccolo, two oboes, two clarinets, two bassoons, timpani, solo horn in F, and strings.

Movement I is taken moderately fast (mm=88–92) and the horn is first heard in measure 21. The movement begins and concludes in $\frac{4}{4}$ but has six time changes in between. The subject is somewhat syncopated in rhythm and is never really developed.

Movement II is a very fast (mm=152) Scherzo in $\frac{2}{2}$. As with the first movement, it is short. The themes appear un-syncopated before the horn concludes the movement with a short exit fanfare.

Norman Del Mar comments on the third movement in the recording sleeve notes:[34]

> Movement III is palindromic in form with the quickest section in the center. The outer parts are thus slow movements with the effect that the Concerto ends extremely slowly and quietly in a most unconventional way. The sections between the outer and inner parts of the palindrome are gently flowing $\frac{6}{8}$ movements, though on its return this passage is longer and more agitated. The core of the palindrome is itself in two parts, the first a violent *tutti* while the second is a most unusual kind of recitation. The horn declaims a short poem (the words of which are quoted in the score at the beginning of the section) in such a way that the note values correspond with the syllables of the verses. It is not intended that the poem should be additionally recited by a speaker, although in an earlier recording by Franz Koch for Nixa this was actually done. The words are by the composer himself and attempt to translate in terms of definite meaning the curiously nostalgic character of the tone of the French Horn. They run as follows:
>
> Mein Rufen wandelt
> In herbstgetönten Hain den Saal,
> Das Eben in Verschollnes,
> Dich in Gewand und Brauch der Ahnen,

In ihr Verlangen und Empfahn dein Glück.
Gönn teuren Schemen Urständ,
Dir Halbvergessener Gemeinschaft,
Und mir mein tongestaltnes Sehnen.[35]

Heinrich Kaminski

Ballade for Horn and Piano

Score: Bärenreiter-Ausgabe 2099, Barenreiter-Verlag Kassel, obtained from the Heinrich Kaminski Gesellschaft

German composer Heinrich Kaminski (1886–1946) was born in Tiengen in the upper Rhine, the son of a Catholic priest of Jewish parentage. After a short period working as a trainee bank clerk, he moved to Heidelberg to study National Economy. In 1907 he met Martha Warbung from Hamburg, who encouraged him by recognizing and supporting his musical talent. In 1909 he moved to Berlin to study music at the Stern Conservatory. (*Pl. 5*)

Following his studies and a brief period in Munich, he began work as a piano teacher in upper Bavaria, where he found near-ideal working conditions. He married Elfriede Jopp, a singer with the Munich Choir. In 1930, he attained the title of Professor and became Director of the master class at the Prussian Academy of the Arts in Berlin, then added the job of State Music Director in Bielefeld.

Kaminski's teaching contract was not renewed in 1933 because of his political views. A check of his ancestry revealed that he had been categorized in 1938 as a "half-Jew," and in 1941 declared a "quarter-Jew." In 1937, his music was forbidden in Germany. Kaminski moved his family to Munich. Between 1939 and 1945 he lost three children, and he died in 1946 at Ried in Upper Bavaria.

Kaminski composed his Ballade for Horn and Piano in about 1943 for Georg Reinhart, a coffee consignment financier.[36] Brain performed the work in a live broadcast from Berlin on RIAS (Radio in the American Sector) with Klaus Billing, piano, on September 18, 1950.[37] Little information is available about Kaminski's works as many of them were destroyed during the war years. A copy of the score was obtained from the Heinrich-Kaminski-Gesellschaft eV., Waldshut-Tiengen, Germany by the authors for analysis.

The single movement structure is simplistic in form as typical of a Ballade. Kaminski wrote his work for the E-flat horn and it is approximately 6:43 in duration. The time signature varies accordingly to each of the short verses comprising the stanzas beginning in $\frac{9}{8}$ time and progressing for a total of thirty-seven time signature changes throughout the composition to complete all three stanzas. The dominant theme is built upon short recurring verses and is well suited for the horn with moderate exploitation of the instrument's mid to upper range. The second stanza is introduced at the end of measure 65 following the refrain (*poco a poco retard. molto*) with the third stanza, the shortest, introduced in measure 94 following the second stanza refrain by the piano (*poco a poco retard.)*

A studio tape of Brain's live RIAS broadcast performance was discovered by the authors at the Deutschlandradio Kultur, Dokumentation und Archive in Berlin, Germany. A digital formatted copy of the broadcast tape was obtained from Deutschlandradio for author review and analysis.

A review of Brain's recording of the Ballade indicates Brain likely performed the work on his 1818 Raoux hand horn (with the valve body attachment) using a B-flat crook based upon the lightness of tone and the distinctive clarity articulating the many staccato triplet passages which are so prominent throughout this intricate, but magnificent work. (From 1948 to 1951, Brain used his 1818 Raoux horn almost exclusively for solo work engagements.) One cannot help but to be reminded of the similarity of tone and phrasing heard in the Kaminski work to that found in his earlier May 21, 1947, recording of the Strauss Horn Concerto No. 2 conducted by Galliera in which he also performed with a B-flat crook but on his Raoux Millereau horn given to him by Aubrey Brain in 1936. He takes no exceptions to the composer's writing as he at times did to fit his own style and interpretation and performs the work exactly as written. Perhaps one noteworthy observation is cited in the eleventh measure of Stanza 2. The score calls for a series of repeated c'''notes briefly sustained followed by a break then an immediate transition to the eight note g''. However Brain executes the transition with a slur rather than the break as called for which is atypical of his manner of articulation suggesting he may have incurred some difficulty in precisely making the four-step transition to g''. Aside from this, Brain does not deviate from Kaminski's instructions in the score providing the listener a flawless performance of this rare work for which no recording by any other performer is known to exist. There is no supporting documentation indicating Brain ever performed the Ballade again. His RIAS broadcast of this rare work was never commercially released.

Gordon Jacob

Concerto for Horn and Strings

Score: Stainer & Bell Ltd, Horn in F

Gordon Jacob (1895–1984) was a prolific British composer known for his wind instrument compositions and instructional writings. He studied music at the Royal College of Music in London, preferring the Baroque and Classical styles to the Romanticism of his peers. Jacob returned to the RCM in 1924, teaching until his retirement in 1966. He reached the pinnacle of his fame in the 1950s. His students included Malcolm Arnold.

Jacob was one of the most musically conservative composers of his generation. Following his retirement, he supported himself by composing, frequently on commission. He published more than seven hundred works, four books, and numerous essays on music. He composed the horn concerto in 1951, dedicated to Brain. Brain gave the first performance on May 8, 1951, at Wigmore Hall, London, with the Riddick String Orchestra conducted by Kathleen Riddick for an event titled "A Festival of Britain Concert" (see Chapter 4). The *Musical Times* critic wrote:

> Dr. Gordon Jacob was fortunate in having Dennis Brain to introduce his new horn concerto with the Riddick String Orchestra at Wigmore Hall on 8 May. It is music designed for entertainment rather than edification, thrown off with the sure, light touch of a master craftsman, but though it in no way taxes the listener, it makes phenomenal demands on the soloist. Dennis Brain's effortless agility in the opening movement, and still more in the busy finale, left the impression that it was as easy to get about at high speed on a horn as on a clarinet, while his phrasing in the imaginative slow movement was in every way as subtle as that obtainable on a stringed instrument.[38]

Marshall lists a BBC broadcast of the work with Brain and the Riddick Orchestra conducted by Gordon Jacob on July 3, 1951. Brain performed it on September 8, 1952, at a Promenade Concert with the London Philharmonic Orchestra conducted by Basil Cameron. Another performance took place in Edinburgh, November 18, 1954, with the University of Edinburgh's Reid Orchestra, conducted by Sidney Newman. The BBC also identifies a broadcast of the work with Brain on March 22, 1955, with the Goldsbrough String Orchestra, Norman Del Mar conducting. A photograph of Del Mar with Brain was taken two days later at Banbury, Oxfordshire.[39] (*Pl. 6*)

Jacob's concerto is brilliant for the horn from beginning to end. Yet it has not received the recognition it merits, perhaps in part due to the technical demands. Brain's performance is heard as best as one will ever hear him play, noting in particular that he performed it live, without retakes or studio recording corrections. Brain breathes expression and tone into each note of every measure weaving these qualities throughout each of the three movements with an absolute sense of phrasing portraying both the performer and composer as one voice. The haunting distant cries of the horn heard in the slow legato passages of the all too brief Adagio movement are played so expressively that the listener finds oneself transported into a distant far world.

The concerto's three movements are:

I Allegro Moderato

II Adagio

III Allegro con spirito, quasi presto

Movement I begins in ¾ (mm=112), changing to 4/4 and back to ¾. This pattern continues throughout. The movement is lively. The horn part has a three-octave range from C to c'''. The *Allegro* changes to *Cantabile* at [D] in ¾ time and to *Allegro moderato* at [F], which calls for six measures in the low register followed by a series of rapidly ascending sixteenth-note arpeggios masterfully articulated by Brain. A brief five-measure *pianissimo* muted passage appears at [J:15]. A demanding twenty-five-measure cadenza beginning at [N:16] leads towards the conclusion of the movement. In measure 15 of the cadenza, Brain deviates from the composer's writing by not ascending from the lower quarter note to a half note as called for, but rather holds the lower quarter note an additional count followed by a rest and then proceeds into the *Piu vivo* with a crescendo.

In the beautiful *Adagio molto* of Movement II (mm=60), Brain performs serenely, employing his sensuous style accompanied with subtle shading of tones and phrasing throughout the movement's haunting melody. As with the first movement, he diverges from the composer's writing; at [B:8], rather than following the progression from a' to e' to b', he repeats the previous measure with the progression a' to e' to d'' for a more positive effect.

Movement III is in ½ (mm=132), then in 4/4 at [N] and returning to ½ at [O]. In listening to this movement, one is reminded of the Jacques-Francois Gallay Studies, Op. 13, due to the movement's numerous intricate rapid ascending and descending arpeggio passages and a glissando at [G:34], all of which Brain dispatches with no apparent effort. A brief muted passage, as in Movement I, appears at [N:14]. The *Allegro con spirito, presto possible*, beginning at [O:7] to the end of the movement, was likely intended as a challenge.

Mátyás Seiber

Notturno for Horn and String Orchestra

Score: Schott, ED 10336, Piano Reduction

Julia Seiber Boyd, daughter of Mátyás Seiber, provides this biography of her father.

> Born and educated in Budapest in 1905, Mátyás Seiber graduated from the gymnasium, reported as "outstanding" in mathematics and Latin. He then

studied his first instrument, cello, and then composition with Kodály at the Music Academy. During this period, his "class of 25" toured—with Kodály, studying and helping him notate the rural traditional folksongs. Seiber's interest in carrying on this enterprise benefited from his facility for foreign languages—and this has created many folk song [*sic*] settings, as well as other works for choral and solo performances, the best regarded being *Ulysses*. While still in Hungary, he submitted a sextet in 1925 for a competition in which Kodály and Bartók were on the jury. The counter-movement to the "progressive" music he personified did not allow him to win—the subtext being that he was Jewish; Bartók, furious, resigned from the jury.

In 1927 Seiber left Hungary and settled in Germany where he was the first Professor of Music and Jazz in Frankfurt. In 1933, the Nazi disapproval of jazz and Jews (however secular) forced his emigration to England after a period of travel as part of a ship's string quartet and some time back in Hungary. He settled in London in 1935 and taught composition at Morley College, where he was invited to fill a vacancy by Michael Tippett in 1942. During this period, he created and trained his own choir, the Dorian Singers. In 1947 he married Lilla Bauer, a fellow exile from Hungary, a dancer who taught Modern Dance at Goldsmith's College in London, and they settled in Caterham, Surrey, where Mátyás also taught at home.

Seiber continued to build his reputation as a composer and outstanding teacher, attracting pupils from all over Europe, including Hugh Wood, Anthony Gilbert, Peter Racine Fricker, and Ingvar Litdholm. His works were performed at Cheltenham and other national music festivals including the 1956 Hoffnung Festival in London. He had many friendships and often worked with soloists, including the guitarist Julian Bream, tenor Peter Pears, and of course Dennis Brain, for whom he composed and dedicated his Notturno for Horn and Strings. He also composed film music, mainly for his friends, the progressive animation couple Halas & Batchelor, the best-known being *Animal Farm*. He continued to write Jazz also—often under the pseudonym G S Mathis.

Seiber's correspondence with many of his contemporary composers, some pupils, and Kodály has recently been donated to the British Library, where his manuscripts are also held. Tragically, he was killed in a car accident in South Africa while on a concert tour in 1960, aged only 55: he was being driven through the Kruger National Park when the car hit a pothole and the axle broke.[40]

Seiber composed the Notturno in 1944. On the face of the score, he wrote, "Written for Dennis Brain and dedicated to the memory of Brahms." Brain first performed the work on December 3, 1945, with the Boyd Neel

Orchestra at London's Wigmore Hall, conducted by the composer.[41] It appears that the work was never recorded and we know of no commercial issue of the concert.

Brain performed the Notturno again at a Promenade concert on July 29, 1955, which was broadcast live by the BBC with the London Symphony Orchestra conducted by Cameron. Although the performance was not recorded by the BBC, it can be heard on the Italian label ASDISC 356. The work is a relatively difficult piece for the horn, but Brain dispatches it effortlessly.

Music critic C. B. Rees relates his meeting with Brain at the July Promenade concert:

> His control is phenomenal and his kind of virtuosity creates the illusion that the diabolically difficult is really absurdly easy. Those of us who never even managed a penny whistle can only gape in amazement.
>
> At a Prom in July of this year I heard him play with great brilliance Matyas Seiber's Notturno, for horn and strings. I met him in the artist's room just before he went on to the platform where he was doing a little casual "warming up" in a genial and imperturbable manner.[42]

The recording reviewed is from the 1955 Promenade concert and is 8:36 minutes in length, in a single movement of 192 measures in various time signatures. The score is well annotated by the composer with directions to the performer. For example, at the bottom of the first page, he gives instructions on how to play the half-tones found in measures 70 to 75: "Open and close without altering the fingers." Another note, on the second page, reads, "Horn may take a breath anywhere between 185 and the end."

The horn is first introduced against a light string background in measure 2 (*Andante moderato*, mm=116) with a short series of ascending and descending legato phrases played expressively by Brain, lasting for eleven measures followed by a thirteen-measure muted passage from measure 25 through 37. From measure 70 through 74 (*Lento*), a short series of half-tones are heard played according to the composer's instructions. This is followed by a *Presto* passage played by the horn beginning at measure 86, which is executed in that clean characteristic Brain style of "tut-tut" tonguing. Brain does not complete the three-measure sustained low F in 9/8 time beginning at measure 97, but rather holds the note for several short counts. Starting at measure 104, Brain again executes a series of difficult rapidly ascending and descending staccato triads beginning in bass clef C and reaching high b'' before descending ultimately to a sustained bass clef G-flat. A seven-measure muted passage is again heard beginning at 150 following a brief *Andante* by the strings. The work concludes with a long series of sustained notes played by the horn against a light string background as in the introduction. Although a difficult work for the horn, Seiber's Notturno is a magnificent composition, receiving less attention than it deserves.

Othmar Schoeck

Concerto for Horn and String Orchestra Op.65

Score: Hawkes & Son (London) Ltd., Horn in F

Othmar Schoeck (1886–1957) was born in Brunnen, Switzerland, and spent his adult life in Zurich, acquiring his musical education at the Zurich Conservatory. He worked briefly in Leipzig as a pupil of Max Reger, a popular German composer. Upon returning to Zurich in 1908, he became one of the leading composers of his generation in Switzerland. His music is considered to be from the modern period (1910–1949) and his compositions consist primarily of vocal music and lieder settings. Schoeck's works were later forgotten; however, interest now appears to be renewed.

Schoeck composed his concerto in 1951 on commission from Dr. Willi Aebi (1901–1986), an amateur horn player and physicist who financed both the composition and its performance. The work was first performed in Switzerland by Hans Will on February 6, 1952, with the Winterthur City Orchestra conducted by Victor Desarzens.

Hans Pizka's CD *Grosse Hornisten Vol. 2* includes a recording of the concerto performed by Brain with the Paul Sacher Chamber Orchestra, conducted by Paul Sacher, on May 4, 1956. The accompanying notes state that the work was "premiered" by Brain on this date; however, *Musical Times* reports the work was performed by Brain two years earlier at the 1954 Edinburgh Festival. The Edinburgh performance was also reported by *Radio Times* of London. Although the 1954 Edinburgh performance, believed to be the first British performance, was broadcast by the BBC Home Service, the BBC did not record it.[43]

Gunther Schuller relates his discussion with Brain following the performance at the 1954 Edinburgh Festival.

> Schoeck, one of the most respected of Switzerland's older generation of composers, wrote this concerto in 1952, I believe, at the instigation of Dennis Brain [actually, it was Dr. Willi Aebi, as noted above], whom I heard in a superb performance of the work at the last Edinburgh Festival. The concerto is a thoroughly charming work, very lyrical in content, and offers no serious problems for the listener, as it is music that springs out of the past—the past of Strauss's and Schoeck's teacher Reger. When I asked Dennis Brain

> after the performance what he thought of the concerto, his first reaction was: "It's rather tiring." His remarkable easy rendition belied this, but I'm inclined to take his word for it, and it did seem that the horn was playing rather constantly. A great deal of the part lay in the upper middle register with occasional forays to high E-flats [concert pitch] at the end of a long phrase.[44]

The concerto is in three movements for horn in F:

I Lebhaft, energisch bewegt 5:41
II Ruhig fliessend 5:50
III Rondo: Ausserst schnell und leicht 3:48

The horn is heard for 523 measures of the total 599 measures. It is perhaps Schoeck's finest and most recorded work.

The first and third movements are reminiscent of Strauss's horn concertos particularly the Rondo movement, which, as with the Strauss works, is written in $^6/_8$ time with rapid staccato passages in triplets reaching high c''' in measure 197.

The second movement, in $^3/_4$, is both lyrical and romantic, again similar to Strauss but far more lyrical (like Britten's Serenade) owing to Schoeck's immersion in vocal writing. Here, Schoeck exploits the wide range of the horn in this taxing movement as Britten does in the Elegy of the Serenade. Brain retains his composure in this performance, which was broadcast live by Swiss Radio and can be heard on a private recording.[45]

York Bowen

Concerto for Horn, String Orchestra, and Timpani (Op. 150)

Score: Emerson Edition Ltd., Windmill Farm, Ampleforth, North Yorkshire, England, Horn in F

York Bowen (1884–1961), a talented horn player as well as a prolific composer whose compositions are now increasingly recognized, was inspired to compose his concerto for Brain in 1955. Brain performed this exciting work with the Welbeck Orchestra, conducted by Maurice Miles, pre-recorded on June 24, 1956, and broadcast in July 1956, by the BBC.

Radio Times reported:

> Dennis Brain is the soloist in York Bowen's new Concerto for horn, string orchestra and timpani (Sunday, Home). The Concerto, which makes use of the entire normal compass of the horn, is mainly romantic and lyrical in style, with a lovely finale. It was written with intimate knowledge and

understanding of the instrument, since York Bowen, who is best known as a brilliant pianist and composer, himself played the horn early in his career, and has been associated with three generations of the Brain family. Dennis Brain, the inheritor of a great tradition and the finest horn player of the day, is the subject of a Musical Profile in "Music Magazine" on Sunday. Joan Chissell.[46]

The composition is in three movements for horn in F:

I Allegro, non troppo—poco tranquillo 8:02

II Poco Lento e Serioso 3:54

III Finale: Allegro molto, con spirto 5:22

Bowen places moderately difficult demands on the soloist, reminiscent of the Strauss concertos. The work is well suited to Brain's style of playing, containing both lyrical and rapid ascending and descending arpeggio passages. The horn is first heralded in measure 6, followed by a short expressive passage that is interwoven by spirited arpeggios articulated brilliantly by Brain.

The pitch range of the complete work encompasses A1 below pedal C (measure 158, first movement) to d-flat''' above high c''' (measure 225, third movement). In this performance, Brain used his B-flat Alexander horn; however, since the lower notes of the work cannot be played with a B-flat horn, he must have also used an F-extension.

The final movement consists of a delightful swinging rhythm in 6/8, which later changes to 4/4. The scurrying arpeggio passages, reaching to a'' above the staff, employ Brain's characteristic "tut-tut" style of tonguing with its highly articulated, clean, and focused sound.

Brain's tone in the Bowen work merits comment. In 1951, he abandoned his French Raoux horn in favor of the wider-bore German Alexander. How he was able to retain the same characteristic pure, light, and clean tone on the German instrument remains an enigma. Brown Meggs (1930–1997), former Chief Operating Officer of Capital Records and later President of EMI/Angel Records, and by avocation a horn player, comments:

> One of the miracles of Brain's playing was the fact that he was able to extract from the more agile and secure B-flat Alexander the more desirable sound quality—robust, darker and more "horn-like"—of the horn in F.[47]

Sir Anthony Lewis

Concerto for Horn and String Orchestra

Score: Alfred Lengnick & Co. Ltd. London, Horn in F

Anthony Lewis (1915–1983) was a British musicologist and conductor who revived neglected works by Handel, Purcell, and Rameau. In 1946, he helped to found the BBC classical music radio network. Lewis was principal of the Royal College of Music from 1968 to 1982, was knighted in 1972, and spent the last part of his career at the Royal Academy of Music.

The Concerto was composed in 1956 with Brain in mind. He gave the first performance with the Boyd Neel Orchestra on April 29, 1956, at the Victoria and Albert Museum with guest conductor Brian Priestman. (*Pl. 7*) Pettitt reports:

> Anthony Lewis had earlier written a trumpet concerto for the Proms and he wanted to write a work for the horn. Dennis was the obvious choice for its first performance and gladly accepted the dedication. He asked for no alterations to Lewis's score except to the long note at the end of the slow movement, for which he needed time to take a breath. The concerto in fact received two "first" performances: Stravinsky's Concerto in D for strings was withdrawn from the programme at the last moment and this gave an ideal opportunity for Dennis to play the new horn concerto again in the second half.[48]

Anthony Wright wrote in *Music and Musicians*: "Anthony Lewis's Horn Concerto contained a monotonous solo part, and all Dennis Brain's skill could not make it more than occasionally interesting. The orchestral part held one's attention more easily and the second movement was full of invention opening with a striking recitative."[49]

Another review, by Donald Mitchell, appeared in the *Musical Times*:

> Professor Lewis's concerto flowed along very professionally and very refreshingly un-professorial. But the work failed to disclose any very striking invention, and was particularly deficient in compelling melody, a want that disfigured the slow movement, devised as a "Recitative and Aria," a structure that might have turned out to be interesting had the aria, in fact materialized; here, no amount of good craftsmanship could compensate for the absence of real inspiration. Perhaps the most hopeful aspect of the concerto was its eclecticism, which ranged well outside the current academic models.[50]

Brain recorded the work on January 18, 1957, in a live Home Service broadcast for its Orchestral Hour with the BBC Midland Orchestra, conducted by Gerald Gentry.

The Lewis concerto is in three movements:

I Allegretto un poco sostenuto 8:40

II Recitative and Aria 5:42

III Allegro con spirito 4:21

The first movement begins in $\frac{6}{8}$ time, alternating throughout between $\frac{9}{8}$, $\frac{10}{8}$, $\frac{8}{8}$, and $\frac{5}{8}$, and places only modest technical demands on the performer. The horn part appears constrained by the composer to a single theme, providing little opportunity for expressiveness. Nevertheless, Brain executes the *animato* passages with delicacy and accuracy. The string orchestra heard in the background is light, reminiscent of cinema music.

The second movement is more melodic, beginning in $\frac{3}{4}$ time with changes to $\frac{4}{4}$, $\frac{5}{8}$, $\frac{3}{8}$, and $\frac{4}{8}$. At the beginning of the movement, the horn is heard in a series of recitatives to measure 16, followed by an expressively written *andante cantabile* in $\frac{5}{8}$ with a supportive string orchestra background.

The third movement alternates between $\frac{2}{4}$, $\frac{3}{4}$, and $\frac{4}{4}$ throughout the movement, which is spirited and to an extent is similar to the first movement. Brain deviates from the composer's score; he combines the two high g'' eighth notes in measure 267 into a single quarter note, and in measures 268 and 270 combining the two d'' eighth notes into a single quarter note.

Lewis's concerto has received little attention since the BBC broadcast. We know of no commercial recordings with Brain.

Ernest Tomlinson

Rhapsody and Rondo for Horn and Orchestra

Score: Mills Music Ltd., London. Horn in F

British composer Ernest Tomlinson (b. 1924) composed the Rhapsody and Rondo in 1956 in response to a request from the BBC to write a work for the 1957 Light Music Festival. Tomlinson responded that he wished to write a work for Brain, to which the BBC agreed with the proviso, "but don't make it so difficult only Dennis Brain can play it," which Tomlinson promptly ignored.

After the BBC had confirmed Tomlinson's proposal, Tomlinson contacted Brain, who asked "Please Ernest, don't write me another $\frac{6}{8}$ rondo." Tomlinson sent the manuscript of the main themes to Brain, who responded on January 28, 1957, stating his hesitation over the two-octave leaps in measure 27. Tomlinson later noted that Brain "managed them without apparent difficulty."

In correspondence with Gamble, Tomlinson recalls:

> It was a great relief to me when I eventually met up with Dennis during a recording session in Walthamstow Town Hall, when he played my cherished themes with aplomb, only suggesting a few minor modifications. The one leap he did fight shy of in the Royal Festival Hall performance was that on the 4th bar of 10, which he played down the octave.[51]

Tomlinson further relates:

> The speed the orchestra started the rondo at (I'd had a rehearsal without soloist on the previous day) which sounded great to me, was too slow for Dennis. As I recall, he stopped playing quite soon so I had to stop the orchestra and Dennis said, "Ernest, you'll have to go a lot faster than that, I've been practicing at this speed." He proceeded to play it thus. The body language of the players was quite something! The off-the-air recording I have of that first performance brings it all back.
>
> I do remember Dennis's words when we were waiting in the wings for our entry. My trepidation must have been very obvious. "At least I do this every day," he said!
>
> The Mozart quote towards the end of the rondo needs a word or two. The idea came to me when I was planning the mock fugue in the final build-up, whereby each entry presents a different theme. With all the themes used there was none left for the horn to enter with, so I decided as a private joke to give him a $^6/_8$ one, with the passage at 42 to express his distaste for the idea. Having written this $^6/_8$ theme I then heard that he was to play the Mozart Rondo in the first half of the concert. Its frequent airings on request programs had made Dennis Brain a household name. So, as a one-off for this concert, I substituted this instead of my own theme. This was a joke that was turned on its head when Dennis was so tragically killed only a few weeks later.
>
> It was at least two years before it seemed appropriate for another horn player to play it. Alan Civil broadcast the piece three times and for at least one of these, after much deliberation with Alan and the publisher, I returned to my own theme for this section. Ifor James was another horn player who broadcast the work. When I heard Richard Watkins play the work in 1992, I said to myself, "at last, someone who can match Dennis Brain's speed."
>
> Dennis Brain never did play the complete Rhapsody and Rondo. The BBC didn't allow me enough time for the full-fledged rhapsody, so I wrote it so that the first and last part put together (i.e. a cut from 4 to 9) made

> an effective introductory section. So for its first performance the work was named Romance and Rondo. Alan Civil referred to the stamina needed to play the rondo after the demanding rhapsody, which of course Dennis never encountered.

The Rhapsody (Romance) and Rondo was broadcast live by the BBC with the BBC Concert Orchestra at Royal Festival Hall on June 22, 1957.[52] We know of no commercial recordings of the performance.

The work is for horn in F. The Rhapsody (4:24), is in $\frac{4}{4}$. Because of the BBC timing constraint, this performance takes the cut mentioned by Tomlinson. In both the rehearsal and the broadcast, Dennis appeared to have had difficulty ascending from the f'' to a'' above the staff. For the rehearsal on June 22, taped by the composer, Brain performs measure 4 (at 10) as written, playing the high a-flat'' and b-flat''. However, in the actual broadcast, he plays the passage an octave lower.

The Rondo begins at rehearsal number 10, measure 9, and is in $\frac{2}{2}$. The composition is technically challenging even for an above-average player. The difficulties of the Rondo consist of two-note octave jumps and rapid ascending and descending passages encompassing extremes of range, from low G [27:7] to high d''' [29:8], requiring extreme virtuosity.

Tomlinson's extraordinary contemporary composition remains, along with the Gordon Jacob's, undoubtedly one of the most technically challenging works for horn in modern times.

Francis Poulenc

Sextet for Piano and Wind Quintet

Score: Wilhelm Hansen, Copenhagen, 25745a, Horn in F

Francis Poulenc (1899–1963) was a French composer of chamber music, song, opera, ballet music, and orchestral compositions. He first learned music from his mother, an amateur pianist. In 1921 he studied with Charles Koechlin, a French composer, teacher, and writer on music who had assisted Fauré in teaching counterpoint while he was still a student in the 1890s.

Poulenc was a featured pianist in several recordings, including some of his own songs. His last major works included compositions for wind instruments and piano. He was particularly fond of winds and planned a series of compositions for them, living to complete only sonatas for flute, oboe, and clarinet, and the *Elégie*.

Work on the Sextet began in 1932 and took seven years to complete. It was performed at Wigmore Hall on March 4, 1947, with Poulenc himself playing the piano, as described in Chapter 3. No recorded broadcasts of the Poulenc Sextet with Brain were known to have existed until October 2005, when the authors discovered a recorded performance in the archives of the ORF-Publikumsservice, Salzburg. The Sextet was recorded and broadcast with the Dennis Brain Wind Ensemble on July 30, 1957, at the Salzburg Festival in the Mozarteum Large Hall with Wilfrid Parry as the pianist.[53]

The Sextet is in three movements:

I Allegro vivace—Très vite et emporté

II Divertissement—Andantino

III Finale—Prestissimo

It is a challenging work for all the players. The horn part, in particular, challenges the best of players; however, Brain keeps things clean, simple, and well articulated even in the most rapid passages.

The first movement begins in $\frac{4}{4}$ for one measure, changing to $\frac{3}{4}$ for the next three measures, back to $\frac{4}{4}$ for a single measure, then to $\frac{2}{4}$, this pattern repeated throughout the remainder of the movement. The tempo is very quick to rehearsal number [9], at which point the bassoon transitions both theme and tempo to a much slower pace, followed by a lively three-measure statement by the horn, which is then carried forward by the piano. An eight-bar bassoon solo precedes a beautiful but brief solo passage by the horn sixteen measures into [10], echoing the previous melodic woodwind theme. The horn is again heard in three combined solos beginning at [12] and closing six measures before [15]. Brain shapes the phrasing and shading of notes. The *vivo* tempo resumes at [16], continuing to the end of the movement. Brain's clear, confident, and highly articulated execution of the rapid horn passages is phenomenal.

The second movement is introduced by the oboe, augmented by the bassoon, followed by the piano and then the horn. It is written with an expression of calmness and serenity and is the shortest of the three movements. The movement is in $\frac{4}{4}$ except for the next to the last measure and contains several magnificent horn passages. An impressive solo horn passage consisting of staccato eighth-note octave leaps from middle g' to high g'' begins at [4], lasts two measures, and is repeated again two measures later. A haunting, calming horn solo is heard at [6] for eight measures. Although not written into the score, Brain fills in the third from the last measure with a repeat of the prior measure, but this time stopped.

The third movement begins with a stunning arpeggio horn passage of accented eighth notes played at lightning-fast speed. As with the earlier movements, Poulenc makes extensive use of changing time signatures throughout.

Beginning in $^3\!/_2$ time, the movement later changes meter every measure or so. The solo horn passages are extraordinary, suggesting that Poulenc understood the possibilities of the horn, which he fully exploited for its range and tonal beauty. Brain's delivery of long legato passages attains a beauty of phrasing and tonal shading, complementing technical skill and agility combined with a rare musicianship.

Francis Poulenc

Elégie for Horn and Piano (In Memory of Dennis Brain)

Score: Chester Music, Limited, No.CH01607, Horn and Piano

Although the *Elégie* was composed after Brain's death, it is included as it enshrines the memory of Brain by a composer who knew and worked with him. Poulenc composed the *Elégie* to commemorate Brain's death. Neill Sanders premiered the work on September 1, 1958, for BBC Radio, exactly one year after Brain's death, with the composer at the piano. Sanders described this performance at the 1991 International Horn Symposium:

> Poulenc was so affected (by Dennis' death) that he decided to write this *Elégie* for Dennis. . . . These were the very early days of taping for the BBC. In those days they kept the tape for a month and if it wasn't played again that month they destroyed them! So there's no record of this one but fortunately as it was going out at the same time as the Sextet, which we were doing with another pianist, I had asked a firm to make a disc of it for me and it's the tape from this disc which we will hope to play now for you.
>
> I think what is interesting in the tape is Poulenc's piano playing, because particularly in the duplets you realize what he is doing is getting Dennis' heartbeat going through it. He does it very well. He naturally has to move a little bit but he gets the overall feeling. You suddenly feel the pulse of body in it. It was a pretty grim thing for me to do because Dennis' death didn't seem long ago.
>
> I had taken over in the Dennis Brain Wind Quintet (from Dennis) which was also quite a grisly experience because Dennis' brother Leonard was the oboe player. Of course Leonard had known Dennis all his life. The flute player was Gareth Morris who had been in the Academy and the Air Force with him. The same with Cecil James, the bassoon and Stephen Waters the clarinet player. They had to look at me! They also had lost their leader and so it was a very difficult job to take over.
>
> Anyhow, we did it! Thank God there is always something amusing in these terrible things at times. I can't remember what horn I was playing at the time (of the broadcast) or mouthpiece but I know . . . I couldn't get

> through the *Elégie* without the start of a bubble and we had just rehearsed it twice and after the first rehearsal I said to Poulenc, "If you give me just the slightest of time that I can empty the water out." [Poulenc] "Yes, I will." The next, he came up to me and said, "I think I have just found the answer for you." What he had done was taken out a measure's rest.[54]

Benjamin Ivry, in his book *Francis Poulenc*, provides a summary of the *Elégie.*

> This is mournful music, with elegant writing for the high range of the horn. The *Elégie* embraces the convention of death as cloud or fog, and England, as a foggy land, becomes by extension a land of death for young Dennis Brain.[55]

Wilfrid Mellers, in his book *Francis Poulenc*, reviews the work.

> This strangely moving piece unexpectedly (and for Poulenc uniquely) opens with a 12-note row, with no tone repeated, magisterially chanted by unaccompanied horn, but brutally dismissed by a Stravinskian *molto agitato* passage in which both instruments utter aggressively false-related triads of C major and minor.[56]

Humphrey Searle

Aubade for Horn and String Orchestra, Op. 28

Commentary

The Humphrey Searle (1915–1982) *Aubade* is included for two reasons. First, it is the only work known to have been commissioned by Brain for himself. Brain referred to it as the finest work ever composed for him.[57] Second, the authors believe that a recording of the work by Brain (official or otherwise) does exist, although, despite exhaustive investigation, it has yet to be found. Regrettably, the work was not recorded by the BBC. It is an exceptionally difficult work for the horn, particularly with regard to its taxing range. The work has been recorded more recently, most notably by Barry Tuckwell.

Brain gave the first performance of *Aubade* on June 13, 1955, at the Aldeburgh Festival with the Aldeburgh Festival Orchestra, conducted by Walter Goehr. The performance was broadcast live; however, the authors have confirmed with the BBC that the broadcast was not recorded.

Radio Times reported:

> Orchestral Concert. Olive Zorian, Violin, Suzanne Rozsa, Violin, Dennis Brain, Horn, Aldeburgh Festival Orchestra, Conductor, Walter Goehr. Part 1: Divertimento for chamber orchestra (Sellinger's Round)—Michael

> Tippett; Horn Concerto No. 2 in D—Haydn; Ten sketches for strings—Skalkottas (1st performance in this country). Part 2 10.05 p.m. Double Concerto Op. 49 for two violins and orchestra—Holst; Aubade for horn and string orchestra—Humphrey Searle (1st performance.); Symphony No. 5 in B-flat—Schubert.[58]

Humphrey Searle commented on hearing a radio broadcast of the work: "How marvelously he played it for it is not at all easy." In 1958, Searle composed a chamber work, *Variations and Finale, Op. 34, for Ten Instruments*, for the Virtuoso Chamber Ensemble. Each of the ten variations is centered on a specific instrument and was written for a specific member of the Virtuoso Chamber Orchestra; then all instruments are heard in unison in the Finale. Although composed after Brain's passing, the variation for the horn part was written in memory of Dennis Brain.[59]

ROYAL FESTIVAL HALL
General Manager: T. E. Bean
1953-1954 Season
The London Chamber Orchestral Society Ltd. presents
Royal Philharmonic Orchestra
LEADER: DAVID McCALLUM
CONDUCTOR: Anthony Bernard
THIRD CONCERT MONDAY FEBRUARY 22 at 8 p.m.
SOLOISTS: Richard Lewis
Dennis Brain
Geoffrey Gilbert

PROGRAMME

MENDELSSOHN	Symphony No. 4 in A (Italian), Op. 90
BRITTEN	Serenade for Tenor, Horn and Strings, Op. 31
NIELSEN	Flute Concerto First public performance in England
BEETHOVEN	Symphony No. 4 in B flat, Op. 60

FURTHER CONCERTS IN THIS SERIES AT 8 p.m.
ON MONDAYS: MARCH 29 · APRIL 26
TICKETS: 12/6 · 10/- · 7/6 · 5/- · 3/6 · 2/6
From Festival Hall Box Office (WAT. 3191) and usual agents

Plate 1 The Royal Philharmonic Orchestra program of Britten's Serenade for Tenor, Horn and Strings conducted by Anthony Bernard for the 1953–1954 concert season at Royal Festival Hall. *Author's private collection.*

Plate 2 The open harmonic series of the F-natural horn contains (16) partials beginning at the fundamental C (1) to c''' (16). Characteristics of the those partials of interest written for in the mid-upper register of the F-horn appearing in the Prolog and Epilog expositions of the Britten Serenade for Tenor, Horn and Strings, Op. 31 are as follows:

7th (B-flat'): Very flat, a very narrow/ flat minor 3rd above the 6th
11th (F/F # ''): Farthest removed from 'true' or tempered intonation thus far in the series sounding halfway between an F and an F#. This is surely the pitch that would have caused critics to note Brain sounded out of tune
12th (G''): a perfect 5th above the 8th partial
13th (A''): Sounds as a sharp a-flat''
14th (B''-flat): a sharp A or a flat Bb depending on how it is used
16th: a true octave above the 8th

The acuity of spacing between partials found in the F-horn's upper register is in part, responsible for the difficulties associated with playing the F-horn. (See R. Morley Pegge, Appendix 1, *The French Horn*, 2nd ed., London: Ernest Benn, 1973, for the partials of horns pitched in keys other than F). *Notes with permission from Tony Halstead.*

Plate 3 English composer Malcolm Arnold (1921–2006) CBE (Order of the British Empire). *Wikipedia website: http://en.wikipedia.org/wiki/Malcolm_Arnold. Released under CC BYSA: http://creativecommons.org/licenses/by-sa/3.0/*

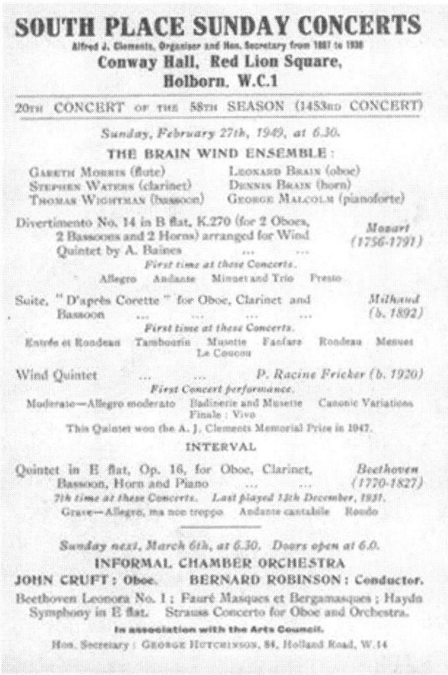

SOUTH PLACE SUNDAY CONCERTS
Alfred J. Clements, Organiser and Hon. Secretary from 1887 to 1938
Conway Hall, Red Lion Square,
Holborn, W.C.1

20TH CONCERT OF THE 58TH SEASON (1453RD CONCERT)

Sunday, February 27th, 1949, at 6.30.

THE BRAIN WIND ENSEMBLE:

GARETH MORRIS (flute)	LEONARD BRAIN (oboe)
STEPHEN WATERS (clarinet)	DENNIS BRAIN (horn)
THOMAS WIGHTMAN (bassoon)	GEORGE MALCOLM (pianoforte)

Divertimento No. 14 in B flat, K.270 (for 2 Oboes, 2 Bassoons and 2 Horns) arranged for Wind Quintet by A. Baines ... ... — *Mozart (1756-1791)*
First time at these Concerts.
Allegro Andante Minuet and Trio Presto

Suite, "D'après Corette" for Oboe, Clarinet and Bassoon ... ... — *Milhaud (b. 1892)*
First time at these Concerts.
Entrée et Rondeau Tambourin Musette Fanfare Rondeau Menuet Le Coucou

Wind Quintet ... ... — *P. Racine Fricker (b. 1920)*
First Concert performance.
Moderato—Allegro moderato Badinerie and Musette Canonic Variations Finale: Vivo
This Quintet won the A. J. Clements Memorial Prize in 1947.

INTERVAL

Quintet in E flat, Op. 16, for Oboe, Clarinet, Bassoon, Horn and Piano ... ... — *Beethoven (1770-1827)*
7th time at these Concerts. Last played 13th December, 1931.
Grave—Allegro, ma non troppo Andante cantabile Rondo

Sunday next, March 6th, at 6.30. Doors open at 6.0.
INFORMAL CHAMBER ORCHESTRA
JOHN CRUFT: Oboe. BERNARD ROBINSON: Conductor.
Beethoven Leonora No. 1; Fauré Masques et Bergamasques; Haydn Symphony in E flat. Strauss Concerto for Oboe and Orchestra.
In association with the Arts Council.
Hon. Secretary: GEORGE HUTCHINSON, 84, Holland Road, W.14

Plate 4 Concert Program for the first concert performance of the Fricker Quintet performed at Conway Hall by the Dennis Brain Wind Ensemble on February 27, 1949, for the South Place Concert Series. *With permission from Mrs. Patricia Morris, Gareth Morris family collection*

Plate 5 German composer Heinrich Kaminski (1886–1946) who was largely self-taught and whose works included chamber music, orchestral, choral, sonatas, and opera. *http://www.bach-cantatas.com/Lib/Kaminski-Heinrich.htm contributed by Aryeh Oron, March 2008, to the Wikipedia website. Released under CC BYSA: http://creativecommons.org/licenses/by-sa/3.0/*

TWO CONCERTS BY THE

BOYD NEEL ORCHESTRA

Director : THURSTON DART

ROYAL FESTIVAL HALL

TUESDAY, APRIL 17 at 8 p.m.

—THE BACHS—

Solo Violin : ERICH GRUENBERG
Solo Harpsichord : THURSTON DART

Overture in D major	J. B. Bach
Harpsichord Concerto in C minor	W. F. Bach
Violin Concerto in A minor	J. S. Bach
Harpsichord Concerto in F major	C. P. E. Bach
Harpsichord Concerto in A major	J. C. Bach
Sinfonia No. 3 in C	C. P. E. Bach
Brandenberg Concerto No. 3 in G	J. S. Bach

12/6, 10/-, 7/6, 5/-, 3/6, from Hall (WAT. 3191), Agents and IBBS & TILLETT Ltd., 124, Wigmore St., W.1. (WEL. 8418).

VICTORIA and ALBERT MUSEUM,
S.W.7

SUNDAY, APRIL 29 at 8 p.m.

Concerto Grosso, Op. 6, No. 6	Handel
Concerto for 2 Violins, D minor	Bach

Solo Violins: ERICH GRUENBERG, JACK ROTHSTEIN
Guest Conductor: BRIAN PRIESTMAN

Concerto for Horn (First performance)	Anthony Lewis

Solo Horn : DENNIS BRAIN

Concerto in D for Strings	Stravinsky

9/-, 6/-, 3/-, from Chappell's (MAY. 7600), Agents and IBBS & TILLETT Ltd., 124, Wigmore St., W.1. (WEL. 8418) (at Museum only from 6.15 on Concert night).

Plate 7 Concert program for the first performance of Lewis's Concerto for Horn and String Orchestra, April 29, 1956, at the Victoria and Albert Museum with guest conductor Brian Priestman and the Boyd Neel Orchestra. *With permission from the Kjell Moseng family by Sisse Moseng.*

Plate 6 Dennis Brain and conductor Norman Del Mar, March 24, 1955, at Banbury, Oxfordshire following the performance of the Jacob Concerto for Horn and Strings. *The Norman Del Mar family with permission from Jonathan Del Mar.*

CHAPTER

11

Horns, Mouthpieces, and Embouchures

Dennis Brain owned and experimented with no fewer than eleven horns varying in form, functionality, and tonal characteristics, most of which he ultimately disposed of for one reason or another. He often visited the Alexander firm in Mainz, Germany, which built a number of horns for him to his specifications. In 1951, he adapted an Alexander single B-flat Model 90 that he had earlier purchased and experimented with, replacing his French-type Raoux-Millereau. He used the Alexander almost exclusively for the remainder of his life.

Brain reveals his relentless pursuit of the ideal horn in his publication *The French Horn*, printed after his death: "As a point of interest, I must confess that I am at the moment negotiating for the manufacture of a five-valved instrument of my own design."[1]

Alexander ceased manufacturing this horn after Brain's death. The instrument, termed the "Brain Model," was kept in a warehouse for several years until a player in the Munich Bach Orchestra worked with Alexander and completed the instrument. The horn was a B-flat/high E-flat descant, thus with a secure high range. The leadpipe reportedly fit directly into the inner rotary valve. The bell was yellow brass and the main body was gold brass. The stopping valve was operated by the little finger. Although fabrication of the horn was finally completed, its design differed significantly from that intended by Brain, and it is doubtful that he would have liked the result.[2]

Brain's transformational move from the narrow-bore, small flare bell French instrument to the wider-bore, larger flare bell German instrument in 1951 effectively closed an era of British horn playing characterized by the clean, pure, light, yet softer tone so characteristic of the French instrument. However, to most, Brain retained the same musical quality of tone and technical prowess on his German Alexander as he did on his French Raoux horn.

Brain's "All-Risks" Policy (No. 51136728) listed several of the many horns he owned at the time of his death. (*Pl. 1*) He purchased other horns from Alexander during his lifetime for experimental purposes and promotional interests through his association with the firm. The instruments discussed here belonged to him at some time during his life.

Raoux-Millereau Horn

The type of horn that Brain used during his student days and the years with the RAF was undoubtedly influenced by his father's preference for the French-style horn. Aubrey Brain gave Dennis a French Raoux piston horn similar in design to his own, an 1865 Raoux manufactured by Labbaye. Pettitt reports:

> When, in 1933, the London Philharmonic replaced the London Symphony as the "pit" orchestra at Covent Garden, a number of brand-new Raoux horns were found under the stage. They were no use to the LPO so they were sold; Aubrey bought two of them—one for himself and one as a spare, possibly for either of his two sons should they want to take the instrument up. He found a use for one of them sooner than he imagined when he succeeded in backing his car over his original instrument, completely flattening the crook.[3]

When Dennis was still a student at St. Paul's School in London, already beginning to consider a career in music, Aubrey, recalling the "spare" Raoux horn, said, "I've found another instrument; would you like to see what you can do with it?" It was the "twin" of Aubrey's own, which he had bought from Covent Garden in 1933.[4]

The reference to the "twin of Aubrey's" is more correctly interpreted to mean a Raoux-Millereau and not another Raoux-Labbaye, the manufacturer of Aubrey's horn. The fact that Brain's instrument prior to 1951 was a Raoux-Millereau is documented by Alan Civil when meeting Brain in the early 1940s and comments by Morley-Pegge, Cousins, and Meggs (an officer at Capital Records).[5] (*Pl. 2*)

The Raoux design is of the early French school. It originally appeared as a natural horn, to which fixed and detachable pistons were later added. The instrument has a small-to-modest bore diameter typically in the order of about 11mm as measured at the tuning slide. It also has a smaller bell flare than its German counterpart.

Brain was instructed on a Raoux-Millereau horn crooked in F, which was his father's favored key for most orchestral and chamber works. On occasion, his father employed a B-flat crook in some works scored for the horn in the upper registers. The French instrument in F is notoriously difficult to play. The modern double horn, with the F/B-flat combination and wider German bore, is far easier to play and considerably more reliable than the French horn in F.

As he matured musically, Brain realized the benefits (with some compromises perhaps) of the B-flat horn, much more so than his father. Gradually he used a B-flat crook on his Raoux almost exclusively. In 1948, he had it modified by Paxman in London, placing the instrument permanently into the key of B-flat with the addition of a descending rotary valve to compensate for muting. (*Pl. 3*)

Farquharson Cousins recalls:

> When Dennis Brain had his Raoux-Millereau "done up" (it had a mass of dents and was held together with sticking plaster) it returned to him looking like new. But to his horror the horn had a "roll" (as he called it) on the B-flat, E-flat and top G—which was a disaster, as his first really big date after the war was due in a week's time: Strauss 1, in the Albert Hall Proms. Dennis was understandably alarmed! Some years previously I had sold him my 1818, black and gold-painted bell, Raoux. He had not intended to use the instrument in his work as it had an undeniable wolf-note F sharp at the top of the stave.
>
> In desperation Dennis tried it with a B-flat crook, and to his delight found that all the notes seemed sound. I heard this broadcast in a pub over the road from the Leeds Town Hall. All we YSO [Yorkshire Symphony Orchestra] horn players were present as fortuitously our concert's first half was for strings only. We listened enthralled to a matchless performance. It was not until later when Dennis wrote to me that I learned the full story. It was a measure of Dennis Brain's flexibility that he was able to switch almost overnight from F fingering to B-flat fingering. Added to which marvel he played the Strauss from memory![6]

During the 1950 US tour with the Royal Philharmonic Orchestra, Brain carried both his Raoux horn (believed to be the Raoux-Millereau and not his 1818 Raoux hand horn) for solo work, and a single Alexander B-flat horn that he had purchased in April. Although he would use the Alexander B-flat horn almost exclusively the following year, he still favored the sound of the French-style instrument for legato playing. After returning from the tour, he returned his Raoux-Millereau to Paxman in London to have a second rotary valve added, enabling the instrument to switch to the key of C-alto, improving reliability and accuracy in the higher register.[7]

Brain describes this horn on February 3, 1953, when acknowledging an inquiry by Gordon Grieve. (*Pl. 4*)

> Just a line to give you a few details of the instrument.
>
> It was a hand horn with crooks made by Raoux, and which later had three detachable piston valves added, and in that form, in F, I made most of my recordings including the Strauss Concerto and Britten Serenade, etc. There is an inscription on the uppermost flange of the bell. I then changed to the B-flat horn and played for a while on a B-flat crook, until I had it built into that key with one rotary valve for A (natural) muting. Then, bearing in mind that the modern French players use an ascending third valve with good effect, I added another rotary, putting the whole instrument in C alto, and providing, in addition to very good high notes, A, B, C, D, the pedal G, and low G which feature so much in the Schubert Octet.
>
> One reason why I preferred it to the big German horn was the softer and more legato tone obtained, partly due to piston action and partly the quality of old, soft metal. Now I use an Alexander B-flat with a narrow mouthpipe and small mouthpiece, which gives, I think, even better results though it is less easy to play so smoothly. However, I do not want to bore you with details, though if there is anything else you wish to know do not hesitate to drop me a line, and even though, as Tom will testify, I am a bad correspondent I will eventually get round to replying.[8]

Raoux 1818 Horn

Cousins sold Dennis an 1818 Raoux hand horn before 1948.[9] It had a decorated floral bell and a set of detachable valves (Sauterelle, or Grasshopper as it is called) making it possible to alternately convert the instrument between a natural horn and a valve horn. (*Pl. 5*) Brain's first public performance with this instrument was at a 1948 performance of the Strauss Concerto No. 1 at a Promenade concert at Royal Albert Hall.

Cousins discusses the horn in his article "The Degenerate Horn": "He plays on a French horn made by Raoux in 1818 and once owned by Puzzi. It has a black and gold painted (lacquered) bell. Mr. Brain plays it with a B-flat crook." [10]

Paul Kampen reported that following Giovanni Puzzi, "the instrument was owned by Alf Button, one of the older players whom Aubrey Brain worked with at the start of his own career."[11] Morley Pegge discusses two, if not three instruments once belonging to Puzzi that remain in existence:

> One, a very fine silver-mounted *cor-solo*, by M. A. Raoux, is said to have been given to Puzzi by Louis XVIII. The appearance and workmanship of the instrument, however, lead the present writer to believe that the giver is more likely to have been Charles X, the erstwhile patron of Punto, whose passion for the horn was notorious, and that it was made about 1826 or 1827. A second instrument is an orchestral horn by L. J., dated 1821. It was used for many years by the late Adolf Borsdorf and is now in the possession of his son, Francis Bradley. The third is also a silver-mounted cor-solo, but by L. J. Raoux and dated 1814. The horn first mentioned is now in the Victoria and Albert Museum, and the last is in the Horniman Museum (No. 166 in the Carse Collection).[12]

It is questionable if the 1818 Raoux horn Brain acquired from Cousins was, in fact, once owned by Puzzi. The date of the 1818 horn indicates that it was manufactured by the L. J Raoux firm (1775–1857) prior to the firm's acquisition by J. C. Labbaye in 1857. Since the horn predates the Labbaye period, and since the instrument is brass and not silver-mounted, the 1818 horn does not appear to be either the first or third instrument once owned by Puzzi as discussed by Morley-Pegge. We preclude the possibility that the 1818 horn is actually the second instrument (1821) referred to and reported to be in the possession of Francis Bradley. This instrument, originally a *cor d'orchestre*, was fitted with valves by Adolf Borsdorf and remains on loan from Bradley to the Royal Academy of Music museum collection in London. The 1818 hand horn is currently owned by Andrew Clark, who joined the Orchestra of the Age of Enlightenment in 1987 and is also a member of the London Gabrieli Brass.

Raoux-Labbaye 1855 Horn

A Raoux-Labbaye horn, currently belonging to Graham Melville-Mason, is reported to have been owned by Dennis Brain. Melville-Mason describes his horn in correspondence with Gamble dated October 9, 2005.

> Incidentally, my old Raoux horn (M. A. Raoux c.1855 with three valves added by Hawkes later) is on loan to the Collection of Historic Musical Instruments at Edinburgh University. Earlier it had come from the Nettlefold Collection and was used by Dennis for a short while before passing to the Walton family (Bob [Richard] being Dennis's colleague as principal trumpet in both the RPO and Philharmonia and Bernard as principal clarinet in the Philharmonia). The mouthpiece is the one which had remained with the instrument and the one which was subject to our mouthpiece discussion in the Beehive Restaurant in Edinburgh![13]

According to University of Edinburgh, the silver-plated brass instrument was manufactured between 1857–1871 by J. C. Labbaye. This falls within the period during which Labbaye acquired the Raoux firm (1857) along with the Raoux design patterns and trademark from Marcel-Auguste Raoux, the third generation owner of the Raoux firm. However, Melville-Mason states in his letter that his instrument is an M. A. Raoux c. 1855, which is contrary to that reported by University of Edinburgh.

The Edinburgh report further states the bell garland is inscribed:

> RAOUX RUE SERPENTE A PARIS / FOURNISSEUR DE S.M. L'EMPEREUR ET DE S.A. LE VICE-ROI-D'EGYPTE
>
> on the bell with poincon [stamp] MAR; inscribed on 2nd valve housing . . .

This suggests that the bell was likely manufactured by Raoux prior to the firm's acquisition by Labbaye and used as a manufacturing component along with the Perinet valves by Hawkes and Son for the instrument by Labbaye. It was common practice for the successors of Raoux to stamp their instruments with the Raoux poincon "MAR" (Marcel-Auguste Raoux) as an advertising trademark. Except for the bell and the valve body assembly, the remainder of the instrument was likely manufactured by Labbaye using the Raoux design pattern, which University of Edinburgh was able to discern during its analysis of the instrument. The approximate date of the instrument (1855) provided by Melville-Mason is in agreement with that determined by University of Edinburgh. The instrument therefore is more correctly a hybrid of the two manufacturers.[14]

Sansone Five-Valve Horn

Lorenzo Sansone (1881–1975), a professional horn player and founder of Sansone Musical Instruments of New York City, sold a five-valve horn to Brain while he was on tour with the RAF Symphony Orchestra in 1944–45. Sansone's son, Lawrence Sansone Jr., wrote to Pettitt on November 15, 1971, about this horn:

> I remember when Dennis came to Los Angeles with the RAF Orchestra because Alfred gave him a special party and invited all the Horn players here in Los Angeles. It was one of the best parties that was possible. Dennis had his old Raoux French Horn and I remember that it was an F Horn and all taped up and leaked like a sieve and we all took turns trying to play it and we could not. Dennis was playing all the Bach Fugues on it and it was wonderful so when everyone else tried to play it and could not Alfred took the horn and played as well as Dennis on it and Alfred said it was the same

horn that he started on and also played many concerts in England on it. Dennis was a wonderful person. I told him to go to New York to meet my Father who was the First Horn with the New York Symphony and also was in the business of manufacturing French Horns and specialized in his own model the Sansone five valve B-flat Horn. Dennis did meet my father and was so impressed with the Sansone Model Horn that he purchased one and used it many times. [15]

Alexander Single B-flat Horn

Brain continued to experiment with his Raoux horn using a B-flat crook and also with the single B-flat Alexander Model 90 he acquired while in Germany in April 1950. (Pl. 6) Pettitt reports: "He still favored the purer tone of his old Raoux instrument too much to consider abandoning it completely for the German horn."[16]

Brain continued to play on the 1818 Raoux until October 1951, when he made the decision to change to the Alexander horn for several reasons. First, the number of new works being written for him increasingly exploited the upper register in which the Alexander horn performed more reliably. Second, technology of the recording industry during this era was maturing rapidly. The recording industry was becoming less tolerant of mistakes that necessitated retakes, which impacted cost and schedule. Third, for some time, Dennis had become increasingly conscious of critical reports that considered his use of a B-flat crook with the French Raoux horn as detracting from the natural beauty and pureness of its tone. He wished to appease those critics, who were aware of the increasing popularity of the German versus French instrument.

Critics who allude to the popularity of the German instrument include a correspondent to the *Strad* magazine: "But Mr. Brain was not a good example to have chosen since he has only recently changed over to wide bore. . . . A new generation is now growing up which has never played and perhaps never heard the French instrument, and already a very marked deterioration is apparent."[17]

Cousins recalls in 1992:

> Dennis Brain made no secret of his change to the German horn in 1950 [1951]. His friends chided him. His father went so far as to say that he had given up the horn! Dennis Brain told me quite openly that he did not like the sound ("noise" he called it) but that he was paid to get the notes. The new instrument was virtually foolproof whereas he had to "nurse" certain notes on his old French horn in F. It always seemed to me that he was foolproof on both instruments.[18]

A letter from Alexander to Richard Kittrell in 1965 concerning the Alexander purchased by Brain provides further details about the instrument.[19] (*Pl. 7*)

Several letters from professionals offer differing views on the matter of the B-flat versus the F-horn in *Music and Letters* around this time associated, in part, with Brain's use of the B-flat crook on his French Raoux instrument. In extracts from his correspondence to the editor of *Music and Letters*, titled "The Degenerate Horn," Cousins wrote:

> The orchestral horn evolved as an instrument in F, trial and error having proved the F tubing to produce the most beautiful sound. But nowadays, the instrument is frequently played in B-flat, with a larger bore. These two modern devices have greatly eased the difficulties of horn playing. Yes, but they have robbed the horn of its all-important characteristic, namely, magical tone.[20]

In response to Cousins' letter to the editor, Morley-Pegge wrote:

> Your correspondent would have us believe that, while the German horn embodies every vice known to Satan and his minions, the French horn with what he rather cryptically calls its "natural bore in F" is an epitome of all virtues. But no sooner has his eloquence begun to win us over to his side than he proceeds carefully to demolish his own argument by telling us that Mr. Brain has to use a B-flat crook because of the deficiencies of the F.[21]

Following Brain's accident, the horn was repaired by the Paxman firm (then located in Covent Garden, London) reusing its original parts as best as possible. The rebuilt horn remained on display in the window of the Paxman shop for several years.

The Royal Academy of Music in London sponsored an event called "Dennis Brain: A Celebration" on November 15, 2002. It would be the first time in forty-five years that Brain's B-flat Alexander horn was to be heard in public. The program commenced with a performance by the RAM Concert Orchestra in Duke's Hall performing works by Artem Vassillev (*Stanza*, in memory of Dennis Brain), David Matthews (*Capriccio* for two horns and strings, Op. 54), Mozart (Fragment of E-Major Horn Concerto), and Haydn's Symphony No. 31 "Hornsignal." The performers included Michael Thompson, conductor and horn player, and horn players Richard Watkins and Alexandra Carr.

The celebration continued in the St. Marylebone Church Crypt with the Anvil Film (in association with John Wates) featuring Dennis Brain and Denis Matthews in a video performance of the Beethoven Sonata. John Humphries, horn historian and author of *The Early Horn: A Practical Guide*, led an illustrated discussion and played recorded examples of historic horn recordings by some of Brain's early predecessors and lesser-known examples by Brain himself. A concert followed at St. Marylebone Parish Church, which included works by Johann Kvandal (*Salmetone*), Norman Del Mar (Sonata for Organ; Duets for horns), Arnold Cooke (Arioso and Scherzo), Francis Poulenc (*Elégie*), and Johannes Fredrick Froehlich (Nonet for horns). Performers included Michael Thompson and Richard Watkins (horns), David Titterington (organ) and the RAM Horn Ensemble. (Pl. 8) The event is reported in *The Horn Magazine*.[22]

The following article by Dalya Alberge, Arts Correspondent, appeared in *The Times*.[23] It discusses how the horn was acquired by the Royal Academy of Music as an addition to its York Gate Collections along with other famous horns, now including Aubrey Brain's 1865 Raoux Labbaye, which is on loan to the collection by the Leonard Brain family:

> The horn played by the legendary virtuoso Dennis Brain until it was crushed in the car crash that killed him 44 years ago has been restored and acquired by the Royal Academy of Music. Brain, arguably the greatest horn player in musical history, inspired Britten, Hindemith and other composers to write works for him, and many of his recordings on that instrument remain unsurpassed 36 years after his death.
>
> His widow, Yvonne, wanted the instrument to go to the Royal Academy, where Brain studied. She could not afford to donate it and the Royal Academy launched an appeal for £15,000 to add it to its collection. Curtis Price, the academy's principal, said that Brain remains "one of the prime icons of British music history." So many people responded to the appeal that they had to turn away thousands of pounds because they reached the target so quickly.
>
> Brain, whose grandfather was also a horn player and whose father was first horn in the BBC Symphony Orchestra and a professor at the Royal Academy, was principal horn of the Royal Philharmonic and later the Philharmonia Orchestra. Britten wrote his Serenade for him, while Malcolm Arnold and Hindemith composed concertos. Brain's recordings of concertos by Mozart and Strauss, among others, show an astonishing mastery, a delicacy of rapid staccato passages and subtlety of phrasing. It was once said that no technical difficulties ever appeared to cause him the slightest apprehension.
>
> He was returning home from a concert in Edinburgh when he lost his life. Bob Paxman, former owner of Paxman Musical Instruments which restored the German-made instrument, said that the horn would have been written off as worth just a few pounds of scrap metal had it not been for its association with a musical genius. Chris Huning, Paxman's managing director, said that the horn was rebuilt by hammering and smoothing the metal of the existing materials.

The Royal Academy, which boasts one of the world's finest collections of historic instruments, will add the horn to the display in its newly opened museum, the York Gate Collections next to its home in Marylebone Road. Like other exhibits, it will be played by staff and students. The traditional museum approach, with instruments propped up forlornly in glass cases, has been scrapped so that the public can see and hear the finest instruments being played." (© Dalya Alberge / *The Times* / *nisyndication.com*)

The RAM's acquisition of Brain's rebuilt B-flat Single Alexander will enable students to observe first-hand how specialized Dennis's own horn was, and how it was unsuited to other players.

Alexander B-flat/D Five-Valve Horn

Pettitt reported:

> During the summer of 1953 he tried out a five-valve horn: it was pitched in B-flat and A as before but with an ascending D valve in addition, which gave a very wide range. (Pl. 9) He was never happy with it and soon returned to his original Alexander B-flat.[24]

Douglas Elliot describes how he came to be the current owner of this horn.

> This particular horn that I own is of course an Alexander that Dennis Brain owned. It was specially made for him and as far as I know this is the only horn of this type in the world. It has five valves, a stopping valve, and a D valve which cuts out about two feet of tubing and raises it to the pitch of high D horn, which makes it very easy to hit the higher notes—you can hit very easily on this horn.
>
> I bought it in 1968 from Don Burbank who during the War was band director at Sheppard Air Force Base in Wichita Falls. He had a horn-player in his band, Joe Henderson, and they were assigned to England during the War. Joe Henderson met Dennis Brain and took some lessons from him. So it was Joe Henderson that originally got the horn from Dennis and then Don Burbank got the horn from Joe in about 1950 and I think the horn was made in about 1944 to 45.
>
> I've enjoyed playing it because when I started playing horn, I had an old F horn and then when I went into college, I started playing on a double horn and it was an old German model of some sort (I don't even know what kind it was) but the F side was terrible and so I got used to playing on the B-flat side and so during the time I spent in the Army, I played on a double horn but I used the B-flat side mostly so when I had the opportunity to buy this single B-flat, well, I jumped at it![25]

Elliot related this information about the horn:

> The Alexander horn is one of a kind that I know of. It is a five valve single B-flat. It has the normal three valves and a stopping valve. A 5th valve cuts out about 23 inches and raises the pitch to D horn. The D valve is very helpful in playing the A above the treble clef. I also have learned that I could pull out the stopping valve slide and use both thumb valves [which] puts the horn in C. I also cut the 2nd valve slide of an old F horn to insert in the stopping valve to lower to A horn. I can also play bass notes using the D valve to play notes not available on a regular single B-flat horn.[26]

The horn currently owned by Douglas Elliot presents an interesting dilemma. Elliot states he acquired the horn in 1968 from Don Burbank who in turn had acquired the instrument from Joe Henderson in 1950 who had acquired the horn from Brain during the war years while in England. It would be interesting to determine if the horn in Elliot's possession is indeed an Alexander and not the five-valve Sansone acquired by Brain while in the RAF.

A statement was recorded during the 1991 Brain symposium that the instrument owned by Elliot was the horn on which Brain recorded the Mozart and Strauss concertos on the Angel label.[27] This is unlikely as the Mozart and Strauss concertos were recorded in November 1953 and September 1956, and Elliot stated that the instrument was in possession of Don Burbank by 1950. A photograph of Brain playing a five-valve horn in 1956 indicates that he was in possession of one or more five-valve horns even at this late date. (Pl. 10) When the photograph is enlarged near the area of the bell engraving, it shows the Alexander trademark. (*Pl. 11*).

Double F/B-flat-alto Horn

Brain purchased an F/B-flat-alto double horn about the same time he purchased his five-valve Alexander, more than likely to experiment with. He never used it in performance, and in 1954 he sold it to Alfred Cursue, a colleague in the Philharmonia. In conversation with composer Ernest Tomlinson, Brain spoke unfavorably about the use of a double horn because of its weight. The horn remained listed on Brain's All-Risks Insurance Policy at the time of his death.[28]

Tony Fairley, a semi-professional horn player who studied under Ifor James, related that he was once in possession of a four-valve, B-flat/F-alto Alexander horn built around 1950 that was once owned by Brain. He acquired the horn around 1963 from Arthur Bevan for use as a spare instrument. Bevan assured Fairley that he had purchased the instrument from Yvonne Brain after Brain's death. Fairley describes the instrument:

> It was a 4 valve, slightly smaller than the Alex B-flat/A single horn I was playing then. It was I remember very "bugle like" on the F alto side, not really pleasant, and I only used it after I had sold the Alex single. After I moved back to the North East in the 80s I was persuaded to sell it to a lady hornist, Val Williams, who lived in the Hemel Hempstead/Watford area and whom I had known and played with during the mid 70s. After the sale I lost contact with her and have no idea where she is now. She may of course have sold it on, so God only knows who owns it now. . . .[29]

Fairley's account shows that Brain continued to experiment with various types and configurations of horns with the Alexander firm during his mid-career.

Selmer Double Horn

The Selmer double horn listed in Brain's All-Risk Policy is likely the instrument Aubrey Brain purchased from a colleague to facilitate playing low horn with the Philharmonia Orchestra from October 1948 until May 1950. According to Pettitt:

> During the winter of 1948–9, Aubrey [Brain] returned to horn-playing. For the moment he did not go back to the BBC Symphony Orchestra; they had appointed Aubrey Thonger, principal horn after his [Aubrey Brain's] illness in 1945 and, in any case, his health would not allow him to undertake any strenuous playing. Dennis arranged for him to play in the Philharmonia as fourth horn from October 1948, and until May 1950 he played fairly regularly with them—usually as fourth or fifth horn, occasionally as second horn, and for a spell in February and March 1950 as sixth horn. His main activity was teaching at the Royal Academy, but his health made even that difficult at times. To make blowing easier he had bought, from a colleague, a second-hand Selmer four-valve horn. . . .[30]

The Selmer double horn listed in Brain's All-Risks Policy was most likely inherited after his father's death.

Correspondence

Brain wrote in July 1953 to Caswell Neal (1923–2007), an engineer and a lover of the horn.

> First an apology for not replying to your letter before, but I expect you know how things pile up, and how one puts off attending to them until suddenly finds one needs a month or so to catch up on correspondence etc.
>
> In England, Conn and Kruspe horns are hardly known, most players using either double Alexander or single Bb, with an occasional Lehman etc.

Before the war my father, Aubrey, brother of Alfred in Los Angeles, played a narrow bore French type horn in F with three valves and recorded almost everything on that, including the Brahms Trio. He probably used a B-flat crook for the Brandenburg No. 1 Concerto. This type of instrument has a small, very refined, smooth tone which develops into an edgy sound when blown hard though of great penetrating quality. Since the war the advantages of a big bore double have become more apparent and I believe I was the last player, except for the service bands, to play a narrow bore horn. Incidentally all my recordings, except the last two, the Schumann "Adagio & Allegro" & "Villanelle" of Paul Dukas, were made on that type of instrument in F.

I then changed to a B-flat crook on the same instrument and then Mr. Alexander of Mainz made me a single B-flat with an A valve (or muting) which I have been using ever since. My only concession to the French horn being, that although the bell and bore are normal size, large, the mouthpipe is narrower than normal, though still larger than the French. I use my ordinary French mouthpiece which is smaller than the big bore one.

My father recorded Mozart No. 2 for Edison Bell pre-electric and I have not recorded No. 3 though there is a possibility that I may do all for long playing. My father did not record the Beethoven and any attempts to obtain continental recordings, Freiburg, Beethoven, and Max Zimalong Mozart have been unsuccessful.

I hope you will forgive this rather hasty scribble, perhaps one day we will meet—and get down to the interesting study of horns—and players![31]

Brain wrote on August 15, 1953, to his uncle and aunt in Los Angeles, Alfred and Straussie Brain:

Doubtless you will be surprised to hear from me after eight years, but I thought a note to let you know how things are over here might interest you. . . .

I still use your mouthpiece that you gave me and in fact have virtually no other and the copy I have had made is not really exact. As soon as I could get to Germany after the war I had Alexander make me a B-flat/A gold brass, narrow mouth pipe, which I changed to when it was blown in and which I have used since, recording the Schumann "Adagio & Allegro" and Dukas "Villanelle" on it. In the past five months I have been using another Alexander specially made in the following manner, B-flat & A (or muting) & ascending D, five valves in all, which gives me everything, particularly low notes and in fact with lower notes and fundamentals, I have the best of two worlds. My second in the Philharmonia, which orchestra I am regularly with, uses a B-flat & high F. . . .[32]

The letter reveals the affinity Dennis had for Alfred and how much the two of them had in common, particularly the use of a mouthpiece that had a much smaller cup and rim than the one used by Aubrey.

Mouthpieces

The design and style of a mouthpiece is important. First, the mouthpiece determines the physical sensation of comfort in playing: namely, what feels best to the lips and embouchure. Second, the mouthpiece can readily be modified or changed out entirely with minimal effort and financial investment. Until recent times, few horn players had considered, or been aware of, the significant differences in tone color and playing qualities that can be achieved from playing on mouthpieces tailored to their specific style of playing.

Orchestral horn players are, in general, classified as either high or low horn performers, and the mouthpieces they use reflect these differences. The low horns typically use a mouthpiece with a relatively large inner rim diameter and large volume. Conversely, the high horns use a mouthpiece with a smaller inner diameter and less volume, which favors the upper register but makes the lowest range less manageable. The soloist faces a more challenging situation as solo parts typically use the entire range of the instrument, often to the extreme.

Cousins comments on Brain's mouthpieces.

> We do well to observe that the famous Brain family, Aubrey, Alfred and Dennis Brain, all used small thin-rimmed mouthpieces. Their bottom registers were strong and powerful. Their consistency and agility have never been challenged. And for sheer beauty of orchestral sound Aubrey Brain's playing in the 1930s has never been equalled. He had, of course, the advantage of a Raoux horn in F.
>
> Dennis Brain's mouthpiece was, by modern comparison, a small affair. The old silver three-penny bit (which horn players used to carry as a measuring device) would not even lie in the cup, but stood, so to speak, half out of it. This I verified on several occasions as Dennis sometimes experimented with different mouthpieces, but (let me hasten to add!) always with the same rim. (The type that used to be known as the "Busby" mouthpiece—named after Tom Busby, a well-known London horn player of the 1920s.)
>
> On examining the mouthpieces of the old French horns we find that they are almost exclusively thin-rimmed with narrow diameters and with a "lager-glass" shaped interior. The modern large-bore German horn is usually supplied with a mouthpiece which has a fatter rim, a wider diameter, and a cupped interior. As the German horn has the wider bore and the shorter

tube (when in B-flat) this makes sense. It is a recognised principle that as a brass instrument gets bigger so does the mouthpiece.

But is this departure from the old tried and proved mouthpiece either necessary or good? The evidence is not in favour. When Dennis Brain changed over to the large-bore German horn in B-flat and A (c. 1950) he retained his old French horn mouthpiece which had served him so well on his Raoux French horn in F. He never changed his mouthpiece and played on it right up until his untimely death in 1957. This writer carefully observed the mouthpieces of Dennis Brain and his father, Aubrey, and can vouch that they were practically identical. They were smaller and narrower in rim than any mouthpiece issued with today's German model.

This is a fitting moment to mention that the Brain embouchures were both of the "stretched" variety. I observed this on many occasions and on one occasion talked with Dennis Brain about it. He admitted that he had never really thought about it, as his father had fixed his embouchure at the age of seven and that was it! On reflection, Dennis was adamant that he "stretched" the lips at the mouthpiece and did not "purse" or "bunch" the vibrating part. What are we to conclude? Perhaps we should tend to "stretch" with a small mouthpiece and tend to "bunch" when using a larger one. We might also suggest that concave embouchures (like the Brain family's) are best suited to thin rims and stretched lips, whereas convex embouchures might need a larger mouthpiece with a tendency to "purse." There can be no solid rule.[33]

Nancy Jordan Fako quotes correspondence between Philip Farkas and Brain regarding a possible business venture centered about Dennis's mouthpiece. The first letter is from Farkas to Brain on December 1, 1950.

We are still recalling with pleasure your visit with Mrs. Brain to our home after that wonderful concert. Your performance of the concerto will remain a model of inspiration for us all for many years to come. It has already made considerable change in the local horn players' practice habits, without, however, causing enough improvement to give you the slightest qualm.

It never occurred to me during our conversations that we perhaps have the elements of a mutually beneficial manufacturing venture. Here is an idea I had yesterday which I would like to submit for your consideration.

Mr. Schilke (the trumpeter you met at my home) and myself own a little manufacturing company called Music Products, Inc. One of the products is a line of brass mouthpieces. They are highly precision-made and we take great pride in their high quality. Of each instrument we have taken the mouthpieces of several of our country's best known players. With their permission, of course, we have made very precise copies of their mouthpieces and advertised them for sale. The copy is exact and each mouthpiece is stamped with the name of the player whose design it is. We have ordinarily given a royalty to the owner of $.50 per mouthpiece sold, which naturally results in very modest amounts, although some of the popular models can result in royalties of $100 or more yearly. In view of your popularity in our country we think that the royalty offered you should be $1.00 a mouthpiece, if you are at all interested. This might mean a pleasant sized check to you each year for a surprising number of years to come. It would give our players here the opportunity of using a mouthpiece that we know can produce astounding results (at least with Mr. Brain behind it) and would result in a quality of mouthpiece which I know you would be proud to have your name on. The way your playing has taken us by storm it might be that we could sell several hundred a year although this is just a guess.

If the idea should appeal to you at all we would need an exact copy of your mouthpiece which we would have to finally destroy in our dissecting for accurate tooling. When, and if, you play Boston there is a mouthpiece maker who could make such a duplicate for us. His name is Archie Smith and he does beautiful work and would need your own mouthpiece for perhaps only a half hour. Of course he should send the bill to me. The only other thing we would need is a letter from you permitting us to use your name on this model and to advertise it. All the rest would be taken care of by our corporation. An accurate account would be kept of the number sold and we would arrange to get your check to England in some manner. I will have to ask the advice of a banker on this procedure.

I would like to hear your reaction to this idea if you can find the time to drop me a line.

Please accept my apology for the commercial tone of this letter. I know that a player such as you has to avoid cheap commercialism but I assure you that our manner of advertising the mouthpieces (they are only advertised in music magazines) would be most dignified.

It seems like such a "natural" that I just had to approach you with my idea.[34]

Brain replied on March 23, 1952:

Doubtless you will be surprised to hear from me after over a year, but I hasten to assure you that only the unbelievable difficulty of getting a mouthpiece made over here has made me postpone writing to you until now, when you should have received a copy through Mr. Kubelik.

> In this country there are instrument makers, repairers, etc., but to get them to copy a mouthpiece, which is near enough to be practical, let alone exact, seems to be beyond them. In the end a friend of mine made a copy, which I tried for a few days to see if it was as comfortable as my own, and, on being satisfied that it was, passed it on to Mr. Kubelik for you.
>
> Naturally, I quite realize that after all this time the mouthpiece may not be of any use to you, in which case I can only say how sorry I am that you should have been delayed in this way, but if it is, I shall be only too delighted to hear from you.
>
> However, rumor has it that we may be touring America again in, perhaps, 1953, with, of course, Sir Thomas, and it would give me great pleasure to meet you there again.[35]

As it turned out, the second planned RPO tour did not occur. Brain did, however, tour the US in 1955 with the Philharmonia Orchestra, performing in Chicago on November 5 and 6 at Orchestra Hall. No confirmation has been found that Brain and Farkas met on that occasion. As to the future of their plans for the reproduction of Brain's mouthpiece, Farkas described (at the 1991 symposium) riding with Brain in a car in London and subsequent events:

> So during that time [May 11, 1957] we had discussed the fact that Renold Schilke and myself were making mouthpieces here in America and he expressed an interest in having his mouthpiece duplicated for sale, so we talked about it and nothing actually came about, but I'll explain that a moment later. . . .
>
> On September 1st, I was about to teach a lesson back in Evanston, Illinois and my student came up and said "I've been driving and the car radio just announced that a horn player in London had been killed—do you know of a Dennis Brain?" Right then I almost fell through the floor and I said, "There'll be no lesson today," and I collapsed—really. During the time that we had discussed the making of a mouthpiece, he wrote me a letter . . . [the letter quoted above]
>
> He sent me his extra mouthpiece—obviously he didn't send his regular mouthpiece. This was a copy and he reassured me that it was a perfect copy. I have it here somewhere. You are welcome to come up and see it when the program's over. Can you see the size of the hole? It's terrific! Very narrow rim—very sensitive. I think you'd be interested in seeing that. At any rate, nothing ever came of the mouthpiece while we were discussing it, unfortunately (during the time he was killed) so the mouthpiece never was manufactured by us, but it's a very interesting one to see and once you see it you'll either wonder why he could play on it at all or you'll say maybe that's the secret of his success.[36]

Embouchure

Brain's embouchure has been described in many papers by colleagues and scholars of the horn who carefully observed him while playing. Perhaps the finest preserved visual example is that which can be seen in the 1952 Anvil Film of Dennis' performance of the Beethoven Sonata with Denis Matthews.

Cousins discusses Brain's embouchure:

> Many tributes have been paid to Dennis Brain since his tragic death at the age of 36. No doubt many more will be paid in the future as the musical world comes to realise that he was not just a great player of his time but probably the greatest player of all time.
>
> Anyone who has listened to Delius's *Appalachia* recorded by the Royal Philharmonic Orchestra with Sir Thomas Beecham conducting will marvel at Dennis Brain's controlled piano-subitos, graded dynamics, and complete overall mastery. Brain had all the hallmarks of the outstanding artist. The magnificent players of today such as Civil, Tuckwell, Baumann and Berger all pay homage to Dennis Brain. He was peerless.
>
> The following analysis of Dennis Brain's embouchure, mouthpiece and breathing-style is by the way of being not only my (albeit humble) tribute, but something which could be of interest, and probably of help, to any young aspiring horn player. As a contemporary of Dennis Brain at the Royal Academy of Music, I was one of the lucky ones who could observe at close quarters. Sometimes I was privileged to play beside him.
>
> We are very much the victims of tooth formation. The best top register horn players have usually been endowed with a "concave" embouchure. Presumably this has enabled the muscles to grip the mouthpiece, rather than the mouthpiece gripping the muscles.
>
> The almost incredible consistency of the Brain family (Alfred, Aubrey and Dennis) probably lay basically in their concave embouchures. Certainly my own impression gained by close observation of Aubrey Brain (my teacher) and later of his son Dennis, was that of a stretched embouchure gripped at the mouthpiece rather than a gripped embouchure trying to stretch at the mouthpiece.
>
> This does not mean to say that a "convex" embouchure spells doom. Far from it. But it may well suggest that those with such an embouchure would be wiser to specialize as a cor-bass rather than strain helplessly and gather complexes in the top octave. "Know thy limitations" advised Emerson. Indeed, we do well to accept Nature's endowment and Emerson's wisdom, with good grace.

Dennis Brain's mouth was concave. That is, his teeth were small and set well back into his head. His lips were nonetheless "full" and obviously sensitive. When Dennis laughed, which he did often, his lips would appear to take up his playing position. Certainly his face in repose and when playing were unrecognisably different. Dennis's concave embouchure made him appear to play much more on the edge of his top lip than in fact was the case. His lower lip position was more "einsetzen" than "ansetzen." One could say that his was a definitely "inset" embouchure.

Dennis Brain's lowest jaw muscles were braced extremely firmly. His whole embouchure gave the impression of a triangle composed of the two corner "whorls" and the point of the chin . . . each of the three appearing to be straining to be getting away from the others. He used considerable pressure, but this was supported by tremendous muscular contraction emanating from the whorls at the corners of the mouth. These whorls were above the line of the mouth. In fact, Dennis Brain could be said to have had a "smiling embouchure," and there was none of the "pursing" which is sometimes (and probably rightly, for some embouchures) recommended today.

Behind the embouchure was a powerful air-pressure. Not the "red-in-the-face" momentary effort, but the "power-house" of an immensely well-trained breathing apparatus. Dennis Brain, in common with all good wind players, practised breathing, and lung-power-building, as seriously as he practised the horn. We do well to carve that sentence over our mantelpiece.

As a student at the RAM, Dennis Brain practised the horn for hours on end. I well remember an almost permanent "whitish" corn on the centre of his lip where the mouthpiece was punishing the muscles. At the time I was misguided enough to be following that will-o'-the-wisp—"the non-pressure-system" oblivious of the fact that there is no such thing, since the moment one surface touches another then some pressure must be exerted. I did not realise that mouthpiece pressure is relative to the muscles which support it—and Dennis Brain was in the process of growing those muscles! In later years I looked closely at Dennis Brain's top lip and noticed that he had moved the mouthpiece up somewhat since our student days. Although there was a distinct roughish mark, the "whitish" corn of his compressed-lip era had gone. In its place was a "roughish" or "toughened" area which seemed to say—"I'm tough enough to take any pressure!"

In summing up, I believe that Dennis Brain's unique standard of playing lay not only in his psychological suitability for the instrument, but in the physical attributes which I have tried, however haltingly, to describe. Dennis Brain attained a greater perfection than anyone else. Could this have been his secret?[37]

In October 2010, eBay.co.uk posted a Seller offering titled "*Dennis Brain's Original 2 French Horn Travel Case—1950*" which Brain carried with him on his 1950 American tour with Beecham and the Royal Philharmonic Orchestra.[38] The case was manufactured for Brain by Paxman, known at that time as Paxman Bros. Ltd at their former London, WI location, 36 Gerrard Street. It enabled Brain to carry both his Alexander B-flat/A and the Raoux Millereau horn on the tour, the latter which he used for solo performances.

The Travelling Box is believed to be that referred to as "Travelling box for above" in his "All-Risks Policy" at the time of his death. The eBay.co.uk website included ten photos of the travel case depicting it to be excellent condition. (*Pl. 12 and Pl.13*) The seller's initial asking price was listed as $6,960.00 USD. On November 1, 2010, the bidding ended with a final accepted offer of $2,990.00 plus a shipping cost. A more detailed description of the travel case posted after its sale can be found at the following site address:

> http://cgi.ebay.co.uk/DENNIS-BRAINs-ORIGINAL-2-FRENCHHORN-TRAVEL-CASE-1950-/300487005951?pt=Brass_Instruments&hash=item45f66bd6ff

"All-Risks" Policy No. 51136728 - Dennis Brain

Single German horn (Alexander)	£250.
Double " " "	£250.
Travelling box for above	£25.
Hand horn (Raoux 1818)	£250.
French hand horn (Raoux 1862)	£50.
Selmer double horn	£100.

Plate 1 Dennis Brain's All-Risks Policy identifying horns that he was known to have had at the time the policy was written. He was in possession of several other horns not listed which he experimented with and, for one reason or another, passed them on to others. *With permission from Audrey Brain L.R.A.M.*

Plate 2 Brain is shown performing with the Raoux Millereau horn given to him by Aubrey Brain in 1936 just prior to his entry into the Royal Academy of Music in London. The photograph shows Brain leading the Royal Philharmonic Orchestra horn section and was likely taken between late 1946 and 1948. The horn section members left of Brain are Ian Beers, Roy White, Frank Probyn, Alan Hyde and Alfred Cursue. *With permission from Siva Oke, Somm Recordings.*

Plate 3 The first modification of the rebuilt Raoux Millereau horn included the addition of the A-descending rotary valve for muting compensation ca. 1948. *With permission from Hale Publishing.*

Plate 4 A later modification to the Raoux Millereau included the addition of a second rotary valve to permit placing the horn in the key of C-alto c.1951. *With permission from The* Horn Call, *the Journal of the International Horn Society.*

Plate 5 Brain acquired an 1818 Raoux horn from Farquharson that reportedly was once owned by the great horn player, Puzzi. It is shown here without the detachable valve body in place permitting it to be played as a natural horn. Note the artistic painting design inside the bell flare. The instrument is now owned by Andrew Clark. *With permission from Chris Larkin and from The British Horn Society journal, The Horn Player, with permission from Paul Kampen.*

Plate 6 Dennis Brain's Alexander B-flat/A model 90 horn (modified) is now on display in the York Gate Collections at the Royal Academy of Music, London. *Wikipedia website:* http://en.wikipedia.org/wiki/Dennis_Brain. Released under CC BYSA: http://creativecommons.org/licenses/by-sa/3.0/

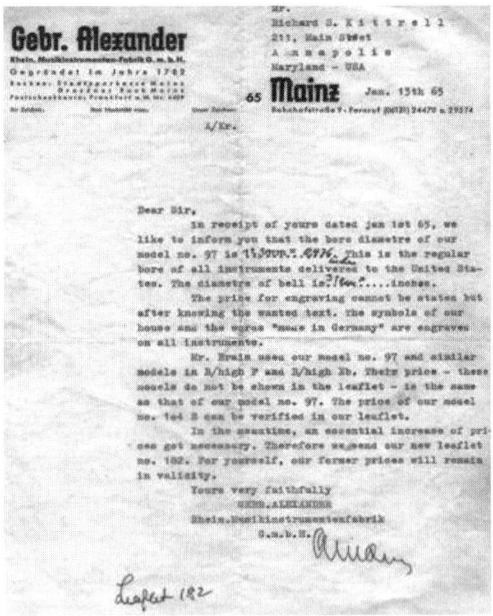

Gebr. Alexander
Rhein. Musikinstrumenten-Fabrik G.m.b.H.
Gegründet im Jahre 1782

Mr.
Richard S. Kittrell
211, Main Street
Annapolis
Maryland – USA

65 **Mainz** Jan. 15th 65

A/Kr.

Dear Sir,

In receipt of yours dated jan 1st 65, we like to inform you that the bore diametre of our model no. 97 is [illegible]. This is the regular bore of all instruments delivered to the United States. The diametre of bell is [illegible]....inches.

The price for engraving cannot be stated but after knowing the wanted text. The symbols of our house and the words "made in Germany" are engraved on all instruments.

Mr. Brain used our model no. 97 and similar models in B/high F and B/high Eb. Their price – these models do not be shown in the leaflet – is the same as that of our model no. 97. The price of our model no. 104 B can be verified in our leaflet.

In the meantime, an essential increase of prices got necessary. Therefore we send our new leaflet no. 182. For yourself, our former prices will remain in validity.

Yours very faithfully
GEBR. ALEXANDER
Rhein. Musikinstrumentenfabrik
G.m.b.H.

Leaflet 182

Plate 7 In correspondence to Richard S. Kittrell, Gebr. Alexander of Mainz, Germany, identifies the model of one of Dennis Brain's B-flat/A Alexander horns. The model 97 is a five-valve instrument (with an F-extension) and is one of several five-valve Alexander horns which Brain experimented with. *With permission from Richard Kittrell.*

Dennis Brain

- a celebratory day of events at the Royal Academy of Music

Friday 15th November 2002

3.30pm: film & talk St Marylebone Church Crypt

Screening of archive film of Dennis Brain and Dennis Matthews performing Beethoven's Sonata in F

Illustrated talk on historic horn recordings presented by John Humphries, author of 'The Early Horn'

5.05pm Early-evening concert
St Marylebone Parish Church

Michael Thompson & Richard Watkins horns
David Titterington organ
Royal Academy of Music Horn Ensemble

Johann Kvandal Salmetone
Norman Del Mar Sonata for Organ; Duets for horns
Arnold Cooke Arioso & Scherzo
Francis Poulenc Elégie
Johannes Frederik Froehlich Nonet for Horns

Plate 8 The mid-afternoon program on November 15, 2002, at the St. Marylebone Church Crypt was sponsored by the Royal Academy of Music, London, in memory of Dennis Brain. *With permission from the Royal Academy of Music, London.*

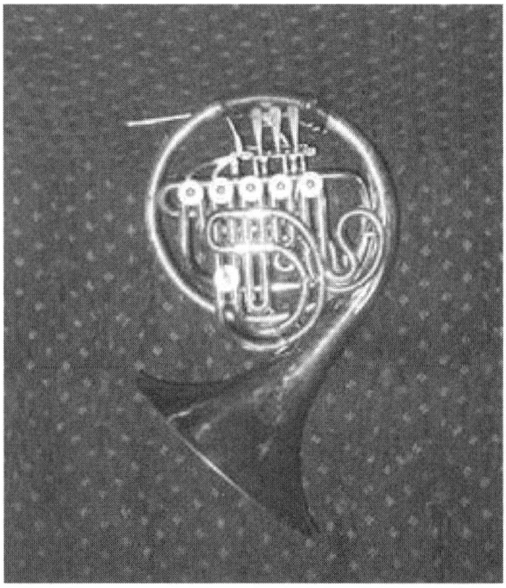

Plate 9 The five-valve B-flat/D Alexander horn once believed to have been owned by Brain. *The Douglas A. Elliot Collection with permission from the Douglas A. Elliot family by Martha Elliot Stallard.*

Plate 10 Shown is a rare photo of Brain with a five-valve B-flat/A Alexander horn. The higher key of this Single B-flat/A Alexander instrument is unknown. *With permission from Mrs. Annetta Hoffnung and the Tony Catterick Collection.*

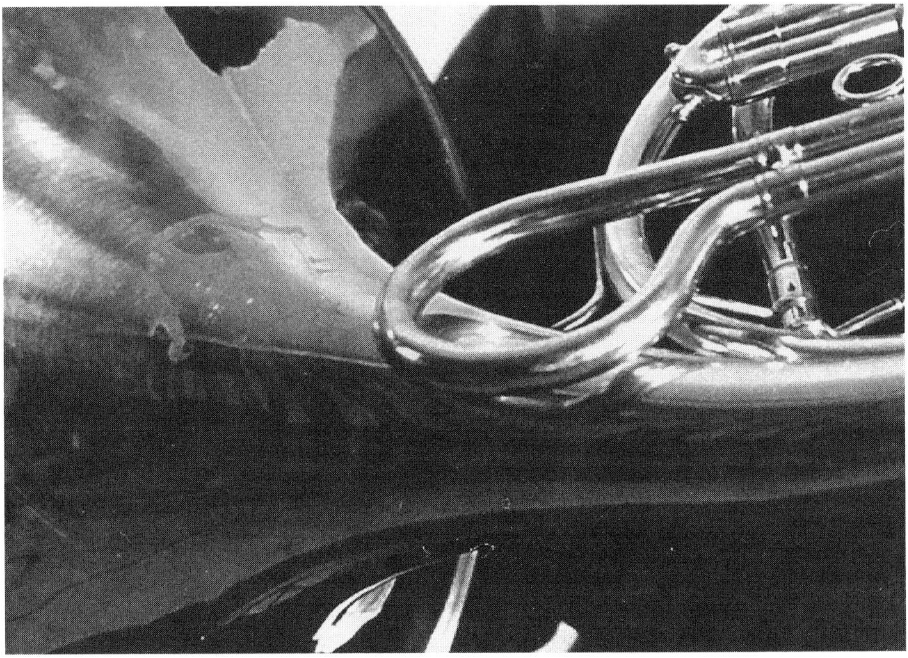

Plate 11 Photo enlargement of the bell area of the 5-valve horn being played by Brain confirms it was manufactured by Alexander Mainz. *With permission from Mrs. Annetta Hoffnung and from Tony Catterick, The Tony Catterick Collection*

Plate 12 The two horn travel case sizes are given as follows: height 1.591 ft, width 1.164 ft, base length 2.887 ft, weight 26.45 pounds. *Germain Poirier MD CM, FRCPC; Ensemble Sinfonia de Montreal.*

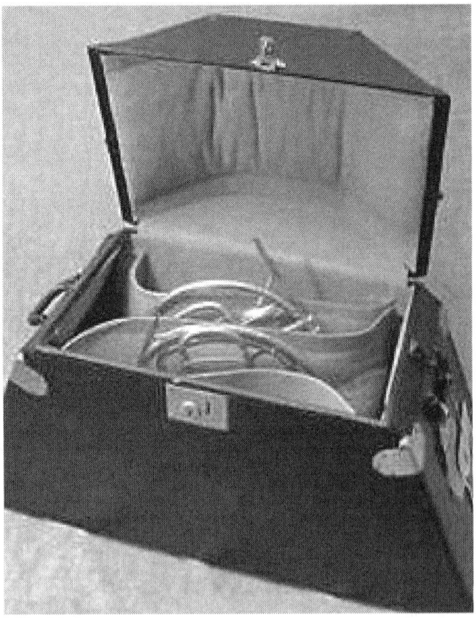

Plate 13 The forward compartment accommodates the larger Alexander horn and the rear compartment is sized only to accept the smaller Raoux horn. *Germain Poirier MD CM, FRCPC; Ensemble Sinfonia de Montreal.*

CHAPTER

12

New Directions

In the last ten years of his life, Brain scheduled engagements well into the future with the Dennis Brain Wind Ensemble and Chamber Orchestra, the Brain-Pougnet-Parry Trio, and as a soloist, as well as prospective opportunities to conduct, compose, and arrange. How might his career have developed, given an average lifespan ahead of him and taking into consideration his extraordinary achievements at the age of thirty-six?

Donald Froud, a professional horn player, remembered Brain in his last year, and it is clear from his recollections and from those of other colleagues, that Brain was searching for new ways to express himself musically.

> I spoke to Dennis in the summer of 1957. He was sitting in his beloved TR2 outside the V&A [Victoria & Albert] in Kensington where he was due to give a recital, but was not anxious to go in until the last minute. That was always his way with solo engagements. He said to me, "You know, Donald, I've got a reputation in the business for never cracking a note, but every morning I wake up I'm one day older and it's one day harder to live up to that. My ambition now is to take up conducting and let others do the playing!"[1]

It is interesting that Brain had concerns about diminishing powers as a player. He had, of course, seen his father declining (due to ill health) as one of the world's top horn virtuosi, so perhaps he had that in mind. This concern may have been one reason for his desire to make conducting his main activity. Yet Brain's health was one of the most robust. According to his wife, he was never sick in the twelve years they were married. His energy was phenomenal. Another reason for turning to conducting has been suggested by Norman

Del Mar (see Chapter 9). He had achieved the pinnacle as a horn player and musically had nothing more to achieve.

Conducting

At a very early age, Brain would have learned a great deal through observation of how the orchestral repertoire could be treated by some of the world's top conductors. A photograph by Georges Maiteny (*Pl. 1*) shows Brain pointing to a passage in a music score that he and Sir Thomas Beecham are studying in an empty concert hall. Clearly, he was interested in aspects of music-making that were not merely about performing as soloist or in the orchestra. No doubt also inspired by horn-playing colleagues who had made a success of conducting (notably Sir Edward Downes and his friend Norman Del Mar, Sir Thomas Beecham's protégé), Brain was searching for a role that would give him greater control over music-making.[2]

A conducting career would have been hugely competitive, however, with so many outstanding conductors in those days. Perhaps he was not looking for a career as a conductor of the fame of Toscanini or Furtwängler or Klemperer, but rather was looking for ways to escape from the increasingly demanding position of being the world's most outstanding horn virtuoso.

The plans that Brain was making in his final months are clear indication that he was expanding his musical interests, developing his Trio, promoting and arranging tours for the Chamber Orchestra (Scotland), Quintet (Italy) and solo tours abroad, including an Australian tour, and a six-week tour to Canada (with Denis Matthews) after the Edinburgh Festival of 1957. He was booked to appear in Los Angeles for two solo appearances in February 1958.[3]

Brain's engagements advertised in the weeks after his unexpected death show no diminishing of solo or orchestral commitments. For example, a concert bill for September 24, 1957, advertises a performance of Mozart's Concerto No. 4 at the Royal Festival Hall with pianist Nina Milkina. On the same day, he was to have performed the Roberto Gerhard Nonet for the BBC with the Brain Ensemble. The BBC had sent him the unpublished score of the Nonet on June 13, 1957. He was also to have recorded the Haydn Concertos for EMI in the winter of 1957 (see his letter of April 19, 1956, to Walter Legge in Chapter 6). In that letter, he also promoted his own Chamber Orchestra, inviting Legge and Elisabeth Schwarzkopf to their third concert on April 27 at Wigmore Hall.[4]

Brain spoke of retiring from the Philharmonia, but whether that would also have meant retiring from orchestral playing generally is doubtful. Morris commented that Brain loved playing the symphonies and would not have left orchestral playing had he lived. Certainly, by 1957 Brain had withdrawn from the other orchestras, but perhaps retirement from the Philharmonia would have enabled him to join new orchestras being formed in the 1950s, including light orchestras. His love of light music found expression as first horn of Jack Coles's Orchestre Moderne during the 1950s. This was exclusively a light music broadcasting orchestra. According to Coles, Aubrey Brain played second horn. Also in the 1950s, Brain was first horn in "Sympathy" (Friml) and "Will You Remember" (Romberg) on a stereo Decca long-playing record entitled *Contrasts in HiFi* made in December 1956 and the first two months of 1957 with the Bob Sharples Orchestra.[5]

Brain's interest in jazz and popular music (Frank Sinatra, Tommy Dorsey, Geraldo and his Orchestra) has been touched on in Chapter 2. Continuing his interest in jazz after the war, he played what was usually a trombone solo in Duke Ellington's "Sophisticated Lady" for BBC Light Programme's *Downbeat* on November 16, 1949, with Ted Heath and his Orchestra. Opportunities to develop his interest in jazz appear to have been few, but in 1956 he talked about the use of the horn in jazz music for *Desert Island Discs.* One of the records he chose was of hornists James Buffington, John Barrows, Ray Alonge, and Gunther Schuller with Mitch Miller (rhythm) and Stan Freeman (harpsichord) performing Alec Wilder's "Horn Belt Boogie." He introduced it as follows: "It's a little piece for Four Horns and Harpsichord, pure Chamber Music, music of the size of a combination to be performed in a chamber or small room, and it's called 'Horn Belt Boogie,' recorded by Mitch Miller."[6]

Plomley responded to this record by asking Dennis whether he played that sort of music himself and Brain replied:

> I have done; I used to play with Geraldo at the end of the war, when he had horns in his orchestra and for the fun of it, we did an arrangement of "Where in the World" and one or two other little things like that. The only thing is, of course, that the trombone is so much better at performing that sort of music than the horn . . . except perhaps for Mitch Miller.[7]

Brain also mentioned the above record, with "The Yellow Rose of Texas" played by Mitch Miller (1955), in his article on the horn published in *Brass Today* (1957), a transcript of which is reproduced in Appendix D. Could jazz horn have been a new direction for him in the late 1950s, with fewer orchestral commitments? It probably would not have been more than an occasional performance.

Brain enjoyed the first Hoffnung Music Festival of November 13, 1956. In his letter (see Chapter 6), it is clear he looked forward to another opportunity for such a concert. After his death, Hoffnung concerts in 1958 and 1961 continued with the same comic, light-hearted approach to music-making. It is likely that, had he lived, he would have found a role to play in those concerts.

The Hoffnung Music Festival of 1956 was televised live, although we have found no copy of the program. Brain played a length of garden hose-pipe, to which he attached his mouthpiece at one end and a funnel at the other (*Pl. 2*). In this photograph his facial muscles are very clearly shown as well as his embouchure. During that concert, the leader of the Morley College Orchestra, John Davies, recalled Brain saying to him after the performance of the movement of the Leopold Mozart Concerto for Alphorn. "Phew! Now I can go back to some real playing!" Also in the same concert, Brain was given the opportunity to play the organ in a piece written for the occasion by Sir Malcolm Arnold, his *Grand, Grand Overture.* Apart from the organ, it contains solo parts for three vacuum cleaners, one electric floor polisher and three rifles—firing blanks, of course![8]

Brain's lecturing about the horn had begun in about 1950 and remained one of his activities, as shown in Chapter 7. He appears to have been taking an increasing interest in educating the young about the horn, two occasions being visits to Portora Royal School in Northern Ireland and George Watson School in Edinburgh in 1956. During the 1950s, he had also taken an active interest in the National Youth Orchestra, giving recitals and, during Easter of 1957, coaching the horn section, as recalled by Dame Ruth Railton: "Dennis Brain arrived by surprise, went straight up to help the horns, then stayed to give a very memorable recital. 'He would speed in, give an exhilarating recital, take a cup of cocoa with us and dash away in the night,' writes one of our horn players."[9]

This horn player was a former pupil of Aubrey Brain's, Timothy Reynish, now a distinguished conductor. He remembered that night going to see Brain into his car and to thank him. Brain replied, "I love coming, the atmosphere breathes excitement."[10]

Had he lived, Brain's talents as a lecturer would almost certainly have matured and his teaching skills would have had time to develop, as indeed would have other projects such as conducting. Conducting and performance in chamber music appear to have been the two principal activities that he was planning to focus on in the future.

Dennis Brain Chamber Orchestra

Brain gathered together a chamber orchestra in 1956 that included friends, some family, and colleagues from the Philharmonia Orchestra. They played only a handful of concerts. Brain wrote to Maurice Johnstone of the BBC in March 1956, enclosing a notice for one of them:

> You may remember that a few years ago I wrote to you on the subject of conducting, which I am sure must have caused you some surprise if not amusement.
>
> However, as you see from the enclosed notice, I am going to have a shot at doing some on my own, and I wondered if you would be interested in coming along.
>
> As I shall be abroad until April 14th I will arrange for Ibbs & Tillett to send you two tickets for each concert in the hope that your commitments will enable you to come to at least one.[11]

Johnstone was out of the office when the letter arrived, so his secretary replied, thanking Brain for his letter and the tickets. We are not told if Johnstone attended the concerts. Johnstone did not like people doing more than one thing and about ten years previously had discouraged Del Mar from taking up a conducting career. Such discouragement did not deter Del Mar from establishing a successful career as one of the world's finest conductors. It is also doubtful that such discouragement could have deterred Brain from making an equally successful career as a conductor. It was early days and impossible to know whether it would have become his chief activity.[12]

The first appearance of the Dennis Brain Chamber Orchestra (*Pl. 3*) at Wigmore Hall on April 18, 1956, received a positive critique from *The Times*:

> It is almost 10 years since Mr. Dennis Brain decided to extend his musical abilities beyond a genius for playing the horn; last night he brought forward his own chamber orchestra which devotes much of its first two programmes to the less familiar Mozart.
>
> This first programme contained several rarities. There was Mozart's first horn concerto, a puzzling torso, complete and characteristic as it stands. . . . Yet the music is as full of jokes as the manuscript—better jokes—and the whole piece has the characteristic of unbuttoned floridity, bravura that wears a swagger grin, which we notice in the other three horn concertos, a quality conveyed to perfection in Mr. Brain's virtuosity and sense of humour.
>
> Alfred Einstein, who edited Köchel's Mozart catalogue, at one time believed that the intended middle movement was to hand in a fragment in

> E major, though he later repented, deciding that the key and the style would not fit this concerto.
>
> Mr. Brain played such of the fragment as remains, and must have convinced all his listeners too: it is patently an allegro—the behaviour of the bridge passages makes that plain—but, most decisively, it belongs elsewhere because the orchestral exposition is serious and experimental as nothing in Mozart's extant horn concertos is. What remains augurs a great concerto by Mozart, and when Mr. Brain shrugged his shoulders sadly as the manuscript petered out unaccompanied, posterity could only weep with him.
>
> For the rest, Mr. Brain conducted an early symphony (No. 17) and a divertimento (K.247) by Mozart, and accompanied his own brother, Mr. Leonard Brain, in Fricker's Concertante for Cor Anglais and Strings. A more experienced conductor would have controlled the flow of Fricker's piece so that its shape was more clearly shown; otherwise Mr. Brain was content to beat time modestly for his skilful players.[13]

Donald Mitchell in *Musical Times* also wrote about this concert, devoting much of his article to an analysis of the Mozart Concerto fragment in E major. He wrote, in part:

> Mr. Dennis Brain has now formed his own chamber orchestra, and the ensemble made its first appearance at Wigmore Hall on 18 April. Mr. Brain served as both conductor and soloist in two works for solo horn and orchestra by Mozart, one the horn concerto in D, K.412, the other a fragment of a horn concerto in E, K.Anh.98a. . . . Mr Brain kept blowing until there was nothing left to blow. It was an eerie experience, this gradual dissolution of what promised to be a masterpiece.[14]

A second concert took place at South Place, Red Lion Square, on April 22, 1956. The Orchestra returned to Wigmore Hall for their third concert on April 27. Frank Hawkins wrote about the South Place concert:

> The orchestral concert this season was given by the Dennis Brain Chamber Orchestra. As well as conducting, Dennis played the Mozart horn concerto K. 447. This supreme horn player was never to play for us again. . . . His brother, Leonard, played the Fricker Concertante for cor anglais and strings.[15]

The following year, they played at the Tenth Aldeburgh Festival in Jubilee Hall. The program included Sir Malcolm Arnold's *Sinfonietta* No. 1, Fricker's Concertante for Cor Anglais (Leonard Brain soloist), and Stravinsky's Concerto in E-flat, *Dumbarton Oaks*. Brain appeared with them as soloist in Haydn's Concerto No. 1 and Mozart's Fragment in E major K.Anh.98a.[16]

During his last Edinburgh Festival (1957), Brain spent many hours at the Scottish Arts Council offices preparing for a tour of Scotland with his orchestra. Seven concerts were planned between September 25 and October 3, 1957. He was working on an arrangement of the National Anthem to play with them, and in his last conversation with Hugh Bean on August 31, he asked "Do you want to see the new National Anthem arrangement?" Bean declined, no doubt tired after that evening's concert and said, "See you about it Monday."[17]

The orchestra (*Pl. 4* partially reproduced on the jacket of this book) played a memorial concert, conducted by Britten, Del Mar, and Fricker, at Chelsea Town Hall, on December 10, 1957, months after Brain's death. Leonard Brain was soloist in Fricker's Concertante for Cor Anglais, and Pears was soloist in songs from Purcell's *Orpheus Brittanicus* and the Sonnet from Britten's Serenade. That evening, as a silent tribute, the Epilogue was not played and the concert ended with no applause. The cover of the program is signed all over by most of the Orchestra, the soloists, and the three conductors.[18]

Brain-Pougnet-Parry Trio

In 1952, Dennis formed a trio (*Pl. 5*) for occasional tours and concerts, which came to be known, in its brief existence, as the "Brain-Pougnet-Parry Trio."[19]

In Brain's first letter to the BBC mentioning his Trio, dated October 24, 1956, he says, "As you know I have a Trio with Jean Pougnet and Wilfrid Parry." In fact, Miss Nisbett had not been informed of this Trio's existence, as indicated by her notes on the back. The next letter from Brain, on November 29, mentions this, with an apology:

> Thank you so much for your answer to my query concerning my broadcast with Max Salpeter and Cyril Preedy on 15th February.
>
> I am so sorry that you have not in your books the Brain-Pougnet-Parry Trio, as it is now called, but as we joined forces under a year ago the occasion has not arisen until now.
>
> However, since then we have performed some twenty or so concerts and have in our repertoire one or two works which I believe have not yet been broadcast.[20]

His statement that they had only joined forces "under a year ago" is puzzling. Perhaps it was not an official trio until then.

As part of their tour of Yorkshire and Lincolnshire in October 1956, the BBC recorded one of the concerts at Barton-on-Humber on October 25, 1956, and broadcast it on November 28. The recording does not appear to have been preserved. We know of no existing recordings by the Trio.[21]

Another concert at York in October 1956, received the following review:

> The Brain-Pougnet-Parry Trio were the artists at the second of the winter concerts arranged by the British Music Society of York in the Tempest Anderson Hall, and they presented a well-balanced and skillfully contrasted programme of works by Beethoven, Mozart and Brahms.
>
> The Trio comprises Dennis Brain (horn), Jean Pougnet (violin), and Wilfrid Parry (piano). All of them are well-known as artists individually at the top of their profession, and collectively they proved a notable combination. Their work as a unit was best shown in the Brahms Trio in E-flat Op. 40, where the contrasting tempo was always effectively played.
>
> The other main work was Beethoven's familiar Kreutzer Sonata in A major, which was given a spirited performance and the rest of the three part programme was devoted to an expressively played performance of Neumann's arrangement of Mozart's Trio in E-flat.[22]

The Trio appeared in concert again on January 17, 1957, at St. George's Hall, Bradford. It was a lunchtime concert that included Neumann's trio arrangement of Mozart's Quintet K. 407 and the Brahms Horn Trio. These works were frequently a part of the Trio's programs from 1952 to 1957.[23]

The Trio toured Scotland in March 1957. Brain took his camera with him and experimented with color photography. The works performed with horn included the Brahms Trio, Neumann's arrangement of Mozart's Quintet K. 407, the Beethoven Sonata, Dukas's *Villanelle*, and (only for the last concert) Strauss's Concerto No. 1 arranged for horn and piano. The trio's final appearance together was at Welwyn Garden City on March 28, 1957.[24]

The Accident

Brain said goodbye to his colleagues outside Usher Hall on the evening of August 31, 1957. He asked several if they would accompany him back to London, but for one reason or another they declined, and so he faced a long journey alone after a very tiring ten days of concerts and traveling. His journey cannot have taken him longer than usual. He had probably stopped for a rest and perhaps some sleep to break the journey. He had always done this for long journeys, whether he had a passenger with him or not. He told Neill Sanders at Usher Hall after the last concert that if he felt sleepy, he would stop and he had his coffee and sandwiches. He was always very safety-conscious.[25]

At about five to six in the morning of September 1, in poor visibility and rain, Brain's car was seen coming very fast round a bend near Wellfield Road on the Barnet Bypass. The car suddenly left the road and traveled some distance at high speed before it crashed into a tree. In an instant, Brain was killed.[26]

The loss was felt acutely by everyone who knew him, especially his wife, Yvonne, and his family, and the world of music was in shock. The crash was widely reported in the newspapers, and the world media carried many tributes and obituaries. His friend Gareth Morris remembered the shock of losing his friend on that terrible day:

> It was dreadful! Particularly extra (if you could possibly say it could be) because I was with him that night in Edinburgh. It was the last night of the Festival. I was playing in the concert and so was he. He always liked to drive, whenever he could, at night. . . .
>
> He said, "Would you like to come back in the car with me?" So I said, "No, I don't think so. I've got my hotel room and everything. It's so late I think I'll go to bed." So he said, "All right, I shall go." That's when he was killed . . . so it was a terrible shock but as it went on perhaps worse. You don't take it in immediately, do you? We did have a great lot of fun together.[27]

Brain's last concert was an all-Tchaikovsky program conducted by Eugene Ormandy. In the rehearsal, Brain had been so tired, he fell asleep. His colleague, clarinetist Basil Tschaikov, remembered that last concert: "He (Dennis) had been sitting just behind me on the platform of the Usher Hall and I remember thinking at the time how extraordinary it was that when, near the beginning of the symphony, the horn has just a single held note, by some magic Brain made it sound like a melody."[28]

Alan Civil recalled the final concert and the last conversation outside Usher Hall. He also summed up Brain's outstanding qualities and influence:

> Dennis had tremendous energy and would drive home immediately after recitals and concerts even if it meant travelling several hundred miles. At the Edinburgh Festival in 1957 we stood outside the Usher Hall after performing Tchaikovsky's Sixth Symphony with Eugene Ormandy. With the engine of his green (Triumph) sports car ticking over gently he asked me if I would care for a lift back to London. "You'll be in before the train," he said.
>
> Declining graciously, I joked that I really must check the matchstick in my first valve and lubricate the instrument with a pint of "heavy" before catching the sleeper.
>
> "See you Monday morning, Dennis."
>
> "What's on?"
>
> "Strauss, Capriccio with Sawallisch."
>
> "Anything to play?" he chuckled.
>
> "Yes," I said, "Horn concerto from beginning to end, all impossible on Monday morning even for you."

> Still chuckling he drove off on the 400-mile journey to London. His death on the Barnet by-pass some 17 miles from home that Sunday morning, September 1, 1957, tore at the heart of every musician and music-lover in the land. As a horn player par excellence he was admired by everyone—his fabulous technique and gracious sense of style were combined with a reliability that was absolute.
>
> His personality acted as a stimulus on the young generation of players who emulated his achievements, and made the public accept the horn as a major solo instrument. His charm and even a certain naïveté to the ways of the modern world were so appealing to all who had the good fortune to meet him. I feel extremely honoured to have known him and thrilled to have played the horn alongside this great artist.[29]

Leonard Brain was among the most affected by his brother's death. He received the following letter of condolence from Florence, Italy, dated September 10, 1957, from conductor Vittorio Gui:

> Some days ago, I was coming back from my rest from the mountains when I received, from John Pritchard (who was in Italy), the tragic news of your brother's death. What a terrible event! I cannot yet believe it. How did it happen? It seems it was a car accident—is it true? And coming back from Edinburgh? My God! How dangerous modern life is getting. I hope that you feel my sympathy for you at this sad moment. It is too difficult to express in words but you can understand my feelings. All my love, Vittorio Gui[30]

Tributes

Memorial concerts and tributes flowed all around the world, not least in the UK.

The Royal Philharmonic Orchestra gave one of the first tributes at the Royal Albert Hall on September 2. In each program was a note stating that Basil Cameron and the Orchestra would play the last movement of the Tchaikovsky "Pathétique" in his memory and afterwards the audience was requested to remain silent. *The Guardian* for that day carried an obituary tribute by Neville Cardus, entitled "Dennis Brain, A Distinguished Horn Player":

> Dennis Brain was unanimously regarded, here and abroad, as the most artistic and most technically gifted player of the horn of his day. It is not often that inherited gifts are improved on, but Dennis even surpassed his father in mastery of the horn and in his truly musical treatment of it. His secret was a rounded tone, never unsteady, which he could phrase in legato passages with the easeful curve of a cellist. In staccato passages he was equally felicitous;

every note, no matter how rapid the figuration, was clean with no waste of breath. The tone was concentrated yet never forced or too emphatic. His lips seemed to have the sensitive touch of a pianist's finger. . . .

Brain could arrest the ear without in any way disturbing poise and evenness of orchestral texture. He had a natural musician's ear for tone values and the blending of tone. By playing proportionately in orchestras, Dennis Brain made his genius felt.

There was no surprise when he first played as a soloist and at once took his place among instrumental masters. Whether of piano, cello, or violin. The bubbling humour of his quick notes in the Horn Concerto of Strauss is a memory to preserve. Perhaps the best of all tributes to him is that in Mozart especially he was without a peer on his instrument. The vacancy caused in English music by his death in the full flower of his art is as irreparable as it is grievous.[31]

The Times critic gave the following obituary on September 2:

Mr. Dennis Brain, the justly renowned hornist, was killed on the Barnet by-pass early on Sunday morning as he was returning from the Edinburgh Festival. . . . The son was a better player than his father, on his father's own testimony, which is saying a lot. . . .

The traditional uncertainties of the instrument never seemed to have occasioned a fluffed note from him and no technical difficulties ever appeared to cause him the slightest apprehension. He professed to have no nerves, though his playing lacked nothing in musical sensitiveness . . . and English music will be poorer by the loss of so brilliant an executant at the early age of 36.[32]

Brain had been scheduled to play Strauss's Second Concerto at Edinburgh with the Concertgebouw Orchestra, conducted by Eugene Ormandy, on September 6 at Usher Hall. *The Times* critic reported:

The Concertgebouw Orchestra will play Schubert's "Unfinished" Symphony at the Edinburgh Festival concert tomorrow as a tribute to Dennis Brain.

At a press conference at Edinburgh yesterday Mr. Eugene Ormandy, the conductor, had difficulty in controlling the emotion of his voice as he made this announcement. Several times he had to clear his throat as he said:

"We had several plans when making arrangements for altering the programme in which Dennis Brain was to have been soloist. The news of his death was so shocking we did not know what the right thing would be to do. The suggestion was made that since his life was unfinished we should play the 'Unfinished' Symphony by Schubert. We request the public not to applaud.

"We are paying our last respects to a very great artist and a very great Englishman, whose loss will be felt not only in this country, but throughout the whole world. As a soloist Dennis Brain had no peer."[33]

The *Musical Times* critic wrote:

That Dennis Brain's astonishing career should have been cut short at the age of thirty-six is both shocking and tragic. He once told me that his chief interest, apart from music, was driving fast cars; preferably, he said, abroad, "where the roads are better." It has been conjectured that he may have fallen asleep before his accident: he had, after all, been driving most of the night. But he was certainly a first-class driver, as his brother Leonard has testified.

Sir Thomas Beecham described him as a prodigy. And a friend of mine, who also played the horn with him in the R.A.F. Band during the war, called him a phenomenon, and confessed that it was almost alarming to sit near him during a performance. Whereas most horn players prepare themselves and their instrument in good time before they are called upon, Dennis Brain would sit there quite imperturbably until the time came for him to play, when he would raise the instrument to his lips only a few seconds before, and exactly the right sound would come out at the right moment, without any apparent effort. He himself said, in his unassuming way, that he had simply been lucky. He was certainly lucky to be born into the right kind of family.[34]

Gramophone, which had reviewed nearly two decades of recordings of Brain, gave the following obituary notice:

The death of Dennis Brain, at the early age of thirty-six, is an irreparable loss to music.

Like his famous father, Aubrey Brain, whose great skill and artistry he even surpassed, Dennis Brain used a French horn in preference to the German instrument and, perhaps unlike most horn players, never knew the meaning of nerves. His mastery of the entire compass, his delicacy in rapid staccato passages, were truly phenomenal, and his tone in lyrical passages was of unbelievable beauty.

I did not have the privilege of knowing him well but, whenever we met, always found him a most engaging and modest personality. We feel sure our readers would like to join us in sending our deepest sympathy to Mrs. Dennis Brain and family.[35]

Among string players, his loss was also keenly felt and *The Strad* gave the following obituary:

The tragic death of Dennis Brain was a shock to everyone connected with music. All those who had known and worked with him have been

> overwhelmed by a sense of personal loss, and it is only on calmer reflection that the extent of our national loss becomes apparent.
>
> Dennis's father, the late Aubrey Brain, had during the nineteen twenties and thirties a supreme position among horn players in this country by reason of his exquisite tone quality, his perfect command of the instrument in all its registers and his general musicianship. He was surpassed by his own son and Dennis Brain raised, or restored, his instrument to the position of a popular soloist in concerto work.
>
> The conventional terms "unique" and "irreplaceable" become in his case the quite literal truth. It is difficult to believe that his phenomenal ability can be matched either in this country or elsewhere and it is doubtful if it ever will. He died at the age of thirty-six, too young to have founded a school, but it is to be hoped that his example, while it is still fresh in the memory, will inspire others to carry on the tradition of English horn playing.[36]

He had been expected to tour in Canada later in October and November 1957 with Wilfrid Parry, and his death was keenly felt by concert-goers who had been looking forward to his first tour to Canada as a soloist. In *The Toronto Daily Star*, Peter Civil of the Irish Guards, a cousin of Alan Civil, gave a short tribute:

> The French horn with its narrow, funnel-shaped mouthpiece is one of the most difficult instruments to master and listeners have become used to accepting strained tone and occasional cracked notes even from top ranking players. With Dennis Brain, there was none of that. Everything sounded so simple in his hands. He had a complete mastery of the full range of the instrument. His tone was magnificent and his technical skill absolutely unbelievable.

Peter Civil had heard the news on September 2, during a concert with the Irish Guards in the CNE Bandshell: "it cast a pall of gloom over the Guardsmen." A performance of Mozart's Concerto K.447 (No. 3), scheduled for the evening's concert, was cancelled.[37]

At Kitchener, Ontario, CKCR Continuity Radio broadcast a program, *Tribute to Dennis Brain*, in which extracts from his recordings were played:

> Today . . . October 23rd . . . our city was scheduled to hear the greatest French Horn player in the world perform with the Kitchener-Waterloo Symphony. The world suffered a great loss when he was killed in an auto crash while driving from the Edinburgh Festival last September . . . Everywhere Dennis went he impressed his audience with his sincere, friendly personality. People who have only seen Dennis perform but once have written letters of sympathy to his brother expressing their own feeling of personal loss. . . .[38]

The two Strauss horn concertos, recorded with Wolfgang Sawallisch and the Philharmonia Orchestra in 1956, were first reviewed in November 1957 in *Gramophone* by Lionel Salter:

> This disc cannot but bring home to us the irreparable loss caused by the untimely death of Dennis Brain. Hearing again that easy, effortless virtuosity, that sensitive, musicianly phrasing and range of tone, that uncanny, unfailing assurance on a notoriously treacherous instrument, we realize that his mastery in this sphere was unique. With these performances saved for posterity, there is probably no need for anyone to record the Strauss Concertos again.[39]

In America, where Brain was to have appeared as soloist at Los Angeles in 1958, a memorial concert was given with Sinclair Lott as the soloist. It was reported in *Woodwind World*:

> A memorial concert to the artistry of the late Dennis Brain, the British horn player, was performed recently by the Los Angeles Philharmonic with Sinclair Lott as soloist. Mr. Brain was to have appeared with the Orchestra as soloist in a performance of the Richard Strauss Horn Concerto Number One. Due to his tragic and untimely end, a gap appeared in the Philharmonia's schedule. Mr. Lott agreed to take over the solo assignment if the concerto was designated a memorial to Brain. This was done, and some fine horn artistry was displayed by Mr. Lott.[40]

Joseph Eger wrote an article in May 1958 about the increasing popularity and acceptance of the horn as a solo instrument, paying tribute to Brain's supreme example: "The 'four-minute mile' for hornists has been breached. The magnificent Dennis Brain, whose tragic and untimely death last year was a severe loss to the musical world, set the pace, and now the horn is being featured as a solo instrument ever more widely."[41]

Leonard Brain decided with agreement from Yvonne Brain that the Dennis Brain Wind Ensemble would be continued in his name with Leonard as the leader. For thirteen more years, they broadcast, gave concerts, and produced a few recordings. Horn players included Neill Sanders, Barry Tuckwell, and James Brown.

The Ensemble and their new horn player, Neill Sanders, gave a memorial concert of special significance at Brain's old school, St. Paul's, in the Great Hall on November 21, 1958. The back of the program for that concert gives the following tribute:

> **Dennis Brain Memorial Scholarship Fund**
>
> The tragic and early death of Dennis Brain has come as a great shock to musicians and music lovers throughout the world. At School, Dennis Brain was very mindful of the encouragement which should be given to music

> making. We felt that the best memorial which could be raised to him would be a Music Scholarship at his School bearing his name in perpetuity. With the permission of his Executors we propose that a Fund be raised sufficient after investment to meet the cost of the musical education of one musician of promise during his time at the School.
>
> Contributions even as small as the cost of a gramophone record will be welcomed, and should be sent to: R. Dowswell, Esq., St. Paul's School, London W.14.
>
> We hope that our proposal will commend itself to all who would wish to honour the memory of a great musician, at the same time furthering the cause of music at St. Paul's School.[42]

This concert was the occasion of the first public concert performance of Poulenc's *Elégie*. It is a work that continues to be played all over the world, a lasting memorial. The program mentioned the first broadcast of the *Elégie* on February 17, 1958, with Sanders and Poulenc. The other works at this memorial concert included Jacob's Sextet, Danzi's Quintet Op. 56 No. 1, and Brain's quintet arrangement of Mozart's Adagio in F minor and major K. 594.[43]

Further recordings appeared for the first time. *Gramophone* reviewed the Hindemith Concerto, conducted by the composer, in December 1959:

> It enshrines what, as far as we know, is Dennis Brain's last record to be issued (though I believe a recording of Britten's third Canticle exists, and this should certainly be published, even if it has technical shortcomings); he is heard playing the short but superb concerto which Hindemith wrote for him.
>
> Only Dennis Brain could do justice to both the technical and interpretative demands of the piece; it seems now like a portrait of his horn-playing. The comical, faster-faster, syncopated tone of the second movement, the deep, frightening, kraken-like sounds that stir and burst upward in the coda of that movement, and the astonishing variety of cantabile and declamatory tone with which the finale variations presented him (those with the cadenza set wordlessly to some lines of evocative poetry)—all these are typical, Dennis Brain to the life. It is not a great concerto, but a very endearing one, and it is as marvelously played as it deserves.[44]

It was to be the last commercial solo recording issued, but a rich archive of BBC and other radio broadcast recordings remained, most of which, over the next half-century, have been made commercially available. The first of these was a long-playing record issued by EMI (Columbia 33CX 1687) of the last BBC broadcast of the Dennis Brain Wind Ensemble, which had been broadcast on September 5, 1957. Royalties for the record were given towards the Dennis Brain Scholarship Fund at St. Paul's School.[45]

One of his closest colleagues, pianist Denis Matthews, gave a tribute in 1974 to mark the first issue of Brain's recording of the Brahms Horn Trio, from a BBC broadcast with Max Salpeter and Cyril Preedy, together with a handful of other broadcasts:

> Dennis Brain was killed tragically in 1957 when driving himself back to London after a concert at the Edinburgh Festival. He was only thirty-six, and there may be some who suspect that sentiment has led us to exaggerate his qualities. This is not so. If the standard of horn-playing is high in Britain today it is largely due to his example. It may or may not be true that as an infant he picked up a French horn and played a scale on it, but he did seem a perfect illustration of the inheritability of instrumental gifts. . . .
>
> He could articulate pieces like "The Flight of the Bumble Bee" or Paganini's "Moto Perpetuo" at a speed that would have left most fiddlers at the starting-post, yet he had a charm of personality that was reflected in every sound he made. No-one who heard Toscanini conduct the Brahms symphonies in London in 1952 will ever forget the way Dennis Brain rose to the occasion and played those famous horn solos with an unmatchable warmth and nobility.
>
> In the post-war years, helped by recordings, Dennis Brain's international reputation was unique. He could, if he had wished, have become first horn of almost any orchestra in the world, and in London both the Philharmonia and the Royal Philharmonic competed for his presence. Composers too were inspired, and not only in Britain.... Yet Dennis remained the most approachable of people: he would approach *you*, whether an amateur horn-player seeking advice or an ordinary music-lover in search of an autograph. If one caught his eye in the orchestra it would somehow smile and convey his delight in the music.
>
> This human quality was part of his secret. To master the most notoriously intractable of instruments was one thing, but to convey—on the French horn—brilliance, charm, serenity, tragedy or humour, was phenomenal. Dennis Brain just seemed to know how music should be played. He was an ideal colleague in chamber music. During student days we would play the wind-and-piano quintets by Mozart and Beethoven, with Dennis's brother Leonard as oboist. There was the Beethoven Sonata for horn and piano, recorded during the war, and in later years Dennis Brain formed his own ensemble, exploring a large repertory.
>
> One important item, the Brahms Horn Trio, he took part in on many memorable occasions. Yet at his death there was no published recording available, which gives a special value to the present release.[46]

Clarinetist Jack Brymer was another colleague who kept alive his friend's memory and broadcast several tributes to him on BBC radio over the years. The following is from a broadcast in 1979, for Radio 3, "At Home, A Profile of Dennis Brain":

> It gives me particular pleasure to give to you now, incidents, experiences and impressions of one of my greatest personal friends of the past, the incomparable horn player, Dennis Brain. Alas, always a young man but one who brought to music something quite special and individual and who is remembered as much as a man, a delightful and modest one, as he is an artist without equal even to this day.
>
> It's no more than a plain statement of truth to say that when Dennis died in a car crash in September 1957 at the age of 36, music suffered an irreparable loss. There have been other fine horn players but there was only one Dennis Brain.[47]

Flutist Richard Adeney, who worked with him on recordings made by Karl Haas and the London Baroque Ensemble, remembered Brain in his unpublished memoirs:

> I knew Dennis quite well and liked him very much; he was pleasant and friendly, but reserved and quiet, unlike the traditional boozy and extrovert brass-player. I worked with him often and enjoyed his playing enormously, for it was full of joy and vitality. I think he'd have gone on from horn-playing to some other form of musical expression if he'd lived longer, for he was a competent organist and was interested in conducting. . . .[48]

William Waterhouse, who had played regularly as fourth bassoon in the Philharmonia from 1952 to 1953, remembered how Brain's influence left its mark later in his career. After Brain's death, he joined the Melos Ensemble, where he remembered playing next to Neill Sanders: "Whenever we got to play a Mozart Divertimento (KV334, or 247, 251, 287) as ersatz second horn I sat next to him. He'd played all these with Dennis Brain and I remember him telling me that he wanted me to phrase with him just how they used to do it. This meant curtailing the ends of certain phrases, emphasizing certain down-beats &c. . . ."[49]

The Continuing Legacy

Brain's place as the supreme executant of the horn is assured, at least until another soloist comes forward to equal his achievements, if not to surpass him. It is unlikely that such a player will be possible. He or she would need to possess the rare combination of gifts: an outstanding technical command of the compass as well as sensitivity to the nuances of anything musical; a good sense of rhythm and a balanced temperament that can overcome nerves in public performance, allied with a warm and delightful personality, able to get on with anybody.

Although Brain was the most gifted horn player in his family, he is not the last member of the family to play the instrument professionally. His niece, Tina (born 1960), youngest daughter of Audrey and Leonard Brain, specialized as fourth horn in various orchestras, including eleven years in the Hong Kong Philharmonic. She studied horn at the Royal Academy of Music with Derek Taylor, and two years prior to attending (1977–1982). The following year, she received a few lessons from Ifor James, who was a great inspiration. James was one of Aubrey Brain's most distinguished pupils in his last few years as professor at the Academy. Tina continues to love playing the harmonies in the orchestral repertoire; she freelances and teaches in Sydney, Australia.[50]

Tributes have not stopped since Dennis Brain's death. In addition to programs broadcast by the BBC and other broadcasting corporations, musicians continue to give commemorative concerts in his honor. They have included concerts at the Royal Academy of Music (July 7, 1988, November 15, 2002), Wigmore Hall (May 20, 1991), and at Queen Elizabeth Hall, South Bank and Bedford Corn Exchange, November 6 and 7, 2007. (See Chapter 11 for details of the tribute in November 2002.) The British Horn Society has given a 50th Anniversary tribute, October 27–28, 2007, at the Royal Academy of Music. Other fiftieth anniversary tributes were held at RNCM, Manchester (October 7, 2007), Nottingham's East Midlands Horn Festival (March 25, 2007), and in Japan and Switzerland on September 1.

These tributes have generated a number of works in memory of Brain, including David Matthews's *Capriccio* for two horns and strings (premiere May 20, 1991), Peter Maxwell Davies's *Fanfare—Salute to Dennis Brain* (premiere March 25, 2007, at the East Midlands Horn Festival with soloist Michael Thompson and conducted by Richard Watkins), and a piece written by Robin Wedderburn, Peter Gritton, and Ben Parry, *Sequence for Dennis Brain*. The last piece in three movements was composed by three members of the music staff at St. Paul's School, London, where it was first performed on March 9, 2008. This is how the composers described it in their program:

> *Sequence for Dennis Brain* is our collective musical response to Richard Watkins's idea to have a piece written specially to celebrate the life of Dennis Brain. . . .
>
> The pertinence of this unusual joint venture lies in the fact that we are the three full-timers responsible for the direction of music at Dennis Brain's old

> school, St. Paul's. The concept of having an optional instrumentation—two solo horns accompanied instead by organ—stems from the fact that Dennis Brain was also a fine organist. Tonight, you will hear the horn-only version.[51]

Richard Watkins, also educated at St. Paul's School, was a soloist on the March 9, 2008, tribute, performing Dukas' *Villanelle* for horn and piano, and he also conducted another performance of Peter Maxwell Davies's *Fanfare*.

Record companies, including BBC Worldwide Limited, EMI, Decca, Beulah, Dutton, Testament, Symposium and Pearl, have taken an increasing interest in making available recordings that are not only reissues but also of recordings not previously issued. Through his recordings, Brain's legacy is assured for many more years to come.

Right: ***Plate 1*** Sir Thomas Beecham Bart. C. H., and Dennis Brain, studying a score in a concert hall. Photo by Georges Maiteny. *With permission from Shirley Lady Beecham and Mrs. Siva Oke.*

Below: ***Plate 2*** Dennis Brain playing a hose-pipe in 1956, at an unknown venue. *Tony Catterick Collection. With permission from Annetta Hoffnung.*

WIGMORE HALL
WIGMORE STREET, W.1

FIRST APPEARANCE
OF THE

DENNIS BRAIN CHAMBER ORCHESTRA

WEDNESDAY, APRIL 18, at 7.30 p.m.
FRIDAY, APRIL 27, at 7.30 p.m.

THE TENTH ANNIVERSARY
OF THE

DENNIS BRAIN WIND ENSEMBLE

MONDAY, APRIL 30, at 7.30 p.m.

In aid of the AUBREY BRAIN MEMORIAL TRUST
(to promote a Wind Scholarship)

TICKETS (including Tax): Reserved 9/- and 6/-; Unreserved 3/-
(All bookable in advance)
May be obtained at the BOX OFFICE, WIGMORE HALL (Wel. 2141), usual Ticket Offices, and from
IBBS & TILLETT LTD., 124 WIGMORE STREET, W.1
Ticket Office Telephone: WELbeck 8418 Hours: 10 - 5; Saturdays 10 - 12

For Programmes P.T.O.

Plate 3 Dennis Brain Chamber Orchestra, concert bill for Wigmore Hall concerts April 18 and 27, 1956. *Tony Catterick collection.*

Above right: ***Plate 4*** Memorial concert, Town Hall, Chelsea, December 10, 1957. Inscribed by the members of the Dennis Brain Chamber Orchestra, by Peter Racine Fricker, Norman Del Mar, Benjamin Britten, and Peter Pears. *Gamble collection.*

Right: ***Plate 5*** Brain-Pougnet-Parry Trio, Auchinleck House, March 3, 1956. *With permission from Robert Hale Limited and Stephen Pettitt.*

Acknowledgments

William Lynch and I (Stephen Gamble) had both been researching Dennis Brain independently for many years when we first came in contact in July 2001 because of an advertisement I had placed in *The Horn Magazine* offering some of my collection of Brain recordings for sale. We first discussed co-authoring a biography in November of the same year and started work the following year, shortly before the Royal Academy of Music in London celebrated the eightieth year since Brain's birth with a performance on November 15, 2002 (more than a year after the actual anniversary). This was also the first occasion at which his B-flat Alexander was to be played in public since August 31, 1957.

When we began our collaboration, it soon became apparent what a wealth of new material was available, untapped and waiting to be gathered. At the end of this project, much material about Brain's career still waits to be explored. We do not know the full extent to which private enthusiasts recorded his performances off-the-air from broadcasts. We have not been able to search many music archives around the world, in part due to limited accessibility, and in part due to lack of institutional funding to catalog archive inventories. We hope that subsequent editions of this book will add to the list of known recordings.

◆ ◆ ◆

The authors agreed at the outset that this book had to be as accurate and thorough as possible. We have been driven by enthusiasm for faithfully documenting Brain's life and career. Although both authors have published articles on aspects of Brain's career, we have not previously produced a book. Many minds and hands have been involved and, wherever possible, we have sought the personal accounts of colleagues, family members, institutions, archives, and others fortunate enough to have known Brain or heard him perform. Most people approached responded enthusiastically and with generosity.

Special thanks to the following contributors who have given so generously of their time and resources, which greatly facilitated the writing of this book: above all, to Mrs. Yvonne Brain for answering many questions about her husband's life and career and for her generosity in permitting the publication of his letters and other documents. We are especially grateful to Stephen Pettitt, whose comprehensive research and documentation on Brain in the earlier years served as a constant inspiration to us, and for his permission to quote results of his research from his excellent books, *Dennis Brain: A Biography* (Hale, 1989) and *Philharmonia—Complete Discography* (Hunt, 1987). We also thank Stephen Pettitt for providing the photographs, and for generously allowing access to his private archives.

Special appreciation also to Mrs. Audrey Brain, for her hospitality and donations of family photographs and other invaluable documents.

And thanks to the following:

Gareth Morris, for spending a long day and subsequent telephone calls and correspondence, talking enthusiastically about his friendship and work with Brain and for lending photographs for illustrations. Mrs. Patricia Morris for giving her time to look up Quintet engagements in her husband's diaries and for providing concert programs and newspaper cuttings.

The authors thank Dr. Edwin Glick for writing the Foreword, promoting the project, contributing his reminiscences, reading the manuscript near its completion, and proofreading the edited chapters. His helpful suggestions, together with those of all involved with the editorial process, have significantly enhanced the format and accuracy of the book. James Diack, for writing the Preface, for his contribution to Chapter 9, and the account he gave of his lessons in Chapter 7. Farquharson Cousins for his permission to quote at length from *On Playing the Horn* in Chapter 11. Composer Ernest Tomlinson for contributing a wealth of detail about the origins and performance of his *Rhapsody and Rondo* for horn and orchestra and providing a copy of the score, bound with a postcard from Brain.

Tony Catterick, Historian of the British Horn Society, for his wholehearted support and contribution of a number of key documents, including a copy of Norman Del Mar's BBC tribute to Brain, which Del Mar had given to him. Wing Commander Gilbert A. Singleton, who brought his unique Royal Air Force scrapbook of the United States tour to York in August 2006. Photographs from this scrapbook are reproduced in Chapter 2.

Erin O'Neill, Archives Researcher at BBC Written Archives, Caversham, who greatly assisted our research by verifying numerous entries in the "program as broadcast" files and making each research visit a joy and not a chore.

◆ ◆ ◆

The authors wish to thank and acknowledge the musicians who offered their reminiscences in Chapter 8, including Richard Adeney, Colin Horsley, Roger Lord, Basil Tschaikov, Wolfgang Sawallisch, William Waterhouse, Arthur Wilson, and Denis Wick.

Horn players, professional, semi-professional, and amateur, have contributed generously to the book, including Mark Biondolillo, John Burden, Peter Civil, Andrew Clark, James Decker, James Diack, Douglas A. Elliot, Tony Fairley, Donald Froud, Bob Gibson, Anthony Halstead, Walter Hecht, Christopher Hortin, Aileen Hunter, Paul Kampen, Richard Kittrell, Richard Mackey, Norman Del Mar, Andrew McGavin, Douglas Moore, Stephen F. Pearce, Martin J. Prowse, Lucien Thevet, Michael Thompson, Barry Tuckwell, Ian Wagstaff, and Frank B. Zimmerman. Together they have offered personal perspectives of the character and career of the subject.

The authors thank Marilyn Bone Kloss, Assistant Editor of *The Horn Call*, for many months patiently editing the manuscript. William Scharnberg, Editor of *The Horn Call* and Regents Professor of Horn at the University of North Texas, assisted Marilyn and facilitated the publication of this book. Special thanks to our editor at the University of North Texas Press, Karen DeVinney.

◆ ◆ ◆

The authors acknowledge help from a number of people, including Lady Evelyn Barbirolli. Lyndon Chapman, Agent for Besson for permission to reproduce Brain's articles published by Besson & Co. (1957 and 1961) and Chris Helme, Editor of *The Conductor Magazine*, for permission to reproduce Brain's 1954 article. Dorothy Beers, for permitting the publication of the photograph in Chapter 4 of Brain, Dorothy, and Ian Beers. Tina Brain, daughter of Audrey and Leonard Brain. Mary Bean, wife of Hugh Bean, Leader of the Dennis Brain Chamber Orchestra and a colleague in the Philharmonia Orchestra, for permission to publish extracts of her husband's writings. Alan Blyth, music critic, for his reminiscence of a performance of Mahler's *Das Lied von der Erde* at the 1957 Edinburgh Festival. Theo Booy, former Stage Manager of the Radio Philharmonic, Hilversum, Holland, whose private collection of Brain recordings was always available for reference and, in particular, for the recording of Borodin's *Prince Igor Suite* (with the Overture), conducted by Walter Susskind, listed in the Discography. Julia Seiber Boyd, daughter of Mátyás Seiber, for permission to use materials pertaining to her father's biography and career.

Also: Nathan Brown, former Archivist of the Western Sound Archives, for his assistance. Timothy Brymer, for permission to use the broadcasts and writings of his father, Jack Brymer. Piers Burton-Page, for permission to quote his book *Philharmonic Concerto*. Reiko Honshoh-Chiba, widow of Kaoru Chiba, for permission to quote from her husband's interviews with Genri Nakagawa and Satoshi Kuwahara. Thanks are also due to the editors and staff of Sankei Shimbun, Ongaku-no-tomo-sha Corp, William Scharnberg the editor of *The Horn Call*, Yukihiro Okitsu, for making his translations of these articles available and to Mrs. Miyuki Nakagawa. Simon Rooks, Multi-Media Archivist, BBC Information and Archives, for permission to list Brain's BBC recordings in the Discography. Jonathan Summers, Curator of Classical Music, British Library Sound Archive, and Richard Ranft, Head of Sound Archive, permission to list all the Sound Archive's recordings of Brain in our Discography. Simon Gurney, Licensing and Synchronisation Manager, BBC Worldwide. The authors also wish to thank Denis Matthews's widow, Beryl Chempin, for her kind permission to quote his article. Oliver Condy, Editor of BBC Music Magazine for permission to quote Michael Thompson's article. James Codd, Head of BBC Written Archives and Vicky Mitchell, Copyright Executive of BBC Commercial Agency for permission to quote BBC Written Archives documents and BBC recorded programs and talk scripts of musicians. Dr. Nicholas Clark, Librarian of Britten Pears Foundation, Aldeburgh, Suffolk, for kind permission to include listings of Dennis Brain's recordings from the archives. Roy Douglas, for his reminiscence of Brain and Del Mar on film soundtracks at Denham Studios. John C. Dressler for his support of the project, suggestions, and for drawing secondary literature to the authors' notice. Gerald Gentry, for first-hand accountings of Brain in performances of the Lewis and Essex Concertos and who gave the authors information not otherwise available concerning Kenneth Essex and his Horn Concerto.

Also: Douglas Hill, University of Wisconsin-Madison and staff members for information about Sir Malcolm Arnold's Horn Concerto No. 2. Martyn Jones, Archivist of the Philharmonia, for assisting in contacting the families of past members of the orchestra. Paul Kampen, Editor of *The Horn Player*, for permission to reproduce James Decker's tribute to Brain and other articles from *The Horn Player*.

Also: Beryl Kenworthy, for the generous gift of concert programs. Yoko Kono, first wife of Kaoru Chiba, for correcting factual information about his career. Moura Martin, daughter of Terence MacDonagh, for concert programs of the Royal Philharmonic Orchestra. Robert Marshall, for his encouragement and support, and for the use of his *Dennis Brain on Record*. Amy McBeth for permitting the use of her *Discography of 78 RPM Era Recordings of the Horn*. Ann Meade-Sanders, wife of Neill Sanders, who gave her permission to quote from her husband's talk to the 1991 International Horn Society meeting and for providing a photograph. Mrs. R. Mellers for permission to quote from her husband's biography of Poulenc.

Also: Mrs. Annetta Hoffnung for permission to reproduce a letter from Brain, which she quoted in her biography of Gerard Hoffnung. Pauline Del Mar, for answering questions and providing the photograph of Norman Del Mar and Brain. Jonathan Del Mar and Tony Catterick for their permission to reproduce Norman Del Mar's BBC tribute to Dennis Brain. Dr. Graham Melville-Mason for his encouragement, introduction to a number of contributors, permission to quote his sleeve-notes and for describing a Labbaye horn in his possession, referred to in Chapter 11. The authors also wish to especially thank Shirley Lady Beecham and Mrs. Siva Oke, for permitting the publication of photographs. Special thanks are due to Norman Morrison, who has been an encouragement throughout, correcting information about Sir Thomas's recordings and contributing quotes from a talk given by Jack Brymer, which he recorded. Michael Gray, for his kind permission to quote from his research into Brain's unissued Columbia recordings and his excellent book. Lyndon Jenkins, for kind permission to quote his sleevenotes to the CD issue of Beecham's recording of Haydn's Symphony no. 40.

Also: Herbert Müller-Lupp, Archivist of the Heinrich Kaminski Gesellschaft, at Waldshut-Tiengen, Germany, for sending a copy of the score of Kaminski's *Ballade* for horn and piano. Len Mullenger, webmaster of *Musicweb International*, for use of his "List of Compositions" of Humphrey Searle. Patricia Naylor, for a copy of her concert program of the Brain-Pougnet-Parry Trio concert in Bradford. Harry Newstone, founder and conductor of the Haydn Orchestra, for his reel-to-reel copy of *The Early Horn*. Yukihiro Okitsu, author of the Brain website *An Enthusiasm for Dennis Brain*, has drawn our attention to additions to the recorded legacy, in particular the Ethel Smyth Concerto (incomplete) at the British Library Sound Archive, and the Kenneth Essex Concerto, a BBC broadcast recording of the only performance.

Also: Gunther Schuller for permitting the use of his article about Othmar Schoeck in *Woodwind* (March 1955). John Shackleton, for alerting us to Brain's visit to the Portora Royal School in 1956. David Robertson for a copy of the anonymous article that appeared in the Portora School's magazine in March 1956. Robert Northridge, Vice Principal of Portora Royal School, for his recollection of Brain's lecture-recital at the school, and for permission to quote the article. Jill Sutcliffe, daughter of Sidney "Jock" Sutcliffe, for permission to quote his letter to Martin Prowse. Lynn Weddle, daughter of Philip Farkas, and also Nancy Jordan Fako, for permission to reproduce Farkas's letter to Brain. David C. F. Wright, for permission to quote his correspondence and articles about Humphrey Searle. Jun Yamada, for the quotation of his English translation, *Kaoru Chiba on Dennis* Brain, that appeared on the Horn List.

◆ ◆ ◆

The authors would also like to thank the staff of many archives and other institutions who assisted the authors. They include staff at the BBC Written Archives (Caversham), Borthwick Institute (University of York), British Library Sound Archive, York Public Reference Library, West Deutsche Rundfunk (Cologne), British Library Sound Archive (London), the International Horn Society, the British Horn Society, the Hoover Institution Library at Stanford University (California), Martin Luther King Library (San Jose, California), Stanford Music Library and Archive of Recorded Sound—The Braun Music Center (Stanford, California), and Scottish Screen Archives (Glasgow). We thank the following archivists and archives for their assistance: Irene Strong, for information about Brain's BBC transcription service recordings preserved by Radio New Zealand Archives, Christchurch; Susanne Paulukat and staff of Deutschland Radio Kultur (Berlin); Jörg Wyrschowy, Deutsches Rundfunkarchiv, Frankfurt; Susanne Schiek-Ernau, SWR (Stuttgart), Alexander Eisenreich, Dua/ Schallarchiv, Norddeutscher Rundfunk, Hamburg; Ruurd Blom, the Institut Beeld en Geluid, Holland. Joanna Hughes, EMI Archives, Hayes, Middlesex. Matthew A. Harris, Editor in Chief of *The Kentucky Kernel*, and staff of University of Kentucky, Yuien Chin and Kevin Bianchi at NBC News Archives.

◆ ◆ ◆

Discography

Introduction

The intent of this discography is to give as comprehensive a listing of Brain's solo and chamber recordings as possible, together with a selection of orchestral recordings, and to reveal newly discovered recordings that have not been featured in any previously published discography. It includes quotations from *The Gramophone*, *Monthly Musical Record*, *Radio Times*, and other sources, but it is not a complete list of every recording that Brain is known to have made.

New works include six solo works for horn and orchestra, two for horn, violin, and piano, three for wind quintet, eight chamber music works for various combinations, fourteen orchestral works, five performances in international archives collections (solo and chamber works), and two of film media. The new items are marked with an asterisk (*).

This list includes commercial recordings (published and unpublished) as well as radio archive recordings and off-the-air recordings. Matrix numbers for recording takes are given only if a recording is unpublished, for example, the British Library Sound Archive takes of the Britten Serenade. Unpublished and incomplete Columbia HMV and EMI recordings are listed even though they may not all be preserved by EMI Archives at Hayes, Middlesex, England. The authors do not have matrices for all these unpublished recordings. Section I lists those recordings referred to or discussed in detail in the chapters of this book as well as new items not listed in any previous Brain discography.

Section II lists international archives with all applicable known recordings in each archive. Many of Brain's recordings are no longer available commercially and are found only through second-hand record dealers or from these archives. One exception is the Stanford Library of Recorded Sound, which has the holdings of the former Western Sound Archive. Stanford University has not yet completed work on a listening and transcription service, which, when available, will be invaluable for the study of their substantial Brain holdings. Many of these recordings originate from the BBC (Information and Archives) and are listed under that heading; only those recordings no longer available at the BBC are listed under the Stanford collection.

Robert Marshall's book *Dennis Brain on Record* lists Brain's orchestral recordings comprehensively (though not exhaustively). This discography focuses on a few orchestral recordings that are especially soloistic and where Brain can easily be identified. Where possible, booking sheets have been used to confirm his presence or absence.

Little documentation exists for Brain's work with the London Chamber Orchestra, also occasionally known as the London Chamber Players. Recordings are represented by only four works, all conducted by Anthony Bernard.

Although Brain was principal horn of several other orchestras, the numerous recordings with them remain obscure and require further investigation, which is beyond the scope of this book. They include recordings with the New London Orchestra, conducted by Alec Sherman, and the RAF Symphony Orchestra, conducted by Wing Commander O'Donnell during wartime. Many of the RAF Symphony Orchestra recordings do not have exposed solos but a few are included because otherwise little documentation exists for this orchestra during Brain's tenure.

Section III lists the few films with Brain recording, including modern reissues. This does not include the enormous quantity of material in the form of music for film sound-tracks recorded at various British film studios, including Gainsborough Pictures, Ealing, Denham, etc., with the National Symphony Orchestra, Philharmonia Orchestra, and the Royal Philharmonic Orchestra.

Key to Abbreviations

45 rpm	A record that plays at 45 revolutions per minute. Sometimes these were issued in "extended play" format, including the London Chamber Orchestra's recording of Faure's Pavane on EMI, 7EP 7701. See Discography I. 7. *London Chamber Orchestra.*
78 rpm	Shellac 10-inch or 12-inch record, that plays at 78 revolutions per minute. Several modern manufacturers make a turntable that will play 78 rpm discs, as part of Hi Fi systems but it is a specialist market and readers are advised to consult specialist dealers to obtain the best equipment to play these records. Not all recordings of Brain issued on 78 rpm are available on compact disc and, in some instances, they are not otherwise obtainable. Second-hand dealers are still a source of recordings.
Alt.	Contralto
AR	Abbey Road Studios, London
B	Bass
Bsn	Bassoon
b/c	Broadcast
BBC	BBC Information and Archives
BBC SO	BBC Symphony Orchestra
BBC TS	BBC Transcription Service
BPL	Britten-Pears Library, Snape Maltings, Aldeburgh, Suffolk, England (Britten-Pears Foundation)
Brain source file	RCONT1, 910, Aubrey, Leonard and Dennis Brain Source File, BBC Written Archives, Caversham, England.
C	Clarinet
CA	Cor Anglais
Cat. No.	Catalogue Number
CHARM	AHRC Research Centre for History and Analysis of Recorded Music; a partnership between Royal Holloway College, University of London (host), King's College, London, and University of Sheffield. The entries in this listing are Columbia recording (HMV) researched by Michael Gray.
Cond.	Conductor

DB	Double Bass
DBWE	Dennis Brain Wind Ensemble (Gareth Morris, Leonard Brain, Stephen Waters, Dennis Brain, Cecil James). If different players than these, they are named.
DRA	Stiftung Deutsches Rundfunkarchiv, Frankfurt, Berttramstraße 8, D-60320 Frankfurt am Main, Germany; it does not preserve recordings but has a database listing Brain's recordings in various German archives.
DRK	Radio in the American Sector (RIAS), now held in the archives of Deutschlandradio Kultur, Berlin
EMI Classics 2008	4-CD set Dennis Brain The Horn Player 50999 2 060102 7 (mono), published in 2008. This set includes a large number of Brain's EMI recordings
F	Flute
FBP	First broadcast performance
FBBP	First British broadcast performance (Northern Ireland, Scotland, England, or Wales)
FP	First performance
FPP	First public performance
FEBP	First English broadcast performance
GOS	General Overseas Service broadcast recording
H, 1stH, 2ndH	Horn, First Horn, Second Horn
Hp	Harp
HS	BBC Home Service broadcast
IGI 370	Discocorp long-player (USA, 1979), Educational Media Associates, Berkeley, California. The Dennis Brain Wind Ensemble, Aldeburgh Festival recital with Benjamin Britten (piano), June 22, 1955, omitting Britten's Canticle III, which remains unpublished. This record included Beethoven's Sonata with Conrad Hansen, recorded for "Radio in the American Sector" Berlin, April 20, 1950
KH London	Kingsway Hall, London
LBE	London Baroque Ensemble
Leader	Concertmaster
Leech no or nos.	Catalogue numbers assigned by Kenneth Leech, who made the recordings off-the-air from radio broadcasts, given to the British Library Sound Archive
LtP	BBC Light Programme
LSO	London Symphony Orchestra
M-S	Mezzo-soprano
NDR	Norddeutscher Rundfunk (North German Radio), Rothenbaumchausee 132, D-20149 Hamburg, Germany
O	Oboe
ORF	Östereichischer Rundfunk
P	Piano

"P as B"	Program as broadcast by the BBC in manuscript files at BBC Written Archives, Caversham. Each service (Third Program, Home, General Overseas, etc.) is bound in volumes chronologically. These files are unique and are the best evidence for the content of actual broadcasts.
Pre-rec	Pre-recording date of a broadcast
RCONT1	Contributors to BBC broadcasts. Each correspondence file has "RCONT1" in its title
RZN	Radio New Zealand, Christchurch
S	Soprano
SDR	Süddeutscher Rundfunk (South German Radio), Stuttgart; now amalgamated with SWR.
SLRS	Stanford Library of Recorded Sound, Stanford University
SWR	Südwestrundfunk (Southwest German Radio) Archives, Neckarstraße 230, D-70190 Stuttgart, Germany (formerly Südwestfunk Archives)
T	Tenor
TP	BBC Third Programme
Tpt	Trumpet
V	Violin
Va	Viola
VC	Cello
UK	Recording issued in United Kingdom
UWM BC	University of Wisconsin-Madison, Blake Collection
WAC	BBC Written Archives, Caversham, England
WDR	West Deutscher Rundfunk (West German Radio), Cologne
WSA	Western Sound Archives, now at Stanford Archive of Recorded Sound, Stanford University, California

I. Selected Discography

1. Solo Horn With Orchestra

Bowen: Concerto for Horn and Strings op. 150. FP, Pre-rec. June 24, 1956; HS, July 1, 1956, 2:30 p.m. Welbeck Orchestra, cond. Miles. Private recording. Unpublished.[1]

Britten: Serenade for Tenor, Horn and Strings op. 31. Pears (T), Boyd Neel String Orchestra, cond. Britten. May 25, 1944, October 8, 1944. UK: 78 rpm: Decca K 1151-3; UK: LP: Decca Eclipse ECM 814; Decca 417 183-1 (1986). UK: CD: Pearl GEMM CD 9177 (1995)[2]

***Britten: Serenade for Tenor, Horn and Strings op. 31.** May 25, 1944. Unpublished takes. Pears (T), Boyd Neel Orchestra, cond. Britten. British Library Sound Archive. The following is a mixture of published and unpublished sides that have been placed on a CD for listening purposes. Unpublished takes were given by the Britten-Pears Foundation. Published sides are underlined and matrix numbers omitted.[3]

Prologue. Pastorale (Cotton) Part 1. October 8, 1944. K 1151

AR 8462-2. Prologue. Pastorale (Cotton) Part 2 "And now on benches all are sat . . ." May 25, 1944.

Nocturne (Tennyson) "The splendour falls on castle walls . . ." May 25, 1944. K 1151

AR 8462-4. Pastorale (Cotton) "And now on benches all are sat . . ." May 25, 1944

AR 8463-1. Elegy (Blake) "O rose thou art sick . . ." May 25, 1944

Elegy (Blake) May 25, 1944. K 1152

AR 8464-1. Dirge (Anonymous 15th-century) "This ay night every night and all." May 25, 1944

AR 8464-2. Dirge (Anonymous 15th-century) "This ay night every night and all." May 25, 1944

Dirge (Anonymous 15th-century) "This ay night every night and all." October 8, 1944. K.1152

Hymn (Ben Jonson); Sonnet (Keats). Part 1. May 25, 1944 K 1153

AR 8466-1. Sonnet (Keats). Part 2. Epilogue. May 25, 1944

Sonnet (Keats). Part 2. Epilogue. Published side. October 8, 1944. K 1153

***Essex: Horn Concerto (1948). FBP.** BBC Scottish Orchestra, cond. Gentry. TP, April 20, 1955, 6–7 p.m. Collections: BBC cat. no. MX40; T 39817; British Library Sound Archive call nos. 1CDR0000565 BD2; 2CDR001298; cat. no. 25A1984. Unpublished; whereabouts of the manuscript score unknown. Listed among the works from Dennis Brain's music library (Chapter 6 and Appendix A). See also Chapter 10.[4]

Hindemith: Concerto for Horn and Orchestra (1949). Philharmonia Orchestra, cond. Hindemith. KH, London, November 19, 1956. UK: LP: Columbia 33CX 1676; RLS 7701; US: LP: Angel S 35491 (stereo); UK: CD: EMI CDC 747834 2; EMI Classics 7243 5 67782 2 1 (2002), tracks 7-9; EMI classics 2008, CD 3, track 7-9. Collections: British Library Sound Archive call no. 1LP000509 D1 BD2; 1CD0296494 SEQ5.[5]

Hindemith: Concerto for Horn and Orchestra (1949). Incomplete recording. Philharmonia Orchestra, cond. Klemperer. KH, London, October 7–8, 1954. Columbia EMI, unpublished.[6]

Jacob: Concerto for Horn and Strings. Riddick String Orchestra, cond. Riddick. TP, July 3, 1951, 6:50 p.m. Private recording. Unpublished.[7]

Lewis: Concerto for Horn and String Orchestra. BBC Midland Orchestra, cond. Gentry. HS, January 18, 1957, 3:30 p.m. Private recording. Unpublished.[8]

Schoeck: Horn Concerto op. 65 (1951). Zürich Tohnhalle, live, May 4, 1956. Collegium Musicum, Zürich. cond. Sacher. Radio Swiss Archives, Basel. Austria: CD: Hans Pizka HPE CD 02 (1994), tracks 10–12; Switzerland: CD: Jecklin-Musikhaus, CH-8024, Zürich JD 715-2 (1997, June 2004).[9]

Brain gave a performance at the Edinburgh Festival, September 3, 1954, also with Collegium Musicum, Zürich, conducted by Sacher. This was broadcast live on the Home Service.[10]

Seiber: Notturno for Horn and Strings. LSO, cond. Cameron. Royal Albert Hall Promenade concert, July 29, 1955. Live concert. TP, July 29, 1955, 9.15–9.55 (Part 2 of the concert). Private recording. Italy: CD: ASDisc 356 (1991), track 9; Legend LGD 192 (1994), track 9.[11]

***Smyth: Concerto for Violin and Horn.** Philharmonic Hall, Liverpool. Grinke (V), Liverpool Philharmonic Orchestra, cond. Goossens. TP, November 5, 1946, 6:45 p.m. Part 1 of the concert. Incomplete recording made off the air from the original transmission. British Library Sound Archive list nos. 30B 5872-5874; C738/325-327. Leech collection nos.1209–1211; dubbing nos. T11571WR; T11573WR; call no. 2CDR0000482 BD2.[12]

***Strauss: Concerto No. 1 in E Flat Major for Horn and Orchestra op. 11.** HS, 3 p.m., Maida Vale Studio No. 1, March 18, 1956. Concert Hour. BBC SO, cond. Boult. Simultaneous broadcast on SB/OB Television with an invited audience. Private recording. Unpublished. No BBC recording was made.[13]

Strauss: Concerto No. 1 in E Flat Major for Horn and Orchestra op. 11. Radion sinfoniaorkesteri, cond. Nils-Fougstedt. Studio recording, Heslinki, October 5, 1956. Radio Finland Archives, Helsinki. Unpublished.[14]

Strauss: Concerto No. 2 in E-flat major for Horn and Orchestra (1942). Incomplete recording. KH London, September 23–24, 1947. Matrix nos. CAX 10051, 10052, 10053. Philharmonia Orchestra, cond. Galliera. EMI Columbia unpublished.[15]

Strauss: Concerto No. 2 in E-flat major for Horn and Orchestra (1942). BBC Welsh Orchestra, cond. Jenkins. Lt.P, February 5, 1951, 12:45–1:45 p.m. *Concert Hour.* Italy: CD: ASDisc356 (1991), track 7; Legend LGD 192 (1994), track 7; Andromeda ANDRCD 5065 (2006), CD2 tracks1–3.[16]

***Tomlinson:** Romance and Rondo for Horn and Orchestra. Complete rehearsal recording. Royal Festival Hall, June 22, 1957. Private recording. Not to be confused with "rehearsal sequences" recorded from the same rehearsal that day.

***Tomlinson: Romance and Rondo for Horn and Orchestra.** BBC Commission. BBC Concert Orchestra), cond. Tomlinson. Rehearsal sequences. Royal Festival Hall, June 22, 1957. Private recording.[17]

2. Horn and Piano

Fricker: Sonata. Parry. TP, August 1, 1956, 10:45 p.m. Private recording. Not preserved by the BBC, although *Radio Times* indicates it was recorded. Pettitt and Marshall give August 4 as the broadcast date, but both *Radio Times* and the P as B file state it was the first. Meckna briefly compared this recording and one with Ifor James.[18]

3. Horn, Violin, and Piano

***Brahms: Trio in E-flat op. 40.** Incomplete. Fragment of the first movement only. Blech and Matthews. Columbia unpublished. Abbey Road, Studio no. 3, January 5, 1944. Matrix no. CAX 9147.[19]

***Brahms: Trio in E-flat op. 40.** Complete. Matrices destroyed in 1955. Grumiaux and Matthews. Columbia unpublished, November 20, 1947. Matrix nos. CAX 10127, 10128, 10129, 10130, 10131, 10132, 10133, 10134.[20]

4. Horn, Piano, and Voice

Britten: Canticle III Still Falls the Rain—The Raids, 1940, Night and Dawn, op. 55. FBP. Pears (T), Britten (P). Aldeburgh Festival, June 22, 1955. TP, BBC TS. Introduction by Britten. Collection: WSA no. 695D. Unpublished. SLRS appears to be the only public collection with a copy of this first broadcast performance.[21]

5. Wind Quintet

Fricker: Quintet op. 5. DBWE. Usher Hall, Edinburgh, HS live August 24, 1957, 11:00–11:40 a.m. UK: CD: BBC Legends BBCL 4192-2 (2006), tracks 17–19.[22]

***Hindemith: Kleine Kammermusik op. 24 no. 2.** DBWE. Salzburg Festival, Mozarteum, July 30, 1957. Collection: Östereichischer Rundfunk (ORF). RM 50/3. This recording (and the rest of the recordings of the recital) was discovered by Lynch. For the other works on this recital, see next entry and Poulenc Sextet and Mozart Quintet K.452 in section 6.

***Mozart: arr. Baines: Divertimento No. 15 in B-flat K.270.** DBWE. Salzburg Festival, Mozarteum, July 30, 1957. Collection: Östereichischer Rundfunk (ORF). RM 50/2.

***Williams: Incidental music, Open House.** Recording takes for the sound track of British Transport Films, *Open House*, 1951, a short film about the stately homes of Britain. Morris (F), James (O), Walton (C), James (Bsn). Archives of British Transport Museum, Covent Garden, London. UK: CD: Beulah *The World of Dennis Brain* 1PD35 (released June 2009). This first issue is not the sound track from the *Open House* film but the takes from the British Transport Film archives.

The film (now unavailable) has been issued on VHS video, "Yesterday's Britain No. 24 London's Country." Copyright, London Transport Museum, 1997. This video contains three British Transport Films, including *Open House*.

6. Chamber Music with Other Combinations

Beethoven: Viennese Dances WoO 17 (1819). LBE, cond. Haas. Adeney, Solomon (F), Brymer, Waters (C), James (Bsn), Sanders (2nd H). St. Gabriel's Church, Cricklewood, London NW2, 9 a.m.–noon, May 17, 1957. UK: LP: Pye CEC 32027. Only five of the eleven dances were recorded: no. 2 in B-flat, no. 1 Waltz in E-flat, no. 3 Waltz in E-flat, no. 10, Waltz in D, no. 11, Waltz in D. UK: CD EMI CDM 7 64135-2 (stereo) 1991.[23]

Dittersdorf: Sinfonia Concertante in D major for Double-Bass and Viola. Soloists: J. W. Merrett (DB) and Riddle (Va); Sutcliffe and James (O), Sanders (2nd H) and other unnamed players, LBE, cond. Haas. AR, October 26, 1953, 10 a.m.–1 p.m. UK: LP: EMI Parlophone PMC 1078.[24]

***Dohnanyi: Sextet in C major for Piano, Clarinet, Horn and Strings op. 37.** FEBP. Loveridge (P), Thurston (C), Philharmonic String Trio (Martin, V; Gilbert, Va; Whitehead, VC). TP, December 30, 1949, 10:56 p.m. Collection: British Library Sound Archive list nos. 30B 6289, 6290, 6291; C 738, C 762-764; Leech nos. 1378-80; dubbing no. T11741WR. Recording incomplete. 3 Nitrate discs, 6 sides, 30 cm. 78 rpm. Duration: 30:50.[25]

***Enesco, Dixtuor in D major op. 14 (1906)** for two flutes, oboe, cor anglais, two clarinets, two horns, and two bassoons. Edition: Enoch. London Wind Players, cond. Blech. FEBP. TP, April 11, 1951, 6:00–6:27 ½ p.m. Collection: British Library Sound Archive, call no. T 9754W; cat. no. 30B1281. Complete recording from a repeat broadcast on August 19, 1951.[26]

***Fibich: Quintet for clarinet, horn, violin, cello and piano op. 42 in D.** Thurston (C), Wilson (V), Whitehead (VC), Fuchsova (P). TP, February 1, 1948, 6:30–7:10 p.m. UK: CD: Symposium 1259 (2003).[27]

Haydn: Concert Trio Pietà di Mé, benigni Dei, Hob. 25b:5 (1791). FBP. Sutherland and Cantelo (S), Nilsson (T), Graeme (CA), Alexandra (Bsn), Goldsbrough Orchestra, cond. Mackerras. TP December 17, 1956, 8:42 p.m. Pre-rec. live December 16, 1956. Portugal: CD: Bella Voce BLV107 001 (1998).[28]

***Haydn: Piano Concerto in D Hob. 18:11.** Scherzer (P), LBE Haas. AR, August 19–20, 1953. UK: LP: EMI Parlophone PMC 1078. British Library Sound Archive, call no. 1LP0110425; 2LP0062233.

***Hindemith: Sonata for Four Horns.** Brain. Columbia EMI unissued, October 15, 1953.[29]

Mozart: Divertimento no. 3 in E-flat, K.166. London Wind Players, cond. Blech. UK: 78rpm Decca AK 2225-2226. September 27, 1946.

Side-filler: **Mozart: Serenade No. 11 in E-flat K.375:** Minuet and Trio only. Played by the "London Symphony Players" cond. Blech. September 28, 1946. AK 2225.[30]

***Mozart: Quintet for piano and winds K.452.** Four members of DBWE and Parry (P). Salzburg Festival, Mozarteum, July 30, 1957. Collection: ORF. PM 50/1005.

***Poulenc: Sextet for piano and winds.** DBWE. Salzburg Festival, Mozarteum, 30 July 57. Collection: Östereichischer Rundfunk (ORF). PM 50/10006.

***Strauss: Symphony in E-flat for sixteen wind instruments, *Fröliche Werkstatt* op. posth. (composed 1943–45).** FEBP. TP, January 28, 1953, 8:20–9:00 p.m. LBE cond. Karl Haas. Recording incomplete. The horn players in the broadcast, in addition to Brain, were Beers, Burden, and Cursue. The same players with Haas gave the first performance in England on January 23 at Royal Festival Hall and recorded with Haas on January 29–30, 1953.[31]

7. Selected Orchestral Recordings

London Chamber Orchestra/ London Chamber Players[32]

Berkeley: Divertimento for Orchestra in B-flat major op.18. First recording. London Chamber Orchestra. UK: 78rpm: Decca K 1882-83. March 25, 1948.[33]

***Bowyer: *Look to This Day* a song for chorus, horn and strings.** FP. London Chamber Players and London Chamber Singers. TP, February 4, 1951, 10:20–10:55 p.m. Levy's Recording Studio, London. A single disc, 2 sides. British Library Sound Archive list no. 30B 4923; dubbing no.NP10682WR. Not listed in the Brain source file at BBC WAC.

Brain is mentioned as the horn soloist by the BBC announcer. The horn plays a phrase at the beginning and the same phrase is repeated at the end. Harold Rutland gives the few facts that are known about this composer:

> After Butterworth's delicate pastel, "The Banks of Green Willow," we shall be able to hear, for the first time, "Look to this Day," for chorus, horn and strings, by R. W. Bowyer, who was a pupil and friend of Butterworth and who died in 1943 when he was in his middle-forties. Like Butterworth, he served in the First World War, in which he was twice wounded; he lived most of his life in Staffordshire, and taught at Cranleigh. He had an abiding love of the English countryside, and a great deal that he wrote took the form of music for plays and pageants. "Look to this Day" is a setting of some inspiring words translated from the Sanskrit.[34]

***Fauré: Fantasie for piano and orchestra.** Fevrier, London Chamber Orchestra. Parts of movements are missing. TP, January 18, 1949, 10:10–11:10 p.m. Recorded Productions of London Ltd. 2 discs, 4 sides, 78 rpm. British Library Sound Archive call no. 33C 115-116; dubbing no. T11448WR, tracks R3, R4.[35]

***Fauré: Pavane op. 50 (1887).** With Morris (F) and Chorus. UK: 78rpm: HMV C 4197; 45 rpm: 7EP 7701. October 16, 1952.[36]

London Mozart Players[37]

Haydn: Symphony No. 49 in F major Hob. 1:49 (1768) "La passione." April 21, 1952. UK: LP: Decca LXT 2753.[38]

Mozart: Symphony No. 40 in G Minor K.550. December 22, 1952. UK: LP: HMV CLP 1009; US: LP: RCA Victor LBC 1069.[39]

National Symphony Orchestra

Tchaikovsky: Symphony No. 5 in E Minor op. 64. Cond. Beer. KH, London, June 8, 1944. UK: 78 rpm: Decca K 1032-36. Andante only: UK: CD: Beulah *The World of Dennis Brain*, 1PD35, track 1.[40]

In addition to the published sides, an unpublished take of the second movement exists:

AR-8430-1-2. Andante cantabile Part 1, May 12, 1944

AR-8431-1-2. Andante cantabile Part 2, May 12, 1944

AR-8432-1-2. Andante cantabile Part 3, May 12, 1944[41]

Thomas: Mignon Overture (1866). Cond. Fistoulari. September 7, 1945. UK: 78 rpm: Decca K1166. Yukihiro Okitsu, Japan: CD: *A Resurrection of Dennis Brain* (2002).[42]

Wagner: Götterdämmerung—Siegfried's Rhine Journey. Cond. Beer. KH, London, October 12, 1944. UK: 78 rpm: Decca K 1284. A full frequency range recording. CD: Dutton CDK 1200 (1995), track 9. Duration: 9:15.[43]

Weber: Oberon Overture J. 306 (1826). Cond. Braithwaite. March 22, 1945. UK: 78 rpm: Decca K 1322. Japan: CD: *A Resurrection of Dennis Brain* (2002).[44]

Philharmonia Orchestra

Bach: Mass in B Minor BWV 232: Quoniam tu solus sanctus. AR, July 16, 1953. Rehfuss (B). Cond. Karajan UK: LP: 33CX 1121-23; EMI RLS 746; EMI 29 09743; World Records T 854-856; CD: US: Angel CHS 763505-2; UK: CHS 567207-2. Archive collection: British Library Sound Archive call no. 1LP014099501.[45]

Beethoven: Fidelio Op.72c (1814): Abscheulicher—Komm Hoffnung. Schwarzkopf (S). Cond. Karajan. Watford Town Hall, September 20, 1954. UK: LP: Columbia 33CX 1266; RLS 7715; Japan: LP: Toshiba EAC 37001-19; UK: CD: EMI CDH 763201-2 (1990).[46]

Beethoven: Symphony No. 3 "Eroica" in E-flat major op. 55. Cond. Karajan. KH, London, November 20–22, December 1, 1952. UK: LP: Columbia 33CX 1046; EMI SLS 5053; World Records SM 143-149; Japan: LP: Toshiba EAC 37001-19; UK: CD: EMI CDM 762 2112; EMI CDM 763 3112; EMI CMS 763310-2.[47]

Beethoven: Symphony No. 3 "Eroica" in E-flat major op. 55. Cond. Klemperer. KH, London, October 3–4, December 17, 1955. UK: LP: Columbia 33CX 1346; EMI SLS 873; EMI EX 29 04573; UK: CD: EMI CDM 763868-2; CDM 763855-2.[48]

Beethoven: Symphony No. 5 in C Minor op. 67. Cond. Kubelik. Usher Hall, Edinburgh, August 30, 1957. Edinburgh International Festival. BBC live TP, August 30, 1957. CD: UK: Testament SBT 1421.[49]

Beethoven: Symphony No. 6 in F Major op. 68 "Pastoral." Cond. Karajan. KH, London, July 9-10, 1953. UK: LP: Columbia 33CX 1124; EMI SLS 5053; World Records SM 143-149; Japan: LP: Toshiba EAC 37001-19; UK: CD: EMI CDM 763 3142; EMI CMS 763310-2.[50]

Beethoven: Symphony No. 9 in D minor op. 125 "Choral." Schwarzkopf (S), Cavelti (M-S), Häfliger (T), Edelmann (B), Lucerne Festival Chorus. Cond. Furtwängler. Kunsthaus Lucerne. Live recording. August 22, 1954. Italy: LP: Fonit Cetra LO 530; LP: Discocorp RR 390; Seven Seas K35Y 41; Classica COLSMH 34006; CD: FURT 1003; FURT 1054-7.[51]

Beethoven: Symphony No. 9 in D minor op. 125 "Choral." Schwarzkopf (S), Höffgen (Alt.), Häfliger (T), Edelmann (B), Vienna Singverein, Vienna Gessellschaft der Musikfreunde. Cond. Karajan. Musikvereinsaal, Vienna, July 24, 25, 27, 28, and 29, 1955. UK: LP: Columbia 33CX 1391-92; EMI SLS 5053; World Records SM 143-149; Japan: LP: Toshiba EAC 37001-19; CD: EMI CMS 763310-2; EMI CDM 763315-2.[52]

Brain is heard playing the Fourth Horn solo in the *Adagio*. Speaking to music critic C. B. Rees after a concert of Seiber's *Notturno* at Royal Albert Hall, July 29, 1955, Brain said he'd just got back from Vienna where he was with the Philharmonia recording Beethoven's "Choral" Symphony.[53]

Bizet: Carmen: Je dis que rien ne m'épouvante. Steber (S). Cond. Susskind. AR, September 17, 1947. UK: 78 rpm: DB 6514; LP: EMI EX 769741-1; US: LP: RCA Victor 60251 2 RG; UK: CD: CHS 769741-2; BMG GD 60521.[54]

Borodin: In the Steppes of Central Asia op. 7 (1880). Cond. Lambert. KH London, January 24, 1946. UK: 78 rpm: Columbia DX 1449.[55]

Borodin: In the Steppes of Central Asia op. 7 (1880). Cond. Collingwood. AR, March 9, 1953. UK: 78 rpm: Columbia DX 1879.[56]

Borodin arr. Glazunov: Prince Igor Overture. Cond. Dobrowen. AR, May 18, 26–28, 1949. UK: 78 rpm: HMV C 3979-3980; US: LP: RCA Victor LBC 1026; UK: CD: EMI CZS 569743-2.[57]

The recording demonstrates Brain's cantabile playing. The conductor slowed down the tempo just prior to the horn's entry.

Borodin: Prince Igor: Suite. Overture; Polovtsian March, Act 3, Polovtsian Dances, Act 2. Cond. Susskind. KH, London, June 25, September 1, 1952. UK: LP: Parlophone PMD 1023 (ten-inch LP).[58]

Borodin: Symphony No. 1 in E-flat major (1867). Cond. Galliera. AR, April 6–8, 1955. UK: LP: Columbia 33CX 1356; EMI XLP 30107. US: LP: Angel 35346. Edmund Chapman played first horn at the session on April 6.[59]

Borodin: Symphony No. 2 in B minor (1876). Cond. Malko. AR, February 19, 23, March 4, 1948. UK: 78 rpm: HMV C 3971-3974; auto C 7781-7784; US: LP: RCA Victor LBC 1024.[60]

Borodin: Symphony No. 2 in B minor (1876). Cond. Kletzki. KH London, February 3, 1954. UK: LP: Columbia 33CX 1167. UK: CD: Testament SBT 1048; CZS 575121-2.[61]

Borodin: Symphony No. 2 in B minor (1876). Cond. Malko. KH, London, September 23, 1955. UK: LP: HMV CLP 1075; EMI Concert Classics (mono) XLP 30010; UK: CD: EMI CZS 575121-2.[62]

Borodin arr. Tcherepnin: Nocturne (String Quartet No. 2). Cond Fistoulari. KH, London, July 27, 1956, March 14, 1957. UK: LP: HMV ALP 1582; XLP 30119; SXLP 30119; US: LP: Capitol G 7119.[63]

Brahms: Haydn Variations, op. 56a. Cond. Toscanini. Royal Festival Hall, October 1, 1952. TP live. LP: LO 511; Doc 52; THS 65027-30; Hunt Productions DC 524; UK: CD: Testament SBT 3167 (CD2 of 3), tracks 6-15.[64]

Brahms: Haydn Variations, op. 56a. Cond. Karajan. KH, London, May 17–18, 1955. UK: LP: Columbia 33CX 1349 (with Schubert Symphony No. 8); Japan: LP: Toshiba EAC 37001-19. CD: Angel CMS 763456-2.[65]

Brahms: Piano Concerto no. 1 in D minor op. 15. Solomon. Cond. Kubelik. KH, London, September 3–5, 1952. UK: LP: HMV ALP 1172; EMI 1C 147 03081/2M; EMI SLS 5094: UK: CD: Testament SBT 1041.[66]

Brahms: Piano Concerto No. 2 in B Flat Major op. 83. Solomon. Cond. Dobrowen. AR, April 29-30, May 1, 1947. UK: 78 rpm: HMV C 3610-3615 (auto: C 7688-7693). UK: LP: EMI XLP 30093; EMI SLS 5094; EMI 1C 147 03081-03082M. UK: CD: Testament SBT 1042.[67]

Brahms: Symphony No. 1 in C Minor op. 68. Cond. Karajan. KH, London, May 5, 7, July 26, 28, 31, 1952. UK: LP: Columbia 33CX 1053; Japan: LP: Toshiba EAC 37020-38; CD: Angel CMS 763456-2.[68]

Brahms: Symphony No. 1 in C Minor op. 68. Cond. Toscanini. Royal Festival Hall concert, September 29, 1952. TP live. Italy: LP: Toscanini Society ATS 1030-33; Turnabout THS 65027-30; Fonit Cetra LO 511; Hunt Productions: DC 524; Italy: CD: Fonit Cetra CDE 1016; UK: CD (3 CD set): SBT 3167 (2000).

Brahms: Symphony No. 1 in C Minor op. 68. Cond. Cantelli. KH, London, May 21–22, 1953. UK: LP: HMV ALP 1152; EMI "Encore" ENC 116; EMI XLP 30023; World Records SH 314; UK: CD: Testament SBT 1012.[69]

Brahms: Symphony No. 1 in C Minor op. 68. Cond. Klemperer. KH, London, October 29, 31, 1956, March 28, 1957. UK: LP: Columbia 33CX 1504; Columbia SAX 2262; EMI ASD 2705; EMI SLS 804; EMI SXLP 30217; UK: CD: EMI CDH 769651-2; EMI CDM 567029-2.[70]

Civil's letter (quoted in Chapter 4) mentioned that Brain played first in Brahms Symphony no. 1 and 2 with Klemperer and Civil played first in the other two symphonies with the same conductor.[71]

Brahms: Symphony No. 2 in D Major op. 73. Cond. Toscanini. Royal Festival Hall concert, September 29, 1952. TP live. Italy: LP: Toscanini Society ATS 1030-33; Turnabout THS 65027-30; Fonit Cetra LO 511; Hunt Productions: DC 524; Italy: CD: Fonit Cetra CDE 1040; UK: CD: Testament SBT 3167 (2000).

Brahms: Symphony No. 3 in F Major op. 90. Cond. Toscanini. Royal Festival Hall concert, October 1, 1952. TP live. Italy: LP: Toscanini Society ATS 1030-33; Turnabout THS 65027-30; Fonit Cetra LO 511; Hunt Productions: DC 524; Italy: CD: Fonit Cetra CDE 1040 (1988); UK: CD: Testament SBT 3167 (2000).

Brahms: Symphony No. 3 in F Major op. 90. Cond. Cantelli. KH, London, August 8, 9, 12, 16, 18, 1955. UK: LP: HMV BLP 1083; EMI XLP 30030; World Records SH 315; EMI 29 05761. UK: CD: EMI CDH 763085-2; Testament SBT 1173 (1999).[72]

Brahms: Symphony No. 4 in E Minor op. 98 Cond. Toscanini. Royal Festival Hall concert, October 1, 1952. TP live. Italy: CD: Fonit Cetra CDE 1031; Hunt DC 524; UK: CD; Testament SBT 3167 (2000).

Brahms: Tragic Overture in D op. 81. Cond. Toscanini. Royal Festival Hall concert, September 29, 1952. TP live. Italy: LP: Toscanini Society ATS 1030-33; Turnabout THS 65027-30; Fonit Cetra: LO 511; Hunt Productions: DC 524; Italy: CD: Fonit Cetra CDE 1016 (1987); Testament SBT 3167 (2000).

Bruckner: Symphony No. 4 in E-flat major "Romantic" WAB. 104. Cond. Matačić. KH, London, October 12–13, December 11, 14, 1954. UK: LP: Columbia 33CX 1274-75; US: LP: Angel 3548. CD: UK: Testament SBT 1050 (1994). For session on October 12, Edmund Chapman was First Horn.[73]

Butterworth: Banks of Green Willow in A major (1913). Cond. Miles. AR, February 18, 1946. UK: 78 rpm: HMV C 3491.[74]

Delibes: Sylvia. Cond. R. Irving. KH, London, April 27, 29, 1954. UK: LP: HMV CLP 1058.[75]

Dvořák: Cello Concerto in B Minor, op. 104, B. 191. Tortelier. Cond. Sargent. AR, June 16–17, 1955. UK: LP: HMV ALP 1306; EMI XLP 30018 (Mono); EMI SXLP 30018 (Stereo); UK: CD: EMI CMS 764069-2.[76]

Dvořák: Legend op. 59, no. 10, B. 117. Cond. Kubelik. AR, May 10, 1950. UK: 78 rpm: HMV C 7822; HMV DB 4317-4328; UK: CD: Testament SBT 1181.

> A beautiful horn solo blooming out of the colors of the orchestra and merging with it again seamlessly.[77]

Dvořák: Scherzo Capriccioso, op. 66, B. 131. Cond. Kubelik. AR, August 26, September 17, 1949. UK: 78 rpm: HMV C 7822-23; HMV DB 4316-17; UK: CD: Testament SBT 1181.[78]

> Alec Robertson wrote in *Gramophone*: "The beautifully articulated horn call at the opening . . . give us at once the feeling that this is going to be an outstanding recording—and it is. . . . The recording captures the full dreaming beauty of the soft and most poetic section that succeeds. It ends with a harp cadenza over a long-held horn note . . ."[79]

Dvořák: Scherzo Capriccioso, op. 66, B. 131. Cond. Sawallisch. KH, London, June 15, 1954. UK: LP: Columbia 33SX 1034; US: LP: Angel 35214.[80]

Dvořák: Symphonic Variations, op. 78, B. 70. Cond. Kubelik. Usher Hall, TP live, August 30, 1957, 8:00–8:50 (Part 1). Edinburgh International Festival. UK: CD: Testament SBT 1421.[81]

Dvořák: Symphony No. 8 in G Major op. 88 ("4") B. 163. Cond. Sawallisch. KH, London, June 12, 14, 15, 1954. UK: LP: Columbia 33SX 1034; US: LP: Angel 35214.[82]

Dvořák: Symphony No. 9 (No. 5) "New World" in E Minor, op. 95, B. 178. Cond. Galliera. KH, London, October 7–8, 1953. UK: LP: Columbia 33SX 1025; US: LP: Angel 35085.[83]

Dvořák: Symphony No. 9 (No. 5) "New World" in E Minor, op. 95, B. 178. Cond. Malko. KH, London, February 16–17, 1956. UK: LP: HMV CLP 1125; EMI MFP 2004; US: LP: Musica Classica 2012; UK: CD: EMI CZS 575121-2.[84]

Falla: El Sombrero de Tres Picos—Suite. Cond. Galliera. AR, June 5, 1946. UK: 78 rpm: Columbia DX 1258-59.[85]

Falla: El Sombrero de Tres Picos—Dances. Cond. Markevitch. AR, November 14, 1951, September 13, 1952. UK: LP: Columbia 33CX 1049; Columbia 33CX 1198 (Miller's

Dance only); HMV Concert Classics Mono XLP 30001; Angel 35008; UK: CD: Testament SBT 1105 (1997).[86]

Falla: El Sombrero De Tres Picos—Dances. Cond. Cantelli. KH, London, June 1, 1954. UK: LP: ALP 1207; UK: CD: Testament SBT 1017.[87]

Fauré: Pavane op. 50 (1887). Philharmonia Chorus. Cond. Sargent. AR, May 8, 1947. UK: 78rpm: Columbia DX 1369.[88]

Glinka: Valse-Fantasie in B, G. ii:13. Cond. Malko. AR, November 8, 1948. UK: 78 rpm: HMV C 3949; US: LP: RCA Victor LBC 1021.[89]

Anon arr. Grainger: Londonderry Air. Cond. Weldon. KH, London, March 14, 1956. UK: LP: Columbia 45 rpm: SED 5547.[90]

The record sleeve describes the horn solo right at the end as played by the "inimitable Dennis Brain."

Gruber arr. Salter: Silent Night. Schwarzkopf (S), Covent Garden Chorus, Hampstead Parish Church Choir. Cond. Pritchard. KH, London, October 3, 1952. UK: 78 rpm: Columbia LB131.[91]

Handel arr. Harty: Water Music: Suite. Cond. Karajan. KH, London, April 26, July 31, 1952. UK: 78 rpm: Columbia LX 8945-8946; UK: LP: Columbia 33CX 1033; Japan: LP: Toshiba EAC 37001-19; US: CD: Angel CMS 763464-2.

Hindemith: Symphonia Serena (1946). Cond. Hindemith. KH, London, November 19–21, 1956. UK: LP: Columbia 33CX 1676; US: Angel (Stereo) S 35491. UK: CD: EMI 7243 5 55032; CDC 555032-2.

Morris, speaking to Gamble on March 1, 2006, said that Brain was playing in this recording. The horn solo occurs in the first movement, marked "Moderately fast."[92]

Humperdinck: *Hänsel und Gretel* (1891–92). Schwarzkopf (Gretel), Grümmer (Hansel), Metternich (Peter, broom maker), von Ilosvay (Gertrud, wife), Schürhoff (the Witch), Felbermayer (Dew Fairy). Cond. Karajan. KH, London, June 27–30, July 1, 2, 16, 1953. UK: LP: Columbia 33CX 1096-97; EMI SLS 5145; World Records OC 187-88; UK: CD: EMI CMS 769293-2.[93]

Kodály: Háry János Suite op. 15. Cond. Schüchter. KH, London, December 31, 1952, January 1, 1953. UK: LP: Parlophone PMC 1017; MFP 2042.[94]

The principal horn solo is in no. 3: "Song."

Lambert: Music for Orchestra (1927). Cond. Lambert. BBC Maida Vale, July 2, 1948. UK: CD: Dutton CDBP 9761 (2005), tracks 11–12.[95]

Liszt: Les Préludes, S. 97. Cond. Fistoulari. AR, November 10, 1952. UK: LP: Parlophone PMD 1019; US: LP: MGM E 3014.[96]

Mendelssohn: Nocturne op. 61 No. 7 from *A Midsummer Night's Dream*. Cond. Kubelik. AR, February 16, 1952. UK:LP:ALP 1049.[97]

Mendelssohn: Nocturne op. 61 No. 7 from *A Midsummer Night's Dream*. Cond. Kletzki. KH, London, February 5, 1954. UK: LP: Columbia 33CX 1174; EMI XLP 30025; EMI RLS 7701; UK: CD: EMI Classics, 2008, CD1, track 15. Other collections: British Library Sound Archive call no. 1CD0289393 D1 BD 15.[98]

Mozart: Concert Aria: Ch'io me scordi te? K.505. Schwarzkopf (S). Cond. Ackermann. AR, May 9, 1955. UK: CD: Testament SBT 1178.[99]

Mozart: Cosi fan tutte (trans. Dr. M Browne) K.588: Ah! My love, forgive my madness; Ah! Mine own, so true, so tender. Cross (S). Cond. Collingwood. AR, January 2, 1947. UK: 78 rpm: Columbia DX 1353; UK: CD: Dutton CDLX 7018; Beulah *The World of Dennis Brain*, 1PD35 (issued June 2009), track 2.[100]

Mozart: Cosi fan tutte K.588: Act 2: Per pietà ben mio. Schwarzkopf (S). Cond. Karajan. The complete opera was recorded at the following venue on the following dates: KH, London and AR, July13, 14, 15, 16, 17, 19, 20, 21, November 6, 1954. UK: LP: Columbia 33CX 1262-64; EMI: RLS 7709; EMI: 1C 147 01748-50M; LP (excerpts) World Records OH 198; World Records SOC 195-7; UK: CD: EMI CHS 769635-2.[101]

Mozart: Musikalischer Spass, K.522 in F major (1789). Cond. Cantelli. KH, London, August 18, 1955. UK: LP: HMV ALP 1461; EMI XLP 30034; EMI 2C 027 03748; EMI RLS 7701; UK: CD: EMI 7243 5 6821729; CZS 568217-2 (Stereo); EMI Classics 2008, CD4, tracks1-4.[102]

Mozart: Symphony No. 40 in G Minor K.550. Cond. Klemperer. KH, London, July 21, 23, 1956. UK: LP: Columbia 33CX 1457; Columbia SAX 2278; US: LP: Angel 35407; UK: CD: EMI 763272-2; EMI 724356733220.[103]

Ravel: Pavane pour une Infante defunte in E minor (1899). Cond. Cantelli. Royal Festival Hall, October 25, 1952. UK: 78 rpm: HMV DB 21553; UK: LP: HMV ALP 1207; EMI XLP 30092; UK: CD: Testament SBT 1017.[104]

Rimsky-Korsakov: May Night: Overture. Cond. Fistoulari. AR, August 30–31, 1951. UK: LP: Parlophone: PMC 1031; EMI XLP 30031; US: LP: MGM E120.[105]

Rossini: La Semiramide: Overture (1823). Cond. Galliera. KH, London, January 21, 1953. UK: LP: Columbia 33SX 1006; EMI MFP 2031; US: LP: Angel 35011.[106]

Sibelius: Symphony No. 2 in D Major, op. 43. Cond. Kletzki. KH, London, July 15–16, 1955. UK: LP: Columbia 33CX 1332; HMV SAX 2280; HMV Concert Classics SXLP (Stereo) 30061; XLP 30061 (Mono); Angel 35314; CD: EMI 767727-2; UK: CD: EMI CZS 767726-2.[107]

Sibelius: Symphony No. 5 in E-flat Major op. 82. Cond. Karajan. KH, London, December 1, 1951, July 28, 29, 1952. UK: LP: Columbia 33CX 1047; Japan: LP: Toshiba EAC 37020-38; US: LP: Angel 35002; UK: CD: EMI Classics 7243 5 66600 2 1 (1998).[108]

Strauss: Capriccio op. 85 (1942): Final Scene. Schwarzkopf (S). Cond. Ackermann. Watford Town Hall, September 26, 1953. UK: LP: Columbia 33CX 1107; EMI RLS 751; EMI 10 38651; Angel 38266; UK: CD: EMI CDH 761001-2; NotaBlu 935.0932.[109]

Strauss: Vier Letzte Lieder (1948). Live recording of final rehearsal. Royal Albert Hall, London, May 22, 1950. Flagstad (S), Cond. Furtwängler. LP: Ed Smith Records EJS 432; Italy: LP: Fonit Cetra LO 501; Turnabout TV 34830; Fonit Cetra FE 41; CD: PSC 1823; JGCD 0019; UK: CD: Testament SBT 1410 (2007).[110]

***Strauss: Vier Letzte Lieder (1948).** Jurinac (S). Cond. Rankl. TP, July 12, 1952. 9:25–10:10 p.m. (Part 2) Part 2 only for Vier Letzte Lieder. British Library Sound Archive, list no. 30B 7048; 30B 6861/6862; Leech nos. 1442-1444. call nos. 1CDR0006469 BD2, 1CDR0004386 BD2; 2CDR0004386 BD2-BD5; dubbing nos. 1CDR0006469; 1CDR0004386; 1CDR0004476. Incomplete recording, although only a second or two is missing from the end of the "September" and all of Brain's solo is captured. Discovered by Lynch.[111]

Strauss: Vier Letzte Lieder (1948). Schwarzkopf (S). Cond. Ackermann. Watford Town Hall, September 25, 1953. UK: LP: Columbia 33CX 1107; EMI 10 38651; EMI RLS 751; Angel 38266; US: LP: Angel 35084; UK: CD: EMI CDH 761 0012; NotaBlu 935.0932.[112]

Strauss: Vier Letzte Lieder (1948). Schwarzkopf (S), Cond. Karajan. Royal Festival Hall, June 20, 1956. CD: EMI CDM 763655-2 (1990). Karajan changed the order so that the last song was "September." Sanders remembered Brain playing the solo (see Chapter 5).[113]

Strauss: Der Rosenkavalier op. 59 (1911). Schwarzkopf (Feldmarschallin) and other soloists. Chorus of children from Loughton High School for Girls and Bancroft's School. Cond. Karajan. KH, London, December 10–15, 17–22, 1956. UK: LP: Columbia 33CX 1492-1495; Columbia SAX 2269-2272; EMI SLS 810; EMI EX 29 00453; UK: CD: EMI CDS 749 3548 (Excerpts); EMI CMS 567605-2.[114]

Gramophone critic Alec Robertson disliked the effect in the Prelude that had been particularly commented on by Brain's colleague Hugh Bean. Of Karajan's direction of this part, Robertson wrote: "I wish he had not emphasized, in the Prelude, one of Strauss's grossest errors of taste, the whooping horns passage—but it is full of beautifully wrought detail, abundant vitality and sensitivity."[115]

As quoted in Chapter 5, Bean remembered Brain leading the horns in the first act.

***Strauss: Symphonia Domestica op. 53 (1902–3).** Cond. Strauss, Royal Albert Hall, London. TP, October 19, 1947, 7:55–8:40 p.m (Part 2). British Library Sound Archive, list nos. 30B 6254; 30B 6260; dubbing nos. T11737WR; T11739W1-W2 C2. Incomplete recording. UK: CD: Testament SBT 21441.

The critic of *Monthly Musical Record* wrote:

> A memorable concert was that of October 19th at the Albert Hall at which Richard Strauss conducted an enormously long programme of his works, including the "Symphonia Domestica." The Philharmonia Orchestra, led by Thomas Carter, played very finely under the veteran's restrained but decisive beat. . . . The audience listened with pleasurable surprise to the "Domestic," a work the world had been led to believe was a freakish absurdity. Strauss can hardly fail to have been touched by the warmth of greeting he received at this and other occasions during his visit.[116]

Strauss: Till Eulenspiegels Lustige Streiche op. 28 (1895). Cond. Karajan. KH, London, December 4, 1951. UK: 78 rpm: Columbia LX 8908-09; UK: LP: Columbia 33CX 1001; EMI RLS 7715; Japan: LP: Toshiba EAC 37020-38; CD: Angel CMS 763316-2.[117]

Tchaikovsky: Evgeny Onegin op. 24 Act 1: Tatiana's Letter Scene. Welitsch (S). Cond. Susskind. AR, May 22, 1948. UK: 78 rpm: Columbia LX 1108-1109; UK: LP: Columbia 33C 1011; EMI HLM 7006; EMI: HMV Treasury, 1172; EMI 101 2671; US: Columbia ML 2048; ML 4795; Angel 60202; World Records SH 289; UK: CD: EMI CDH 761007-2; EMI CHS 764855-2.[118]

Tchaikovsky: Manfred Symphony op. 58. Cond. Kletzki. KH, London, January 29, February 12, 1954. UK: LP: Columbia 33CX 1189; HMV Concert Classics XLP 30015; CD: UK: Testament SBT 1048.[119]

Tchaikovsky: Symphony No. 5 in E Minor op. 64. Cond. Karajan. KH, London, May 1, 8, July 25, 31, 1952, June 19, 1953. UK: LP: Columbia 33CX 1133. CD: Angel CMS 763460-2. NB. Edmund Chapman was booked as principal horn on June 19, 6–9 p.m.[120]

Traditional arr. Salter: The First Noel (Nowell). Schwarzkopf (S), Covent Garden Chorus, Hampstead Parish Church Choir. Cond. Pritchard. KH, London, October 3, 1952. UK: 78 rpm: Columbia LB131.[121]

This rare ten-inch 78 rpm recording is long-overdue for a CD release.

Wagner: Götterdämmerung: Brünnhilde's Immolation. KH, London, June 23, 1952. Flagstad (S). Cond. Furtwängler. UK: LP: HMV ALP 1016; EMI HQM 1057; EMI 1C 147 01149M; EMI 29 10373 UK: CD: EMI CDHB 64935.[122]

***Wagner: Götterdämmerung: Dawn and Siegfried's Rhine Journey.** Royal Albert Hall London, May 22, 1950. Cond. Furtwängler. UK: CD Testament SBT 1410 (2007). Duration: 11:09.[123]

***Wagner: Götterdämmerung: Act 3: Starke Scheite schichtet mir dort.** Royal Albert Hall, London, May 22, 1950. Flagstad (S), cond., Furtwängler. UK: CD Testament SBT 1410 (2007). Duration: 18:59.[124]

Wagner: Siegfried Idyll. Cond. Kletzki. KH, London, May 27, 1948. UK: 78 rpm: Columbia LX 1296-97.[125]

Wagner: Siegfried Idyll. Cond. Cantelli. AR, October 16, 1951. UK: 78 rpm: HMV DB 9746-47; UK: LP: HMV ALP 1086; World Records SH 287; UK: CD: Testament SBT 1012.[126]

***Wagner: Tristan und Isolde: Prelude und Liebestod.** Flagstad (S), Cond. Furtwängler. Royal Albert Hall London, May 22, 1950. UK: CD Testament SBT 1410 (2007).

Waldteufel: Les Patineurs: Waltz op. 183 (1882). Cond. H. Krips. KH, London, January 5, 1956. UK: LP: Columbia 33SX 1048; Columbia SCX 3251; EMI XLP 30035 (Mono); EMI SXLP (Stereo) 30035; EMI CFP 40305; CD: CZS 586289-2.[127]

Walton: Scenes from Shakespeare's Henry V. Olivier (Speaker) with chorus. Cond. Walton. AR, August 27–28, October 12–13, 1946. UK: 78 rpm: HMV C 3583-86 (auto C 7678-81); UK: LP: ALP 1375; US: LP: RCA Victor RB 16144; CD: EMI CHS 565003-2; EMI Classics CDM 565007-2 (2000).[128]

Weber: Der Freischütz Overture, op. 77, J. 277. Cond. Susskind. AR, March 12, 1946. UK: 78rpm: Columbia DX 1244; Japan: CD: *A Resurrection of Dennis Brain* (2002).[129]

RAF Symphony Orchestra[130]

***Coates: March "Over to You" (1942).** HMV RAF 7. Recorded 1942. UK: CD: The Golden Age of Light Music. Four Decades of Light Music, Volume 2, 1940s and 1950s. Guild Light Music GLCD 5135. This is one of a set of ten 10-inch 78 rpm discs, recorded in 1941, and produced in aid of the RAF Benevolent Fund: HMV 1-10, of which this is the seventh disc. They were favorably reviewed by "W.A.C." in *The Gramophone* 19, no. 225 (February 1942): 14.

***Coates: "Song of Loyalty" (1935).** HMV RAF 7. Recorded 1942.

***Handel arr. Harty: *Water Music*.** Excerpts. HMV unpublished test pressing recorded circa 1944.Air, Bourée, Alla Hornpipe. Private collection.

***Rossini arr. Respighi: La Boutique Fantasque.** HMV unpublished test pressing. Recorded circa 1944. Private collection.

Royal Opera House Orchestra, Covent Garden[131]

Wagner: Siegfried. The 100th Performance at the Royal Opera House. Excerpts. Soloists: Svanholm (Siegfried), Kuen (Mime), Franz (Wanderer), Krauss (Alberich), Sutherland (Woodbird), Langdon (Fafner), cond. Stiedry. TP, June 25, 1954. UK: CD: Pearl GEM 0230 (2005). Brain has been identified by Del Mar as the horn soloist in the Horn Call, Act 2.[132]

Royal Philharmonic Orchestra[133]

Beethoven: Symphony No. 3 in E-flat major op. 55 "Eroica." AR, December 20–21, 1951, August 13, 1952. UK: LP Columbia 33CX 1086; Phillips SBL 5233; US: Columbia ML 4698; UK: CD: Sony SMK 89887.[134]

Malcolm Macdonald wrote in *Gramophone*:

> At the famous clash of implied harmony in the first movement, for example, the horn entry is refined away almost to inaudibility; and a very leisurely and seemingly tentative Scherzo is redeemed by fine horn-playing in the Trio. . . . But even so, I think that Karajan and the Philharmonia on Columbia 33CX1046 (July, 1953) must remain, to date, the preferred version; they give a fine performance, recorded with verve if not always with extreme clarity.[135]

Beethoven: Symphony No. 5 in C minor op. 67. Rehearsal excerpts, third and fourth movements. July 14, 1951. CD: UK: EMI CDM 7 64465-2.[136]

Beethoven: Symphony No. 6 in F Major op. 68 "Pastoral." AR, December15, 18, 19, 1951, May 5, 1952. LP: UK: Columbia 33CX 1062; US: Columbia ML 4828. CD: Sony SMK 89888.[137]

See Civil's letter, quoted in Chapter 4.

Berlioz: The Trojans H. 133a, op. 5: Act 2: Royal Hunt and Storm. TP, July 4, 1947. World Records: LP: WSA (Western Sound Archive) 513-516; MEL 303. France: CD: Malibran CDRG 162 (3); SOMM-Beecham 26-8 (2010). Duration: 9:43.

The BBC broadcast Act 2 on July 2 and 4, 1947, but they recorded the performance only on July 4. Stephen Pettitt gives July 2 as the date of the only recording he lists. This other recording (if indeed it is and not the July 4 BBC recording) must have been recorded from the transmission privately. See Chapter 4 for more about this performance.[138]

Delius: Appalachia (1896). Royal Philharmonic Chorus. AR, October 29, November 6–7, December 13 and 18, 1952. LP: UK: Columbia 33CX 1112; Phillips GL 5690: GO3634L. US: Columbia ML 4915. CD: Sony SMK 89429 (2001) *Sir Thomas Beecham Conducts Delius*, tracks 6–22.

See Civil's letter quoted in Chapter 4 that states Brain, Civil, and Hyde shared the principal horn parts for this recording.[139]

Delius: Brigg Fair an English Rhapsody (1907). AR, November 26, 1946. UK: 78 rpm: HMV DB 6452-53; US: 78 rpm: RCA Victor set M 1206 (12-02-2/3,12-0204/5); World Record Club: LP: SHB 54; CD: UK: Dutton CDLX 7028.

At one of the rehearsals for a Delius Festival concert, Brain and Del Mar asked Beecham if he would attend a concert at Chelsea Town Hall on November 26, 1946. Del Mar conducted and Brain was the soloist in Strauss's Concerto No. 1. Also in the concert was Act 2 of Wagner's *Siegfried*. Beecham was in the audience.[140]

Delius: Evening Voices (1889–90). Suddaby (S). AR, April 3, 1951. LP: World Record Club SHB 54; US: RCA Victor LHMV 1050.[141]

Delius: In a Summer Garden (1908). AR, October 27, 1951. LP: UK: Columbia 33C 1017; CD: UK: *Sir Thomas Beecham Conducts Delius* Sony SMK 89429 (2001).[142]

Delius: Eine Messe des Lebens (1905) Part 2, Prelude "On the Mountains" AR, May 8, 1948. Matrix 2EA 13033-1-2. White (2nd H). First issued on LP, World Record Club SH 325 in set SHB 32; Issued in Japan on LP: EMI Toshiba EAC 60060-64. CD: UK: EMI CDM 764054-2. CD (Japan) EMI Toce 9332.[143]

Delius: Eine Messe des Lebens (1905). Soloists: Fisher, Raisbeck (S), Sinclair (Alt), Craig (T), Boyce (Bar), LPO Choir. AR, November 8, 11, December 8–10, 12–13, 1952, January 1 and 20, April 10, May 14, 1953. UK: LP: Columbia 33CX 1078-79; US: LP: SL 197; UK: CD: Sony SM2K 89432. See especially Part 2: Prelude "On the Mountains."[144]

Delius: Over the Hills and Far Away (1895–97). AR, February 7, 1950. LP: UK: Columbia 33C 1017; Phillips GL 5713; US: LP: ML 2133, ML 5268; UK: CD: Sony SMK 89430 (2001) *Sir Thomas Beecham Conducts Delius*, track 1. Duration: 14:05.[145]

Delius: Song of the High Hills (1911). Hart (S), Jones (T), Luton Choral Society. AR, November 22, 1946. UK: 78 rpm: HMV DB 6470-2; US: 78rpm: RCA Victor: set M 1185 (12-0031/3, 12-0034/9); UK: LP: ALP 1889; UK: CD: EMI CDM 764054-2.[146]

Delius: A Village Romeo and Juliet (1900). Soloists and BBC Theatre Chorus (Chorus Master: John Clements), Dawson (Organ), Repetiteur: Del Mar. TP, April 23, 1948, 6:55–9:15 p.m. CD: UK: SOMM-Beecham 12-2.[147]

Dvořák: Symphonic Poem: The Golden Spinning Wheel, op. 109, B. 197 (1896). AR, September 15, November 6 and 29, 1947. UK: 78 rpm: HMV DB 6656-58; US: 78 rpm: RCA Victor set M 1291 (12-0797/9, 12-0800/2); LP: World Record Club SHB 100 (SH 1003); UK: CD: Dutton 2 CDEA 5025-5026 (2000). Duration: 24:48.[148]

Goldmark: Rustic Wedding Symphony op. 26. AR, May 5, 6, 7, and 8, 1952. UK: LP: Columbia 33CX 1067; US: LP: Columbia ML 4626; UK: CD: Sony Classical SMK 87780 (2002), tracks 9–13.[149]

Gounod: Faust (1856–58). Géori-Boué (S), St. Arnaud (M-S), Bannerman (M-S), Nore (T), Bourdin (Bar), Rico (B), Frank (B), RPO Chorus. AR, November 25–27, and 29, 1947, December 12, 1947, January 5–8, and 10, June 30, 1948. UK: 78 rpm: auto couplings only: HMV DB 9422-37; US: 78 rpm: RCA Victor set M 1300 (12-0821-28; 12-0829-36), M 1303 (12-0837-44, 12-0845-52); LP: Collector's LCT 6100; WCT52; MC 124. CD: Presier 90355.[150]

Handel adapted by Beecham: *The Faithful Shepherd Suite*. KH, London, April 25, May 1, September 28, 1950. UK: 78 rpm: LX 1517-19; UK: LP: Columbia 33CX 1105; UK: CD: Sony Classical SMK 87780 (2002), tracks 1–8. According to Michael Gray, the Introduction and Fugue were recorded on April 25 and May 1.[151]

Handel: Amaryllis: Scherzo. AR, May 12, 1947. UK: 78 rpm: HMV DB 6821; US: 78 rpm: RCA Victor M 1264.[152]

Haydn: Symphony No. 40 in F major, H.1:40. AR, April 20, 1948. UK: 78 rpm: HMV DB 6823-24; UK: 45 rpm: EMI 7ER 5093; LP: World Record Club SH1002; UK: CD: Dutton 2 CDEA 5025-5026 (2000). Duration: 14:19.[153]

Lyndon Jenkins writes in his CD notes to the Dutton first CD issue:

> But then would come a day when everything went smoothly, as with Haydn's Symphony No. 40, completed in one session with three of the four movements able to be published as first "takes." Only in the case of the Minuet and Trio, where Dennis Brain and his colleague demonstrate their fabulous playing, was a second attempt preferred.[154]

Méhul: Le Jeune Henri Overture: "La Chasse de Jeune Henri" (1797). Walthamstow Town Hall, December 7–10, 14–15, 17–18, 1953. UK: LP: Phillips ABR 4056; GL 5714; GO3625L; US: LP: Columbia ML 5029; US: CD: Sotone 103; UK: CD: Sony SMKL 91167.

Phillips's files for session dates do not survive for December. They were accidentally destroyed. Peter Sermon, a retired viola player from the orchestra, added the dates from his diaries and from diaries of former colleagues, as well as the orchestra's own recording schedules. The dates are quoted from an unpublished discography of the Royal Philharmonic Orchestra that he was compiling before his death. Civil has confirmed that Brain was leading the section for this recording. See his letter quoted in Chapter 4. *Le Jeune Henri* is the correct title of Méhul's opera but the Overture has been long-known as "La Chasse de Jeune Henri."[155]

Moeran: Sinfonietta (1944). Live Royal Albert Hall concert, HS, April 26, 1947, 3:30–5:00 p.m. Royal Philharmonic Society concert. Private recording made on 78 rpm discs direct from the first broadcast. UK: CD: SOMM-BEECHAM 24 (2008), tracks 1–3. Only the Sinfonietta appears to have been recorded. The order of the concert, according to *Radio Times*, was:

Sinfonietta—Moeran

Symphony No. 3 in D—Tchaikovsky (not recorded)[156]

Mozart: *Cosi fan tutte* K.588: *Per Pietà ben mio, perdona.* Jurinac (S), Glyndebourne Festival Orchestra (RPO). Cond. F. Busch. July 12, 1950. UK: 78 rpm: HMV DB 21120; DBZ 1120; LP: World Record Club SH 397; UK: CD: Testament SBT 1040 (1994), track 13.[157]

Testament SBT 1040 gives recording dates July 12, 14, and 15, 1950, for excerpts of *Cosi fan tutte* but does not give a date for the aria. Pettitt (1989), 199, gives August 21, 1950.

Mozart: *Cosi fan tutte* K.588: (rehearsal) *Per Pietà ben mio, perdona.* Jurinac (S), Glyndebourne Festival Orchestra (RPO). Cond. F. Busch. July 1950. UK: CD: Testament SBT 1040, track 16. The RPO was the pit orchestra at Glyndebourne this year. See previous entry for the recording dates in July.

Mozart: *Cosi fan tutte* K.588: *Per Pietà ben mio, perdona. Jurinac (S). Glyndebourne Festival Orchestra (RPO), cond. F. Busch. Live concert, July 5, 1951. First release: Guild Historical GHCD 2304 (set, 2303-2304) track 12.[158]

Mozart: Divertimento no. 2 in D major K.131. AR, November 28–30, 1947, January 4, 1948. UK: 78 rpm: HMV DB6649-51; automatic: DB9354-5; UK: CD: Dutton CDLX 7037 (1999), tracks 5–8, 10.[159]

***Mozart: Divertimento no. 15 in B-flat major for two horns and strings, K.287 (K.2871H).** AR, July 12, 1947. Second and third movements only.

2nd mvt. Tema con variazioni. Andante grazioso 2EA 12173-1-2. Duration: 4:55.

3rd mvt. Menuetto—Trio. 2EA 12174-1-2. Duration: 4:09. UK: CD: IMG Artists 7 24357 59382 *Great Conductors of the 20th Century: Sir Thomas Beecham* (2003).[160]

Dr. Graham Melville-Mason writes in his sleeve notes to the first issue on CD:

> The two movements recorded here demonstrate that graceful elegance which Sir Thomas's character could draw from this music. Here the grazioso qualification of the andante of the second-movement theme and variations is eloquently judged, supported by the deft touches he imparts to the two horns, played by Dennis Brain and Ian Beers. Sir Thomas omits the fifth of the six variations and abandons their repeats, presumably to accommodate the work on the 78-rpm sides, but he includes the repeats in the shorter third movement, a Minuet and Trio.[161]

Paisiello: Overture, *Nina, o sia La Pazza per amore.* AR, July 7, 1947. UK: 78 rpm: HMV DB 6499; US: 78 rpm: RCA Victor set M 1264 (12-0591, 12-0595/6); UK: CD: Dutton 2CDEA 5025-5026 (2000). Duration: 6:31.[162]

Rossini: Overture: La Cambiale di Matrimonio. KH, London, September 28, 1950. UK: 78 rpm: Columbia LX 1458; UK: 45 rpm: EMI SEL 1509; UK: LP: Phillips GL 5693; Fontana CFL 1033; US: LP: Columbia AAL 11; UK: CD: SMK 91185.[163]

Strauss, R.: Bourgeois Gentilhomme op. 60: Incidental Music (1912). AR, February 24, March 29, November 5, 1947. UK: 78 rpm: HMV DB 6646-48; LP: World Record Club SH 378; UK: CD: EMI CDM 763106-2; EMI 3 71502 21.[164]

Strauss, R.: Ein Heldenleben op. 40 (1898). Oscar Lampe (V). AR, November 21, 28, December 14, 1947. UK: 78 rpm: HMV DB 6620-24; World Record Club: LP: SHB 100; UK: CD: Testament SBT 1147.[165]

In the coda, Brain plays the solo inimitably. See Basil Tschaikov's remarks quoted in Chapter 4.

Strauss, R.: *Intermezzo* op. 72: *Entr'acte* (1924). BBC Third Programme, live from Drury Lane Theatre, London, October 12, 1947. Private recording from the original transmission.

Tchaikovsky: Symphony No. 2 in C minor, op. 17, "Little Russian." Walthamstow Town Hall, December 7–10, 14–15, 17–18, 1953. UK: LP: Philips ABL 3015; Philips GL 5636; US: LP: Columbia ML 4872; UK: CD: Sony 89875.[166]

Tchaikovsky: Symphony No. 3 in D op. 29 "Polish." AR, April 8, 11, and 18, May 12, 1947. UK: 78 rpm: HMV DB 6583-87; US: 78 rpm: RCA Victor set M 1279 (12-0693-97; 12-0698-06702); UK: CD: EMI Beecham 1 (1988) tracks 2-6.[167]

Wagner: Götterdämmerung: Siegfried's Funeral Music. Walthamstow Town Hall, December 7–10, 14–15, 17–18, 1953. UK: LP: Phillips A02113L; ABL 3039; GL 5635; US: LP: Columbia ML 4962; UK: CD: Sony SMK 89889. Duration: 7:48.

According to Civil's letter (quoted in Chapter 4), the "Siegfried" was recorded with himself and Brain. This must refer to either this recording in December 1953, or it could refer to the recording of *Götterdämmerung*: *Siegfried's Rhine Journey*, made at Walthamstow Town Hall on April 20, 1954. Beecham and the RPO did not record Wagner's opera *Siegfried*.[168]

Wagner: Parsifal: Good Friday Music. Walthamstow Town Hall, December 7–10, 14–15, 17–18, 1953. UK: LP: Phillips ABL 3039, Phillips A02113L; GL 5635. US: LP: Columbia ML 4962; UK: CD: Sony SMK 89889. Duration: 11:45.[169]

Wagner: Das Rheingold: Entry of the gods into Valhalla. Furmedge (S), Field-Hyde (S), Garside (M-S), Evans (Alt.), P. Jones (T), Chitty (T), Schöffler (B). EMI unissued. AR, September 22, 1947. Matrices: 2EA 12315-1-2-3; 12316-1-2-3. UK: CD: SOMM-Beecham 9. Duration: 8:09.[170]

Wagner: Tannhäuser: Act 3 Introduction. Matrices: 2EA 11645-1-2; 11633-1-2.AR, February 5 and 8, 1947. UK: CD: SOMM-Beecham 9. Duration: 9:44.[171]

Wagner: Tristan und Isolde: Prelude und Liebestod. Flagstad (S). BBC, Maida Vale, December 21, 1952. CD: SOMM-Beecham 20.

Wagner: Wesendonck Lieder. Flagstad (S). BBC, Maida Vale, December 21, 1952. CD: SOMM-Beecham 20.

II. International Archives Collections

1. United Kingdom

BBC Information and Archives, London[172]

Beethoven: Quintet in E-flat for piano and winds op. 16. DBWE with Parry. Usher Hall, Edinburgh, HS live, August 24, 1957, 11:00–11:40 a.m. UK: LP: REGL 352 (1979), side 2, band 1; US: LP Arabesque 8071 (1981). UK: CD: BBC Legends 4048-2 (2000) tracks 1–3. BBC cat. no. MX30; LP 23831-2. Other collections: British Library Sound Archive call no. 1LP0058897 S2 BDS 1-3 (BBC Artium REGL 352); 1CD0181595 BD1-3.[173]

Beethoven: Sextet in E-flat major op. 81b for two horns and strings. Civil (2nd H), English Quartet: Pearl (V), White (V), Lempfert (Va), Just (VC). TP, February 18, 1957, 8:20–7:05 p.m. UK: CD: BBC Legends 4066-2 (2001), tracks 1–3. BBC cat. no. MX30; LP 26847. Other collections: British Library Sound Archive call no. 1CD0242900 BD1-3; B8236/06. BPL. WSA no.1089.[174]

Brahms: Trio for violin, horn and piano in E-flat op. 40. Salpeter (V), Preedy (P). HS, February 15, 1957. UK: LP: REB 175 (1974), side 1, bands 1–3; side 2, band 1; CD: BBC Legends 4048-2 (2000), tracks 9–12. BBC cat. no. MX30; LP 24099. Other collections: British Library Sound Archive call no. 1CD0181595 BD9-12. WSA no.1089. University of Wisconsin-Madison: Blake Collection: accession no. ARE3424UW, call no. LP 73245 (Perennial long-player PER2007, New York, 1971.)[175]

Britten: The Heart of the Matter: Poetry and Music. Sitwell (poet and narrator), Pears (T), Britten (P). Aldeburgh Festival, June 21, 1956. BBC TS. Not broadcast in Brain's lifetime. BBC cat.no. MX 80; LP 23044-45. Other collections: BPL Shelf mark 10ca6. R0217; ID: 3-9700591. British Library Sound Archive list no. T11777WR. Dubbing of BBC Sound Archive discs: LP 23044; 23045. See also British Library Sound Archive for Canticle III from this concert: call no. 1CD0171154 BD3, cat. no. B8236/05 1. RNZ, for the whole recital.

Only Canticle III has been issued on CD: BBCB 8014-2. The music comprises:

Prologue

Fanfare. For horn and piano. First performance. Unpublished.

Where are the seeds of the Universal Fire to burn the roots of Death in the World's cold heart? For tenor, horn, and piano. FP. Unpublished.

Canticle III Still Falls the Rain—The Raids, 1940, Night and Dawn, Op.55. For tenor, horn and piano. UK: CD: BBCB 8014.

Epilogue

So Out of the dark, see our great Spring begins. For tenor, horn, and piano. FP. Unpublished.[176]

Cooke: Arioso and Scherzo for horn, violin, two violas and cello. FBP. TP, November 3, 1956; pre-rec. October 30, 1956. Carter Trio: Carter (V), Mines (Va), McCarthy (VC), and Grainger (2nd Va). BBC cat. no. MX 30; LP 27178. Other collections: British Library Sound Archive call no. 1CD0242900 BD12-13, dubbing no. NP10738WR. Unpublished.[177]

Cooke: Arioso and Scherzo for horn, violin, two violas and cello. HS, March 5, 1957; pre-rec. March 1, 1957. Carter String Trio and Lempfert (2nd Va). BBC single-sided LP: 24156; CD: BBC Legends BBCL 4066-2 (2001), tracks 12–13. BBC cat. no. MX31; LP 24156 (single-sided) band 2.[178]

Dukas: Villanelle for horn and piano. Parry (P). Usher Hall, Edinburgh, August 24, 1957. HS live. UK: LP: BBC Artium REGL 352 (1979), side 2, band 3; US: LP: Arabesque 8071 (1981); UK: CD: BBC Legends 4048-2 (2000), track 4. BBC cat. no. MX30; LP 2383-2. Other collections: British Library Sound Archive call no. 1LP0058897 S2 BD5 (BBC Artium REGL352); 1CD0181595 BD4. WSA no.1089.[179]

Haydn: Horn Concerto No. 1 in D major, Hob. 7d:3. BBC Midland Light Orchestra, cond. Wurmser. Nuffield House, Queen Elizabeth Hospital, Edgbaston, HS, January 21, 1957. UK: CD: BBC Legends 4066-2 (2001), tracks 9–11. BBC cat. no MX 40; LP 26503 (back of the LP only). Other collections: British Library Sound Archive call no.1CD0242900 BD9-11, list no. NP10738WR.[180]

Hindemith: Sonata for horn and piano (1939). Mewton-Wood (P). TP, January 28, 1953. UK: CD: BBC Legends 4164-2 (2001), tracks 9–11; Pearl GEM 0227 (2005), tracks 3–6. BBC cat. no. MX 31; T27618. Other collections: British Library Sound Archive call no. 1CD0242890 SEQ3, cat. no. H9070/3. WSA no. 1150.[181]

Ibert: Trois Pièces Brèves. DBWE. TP, September 5, 1957; pre-rec. July 22, 1957, Memorial Hall Studio, Farringdon Street, London. UK: LP: Columbia 33CX 1687; EMI RLS 7701; US: LP: Seraphim 60169. UK: CD: BBC Legends BBCL 4066-2 (2001), tracks 14–16; EMI Classics 2008, CD4, track 13. BBC cat. no. MX 30; LP 24110. Other collection: British Library Sound Archive call no. 1CD0242900 BD14-16.[182]

Jacob: Sextet for piano and winds op. 3. DBWE and Malcolm (P). TP, September 5, 1957; pre-rec. July 22, 1957, Memorial Hall Studio, Farringdon Street, London. UK: LP: EMI Columbia 33CX 1687; US: LP: Seraphim 60169; UK: CD: BBC Legends BBCL 4164-2 (2001), tracks 4–8; EMI Classics 2008, CD4, tracks 14–18. BBC cat.no. MX 30; LP 24110. Other collections: British Library Sound Archive call no. 1CD0289393 D4 BD14-18. WSA no.235.[183]

Marais: Le Basque for horn and piano. Parry (P). Usher Hall, Edinburgh, August 24, 1957. HS live. UK: LP: BBC Records REB 175 (1974), side 2, band 3; US: LP: Everest 3432 (1978); Arabesque 8071 (1981); UK: CD: BBC Legends 4048-2 (2000), track 5. BBC cat. no. MX30; LP 2383-2. Other collections: British Library Sound Archive call no. 1LP0058897 SI BD1 C1-2 (BBC Artium REGL 352); 1CD0181595 BD5; cat. no. B8236/07. WSA no.1089.[184]

Malipiero: Dialogue No. 4 for wind quintet (1956). FBBP. DBWE. Usher Hall, Edinburgh, August 24, 1957. HS live. UK: LP: BBC Artium REGL 352 (1979), side 1, band 3; US: LP: Arabesque 8071 (1981); CD: Italy: ASDisc 356 (1991), track 4. BBC cat. no. MX30; LP 2383-2. Other collections: British Library Sound Archive call no. 1LP0058897 S1 BD3 (BBC Artium REGL 352). WSA no.1089.[185]

Mozart arr. Baines: Divertimento no. 14 in B-flat K.270. DBWE. TP, September 5, 1957; pre-rec. July 22, 1957, Memorial Hall Studio, Farringdon Street, London, England; UK: LP: Columbia 33CX 1687; US: LP: Seraphim 10169; UK: LP box set EMI HMV Treasury *The Art of Dennis Brain*, RLS 7701; UK: CD: BBC Legends 4066-2 (2001), tracks 5–8; EMI Classics 2008, CD4, tracks 5–8. BBC cat. no. MX 30; LP 24110. Other collection: British Library Sound Archive call no. 1CD0289393 04 BD5-8; 1LP0181606 3 (Columbia 33CX 1687)[186]

Mozart: Quintet for horn and strings K.407 (K.386c). TP, November 3, 1956; pre-rec. October 30, 1956. Carter String Trio and Grainger (2nd Va). UK: LP: BBC Records REB 175 (1974), side 2, band 2; BBC cat. no. MX 30; LP 27178. Other collection: WSA no.1089.[187]

Mozart: Quintet for horn and strings K.407 (K.386c). TP, February18, 1957. Three members of English String Quartet and Mines (2nd Va). UK: CD: BBC Legends 4048-2 (2000), tracks 6–8. Other collections: British Library Sound Archive call no. 1CD0181595 BD 6-8; B8236/04. WSA no.1089.[188]

Robertson (arranger): Theme music and hunting scene from radio play, *Bayeux Tapestry*. HS, November 27, 1944. The broadcast date is taken from the "Alphabetical Index to Recorded Programmes Permanent Library Catalogue," p. 298 and "Supplement 2," p. 360. This is confirmed by *Radio Times*. This date differs from the one given by Pettitt (1989, p. 191). Another date in the BBC's Catalogue is "26 September 44" but this is probably a pre-recording date. Unpublished. BBC cat. nos. MT1 7306-9; T/28105.[189]

Schubert: *Auf dem Strom* for tenor, horn and piano op. posth. 119, D. 943. TP, January 28, 1953. Pears (T), Mewton-Wood (P). CD: UK: BBC Legends BBCL 4066-2 (2001), track 4; Pearl *The Age of Gold*, GEM 0227 (2005), track 1. BBC cat. no. MX31; T27618. Other collections: British Library Sound Archive call no.1CD0242900 BD4; H2302/07; M557W BD1; M4366W BD1. WSA no.1150.[190]

Seiber: Fantasy for flute, horn and string quartet. Morris (F), Allegri Quartet: Goren, Barton, Ireland, Pleeth. TP, February 6, 1957; pre-rec. February 3, 1957. BBC cat. no. MX 30; LP 26963. Unpublished. Other collections: British Library Sound Archive list no. NP10738WR.[191]

Vinter: Hunter's Moon for horn and orchestra. BBC Concert Orchestra, cond. Tausky. HS, June 16, 1957. UK: CD: BBC Legends BBCL 4164-2 (2001), track 12. Duration: 5:14. BBC cat. no. MRJ 11; LP 24156, band 1 (single-sided). Other collection: British Library Sound Archive call no. 1CD0242890 SEQ4.[192]

Britten-Pears Library, Snape Maltings, Aldeburgh, Suffolk[193]

Beethoven: Quintet in E-flat for piano and winds op. 16. DBWE, Britten (P). Aldeburgh Festival, June 22, 1955. UK: CD: BBCL 4164-2 (2001), tracks 1–3. Other collections: British Library Sound Archive call no. 1LP0132771 S1 BD2-4; 1CD0242890 SEQ5. WSA no.695D. UWM BC, accession no. AQR3568UW, call no. LP 73045 (IGI 370);

Music Preserved archive (formerly Music Performance Research Centre), Barbican, London. Cat.no. BCT 0204 (Pearsall-Pollard donation). RNZ.

Britten: Serenade for Tenor, Horn and Strings op. 31 (1944). Pears (T), Boyd Neel Orchestra, cond. Britten. Unpublished test pressing. Audio-cassette, dated April 29, 1992. Shelf mark 10E8.k1339; ID 3-9601394. Catalogue: *Sound and Video Recordings.*

Britten: Serenade for Tenor, Horn and Strings, op. 31. Pears (T), Boyd Neel Orchestra, cond. Britten. 1944. Decca test pressing. 2 sound discs: analogue, 78 rpm, 12-inch. Shelf mark 10GL5; ID: 3-01052226. Catalogue: *Sound and Video Recordings.*

Milhaud: La Cheminée du Roi René for wind quintet op. 205. The recording omits the third movement. DBWE. Aldeburgh Festival, June 22, 1955. TP live. BBC TS. US: LP: IGI 370; CD: BBC Legends 4066-2 (2001), tracks 17–22. Other collections: British Library Sound Archive call no. 1LP0132771 S1 BD3 C1-3 (IGI 370).; 1CD0242900 BD17-22 (BBC Legends 4066-2). WSA no.695D. UWM BC, accession no. AQR3568UW; call no. LP 73045 (IGI 370)

Mozart arr. Baines: Divertimento no.14 in B-flat K.270. DBWE. Aldeburgh Festival, June 22, 1955. TP live. BBC TS. US: LP: IGI 370. Other collections: British Library Sound Archive call no. 1LP0132771 S1 BD1 (IGI 370). WSA no.695D. UWM BC, accession no. AQR3568UW; call no. LP 73045 (IGI 370)

Schumann: Adagio and Allegro in A-flat major op. 70 for horn and piano. Britten (P). Aldeburgh Festival, June 21, 1956. BBC TS. Not broadcast. Recording from the morning concert, made by BBC Transcription Service. UK: CD: BBC Legends 4192-2 (2006), tracks 12–13. Shelf mark: 10Hc3.V087; ID no. 3-920022. Catalogue: *Sound and Video Recordings*. Other collection: British Library Sound Archive call no. 1CD0276751 SEQ3.

British Library Sound Archive, London[194]

Arnell: Serenade for 10 winds and double bass op. 57 (1949). LBE, cond. Haas. Adeney, Solomon (F), Dobson, James (O), Brymer, Waters (C), Draper, Kennedy (Bsns), Sanders (2nd H), J. W. Merrett (DB), cond. Haas. St. Gabriel's Church, Cricklewood, May 17, 1957, 10:00 a.m.–1:00 p.m.; 2–5 p.m. UK: LP: Pye CCL 30120; Pye Golden Guinea GGC 4040; GSGC 14040 (stereo). Call no. 1LP0113782 2.

Bach C. P. E.: Sonatinas for winds Wq. 184 (H629-34). LBE cond. Haas. Morris and Adeney (F), Walton and de Peyer (C), Sanders (2nd H), James (Bsn). AR, June 18, 1953. UK: LP: Parlophone PMB 1004. Call no. 1LP016497; 2LP0083616.

Sonata no. 1 in E-flat. Allegro ma non troppo. Haas states in his notes to Parlophone PMB 1004: "In Sonata no.1 the horns have their difficult high-pitched duet passages connecting up phrases played by the flutes, clarinets and bassoon."

Sonata no. 2 in G. Allegro

Sonata no. 3 in C. Allegretto grazioso

Sonata no. 4 in F. Andante. Haas states: "No. 4 has flutes and clarinets first, then horns and bassoon as solo groups."

Sonata no. 5 in D. Allegretto. Haas states: "No. 5 features in general two clarinets and two flutes against a tutti in which the treble instruments play in unison accompanied by bassoon and horns."

Sonata no. 6 in A. Allegro assai

Bach J. S.: Brandenburg Concerto No. 1 in F major BWV 1046. Grinke (1st V), Del Mar (2nd H), Goossens (1st O), James (1st Bsn), Boyd Neel Orchestra, cond. Boyd Neel. UK: Decca 78 rpm: K 1541-43. June 22, October 29, 1945. Japan: CD: *A Resurrection of Dennis Brain* (Yukihiro Okitsu, 2002). Call no. H1249/1. The players could not be named for contractual reasons.[195]

Bach J. S.: Brandenburg Concerto No. 1 in F major BWV 1046. Hurwitz (1st V), Sanders (2nd H). Other players unidentified. Boyd Neel Orchestra, cond. Boyd Neel. July 26, 1956. Canada: LP: UNLP 1040; Internationale Guilde du Disque, MMS 2097-98; UK: LP: Concert Hall BM 2097-98 (published 1962). The players could not be named for contractual reasons. Call no. 1LP0071466 D1 S1.

Beethoven: Quintet in E-flat op. 16 for piano and winds. Gieseking (Piano), and Philharmonia Wind Ensemble: Sutcliffe (O), Walton (C), James (Bsn). AR, September 15–16, 1955. UK: LP: Columbia 33CX 1322; US: LP: Seraphim 60368; France: LP: EMI References 1017831 (PM 322). The EMI References LP gives April 15–16, not September15–16. Call no. 1CD0257751 SEQ17.

Beethoven: Sonata in F major for horn and piano op. 17. Matthews (P). EMI Studio no. 3. February 21, 1944, and April 3, 1944. UK: 78 rpm: Columbia DX 1152-3; UK: 45 rpm: SEL 1669; SEB 3514; UK: LP: HQM 1033; LP: EMI RLS 7701; US: LP: Seraphim 60040; CD: Andromeda (2CD) ANDRCD 5065/2 (2006), track 7; EMI Classics 2008, CD1, tracks 10–11. Call no. 1LP0143821 3; 1CD0070400 BD12-14; other copy (SEB 3514) call no. 1SE0085762.[196]

Brahms: Songs for female chorus, two horns and harp op. 17. Sung in English in Rev. Troutbeck's edition. Del Mar (2nd H), Mason (Hp), Nottingham Oriana Choir, cond. Henderson. December 30, 1943. UK: 78 rpm Decca (10-inch) M 560-62; Japan: CD: *A Resurrection of Dennis Brain* (2002), tracks 5–8. Call no. 1CS0042897 S1.[197]

1st mvt. *When e'er The Sounding Harp Is Heard*, op.17, no. 1 (Friedrich Ruperti: Es tönt ein voller Harfenklang) M-560

2nd mvt. *Come away, Death*, op.17, no. 2. (Komm herbei Tod, song setting from Shakespeare's *Twelfth Night*) M-561

3rd mvt. *The Gardener*, op.17, no. 3. (Eichendorf, *Der Gartner*) M-561

4th mvt. *The Death of Trenar*, op.17, no. 4. (*Gesang aus Fingal*, from Macpherson's "Ossian") M-562

Britten: Serenade for Tenor, Horn and Strings op. 31. Pears (T), BBC SO, cond. Hollingsworth. Live, Royal Albert Hall Henry Wood Promenade Concert, July 30, 1953. TP, recorded for BBC TS. UK: CD: BBC Legends BBCL 4192-2 (2006), tracks 4–11. Call no 1CD0276751 SEQ4.[198]

Britten: Serenade for Tenor, Horn and Strings op. 31. Pears (T), New Symphony Orchestra of London, cond. Goossens. November 25-27, 1953. UK: LP: Decca LXT 2941; Decca ECM 507; US: LP: LL994; CD: Decca Eloquence 0289 476 847-0 (2006). Call nos. 1LP0046780 S2; 1LP0075986 1; 1CD0298706 SEQ1.

Dittersdorf ed. Haas: Partita in D major for winds (MS). LBE cond. Haas. Sutcliffe, James (O), Sanders (2nd H), James (Bsn). AR, July 20, 1953. UK: LP: Parlophone PMB 1008; Japan: EMI Toshiba TOCE 9335 (all movements). US: LP part-issued on Seraphim 60040 (side 1, band 4, minuet and trio); CD: part-issued (minuet and trio) EMI Classics 2008, CD4, track 11. Call no.1CD0289393; 2CD0076165 (minuet and trio only).

Dukas: Villanelle for horn and piano. Moore (P). EMI Studio No. 1A, April 19, 1952. UK: 78 rpm HMV DB 3300; LP: HQM 1033; LP: RLS 7701; Seraphim 60040; Da Capo 1C 047-01-242; CD: Testament SBT 1022; Andromeda (2CD) ANDRCD 5065/2 (2006), track 9; EMI Classics 2008, CD4, track 19. Duration: 6:10. Call no. 1CD0070400 BD15.

Dvořák: Serenade in D minor op. 44. LBE cond. Haas. Sutcliffe and James (O), Brymer and Tschaikov (C), James, Wilson and Parry (Bsns), Sanders (2nd), Beers (3rd H), Shinebourne (VC), J. W. Merrett (DB). AR, December 6–7, 1951. UK: 78 rpm: Parlophone R 20604-6; Parlophone SW 8132-34; LP: Parlophone PMB 1001; EMI XLP 30011. UK: CD: Testament SBT 1180. Call no. 1CD0209323.

Ferguson: Octet for winds and strings op. 4. First recording. Griller Quartet: Griller and O'Brian (V), Burton (Va), Hampton (VC), Juler (C), James (Bsn), J. E. Merrett (DB). April 7, May 24, 1943. UK: 78 rpm: Decca K 1095-97; UK: CD Dutton CDAX 8014. Call no. 1CD0092935 D1 S1 BD2.[199]

Gounod: Petite Symphonie. LBE cond. Haas. Morris (F), Sutcliffe, James (O), Brymer, de Peyer (C), James, Parry (Bsns), Sanders (2nd H). AR, November 24, 1953, 2–5 p.m. UK: LP: XLP 30011. Call no. 2LP0074119; 1LP0142337.

Handel: Arias for Winds no. 1 & 2. LBE cond. Haas. Dobson, Selwyn, James and Smith (O), Cursue (2nd H), James and Wilson (Bsns), Clift (Tpt), Bradshaw (Tenor Drum). AR, July 15, 1952, 2 and 5 p.m. UK: 78 rpm Parlophone R 20617. Call nos. 1CL0022305; 1CL0022306.

Harback and Friml arr. Sharples: *Sympathy*. UK: LP: Decca Contrasts in HiFi LK 4213; CD UK: Dutton Vocalion CDLK 4169 (2003). December 7, 1956. Brain's two contributions to this long-playing record, "Sympathy" and "Will You Remember" (see Young-Romberg below) were recorded first. The rest of the LP was recorded on February 9 and 19, 1957. Pettitt (1989, p. 197) gives February 1, 1957, as the date. Call no. 1LP0169963 8; list no. M4383R BD 1.[200]

Haydn: Divertimento in C major "Feldparthie" Hob. II:7 (1761). LBE cond. Haas. Sutcliffe, James (O), James, Wilson (Bsn), Sanders (2nd H). AR, September 24, 1953. UK: LP: PMA 1013; XLP 30016. Call no. 1LP0144922; 2LP0071836.

Haydn: Notturno in C major no. 3 Hob. II:32 (1792). LBE, cond. Haas. Morris and Adeney (F), Walton and de Peyer (C), Sanders (2nd H), Glazier and Dyer (V), Clark (VC), J. W. Merrett (DB), Malcolm (Harpsichord). AR, September 24, 1953. UK: Parlophone: LP: PMA 1013; EMI XLP 30016. Call no.2LP0071836; 1LP0144922.

Haydn: Symphony No. 22 in E-flat Hob. 1:22 (1764) "Philosopher." London Baroque Orchestra, cond. Haas. Salter (Continuo). AR, July 4, 1951. UK: 78 rpm: Parlophone SW 8122-3; LP: Parlophone PMA 1004. Call no. H1628/20.

Haydn: Symphony No. 31 in D major Hob. 1:31 (1765) "Horn Signal" Movements 1 and 4 only. September 17, 1952. "Orchestra" including Hurwitz (V), Weil (VC), Sanders, Chapman, Cursue (H), Morris (F), cond. Westrup. UK: 45 rpm EMI HMS 76; HLP18; EMI 7ER 5096; HQM 1033; US: LP: Seraphim 60040 (1st mvt. Only); UK: CD: EMI Classics 2008, CD4, track 12. The EMI CD also only issues the first movement and not the first and fourth, issued on 45 rpm 7ER 5096. Call no.1CL0018987 1.

Jacob: Sextet op. 3 for piano and winds. DBWE and Malcolm (P). TP, September 5, 1957, 6:20–7:00 p.m. Pre-rec July 22, 1957, Farringdon Street, London. UK: LP: EMI Columbia 33CX 1687; US: LP: Seraphim 60169; UK: CD: BBC Legends BBCL 4164-2

(2001), tracks 4–8; EMI Classics 2008, CD4, tracks 14–18. Call no. 1CD0289393 04 BD14-18.[201]

Kay: Miniature Quartet (1950). First recording. Adeney (F), Waters (C), James (Bsn), cond. Haas. St. Gabriel's Church, Cricklewood NW2, May 18, 1957, 2–5 p.m. UK: LP: Pye CCL 30120; GGC 4040 (mono); GSGC 14040 (stereo); GSGC 7054. Call no. 1LP0113782 1.

Mascagni: Intermezzo from Cavalleria *Rusticana*. Organ. Philharmonia Orchestra, cond. Karajan. KH, London, July 24, 1954. UK: LP: Columbia 33CX 1265; US: LP: Angel 35207; CD: UK: EMI CDM 56603-2. Call no. 2LP0032530 1.

Milhaud: *La Cheminée du roi René* op. 205: 6th mvt: Chasse a Valabre only. DBWE. GOS, June 19, 1956. BBC TS. CD: UK: BBC Legends BBCL 4192-2 (2006), track 16. Call no. 1CD0276751 SEQ6A.

Mozart, Leopold: Concerto for alphorn and strings (played on a garden hose-pipe). One movement only. Morley College Symphony Orchestra, cond. Del Mar. Hoffnung Music Festival concert, Royal Festival Hall, November 13, 1956. UK: LP: Columbia 33CX 1406; RLS 7701; UK: CD: EMI Classics 2008, CD4, track 20. Call no. 1LP0140103 S6 BD6; 1CD0015435 D1 S1 BD4.

Mozart: Concerto for Horn No. 1 in D major K.412. Philharmonia Orchestra, cond. Karajan. KH, London, November 12–13, 1953. UK: LP: Columbia 33CX 1140; EMI Classics 7243 5 66898 2 4 (1997); Andromeda (2 CD) ANDRCD 5065/1 (2006), tracks 1–2; Naxos CD 8 111070 (2007), tracks 1–2; EMI Classics 2008, CD 2, tracks 1–2. Call no. 1CD0141461.

Mozart: Concerto for Horn No. 2 in E-flat K.417. Philharmonia Orchestra, cond. Susskind. AR, March 27, 1946. UK: 78 rpm Columbia DX 1365-6; LP: HQM 1033; EMI box set RLS 7701; US: LP: Seraphim 60040; Japan: LP: EMI Toshiba GR-70036; South Korea: CD: Grammofono AB 78 881 (1998), tracks 1–3; EMI Classics 2008, CD1, tracks 4–6. Call no.1LP0140103 S2 BD1.

Mozart: Concerto for Horn No. 2 in E-flat K.417. Philharmonia Orchestra, cond. Karajan. KH, London, November 12, 1953. UK: LP: Columbia 33CX 1140; CD: EMI UK: LP: Columbia 33CX 1140; CD: EMI Classics 7243 5 66898 2 4 (1997); Andromeda (2CD) ANDRCD 5065/1 (2006), tracks 3–5; Naxos CD 8 111070 (2007), tracks 3–5; EMI Classics 2008, CD 2, tracks 3–5; Call no.1LP0140399 S2 BD1-3; 1CD0005930 D1 S1 BD3.

Mozart: Concerto for Horn No. 3 in E-flat K.447. Philharmonia Orchestra, cond. Karajan. KH, London, November 13, 1953. UK: LP: Columbia 33CX 1140; CD: EMI UK: LP: Columbia 33CX 1140; CD: EMI Classics 7243 5 66898 2 4 (1997); Andromeda (2 CD) ANDRCD 5065/1 (2006), tracks 6–8; Naxos CD 8 111070 (2007), tracks 6–8; EMI Classics 2008, CD 2, tracks 6–8. NSA, Call no. 1CD0005930 S1 BD3.

Mozart: Concerto for Horn No. 3 in E-flat K.447. BBC SO, cond. Sargent. Royal Albert Hall, London. TP, July 30, 1953. BBC TS. CD: BBC Legends BBCL 4192-2 (2006), tracks 1–3. Not in the BBC Sound Archives. Call no. 1CD0276751 SEQ1A.

Mozart: Concerto for Horn No.4 in E-flat K.495. Philharmonia Orchestra, cond. Karajan. KH London, November 23, 1953. UK: LP: Columbia 33CX 1140; CD: EMI Classics 7243 5 66898 2 4 (1997); Andromeda (2CD) ANDRCD 5065/1 (2006), tracks 9–11; Naxos CD 8 111070 (2007), tracks 9–11; EMI Classics 2008, CD 2, tracks 9–11. Call no.1LP0140399 S2 BD4-6; 1LP0010770 D1 S2 BD2;1CD0011778 D1 S1 BD14.

Mozart: Concerto for Horn No. 4 in E-flat K.495. Hallé Orchestra, cond. Sargent (1st mvt) and Turner (2nd and 3rd mvts.). Houldsworth Hall, Manchester, June 21, 1943. UK: 78 rpm. Columbia DX 1123-4; Japan: LP: EMI Toshiba GR-70036. UK: CD: EMI Classics 2008, CD1, tracks 1–3. Call no. 1LP0140103 S1 BD-3; 1CD0135963 BD04-06.[202]

Mozart arr. Baines: Divertimento No. 14 in B-flat major K.270. Arranged for flute, oboe, clarinet, horn, and bassoon. Movements 1 and 4 only. DBWE. GOS, March 19, 1956. BBC TS. UK: CD: BBC Legends BBCL 4192-2 (2006), tracks 14–15. Call no. 1CD0276751 SEQ4A; 1CD0276751 SEQ4A, SEQ5A.

Mozart: Divertimento no. 16 in E-flat K.289 (K.271g). DBWE: Brain, Sutcliffe (O), Sanders (2nd H), Alexandra and Draper (Bsn). AR, November 5, 1952. UK: 45 rpm EMI 7ER 5096; LP: EMI HQM 1033; US: LP: Seraphim 60040. Palladio PD 4125; UK: CD: EMI Classics 2008, CD4 tracks 9–10. Call no. 1CD0289393 D4 BD9-10; 1SE0092048 S2 BD2 HMV; Call nos. 1CL0018995 2 HMV; 1CL0018996 2 HMV.

Mozart: Divertimento in D major K.334 (K.320b) for two horns and strings. Aubrey Brain (1st H), Léner Quartet: Léner and Smilovits (V), Roth (Va), Hartman (VC). AR, February 16, 1939. UK: 78 rpm: Columbia LX 841-845; CD: UK: EMI CDH 7 64198 2 (1992); Call no. 9CL0019440 1; 1CD0043082 D1 S1 BD1.

Mozart: Quintet K.407 (K.386c) for horn and strings. Three members of the Griller Quartet with Gilbert (2nd Va). Decca Studios, Broadhurst Gardens, West Hampstead, London, October 6, 1944. UK: 78 rpm: Decca K 1138-39; UK: CD: London 425960-2 LM; Dutton: CDBP 9717 (2001), tracks 10–12. Call no. 1CD0201704 BD3; 1CD0029614 D1 S1 BD3; 1CD0134067 D1 S1 BD9.[203]

Mozart: Quintet in E-flat for piano and winds K.452. DBWE, Horsley (P). May 19 and 23, 1954. UK: LP CLP 1029; CD: EMI Classics 7243 5 66898 2 4 (1997); EMI Classics 2008, CD2, tracks 12–14. Call no. 1LP0144911 1; 1CD0141461 BD5.

Mozart: Quintet in E-flat for piano and winds K.452. Philharmonia Wind Quartet, Walter Gieseking (P). April 15, 1955. UK: LP: 33CX 1322; UK: CD: Naxos Historical 8 111070 (2007). Call no. 1CD0257751 SEQ17.

Mozart: Serenade no. 11 in E-flat major, K.375. LBE cond. Haas. Sutcliffe and James (O), Brymer and Tschaikov (C), James, Wilson (Bsn), Sanders (2nd H). AR, January 3–4, 1952. UK: 78rpm: Parlophone R 20610-2; SW 8142-44; LP: Parlophone PMB 1002. Call no.1CD0209323 BD1.

Mozart: Serenade no. 11 in E-flat major, K.375. LBE cond. Haas. Dobson and James (O), Brymer, (1st C), Walton (Alternating 1st C), Waters (2nd C), James and Kennedy (Bsn), Sanders (2nd H). St Gabriel's Church, Cricklewood, May 15, 1957, 2–5; May 16, one hour. UK: LP: Pye CCL 30119; Golden Guinea Collector GGC (Mono) 4062; GSGC (Stereo) 4062. Call no.1LP01113484 1

Mozart: Serenade no. 12 in C minor, K.388 (K.384a). LBE cond. Haas. Sutcliffe, James (O), Brymer, Tschaikov (C), James and Wilson (Bsn), Sanders (2nd H). AR, June 23–24, 1952. UK: LP: Parlophone PMA 1013; EMI XLP 30016. Call no.1CD0209323 BD2.

Mozart: Serenade no. 12 in C minor, K.388 (K.384a). LBE cond. Haas. Sutcliffe and James (O), Brymer and Waters (C), James and Wilson (Bsn), Sanders (2nd H). St. Gabriel's Church, Cricklewood, May 13, 1957, 2–5 p.m. UK: LP: Pye CCL 30119; Golden Guinea Collector GGC 4062 (Mono); UK: CD: Testament SBT 1180. Call no. 1CD0031920 D1 S1 BD2.

Mozart: Sinfonia Concertante K.297b (K.320d). Sutcliffe (O), Walton (C), James (Bsn), Philharmonia Orchestra, cond. Karajan. AR, November 17–18, 1953. UK: LP: Columbia 33CX 1178; EMI XLP 60004; EMI RLS 7715; US: LP: Angel 35098; Japan: EMI Toshiba EAC 37001-19. Call no.1CD0015296 D1 S1 BD1; 1CD0116380 BD3.

Romberg arr. Sharples: "Will You Remember." Bob Sharples Orchestra, cond. Sharples. UK: LP: Decca Contrasts in HiFi LK 4213; UK: CD: Dutton Vocalion CDLK 4169 (2003). December 7, 1956. See note for Harback-Friml above, recorded by Brain for this LP. Call no. 1LP0169963-4.

Schumann: Adagio and Allegro in A-flat major op. 70 for horn and piano. Moore. AR, April 22, 1952, January 13, 1953. UK: 78 rpm: Columbia DX 1867; UK: LP: EMI HQM 1033; US: LP: Seraphim 60040; HMV Electrola 1C 047 01 242; LP: World Record Club 3115; UK: CD: Testament SBT 1022; Andromeda (2CD) ANDRCD 5065/2 (2006), track 8; EMI Classic.[204]

Strauss: Concerto No. 1 in E Flat Major for Horn and Orchestra op. 11. Philharmonia Orchestra, cond. Galliera. KH, London, May 21, 1947. UK: 78 rpm: Columbia DX 1397-98; LP: EMI HQM 1033; EMI HMV Treasury LP box set EMI RLS 7701: Japan: LP: EMI Toshiba GR-70036; CD: Pearl GEMM 0026; Testament SBT 1009; EMI Classics 2008, CD1, tracks 7–9. Call no.1CD0051547 D1 S1 BD1.[205]

Strauss: Concerto No. 1 in E Flat Major for Horn and Orchestra op. 11. Philharmonia Orchestra, cond.,Sawallisch. AR, September 22, 1956. UK: LP: Columbia 33CX 1491; US: Angel 35496; UK: CD: EMI Classics 7243 5 67782 2 1 (2002), tracks 1–3; EMI Classics 2008, CD3, tracks 1–3. Call no.1CD0001933 BD1.

Strauss: Concerto No. 2 in E-flat major for Horn and Orchestra (1942). Philharmonia Orchestra, cond. Sawallisch. AR, September 22–23, 1956. UK: LP: Columbia 33CX 1491; CD: EMI Classics 7243 5 67782 2 1 (2002), tracks 4–6; EMI Classics 2008, CD3, tracks 4–6. Call no.1CD0001933 D1 S1 BD2; 1CD0001933 BD1.

Strauss: Symphony in E-flat for sixteen wind instruments, *Fröliche Werkstatt* Op. Posth. (1943–45). LBE cond. Haas. Gilbert and Adeney (F), MacDonagh and James (O), Brymer, Tschaikov and Waters (C), Whewell (Bassett-horn), Lear (Bass C), Beers, Burden, and Cursue (H); James and Wilson (Bsn), O'Loughlin (Contra-bassoon). AR, January 29–30, 1953. UK: LP: Parlophone PMA 1006; XLP 30021. Call nos. 1LP0110322; 2LP0062155.[206]

Strauss: Suite in B-flat op. 4 for thirteen wind instruments. LBE cond. Haas. Solomon and Ellory (F), Dobson and James (O), Waters and King (C), Sanders, Bradley, and Borsforf (H), Draper and Kennedy (Bsn), Waller (Contra-bassoon). St. Gabriel's Church, Cricklewood, 10 a.m.–1 p.m.; 2–5 p.m. May 18, 1957. UK: LP: Pye Golden Guinea GSGC 14040 (Stereo) GGC 4040 (Mono); CCL 30120; Precision Records and Tapes GSGC 7054 (1984); audio-cassette: Precision Records and Tapes ZCGC 7054. Call nos. 1LP0113782; 2LP0061437; 1LP0113310; 1LP0113465; 2LP0061516.[207]

Wagner: Siegfried: Horn Call (one of set of 78 rpm records entitled *Instruments of the Orchestra*) cond. Sargent. AR, May 14, 1947. UK: 78 rpm: C3622. UK: CD: Testament SBT 1012; EMI Classics 2008, CD1, track 12. Call no.1LP0140103 7; 1CD0051548 D1 S1 BD1 (Testament SBT 1012).

2. Germany

Deutschlandradio Kultur, Berlin

Hans-Rosenthal-Platz 10825 Berlin

This organization inherited the archives of the former RIAS (Radio in the American Sector). The RIAS recordings include the following which have been transcribed from the original index cards in the archives of Deutschlandradio Kultur:

Beethoven: Sonata in F major for horn and piano op. 17. Hansen (P). April 20, 1950. Duration: 13:59. Archive no. Bd. 34-044/I; other catalogue ref. B II 2f; P 41-466. US: LP: IGI 370. Other collections: BPL. LP issue: IGI 370. British Library Sound Archive call no. 1LP0132771 S2 BD1-2 (IGI 370). WSA no.1631. University of Wisconsin Madison, Blake Collection. Accession no. AQR3568UW; Call no. LP 73045 (IGI 370)

Dukas: Villanelle for horn and piano. Billing (P). May 4, 1953. Edition: Durand. Duration: 5:47. Archive no. Bd. 82-882 U; other catalogue ref. B II 2a; R 40-820. Unpublished.

Hindemith: Sonata for Horn and Piano (1939). Hansen (P). April 20, 1950. Duration: 16:08. Edition: Schott. Archive no. Bd. 34-044/II; other catalogue ref. B II 2a; R 41-467. Unpublished.

Kaminski: Ballade for horn and piano. Billing (P). September 18, 1950. Duration: 6:30. Catalogue ref. B II 2f; P 41-468. Unpublished.

Mozart: Concerto for Horn in E-flat K.447. RIAS-Symphonie Orchester, cond. van Kempen. May 4, 1953. Duration: 14:20. Edition: Breitkopf & Hartel. Archive no. Bd. 82-798/III; other catalogue ref. B I, 7f; St 31-972. LP: Longanesi Periodici GCL 53. NB. The last movement on the LP contains an unknown splice from another recording with another player. The reason for this splice is not clear. In the original archive recording, the whole is played by Brain. The catalogue states the conductor is Paul van Kempen not Rudolf Kempe, as on the Longanesi Periodici LP. Other collections: British Library Sound Archive call no. 1LP0095952 S2.

Mozart: Quintet for Piano and Winds K.452. DBWE, Hansen (P). September 22, 1951. Edition: Peters. Duration: 20:40. Archive no. Bd. 55-755 U; other catalogue ref. BII, 2b; R 41-478. Unpublished.

Schumann: Adagio and Allegro A-flat major op. 70 for horn and piano. Billing. May 4, 1953. Duration: 8:04. Edition: Breitkopf. Archive no. Bd. 82-881 U; other catalogue ref. B II, 2a; R 40-876. Unpublished.[208]

Norddeutsches Rundfunk (NDR), Hamburg[209]

*__Beethoven: Sonata in F major for horn and piano op. 17.__ Conrad Hansen. April 18, 19, 1950. Archive no. 00-30216, take 100. Duration: 14:25. Unpublished. Not to be confused with the performance for RIAS, Berlin, with Hansen, April 20, 1950.

*__Dukas: Villanelle for horn and piano.__ Alfred Westphal. May 6, 1954. Archive no. 00-72561, take 200; Production no. S-543. Duration: 5:40. Unpublished.

*__Hindemith: Sonata for horn and piano (1939).__ Conrad Hansen. April 18, 1950. Archive no. 00-30207, take 100. Duration: 17:20. Unpublished. Not to be confused with the performance for RIAS, Berlin, with Hansen, April 20, 1950.

Mozart: Concerto for Horn in E-flat K.417. Norddeutsches Rundfunk Sinfonieorchester, Hamburg cond. Schmidt-Isserstedt. May 7, 1954. Archive no. 00-72629, take 200; production no. S-533.Duration 13:35. France: CD: Tahra 59598 (2007). Other collections: British Library Sound Archive call no.1CD0270267 SEQ4A (Tahra 59598).

Schreiter: Sonatine for Horn and Piano op. 12. FBP. Westphal (P). May 6, 1954. Archive no. 00-72561, take 100; production no. S-543. Unpublished.

Strauss: Concerto No. 1 in E Flat Major for Horn and Orchestra op. 11. Norddeutsches Rundfunk Sinfonieorchester, Hamburg cond. Schmidt-Isserstedt. May 7, 1954. Archive no. 00-72629, take 100; production no. S-533. Duration: 15:05. US: CD: Green Hill GH-0015/16 (1996).[210]

Südwestrundfunk Archives (SWR), Stuttgart. (Formerly Süddeutscher Rundfunk Archives (SDR), Stuttgart)

Beethoven: Sonata in F major for horn and piano op. 17. Hansen (P). April 19, 1951. Archive no. 40-03957, take W00 (001-003). Duration: 11:58. Unpublished.

Hindemith: Sonata for horn and piano (1939). Hansen (P). April 19, 1951. Archive no. 40-03958, take W00 (001-003). Duration: 16:50. Austria: CD: HPE CD02 (1994), tracks 4–6.

Mozart: Concerto for Horn in E-flat K.447. Radio-Sinfonieorchester Stuttgart des SWR, cond. Hans Müller-Kray. Villa Berg, April 20, 1952. Archive no. 41-16000, take W00 (001-003). Duration: 14:28. Unpublished.[211]

Südwestrundfunk Archives (SWR), Baden-Baden (Formerly, Südwestfunk (SWF)

*__Hindemith: Sonata for horn and piano (1939).__ Mewton-Wood (P). June 8, 1950, Baden-Baden, Hans Rosbaud Studio. Archive no. 56-01703, take W00 (001-003); production no. 0101691. Duration: 16:56. Unpublished.

Mozart: Concerto for Horn in E-flat K.417. Südwestfunk Orchestra, Baden-Baden, cond. Hindemith. Kursaal, Baden-Baden, October 10, 1948. Archive no. 01-24306; take 000; production no. 0130820. Duration: 13:30. Austria: CD: HPE CD02 (1994), tracks 1–3.

Mozart: Concerto for Horn in E-flat K.417. Südwestfunk Sinfonieorchester, Baden-Baden und Freiburg, cond. Rosbaud. Hans Rosbaud Studio, Baden-Baden, May 6, 1953. Archive no. 56-05957, take W00 (001-003); production no. 0130820. Duration: 13:45. Italy: CD: Arkadia GI 772.1 (1994), tracks 5–7; CD: Germany: Archipel ARPCD 0202 (2003); Hänssler HAN 093129 (2006). Other collections: British Library Sound Archive call. no. 1CD0284025 SEQ4A.

Mozart: Concerto for Horn in E-flat K.447. Südwestfunk Sinfonieorchester, Baden-Baden und Freiburg, cond. Rosbaud. May 6, 1953. Archive no. 56-05958, take 000; production no. 0130820. Duration: 15:00. Italy: CD: ASdisc 356 (1991); CD: Germany: Hänssler HAN 93064 (2002); HAN 093129 (2006). Other collections: British Library Sound Archive call no. 1CD0284025 SEQ9A; 1CD0220539 BD8-10 Hänssler Classic. WSA no.1386.[212]

*__Mozart: Concerto for Horn in E-flat K.447.__ Südwestfunk Sinfonieorchester, Baden-Baden und Freiburg, cond. Rosbaud. Hans Rosbaud Studio, Baden-Baden, May 6, 1953. Stereo. Archive no. 35-00850, take W03 (008-010); production no. 1000815. Duration: 15:05. Unpublished. Not the mono recording broadcast on the same date (see above) but another performance.

West Deutscher Rundfunk, Köln (WDR)

Hindemith: Concerto for Horn and Orchestra (1949). Westdeutscher Rundfunk Orchester, cond. Keilberth. January 22, 1951. Preserved by WDR but no longer in their archives. It exists as a rare archive copy in a private collection. Unpublished.

Mozart: Concerto for Horn in E-flat K.447. Westdeutscher Rundfunk Orchester, cond. Wand. January 23, 1951. Archive no. 5125013. Duration: 13:48. US: CD: Treasure of the Earth TOE 2004 (2001).[213]

Stiftung Deutches Rundfunkarchiv (DRA), Frankfurt

This archive does not preserve recordings but lists the recordings preserved by German radio archives and lists additional takes for broadcasting that appear not to have been preserved. These extra recordings (if they still exist) have the same dates, personnel, and pieces as listed separately above, under the relevant radio archive, but have different computerized database numbers, durations and take numbers. We have not been able to verify if these recordings have been preserved.

Beethoven: Sonata in F major for horn and piano op. 17. Hansen (P). NDR, April 18, 1950. Archive no. M8-06689, take 001. Duration 14:33.

Dukas: Villanelle for horn and piano. Alfred Westphal. NDR, May 6, 1954. Archive no. M8-13690, take 002. Duration: 5:44.

Hindemith: Sonata for horn and piano (1939). Hansen (P). NDR, April 18, 1950. Archive no. M8-06688, take 001. Duration: 17:26.

Hindemith: Sonata for horn and piano (1939). Mewton-Wood (P). SWR, June 8, 1950, Baden-Baden, Hans Rosbaud Studio. Archive no. 71-09524, take 000. Other catalogue data: "Bem. Allgemein Umschnitt BB (M1703)." Duration: 17:00.

Mozart: Concerto for Horn in E-flat K.417. NDR. Norddeutsches Rundfunk Sinfonieorchester, Hamburg cond. Schmidt-Isserstedt. May 7, 1954. Archive no. M8-12869, take 002. Duration: 13:42.

Schreiter: Sonatine for horn and piano op.12. Alfred Westphal. NDR, May 6, 1954. Archive no. M8-13690, take 001. Duration: 6:38.

Strauss: Concerto no. 1 in E-flat for Horn and Orchestra op.11. Norddeutsches Rundfunk Sinfonieorchester, Hamburg cond. Schmidt-Isserstedt. NDR. May 7, 1954. Archive no. M8-12869; take 001. Duration: 15:09.

3. Netherlands

Sound and Vision (Nederlands Institut voor Beeld en Geluid), Postbus 1050-1200 BB, Hilversum.

This organization now preserves these archive recordings made by the Dutch broadcasting company, AVRO, from a concert in the Amsterdam Concergebouw. [214]

Britten: Canticle III Still Falls the Rain—The Raids, 1940, Night and Dawn, Op. 55. Pears (T), Britten (P). Amsterdam, July 6, 1956. HM-11160; 1L-1; duration: 14:15. Unpublished.

Dukas: Villanelle for horn and piano. Britten (P). Amsterdam, July 6, 1956. HM-11160;11-1; duration: 06:30. Unpublished.

Schubert: *Auf dem Strom* for tenor, horn and piano op. posth. 119, D. 943. Pears (T), Britten (P). Amsterdam, July 6, 1956. HM-22260; 1K-1; duration: 11:50. Unpublished.

Schumann: Adagio and Allegro A-flat major op. 70 for horn and piano op. 70. Britten (P). Amsterdam, July 6, 1956. HM-11160; 1J-1; duration: 08:20. Unpublished.

4. Sweden

Swedish Radio Archives

Mozart: Concerto for Horn in E-flat K.417. Swedish Radio Orchestra, cond. Frykberg. October 7, 1956. Sweden: LP: BIS 331-333 (1986).[215]

5. United States

Stanford Archive of Recorded Sound

Braun Music Center, Stanford University, California

Since the late 1970s, the location of the Western Sound Archives (WSA), whose vast library was alleged to include a significant collection of Brain BBC radio broadcasts, has remained a mystery. Documents dating back to that period placed its location near San Luis Obispo in southern California. However, in the mid-1980s, it mysteriously ceased to exist. A breakthrough occurred when we located the former archivist for the WSA, Nathan Brown, and with his assistance uncovered Brain solo, orchestral, and chamber works, plus a collection of European festival studio tape recordings from that period.

WSA re-emerged as the Classical Recordings Archive of America (CRAA) in the early 1980s in El Cerrito, northern California. CRAA specialized in classical orchestral and instrumental recorded music. In 1993, it relocated to Cottonwood, Arizona, retaining its name. Before relocating, CRAA donated a large portion of its original classical archives to the Stanford Archive of Recorded Sound, with the stipulation that the donation be open to access for research. After contacting CRAA, written authorization was granted by CRAA to Lynch permitting full access to the donated collection. The Braun Music Center plans to catalog the entire WSA and transfer it to modern digital media.

If a recording is kept by the Braun Music Center CRAA collection and is currently preserved by the BBC (BBC Information and Archives) or other archive collections, it is not listed here. Rather, it is listed in the relevant section, with a catalog reference number to its location in the Braun collection. Thus the following are not representative of the entire Brain holdings in the Braun collection. The bulk are also preserved by the BBC and British Library Sound Archive in London.[216]

The Early Horn.* Sub-title: *A Programme About the Horn and Its Music in the Eighteenth Century. TP, July 23, 1955. Sanders (2nd H), Delman (S), Helliwell (Harpsichord and Continuo), The Haydn Orchestra, cond. Newstone. WSA no.1150. Other collections: British Library Sound Archive call no. 1LP0058897 S1 BD5. Excerpt.[217]

This archive recording preserves more of this broadcast than the BBC. It includes, for example, the movement of Rosetti's Concerto in E-flat and Mozart's Fragment K.494a (K.98a)., as well as speech links not available anywhere else.

Hindemith: Sonata for four horns. Sanders, Chapman, and Cursue. TP, January 5, 1956. Italy: CD: ASDisc 356 (1991); Andromeda ANDRCD 5065 (2006). WSA no.1231. This recording is not preserved in the British Library Sound Archive or by the BBC.

University of Wisconsin-Madison

Mills Music Library: Blake Collection

Schubert: *Auf dem Strom* for tenor, horn and piano, D. 943, op. posth. 119. Lewis (T), Lush (P). BBC TS. BBC TP, April 6, 1954. Taken from the program presenting works performed at Schubert's Invitation Concert, March 26, 1828. No longer preserved by the BBC sound archives and not located in any public archive collection, except at this university, on this long-playing record, commercially issued in 1971 by Perennial Long-player (New York) PER 1007.[218]

III. Film Media

Crown Film Unit (Anvil Films). Beethoven Sonata in F major for horn and piano op. 17. Matthews (P). 1952. Released several times since the original film.

Amati Video (in association with John Wates), 1989. VHS. Not available.

Laser disc Toshiba EMI TOLW-3548 (Japan, 1991) See *dennisbrain.net/tributes.html*

Beulah, *Listening to Britain*. VHS RT151. Not available.

Beulah. YB35 *Classical Music of the Forties.* DVD (pal format all regions). May still be available outside the USA from Brian Coward, Beulah, 8 Woods Terrace, Gainsborough, Lincolnshire DN21 2RP. See eavb.co.uk.

Hans Pizka, on DVD in 2007. See *pizka.de/Dennis%20BrainDVDInfo.htm*

***British Pathé. Festival in Edinburgh** (published 1955). Brain appears briefly in this color documentary. The soundtrack, with voice narration by Alistair Sim, covering part of Brain's performance, is of Wagner's *Siegfried Horn Call.* This was dubbed from his HMV recording of May 14, 1947 (C 3622). For the recording, see above, II. British Library Sound Archive. For the Beethoven Sonata with Matthews, Pettitt (1989), 198–99.

The film sequence with Brain has no authentic soundtrack of him playing, but it is useful to see him playing and to study the embouchure. The film can be downloaded from British Pathé's website. It is also available for loan as a VHS archive copy at Scottish Screen Archives. The film is in two parts; Brain features in Part 1, at 4:36.[219]

Halas and Batchelor. *The Magic Canvas: A Story in Movement, Form and Color (UK release 1948, first published in US 1955). Music by Mátyás Seiber: Fantasy for flute, horn and string quartet. Morris (F), Blech Quartet. Directed by Mátyás Seiber. The musicians do not appear in the film. A copy of this video was preserved at Iowa State University, later transferred to the Library of Congress. The Library of Congress catalog number AAFF4 -05041604739-1-1. See above (II. International Archives Collections: I. United Kingdom: BBC Archives and Information Service, London) for another recording with Brain, Morris, and the Allegri Quartet.[220]

IV. Performers and Composers

1. Conductors

Ackermann, Otto
Beer, Sidney
Bernard, Anthony
Beecham, Sir Thomas Bart. C.H.
Blech, Harry
Boult, Sir Adrian Cedric
Braithwaite, Warwick
Britten, Benjamin
Busch, Fritz
Cameron, Basil
Cantelli, Guido
Collingwood, Lawrance
Dobrowen, Issay
Fistoulari, Anatole
Frykberg, Sten
Furtwängler, Willem
Galliera, Alceo
Gentry, Gerald

Goossens, Eugene
Haas, Karl
Henderson, Roy
Hindemith, Paul
Hollingsworth, John
Irving, Robert
Jenkins, Rae
Karajan, Herbert von
Keilberth, Josef
Klemperer, Otto
Kletzki, Paul
Krips, Henry
Kubelik, Rafael
Lambert, Constant
Mackerras Charles (Sir)
Malko, Nicolai
Markevitch, Igor
Matačić, Lovro von
Miles, Maurice
Müller-Kray, Hans
Neel, Boyd
Newstone, Harry
Nils-Fougstedt, Erik
O'Donnell, Rudolph P., Wing Commander, MVO
Patane, Franco
Priestman, Brian
Pritchard, John (Sir)
Rankl, Karl
Riddick, Kathleen
Rosbaud, Hans
Sacher, Paul
Sargent, Sir Malcolm
Sawallisch, Wolfgang
Schmidt-Isserstedt, Hans
Schüchter, Wilhelm
Seiber, Mátyás
Sharples, Bob
Stiedry, Fritz
Susskind, Walter
Strauss, Richard
Tausky, Vilem
Tomlinson, Ernest
Toscanini, Arturo
Turner, Laurence
Van Kempen, Paul
Walton, Sir William
Wand, Gunther
Weldon, George
Westrup, Jack A.
Wurmser, Leo

2. Orchestra Leaders (Concertmasters)

Armon, William (BBC Concert Orchestra)
Beard, Paul (BBC Symphony Orchestra)
Hutcheon, James (BBC Midland Orchestra)
Jones, Granville (London Symphony Orchestra)
Kantrovitch, Vera (Welbeck Orchestra, Riddick String Orchestra)
Lampe, Oscar (Royal Philharmonic Orchestra)
McCallum, David (National Symphony Orchestra, Royal Philharmonic Orchestra)
Mouland Begbie, J. (BBC Scottish Orchestra)
Parikian, Manoug (Philharmonia Orchestra)
Taylor, Charles (Royal Opera House Orchestra, Covent Garden)
Whiteway, Philip (BBC Welsh Orchestra)

3. Singers

Baritone
Bourdin, Roger
Boyce, Bruce
Krauss, Otakar
Metternich, Josef
Langdon, Michael
Rehfuss, Hans
Rico, Roger
Schöffler, Paul

Bass
Edelmann, Otto
Frank, Ernest
Franz, Ferdinand

Contralto
Evans, Nancy
Höffgen, Marga
Ilosovay, Maria von
Sinclair, Monica

Mezzo-Soprano
Bannerman, Betty
Cavelti, Elsa
Garside, Gwladys
Schürhoff, Else
St. Arnaud, Huguette

Soprano
Cantelo, April
Cross, Joan
Delman, Jacqueline
Felbermeyer, Anny
Fisher, Sylvia
Flagstad, Kirsten
Field-Hyde, Margaret
Furmedge, Edith
Geori-Boue,
Grümmer, Eliszabeth
Hart, Freda
Jurinac, Sena
Raisbeck, Rosina
Schwarzkopf, Elisabeth
Steber, Eleanor
Suddaby, Elsie
Sutherland, Joan (Dame)
Welitsch, Ljuba

Tenor
Chitty, George
Craig, Charles
Häfliger, Ernst
Infantino, Luigi
Jones, Leslie
Jones, Parry
Kuen, Paul
Lewis, Richard
Nilsson, Raymond
Nore, George
Pears, Peter
Svanholm, Set

4. Instrumentalists

Bassoon
Alexandra, John
Draper, Paul
James, Cecil
Kennedy, Valentine
Parry, Peter
Wilson, Edward

Cello
Cameron, Douglas (Blech String Quartet)
Clark, Raymond
Hampton, Colin (Griller Quartet)
Hartman, Imre (Léner Quartet)
Just, Helen (English Quartet)
McCarthy, Eileen (Carter Trio)
Pleeth, William (Allegri Quartet)
Shinebourne, J.
Tortelier, Paul
Weil, Terence
Whitehead, James (Philharmonic String Trio; see also Fibich Quintet)

Clarinet
Brymer, Jack
De Peyer, Gervase
Juler, Pauline
King, Thea
Tschaikov, Basil "Nick"
Thurston, Frederick "Jack"
Walton, Bernard
Waters, Stephen

Continuo
Helliwell, Clifton
Salter, Lionel

Contra-bassoon
O'Loughlin, James
Waller, Ronald

Double Bass
Merrett, James W. (see Arnell Serenade, Dittersdorf Partita, Dvorak Serenade)
Merrett, James E. (see Ferguson Octet)

Cor Anglais
Graeme, Peter

Flute
Adeney, Richard
Ellory, Jack
Morris, Gareth
Solomon, Lionel

Harp
Mason, Gwendolen

Harpsichord
Helliwell, Clifton
Malcolm, George

Horn
Beers, Ian
Borsdorf, Emil
Bradley, Francis
Brain, Aubrey
Burden, John
Civil, Alan
Cursue, Alfred
Chapman, Edmund
Del Mar, Norman
Sanders, Neill
White, Roy

Oboe
Brain, Leonard
Dobson, Michael
Goossens, Leon
James, Natalie
Selwyn, Edward
Smith, Stan
Sutcliffe, Sidney

Organ
Brain, Dennis
Dawson, Herbert

Piano
Billing, Klaus
Britten, Benjamin
Crowson, Lamar
Cutner, Solomon (known as Solomon)
Fevrier, Jacques
Fuchsova, Lisa
Gieseking, Walter
Hansen, Conrad
Horsley, Colin
Long, Kathleen
Loveridge, Iris
Lush, Ernest
Malcolm, George
Mason, B.
Matthews, Denis
Mewton-Wood, Noel
Moore, Gerald
Parry, Wilfrid
Preedy, Cyril
Salter, Lionel
Scherzer, Grete
Westphal, Alfred

Spoken Voice
Olivier, Laurence (Sir)
Sitwell, Edith (Dame)

String Ensembles
Allegri Quartet: Eli Goren, James Barton, Patrick Ireland, William Pleeth
Blech Quartet: Harry Blech, Lionel Bentley, Keith Cummings, Douglas Cameron,
Carter String Trio: Mary Carter, Anatole Mines, Eileen McCarthy
English String Quartet: Ruth Pearl, Lesley White, Marjorie Lempfert, Helen Just
Griller Quartet: Sidney Griller, Jack O'Brian, Philip Burton, Colin Hampton
Léner Quartet: Jenö Léner, Joseph Smilovits, Sandor Roth, Imre Hartman
Philharmonic String Trio: David Martin, Max Gilbert, James Whitehead

Tenor Drum
Bradshaw, James

Trumpet
Clift, Denis

Viola
Aronowitz, Cecil
Burton, Philip (Griller Quartet)
Cummings, Keith (Blech Quartet)
Gilbert, Max (Philharmonic String Trio; with Griller Quartet)
Grainger, Eileen (accompanying Carter Trio as Second Viola)
Hurwitz, Emanuel
Ireland, Patrick (Allegri Quartet)
Lempfert, Marjorie (English Quartet; and accompanying Carter Trio as Second Viola)
Mines, Anatole (Carter Trio; members of the English String Quartet)
Riddle, Frederick
Roth, Sandor (Léner Quartet)

Violin

Barton, James (Allegri Quartet)
Bentley, Lionel (Blech Quartet)
Carter, Mary
Dyer, John
Griller, Sidney (Griller Quartet)
Glazier, Joshua
Grinke, Frederick
Goren, Eli (Allegri Quartet)
Hurwitz, Emanuel
Léner, Jenö (Léner Quartet)
Martin, David (Philharmonic String Trio)
O'Brien, Jack (Griller Quartet)
Parikian, Manoug
Pearl, Ruth (English Quartet)
Salpeter, Max
Smilovits, Joseph (Léner Quartet)
White, Lesley (English Quartet)
Wilson, Marie

5. Composers

Arnell, Richard Anthony Sayer
Bach, Carl Philipp Emanuel
Bach, Johann Sebastian
Baines, Anthony (arranger)
Beethoven, Ludwig van
Berkeley, Sir Lennox Randal Francis
Berlioz, Hector
Bizet, Georges
Borodin, Aleksandr Porfir'evič
Bowen, York
Bowyer, R.B.
Brahms, Johannes
Britten, Baron OM CH, Edward Benjamin
Bruckner, Anton
Butterworth, George Sainton Kaye
Campese, G.
Cardillo, Salvatore
Coates, Eric
Cooke, Arnold Atkinson
Crescenzo, Vincent de
Curtis, Ernesto de
Delibes, Clément Philibert Léo
Delius, Frederick Albert Theodore
Dittersdorf, Karl Ditters von
Dohnanyi, Ernö (Ernst von)
Dukas, Paul Abraham
Dvořák, Antonin Leopold
Enesco, Georges
Essex, Kenneth
Falla Manuel de
Fauré, Gabriel Urbain
Ferguson, Howard
Fibich, Zdeněk
Fricker, Peter Racine
Friml, Rudolph
Glazunov, Alexander Constantinovich (arranger)
Glinka, Mikhail
Gounod, Charles François
Goldmark, Karl
Grainger, Percy George
Gruber, Franz Xavier
Handel, George Frederick
Harback, Otto
Harty Hamilton, Sir Herbert (arranger)
Haydn, Franz Josef
Hindemith, Paul
Humperdinck, Engelbert
Ibert, Jacques François Antoine
Jacob, Gordon Percival Septimus
Janáček, Leoš
Kaminski, Heinrich
Kay, Norman Forber
Kodály, Zoltán
Lambert, Constant
Lewis, Anthony, Sir
Liszt, Franz
Malipiero, Gian Francesco
Mascagni, Pietro
Méhul,, Étienn-Nicolas
Mendelssohn-Bartholdy, Jakob Ludwig Felix
Milhaud, Darius
Moeran, Ernest John
Mozart, Leopold Johann Georg
Mozart, Johannes Chrysostomus Wolfgangus Theophilus Gottlieb Amadeus
Paisiello, Giovanni
Poulenc, Francis Jean Marcel
Ravel, Joseph Maurice
Respighi, Ottorino (arranger)

Rimsky-Korsakov, Nikolai Andreyevich
Robertson, Alec (arranger)
Romberg, Sigmund
Rossini, Gioacchino Antonio
Salter, Lionel Paul (arranger)
Schoeck, Othmar
Schreiter, Heinz
Schubert, Franz Peter
Schumann, Robert
Seiber, Mátyás György
Sharples, Robert (arranger)
Sibelius, Jean
Smyth, Dame Ethel Mary DBE
Strauss, Richard Georg
Tchaikovsky, Pyotr Il'yich
Thomas, Ambroise
Tomlinson, Ernest
Vinter, Gilbert
Wagner, Richard Wilhelm
Waldteufel, Charles Émile Lévy
Walton, William Turner, Sir OM
Weber, Carl Maria Friedrich Ernst von
Williams, Edward Aneurin

APPENDIX

A

Brain Ensemble Music Library

Audrey Brain has stated that the music scores used for the Quintet's engagements were divided equally between the Brain brothers. This may have been a precaution in case one or the other was indisposed at the last minute and a deputy was required for either.[1]

Some of the scores are handwritten copies; a few appear to be autograph manuscripts of composers, including Fricker's Quintet, with instruction on the oboe part, and an unknown quintet (composed in 1946) by a pupil of Paul Hindemith, Heinrich Jacoby (b.1909–d.1990), also known as Hanoch Jacoby. Poulenc's Sextet (minus the piano part) has Brain's signature and that of Poulenc on each of the parts. This is probably the score used for the performance with Poulenc at Wigmore Hall in the winter of 1947. Poulenc does not appear to have played with them on any other occasion. Mozart's Serenade K388 also has Brain's signature on each part. The Serenade K375 has Leonard Brain's initials on each part.

The following are what remains of that collection. Scores used by the Quintet after Brain's death are not listed. How extensive the repertoire may have been originally can only be judged from the works performed and also from the works for quintet that were in Brain's music library. Evidence of these is contained in a letter to Denis Stevens, dated November 3, 1951 (with Brain's approximate timings after each piece).[2]

Works with Piano

Francis Poulenc: Sextet. 20'
Ghedini: Quartet for flute, oboe, clarinet, bassoon and piano. 20'
Reinhard Schwarz-Schilling:3 Variations for oboe, clarinet, horn, bassoon, and piano. 20'
Carl Reinecke: Trio for oboe, horn, and piano. 20'
Robert Schumann: Adagio and Allegro for horn and piano. 10'
Samuel H Adler: Sonata for Horn and Piano. 20'

Trios for Oboe, Clarinet, and Bassoon

Henri Tomasi: Concert Champêtre. 15'
Darius Milhaud: L'après Corelli 15'

Wind Quintets

Darius Milhaud: The Chimney of King Renée. 15'
Peter Racine Fricker: Quintet. 20'
Denis Matthews: Quintet. 15'
Franz Reizenstein: Quintet. 15'
Fleming Weiss: Serenade. 5'
Kenneth Essex: Quintet. 10'
Carl Nielsen: Quintet. 15'
Roy Douglas: Six Dance Caricatures. 15'
Gilbert Vinter: Two Miniatures. 10'
Henri Tomasi: Variations on a Corsican Theme. 10'
Eugène Bozza: Variations sur un thème libre. 11'
Schmid: Quintet. 20'
Percy Grainger: Walking tune. 5'
Leo Sowerby: Pop Goes The Weasel. 5'
W. A. Mozart: Organ Fantasia in F minor & major K. 594. Arr. Dennis Brain. 10'

Other Combinations

Mátyás Seiber: Sextet, 2 clarinets, 2 horns, and 2 bassoons. 10'

Carl Reinecke: Octet, flute, oboe, 2 clarinets, 2 horns, and 2 bassoons.

"Various Mozart Divertimenti for various combinations"

G. F. Handel:4 Trio (Overture in D) for 2 clarinets and horn or oboe, clarinet and horn. 10'

At the present, a complete list of the Quintet's repertoire and of their concert engagements has not been compiled. The following scores include works for different combinations other than wind quintet, and this is reflected in the works performed at concerts.

Peter Racine Fricker: Quintet Op.5

Composer's manuscript parts, with his handwriting on the oboe part. Five parts with alternative Finale for each instrument. Gamble collection. Provenance: Given by Audrey Brain in October 2003.

The parts are heavily corrected in places with different colored pencils and some pages have been crossed through. The oboe part is inscribed with the following instruction:

(Finale, alternative notation)

This movement is written in ordinary $^{12}/_{8}$ time for the convenience of the players. It is emphasized that the rhythm is $^{3}/_{8}$ + $^{3}/_{4}$ + $^{3}/_{8}$, (as in the score), and the accents are (to) be observed carefully.

Heinrich Jacoby: Quintet op.19 for Flute, Oboe, Clarinet in B-flat, Horn in F, and Bassoon (20.4. – 1.5.1946)

Manuscript score and parts. Gamble Collection. Provenance: see Fricker Quintet above.

This appears to be one of the earliest works written for the Brain Quintet. No performance of this work has yet been found.

This composer changed his name from Hanoch to Heinrich and is not to be confused with Heinrich Jacoby, educational psychologist and composer (1889–1964). Hanoch Jacoby (1909–1990) was a pupil of Hindemith in Berlin from 1927 to 1930 and emigrated to England in 1933.

Francis Poulenc: Sextuor pour piano-flute-hautbois-clarinette-basson et cor. Copyright 1945 by Wilhelm Hansen, Copenhagen 25745a. Provenance: see above.

The piano part is missing. All parts are signed in blue ink by Brain and Poulenc (top right corners of each part). Poulenc and the Dennis Brain Wind Quintet performed this work together at the Wigmore Hall on March 4, 1947.

W. A. Mozart: Serenade No. 12 in C minor K. 388. Leipzig, Breitkopf & Hartel, [n.d.]

Signed in ink (top right corner on the front of each part) by Brain. Gamble collection, Provenance: see above.

W. A. Mozart: Serenade No. 11 in E major K. 375. Leipzig, Breitkopf & Hartel, [n.d.]

Initialled on each part (top right corner) “L B” (Leonard Brain). Collection and provenance: see above.

Ludwig van Beethoven: Quintet in E-flat, Op.16 for Pianoforte, Oboe, Clarinet, Bassoon and Horn. Leipzig, Breitkopf & Hartel, series 10, no. 74 [n.d.] Collection and provenance: see above.

Albert Roussel: Divertissement Op.6. pour Flute, Hautbois, Clarinette, Basson, Cor et Piano. A la société Moderne d’Instruments à vent. R.L.5982 & Cie.

The piano part is missing. Only the parts for flute, oboe, clarinet, bassoon and horn. Collection and provenance: see above.

Carl Nielsen: Kvintet for Flojte, Obo, Klarinet, Horn og Fagot (op.43). Copyright 1923 by Wilhelm Hansen, Copenhagen.

This is a very brittle, yellowing, and incomplete set (only the flute, oboe and bassoon parts). Collection and provenance: see above.

Literature

Israel Music Instutute (IMI) website which has biographical information and a photograph of the composer. *www.imi.org.il/site/*

Traber, Weingarten, eds. *Verdrängte Musik Berliner Komponisten Im Exil*, Berlin 1987.

APPENDIX

B

The Early Horn

The script for "The Early Horn" is preserved on microfilm at the BBC Written Archives near Reading. Private recordings of most of the actual broadcast have been preserved by enthusiasts. The following is a reconstruction of this program, using the surviving tape fragments from private sources, and Brain's BBC script. The BBC did not preserve the recording made on July 6 and 11, 1955. Nearly all the music is preserved on the tapes, but some of the extracts and scales Brain played, as well as part of his talk, are missing. **For these missing passages, references are to the BBC script and appear in bold.**[1]

Horn Call: Méhul [2]

Hose-pipe

Raoux 1818 hand horn

Alexander B-flat single horn with valves

The instruments that you've just heard range from 1818 up to the present day—in fact, from the sublime to the ridiculous—the first being the most modern and cheapest; the second an old French hand-horn with the date 1818 and floral pattern inscribed on the bell; the third being my usual every-day instrument, an Alexander. In case you're curious about the first example, the reason is simple, that I have included it to show that on any tube containing a column of air a series of notes, determined by nature, can be produced. And as that fact is almost the point of this programme, it is not inappropriate that one should begin with a common, or rather garden object, which I imagine has not been broadcast before—a hose-pipe. Here it is again.

(Horn call on hose-pipe)

Even though the notes are more out of tune than with a more normal instrument, the ratio between them is the same. This ratio is called the harmonic series, though the term "upper partials" is perhaps more accurate. Only these notes can be produced, by the correct application of one's own air-stream passing between the lip muscles in tension, on an instrument without valves, such as a hand horn, bugle, etc.—or hose-pipe. Here is the series:

(Play the series on hose-pipe)

As you will have heard, the notes get closer together as one gets higher and in the top octave a scale is possible though somewhat out of tune to our ears today.

(Play scale on hose-pipe)

A modern application of this technique, that is playing the harmonics as they come and not correcting the intonation as one can with the hand, occurs in Benjamin Britten's Serenade where the player is directed to "use the out-of-tune notes to give a particular 'natural' colour and atmosphere to the setting of the six poems." Here is the Prologue from the Serenade which I shall play on my 1818 hand horn.

(Prologue from Serenade played on Raoux 1818 hand horn)

The horn must have been played that way 200 years ago.

Here are two hunting calls of the late 17th century, taken from a French method for "Trompe,"or "Cor de Chasse," which deals not only with the "Emission of Sounds," but also gives a dictionary of hunting terms, on articles describing the art of hunting as well as the ailments of hounds.

(Two hunting calls: two horns)

Here is a later and more sophisticated approach to a pair of horns, the last movement of Mozart's 12 duos. These Duos are interesting in that in some of the movements he writes up to the 24th harmonic, that is G above top C, not specifying a crook to be used, which is just as well, though it has led to the belief that they may have been written for basset-horns.

(Mozart Duo in B-flat No. 12, K.487)

The horn doesn't seem to have been used in the orchestra until the year 1705, when the Hamburg composer Keiser wrote for it in his opera *Octavia*. It's almost certain that Handel, who was twenty that year, was present at the performance. Just eleven years later Bach used two horns in his secular cantata *Was mir behagt*, and this seems to be their first appearance in his music. Now why horn and trumpet players view the parts of Bach and Handel with a certain degree of diffidence is that before the advent of hand-horn technique, of which more later, the only adjacent notes available were in the top octave; and so for florid contrapuntal writing that top octave was almost the only part of the compass that could be used. The sustained playing of parts at that pitch throws a very great tension on the muscles of the lips and make such parts, even in these days, more difficult than almost any modern piece of writing, as the difficulties are in no way solved with the modern instrument. **This cantata was first performed in February 1716 at Weissenfels in honour of the local Duke's birthday. One of the movements in it is the famous "Sheep may safely graze." We shall now play for you the aria for soprano, two horns, and continuo.**[3]

(Bach Cantata No. 208, *Was Mir Behagt*, for soprano, two horns and continuo)

Just one year after that cantata, Handel, here in London, wrote his famous *Water Music*, and this seems to have been the first time the horn was used orchestrally in this country. Most people know, in some form or other, the story of the *Water Music*; less well known, except for the movements in Harty's fine arrangement, is the actual music. Here we have a minuet starting with two horns, or as many more as circumstances allow in which the stateliness of the minuet is balanced by the softness of the trio, well known in Harty's arrangement on other instruments.

(Handel: Minuet from *Water Music*)

And now some music which I think has not been played before in this country: Vivaldi's concerto in F for two horns, possibly the only work of its kind, though I believe there is one by Haydn. There are three movements, the middle being for cello and continuo whilst the horns rest—an excellent idea.

(Vivaldi: Concerto for Two Horns in F RV 538)

All the previous works could have been played on a natural horn. We come now to the works of Mozart, Haydn, Beethoven, etc., and for these a slightly more advanced technique was used—by moving the hand across the bell from the normal position the pitch of the note being played is lowered, which means that it is possible to fill in the gaps, though the more closed the bell the more muffled the sound—as this demonstration will show.

(Play Raoux 1818 hand horn)

By filling in the gaps a complete scale in the middle register can be played—not faked. This was the legitimate method of playing until the advent of valves.

(Play scale on Raoux 1818 hand horn)

Mozart's three concertos in E-flat are all fairly well known. Less known is his first in D. This is interesting for several reasons. It has only two movements. The solo part has a surprisingly small compass, except for one note only one octave sounding A to A. In spite of this limitation, or perhaps because of it and the suitable key for strings, the concerto is very bright, with some exciting fiddling in the first movement and a sombre mood in the second, in which Mozart for reasons unknown uses the plainsong. I shall endeavour to perform this Concerto using a horn in D without valves and with a hand horn technique. You'll notice how the quality of the notes varies.

(Mozart Concerto in D K.412 for horn and orchestra.)

That concerto dates from the year 1782. Amongst its virtues is its brevity. But the great Mozart scholar Einstein thought that it was originally longer than that. There exists a fragment of a movement in E major which Einstein suggests is a missing slow movement. But E is not the relative key for a slow movement in D, and the "tutti" suggests not a slow movement but the beginning of what might have been a very big concerto and this seems as good an opportunity as any for giving it its first performance.

(Mozart fragment in E K.98A, for horn and orchestra.)

And there, alas, the manuscript stops.

Now it is probable that the composer Rosetti had a hand in inspiring Mozart's horn concertos. Rosetti was born Franz Anton Rössler, but took an Italian name because it was good for trade. His horn concerto is of interest because of its likeness to Mozart's. It's in the same key—E-flat; its slow movement is called "Romance," as are all Mozart's, and the finale is of the six-eight hunting call variety that Mozart favoured. Rosetti was not a Mozart writing wonderful music which employs a considerable number of grace notes not usually found in horn music, in spite of the instrument's limitations, but one who went all out to show off every facet of technique possible on that very beautiful instrument, the eighteenth century horn.

(Rosetti: Horn Concerto: Finale)

Well, I'm not pretending I played all that without valves. Though it can be done just with the lips and the hand. But valves have done a lot to soothe horn-players' nerves. Although that movement could have been played on a hand horn I use my modern instrument with valves which fills in the gaps in the harmonic series with good notes instead of muffled. Valves are simply a means of adding length of tubing and so giving the same series of notes in different keys which when combined give a complete chromatic scale throughout three octaves. **Thus with no valves depressed I get (PLAY). With one valve depressed (PLAY). You can use any two valves or all three at once.** Valve-horns seem to have been first used orchestrally in Halevy's "La Juive" in 1830, though they had been invented quite a lot earlier to that.

I'm going to finish the programme with the earliest piece I know which cannot be played on a hand horn. It's not a loud cheerful piece like you usually get at the end of a programme. In fact it's rather slow and quiet, and I think it's very beautiful: it's Schubert's song *Auf dem Strom*, for soprano, horn, and piano, written in 1828. Half of the horn part is possible on a hand horn except for one passage which occurs twice and which suggests it may be the earliest which he played with valves. Here is the passage.

(Play)

And now the whole song sung by Jacqueline Delman with Clifton Helliwell at the piano.

(Schubert: *Auf dem Strom* for soprano, horn and piano D.943)

APPENDIX

C

Talking About the Horn

Talking About the Instrument: No. 7, The Horn

Illustrated Talk by Dennis Brain
General Overseas Service
Pre-Recorded on March 19, 1956
Recorded Talks Reference Number: TOX 39218
Broadcast on Tuesday March 27, 1956, 06:30–07:00 GMT

The second radio talk was "No. 7, The Horn" in the series *Talking About the Instrument* for the General Overseas Service.

The BBC correspondence files describe the stages of its planning. Brain received a contract for this broadcast on March 8, 1956. Rosemary Jellis, Overseas Talks department, wrote to Miss Firth, Music Bookings that "At last we have nailed Dennis Brain down to record his programme in this series on Monday, 19 March . . ." It was broadcast on Tuesday March 27, 1956, at 06.30–07.00 Greenwich Mean Time and repeated the next day (Wednesday, March 28) at 02.30 a.m. GMT and Thursday, March 29, at 19.30 GMT. We do not know whether a recording has been preserved. Most likely, as with an enormous number of his BBC recorded programs, it had a shelf life and after that had expired, it would have been destroyed. The only evidence of it, therefore, is the entry in the "program as broadcast" file for General Overseas Service.[1]

The program included excerpts from the solo, chamber, and orchestral repertoire, played on his 1818 hand horn, on a length of hosepipe, and on a modern instrument with valves. After playing live extracts, he included excerpts of recorded repertoire, featuring mostly his father, Aubrey, in solo, chamber, and orchestral works with the LSO, with "Symphony Orchestra" (Aubrey Brain's name not mentioned), the BBC Symphony Orchestra, and with Rudolf Serkin and Adolf Busch in the famous second recording of the Brahms Horn Trio. For the final recorded excerpt, he chose a recording that features him with Neill Sanders, playing with members of the London Baroque Ensemble, in a work by Ditttersdorf, his Partita No. 3 in D major. The whole of this work was recorded for EMI Parlophone in 1953. As with the other discs, he played only a short fragment of the recording for the program. Even without a script, the program looks interesting enough (see below), and one can only guess at what it would have been like with a script. Alas, the General Overseas Service does not generally preserve the scripts to talks.[2]

Music "Live"

Dennis Brain (1818 Horn)

Four improvised passages 00'09", 00'09", 00'10", 00'07"

Theme from Horn Sonata Beethoven Non copyright A. D. Peters 00'19"

Theme from *Till Eulenspiegel* 00'10". R. Strauss. Wiener Philharmoniker Verlag

Dennis Brain (Hosepipe)

Theme from Mendelssohn's Nocturne from *A Midsummer Night's Dream* 00'20" Mendelssohn. Breitkopf

One improvised passage 00'12"

Dennis Brain (Modern Horn)

Four improvised passages 00'13", 00'11"; 00'07"; 00'08";

Serenade for Tenor, Horn and Strings, Op.31. 01'20"; Benjamin Britten. Boosey and Hawkes

Commercial Discs (Dubbed)

Nocturne from *A Midsummer Night's Dream* HMV DA 1318 01'42"
Aubrey Brain (horn) with BBC Symphony Orchestra

Romanze from 3rd Concerto in E-flat for Horn Koechel No. 447 (Mozart). HMV DB 3974 02'25"
Aubrey Brain and the BBC Symphony Orchestra

Overture to *Prince Igor* (Borodin) HMV D 1210 00'33"
Symphony Orchestra

Till Eulenspiegel (R. Strauss). HMV DB 2187 00'32"
BBC Symphony Orchestra

Partita No. 3 in D Major (Dittersdorf ed. Haas). PARL PMB 1008 00'53"
London Baroque Ensemble

Commercial Disc "Live"

Trio in E-flat Major, Op.40 (Brahms) HMV DB 2106 06'55"
Rudolf Serkin (piano); Adolf Busch (violin); Aubrey Brain (horn)

APPENDIX

D

Articles

French Horn Playing

By Dennis Brain

The Conductor 3, issue 10 (October 1954): 3, 8.

The Quarterly Journal of the National Association of Brass Band Conductors[1]

> Dennis Brain, at the age of thirty-three, stands at the head of his profession. French horn playing and his name are almost synonymous. Son of Aubrey Brain, also a famous horn player, Dennis has been the principal soloist of the Royal Philharmonic Orchestra since 1946. He has played concertos in Switzerland, France, Germany, Holland, Italy and U.S.A. and has recorded most major works for the horn. A number of works has been specially written for him, notably those by Benjamin Britten, Hindemith and Gordon Jacob. He has also been awarded the coveted Cobbett medal of the Worshipful Company of Musicians.
>
> Bandsmen will gratefully recall his wonderful playing at the concert following the "Daily Herald" Contest at the Empress Hall in 1952 when he was accorded a tremendous ovation by the crowded audience.—Ed.

To write an article for a Brass Band Journal on an instrument which does not appear in a Brass Band would seem to give rise to a situation similar to that of Daniel entering the lion's den; but as I had seven years in the R.A.F. Central Band I felt that it was sufficiently similar to give me some knowledge of the differences and difficulties involved.

The most important aspect to be considered for a horn player is tone. Technique, strength of lips and experience come naturally in time if built up on a solid foundation of proper sound, whereas the most facile agility is comparatively worthless if the sound produced does not bear listening to.

What is horn tone? Naturally, I like to think that it is the sound which I myself produce—but is it? After all, each nation has its own idea about quality. The Germans have a thicker and bigger sound than ours; the Viennese, using their Vienna horn, a big-bore instrument in F with a strange system of piston valves, produce a big brassy sound though very imaginative in soft passages; the Italians who rest the horn on their knees and produce a woolly, tubby sound:

and the French with their excessive vibrato, (which I shall return to later) sound often like a bad saxophone, a much maligned instrument.

My ideal is a pure, clear, warm sound which does not lose quality in ff, as quality, not quantity, has more penetrating power; and nothing is worse than woodwind, or strings, being blotted out by the sheer noise of brassy horns.

To revert to the question of vibrato. This, except in France, is hardly used on the horn at all, which is in a way a pity, as it has in musical expression a definite purpose.

But first, what is vibrato?

My colleague, Eric Bravington, in his excellent article on Trumpet Playing which appeared in *The Conductor* in April last, mentioned the wide use of vibrato. If I may re-arrange his words and say—the use of "wide" vibrato, they will convey more clearly my objections to its use.

Wide vibrato is wobbly, whether on a wind instrument, string or voice, and is similar to a bad tremulant on an organ; something which appears to be turned on and too seldom turned off!

The horn-call from Wagner's Opera *Siegfried* would appear to me to be singularly offensive with vibrato; but in some French music the sound without vibrato can be very dull and uninteresting.

It is usually effected by fluctuating the air stream or altering the pitch with the lips or hand, but should only be done in certain kinds of music where one's feelings suggest that the sound should be more coloured and warmer.

Two artists come to mind who use a proper, natural vibrato, on their respective instruments—Jascha Heifetz and Tommy Dorsey. Having been fortunate enough to hear both in person, it seems to me that their use of vibrato makes a magnificent sound, live and human.

May I briefly summarise on this subject, which is, I think, very important. Vibrato should be used to colour the sound and not to cover up deficiencies of tone and intonation.

I cannot advocate too strongly the proper practice of sustained notes for the following reasons: one note alone gives you time to listen to the sound that you are making, whether or not it is in tune, the attack correct and the finish smooth and not abrupt; it strengthens the lip muscles, helps you to breathe correctly and naturally—and drives the neighbours crazy, not a bad total for one note!

But surely, if one cannot play one note properly what hope is there for several?

I do not, however, believe in practising sustained notes up to the limit of the compass, as this tends to harm the sound in the middle of the instrument—the part of the compass one uses most of the time. To increase the range, scales and, particularly, arpeggios, I find a great help as these also develop flexibility of embouchure. They should be played slurred more often than tongued as it is more difficult to slur evenly than to tongue.

My comment on another maligned aspect of brass playing, the trill, is that if one thinks of it as a slur from one note to the next and back, one can then appreciate the need for control rather than speed. Practised slowly the trill will pay great dividends, as a slow, even trill will sound faster than one that is quick and uneven.

A suggestion for the correct embouchure is that the mouthpiece should be placed on the lips in as natural a position as possible, even if it is to one side or inset into one or other or both lips, or more on the top than bottom. When one considers that it is going to be there a long time, it may as well be as comfortable as possible! This can only be achieved by a natural position.

Why do brass players "blob," "fluff," mis-pitch, etc. notes?

Apart from the fact that players are human beings, a thought about the instrument, in my case the horn, may not be out of place.

It is founded on a system, the harmonic series, which is by nature out of tune; so that one is constantly correcting intonation. The narrow bore relative to its length makes for unsteadiness, and the mouthpiece, with its small bore and rim area, is less conducive to "safety" than a larger one. When you consider that the F horn is the same length as the F tuba, the Bb as the Bb trombone, and that the mouthpiece is in area (though I am open to correction on this point) about a third the size, also that the bore is much smaller and that one is playing up on the 12th to the 16th harmonic, it is always a source of amazement to me that horn playing is as accurate as it is in these times.

The nearest equivalent instrument in a Brass Band is the tenor horn. This is pitched in E-flat, nearly an octave higher, or only half as long as the F horn. As it has also a wider bore, its sound is much less refined than the orchestral horn. Learn to appreciate as much as possible about every type of music in order to develop a broad outlook—not always easy for a wind player who has not as large a repertoire to draw on as a pianist or violinist. After all, if you are a professional musician you must be prepared to play in any style required, whether it is symphonic or jazz.

Do not over-practise. I myself started playing at the age of fifteen and practised about one-and-a-half hours a day. I still do the same amount and find it quite enough; it must be done properly and not as a duty whilst thinking of other things. I would emphasize again the value of sustained notes.

Lastly, try to enjoy your playing at all times, sometimes difficult in these days of the virtuoso conductor, who is generally so demanding. If you are able to enjoy your own work, you may be assured that you will be the more able to give the maximum pleasure to others.

About the French Horn

By Dennis Brain, edited by Frank C. F. Wright
Brass Today, published in London by Besson & Co., 1957, pp. 60–63.[2]

The following article, which is based on a manuscript submitted to *Brass Today* by Brain shortly before his death, was first published late in 1957.

The manuscript appears to be lost, but the following extract from it was published in *Brass Today*. It is a sample of Brain's handwriting:

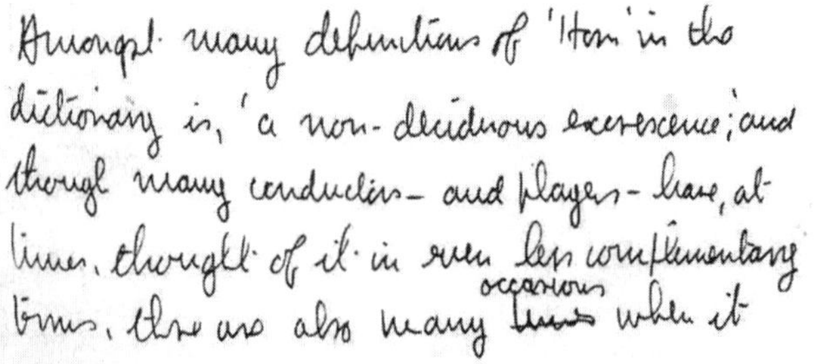
Amongst many definitions of 'Horn' in the dictionary is, 'a non-deciduous excrescence'; and though many conductors – and players – have, at times, thought of it in even less complimentary terms, there are also many occasions when it

Among the definitions of *horn* in the dictionary is, a *non-deciduous excrescence* and though many conductors—and players—have, at times, thought of it in even less complimentary terms, there are also many occasions when it can be described as a musical instrument!

Evolving from the horn of an animal used by hunters, it emerged into the 5-valve and, more rare, 6-valve instrument which, in groups of 4, sometimes 6 or 8 (and on one occasion at least 20, in the *Alpine Symphony* of Strauss) shines so brightly from the back of the orchestra. Between these extremes there has been a great development when one considers that the string family has remained virtually unaltered in 200 years.

Let us trace this development. The instrument began as a brass tube (coiled for convenience), the length varying from 8ft. to 16ft. or 17ft. It had a conical bore, a bell at one end and a mouthpiece at the other. On it could be produced, by passing air between the lips placed across the mouthpiece and causing them to vibrate—the column of air in the tube vibrating in sympathy—a group of notes called the harmonic series, or, more simply, *open* notes. These notes are similar to those on a bugle, but many more are possible because the tube is longer. (A chart of the harmonic series on page 62 shows that, counting the fundamental note as 1, the number of the harmonic doubles at each successive ascending octave, i.e., 1, 2, 4, 8, 16.) On the normal horn in F number 1 is usually unobtainable, 4 is middle C and 16 top C. It will be seen that the higher the octave the more notes are possible; and in the top octave a scale can be played. One of the difficulties of the F horn is that top C is the 16th harmonic whereas on the B-flat trumpet it is the 8th. Hence the notes are much closer together and need a greater adjustment of lip control—and luck.

Incidentally, it can be proved that on any column of air the open notes can be played simply by using an ordinary mouthpiece in a 12 ft. length of hosepipe, or *Gartenschlauch*. A soft but pleasing sound can be produced, and if it does nothing else it at least shows how long the F horn would be if it were straightened out!

Crooks began to appear at about the beginning of the eighteenth century. These pieces of tubing of varying sizes, inserted between the mouthpiece and main body of the instrument, altered the length of the instrument, so enabling the player to produce the series in any one of the twelve keys. This device also enabled the player to carry one instrument and twelve crooks, instead of twelve instruments. Much better. Hand-horn technique was evolved. By moving the hand across the bell it was possible to lower the pitch of each open note and so fill in the gaps, at least in the upper two octaves. This meant that instead of having to play in the top octave, where the notes are adjacent, it was now possible to play tunes in a much more comfortable and pleasant register. From the very high parts of Bach and Handel, with the difficulties due to great tension of the lip muscles to produce these extreme notes—difficulties which are the same now and in no way eased by modern instruments—we come to the more melodious parts of Mozart, Haydn and Beethoven, culminating in probably the greatest writer of all for the hand horn, Brahms.

The right hand nowadays fulfils four necessary duties:

1. Holding up the bell end of the instrument.
2. Softening the otherwise rather blatant sound which is very apparent when the hand is removed.
3. Correcting intonation.
4. Muting

The horn should never be rested on the knee. In this position the sound goes straight into the body, resulting in a muffled noise with no carrying power.

By opening out the hand, or moving the wrist away from the body, the pitch of the note can be raised, or *vice versa*. This is a very essential feature of horn playing as no instrument is perfectly in tune and it is often not possible to alter the pitch with lip adjustment only.

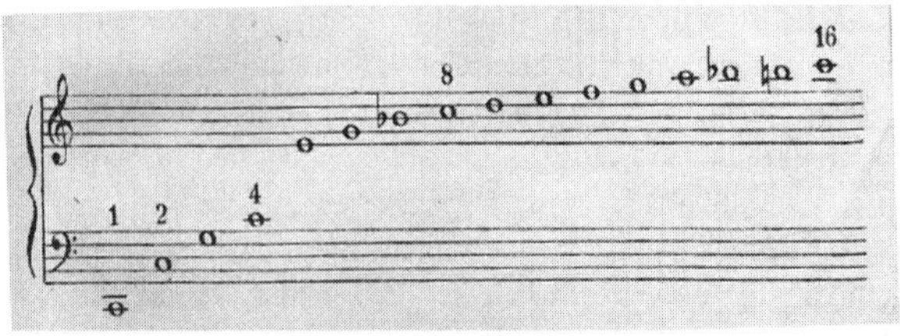

If the hand is forced into the bell so that it is closed almost completely (if it were completely closed it couldn't be blown through) a nasal sound can be produced. This is called muting, and different qualities of muting are also produced with fibre, metal, and other kinds of mutes. A curious feature of hand muting is that the length of tube is shortened, raising the pitch on the F-horn a semitone. In order to compensate for this, any passages so muted have to be transposed down a semitone. Most metal mutes do not affect the pitch, although there is one type which does have very similar characteristics to those of the hand, but it makes the playing a little easier. Hence, the terms *transposing* and *non-transposing* mutes.

Valves, coming on the scene in the nineteenth century, are simply a mechanical means of adding, instantaneously, crooks by the movement of a finger, so giving seven different series of notes (similar to the seven positions of the trombone), and enabling a complete chromatic scale to be played.

There are three reasons why the horn is considered to be more treacherous to play than other brass instruments—a general opinion with which I am not going to disagree. These are that (a) the bore is narrow for its length (a wide-bore instrument such as the euphonium is *much* easier to play); (b) the mouthpiece is very small, allowing for a corresponding small amount of lip muscle to control; and (c) the harmonics being so close together in the top octave, it is very easy to get the "wrong" one. When one considers that in the top octave one can play almost any note with any fingering, it is surprising that any note but the *right* one happens as infrequently as it does. But it has to be admitted that these differences from other brass instruments add up to a most distinctive sound, and one worth the extra trouble—and strain.

One feels that the natural sound is beautiful enough without having to add to it by any artificial means, such as vibrato. On the other hand, vibrato is necessary in certain types of music although it has to be most tastefully employed if it is not to become objectionable.

The repertoire for the French horn, though small, is interesting and varied. It ranges from two Concertos by Haydn, four by Mozart, two by Strauss, to three works by Hindemith—a Concerto, a Sonata with piano, and a Sonata for four horns. Five pieces for five horns by Gunther Schuller (1st horn of the Metropolitan Opera) and a fascinating work by Villa-Lobos for three horns and trombone called Choros No. 4 are very good examples of skilful and imaginative writing. Then there are the unusual Mitch Miller records—"The Yellow Rose of Texas" (juke box favourite of 1955), and "Horn Belt Boogie," to name but two.

The Britten Serenade is perhaps the best example of modern writing. This gives the impression that most of it could be played on a hand horn—but one would have to possess an unusually flexible wrist! The work is suited to the instrument, is "natural" to play, sounds well, and bears out my theory that horn parts which could almost be played on a natural horn without valves (such as the opening phrase in Strauss's *Till Eulenspiegel*) are the most effective and give the listener the greatest satisfaction.

Horn playing of the future will, I suppose, follow the trend and get bigger and better, louder and higher. But the same basic difficulties will always remain, regardless of any advance in instrument making. The most important operative elements are the lip muscles. It is in the lips—which are, after all, part of the body and subject to its ills—that the secret of horn playing might almost be said to lie.

The French Horn

By the late Dennis Brain, edited by Frank C. F. Wright
Variant of the article reproduced above, in *Brass Today*, published in London by Besson & Co., 1961, pp. 19–20.

Amongst other definitions, the dictionary shows the horn to be a non-deciduous excrescence, a branched appendage, and a wind instrument. However, as the orchestral version was originally animal, the definitions have something in common. The horn, as we know it, has something of a reputation for being the most difficult of instruments to play, and because of that it is often thought to be the most complex in design; whereas, along with the tuba, trumpet, and sundry other valved instruments, it is second only to the trombone in simplicity—the trombone being second to the bugle.

The principle of the horn, as with other brass instruments, is based on the harmonic series—whereby the various notes are selected by lip tension, air pressure, and good luck. In the natural horn one can obtain about fifteen notes over the three octaves, and these get closer together as they go higher, which explains why some of the Bach and Handel writing is so treacherous, as only in the top octave can one play consecutive tones and semi-tones. One explanation why these notes are so difficult—even today, with modern instruments—is that the technique of producing the sound has not altered at all; and that to produce a note of a given pitch requires the same lip tension, regardless of the instrument in use. For instance, high F (known as top C) on the ordinary F horn, or on the B-flat alto horn, or on an F alto horn, requires the same lip tension in each case—although one is playing the 16th harmonic on the F horn, the 12th harmonic on the B-flat, and the 8th harmonic on the alto. However, when playing the 16th, the harmonics on either side (i.e. 15 and 17) are a narrow semi-tone apart. When playing the 12th, they are a wide semi-tone. And when playing the 8th they are a wide tone. So the element of risk is reduced by using a shorter crook, though the effort required is the same, and much more care is needed in the attack if the tone is not to be inferior. Therefore, one is faced with the alternatives of accuracy or tone quality; and as with most problems of these times, one adopts a compromise—the double horn.

The Hunting or Natural Horn

Before dealing with this latest instrument, let us glance at its development, starting with the hunting horn, or natural horn. This could be worn over the shoulder for convenience, and is, I believe, still used in French hunting bands. Then came the crooks—coiled tubes of different lengths, which could be inserted into the instrument to alter the total tube length, and of course the pitch, thus enabling the player to play the harmonic series in different keys. Before crooks established themselves, various horns were made with built-in arrangements for changing pitch. None of these was very satisfactory, and the limit was reached with one which earned the nickname of "plumber's nightmare." It was in fact eight horns in one, with a row of tubes into which the mouthpiece could be plugged, and with a slide for connecting the selected plumbing circuit to the bell!

Narrow-bore French Horns

After crooks came valves—various kinds of valves, from square ones to the piston-type, as used on the narrow-bore French horns, to the modern rotary type. The valves, when operated, instantaneously add lengths of tubing which change the pitch by one tone, one semi-tone, and three semi-tones, in that order. These, in their various combinations, provide seven positions—six with valves and one without—which correspond to the seven of the trombone. As one obtains a further set of harmonics in each position, it follows that by combining them one can play a complete chromatic scale. And, of course, the higher one goes up the scale, the more are the fingerings duplicated—so much so that the highest note can almost be played with any fingering. For example, any notes above top G on the horn can be obtained with any fingering, more or less; and contrariwise, of course, any fingering can be used for the production of any particular note. However, lest this be thought to be a good thing, let me point out that the chances of accuracy are much greater if one knows that with certain fingering a certain note will follow—as with most instruments—instead of being able to help oneself to half-a-dozen or so in the vicinity, with the same fingering!

There is an instrument made with six valves, and a lever like the shift key of a typewriter. This is supposed to provide many convenient arrangements of fingering, but in practice it is more likely to confuse one with its theoretically endless number of possible combinations. Whilst such systems are technically interesting, I am convinced that the simplest instrument is the best—that is to say three valves plus a thumb change, as in a double horn, or in the case of the single B-flat Horn, for changing to A or for muting. As a point of interest, I must confess that I am at the moment negotiating for the manufacture of a five-valved instrument of my own design. (Note: Dennis Brain did in fact go to the famous Horn manufacturers Alexander, of Mainz, Germany, who made several 5-valved instruments for him to his own specification.)

Crooked Horns

When crooks came into fashion it was said that the tone of the instruments thus fitted was inferior to that of the natural horn. Again, when valves were introduced, people said that valved horns were not so pure in tone as crooked horns. My own view is that, as it is the player who produces the sound, whether he plays on an Alphorn, or a suitable length of gas-pipe, provided he uses his horn mouthpiece it will sound the same, basically.

On the subject of quality of sound, one reason why the horn is difficult is the number of conflicting conditions that govern the production of sound: first, the narrow bore of tube for its length; second, a small mouthpiece: third, a big range of four octaves, taking one up to the 16th harmonic instead of to the 8th, as in the case of the trumpet and trombone. As narrow-bore instruments seem to be less technically perfect than those with wide bores, and as a small mouthpiece limits the amount of muscle for purposes of lip control, it is not surprising that a certain amount of bubbling occurs at times.

However, returning to the point at which we left the double horn in order to discuss its development, we must not overlook the fact that the double horn is by no means used exclusively. Many American horn players, and also some on the continent, use the single B-flat horn as well. For instance, 1st and 3rd chair men (as they call them across the Atlantic) use the single B-flat, and double instruments are used by 2nd and 4th chairs. The reason for this is that horn parts are written in pairs—a custom which dates from the classical days, when a composer would write for one pair in the tonic and another pair in the dominant, or in the case of a minor key in the relative major; and so the high player of each pair uses an instrument most suited to the parts, and vice versa. And what happens when a high player has to play a very low note?—Liszt had a habit of doing that to the first horn. Well, if the note is not on the single B-flat instrument, it is to be hoped that the player is on good terms with his colleagues, so that one of them will play it for him (and here one must recall some of the stories of musicians who have not spoken to each other for years, and who would only communicate by notes, or through a third party—though today, as a rule, the difficulty is to stop them talking!). An alternative to relying upon the good nature of a colleague for the low note is a search in the instrument case for a suitable length of tube—known to himself as an extension, and to his friends by many other strange names!

So far as the other instruments go, I believe the only orchestra still playing F instruments is in Vienna, where a particular type, called the Vienna Horn, is used. This has a big bore and its own patent valve mechanism.

Why the hand. . . . ?

Leaving till last the question that everyone wants to ask a horn player—why do you put your hand in it?—the answer is four-fold. First, it prevents one from dropping it! Next, it softens the often blatant sound. Again, by blocking the bell it raises the note a semi-tone, and makes a sound known as muting. Finally, by moving it across the bell one can adjust intonation. This latter action is, of course, the principle of the old Hand Horn, whereby one can lower the pitch of a note down to a semi-tone above the next lowest harmonic, and so fill in the gaps. Of course, the tone suffers, but the gaps are filled: and such works as the Beethoven sonata and the Mozart concertos are written for that technique. I have in my possession a Hand Horn dated 1818, by Raoux, on which a Mozart concerto can be played by hand.

Should any reader wish to pursue this subject further, I cannot do better than recommend him, her, to the most comprehensive of all articles on the horn in the Hinrichsen *Annual Music Book*, Volume VII. This is written by R. Morley-Pegge who, in company with W. H. Blandford, knows more about the instrument than anyone else. And if I may offer a word of advice to those who want to learn to play it, start on an F French Horn and learn slowly. It is better to practise sustained notes—that is, one breath per note—than florid parts, for one spends most of one's life playing those anyway: and, of course, what chance is there of being able to play a series of notes well if one cannot play one note correctly?

Portora Royal School, Enniskillen, Northern Ireland, March 1956

Portora Royal School Music Society
Portrora Royal School Magazine, Easter Term, March 1956, page 9

Many of those who were in the audience on 7th March will remember Mr. Brain's recital and talk for a very long time.

First of all, he played Mozart's second horn concerto in E-flat, written in 1782 for the virtuoso Leutgeb. Then came the concerto written by Richard Strauss at the age of nineteen for his father. Like the Mozart, this is brilliant but typical horn music that can scarcely be imagined on any other instrument. It can hardly be called a portent of his later work, but the piano reduction may be to blame for this. No arranger could possibly do justice to Strauss's orchestration within the limits of two hands and piano tone.

In spite of this, Mr. Smith deserves warm praise for his part in the recital. None of his music was written for his instrument, all of it was an attempt by an arranger to cram a quart into a pint pot, and most of it was new to him. In spite of this he played as though there had been ample time for rehearsal.

Mr. Brain then told us the nature and history of the "French" horn. The hunting horns were first brought into the orchestra in France during the seventeenth century. He illustrated their limitations most effectively by blowing horn calls on a fifteen-foot length of garden hose. The early players were encumbered with up to a dozen "crooks," which were the only method of changing the fundamental pitch of the instrument, and so obtaining a fresh series of notes, until the valve mechanism was invented in the middle of the last century.

The recital ended with three shorter works for the modern instrument. *Hunter's Moon*, by Gilbert Vinter, made amusing use of the stopped notes that had just been demonstrated to us, and employed the chromatic notes made available by the valves. *Villanelle*, by Paul Dukas, was a more lyrical piece based on a soft hunting call reminiscent of Berlioz. Mr. Brain played us the "Little French Dance" as an encore because, in his own words, it was short and he enjoyed playing it.

It will be a long time before we forget the matchless perfection of his playing and the charm and wit of his talk and answers to questions. Mr. Brain only failed to explain one thing: the horn is fiendishly difficult to play, and some members of the audience, because of his effortless technique and modest personality, may have been quite unaware that they had been privileged to listen to the finest horn player of our time.

—T. K. D.

A former boarder and current staff member at the school wrote in 2006:

> I was at the concert in the Steele Hall in 1956 . . . I remember his horn and the marvellous sound but above all I remember him playing a piece of hosepipe to the great amusement of all the small boys in the Hall. The boarders were, of course, given no choice as to whether they attended the concert or not.[3]

APPENDIX

E

Extended Bibliography

1. Concert Programs and Souvenir Booklets

Unless otherwise stated, these concert programs are in Stephen Gamble's collection. This is not a complete list of Dennis Brain's concerts. Not all have been referred to in this book but are included for the reader's interest to give a more complete picture of Brain's busy concert schedule.

Souvenir Booklet of the Thirteenth Bristol Music Festival

Colston Hall

October 23-26 1912

Photograph of Marion Beeley and a short article about her career on page 15.

This copy once belonged to Ernest Hall, principal trumpet in the BBC Symphony Orchestra and is inscribed in ink in the front: "Ernest Hall Bristol Festival October 23rd to 26th 1912."

St. Paul's School, London

Musical Society

Thursday, December 19 1935 at Eight p.m.

The program included:

Pianoforte solo: Sonata in G—Beethoven (First Movement) D. Brain

Musical Society

Tuesday, December 21 1937 at Eight p.m.

The program included:

Trio for Oboe, Horn and Pianoforte—Paul Rogers, Leonard Brain, Dennis Brain, and Norman Tucker

Musical Society
Tuesday, December 20 1938 at Eight p.m.

The program included the following for the orchestra whose horn section comprised Dennis Brain and Denis Mason:

Part 1
Fantasia for Chorus and Orchestra "In Honour of the City"—Dyson

Part 2
Minuet from Quintet in A—Boccherini
Air from Suite in D—Bach
Minuet from Symphony in G minor—Mozart

Wathen Hall, St. Paul's School, 7 p.m.
Dennis Brain a Celebration
Sunday March 9, 2008

Feierlicher Einzug der Ritter des Johanniterordens (Solemn Entrance of the Knights of St John)—Richard Strauss
Villanelle—Paul Dukas
Richard Watkins (horn), Peter Gritton (piano)
In Memoriam Dennis Brain—Benjamin Britten
Francesca Moore-Bridger, Hugh Sisley, Richard Watkins, Susie Wedderburn (horns)
String Ensemble (concert master: David Juritz)
Jonathan Jackson (tubular bells)
Peter Gritton (conductor)
En Irlande—Eugene Bozza
Thomas Jackson (horn), Robin Wedderburn (piano)
World Premiere
Sequence for Dennis Brain by Robin Wedderburn, Peter Gritton and Ben Parry
Moderato (Robin Wedderburn), Lento (Peter Gritton), Allegro (Ben Parry)
Richard Watkins, Francesca Moore-Bridger (horns)
St Paul's Horn Day Ensemble
Michael Thompson (conductor)
Romance in E—Camille Saint-Saens
Hugh Sisley (horn), Peter Gritton (piano)
Tribute (Stephen Pettitt)
Fanfare—Salute to Dennis Brain—Peter Maxwell Davies
Michael Thompson (horn)
St Paul's Horn Day Ensemble
Richard Watkins (conductor)

London Baroque Ensemble

National Gallery Concerts
Monday, March 25, 1946

Musical Director: Karl Haas
Soloist: Dennis Brain
David Martin (V), William Pleeth (VC)
Gareth Morris, Edith Schragenheim (F)
Bernard Walton, J. Fell (C)
Dennis Brain, Norman Del Mar (H)
Cecil James, Ronald Waller, Vernon Elliot (Bsns)
Harold Jackson (Tpt)

Four Sonatas for 2 flutes, 2 clarinets, 2 horns and bassoon—C. P. E. Bach (composed 1775)

D major: Allegretto
C major: Allegretto grazioso
F major: Andante
G major: Allegro

Divertimento in E-flat for Horn, Violin and Violoncello (1767)—Joseph Haydn
Moderato assai—Finale, Allegro
Two Marches for the Derbyshire Volunteer Cavalry for 2 clarinets, 2 horns, trumpet, 3 bassoons and side drum (composed 1794)—Joseph Haydn
March for the Prince of Wales (composed 1792)—Joseph Haydn

All first concert performances

Summer Entertainment.
Russell Square, Tuesday, July 27 1948, 1 p.m.

Brass Section of the London Baroque Ensemble.
Musical Director: Karl Haas. Leader: Norbert Brainin

1. Fanfare de la Chasse for 4 Horns. (G. Rossini).
2. [deleted in pencil so perhaps not played] Fantasia (Printed 1601) for treble Trombone and tenor Trombone. Orlando Lassus.
3. Suite for 2 Trumpets, 2 Horns, Trombone and Tuba (1934). Arnold Cooke.
4. Four Pas Redoubles (1814) for Trumpet, 3 Horns and Trombone. L. Cherubini.
5. Sonata in E flat major (1775) for Violin and Viola. Joseph Haydn. Movements: Moderato—Adagio—Minnetio. Violin: Norbert Brainin. Viola: Karl Haas. First public London performance.
6. Morgenmusik (morning music) (1932) for Trumpets, Horns and Trombone. P. Hindemith. Movements: Moderato—Lied—Con moto.
7. Four pieces for Trumpet, 3 Horns, Trombone (or Tuba) (1814). L Cherubini.

Personnel
Trumpets: Malcolm Arnold (who also plays treble trombone)
Wesley Woodage
Horns: Dennis Brain, Francis Bradley, Vincent Burrows, Tony Tunstall.
Trombone: George Maxted
Tuba: John Wilson

Holborn Borough Council present Members of the London Baroque Ensemble.
Director: Karl Haas
In a series of Lunchtime Concerts, Queen Mary Hall, Y.W.C.A
Programme: 3d. No. 47
Friday March 11 1949. Regency Music

1. Sonata in G-major for two Flutes, two Clarinets, two Horns and Bassoon in one movement. Carl Philipp Emanuel Bach (1775).
2. Adagio for Cor Anglais, two Violins and Cllo. W.A. Mozart (1789).
3. Slow Regimental Foot March for the Prince of Wales Light Dragoons for two Clarinets, two Horns, Bassoon and Side-drum.* John Christian Bach (1781).
4. Duet for two Flutes. (Allegro con brio and Minuet)* L. v. Beethoven (1792).
5. Trio in G-major for two Violas and Cello in four movements.* J. Haydn (1792).

* First performance

Artists
Flutes: Edward Walker, Arthur Hedges
Cor Anglais: Natalie James
Clarinets: Frederick Thurston, Gervase de Peyer
Bassoon: Cecil James
Horns: Dennis Brain, Aubrey Brain
Cello: James Whitehead
Violin: Kathleen Sturdy
Double-Bass: James E. Merrett
Violas: Herbert Downes, Kathleen Sturdy
Conductor: Karl Haas.

Holborn Borough Council presents Members of the London Baroque Ensemble directed by Karl Haas. Friday April 29 1949
Programme:

1. Quartet in C Major for Flute, Violin, Viola and 'Cello in two movements. Mozart, K.285B.
2. Divertimento for Horn, Violin and 'Cello in two movements. Haydn, 1767.
3. Short Duets for Clarinet and Violin (first performance in England). Hindemith, 1932.
4. Quartet in E flat Major for Clarinet, Violin, Horn and Cello in three movements (first modern performance). K. Stamitz, 1746–1801.

Artists
Flute: Gareth Morris
Clarinet: Frederick Thurston
Horn: Dennis Brain
Violin: Kathleen Sturdy
Viola: Karl Haas
Cello: James Whitehead

Holborn Borough Council presents Members of the London Baroque Ensemble directed by Karl Haas, Friday May 6 1949
Programme:

1. Notturno in C for two Flutes, two Clarinets, two Horns, two Violas, Cello and Double Bass in three movements. J. Haydn (1792)
2. Sonatina for Mandolin and Harpsichord (first concert performance in England). Beethoven
3. Duet for two Clarinets in two movements. C.P.E. Bach (1775)
4. Five Contradances (K.609) for two Violins, 'Cello, Double Bass, Flute and Side-Drum. W.A. Mozart (1791)
5. Viennese Waltzes for seven instruments (first concert performance of the original version). Beethoven (1819)

Artists
Violin: Kathleen Sturdy, David Martin
Viola: Kathleen Sturdy, Herbert Downes
Cello: James Whitehead
Double Bass: James E. Merrett.
Flute: Gareth Morris, Edward Walker
Clarinet: Frederick Thurston, Gervaise de Peyer
Horns: Dennis Brain, Aubrey Brain
Harpsichord: Dennis Brain
Mandolin: Karl Haas

Royal Festival Hall January 23 1953 at 8 p.m.
London Baroque Ensemble

Conductor, Karl Haas.
Serenade op. 44—Dvorak
Serenade in C minor, K.388—Mozart
INTERVAL
Symphony for 16 wind instruments (1945)—Strauss
First performance in England

The Music and Musicians at The Coronation Service of Her Majesty Queen Elizabeth II in Westminster Abbey
Tuesday, June 2 1953

Director of Music
Dr. Wiliam McKie, M.V.O.

Conductors
Dr. William McKie (during the Service)
Sir Adrian Boult (before and after the Service)

Sub-Conductors
Dr. William H. Harris, C.V.O.
Dr. John Dykes Bower

Organists
W. H. Gabb, Dr. Henry Ley, Dr. O. H. Peasgood

Leader of the Orchestra
Paul Beard, O.B.E.

THE ORCHESTRA

Horns
Dennis Brain
John Burden
Sydney Coulston
Charles Gregory

Hon. Organizing Orchestral Secretary: Eugene Cruft

Tony Catterick collection

London Wind Players

National Gallery Concerts
Wednesday May 26 1943

Angus Morrison (Pianoforte)
Conductor: Harry Blech
Natalie James (O), Peter Newbury (O), Pauline Juler (C), Richard Walthew (C), Cecil James, William Smith, (Bsns), Dennis Brain, Norman Del Mar (H).
Mozart Program
Quintet for Pianoforte and Wind Instruments in E-flat, K.452
Serenade for Wind Octet, No. 12, in C minor, K.388

Monday November 11 1946
Chelsea Town Hall King's Road S.W.3
London Wind Players

Conductor, Harry Blech
Serenade in B flat major K.361—Mozart
Octet in E flat Op.103 – Beethoven

The 1950 Cambridge Summer Festival Of Music and Drama
Promoted By The Cambridge Arts Theatre Trust with the support of The Arts Council of Great Britain
Sunday August 6 1950 at 8 p.m.

Serenade Concert
The London Wind Players
Conductor: Harry Blech
Flutes: Gareth Morris; George Crozier; Oboes: Sidney Sutcliffe, Leonard Brain; Clarinets: Stephen Waters, Jack Brymer; Bassoons: Cecil James, Edward Wilson; Basset Horns: Walter Lear, Michael Whewell; Horns: Dennis Brain, Ian Beers, Neill Sanders, Frank Probyn; Double Bass: James W. Merrett
First Court of Clare College by kind permission of The Master and Fellows
Programme Sixpence

Symphony in E flat for Wind Instruments—J.C. Bach (transcribed and edited by Mr Arthur Campbell)
Scored for two clarinets, two horns and two bassoons
Serenade for Wood-Wind—Gordon Jacob
No horns. Scored for two flutes, two oboes, two clarinets and two bassoons

Serenade in B flat (KV no.361)—Mozart
Scored for two oboes, two clarinets, two basset horns, four horns, two bassoons and double bass

Under The Patronage of their Majesties The King and Queen
Edinburgh International Festival of Music & Drama
Freemasons' Hall Edinburgh
Saturday September 1 1951 at 11 a.m.

The London Mozart Players
Conductor: Harry Blech
Dennis Brain (Horn)
March in F K.248.—Mozart
Symphony no.44 in E minor—Haydn
Horn Concerto (No. 1)—Haydn
Symphony No. 33 in B flat K.319—Mozart
The concert ends about 12.20 p.m.

Tony Catterick collection

London Mozart Players
Wednesday March 2 1955 at 8 p.m.

Haydn-Mozart Society Concert
Royal Festival Hall
Leader: Eli Goren
Conductor: Harry Blech
Solo Horn: Dennis Brain
National Anthem
Symphony No. 83 in G minor ('La Poule')—Haydn
Horn Concerto in E flat, K. 417—Mozart
Symphony No.33 in B flat, K.319—Mozart
Interval
Sinfonia Concertante in E flat, K.297b—Mozart

Tony Catterick collection

The Bach Choir
Founded 1876
Patron–Her Majesty The Queen
Royal Festival Hall
Tuesday, February 16 1954 at 8 p.m.

Mass in B Minor Bach

Soloists
Ena Mitchell, Gladys Ripley
Eric Greene, Stanley Clarkson, William Parsons

Harpsichord: Dr. C. Thornton Lofthouse
Organ: Dr. Osborne H. Peasgood
Flute: Gareth Morris
Oboe: Leon Goossens

Horn: Dennis Brain
The Jacques Orchestra, leader Emanuel Hurwitz
Conductor: Dr. Reginald Jacques
Tony Catterick collection

New London Orchestra

Leader: Leonard Hirsch
Conductor: Alec Sherman
Sunday, August 12 1951
William III Orangery
Hampton Court Palace
(by gracious permission of His Majesty the King)

Eighth Season
Serenade Concerts

[Interleaved note: "Sunday, August 12 In addition to the printed programme, the first performance will be given of Concertante Pastorale for Flute and Horn—Rawsthorne. Soloists: Gareth Morris, Dennis Brain"]
Sinfonia No. 1 in B flat—J.C. Bach
Flute Concerto in D—Gordon Jacob (First Performance)
Romance in F For Violin and Orchestra—Beethoven
The Lark Ascending—Vaughan Williams
Andante in C for Flute and Orchestra K.315—Mozart
Four Diversions on Ulster Airs—Howard Ferguson

Private collection

National Symphony Orchestra

Sunday November 29 1942 at 2:30 p.m.
The Phoenix Theatre, Charing Cross Road W.C.1

Conductor: Charles Hambourg
Soloist: Clifford Curzon
Symphony in D ("Classical")—Prokofiev
Two Aubades—Lalo
Concerto no. 27 in B-flat (K.595) for pianoforte and orchestra—Mozart
Interval
Rondino for Wind Instruments—Beethoven
Symphony no. 8 in F major, op. 93—Beethoven
Horns: Dennis Brain, Alwyn Hart, Norman Del Mar, Leonard Fleming

RAF Symphony Orchestra and Central Band

The Mosque, Richmond, December 27 1944, 8:15 p.m.

RAF scrapbook of the US tour.
Collection of Wing Commander Gilbert Singleton MCGI, FRSA

Gala Concert, Royce Hall, U.C.L.A. Westwood.
Monday January 29 1945, 8:00 p.m.

RAF scrapbook of the United States tour.

Civic Auditorium, San Francisco
January 31, 1945.

RAF scrapbook of the United States tour.

Scottish Rite Cathedral, Saint Louis
February 18 1945, 8:30 p.m.

Constitution Hall, Washington D.C.
February 26 1945, 8:30 p.m.

Waldorf-Astoria Hotel, New York
February 28 1945.

Blue Star Brigade Concert.

Dennis Brain Wind Quintet and Dennis Brain Wind Ensemble

Undated Program
Jesus College Chamber Recital
By Dennis Brain Wind Ensemble

Leonard Brain (Oboe)
Cecil James (Bassoon)
Stephen Waters (Clarinet)
Dennis Brain (Horn)
Wilfrid Parry (Pianoforte)

Divertimento No.4 in B flat, for Obie, Clarinet and Bassoon
Mozart—Oubradous
Sonata for Horn and Pianoforte in F op.17 Beethoven
Trio for Oboe, Bassoon and Pianoforte Poulenc
Interval with refreshments
Trio for Oboe, Clarinet and Bassoon (d'après Corrette) Milhaud
Villanelle for Horn and Pianoforte Dukas
Quintet for Wind and Pianoforte in E flat, K.452 Mozart

South Place Sunday Concerts
Conway Hall, Red Lion Square, Holborn W.C.1
20th Concert of the 58th Season (1453rd Concert)
Sunday February 27 1949, 6:30 p.m.

The Brain Wind Ensemble
Program:
Divertimento No. 14 in B-flat K. 270—Mozart, arranged for wind quintet by Anthony Baines
First time at these concerts.
Suite d'Après Corette [*sic*] for oboe, clarinet and bassoon—Milhaud
First time at these concerts
Wind Quintet (Clements Memorial Price, 1947)—Racine Fricker
First time at these concerts.
INTERVAL
Quintet in E-flat op. 16—Beethoven
7th time at these concerts. Last played December 13, 1931
Mrs. Patricia Morris collection

"Society for Twentieth-Century Music" concert, Hampstead Town Hall
March 3 1952
Program:

Schoenberg: Quintet op. 26. Alfred A. Kalmus Universal Edition.
Bernard van Dieren: Songs:

1. Weep you no more sad fountains (Anon, 16th century)
2. Spring Song of the Birds (King James I of Scotland)
3. Der Asra (Heinrich Heine)
4. Rondel (Charles I de Valois, Duc d'Orléans)

René Soames—tenor; Frederick Stone—pianoforte
Gerhard: Wind Quintet
Notes by Daniel Drew

Mrs Patricia Morris collection. A copy of the program is also preserved at the Britten-Pears Library shelf mark 3E1.2; 1-9204156.

York Festival 1954
York City Art Gallery. Saturday, June 26 1954, 11:00 a.m.
Dennis Brain Wind Ensemble

Wilfrid Parry (Piano)
Divertimento for wind quintet K. 270—Mozart
Quintet for Piano and Wind Instruments K. 452—Mozart
Quintet for flute, oboe, horn and bassoon Op. 5—Racine Fricker
Notes by Ernest Bradbury
INTERVAL
Suite d'Après Corelli—Milhaud
Sonatina for Horn and Pianoforte Op. 12—Schreiter

Mrs Patricia Morris collection

South Place Sunday Concerts
Conway Hall, Red Lion Square, Holborn W.C.1
Twenty-Third Concert of the 64th Season (1621th Concert)
Sunday March 20 1955, 6:30 p.m.
Dennis Brain Wind Ensemble

Harry Isaacs—Pianoforte
Program:
Divertimento No. 14 in B-flat, K. 270—Mozart arr. Anthony Baines
Second time at these concerts. First played, February 27, 1949
Sonata for Horn and Piano, Op. 24—Racine Fricker
First Performance
Interval
Wind Quintet (Clements Memorial Price, 1947)—Racine Fricker
Second time at these concerts. First played February 27, 1949
Quintet in E-flat K. 452 for Piano and Wind—Mozart
9th time at these concerts. Last played, October 13, 1946

Monday, April 30 1956, 7:30 p.m.
Wigmore Hall, Wigmore Street, W.1
Dennis Brain Wind Ensemble

Pianoforte: York Bowen, George Malcolm, Wilfrid Parry
Program
Concerto a Cinque, for Flute, Oboe, Clarinet, Bassoon and Piano—Ghedini
Pianoforte: Wilfrid Parry
Fantasia in F minor and major K. 594—Mozart (arranged for wind quintet by Dennis Brain)
Sonata for Horn and Piano, Op. 101—York Bowen
Pianoforte: York Bowen
Interval
Partita in F major for wind quintet—Denis Matthews
Sextet for Piano and Wind Instruments—Gordon Jacob
Pianoforte: George Malcolm
Written especially for this concert

Newbury and District Arts Society
Concert
Brain Wind Quartet and Pianoforte
Plaza Theatre, Newbury, November 29 1956, 7:00 p.m.

Program
Divertimento No. 4—Mozart arr Oubradous [written "An Oubradous"]. Oboe, Clarinet and Bassoon
Sonata for Horn and Pianoforte in F Opus 17—Beethoven
Trio for Oboe, Bassoon and Pianoforte—Poulenc
Villanelle for Horn and Pianoforte—Dukas
Interval
Quintet in E-flat, K. 452—Mozart
Tony Catterick collection

Edinburgh International Festival 1957. Souvenir Program
August 18 to September 7 1957
Page 25
Usher Hall
Dennis Brain Wind Ensemble
Thursday, August 22 8.00 p.m.

Divertimento for Wind in B-flat major, K. 270—Mozart
Quintet for Piano and Wind Instruments in E-flat major, K. 452—Mozart
Kleine Kammermusik No. 2, Op. 24, No. 2—Hindemith
Sextet for Piano and Wind Instruments—Poulenc

Page 41
Freemasons' Hall
Dennis Brain Wind Ensemble
Saturday, August 24 11.00 a.m.

Quintet for Piano and Wind Instruments in E-flat major, Op. 16—Beethoven
Fourth Dialogue for Wind Quintet—Malipiero
Villanelle for Horn and Piano—Dukas
Wind Quintet—Racine Fricker

Bach Bi-Centenary Concerts
The Brandenburg Concertos
The Boyd Neel Orchestra

Leader: Maurice Clare
Conducted by Boyd Neel
Soloists: Maurice Clare (Violin) Gareth Morris Arthur Hedges (Flutes) Leon Goossens Leonard Brain Donald Bridger (Oboes) Cecil James (Bassoon) Dennis Brain Ian Beers (Horns) George Eskdale (Trumpet) Ernest Lush (Harpsichord)

Sunday, June 11 at 4.20 p.m.

Brandenburg Concerto no. 3 in G Brandenburg Concerto no. 4 in G
Brandenburg Concerto no. 5 in D, Brandenburg Concerto no. 1 in F

Richard Kittrell collection

South Place Sunday Concerts

Conway Hall, Red Lion Square, Holborn, W.C.1
Twelfth Concert of the 65th Season (1637th Concert)
Sunday December 18 1955, at 6.30 p.m.
Aeolian String Quartet
Sydney Humphreys (Violin), Trevor Williams (Violin),
Watson Forbes (Viola), John Moore (Cello)
Dennis Brain, (Horn), Ian Beers (Horn)
Sextet in E flat, Op.81b—Beethoven
First time at these Concerts

Tony Catterick collection

Busch Players
Busch Concerts Tenth Series 1948
Kingsway Hall, Kingsway W.C.2
Friday April 30 at 7.30 p.m.

Cantata No. 140, "Wachet auf ruft uns die Stimme" for soprano, tenor, bass and choir, with two oboes, English horn, horn, strings, continuo and organ—Bach

Wednesday, May 5 at 7.30 p.m.

Brandenburg Concerto No. 1 in F major, for three oboes, bassoon, two horns, solo violin, strings and continuo—Bach

Single Tickets, 12/6, 10/6, 7/6, 5/– and 3/– by post from Miss M. F. Dakyns (Hon. Secretary, Busch Concerts Society), 6 Devonshire Place, W.1 usual Ticket Offices and Ibbs & Tillett Ltd., 124 Wigmore Street, W.1 Tickets on Sale at Kingsway Hall on Evenings of Concerts only

List of Performers
Solo Violin and Leader: Adolf Busch
Solo Singers: Soprano: Jo Vincent; Tenor: William Herbert; Bass: Gordon Clinton, Robert Irwin
Viola: Hugo Gottesmann; Jean Stewart; Kenneth Essex (not the composer); Philip Long
Violoncello: Herman Busch; Helen Just; Bernard Richards
Choir: The St. Michael Singers
Choirmaster and Organ: Harold Darke
Double-bass: James Merrett

Continuo: Thornton Lofthouse; May 5th: Peter Gellhorn
Violin: Bruno Straumann; Blanchette Honegger; Ruth Pearl; Vivian Hind; Irene Richards; Lorraine Du Val; Toni Booth; H. Leyton-Brown; Desmond Fenton; Ernest Scott; Leonard Friedman
Oboe: Evelyn Rothwell; Joy Boughton; Leonard Brain
Bassoon: Paul Draper
Horn: Dennis Brain; Ian Beers
Trumpet: George Eskdale
Harpsichord: Thomas Goff

First Performance of Hindemith's Horn Concerto Bader–Und Kurverwaltung Baden-Baden

Kurhaus Grosser Bühnensaal
Donnerstag, den Juni 8 1950 20 Uhr
Sonder-Konzert
Des Südwestfunkorchesters Baden-Baden
Leitung: Paul Hindemith
Soloist: Dennis Brain, Horn
Paul Hindemith
Sinfonietta (1949)
Konzert für Horn und Orchester (Uraufführung)
Konzert für Holzbläserm Harfe und Orchester (1. Aufführung in Europa)
Soloisten: Kraft Thorwald Dilloo (Flőte)
Horst Schneider (Oboe)
Sepp Fackler (Klarinette)
Helmut Müller (Fagott)
Marie Kindler (Harfe)
Konzertmusik für Streichorchester und Blechbläser
Tony Catterick collection

Royal Philharmonic Orchestra

Royal Philharmonic Orchestra, leader David McCallum
Conductor: Anthony Bernard

Soloists: Richard Lewis, Dennis Brain, Geoffrey Gilbert
Monday. February 22 1954. Programme: One Shilling

Symphony No.4 in A, Op.90 (Italian). Mendelssohn
Allegro vivace; Andante con moto, Con moto moderato; Saltarello: presto
Serenade for Tenor, Horn and Strings. Benjamin Britten. Richard Lewis, Dennis Brain
Concerto for Flute and Orchestra (1926). Carl Nielsen. Geoffrey Gilbert (flute)
Allegro moderato; Allegretto-Adagio ma non troppo-Allegretto; Poco adagio-Tempo di marcia
Symphony No.4 in B flat, Op.60. Beethoven
Adagio—Allegro vivace; Adagio; Allegro vivace; Allegro ma non troppo

Personnel (Horns:)
Alan Civil (Principal), Ian Beers, Andrew Woodburn, Frank Probyn
William C. Lynch collection

Royal Festival Hall
March 27, 1954

General Manager: T. E. Bean
Thomas Beecham Concerts Society Ltd. Presents a Beecham Popular Concert
Sir Thomas Beecham Bart. Conducting
Royal Philharmonic Orchestra (Leader David McCallum)

Program
Symphony No. 97 in C major—Haydn
Concerto for Oboe and Orchestra in G minor—Handel
Soloist: Terence MacDonagh
Air de Ballet (Zemire et Azor)—Gretry, arranged Beecham
Overture, La Chasse du Jeune Henri (Le Jeune Henri Overture)—Mehul
INTERVAL
Scenes from Act II, Irmelin (by request)—Delius
Suite de Ballet, Casse Noisette—Tchaikovsky

List of Personnel (Horns)
Dennis Brain (Principal)
Alan Civil
Ian Beers
Andrew Woodburn
Frank Probyn
Moura Martin, daughter of Terence MacDonagh, collection

Souvenir Tour Booklet
Beecham, Sir Thomas; Thorogood, Horace; Cardus, Neville
The Royal Philharmonic Orchestra of London England, New York,
Program Publishing Company, 1472 Broadway (1950)

Philharmonia Orchestra

Kingsway Hall, Kingsway, W.C.2
Philharmonia Concert Society
(Walter Legge and Victor Schuster)
Autumn 1945

Philharmonia Orchestra
(Leader: Leonard Hirsch)
Sir Thomas Beecham Bart.
Reginald Kell
Mozart Concert
Saturday October 27, 1:00–3:00 p.m.
Program notes by Alec Robertson
Program:
Symphony No. 40 in G minor, K.550
Concerto in A for Clarinet and Orchestra, K.622
Interval
Overture: *Don Giovanni*
Divertimento No. 2 in D major, K.131

Five German Dances
No 1 in C—K.600
No. 5 in G—K.600
No. 3 in B-flat—K.600
No. 2 in F—K.600
No. 3 in C—K.605
Future Concerts in this Series
Saturday, November 17
Ernest Element (Violin), Herbert Downes (Viola), Anthony Pini (Violoncello), Kendall Taylor (Pianoforte), Alec Whittaker (Oboe), Reginald Kell (Clarinet), John Alexandra (Bassoon), Dennis Brain (Horn)
Quartet in G minor, K.478, for Pianoforte and Strings—Mozart
Divertimento Trio in E-flat, K.563, for Violin, Viola and Violoncello—Mozart
Quintet in E-flat, K.452, for Wind and Pianoforte—Mozart

Philharmonia Concert Society
President: H. H. The Maharaja of Mysore
Subscription Series, 1949–1950
Sunday, February 12 1950, at 7:30 p.m.

Royal Opera House Covent Garden
The Philharmonia Orchestra (Leaders: Manoug Parikian and Max Salpeter)
Conductor: Igor Markevitch
Robert Helpmann
Apollo Musagetes—Stravinsky
Suite: "Le Bourgeois Gentilhomme"—Strauss
Nocturne—Andrzej Panufnik
"Peter and the Wolf"—Prokofiev

This program has a personnel list at the back. In addition to Dennis Brain, the horns are Ian Beers, Edmund Chapman, Alfred Cursue, and Aubrey Brain.

Wigmore Hall, Wigmore Street, W.1. Philharmonia Concert Society
Chamber Music Concerts
Friday, May 26 at 7 p.m. Quartet to be announced

Dennis Brain, John Alexandra, Frederick Thurston, J. Edward Merrett.
Beethoven: Septet in E flat major, Op.20
Schubert: Quintet in A major.
Single tickets: 6/– and 9/–

Monday May 22 1950
Royal Albert Hall

Wagner: Meistersinger Prelude, Siegfried Idyll
Strauss: Four Orchestral Songs (First European Performance)
Wagner: Tristan, Prelude and Liebestod
Siegfried's Rhine Journey
Closing Scene: Gotterdammerung
Wilhelm Furtwängler
Kirsten Flagstad

Kingsway Hall Kingsway, W.C.2
Concerts of 20th Century Music
Monday, April 16 1951, 7:30 p.m.

Philharmonia Orchestra
Soloists: Peter Pears, Dennis Brain
Conductor: Norman Del Mar
Richard Strauss: Prelude Capriccio
Hindemith: Horn Concerto
Strauss: Metamorphosen for 23 Strings
Britten: Serenade for Tenor and Horn

Royal Festival Hall
The London City Council
in association with S. A. Gorlinsky and Philharmonia Ltd.
Present
Arturo Toscanini
Conducting The Philharmonia Orchestra
Leader: Manoug Parikian
Monday September 29 1952

Tragic Overture,Op.81—Brahms
Symphony No. 1 in C minor, Op.68—Brahms
Interval
Symphony No. 2 in D major, Op.73—Brahms

Wednesday, 1 October 1952

Variations on a Theme of Joseph Haydn, Op. 56a—Brahms
Symphony no.3 in F major, Op. 90—Brahms
Interval
Symphony No.4 in E minor, Op. 98—Brahms

Horn personnel:
Dennis Brain Principal
Neill Sanders
Edmund Chapman
Alfred Cursue
Aubrey Thonger
Private collection

Kingsway Hall. Kingsway, W.C.2
Philharmonia Chamber Music Concerts

Monday, February 26, 7.30 p.m.
Denis Matthews (Pianoforte)
Dennis Brain (Horn)
Arthur Grumiaux (Violin)
Elisabeth Schwarzkopf (Soprano)
Beethoven: Sonata in A, Op. 47—Kreutzer
Brahms: Folk Songs
Brahms: Horn Trio in E flat, Op. 40

Souvenir Program
Edinburgh International Festival 1957
Page 27
Usher Hall
Philharmonia Orchestra
Thursday, August 29, 8:00 p.m.

Conductor: Otto Klemperer
Soloists: Anton Dermota, Dietrich Fischer-Dieskau
Symphony No. 29 in A major, K.201—Mozart
Das Lied von der Erde—Mahler

Saturday, August 31, 8:00 p.m.
Conductor: Eugene Ormandy
Tchaikovsky Program
Serenade for String Orchestra, Op. 48
Fantasy Overture: *Romeo and Juliet*
Symphony no. 6 in B minor, Op. 74, "Pathetique"

Scottish National Orchestra

Friday January 21 1954, 8:00 p.m.
The Scottish National Orchestra Society Limited

Scottish National Orchestra
Assistant Conductor and Leader Thomas Matthews
Conductor Karl Rankl
Soloists: Peter Pears, Dennis Brain
Usher Hall, Edinburgh
Program
Overture "The Water Carrier"—Cherubini
Horn Concerto No. 3 in E-flat, K.447—Mozart
Arias:
Kommet her ihr armen sunder K.146—Mozart
Per Pieta, None Ricercate K.420—Mozart
Serenade for Tenor, Horn and Strings, Op. 31—Britten
Symphony No. 8 in F, Op. 93—Beethoven

Dennis Brain Chamber Orchestra

First Appearance of The Dennis Brain Chamber Orchestra
Wednesday, April 18 1956, 7:30 p.m.; Friday, April 27, 7:30 p.m.

Tickets (including Tax): Reserved 9/– and 6/–; Unreserved 3/– (all bookable in advance) May be obtained at the Box Office, Wigmore Hall (Wel.2141), usual Ticket Offices, and from Ibbs & Tillett Ltd., 124 Wigmore Street, W.1

Concerto No. 2 in D K.412—Mozart
Dennis Brain
Concerto Fragment K.Anh.98a—Mozart
Dennis Brain
Symphony No. 17—Mozart

Divertimento K.247—Mozart
Concertante for Cor Anglais and Strings—Fricker
Leonard Brain

Tony Catterick collection

South Place Sunday Concerts
Alfred J. Clements, Organiser and Hon. Secretary from 1887 to 1938
Conway Hall, Red Lion Square, Holborn, W.C.1
Twenty-Seventh Concert of the 65th Season (1652nd Concert)
Sunday April 22 1956, 6:30 p.m.
Dennis Brain Chamber Orchestra
Leader: Hugh Bean

Symphony No. 33 in B-flat major, K.319—Mozart
First time at these Concerts
Concertante for Cor Anglais and Strings—Fricker
Leonard Brain
First time at these Concerts
Horn Concerto in E-flat , No. 3, K.447—Mozart
Dennis Brain
First time at these Concerts
Interval
Serenade for Wind in C minor, K.388—Mozart
Second time at these Concerts. First played, 5th February 1899
Encore: Mozart Concerto in E-flat, No. 3 K.447 (last movement)

Tony Catterick collection

Brain-Pougnet-Parry Trio

City of Bradford Libraries, Art Gallery And Museums Committee.
Lunch Hour Recital (no. 610). St George's Hall
Thursday 17 January 1957, 1.10 p.m. to 1.55 p.m.
Jean Pougnet (Violin), Dennis Brain (Horn), Wilfrid Parry (Pianoforte)

Trio in E-flat K.407 Mozart arr. Neumann
Allegro
Andante
Allegro
Trio in E-flat Op. 40 Brahms
Andante
Scherzo-Allegro-Molton meno allegro
Adagio mesto
Finale-Allegro con brio

Mrs. Patrcia Naylor collection

Jacques Orchestra

Royal Festival Hall, Tuesday, September 24 1957, 8:00 p.m.

Nina Milkina, Dennis Brain, The Jacques Orchestra, Leader: Emanuel Hurwitz, Conductor: Dr. Reginald Jacques.

Tickets: 12/6 10/0 7/6 5/– (available from August 24) from Royal Festival Hall Box Office (Waterloo 3191), usual Ticket Offices and Ibbs & Tillett Limited, 124 Wigmore Street, London W.1 (Welbeck 8418)

Programme
Water Music—Handel
Piano Concerto in D minor, K.466—Mozart
Nina Milkina
Horn Concerto in E-flat, K.495—Mozart
Dennis Brain
Symphony No. 94 in G (Surprise)—Haydn

2. Documents preserved by BBC Written Archives, Caversham, Berkshire, England.

1. Program as Broadcast Files for Overseas Services

Afrikaans Program
December 16, 1940
6:45 Greenwich Mean Time. Recorded talks on Dingaans Day by Dr. Von Broekhuizon and Junkhur Beelaerto von Blockland

Background music for the production was played by:
Dennis Brain—Organ
Leonard Brain—Oboe
Reginald Barker—Timps
Mr. Cant—Trumpet

Empire Service, Purple Network
South Africa

20:30. Music Program—Live
Presented by Arnold van Wyk
Soloists: Clement Hardman (Baritone)
Dennis Brain (Horn)
Accompanied by John Wills
Horn Concerto No. 4 in E-flat—Mozart (First Movement. Arr. Francis G. Sanders. 1'35")

European Service
November 20, 1942

Greenwich Mean Time: 10:30 p.m.
Horn and Piano Recital
Dennis Brain (horn) and Denis Matthews (pianoforte)
Sonata for Horn and Pianoforte—Beethoven. Non-copyright
Pre-recorded November 20, 1942. SBU 14684
We do not know if a copy of the recording was preserved.

French Transmission
May 21, 1947

23:00–23:30. Musical Program
Harry Blech (Violin)
Dennis Brain (Horn)
Leonard Isaacs (Piano)
Announced in French and English
Brahms: Trio in E-flat, Op. 40—Brahms. 26'25"

French Transmission
April 6, 1949

Wednesday Concert
20:00–21:00. Written by M. Glock. Presented by M. Belfer. Pre-recorded March 28, 1949. Recording ref. SBU 28648
Quintet in E-flat Op. 16—Beethoven. George Malcolm (piano). Edition: Breitkopf. 21'45"
Six Dance Caricatures for wind quintet—Roy Douglas. Edition: Hinrichsen. 9'05"
Wind Quintet—Roberto Gerhard. Manuscript score. 18'10"

French Transmission
April 20, 1949

20:00–21:00. Concert. Edited by M. Glock
London Baroque Ensemble, Directed By Karl Haas
Pre-recorded March 16, 1949. SBU 28038. 22'30"
Serenade Op. 44—Dvorak. Simrock.
We do not know if the recording for this broadcast was preserved.

French Transmission
March 8, 1950

19:00–20:00. Concert. Presented by P. Forster with the London Baroque Ensemble, Directed by Karl Haas
Five Marches for Louis XIV's Regiments. 06'00. Lully arr. Karl Haas. Mss
Chansons et Danses op. 50. Vincent D'Indy. 16'55" Durand

German Transmission
December 7, 1947

20:00–21:30. Musical Program
Sonata (1st movement) Beethoven SBU 7257/2. Played by Franz Osborn and Dennis Brain. 11'40"
Horn Concerto No. 1—Mozart SBU 7257/1. Played by Franz Osborn and Dennis Brain
Brahms: Trio in E-flat Major Op. 40. Played by Harry Blech, Franz Osborn, and Dennis Brain
Recorded December 1, 1947. 29'08"
First movement. SBU 7257/5
Second movement. SBU 24300/7
Third movement. SBU 7257/7
Fourth movement. SBU 7257/8
We do not know if any of the recordings in this broadcast were preserved.

Latin-American Service
August 9, 1944

02:30 SB7. Dennis Brain (horn), accompanied by B. Mason.
Concerto No. 2 in D major (Haydn) Breitkopf and Härtel.
Pre-recorded August 2, 1944. PLA 386 DAL 15305. Recorded at Aldenham
We do not know if a recording has been preserved.

Brown Network
July 10, 1947

23:45. Dennis Brain, accompanied by Frederick Stone
Horn Sonata Op. 17—Beethoven. Non-copyright. 12'30"

September 2, 1948
00:30 Recital by James Johnston (Tenor), and Dennis Brain
Pre-recorded August 23, 1948. PLA 1788, DLA 12431
Sonata for Horn and Piano—Beethoven. 12'10" Breitkopf & Härtel

December 29, 1949
00:30. Joint Recital. Dennis Brain, accompanied by Arthur Dulay
Pre-recorded December 22, 1949. PLA 2143—DAL 21985
Larghetto—Chabrier. Durand. 07'28"
Villanelle—Dukas. Ed. Costolat 05'49"
We do not know if the recording for this broadcast was preserved.

Eastern Service, Green Network
India, Burma and Indonesia
May 31, 1946

17:30. Horn Recital.
Dennis Brain, accompanied by John Wills
Sonata Op. 17 in F—Beethoven. Breitkopf and Härtel. 12'00"

September 24, 1947
Musical Box. Presented by Narayana Monon
Edited and Produced by Basil Douglas and Narayana Monon
15:30. Live music performed by Gareth Morris, Leonard Brain, Stephen Waters, and Dennis Brain:
Three movements from Divertimento in B-flat (K. 270)—Mozart. 7'00". Non-copyright.
Allegretto from Partita for Wind Quintet—Denis Matthews. 1'35". Manuscript score.
No. 1 of three short pieces for wind quintet—Ibert. 1'55". Durand

Eastern Service, Purple Network
February 15, 1947

Recital by Dennis Brain
Villanelle 6'00"—Paul Dukas. Durand
Reverie 3'30"—Glazunov Belaieff
Allegro Spiritoso 2'00"—Senaille. Ricordi
Pre-recorded December 16, 1946—SOX 79165
We do not know if a recording was preserved.

General Overseas Service
July 29, 1947

20:15. Dennis Brain
Horn Concerto—Haydn
Allegro moderato 5'55"
Adagio 3'50"
Allegro 3'20"
Non-copyright

Green Network
September 27, 1950

19:30. The Royal Philharmonic Orchestra
Leader: David McCallum
Conducted and presented by Sir Thomas Beecham
Concertante for Wind Instruments (K.297b)—Mozart. Breitkopf & Härtel. 27'28"
Soloists: Terence MacDonagah, Jack Brymer, Gwydion Brooke, Dennis Brain

September 2, 1951
15:15. From Manchester.
BBC Northern Orchestra
Leader: Reginald Stead
Conductor: Charles Groves
Dennis Brain
Horn Concerto No. 1 in D, K.412—Mozart 08'00". Breitkopf
Concerto for Horn and Strings—Gordon Jacob. 18'00". Jos. Williams

March 27, 1956
06:30–7:00 a.m. Talking About the Instrument: "No. 7: The Horn"
Illustrated Talk by Dennis Brain
Pre-recorded March 19, 1956, 10:00–11:15 a.m., Studio 2, Maida Vale. Rehearsal: 8:00–10:00 a.m. Recorded Talks reference: TOX 39218

We do not know if the recording for this broadcast was preserved. The program was broadcast again on the General Overseas Service, March 28 at 2:30 a.m. and March 29 at 19:30 Greenwich Mean Time.

2. Television and Radio Scripts and Other Documents

Television

Internal BBC publicity document
T14/485/1.

July 4, 1952. 9:00–9:55 p.m. Music Recital "You are invited . . ."

—*OB Television*

Banqueting House, Goldsmiths' Hall, London. With the Dutch String Quartet: Nap de Klijn (Violin), Johan van Helder (Violin), Paul Godwin (Viola), Carel Boomkamp (Cello), Gerald Moore (Piano) and Max Gilbert (2nd Viola)

T14/485/1

Internal letter, June 6, 1952, from (Sir) Huw Weldon to Mrs. N. G. Bradbury, Lime Grove.

The letter mentions the televised concert at the Goldsmiths' Hall, London, and lists the musicians engaged.

TELI/0421/581/18798

Teleclub No. 6, December 18, 1953, 7:45–8:45 p.m.

With Wilfrid Parry (piano). Marais: "Le Basque"; Saint Saens: "The Swan."

TELI/D421/458/14051

This Is Show Business (episode 5). Vic Oliver (Master of Ceremonies), May 31, 1954. Studio G. Produced by Graeme Muir. Orchestral schedule: Dennis Brain, 2:15–2:40 p.m., cameras 1, 2, and 3. Brain plays the third movement from Mozart's Horn Concerto K.495.

T12/439/A

Internal BBC "Caption and Photographic Requirements" document
Programme title: *Vera Lynn Sings*
Guest artist: Dennis Brain
Orchestra, conducted by Eric Robinson (Leader, David McCallum)
Broadcast, April 7, 1957

T6/111

Matthews, Denis, Introduction, dated August 14, 1958, for Anvil Films, Beethoven Horn Sonata. Script reference T6/111. See Discography, III for further details about this film.

Radio

TLO 93671 (recording reference)

Light Program, series *Say It With Music*, December 17, 1955, 9:00–10:00 p.m. Pre-recorded December 15, 1955, 1:00–2:30 p.m., King's Theatre, Hammersmith. Rehearsal, December 14, 10:30–1:30 p.m.; December 15, 9:30–12:30 p.m. Brain played Dukas's *Villanelle* with Wilfrid Parry.

TLO 23653 (recording reference)

Home Service series, "Call the Tune" no. 1. Producer, Walter Todds. Recorded, February 4, 1957, 4:15–5:00 p.m., Studio 3A. Rehearsal: 1:15 p.m. Broadcast May 22, 1957, 10:15–10:45 p.m. With Joseph Cooper, Joyce Grenfell, Stephen Potter, and Wynford Vaughan Thomas. Duration: 29:37

Brain, Dennis, *The Early Horn*. Transmission: July 23, 1955 6:0–-6:55 p.m. Pre-recorded July 6 on TBS 15752. Speech, July 11 on TLO 82995. Rehearsal, 3:30, recorded 5:30–6:00 in Concert Hall, Broadcasting House. Edited July 19, 9:30–12:30 in H.1 Trial no. TLO 83028. Producer, Roger Fiske. Microfilm talk scripts reference "T51 (BRAD-BRAI)"

Desert Island Discs. With Roy Plomley. Home Service, August 13, 1956, 1:10–1:40 p.m. Produced by Monica Chapman. WAC, telediphone script, band 5a and 6, pp. 5–11. BBC recording reference DLS 9281. Cat. no. S133/18/28—Plomley, Roy: *Desert Island Discs.*—Plomley, Roy: Desert Island Discs."

Del Mar, Norman. BBC hand-corrected script by Norman Del Mar for his BBC tribute, *Dennis Brain*, BBC Home Service, October 9, 1957, 7:00–7:30 p.m. BBC radio talks, microfilm ref.no. T113.

Gareth Morris, BBC Home Service, "Dennis Brain 1921–1957" in *Music Magazine*, May 21, 1961, 10:45 p.m. WAC "Music Magazine" scripts reel 7/8 (14/06/1959–21/12/62)."

Endnotes

Introduction

1. Stephen Pettitt, *Dennis Brain, a Biography* (London: Robert Hale, 1989). Hereafter cited as Pettitt (1989).

Chapter 1. The Early Years (1921–1939)

1. Aubrey's positions in London Orchestras in 1921, Pettitt (1989), 32. Marion Beeley at Covent Garden, from souvenir program of Bristol Music Festival, October 23–26, 1912, p. 14. Sir Edward Elgar's "Hail, Immemorial Ind!" idem. Audrey Brain played for Gamble some of Marion Brain's old shellac records that clearly demonstrate what a fine contralto she was. For Denhof Opera tour, Pettitt (1989), 28.
2. Roger Brain, nephew of Dennis, sent Gamble information about Basil Bernard Beeley (b. Kettleshulme, Cheshire, 1860) and his Beeley relations. Broadstairs, Kent as a favorite holiday destination, Pettitt (1989), 56.
3. Brain speaking to Roy Plomley on *Desert Island Discs*, pre-recorded July 28, 1956, broadcast August 13, 1956, Home Service, 1:10–1:40 p.m. Transcript from an LP issue of the speech links, BBC Artium, REGL 352 (1979). BBC radio program listing in *Radio Times* 132, no. 1709 (August 12–18, 1956): 16, August 13, Home Service 1:10 p.m.
4. The anecdote about playing a perfect note at the age of three is briefly told by Brain in the same *Desert Island Discs* program. Also Arthur C. Payne (1927), 191. Brain playing his father's horn every Saturday, Pettitt (1989), 55.
5. Early schooling, Pettitt (1989), 55–56.
6. Stephen F. Pearce, pupil of Sir Vivian Dunn, related this reminiscence to Gamble in an email, March 25, 2006. For the factory under Waterloo Bridge, Basil Tschaikov *The Music Goes Round and Around* (Peterborough: Fastprint Pub., 2009), Chapter 2, p. 13. He describes it by its nickname "Number 10" situated "more or less under Waterloo Bridge."
7. Piano lessons, school contemporary with Fricker, and singing treble at St. Paul's, Pettitt (1989), 56. St. Paul's School Music Society concert, December 19, 1935, private collection.
8. Lessons with Aubrey Brain after leaving St. Paul's, Pettitt (1989), 57. Old Pauline concerts, December 21, 1937, and December 20, 1938, private collection. Denis Mason, third horn in the RPO, Chapter 4, section, "United States, 1950."
9. Stokes Scholarship and professors at the Royal Academy of Music, Pettitt (1989), 57. Strauss hearing Douglas Moore privately at the Academy, playing *Till Eulenspiegel*, in letter from Douglas Moore to Gamble, November 30, 2005. Douglas Moore, telephone call with Gamble on January 30, 2005.

10. Jack Brymer, *From Where I Sit* (London: Cassell, 1979), 51. Hereafter cited as Brymer (1979). Quoted with permission of Timothy Brymer.
11. Concert program, Richard Kittrell collection. The concert included Fanfare for brass and organ (Purcell-Wood); "Blest Pair of Sirens" for choir and orchestra (Parry); *Overture to Adventure*, first London performance (Arnold Bax), Two Purcell Songs (sung by May Blyth); Beethoven Piano Concerto op.58 (Soloist, Myra Hess); Coronation Anthem: "The King Shall Rejoice" (Handel); A Song of Thanksgiving (Mackenzie); Aria: "Woo Thou Thy Snowflake" from *Ivanhoe* (Sullivan); *Valse Gracieuse* (German); Festival Te Deum (Stanley Marchant); The National Anthem.
12. Gareth Morris, speaking on *Mining the Archives* series, BBC Radio 3, May 17, 1996, presented by Fiona Talkington. British Library Sound Archive call no. H 7135/2. Hereafter cited in Endnotes only as BLSA.
13. Edwin Glick, email to Gamble, November 26, 2009.
14. Douglas Moore recalling the use of Franz's treatise, taped interview with Gamble, June 30, 2005. Aileen Hunter, email to Gamble, February 27, 2005.
15. Douglas Moore, telephone call with Gamble, January 30, 2005.
16. Donald Froud, letter to Gamble, October 14, 2005.
17. Ibid.
18. Christopher Hortin letter to Gamble, October 2005 (undated, received October 12).
19. John Burden, MS "Reminiscenses," 1. Morris, taped interview with Gamble, March 1, 2006.
20. Burden, ibid.
21. Conductor's class with Ernest Read, Pettitt (1989), 61–62. Douglas Moore, in telephone call with Gamble, January 30, 2005. "Academy and College Notes," *Musical Times* 78, no. 1131 (May 1937): 455.
22. John Burden, telephone call with Gamble, February 14, 2005, mentioned that Aubrey Brain sometimes sat in at concerts at Queen's Hall and Duke's Hall "listening a lot."
23. For *Marriage of Figaro*, Pettitt (1989), 59. John Burden, MS "Reminiscenses," 2.
24. Pettitt (1989), 59. Also "Academy and College Notes," *Musical Times* 79, no. 1145 (July 1938): 531.
25. Morris, remembering his student days in *Mining the Archives*, BBC Radio 3, May 17, 1996. Presented by Fiona Talkington. BLSA call no. H 7135/2. Morris taped interview with Gamble, March 1, 2006, recalling Aubrey Brain in radio broadcasts.
26. Morris taped interview with Gamble, March 1, 2006.
27. Ibid.
28. Burden, MS "Reminiscences," 1. Lady Barbirolli recalling the Busch Players concert, in taped interview with Gamble, May 29, 2004. *Daily Telegraph*, October 7, 1938. © Telegraph Media Group Limited, 1938. Aubrey Brain's collection of newspaper cuttings, private collection. Also quoted in Pettitt (1989), 60.
29. Morris taped interview with Gamble, March 1, 2006.
30. Ibid.
31. Morris speaking on BBC Artium LP, REGL 352 (1979).
32. Pettitt (1989), 61–62, on broadcasts and concerts of Mozart's K334.
33. Ibid., 60–61.
34. Morris telephone call with Gamble, March 23, 2006. The concert was mentioned in "Academy and College Notes," *Musical Times* 80, no. 1155 (May 1939): 380.
35. Pettitt (1989), 62. Also "Academy and College Notes," *Musical Times* 80, no. 1156 (June 1939): 462.

36. Gerald Jackson, *First Flute* (London: J. M. Dent & Sons, 1968), 66, remembering a "Monday Night at Seven" BBC broadcast, no date. BBC Empire Orchestra concert, 3:00–4:00 p.m., Regional service, June 21, 1939, WAC *RCONT1, Artists, Brain Dennis, File 1A 1939–1946*, application dated May 1, 1939.

Chapter 2. The RAF Years (1939–1946)

1. The Brain brothers' date of enlistment, Pettitt (1989), 63.
2. Morris speaking on BBC Radio 3, *Mining the Archives,* May 17, 1996. Presented by Fiona Talkington. BLSA call no. H 7135/2.
3. The Brain brothers' invitation to return to the Royal Academy in the spring and summer terms, 1940, Pettitt (1989), 65. Aubrey Brain at Bristol, idem, 65.
4. Del Mar, speaking on BBC Artium LP, REGL 352 (1979).
5. Ibid.
6. Ibid.
7. Burden, MS "Reminiscenses," 3.
8. Del Mar's job as chauffeur to the Commanding Officer and hatred of routine barracks duties, told by Pauline Del Mar to Gamble, November 9, 2005. Morris remembering the routine at RAF barracks, on Radio 4 *Music in Air Force Blue*, April 22, 2005. Also Pettitt (1989), 66. Pam's Pantry, the favorite "greasy spoon," recalled by Pauline Del Mar in taped interview with Gamble, November 9, 2005. Also recalled by Audrey Brain, taped interview with Gamble, October 29, 2003. Also Pettitt (1989), 66–67.
9. Cartoon, reproduced with permission from Patricia Morris.
10. WAC *RCONT 1 Artists File 1A Brain Dennis, 1939–1946*. This is one of the files that survive of Brain's BBC correspondence.
11. Morris taped interview with Gamble, March 1, 2006.
12. Donald Weeks, a violinist in the Philharmonia from 1956, in taped interview with Tony Catterick, second horn of the London Mozart Players and Historian of the British Horn Society.
13. Appearance as soloist in Mozart's Concerto K495 (No. 4), Pettitt (1989), 68.
14. Morris taped interview with Gamble, March 1, 2006. The film of Dame Myra Hess playing a movement from Mozart's Piano Concerto No. 17 has most recently been issued on Beulah DVD (UK), *Classical Music of the Forties* (YB35), together with Brain and Matthews's film of Beethoven's Horn Sonata, Anvil Films Ltd., 1952. The DVD also contains *Steps of the Ballet* with soundtrack of music by Arthur Benjamin (who appears in the film), played by the Philharmonia Orchestra, conducted by Muir Mathieson.
15. Roy Douglas telephone call with Gamble, August 6, 2006. First performance of the *Six Dance Caricatures* (published by Peters) at the National Gallery, The British Music Information Centre shelf mark Hw. *www.bmic.co.uk/collection/searchdetails.asp?id=5861*.
16. Concert details from concert programs, private collection. Personnel for the performance of Mozart's Serenade K.361, August 19, 1942, in addition to Brain were: Natalie James, Peter Newbury, oboes; Pauline Juler, George Anderson, clarinets; Walter Lear, Richard Temple Savage, Bassett horns; Vivian Grey, Norman Del Mar, Livia Gollancz, horns; Cecil James, Tom Wightman, bassoons; James Merrett, double-bass, conducted by Harry Blech. Pettitt (1989), 74.
17. Pettitt (1989), 68. The London Wind Players had also given a broadcast performance of Mozart's Divertimento K166 on Home Service, May 30, 1946. BBC radio program listing in *Radio Times* 91, no. 1182, p. 14, for The Thursday Concert, 7:15–8:15 p.m. Apart from Brain

and Del Mar, the personnel were Natalie James and Aubrey Johnson (oboes), Stephen Waters and Richard Walthew (clarinets), Leonard Brain and Donald Bridger (cor anglais), Cecil James and Thomas Wightman (bassoons), conducted by Harry Blech.

18. Pettitt (1989), 75.

19. Dame Myra Hess, et al., *National Gallery Concerts 10th October 1939–10th October 1944*, printed for the Trustees, London 1944, private collection.

20. Michael Kennedy, 1993, Appendix B, "Classified List of Works: Incidental Music 3. Radio," 291–92.

21. First performance of the Serenade, Pettitt (1989), 182.

22. Alec Robertson, "Analytical Notes and First Reviews: The Great Tradition: Henry Purcell 1658–Benjamin Britten 1913," *Gramophone* 23, no. 271 (December 1945): 79. Timothy Day, *A Century of Recorded Music: Listening to Musical History* (New Haven: Yale University Press, 2000), 243.

23. Burden MS "Reminiscenses," 5.

24. "National Gallery Concert. Octet for Strings and Wind," *The Times*, Late London Edition, February 18, 1943, p. 6, column d. The Octet was issued on CD in 1992 by Dutton Laboratories (CDAX 8104), under license from Decca, and the Brahms work was reissued in 2002 by Yukihiro Okitsu on CD in Japan, entitled *A Resurrection of Dennis Brain*. Pettitt (1989), 72.

25. Sargent and Turner conducting, Pettitt (1989), 72. The cadenza by Del Mar, idem.

26. Alec Robertson, "Analytical Notes and First Reviews," *Gramophone* 21, no. 252 (May 1944): 180.

27. William McNaught, "Gramophone Notes," *Musical Times* 86, no. 1231 (September 1945): 276.

28. Del Mar in a letter to Gamble, September 4, 1990, mentioned he and Brain were the horn players. See Discography II.1, British Library Sound Archive, entry for Brandenburg Concerto.

29. Neill Sanders, speaking at the International Horn Society Symposium, Brain Seminar, at the University of North Texas, May 17, 1991. Private tape.

30. BBC radio program listing in *Radio Times* 73, no. 945 (November 9–15, 1941): 6, Home Service, November 9, 11:30–midnight. BBC radio program listing in *Radio Times* 76, no. 989 (September 13–19, 1942):14, September 17, Home Service 7:15–8:00 p.m. BBC radio program listing in *Radio Times* 77, no. 994 (October 18–24, 1942):18, October 24, Home Service 11:00–11:25 p.m. Concerning Brain's effort to gain a higher fee for Mozart's Quintet K407 commensurate with the fee for solo works, WAC, *RCONT1 Brain Dennis, Artists File III 1953–1956*, contract ref. 01/PC/NC, from Norman Carrell to Brain, January 25, 1956. For November 20, 1942, overseas broadcast, WAC *RCONT1 Brain Dennis, Artists File 1A 1939–1946*, application letter, ref. AP/AW from Arthur Wynn to Brain, November 13, 1942.

31. Purple Network broadcast, information from the P as B file, WAC, provided by Written Archives Researcher Erin O'Neill. BBC radio program listing in *Radio Times* 79, no. 1024 (May 16–22, 1943): 6, May 16, Home Service 6:45–7:30 p.m. For the contract concerning this broadcast, WAC *RCONT1 Artists, Brain Dennis, File 1A, 1939–1946*, ref. 03/PC/AW, April 29, 1943, from Wynn to Brain.

32. "Music This Week," *The Times*, Late London Edition, April 26, 1943, p. 8, col. a; BBC radio program listing in *Radio Times* 80, no. 1034 (July 25–31, 1943): 14, July 29, Home Service 11:00–11:30 p.m. *WAC RCONT1 Artists, Brain Dennis, File 1A, 1939–1946*, ref., 03/PC/AW, from Wynn to Brain, July 5, 1943.

33. Latin American Service broadcast, August 9, 1944, information from the "P as B" file, given to the authors by archives researcher Erin O'Neill. Pettitt (1989), 40; 134–35, for

comments on Dennis and Alfred Brain's difficulties playing this piece. Idem, 53–54 for comparison between the embouchures of Aubrey, Dennis, and Alfred Brain.

34. BBC radio program listing in *Radio Times* 88, no. 1139 (July 29–August 4, 1945): 16, August 1, Home Service 11:15–midnight.

35. *The Times*, Late London Edition, December 3, 1945, p. 7, column c.

36. Eastern Service, Purple Network, May 31, 1946, information from the "P as B" file, given to the authors by Erin O'Neill. BBC radio program listing in *Radio Times* 92, no. 1193 (August 11–17, 1946): 6, August 11, Home Service 10.15–10.30 p.m.

37. Brain speaking to Roy Plomley on *Desert Island Discs*, BBC Home Service, August 13, 1956. BBC Artium LP REGL 352 (1979).). See also WAC, BBC radio talks, microfilm ref.no. T113. BBC hand-corrected script by Norman Del Mar for his BBC tribute, "Dennis Brain," Home Service, October 9, 1957, 7:00–7:30 p.m.

38. National Symphony Orchestra principals, Pettitt (1989) 69. Morris described the National Symphony Orchestra as a session orchestra in conversation with Gamble, March 1, 2006. Concert program, November 29, 1942, private collection. Plate 7 of the NSO horn section, reproduced with permission from Pettitt.

39. Morris taped interview with Gamble, March 1, 2006, about Brain and Morris playing for Walter Goehr's Orchestra during wartime at Wigmore Hall. "Orchestral Concerts," *Musical Times* 84, no. 1201 (March 1943): 95.

40. "Concerts &c" (advertisement), *The Times*, Late London Edition, January 19, 1943, p. 8, col. b. For concert on January 16, 1943, at Wigmore Hall with Gareth Morris (flute solo).

41. BBC radio program listing in *Radio Times* 78, no. 1005 (January 3–9, 1943): 6, January 3, Home Service 4:05–4:45 p.m. WAC, RCONT1 Artists, Brain Dennis, File 1A 1939–1946: letter from Brain to Wynn, March 19, 1942, stating availability.

42. The Brain brothers at 16, The Greenway, Pettitt (1989), 65–66. Letter to the BBC stating Brain was "bombed out," WAC, *RCONT1 Artists, Brain Dennis, File 1A 1939–46*; letter to Wynn, July 15, 1944. This gives Elsworthy Terrace as his new address. For Thomas Carter, Pettitt (1989), 75. Brain's future wife, Yvonne Coles, a pupil of pianist Harold Craxton at the Royal Academy, Pettitt, idem. Pettitt (1989), 75.

43. Hess performing all Mozart's piano concertos, 1943 to 1945, with the New London Orchestra, Pettitt (1989), 70. Morris in conversation with Ian Wagstaff, "Aubrey and Son," *Horn Magazine* 1, no. 2 (Spring 1993): 13.

44. RAF scrapbook, collection of Wing Commander Gilbert Singleton. Plates 8–11 reproduced from the scrapbook. For an account of the tour, Pettitt (1989), 76–79.

45. Morris taped interview with Gamble, March 1, 2006. First concert, Pettitt (1989), 76. Matthews, arranger of the Bach Toccata and Fugue, mentioned by Morris to Gamble, March 1, 2006. NBC radio broadcast, December 18, 1944, Pettitt, idem.

46. First movement of Mozart's Quintet K407, Pettitt (1989), 77.

47. Brain's make of camera, information given to Gamble by Yvonne Brain.

48. Morris taped interview with Gamble, March 1, 2006.

49. Los Angeles visit, Pettitt (1989), 78–79. Party at The Tropics, Leighton Jones, "Alfred Brain—The Forgotten English Horn Virtuoso?" in *Horn Magazine* 10, no. 3 (April 2003): 21.

50. Tour of the chicken farm, Pettitt (1989), 78. Morris remembering the party at Gardena and Alfred on the roof playing his horn, taped interview with Gamble, March 1, 2006. Leonard Brain recalling a "sea of alcohol," quoted from Pettitt (1989), 78. Lawrance Sansone, Jr. remembering the party and Brain playing Bach fugues, mentioned in a letter from Sansone to Pettitt, quoted in Chapter 11. Also Pettitt (1989), 78–79 for account of the party and

Brain playing part of the *Flight of the Bumble-Bee*. Kreisler's *Schön Rosmarin*, Leighton Jones (2003), p. 23. James Decker present at the party at Gardena, idem. For James Decker, see also Chapter 9.

51. Alfred's emigration to the United States, Pettitt (1989), 33. Plates 13–14, private collection. Lady Barbirolli taped interview with Gamble on May 29, 2004, about a party in 1939 or 1940 where Alfred cooked all the food. She also remembered that Alfred welcomed the guests from his roof with excerpts of the big horn solos in the orchestral repertoire: "He played everything—the *Siegfried* Horn Call, bits of Wagner. He was up there for a long time—we were a long time getting anything to eat! I remember that!"

52. Information from concert program, pasted in the RAF scrapbook, collection of Gilbert Singleton.

53. Journey back to Washington via Denver and Omaha, O'Donnell's leg injury and concerts conducted by Hollingsworth, Pettitt (1989), 79. Morris remembering Tommy Dorsey at the 400 Club, telephone call with Gamble, March 23, 2006.

54. BBC radio program listing in *Radio Times* 88, no. 1134 (June 24–30, 1945): 6, June 24, Home Service 9:30–10:00 p.m. For Brain's return to concert life in London, Pettitt (1989), 80.

55. Concert program, private collection. Also Pettitt (1989), 86–87, for a description of the pieces played, in particular the Haydn Divertimento a tré in E-flat for horn, violin, and cello (1767). Brain's student Edwin Glick, Chapter 7, "Teacher and Lecturer."

56. WAC, *RCONT1, Artists, Brain Dennis, File 1A 1939–1946;* letter from Brain to Lewis, March 27, 1946, informing him that he is away in Germany for a month with the RAF Band, touring the camps (military bases).

Chapter 3. The Brain Quintet and Ensemble (1946–1957)

1. First concert, Pettitt (1989), 87. Brain explained several times in his letters to the BBC that he was away in Germany with the RAF Symphony Orchestra until the end of April. Del Mar remembering he played horn in Brain's absence for the first concert of the Dennis Brain Wind Quintet at Chelsea Town Hall on April 30, 1946, WAC, BBC radio talks, microfilm ref. no. T113. BBC hand-corrected script by Del Mar for his BBC tribute, "Dennis Brain" for Home Service, October 9, 1957, 7:00–7:30 p.m. Morris speaking to Gamble on the subject, March 1, 2006. Matthews, engaged as pianist for the first concert, *The Times*, Royal Edition, May 1, 1956, p. 5 column d. A search of *The Times* for April 1946 showed no advertisement or review of the concert.

2. WAC *RCONT1 Artists File I, 1946–1962 Dennis Brain Wind Ensemble*; letter from Brain to Wynn, September 1, 1946. Also Pettitt (1989), 87, for the first broadcast. BBC radio program listing in *Radio Times* 92, no. 1199 (September 22–28, 1946): 14, September 26, Home Service 7:30–8:30 p.m. *The Thursday Concert*.

3. Jacoby Quintet. MS score given to Gamble by Audrey Brain in October 2003.

4. Thomas Wightman and his return to Australia, Pettitt (1989), 106. For John Alexandra, idem. Cecil James as bassoonist in the Quintet, idem, 128.

5. WAC, *RCONT1, Artists, File I 1946–1962, Dennis Brain Wind Ensemble*; repertoire list in letter from Joan Ingpen to E Lockspeiser Esq., February 22, 1947. "Matthews" refers to Denis Matthews; for his Partita, see first performance in Chapter 1.

6. Arnold Quintet, Paul Harris's article, "Lost and Found—The Remarkable Story of Malcolm Arnold's Wind Quintet" in *The Horn Call*, October 2003, p. 80.

7. Date of concert Pettitt (1989), 91. Morris taped interview with Gamble, March 1, 2006.

8. Leonard Brain, *Dennis Brain Wind Ensemble*, BBC Third Programme, September 5, 1960, 10:47 p.m. WAC Brain source file ref. 4(77); also Pettitt (1989), 91, for an account of this

concert that uses this source. Copy of transcript from private tape of the broadcast, given to the authors by Pettitt.

9. BBC radio program listing in *Radio Times* 93, no. 1209 (December 1–7, 1946): 16, December 3, Third Programme 6:15 p.m. Thanks to BBC Written Archives Researcher Erin O'Neill for checking the "P as B" file, which confirms that it was the London Wind Quintet that was engaged for the first British broadcast performance. The concert bill for Wigmore Hall on March 4, 1947, gives Natasha Litvin as the pianist. Information courtesy of Patricia Morris.

10. Parts for the Poulenc Sextet from Leonard Brain's collection of music scores used for the Quintet, now in the possession of the authors. Morris telephone call with Gamble, March 23, 2006.

11. WAC, P as B file: Musical Box, Eastern Service, Purple Network, September 24, 1947. The P as B file does not state the broadcast times of the relevant items, only the start of the program at 15:30. Information supplied to the authors by Erin O'Neill, BBC Written Archives.

12. Morris, speaking on BBC Artium LP, REGL 352 (1979). For the commercial recordings, Discography II. 1, British Library Sound Archives.

13. WAC, *RCONT1, Artists File I Dennis Brain Wind Ensemble 1946–1962*; letter October 20, 1947, to Nisbett, confirming availability to broadcast on November 26, 1947, at 10:05 p.m. and requesting a new set of parts to replace those supplied that were "impossible to play from." Letter from Brain to Wynn, November 17, 1947, declining the contract and requesting a fifty-guinea joint fee for the broadcast instead of the forty guineas offered.

14. David Drew, program notes, in concert program, March 3, 1952, p. 22, private collection.

15. Audrey Brain taped interview with Gamble, October 29, 2003.

16. For the *Bienniale di Venezia Internationale di Musica Contemporanea*, September 12, 1956, Pettitt (1989), 147. Also Christina Thoresby, "Stravinsky at the Venice Festival" in *Strad* 67, no. 799 (November 1956): 248.

17. Audrey Brain taped interview with Gamble, October 29, 2003. Pettitt (1989), 115, for the year Parry became the Quintet's pianist.

18. WAC *RCONT1 Artists File I 1946–1962, Dennis Brain Wind Ensemble;* letter, December 21, 1947, from Brain to Wynn that confirms availability. Contract 03/PC/AW, from Wynn to Brain, January 13, 1948, gives the details of date, time, program, studio, and personnel as well as a joint fee for the broadcast of £52.10s.0d.

19. BBC radio program listing in *Radio Times* 101, no. 1316 (January 2–8, 1949): 15, January 3, Third Programme, 7:35–8:00 p.m. Review of South Place concert, Conway Hall, February 27, 1949, "A Wind Ensemble: New Work Performed," *The Times*, Late London Edition, March 1, 1949, page 6, column e.

20. WAC P as B states this was pre-recorded on March 28, 1949 (recording reference SBU.28648). Rehearsal on March 28 from 10:00 until 11:30 a.m. and recording from 11:30 until 1:00 p.m. It is not known if the recording was preserved. Gareth Morris's diary entry for the broadcast, courtesy of Patricia Morris.

21. BBC radio program listing in *Radio Times* 108, no. 1403 (September 3–9, 1950): 27, September 7, Third Programme 6:20–7:00 p.m.

22. Morris taped interview with Gamble, March 1, 2006. Pettit (1989), 141.

23. Morris taped interview with Gamble, March 23, 2006.

24. Letter from Sidney "Jock" Sutcliffe to Martin Prowse, July 12, 1969.

25. Morris taped interview with Gamble, March 1, 2006. He mentioned that the manuscript was last in the possession of Walter Legge. This quintet is not to be confused with a wind quartet by Lipatti for flute, oboe, clarinet, and bassoon entitled *Aubade*, published by Rongwen, which Morris premiered with Sutcliffe, Thurston, and James on March 5, 1951, at Kingsway Hall. This was reviewed in *The Times,* Late London Edition, March 6, 1951, p. 7, col. e.

26. "Wind Ensemble: Five Modern Works," *The Times,* Late London Edition, January 28, 1952, p. 8, col. b.
27. Mládi, a favorite of Brain's, WAC, *RCONT1, File I 1946–1962, Dennis Brain Wind Ensemble;* letter from Ingpen to E Lockspeiser, Esq., January 22, 1947.
28. Information from concert program, private collection. A copy of the program is also preserved at the Britten-Pears Library, Aldeburgh, Suffolk (shelf mark 3E1.2; 1-9204156). *Radio Times* 114, no. 1478 (March 9–15, 1952): 19, March 9, Third Programme, 10:05–11:10 p.m.
29. WAC *RCONT1, Artists File 2 Brain Dennis, 1950–1952;* letter from Brain to Carrell, February 27, 1952. Leonard Brain (1960).
30. Morris taped interview with Gamble, March 1, 2006.
31. Pettitt (1989), 103.
32. "Radio in the American Sector" no longer exists. It has been replaced by Deutschlandradio Kultur since the fall of the Berlin Wall. Discography, II: *International Archives Collections*: 2.*Germany: Deutschlandradio Kultur* for a list of their Brain archive recordings. Leonard Brain (1960); also Pettitt (1989), 111 for mention of the quintet works they played. Pettitt (1989), 111, using same source Leonard Brain (1960).
33. WAC *RCONT1 Brain, Dennis, Artists File I, 1946–1962, Dennis Brain Wind Ensemble*; letter from Brain to Wallis, June 19, 1951.
34. BBC radio program listing in *Radio Times* 112, no. 1443 (July 8-14, 1951): 29, July 12, Third Programme, 6:00–6:50 p.m. The other players were Frederick Fuller (baritone) and John Cockrill (harp), with the Brain Wind Ensemble.
35. WAC *RCONT1, Artists File 2 Brain Dennis, 1950–1952*; letter from Brain to Denis Stevens, November 3, 1951.
36. The Serenade K388 was not often broadcast with Brain's Ensemble. It had been recorded by Karl Haas and the London Baroque Ensemble (two recordings), both of which have Brain playing. Discography, Section II.1 British Library Sound Archive for those Haas recordings. WAC *RCONT1, Artists, File III 1953–1956 Brain Dennis*; letter from Brain to Middlemiss, February 17, 1953. In the letter, he lists the extra players for octets: Sidney Sutcliffe, Basil Tschaikov, Ian Beers, and Peter Parry. Also WAC *RCONT1, Artists File I, 1946–1962, Dennis Brain Wind Ensemble;* letter from Brain to Bowling, February 27, 1953, concerning this broadcast.
37. WAC *RCONT1, Artists File I, 1946–1962, Dennis Brain Wind Ensemble;* letter from Brain to Carrell, March 10, 1953.
38. WAC *RCONT1, Artists File I, 1946–1962, Dennis Brain Wind Ensemble;* letter from Brain to Bowling, June 24, 1953. BBC radio program listing in *Radio Times* 120, no. 1558 (September 20–26, 1953): 25, September 22, Third Programme 6:00–7:00 p.m.
39. WAC *RCONT1, Composers, Essex Kenneth 1943–1962*; letter from Brain to Wade, July 24, 1953. Essex had written to the BBC Music Department on July 29, 1953, to bring to their attention that his Quintet had been broadcast by "Nederland Radio, Radio Eire, Radio France and Radio New York" and performed all over the world at concerts. In his letter, he expressed the hope that Brain's Quintet would again be able to broadcast it.
40. Morris's diary entry for this engagement has been scored through; information courtesy of Patricia Morris. BBC radio program listing in *Radio Times* 122, no. 1584 (March 21–27, 1954): 31, Third Programme March 24. *The Heritage of Spain. A Survey of Spanish Music*, prepared by Roberto Gerhard and Lionel Salter. Also BBC radio program listing (repeat broadcast) in *Radio Times* 125, no. 1623 (December 19–25, 1954): 19, December 20, Third Programme 10:30–11:00 p.m., which states it was the recorded broadcast of March 24. WAC *RCONT1,*

Artists File I, 1946–1962, Dennis Brain Wind Ensemble; letter from Brain to Carrell, September 22, 1953, stating availability.

41. *York Evening Press*, June 26, 1954; *Northern Echo*, June 28, 1954. For this concert and that at Kenwood Orangery, Hampstead, Pettitt (1989), 129–30. The local press notices are cuttings consulted at York Public Library, York, North Yorkshire.

42. Concert program, private collection.

43. WAC *RCONT1, Brain Dennis, Artists File III, 1953–1956;* letter from Brain to Waller, May 31, 1955. Also in the concert was the first broadcast performance of Britten's Canticle III, *Still Falls the Rain* for tenor, horn, and piano. This had been written for Pears and Brain in memory of a young Australian pianist, Noel Mewton-Wood, who had taken his own life the previous year and who had taken part in many of their chamber concerts. Discography, I.4 Horn Piano and Voice, for the recording of this broadcast recital. Stanford University is the only public archive that preserves a copy of this first broadcast performance.

44. WAC *RCONT1, Brain Dennis, Artists File III, 1953–1956*; letter from Brain to P. V. Gould, May 29, 1955, suggesting two available dates for the pre-recording: June 30 morning and July 1 afternoon. Also WAC *RCONT1, Artists File I, 1946–1962, Dennis Brain Wind Ensemble;* letter from Brain to Carrell, May 11, 1955, confirming availability to broadcast in the J. C. Bach Quintets. For discovery of the Bach quintets, Stanley Sadie, "The Wind Music of J. C. Bach" in *Music and Letters* 37, no. 2 (April 1956): 113–117. Brain sent a letter to P. V. Gould of the BBC on May 29, 1955, saying he would like to see the parts for the J. C. Bach Quintets "if Mr. Sadie can be persuaded to part with the music. . . ." WAC, RCONT1, Artists File III, 1953–1956.

45. Quintet engagements at Farnham, Kent, Brighton, Sussex, and Ireland tour, Pettitt (1989), 141. Broadcast of Octets by Uhl and Mozart, idem. WAC *RCONT1, Brain Dennis, Artists File III, 1953–1956*; letter from Brain to T. M. Whewell, August 15, 1955. Also Whewell's reply in the same file, ref. 38/M/TMW, August 18, 1955. Brain had received the score of the Uhl piece from S. G. Harpner of Alfred H. Kalmus, music publishers.

46. Morris speaking to Gamble, March 23, 2006. Pettitt (1989), 142 for dates and venues of the Italian tour. Anecdote about the crackling sound of a lady's black dress, told by Leonard Brain (1960).

47. Parry, remembering the Italian tour, on BBC Artium LP, REGL 352 (1979). On Stock brandy, Pettitt (1989), 142, quoting Leonard Brain (1960).

48. BBC radio program listing in *Radio Times* 131, no. 1693 (April 22–28, 1956): 36, April 26, Home Service 7:15–8:15 p.m. "City Music Society: Mozart Recital" in *The Times*, Royal Edition, April 26, 1956, p. 3, column c. WAC *RCONT1, Artists File I, 1946–1962, Dennis Brain Wind Ensemble;* letter from Brain to Nisbett, February 18, 1956, confirming availability but asking whether Gareth Morris would be required.

49. Information about the Wigmore Hall 10th Anniversary concert, original program, private collection.

50. "Wigmore Hall: Dennis Brain Wind Ensemble" in *The Times*, Royal Edition, May 1, 1956, p. 5 column d. Information about the Wigmore Hall 10th Anniversary concert, original program, private collection.

51. Morris speaking to Gamble on March 1, 2006, mentioned he still had the flute part. Signed *Memorandum of Agreement*, July 22, 1975, between Sir John Brown, Publisher of Oxford University Press, and Leonard Brain, Esq. concerning publication of Brain's arrangement of Mozart's Fantasy in F minor and major K594; private collection. The MS arrangement by Brain after Mozart's Fantasia in F minor and major K.594 was part of lot 38 that sold at Sotheby's, New Bond Street, London, December 6, 1996, and is now in private ownership.

52. Pettitt (1989), 147.

53. James, recalling the first performances of Malipiero's Dialogue for Wind Quintet, on BBC Artium LP REGL 352 (1979).
54. Morris speaking to Gamble, March 23, 2006. The only occasion that the Quintet played at the Venice Festival was on September 12, 1956.
55. Christina Thoresby, "Stravinsky at the Venice Festival," *Strad* 67, no. 799 (November 1956): 248. Quoted with permission of Ariane Todes.
56. A copy of the concert program with signatures, reproduced with permission from Tony Catterick; Catterick collection. Pettitt (1989), 148, quoting "Oubradous" anecdote.
57. WAC *RCONT1, Artists File I, 1946–1962, Dennis Brain Wind Ensemble;* Brain to P. V. Gould, November 28, 1956.
58. Karajan, Director of Salzburg Festival 1957, Pettitt (1989), 154. For the complete recording of the Salzburg Festival recital, discovered by Lynch in the Archives of Austrian Radio, see Discography, I. 5 *Wind Quintet* and I. 6 *Chamber Music with Other Combinations.* Not listed in any previous discography, including Pettitt (1989) or Robert L. Marshall, *Dennis Brain on Record: A Comprehensive Discography of His Solo, Chamber, and Orchestral Recordings* (Newton Center, MA: Margun Music Inc., 1996).
59. "German Music by Bavarian Orchestra," *The Times*, Royal Edition, London, August 26, 1957, p. 12, column d.
60. Christopher Grier in *The Scotsman*, August 26, 1957. Quoted with permission The Scotsman Publications Library and Syndication Executive.
61. BBC Transcription Service long-playing records of the Edinburgh Festival, August 24, 1957, private collection.

Chapter 4. Royal Philharmonic Orchestra

1. R. C., "Opera and Concerts," *Monthly Musical Record* 76, no. 881 (November 1946): 217–18.
2. For this and other selected orchestral recordings, Discography, I. 7 *Selected Orchestral Recordings: Royal Philharmonic Orchestra.* All the recordings discussed in this chapter are listed.
3. Brain in *Desert Island Discs,* Home Service, August13, 1956, told Roy Plomley he was co-principal in the RPO and the Philharmonia at the same time. Recorded excerpts from this conversation were issued in 1979 on BBC Artium LP REGL352.
4. Basil Tschaikov email to Gamble, January 9, 2006. See also, with slight variation, Basil Tschaikov, *The Music Goes Round and Around,* Chapter 7, 75.
5. For the tour in December 1948 and account of Brain leaving the RPO, Pettitt (1989), 99–100. Brain's return to the RPO early in 1950, idem, 103.
6. Tschaikov writing to Gamble, January 9, 2006. See also, with slight variation, Tschaikov, *The Music Goes Round and Around,* Chapter 7, 75.
7. Brymer speaking to the Sir Thomas Beecham Society, April 26, 1975. Private tape. Hereafter cited as Brymer Talk (1975).
8. Delius Festival concerts, Alan Jefferson, *Sir Thomas Beecham: A Centenary Tribute* (London: Macdonald and Jane's, 1979), 100; for soloists during the Festival and the London debut on October 26, 1946, Pettitt (1989), 90.
9. Maurice Parker, "Sir Thomas Beecham 1946–1953; 1954–1960 Concert and Theatrical Calendar" *Grand Baton,* microfiche, Sir Thomas Beecham Society, 1986, 10. Hereafter Parker (1986.) WAC, *RCONT1, Artists, Brain Dennis, File IB 1947–1949*; Brain to Nisbett, January 21, 1947.
10. Spring concerts at Theatre Royal, Drury Lane, and Mendelssohn centenary concert, Pettitt (1989), 93. *Daily Telegraph,* November 3, 1947, quoted by Pettitt, idem. Strauss Festival

at Theatre Royal, Drury Lane, Jefferson (1979), 100. "Mendelssohn Centenary: A Beecham Concert," *The Times*, Late London Edition, November 4, 1947, p. 6, column g.

11. For the Philharmonia recordings of Mendelssohn's Nocturne, Discography, I. 7 *Selected Orchestral Recordings: Philharmonia Orchestra.*

12. R. C. "Opera and Concerts," *Monthly Musical Record* 77, no. 891(November 1947): 242.

13. Private collection, made from the original transmission, unpublished.

14. Leonard Brain's comment on his brother's playing in *The Trojans* broadcast, Pettitt (1989), 92. Brymer Talk (1975).

15. First appearance of the RPO at Glyndebourne with Beecham, Pettitt (1989), 96. For Brain's appearance at Guildford on July 15, idem. On the first Glyndebourne in July 1948, also Jefferson (1979), 101.

16. Brain sharing first horn, Pettitt (1989), 103. Roy White's return to Australia, ibid. Brain performing the obbligato part in *Per Pietà* with Sena Jurinac and the Glyndebourne Festival Orchestra, idem, 198–99. Also, Discography I. 7, for the recording of August 21, 1950.

17. Brymer (1979), 83.

18. Account of the omission of the minuet and trio of Haydn's Symphony No. 40, Pettitt (1989), 107.

19. Edward Sackville West, "A Quarterly Retrospect," *Gramophone* 30, no. 357 (February 1953): 217.

20. Lionel Salter, "Analytical Notes and First Reviews: Orchestral," *Gramophone* 29, no. 342 (November 1951): 129. For the recording, Discography I. 7.

21. Information on the RPO horn section in a souvenir book of the United States tour entitled *The Royal Philharmonic Orchestra of London England*, published by Program Publishing Company, New York (1950), private collection. For a detailed account of the journey on *Queen Mary*, Brymer (1979), 89–90.

22. Jack Brymer, "Royal Philharmonic," *Symphony*, November 1950, p. 5.

23. Brymer (1979), 89.

24. Brain taking both horns and departure of the RPO for their US tour, Pettitt (1989), 107. Works performed during the tour, information on the tenth page of the aforementioned tour book (no page numbers).

25. Information about the first rehearsal and the bus journey to Hartford, Brymer Talk (1975). Pettitt (1989), 108, citing *Hartford Times.*

26. Jackson (1968), p. 117, in the *Christian Science Monitor.*

27. Maurice Parker (1986), 62.

28. Pettitt (1989), 109. Philip Farkas, speaking at the International Horn Society Symposium, Dennis Brain Seminar, University of North Texas, Denton, May 17, 1991. A private tape.

29. Brymer (1979), 91.

30. Ed Brooks, "Royal Philharmonic Orchestra Warmly Applauded," *Times-Picayune*, November 13, 1950. Also partly quoted by Pettitt (1989), 108.

31. Ed Coffman, "Musicians Impressed by Coliseum," *The Kentucky Kernel*, December 1, 1950, p. 8, columns c, d, e. Curiously, the article was published twelve days after the interview with Brain and Brymer. Quoted with permission of Matt Murray.

32. Hugh Hough, quoted from *The Illini*, November 22, 1950, p. 1.

33. Claudia Cassidy, "On the Aisle. Brilliant Conductor, Orchestra and Soloists, That's Philharmonic," *Chicago Tribune*, November 27, 1950, p. D1.

34. Account of Brain's meeting with Chicago horn players after the concert on November 25, Pettitt (1989), 109–10.

35. Milan Yancich, *An Orchestra Musician's Odyssey* (Rochester, NY: Wind Music Inc., 1995), 207–8. Quoted with permission of Mark Yancich. Wind Music Inc., 974 Berkshire Rd., Atlanta, GA 30324, US.
36. Account of the party at the Farkas home and gifts, Pettitt (1989), 110. Also re-told by Philip Farkas at the International Horn Society Symposium, Dennis Brain Seminar, University of North Texas, May 17, 1991.
37. Solo appearances, Parker (1986), 62, 63. Photograph provided by Dorothy Beers through Tony Catterick.
38. Performance of Mozart's Sinfonia Concertante K297b at Lafayette, Pettitt (1989), 110. Also Parker (1986), 62. Carnegie Hall concerts, information by permission of the archivist, Carnegie Hall.
39. Arrival in Southampton, Pettitt (1989), 111.
40. "Royal Philharmonic Society: Mozart and Sibelius," *The Times,* Late London Edition, March 29, 1951, p. 6, column c. Also R. C., "Opera and Concerts," *Monthly Musical Record* 81, no. 926 (May 1951): 101.
41. Brymer Talk (1975).
42. Parker (1986), 68.
43. For the concert on July 24, 1951, Pettitt (1989), 114.
44. Alan Civil remembering Brain in the RPO, sleeve notes to *The Art of Dennis Brain*, Angel Seraphim 60040 (1966).
45. Alec Robertson, "Analytical Notes and First Reviews: Operatic and Song," *Gramophone* 31, no. 366 (November 1953): 199.
46. Alec Robertson, "Analytical Notes and First Reviews: Choral and Song," *Gramophone* 31, no. 368 (January 1954): 297.
47. A. J., "London Concerts: Eugene Goossens," *Musical Times* 93, no. 1310 (April 1952): 180.
48. "LCC Concert: Goossens and Hindemith," *The Times*, Late London Edition, March 3, 1952, p. 8, column c.
49. Christopher Grier, "Morning Concert: Royal Philharmonic Chamber Orchestra," *Scotsman,* August 27, 1952. Also quoted with slight variation in Pettitt (1989), 121. For rehearsal on August 24, solo rehearsal and concert with the LSO and Stanford Robinson on August 25, and Brain's appearance in Act 1 of Berlioz's, *L'Enfance du Christ,* idem. Quoted with permission of The Scotsman Publications Library and Syndication Exeutive.
50. W. R. Anderson, "The Edinburgh Festival," *Musical Times* 93, no. 1316 (October 1952): 459. For Third Programme studio performance from Edinburgh, August 28, 1952, WAC, *RCONT1 Artists, Brain Dennis, File 2 1950–1952*; contract 01/PC/NC, from Carrell to Brain, May 9, 1952. This gives Brain's first fee of £26.5s.0d (25 guineas) which was his concert fee for playing a solo work in promenade concerts.
51. Irving Rosenthal, "The Edinburgh Festival," *Woodwind,* October 1952, p. 14.
52. A. J., "London Concerts: Two Beecham Concerts," *Musical Times* 94, no. 1324 (June 1953): 276–77.
53. Royal Festival Hall concert information from program, Tony Catterick collection. "Royal Philharmonic Orchestra: More Nielsen," *The Times*, London Royal Edition, February 23, 1954, p. 2, column f.
54. Pettitt (1989), 128–29, gives April 7, 1954, as a leaving date. For the concert, concert advertisement, "Concerts &c" in *The Times,* Royal Edition, March 27, 1954, column c. The Beecham Archives gives May 3, 1954, as the leaving date. Information supplied by Dr. Graham Melville-Mason in letter to Gamble, October 9, 2005. Jackson (1968), 100, gives 1952 as

the year. Discography I. 7, for Brain's participation in recordings. A cut-off date of "December 1953" is given for recordings, but the concerts, on the other hand, show he was present when available as late as December 1956.

55. "A Beecham Concert: Conductor's Return from America," *The Times*, London Royal Edition, March 29, 1954, p. 9, column b. The horn section is quoted from the concert program with permission from Moura Martin.

56. "Philharmonic Concert: Out of a Hat," *The Times*, Royal Edition, London, April 8, 1954, p. 10, column a.

57. "Festival Hall: Beecham Concert," *The Times*, Royal Edition, November 9, 1956, p. 3, column c.

58. "Festival Hall: A Wagner Night," *The Times*, Royal Edition, London, December 7, 1956, p. 3, column d.

59. Thanks to Martin Prowse for providing a copy of this letter and to the Civil family for permission to reproduce it.

60. Martin J.Prowse, "The Unfamiliar Dennis Brain," *Audio-Record Review*, October 1969, p. 679.

61. For these recordings and others, Discography I. 7.

62. Marshall (1996), 17, considers that the first horn in the solos played in Wagner recordings of December 1953 and April 1954 "seems to be that of Dennis Brain." The attribution of recordings by aural means, in the absence of documentary evidence of Brain's presence, is open to question.

63. Brymer Talk (1975). Beecham included *Daphnis and Chloë* Suites 1 and 2 for a Royal Festival Hall concert on December 2, 1953. Parker (1986), 87. Jefferson (1979), 233, gives 1956, but Parker does not list a concert in 1956 for *Daphnis et Chloë*. Brymer described the *Daphnis et Chloë* performance as the last occasion that Sir Thomas played it in his programs. The authors assume, therefore, that the date is not 1956 but December 2, 1953.

64. Jefferson (1979), 233.

65. Jackson (1968), 100.

Chapter 5. Philharmonia

1. Pettitt (1989), 85, quoting a document by Legge that states the Philharmonia would not have one permanent conductor but that it "should have style, not 'a style.'" This document was reproduced in the Philharmonia Orchestra's concert program for September 29, 1952, conducted by Toscanini at Royal Festival Hall. The point about "style" is made in the sixth and last principle defined by Legge in this document.

2. Joan Ingpen, speaking on BBC Radio 3 for series *Philharmonia*, episode 1 of 6: "Beginnings" in the program, *Vintage Years*, January 4, 1997. BLSA call no. H8273/1.

3. Morris taped interview with Gamble, March 1, 2006. For Potsdam concerts, also Pettitt (1989), 84. Concert program, October 27, 1945, private collection.

4. For the wedding at Petersfield, Pettitt (1989), 84.

5. Pettitt (1989), 84.

6. Personnel information for the first concert from concert program, private collection.

7. Legge's first recordings of the Philharmonia in 1945, including the Tchaikovsky Piano Concerto with Moiseiwitsch and Sibelius Violin Concerto with Neveu, Stephen Pettitt, *Philharmonia: A Complete Discography, 1945–1987* (London: John Hunt, 1987), 148–49. Review of Butterworth's *Banks of Green Willow*, "Analytical Notes and First Reviews: Orchestral," *Gramophone,* 23, no. 276 (May 1946): 142. Also Discography I. 7 *Philharmonia Orchestra* (hereafter Discography I.7).

8. Alec Robertson, "Analytical Notes and First Reviews: Orchestral," *Gramophone* 24, no. 277 (June 1946): 5. The recording was reissued in 2002 by Yukihiro Okitsu in Japan on CD, *A Resurrection of Dennis Brain.*
9. Solo concerts in 1946 with Sir John Barbirolli and Walter Susskind conducting, Pettitt (1989), 86. Recording of "Where Corals Lie," Pettitt (1987), 152. First review, *Gramophone,* 24, no. 278 (July 1946): 21."Week-End Concerts: End of Philharmonia Series," *The Times,* Late London Edition, March 25, 1946, p. 8, column b.
10. Brain's recording of Mozart's Concerto No. 2 with Susskind, idem. W. R. Anderson, "Analytical Notes and First Reviews: Orchestral," *Gramophone* 25, no. 289 (June 1947): 4.
11. *Daily Telegraph,* September 20, 1946, cited by Pettitt (1989), 89. © Telegraph Media Group Limited, 1946.
12. Brain quoted by Pettitt (1989), 91.
13. Recording date of *Per Pietà,* Pettitt (1987), 160. Alec Robertson, "Analytical Notes and First Reviews: Operatic and Songs," *Gramophone,* 24, no. 286 (March 1947): 151.
14. Karajan's public début with the Philharmonia, Richard Osborne, *Herbert von Karajan: A Life in Music* (London: Chatto & Windus, 1998), 245. For the first recording sessions with Karajan, April 9 and 10, 1948, Pettitt (1987), 174.
15. Pettit (1989), 95, 96.
16. Morris taped interview with Gamble, March 1, 2006.
17. Karajan recordings, Pettitt (1987), 188. Horn personnel changes in 1950 and the premiere of *Vier Letzte Lieder,* with Flagstad, Pettitt (1989), 103–4. *Musical Quarterly,* quoted idem, 104.
18. Hans Keller, "Mysore Concerts," *Music Survey* 3, no. 3 (March 1951): 205.
19. Furtwängler concert, February 22, 1951, and Brain as soloist in the Hindemith Concerto and Britten Serenade on April 16, 1951, Philharmonia concert programs listed in the Bibliography. Also Pettitt (1989), 112.
20. June 1951 sessions with Karajan, Pettitt (1987), 203; sessions in November and December 1951, idem, 210.
21. Brain's participation in three of the Cantelli concerts, Pettitt (1989), 115. Brahms Symphony No. 3 and Siegfried *Idyll* recordings with Cantelli, Discography, I. 7.
22. Pettitt (1989), 115 (concert conducted by Furtwängler on October 25, 1951), op.cit., 119–20 (concert conducted by Furtwängler on April 24 1952.). Horn personnel from a 1951 concert program, reproduced in Alexander Kok, *A Voice in the Dark*: *The Philharmonia Years* (Ampleforth, North Yorkshire: Emerson Edition E 414, 2002), 169. The date of the concert is not given.
23. Recordings with Karajan during April to July, 1952, Pettitt (1989), 120. Also Pettitt (1987), 220; European tour, May 1952, Pettitt (1989), 118; Schwarzkopf's Hudson saloon, idem; journey via St. Gothard Pass, Morris taped interview with Gamble, March 1, 2006. Celebration of Toscanini's engagement to conduct and bread and butter pudding anecdote, Pettitt (1989), 119.
24. Moore taped interview with Gamble, June 30, 2005.
25. Kok (2002), 251. Kok was one of the cellists in the Philharmonia; he and Brain shared a passion for motoring.
26. For the Toscanini concerts, Pettitt (1989), 121–22; also Discography I. 7.
27. Neville Cardus, "Some Thoughts on Toscanini," *Manchester Guardian,* October 1, 1952, p. 3, column c. Also partly quoted by Pettitt (1989), 122.
28. Private photograph, whereabouts of the original not known. Information, courtesy of Ann Meade Sanders, widow of Neill Sanders. "Festival Hall: Signor Guido Cantelli," *The Times,*

Late London Edition, October 6, 1952, p. 10, column b. For the series of six concerts in October 1952, "Entertainments: Royal Festival Hall," *The Times*, Late London Edition, October 3, 1952, p. 9, column a. The other concerts were October 8, 14, 17, 21, and 23.

29. Karajan recordings, Pettitt (1987), 229. *Vier Letzte Lieder* with Schwarzkopf conducted by Otto Ackermann, Discography I. 7. For the recording date and venue, Pettitt (1987), 246.

30. For an account of the recording sessions of the Mozart Horn Concertos, Pettitt (1989), 126. EMI bestseller, idem. Del Mar remembering Brain playing the Mozart Concertos without a score, on BBC LP: BBC Records, REGL 352 (1979).

31. "Philharmonia Concert: Mr Karajan," *The Times*, Royal Edition, June 25, 1954, p. 10, column b.

32. For a short account of the 1954 European tour, Pettitt (1989), 130; also Kok (2002), 249–52; Brain's cine camera at Aix-en-Provence, Osborne (1998), 363. Live recording of Choral Symphony, Pettitt (1987), 261. Also Discography I. 7.

33. Discography I. 7. Pettitt (1987), does not list the Beethoven Symphony No.5 recording, first issued on Columbia 33CX 1266, coupled with Beethoven's recitative and aria from Fidelio: *Abscheulicher—Komm Hoffnung*. Marshall (1996), 5, lists Beethoven's Fifth Symphony but with no precise recording date. An unpublished recording is listed by Pettitt (1987), 245, for sessions at Kingsway Hall, August 26–28, 1953. Idem, 263, lists *Abscheulicher—Komm Hoffnung* on 33CX 1266 for a session at Watford Town Hall on September 20, 1954.

34. Karajan recording, Pettitt (1987), 276, 278. C. B. Rees, "Impressions . . . Dennis Brain," *London Musical Events*, no. 10 (September 1955): 25.

35. Brain, quoted in "London Philharmonia Arrives on U.S. Tour," *Washington Evening Star*, October 22, 1955.

36. Claudia Cassidy, "The Philharmonia," *Chicago Daily Tribune*, November 7, 1955; Max de Schauensee, "London Philharmonia in First Appearance," *Philadelphia Sunday Bulletin*, November 12, 1955; Samuel L. Singer, "Philharmonia in Phila. Debut: Three Classics," *Philadelphia Inquirer*, November 16, 1955; R. A. Paton, "Philharmonia Orchestra's Artistry 'Electrifying.'" *Kalamazoo Gazette*, November 9, 1955; Irving Kolodin, "Music to My Ears: Philharmonia and Philharmonic," *Saturday Review*, November 12, 1955.

37. Winthrop Sargeant, "Musical Events: Three Cheers," *New Yorker*, November 5, 1955.

38. *New York Nation*, November 12, 1955.

39. Howard Taubman, "Music: Philharmonia: London Orchestra Is Heard in Debut Here," *New York Times*, October 26, 1955; Hugh Thomson, "Britain's Philharmonic Wins All-Out Reception," *Toronto Daily Star*, November 12, 1955; J. Dorsey Callaghan, "London Orchestra Is Great," *Detroit Free Press*, November 11, 1955; Bruce Jacobson, "London Orchestra Enthrals," *Michigan Daily*, November 10, 1955. Quoted with permission from Stephanie Steinberg.

40. Rudolph Elie, "Symphony Hall: London Philharmonia," *Boston Sunday Herald*, November 20, 1955. Reprinted with permission of Boston Herald.

41. Harold Rogers, "Philharmonia Orchestra: London Group Conducted by von Karajan," *Christian Science Monitor*, November 21, 1955. Reproduced with permission © 1955 The Christian Science Monitor.

42. Transcript from programs analysis card, NBC Studio Archives, *Today Show*, October 26, 1955. With permission. Brain's appearance was confirmed through correspondence (July 30, 2004) by Lynch with the NBC Archives database. Unfortunately, the studio recording of his televised appearance cannot be located.

43. Andrew McGavin, telephone call with Gamble, November 9, 2004.

44. Paul Hume, "Postlude: U.S. Debut by London Orchestra," *Washington Post*, October 24, 1955. Also the same passage quoted by Pettitt (1989), 138, and Osborne (1998), 392.
45. Day Thorpe, "Amazing Is the Word for London Orchestra," *Washington Evening Star*, October 24, 1955; Milton Berliner, "Philharmonia Opens to 'Bravos,'" *Washington Daily News*, October 24, 1955.
46. Paul Henry Lang, "Philharmonia Orchestra," *New York Herald Tribune*, October 26, 1955. The same article was printed in *Montreal Star*, October 26. Also quoted by Osborne (1998), 393.
47. G. E. A., "Philharmonia Shows Touch of Greatness," *New Haven Register*, October 28, 1955. Quoted with permission of Jack Kramer.
48. Evans Clinchy, "Philharmonia in New Haven," *Hartford Times*, October 28, 1955.
49. G. A. E., "Philharmonia Orchestra Fine But Too 'Calm, Conventional,'" *Grand Rapids Press*, November 8, 1955. Quoted with permission of Paul Keep.
50. Willard M. Clark, "Famed London Orchestra Gets Ovation at UM: 4000 Hear Philharmonia in Visit as Part of First U.S. Tour," *Springfield Union*, November 17, 1955. The same article was published in *Springfield Republic*, November 20, 1955. Quoted with permission James S. Gleason, *The Republican.*
51. Paul Hume, "2d Concert Given by Philharmonia," *Washington Post*, October 30, 1955. Also quoted by Osborne (1998), 392.
52. For the last rehearsal and concert in Boston, Pettitt (1989), 139; Osborne (1998), 396–97; Kok (2002), 237–39. Karajan's appointments in Berlin and Vienna, Osborne (1998), 399; Kok (2002), 239.
53. Neill Sanders, speaking to the International Horn Society Symposium, Dennis Brain Seminar, University of North Texas, May 17, 1991, private tape.
54. "Philharmonia Concert: Strauss Last Songs," *The Times*, Royal Edition, June 21, 1956, p. 5, column b.
55. "Mysore Concert: Strauss and Hindemith," *The Times*, Late London Edition, April 17, 1951, p. 6, column e.
56. Harold Rutland, "What a Good Orchestra is Like," *Radio Times* 116, no. 1495 (July 6–12): 7; also Discography I. 7. Philharmonia Orchestra.
57. "Festival Hall: Philharmonia Orchestra," *The Times*, Royal Edition, February 25, 1954, p. 10, column a.
58. Alan Blyth email to Gamble on November 24, 2005. Concert information from souvenir program book of the Edinburgh International Festival, 1957, p. 27.
59. Arthur Wilson taped interview with Gamble, November 8, 2005.
60. Joan Ingpen, speaking on BBC Radio 3 for series *Philharmonia* episode 1 of 6: "Beginnings" in program *Vintage Years*, January 4, 1997. BLSA, call no. H8273/1.
61. Hugh Bean, speaking on BBC Radio 3 for series *Philharmonia* episode 2 of 6: "Enter Karajan" in program, *Vintage Years*, January 11, 1997. BLSA, call no. H 8337/1.
62. Morris, remembering Brain on BBC Radio 3 for series, *Philharmonia* episode 1 of 6: "Beginnings" in program *Vintage Years*, January 4, 1997. BLSA call no. H8273/1.
63. Khachaturian sessions, Pettitt (1987), 266. A photograph of one of Khachaturian's recording sessions, conducting his own music, was reproduced in sleevenotes to EMI CDC 555035 2 (1994.) It clearly shows Dennis Brain seated second in from the right of the section.
64. Basil Tschaikov, email to Gamble, January 9, 2006.
65. Hugh Bean, remembering Brain leading the horn section in Strauss's *Der Rosenkavalier* on BBC Radio 3 for series *Philharmonia* episode 2 of 6 "Enter Karajan" in program *Vintage Years*, January 11, 1997. BLSA call no. H 8337/1.

Chapter 6. A Horn Virtuoso's Letters

1. Brain's notebook of times for journeys, recalled by Morris, speaking on BBC Radio 3, May 17, 1996; quoted in Chapter 8. *Desert Island Discs* broadcast, *Radio Times* 132, no. 1709 (August 12–18, 1956): 16, August 13, Home Service 1:10–1:40 p.m. Speech links from this broadcast were partly issued on BBC LP REGL 352 (1979).

2. Transcript by Gamble of tape of James Decker talking to Arthur Frantz, July 1997, Tony Catterick collection. Decker: "Al never used an assistant. He said, 'Just give me the money.' . . . He always got a double check! That followed him for the rest of his life and it taught us all a lesson how to negotiate for higher money."

3. Postcard to Ernest Tomlinson, quoted by permission of Tomlinson.

4. Quoted from Alan Sanders, ed., *Walter Legge: Words and Music* (London: Gerald Duckworth, 1998), 121.

5. Annetta Hoffnung, *Hoffnung: His Biography* (London: Gordon Fraser, 1988), 138–39. With permission. Information on the televised Hoffnung Festival concert, from sleeve-notes by John Amis on the first edition of the EMI Columbia LP, 33CX1406.

6. WAC *RCONT1: Artists, Brain Dennis File 1A, 1939–1946*; letter to Wynn, March 19, 1942; letter to Bliss, July 6, 1942; letter to Murvill, August 17, 1942. See also quoted and reproduced by Jonathan Stoneman, "Dennis Brain and the BBC," *The Horn Player* 4, no. 2 (August 2007): 30. Hereafter cited as Stoneman (2007).

7. WAC *RCONT1: Artists, Brain Dennis, File1A, 1939–1946;* letter to Wynn, July 15, 1944.

8. For Afrikaans service, May 3, 1943, and April 19, 1943, performance of Ferguson's Octet for wind and strings, WAC *RCONT1: Artists, Brain Dennis, File 1A, 1939–1946*; letter to Wynn, March 16, 1943.

9. WAC *RCONT1: Artists, Brain Dennis, File IB, 1947–1949*; letter to Lockspeiser, August 17, 1947.

10. WAC *RCONT1: Artists, Brain Dennis File 1A, 1939–1946*; letter to Wynn, May 18, 1946. Information from the "P as B" file found for the authors by BBC Written Archives researcher Erin O'Neill.

11. WAC *RCONT1: Artists, Brain Dennis File 1A, 1939–1946*; letter to Wynn, July 27, 1946. See also Stoneman (2007), 31.

12. WAC *RCONT1: Artists, Brain Dennis File 1A, 1939–1946*; letter to Wynn, November 24, 1946.

13. WAC *RCONT1: Artists, Brain Dennis, File IB, 1947–1949*; letter to Wynn, November 29, 1947.

14. WAC *RCONT1: Artists, Brain Dennis, File IB, 1947–1949;* letter to Carrell, April 9, 1949; Carrell's reply, ref. 03/PC/NC, April 27, 1949; Brain's reply, May 2, 1949.

15. WAC, *RCONT1: Artists, Brain Dennis, File 1B, 1947–1949*, letter from Brain to Carrell, October 5, 1949; 03/PC/NC, Carrell's reply, October 18, 1949.

16. WAC *RCONT1: Brain Dennis, Artists File 2 1950–1952;* letter to Carrell, August 29, 1950.

17. WAC *RCONT1: Brain Dennis, Artists File 2 1950–1952;* letter to Carrell, August 21, 1952.

18. WAC *RCONT1: Brain Dennis, Artists File 2 1950–1952*; 01/PC/NC from Carrell to Brain, August 25, 1952.

19. WAC *RCONT1: Artists, Brain Dennis, File 1B, 1947–1949;* Brain to Sir Steuart, December 7, 1949. See also Stoneman (2007), 32.

20. *WAC RCONT1: Artists, Brain Dennis, File 1B, 1947–1949*; Brain to Steuart, December 31, 1949.

21. WAC *RCONT1: North Region Artists, Brain Dennis, File N18/305/1, 1948–1955*; letter to Johnstone, November 14, 1951. See also quoted by Gamble, "A Horn Virtuoso's Writings," *The Horn Player* 4, no. 3 (December 2007): 28. Hereafter cited as Gamble (2007).
22. WAC *RCONT1: North Region Artists, Brain Dennis, File N18/305/1, 1948–1955*, letter from Johnstone to Brain, November 21, 1951.
23. WAC *RCONT1: Brain Dennis, Artists File 2 1950–1952*; letter to Nisbett, March 20, 1950.
24. Pettitt (1989), 182, gives the details of the first performance of Gordon Bryan's Concerto. WAC *RCONT1: Brain Dennis, Artists File 2 1950–1952*; letter to Thompson, April 4, 1950.
25. WAC *RCONT1: Artists, Brain Dennis, File III 1953–1956*; letter to Isaacs, December 4, 1953.
26. WAC *RCONT1: Artists, Brain Dennis, File III 1953–1956;* Brain to Carrell, October 17, 1956.
27. Gamble (2007), 28–29. Hugo Cole's Concerto appears not to have been published. His publisher is Chester Novello. Cole (1917–1995) was a British music critic and composer. Driessler is Johannes Driessler (1921–1998). For his Concerto for horn and strings, op. 16 (1950), *klassika.info/Komponisten/Driessler/Hornkonzert*. "Gillman" is Kurt Gillmann (1889–1975), and the Horn Concerto is op. 45. The Kurt Atterberg Concerto, op. 28, was published in a horn and piano reduction by Breitkopf (no. 5408) in 1928. It had been composed, according to this edition, in 1926. In the list of horn and piano pieces, Samuel Adler's Sonata for Horn and Piano was published in 1951, currently available from Robert King Music Co., Editions Musicales Alphonse Leduc, Paris, catalog number AL.28570. Busser is Henri Busser (1872–1973) and the piece is *Cantecor* opus 77. *www.hornarama.com/page24.htm*. G. F. Linstead is George F. Linstead (1908–1974), an organist and composer whose centenary website gives biographical information but does not list the piece. *www.georgeflinstead.org.uk*. Reuchsel, composer of "Reverie & Villanelle" for horn and piano, is one of a family of composers chiefly of organ works. It could be any one of them. The piece has not been traced. A website giving all the Reuchsel composers is at www.organ-biography.info. Paul Vidal's *Pièce de Concert* has been published by Masters Music Publications, Boca Raton, in 2001. Tcherepnin's "Suite for Horn Quartet" is by Nikolayevich Tcherepnin (1873–1945), with six movements.
28. WAC *RCONT1: Brain Dennis, Artists File 2 1950–1952*; letter to Isaacs, November 3, 1951; Isaacs to Brain, November 12, 1951.
29. Reproduced with permission from Martin Prowse.

Chapter 7. Teacher and Lecturer

1. Dame Ruth Railton, *Daring to Excel: The Story of the National Youth Orchestra of Great Britain* (London: Secker & Warburg, 1992), 92–93. Quoted with permissionof Catherine Trippett, Random House Group, London.
2. Accounts of Alfred Brain, Jr.'s teaching have been related on private tapes by students Art Frantz, Vincent De Rosa, and Bob Gibson but are not described in this book.
3. Morris taped interview with Gamble, March 1, 2006.
4. Diack taped interview with Gamble, November 9, 2005.
5. Dr. Edwin Glick email to Gamble, November 29, 2004, on the subject of his lessons with Brain. Diack's lessons, Diack (2005). Cyril Taylor's lessons at the Guildhall School, Tony Catterick, "A Pupil of Dennis Brain," *The Horn Player* 2, no. 3 (December 2005): 35. The little we know of Sten Engström's lessons is from horn player Ib Lanzky-Otto, email to Gamble in February 2006 stating that Engström was a pupil for a few months and that his lessons had been recorded on tapes. The whereabouts of these tapes, if they survived, is not known. The

little information on Joe Henderson is from Douglas A. Eliott, who briefly mentioned him at the IHS symposium, Denton, Texas, May 17, 1991. A five-valve Alexander shown at the IHS symposium by Eliott, once owned by Brain, had previously been owned by Don Burbank and before him by Brain's pupil Joe Henderson.

6. Mention of Karajan's invitation of 1966, Yuichi Iwano, "Kaoru Chiba's 'Bachi's' Biography," *The Horn Call*, October 2008, p. 36. The official quotation of Bachi's reason for declining Karajan's invitation changed the word "sashimi" to "sushi" because "sushi" is better-known to foreigners. The visit to Japan with the Berlin Philharmonic in April 1966 is also briefly described by Osborne (1998), 546. Karajan's tour of Japan in April 1954 for six weeks, idem, 358–59. Bachi's reason for declining the offer quoted from private information. Dr. Arima was a fellow student with Karajan at the Vienna Academy of Music, and they remained good friends.

7. Genri Nakagawa, in conversation with Kaoru Chiba, July 23, 1973, published in Japan by Ongaku-No-Tomo-Sha Corp., March 1, 1975, translated into English by Yukihiro Okitsu; hereafter cited as Bachi interview (1973).

8. Chiba interviewed by Akashi-Minami High School Students Miho Miyamoto and Shizuka Machigashira, translated by Jun Yamada, "Kaoru Chiba on Dennis Brain," October 4, 2004. Internet publication in Horn List, June 24, 2008; hereafter cited as Bachi on Dennis Brain (2004). *www.mailarchive.com/horn@music.memphis.edu/msg26407.html.* Strauss, Rosenkavalier, was recorded in Kingsway Hall on December 10–15 and 17–22, 1956. Pettitt (1987), 301.

9. Kaoru Chiba, "My Teacher Dennis Brain" published in Japan by Ongaku-No-Tomo-Sha Corp., 1989. The article was translated into English by Yukihiro Okitsu. Hereafter cited as, Bachi interview (1989).

10. Bachi on Dennis Brain, 2004.

11. Bachi interview (1973). For the recordings of the Haydn Symphonies, Borodin *Prince Igor* Overture with Dobrowen, and the Haydn Concert Trio *Pietà di Mé*, Discography, I.7 Selected Orchestral Recordings; I 6 Chamber Music With Other Combinations.

12. Bachi interview (1973).

13. This was an interview with Kaoru Chiba in his workshop by Satoshi Kuwahara, entitled "Profile of The Master" first published in The "Seiron" Magazine, Tokyo, Sankei Shimbun, August 1999. Translated by Yukihiro Okitsu. With kind permission from Satoshi Kuwahara, Editor in Chief of The "Seiron" Magazine and Sankei Shimbun.

14. Bachi interview (1973).

15. Bachi on Dennis Brain, 2004.

16. Ibid.

17. Bachi interview (1989). The BBC has now published a performance of Haydn's Concerto No.1 with the BBC Midland Light Orchestra, conducted by Leo Wurmser (BBC Legends 4066-2). The recording was made by the BBC from a Home Service broadcast on January 21, 1957. Also Pettitt (1989), 193.

18. Chiyoshige Matsubara, "Memories of 'Bachi'—Kaoru Chiba (1928–2008)," *The Horn Call*, October 2008, p. 37.

19. Dennis Brain, "French Horn Playing," *The Conductor* 3, issue 10 (October 1954): 3; Dennis Brain, "About the French Horn," *Brass Today*, 1957, p. 60. Both reproduced in Appendix D.

20. James Diack taped interview with Gamble, November 9, 2005, revised by Diack, October 27, 2010. Hereafter cited as Diack interview (2005).

21. Diack interview (2005).
22. Diack interview (2005).
23. Diack interview (2005).
24. Edwin Glick email to Gamble, November 29, 2004. The trio by Haydn is his Divertimento a tré in E-flat for horn, violin, and violoncello (1767) which Brain performed with William Pleeth (cello) and David Martin (violin) at the National Gallery, March 25, 1946. Its movements are: Moderato assai and Finale. Allegro. Glick also recalled that it was a National Gallery concert in 1946 in which he heard Brain play this rare and exceptionally difficult piece. For the National Gallery concert, see Concert Programs in the Appendix E.
25. Tony Catterick, "A Pupil of Dennis Brain," *The Horn Player* 2, no. 3 (December 2005): 35.
26. Scottish Orchestra Club talk, WAC RCONT1, Brain Dennis, File 2 1950–1952; letter from Brain to Robertson, August 27, 1951. Royal Festival Hall lecture-recital, February 1, 1955, Pettitt (1989), 135. Brain's talk, "On a Personal Note," WAC RCONT1 Brain Dennis, Artists File III, 1953–1956; contract July 3, 1956, from Carrell to Brain. WAC RCONT1 Brain Dennis, Artists File 2 1950–1952; L. M. Stapeley, Far Eastern Service, fragment of a letter to Brain, reference, /FES/LS, July 20, 1950; letter from Brain to Morris, August 8, 1950.
27. WAC RCONT1 Brain Dennis, Artists File 2 1950–1952; letter from Stapeley to Brain, August 9, 1950, ref. 07/FES/LS.
28. WAC RCONT1 Brain Dennis, Artists File 2 1950–1952; letter from Brain to Robertson, August 27, 1951.
29. WAC RCONT1 Brain Dennis, Artists File 2 1950–1952; letter from Robertson to Brain, April 24, 1951; letter from Robertson to Brain, September 5, 1951; letter (ref. 03/M/AR) from Robertson to Brain, October 4, 1951.
30. WAC RCONT1, Brain Dennis, File III 1953–1956; letter from Brain to Fiske, June 4, 1955.
31. WAC RCONT1, Brain Dennis, File III 1953–1956; letter from Brain to Fiske, May 5, 1955. See also quoted by Gamble (2007), 28–29.
32. A reel-to-reel recording of "The Early Horn" broadcast was sent to Gamble by the conductor, Harry Newstone, in 2005. Another recording made by Professor Kenneth Mobbs was used with this one for a BBC LP (REGL352) that gave an extract. These two sources preserve all the principal pieces played but miss some of the speech links and some demonstration of the valves prior to playing Schubert's *Auf dem Strom*. A further fragment of "The Early Horn" is preserved at Stanford University Library of Recorded Sound. It had formerly been part of the Western Sound Archive, at El Cerrito in California. WAC, RCONT1, Artists, Brain Dennis, Artists File III 1953–1956; letter from Fiske to Brain, dated May 31, 1955.
33. C. B. Rees, "Impressions Dennis Brain," *London Musical Events*, no. 10, (September 1955): 25.
34. A brief mention of Brain's recital at George Watson School is in Pettitt (1989), 140. Recital at Portora Royal School, Northern Ireland in March 1956, report in Appendix D. Christopher Hortin, letter to Gamble, October 2005.

Chapter 8. Reminiscences by Colleagues

1. Morris, remembering Brain, BBC Radio 3, May 17, 1996. BLSA call no. H7135.
2. BBC Home Service, "Dennis Brain 1921–1957," *Music Magazine*, May 21, 1961, 10:45 p.m., presented by Gareth Morris.
3. BBC Home Service, "Dennis Brain 1921–1957," *Music Magazine*.
4. Morris BBC Radio 3 series, *Mining the Archive*, May 17, 1996. Presented by Fiona Talkington, BLSA call no. H 7135.

5. Morris taped interview with Gamble, Bristol, March 1, 2006.
6. Klemperer's unexpected return to Germany, owing to the death of his wife, and Hindemith's recording sessions with the Philharmonia, Pettitt, sleeve notes to EMI Classics 2 06010 2 (2008), p. 12. Morris speaking to Gamble, March 1, 2006.
7. Morris, speaking on BBC Artium LP, REGL 352 (1979).
8. Morris taped interview with Gamble, March 1, 2006. First performance listed by Pettitt (1989), 183.
9. Brymer, "Profile of Dennis Brain" in BBC Radio 3, series *At Home*, November 7, 1979. The first performance in England of the Strauss Concerto No. 2 was at Chelsea Town Hall, May 31, 1949. R. C., "Opera and Concerts," *Monthly Musical Record* 79, no. 908 (July–August 1949): 157.
10. Brymer, "Profile of Dennis Brain" in BBC Radio 3, series *At Home*, November 7, 1979.
11. Britten Serenade at Brain's first Edinburgh Festival, Pettitt (1989), 96–97. Edinburgh performance with Scottish National Orchestra conducted by Karl Rankl, from concert program, Gamble collection.
12. Brymer, "Profile of Dennis Brain" in BBC Radio 3, series *At Home*, November 7, 1979.
13. William Waterhouse, writing (no date on the letter) to Gamble, February 2006.
14. Basil Tschaikov email to Gamble, January 9, 2006.
15. Basil Tschaikov telephone call with Gamble, October 22, 2005. Discography I. 6 *Chamber Music with Other Combinations*. See also for a detailed personal account of this broadcast, Tschaikov, *The Music Goes Round and Around*, Chapter 23, 312.
16. Basil Tschaikov telephone call with Gamble, October 22, 2005. See also Tschaikov, *The Music Goes Round and Around*, Chapter 23, 312. Discography, II. 1 British Library Sound Archive, for a copy of the commercial recording, December 28, 1949. It is a very charming and beautiful piece which Brain and his colleagues play with great aplomb. A remastering by Yukihiro Okitsu appeared in Japan in March 2002 on the CD *A Resurrection of Dennis Brain*. Okitsu's website is the largest Dennis Brain website in the *world: www.dennisbrain.net*.
17. Basil Tschaikov telephone call with Gamble, October 22, 2005; for the date 1943, Tschaikov, *The Music Goes Round and Around*, 225.
18. Lady Barbirolli taped interview with Gamble, May 29, 2004.
19. Ibid.
20. Denis Wick telephone call with Gamble, March 27, 2005. The Jacob Trombone Concerto was first broadcast on June 22, 1956, on the Home Service. Alan Frank, "Music Diary: Trombone Premiere," *Radio Times* 131, no. 1701 (June 17–23, 1956): 4. Denis Wick, "My Friends on the Left" *The Horn Player* 1, no.1 (April 2004): 27.
21. Arthur Wilson taped interview with Gamble, November 8, 2005.
22. Roger Lord, letter to Gamble, May 24, 2005.
23. Roger Lord, letter to Gamble, July 11, 2005.
24. Felix Aprahamian, speaking on BBC Artium long-playing record, REGL 352 (1979). Reproduced with permission Arabesque Trust for Blind Pipe Organists.
25. Colin Horsley, letter to Gamble, October 23, 2005.
26. Wolfgang Sawallisch, letter to Gamble, July 15, 2006.

Chapter 9. The Legacy–Horn Players Look Back

1. E. D., "Correspondence" in *Strad* 64, no. 764 (December 1953): 250 states: "Dennis Brain's supremacy among contemporary horn players can hardly be questioned and his agility is probably without precedent . . . we must admit that we do not consider his tone quality to equal that of his father."

2. See the Discography for these recordings and many others, including some previously unpublished in any other discography.
3. Career information about James Decker in *Horn Player* 4, no. 2 (August 2007): 28.
4. James Decker "Dennis Brain—The American Perspective: James Decker on Hollywood Musicians," *Horn Player* 4, no. 2 (August 2007): 28.
5. Civil, sleeve notes to Seraphim's long-playing record 60040 *The Art of Dennis Brain* (1966).
6. WAC, BBC radio talks, microfilm ref. no. T113. BBC hand-corrected script by Norman Del Mar for his BBC tribute, "Dennis Brain," BBC Home Service, October 9, 1957, 7:00–7:30 p.m. Also reproduced under the title "A 1957 BBC Radio Script of a Tribute to Dennis Brain, by Norman Del Mar, edited by the BHS Historian Tony Catterick," *The Horn Player* 4, no. 3 (December 2007): 19–20, 25.
7. Del Mar speaking on BBC Artium long-playing record, REGL 352 (1979).
8. Ibid.
9. Neill Sanders, speaking at the International Horn Society Symposium, Dennis Brain Seminar, University of North Texas, Denton, May 17, 1991.
10. Ibid.
11. Andrew McGavin, letter to Gamble, November 26, 2004.
12. Diack interview (2005), as revised.
13. Diack interview (2005) as revised.
14. Diack interview (2005) as revised.
15. Diack interview (2005) as revised.
16. Diack interview (2005) as revised.
17. Diack interview (2005) as revised.
18. Diack interview (2005) as revised.
19. Barry Tuckwell, speaking for BBC Radio 3 program "Dennis Brain 75th Birthday" in the series *Mining the Archives*, May 17, 1996. Presented by Fiona Talkington. BLSA call no. H 7135.
20. Ibid.
21. Anthony Halstead, speaking to George Pratt, BBC Radio 3, *Spirit of the Age*, March 19, 1994, produced by Kate Bolton, private tape.
22. Ibid.
23. Michael Thompson, "Dennis Brain," *BBC Music Magazine* 9, no. 3 (November 2000): 65.
24. Michael Thompson talking to Tommy Pearson in the series *Music Machine*, BBC Radio 3, May 21, 1995, produced by Christina Pritchard, private tape. For the recording of Strauss's *Vier Letzte Lieder* with Schwarzkopf (1954), Discography I.7.
25. Donald Froud letter to Gamble, October 14, 2005.
26. Tony Fairley email to Gamble, October 7, 2003.
27. Christopher Hortin letter to Gamble, received October 12, 2005.
28. Mark Biondolillo email to Gamble, June 25, 2009.
29. Richard Kittrell email to Gamble, June 27, 2009.
30. Martin Prowse, "The Unfamiliar Dennis Brain," *Audio-Record Review*, October 1969, p. 678.
31. Franklin B. Zimmerman in email to Gamble on July 9, 2003. Used with permission.
32. Bob Gibson, in recorded telephone conversation with Walter Hecht, April 12, 2004. A copy provided to the authors with permission by Walter Hecht.
33. Walter Hecht, writing to Stephen Gamble, October 13, 2010. Used with permission.

Chapter 10: Selected Performances

1. Wilfrid Mellers, *Francis Poulenc* (Oxford: Oxford University Press, 1993), 162.
2. Benjamin Britten, "Dennis Brain (1921–1957)," *Tempo* 46 (Winter 1958): 5–6.
3. Lloyd Moore, review of a recording of the Britten Serenade, NAXOS Classical Reviews, *www.naxosdirect.com/title/8557199/*
4. Marshall (1996), 8.
5. BBC WAC *RCONT1: Artists, Brain Dennis, Artists File 2 1950–1952;* letter from Muriel Goodhall to Brain, 03/M/MG, March 3, 1950; contract issued by Carrell to Brain, dated February 17, 1950, ref. 03/PC/NC). The documents do not name the tenor soloist, but the *Radio Times* lists Pears as the tenor (ref., *Radio Times* 106, no. 1378 (March 12–18, 1950): 19, March 12, Third Programme, 6:50–7:55 p.m.). The Reid Orchestra performance on November 18, 1954, Pettitt (1989), 133.
6. Michael Meckna, "The Legacy of Dennis Brain," *The Horn Call* 71, no. 2 (April, 1991): 56.
7. Colin Mathews, "In Memoriam Dennis Brain," Presto Classical NMCD140.
8. Piers Burton-Page. *Philharmonic Concerto: The Life and Music of Sir Malcolm Arnold* (London: Methuen 1994), 32.
9. First performance: Pettitt (1989), 153; BBC broadcast: *Radio Times* (May 13–19, 1951): 30.
10. Hugo Cole, *Malcolm Arnold: An Introduction to His Music* (London: Faber & Faber, 1989), 31. Hereafter cited as Cole (1989).
11. Dyneley Hussey, "Provincial Events: The Cheltenham Festival," *Musical Times* 98, no. 1375 (September 1957): 506.
12. Cole (1989), 82 (extracts).
13. Pettitt (1989), 147.
14. BBC Legends: Dennis Brain (horn), BBCL 4192-2.
15. Correspondence between Lynch and conductor Gerald Gentry, March 25, 2009.
16. BBC radio program listing in *Radio Times* 127, no. 1640 (April 17–23, 1955): 31, gives the first performance as April 20 on the Third Programme, 6–7 p.m. BBC Scottish Orchestra, conducted by Gerald Gentry. Performance available from the British Library Sound Archive, NSA Reference Number 25A1984.
17. BBC WAC, RCONT1 Essex, Kenneth 1943–1962. Copyright subsists with the Executors of Kenneth Essex (1915–1955).
18. WAC *RCONT 1 Artists File R CONT 1, Essex, Kenneth*, July 24, 1953, Brain to BBC.
19. WAC *RCONT 1 Artists File R CONT 1, Essex, Kenneth*, January 24, 1949, Brain to Kenneth Essex.
20. BBC Ref. 38/M/SVG, March 8, 1955, from Maurice Johnstone's secretary to Brain.
21. Gerald Gentry writing to Lynch, March 25, 2009. "I seem to recollect that he [Essex] had dedicated the 2nd movement of the Horn Concerto, without permission, to William Walton."
22. As the whereabouts of this manuscript is unknown, we can not evaluate Brain's interpretation. The duration of the movements is I 4:54, II 5:58, III 5:54.
23. Willie Ruff, "Paul Hindemith and the Sound of the Horn," *The Horn Call* 17, no. 1 (October 1986): 52 (Extracts). The Mozart concerto referenced by Ruff is No. 2 in E-flat Major, K417, performed with the Sudwestfunk Orchestra Baden-Baden conducted by Paul Hindemith in 1948 (Kursaal Baden-Baden). The recorded performance can be heard on the Hans Pizka Edition of *Historic Performances, Grosse Hornisten Vol. 2*, HPE-CD 02.
24. Reported by Norman Del Mar in sleeve notes to Angel Records recording 35491.
25. Hindemith Horn Concerto, Op. 119, Philharmonia, Dennis Brain, horn solo, Paul Hindemith, conducting. EMI CDC-7-47834-2.

26. *Radio Times*, February 25–March 3, 1951, p. 45, March 3, Third Programme. 8:35–9:20 p.m. Orchestral Concert. Dennis Brain—Horn, London Philharmonic Orchestra, Leader David Wise, Conductor Norman Del Mar.
27. Advertisement of forthcoming concert, Kingsway Hall, Kingsway W.C.2, Concerts of 20th Century Music. The concert also included the Britten Serenade with Peter Pears, tenor.
28. Salter, Lionel, "Analytical Notes and First Reviews: Orchestral," *Gramophone* 29, no. 346 (March 1952): 226; *Hindemith Concert Music for Brass and Strings and Concertino for Horn and Orchestra*, Vienna Symphony Orchestra (Prof. Haefner), Franz Koch (horn). NixaSPLP515 "The Horn Concerto (demoted by Nixa, for no apparent reason, to Concertino) is a much later work and is much cleaner and brighter in texture: it was written in 1949 as a tribute to Dennis Brain, who gave the first performance under the composer in Baden-Baden.
29. Gareth Morris in a taped interview with Gamble on March 1, 2006.
30. Elisabeth Schwarzkopf, *On and Off the Record: A Memoir of Walter Legge* (Boston: Northeastern University Press, 1982), 180.
31. Peter Heyworth, *Otto Klemperer: His Life And Times, Vol. 2: 1933–1973* (Cambridge: Cambridge University Press, 1996), 250.
32. Pettitt (1989), 131.
33. David Neumeyer, "University of Texas, Notes," *Blaserkonzert I from Paul Hindemith Samtliche Werk*, Bloomington, Indiana, November 1982. M3 H662 P5. Notes.
34. Movement III notes by Norman Del Mar, sleeve notes (extracts) to Angel LP 35491, "Paul Hindemith Conducts His Own Works, Symphonia Serena for Orchestra, Concerto for Horn and Orchestra."
35. The declamation is translated:

> My call transforms
> The concert hall into a fall-toned grove,
> The present into the unremembered,
> You into the cloth and custom of your ancestors,
> Your fortune into their longing and resignation.
> Permit these dear shadows their resurrection,
> Yourself communion with them, the half-forgotten,
> And me my tone-formed longing.

36. W. Abegg, *Heinrich Kaminski* (Tutzing: Verlegt BEI Hans Schneider, 1986), 172, 67.
37. Pettitt (1989), 192–93.
38. J. O. C., "Gordon Jacob's Horn Concerto," *Musical Times* 92, no. 1301 (July 1951): 324. The article is a review of the first performance (not recorded), not the first broadcast. Lynch reviews a recording of the first broadcast in Chapter 10.
39. Marshall (1996), 51. For the Edinburgh performance: Pettitt (1989), 133. For the BBC broadcast: BBC WAC, *Radio Times* (March 20–26, 1955): 24, March 22, Midland Home Service, 9.15–10.15 p.m.
40. Julia Seiber Boyd, "The Seiber Centenary: 2005 and Beyond," Jewish Music Institute, International Center for Supressed Music, ICSM Online Journal. *www.jmi.org.uk/suppressed-music/newsletter/articles/005.html.*With permission from Julia Seiber Boyd.
41. Pettitt (1989), 182.
42. C. B. Rees, "Impressions . . . Dennis Brain," *London Musical Events,* no.10 (September 1955): 24–25.

43. W. R. Anderson, "The Edinburgh Festival," *Musical Times* 95, no. 1340 (October 1954): 555–56. BBC radio program listing in *Radio Times* 124, no. 1607 (Aug 29–September 4, 1954): 40, September 3, Home Service 11:00 a.m.–noon. Edinburgh Festival Collegium Musicum (Zürich). Paul Sacher, conductor; Andre Jaunet, flute; Dennis Brain, horn. Concertino no. 5 in E-flat by Pergolesi; Concerto for horn and string orchestra (1951) by Othmar Schoeck; Suite No. 2 in B minor for flute and strings by Bach, from Freemasons' Hall, Edinburgh.
44. Gunther Schuller, "Horn Literature: Othmar Schoeck . . . Concerto for Horn and String Orchestra 1952," *Woodwind*, March 1955, p. 10.
45. Review of the Othmar Schoeck Horn Concerto by author Lynch.
46. Joan Chissell, "Music of the Week" (untitled caption to photo by Howard Coster, of Brain, taken in 1956) in *Radio Times* 131, no. 1703 (July 1–7, 1956): 5. The article itself does not mention Brain; only the caption to the photo that illustrates the article gives his name.
47. Brown Meggs, recording sleeve, *The Art of Dennis Brain, Vol. 2,* Seraphim 60073 (1966).
48. Pettitt (1989), 143–44.
49. Anthony Wright, "Anthony Lewis Concerto for Horn," *Music and Musicians* 4 (June 1956): unpaginated.
50. Donald Mitchell, "London Concerts: Orchestral, Choral and Vocal," *Musical Times* 97, no. 1360 (June 1956): 316.
51. Ernest Tomlinson, letter to Gamble, April 7, 2005.
52. Marshall (1996), 26, and Pettitt (1989), 196–97.
53. ORF-Publikumsservice, Salzburg (PM 50/10006), Dennis Brain Wind Ensemble on July 30, 1957, at the Salzburg Festival in the Mozarteum Large Hall with Wilfrid Parry as the pianist. The concert also included Mozart's Divertimento in B-flat major, K270 and Hindemith's Small Chamber Music for Bläserquintett at this event.
54. With permission from Professor John Dressler, Murray State University, Kentucky, to Gamble for use in this publication and with written permission from Ann Meade-Sanders, widow of Neill Sanders. Neill Sanders (1923–1992) briefly led the horn section of the London Symphony Orchestra until he was called up to serve in the Army during World War II. He was principal horn of the London Philharmonic and the BBC Symphony Orchestras and played second horn alongside Dennis Brain in the Philharmonia Orchestra for seven years.
55. Benjamin Ivry, *Francis Poulenc* (London: Phaidon Press, 1996), 195.
56. Mellers (1993), 161–62. Wilfrid Mellers (1914–2008) was for many years Emeritus Professor of Music, University of York.
57. Correspondence between Lynch and David C. F. Wright, May 4, 2009.
58. BBC radio program listing in *Radio Times* 127, no. 1648 (June12–18, 1955): 9, lists June 13 on Third Programme, 8:50–9:45 p.m. (Part 1) and 10:05–10:55 p.m. (Part 2). *Aubade* was performed in Part 2 of the concert.
59. For the Searle comment, David C. F. Wright, "Humphrey Searle," wrightmusic.net. For the chamber work: Len Mullenger, "Humphrey Searle List of Compositions" at Music on the Web. *www.musicweb-international.com/searle/works.htm*, Item no. 34. Regarding the variation, David C. F. Wright, *Humphrey Searle, Part 2.* wrightmusic.net.

Chapter 11. Horns, Mouthpieces, and Embouchures

1. Brain, Dennis, "The French Horn," *Brass Today*, 1961, pp. 19–20. See Appendix D in this book.
2. See discussion notes regarding the "Brain Model Horn" on *facebook.com/people/Dennis-Brain/100000187896810.*

3. Pettitt (1989), 50.
4. Ibid., 57.
5. The reader is referred to the following resources for discussion relative to the history of the Raoux horn: *The New Langwell Index*, London, William Waterhouse, 1993, pp.318–19. *An Index of Musical Wind Instrument Makers*, Lyndesay Langwell, 4th edition, 1974, p.143. Civil: Seraphim 60040, *The Art of Dennis Brain*, recording notes. Reginald Morley-Pegge, *Instruments of the Orchestra: The French Horn*. Second Edition. London: Ernest Benn Limited, 1973, p. 170. Farquharson Cousins, *On Playing the Horn*. 2nd Edition. Caron Publications, 1992, p. 66, note 32. Brown Meggs, recording notes for Seraphim 60073, the *Art of Dennis Brain, Vol. 2*.
6. Cousins (1992), 66.
7. Pettitt (1989), 174. Second rotary valve, idem, p. 111.
8. Alex Grieve, "A Letter From Dennis Brain," *The Horn Call*, August 2000, p. 77, reprinted from original appearing in *The Horn Call*, May 1971, pp. 48-49.
9. Cousins (1992), 66 n32.
10. Farquharson Cousins, "The Degenerate Horn," *Music and Letters* 31, no. 4 (October 1950): 378–79.
11. Paul Kampen in blog at *hornplayer.net/archive/a321.html.*
12. Morley-Pegge (1973), 161–62.
13. Correspondence by letter from Melville-Mason to Gamble, October 9, 2005. Melville-Mason (b. 1933) studied in Edinburgh, where he also devoted himself to practical music-making as a bassoonist, conductor of larger wind ensembles, and organization of the Edinburgh Festival. Melville-Mason headed the department of contracts in the arts at the BBC in London. Since 1990 he has taught at the Prague Academy of Music and has been an advisor to the Prague Spring Festival. He has been Chairman of the Dvorak Society in London and a promoter of Czech music in Great Britain.
14. Refer to *Report on Dennis Brain's horn and mouthpiece*, Dr. Arnold Myers, Edinburgh University, *hornplayer.net/archive/a292.html.*
15. With permission from Pettitt.
16. Pettitt (1989), 98.
17. E. D., "Correspondence," *Strad* 64, no. 764 (December 1953): 250.
18. Cousins (1992), 53.
19. Gebr. Alexander to Richard Kittrell, January 13, 1965.
20. Cousins, "The Degenerate Horn," 378–80.
21. Reginald Morley-Pegge, "The Degenerate Horn," *Music and Letters* 32, no. 1 (October 1951): 94–96.
22. See *The Horn Magazine*, December 2002, pp. 6-10, "Brain Celebration," for a more comprehensive review of the event.
23. Dalya Alberge, "Royal Academy of Music's Horn of Plenty," *The Times*, December 4, 2001, p. 16, columns a–f.
24. Pettitt (1989), 123–24.
25. Taped transcripts of Elliot's discussion provided to Gamble by John Dressler from the International Horn Symposium, Dennis Brain Seminar, University of North Texas, May 17, 1991.
26. Douglas A. Elliot, writing to Gamble, February 10, 2006.
27. John C. Dressler, "Dennis Brain—A Seventieth-Birthday Tribute," *The Horn Call*, October 1991, p. 47.
28. Pettitt (1989), 124. Tomlinson, letter from Tomlinson to Gamble, April 7, 2005, quoted in Chapter 10.

29. Anthony Fairly, in correspondence with Gamble, October 7, 2003.
30. Pettitt (1989), 99.
31. Letter to Dr. Caswell Neal, July 24, 1953, authors' private collections.
32. Letter to Alfred and Straussie Brain, August 15, 1953. This transcript is from a private collection jointly owned by Boston Symphony Orchestra players, including Richard Mackey. Written permission from all the players.
33. Cousins (1992), 17.
34. Nancy Jordan Fako. *Philip Farkas and His Horn: A Happy, Worthwhile Life* (Elmurst, IL: Crescent Park Music Publications, 1998), 69–70.
35. With permission from Lynn Weddle, 95–96.
36. Taped transcripts of Farkas's discussion provided to Gamble by John Dressler from the International Horn Symposium, Dennis Brain Seminar, University of North Texas, May 17, 1991.
37. Cousins (1992), 64.

Chapter 12. New Directions

1. Donald Froud email to Gamble, October 28, 2005.
2. Reproduced from the original photograph lent to the authors by Mrs. Siva Oke, Somm Recordings, with kind permission of Shirley Lady Beecham. Also reproduced in sleeve notes to compact disc, SOMM-BEECHAM 24 (2008). Gamble wrote to Norman Del Mar about horn-playing conductors, mentioning Dennis Brain as well as Barry Tuckwell, and Del Mar's reply, September 4, 1990, stated "With regard to horn playing conductors I was surprised to find no mention of Edward (Ted) Downes (who played 1st horn for me in the first orchestra I ever conducted), or Maurice Handford (Barbirolli's 1st horn in the Hallé) who both became most reputable conductors . . ."
3. Plans for future tours to Scotland (Dennis Brain Chamber Orchestra), and to Australia, Pettitt (1989), 155; solo tour to Canada with Matthews, idem, 161–62.
4. Recording all of the Haydn Concertos, Pettitt (1989), 162; also Brain's letter to Legge, quoted in Chapter 6, reproduced from Alan Sanders (1998), 121. Gerhard Nonet broadcast, WAC, *RCONT1 Artists, Dennis Brain Wind Ensemble, 1946–1962*; letter from Bowling to Brain, ref. 38/M/HM, June 13, 1957; ref. 01/PC/NC contract from Bowling to Brain, July 8, 1957; for the concert on September 24, 1957, Pettitt (1989), 161.
5. Brain speaking of retiring from the Philharmonia, Neill Sanders's talk at the International Horn Society Symposium, Dennis Brain Seminar, University of North Texas, Denton, May 17, 1991, quoted in Chapter 9, private tape. Morris taped interview with Gamble, March 1, 2006. Dennis and Aubrey Brain, the two horns of *Orchestre Moderne*, mentioned in letter from Ernest Tomlinson to Gamble, April 7, 2005. Recording with Bob Sharples Orchestra, Discography II. 1 British Library Sound Archive.
6. BBC appearance on *Downbeat*, Pettitt (1989), 127. Also Chapter 6 for quotation of correspondence about this broadcast. *Desert Island Discs*, Home Service, August 13, 1956, 1:10–1:40 p.m. *Radio Times* 132, no.1709 (August 12–18 1956): 16. Produced by Monica Chapman, WAC, telediphone script, p. 9, band 5a of BBC recording, DLS 9281. The record of Alec Wilder's "Horn Belt Boogie" is Columbia DB 3255.
7. WAC, telediphone script, band 6 of BBC recording, DLS 9281, pp. 10–11.
8. John Davies, leader (concertmaster) of the Morley College Orchestra, anecdote told to Tony Catterick in 1995. Quoted with permission from Tony Catterick. Discography II. 1 British Library Sound Archive for recording of Leopold Mozart's Alphorn Concerto (movement) played on a hose-pipe.

9. Railton (1992), 251.
10. Ibid., 252.
11. WAC *RCONT1 Artists, Brain Dennis, File III, 1953–1956*; letter from Brain to Johnstone, March 28, 1956.
12. WAC *RCONT1 Artists, Brain Dennis, File III, 1953–1956*; Maurice Johnstone's Secretary to Brain, ref. 38/M/SVG, April 3, 1956; Del Mar discouraged by Johnstone, Pauline Del Mar taped interview with Gamble, November 9, 2005.
13. "Wigmore Hall: Dennis Brain Chamber Orchestra," *The Times*, Royal Edition, April 19, 1956, p. 3, column c.
14. Donald Mitchell, "London Concerts: Concerts," *Musical Times* 97, no. 1360 (June 1956): 318.
15. Frank V. Hawkins, *A Hundred Years of Chamber Music* (London: South Place Ethical Society, 1987), 47. Quoted with permission South Place Ethical Society, London.
16. Pettitt (1989), 152. For the Aldeburgh concert, also Burton-Page (1994), 67. Dennis Brain Chamber Orchestra personnel listed in the memorial concert program, Chelsea Town Hall, December 10, 1957, at 8 p.m. private collection. Chapter 12, Plate 4 for the program front cover, signed by the orchestra, soloists, and the three conductors for that concert: Fricker, Britten, and Del Mar. Personnel:

First Violin: Hugh Bean (Leader), Tessa Robbins, Michael Jones, Elizabeth Boenders

Second Violin: Ivor McMahon, Ernest Scott, Ernest Routledge

Viola: Maurice Loban, Eileen Grainger, Muriel Brain

Cello: Raymond Clarke, John Holmes

Double Bass: Adrian Beers, Edmund Chesterman

Flute: Gareth Morris, Clifford Seville

Oboe: Leonard Brain, Natalie James

Clarinet: Stephen Waters

Bassoon: Cecil James, Edward Wilson

Horn: Neill Sanders, Alfred Cursue

Trumpet: Richard "Bob" Walton

17. Scottish tour plans for the Chamber Orchestra in September and October 1957, Pettitt (1989), 155; arrangement of the National Anthem and last conversation with Hugh Bean, idem, 155–56. Bean telephoned Gamble in May 1991 and mentioned that Brain had confided that he intended retiring in 1958.
18. Memorial concert, Chelsea Town Hall, December 10, 1957, at 8 p.m.; Gamble collection.
19. Formation of the Brain-Pougnet-Parry Trio in 1952, Pettitt (1989), 130.
20. Brain's first letter to the BBC mentioning his Trio, WAC *RCONT1 Artists, Brain Dennis, File III, 1953–1956*; letter to Nisbett, October 24, 1956; Brain's second letter to Nisbett, November 29, 1956. Internal memorandum admitting that the Brain Trio is not known to the BBC, idem, notes in ink on the back of Brain's letter of October 24, 1956.
21. Broadcast concert at Barton-on-Humber, Pettitt (1989), 147.
22. York concert, reviewed in "Music in York: Trio's Notable Recital," *York Gazette* and *Herald*, October 26, 1956, p. 1. Quoted with permission of Sarah Hyde, *York Gazette and Herald*. The date of the concert is not clear, although likely to have been October 25, the same day as the concert at Barton-on-Humber. Pettitt (1989), 147, gives October 18, 1956, as the date of the York concert.

23. Patricia Naylor, a young schoolgirl at the time, was in the audience.
24. Tour of Scotland in March 1957, Pettitt (1989), 150–51; Brain experimenting with color photography, works performed, and the Trio's last appearance, idem, 151.
25. Neill Sanders related his last conversation with Brain on August 31, at the International Horn Society Symposium, Dennis Brain Seminar, University of North Texas, Denton, May 17, 1991. Quoted in Chapter 9.
26. The eyewitness account of the car crash was given at the inquest, Hatfield, September 4, 1957. "Brother's Tribute to Musician's Driving," *The Times*, Royal Edition, September 5, 1957, p. 2, column f. Also Pettitt (1989), 157. Other details of the crash in "Mr. Dennis Brain Killed in Car Crash," *The Times*, Royal Edition, September 2, 1957, p. 8, column b. Other newspaper accounts give inaccurate and contradictory information about the accident.
27. Morris, remembering Brain, BBC Radio 3, May 17, 1996. BLSA call no. H7135.
28. Basil Tschaikov email to Gamble, January 9, 2006. See also Tschaikov, *The Music Goes Round and Around*, Chapter 17, p. 207.
29. Alan Civil, sleeve notes to Seraphim long-playing record 60040 (1966).
30. Vittorio Gui (1885–1975), letter to Leonard Brain from Florence, dated September 10, 1957, private collection.
31. Neville Cardus, "Dennis Brain, A Distinguished Horn Player," *The Guardian*, September 2, 1957. A newspaper cutting inserted in Leonard Brain's program of the RPO concert at the Royal Albert Hall that day. Copyright Guardian News & Media Ltd. 1957.
32. "Mr. Dennis Brain, A Renowned Horn Player," *The Times*, Royal Edition, September 2, 1957, p. 10, col. f.
33. "Edinburgh Tribute to Dennis Brain. Dutch Orchestra's Last Respects," *The Times,* Royal Edition, September 5, 1957, p. 4, column e.
34. Harold Rutland, "Notes and Comments, Dennis Brain," *Musical Times* 98, no. 1375 (September 1957): 548.
35. Alec Robertson, "Dennis Brain," *Gramophone* 35, no. 413 (October 1957): 169.
36. Untitled obituary in *The Strad* 68, no. 810 (October 1957): 197. Quoted with permission from Ariane Todes, Editor, *The Strad.*
37. Leslie Bell, "Best on French Horn Killed in Car Crash," *Toronto Daily Star*, September 7, 1957, p. 24, col. a. Leslie Bell was quoting Peter Civil in the article. The cancelled performance, idem. Reprinted with permission Torstar Syndication Services and Peter Civil.
38. Kay Simons, "Tribute to Dennis Brain," CKCR Continuity Radio, Kitchener, Ontario, 250 watts SH. 3-3628. October 23, 1957, 2:30–3:00 p.m. Announcer, Paul Freeman. Original script, private collection.
39. Lionel Salter, "Analytical Notes and First Reviews: Orchestral," *Gramophone* 35, no. 414 (November 1957): 220.
40. Gordon Schonberg, "Sinclair Lott is Horn Soloist in D. Brain Memorial Concert," *Woodwind World*, March 1958, p. 4.
41. Joseph Eger, "Breaking the Endurance Barrier," *Woodwind World*, May 1958, p. 6.
42. Tony Catterick collection.
43. For the first performance of Poulenc's *Elégie*, BBC radio program listing in *Radio Times* 138, no. 1788 (February 16–22, 1958): 31, February 17, Third Programme 9:25–10:10. *Poulenc.* The broadcast also featured the Dennis Brain Wind Ensemble with Neill Sanders, playing Poulenc's Sextet.
44. W. S. Mann, "Analytical Notes and First Reviews," *Gramophone* 37, no. 439 (December 1959): 284–85.
45. For EMI's record of the Dennis Brain Wind Ensemble broadcast of September 5, 1957, Pettitt (1989), 164.

46. Matthews, sleeve notes to BBC long-player REB175 (1974).
47. Brymer, "Profile of Dennis Brain" BBC Radio 3, November 7, 1979, in series *At Home.* WAC Radio Talks script, microfilm reel 398/9 (27/10/1979-09/11/1979).
48. Richard Adeney, unpublished Memoirs, p. 93.
49. William Waterhouse, undated letter to Gamble, February 2006.
50. Tina Brain taped interview with Gamble, June 29, 2005.
51. Robin Wedderburn, Peter Gritton, Ben Parry, notes in concert program, *Dennis Brain: A Celebration*, March 9, 2008, Wathen Hall, St. Paul's School, 7 p.m., private collection.

Discography

1. The only recording that exists was made privately from the first broadcast and has never been commercially available. Norman Del Mar mentioned a recording, possibly this one, in a letter to Gamble, September 4, 1990. BBC radio program listing in *Radio Times*, 131, no. 1703 (June 24–July 1, 1956): 10, July 1, Home Service 2:30–3:30 p.m. *A Concert.* See also Joan Chissell "Music of the Week" (untitled long caption to photo of Brain, dating from 1956, by Howard Coster) in *Radio Times* 131, no. 1703 (July 1–7, 1956): 5. Pettitt (1989), 190–91; Marshall (1996), 7. Emerson music publishers, York, North Yorkshire, have published a horn and piano reduction: Emerson Edition 440 (2006).
2. Archive collection: British Library Sound Archive (hereafter cited as BLSA in notes only) call nos. 2LP0028043 2; 1CD0209536 BD7. William McNaught, "New Music: Britten Serenade," *Musical Times* 85, no. 1219 (September 1944): 275–76; William McNaught, "*Gramophone* Notes: Britten's Serenade," *Musical Times* 87, no. 1235 (January 1946): 16–17; "New Works for Small Orchestra: Wigmore Hall Concert," *The Times*, Late London Edition, October 16, 1943, p. 6, col. d. F. F. Clough and G. J. Cuming, "Diskography," *Gramophone Record Review*, October 1958, p. 153; Prowse (1969), 679; Pettitt (1989), 190–91; Marshall (1996), 8; McBeth (1997), 55–57; Michael Smith, *The Decca Recording Company Limited: Decca 78 rpm Records 1929 to 1954.* 10-inch prefixed A, M and Z series. 12-inch prefixes K, S, T and X series. A Discography. London, City of London Phonograph and Gramophone Society, 2002, p. 578.
3. Archive collection: BLSA call nos. 1CDR 0012286 BD1-12; 2CDR0015599. Day, 2000, p. 243, gives a brief account of these unpublished takes. On May 11, 2004, Dr. Day emailed Gamble the information on matrix numbers for the individual takes.
4. Deryck Cooke, "Music of the Week: New British Works," *Radio Times* 127, no. 1640 (April 17–23, 1955): 5; BBC radio program listing in *Radio Times* 127, p. 31, April 20, Third Programme 6–7 p.m. *Alphabetical Index to BBC Sound Archives Catalogue*. Accessions 1973–April 1984. Vol. 1, A-EVA, p. 318; *Catalogue, BBC Sound Archives: A Chronological List of Sound Recordings from January to December 1955.* HUS 025 348 209 42, Humanities 2 Reading Room, British Library. The latter catalogue gives a recording reference, T39817 and duration of recording: 17:30; Pettitt (1989), 134, mentions the first performance but no recording.
5. Clough and Cuming (1958), 953; Prowse (1969), 679; Pettitt (1987), 300; Pettitt (1989), 192–93; Dressler (1991), 49; Marshall (1996), 14; Lyndon Jenkins, sleeve notes to EMI Classics 7243 5 67782 2 1 (2002), 6; Pettitt, sleeve notes to EMI Classics 2 06010 2 (2008), 9–13; Paul Sawbridge, "CD Reviews—Dennis Brain—The Horn Player EMI Classics—Icon 2 06010 2," *Horn Player* 5, no. 2 (Autumn 2008): 40.
6. Pettitt (1987), 264; Discography data collected by Michael Gray available from the CHARM Discography: *charm.rhul.ac.uk/discography/search/search_simple* (accessed February 13, 2010).

7. The recording of the first broadcast performance exists only as a private recording made with the authorization of the composer. It has never been commercially available. BBC radio program listing in *Radio Times* 111, no. 1442 (July 1–7, 1951): 21, July 3, Third Programme 6:50 p.m. J. O. C., "Gordon Jacob's Horn Concerto," *Musical Times* 92, no. 1301 (July 1951): 324. "Riddick Orchestra," *The Times*, Late London Edition, May 9, 1951, p. 4, column e. Pettitt (1989), 192–93; Marshall (1996), 15. The composer's horn and piano arrangement is published by Stainer & Bell (1951), no. 2627. The score states "For Dennis Brain" on the first printed page.
8. The recording of this BBC broadcast exists only as a private recording and has never been commercially available. BBC radio program listing in *Radio Times* 134, no. 1731 (January 13–19, 1957): 40, January 18, Home Service, 3:30 p.m. Pettitt (1989), 192–93; Marshall (1996), 16. The score was published in a horn and piano reduction by Alfred Lengnick & Co., London, no. 3972.
9. Archives collections: Radio Swiss Archives, Basel; BLSA call no. 1CD0246550 BD01-03. Pettitt (1989), 194–95; Hans Pizka: sleeve notes to CD, HPE CD 02 (1994), 7; Marshall (1996), 25.
10. BBC radio program listing in *Radio Times* 124, no. 1607 (August 29–September 4, 1954): 40, September 3, Home Service, 11 a.m.–noon. Freemasons' Hall, Edinburgh Festival. Collegium Musicum Zurich, cond. Paul Sacher.
11. Archive collection: WSA no. 1231. BBC radio program listing in *Radio Times* 128, no. 1654 (July 24–30, 1955): 42, July 29, Home Service, Part 2: 9:15–9:55 p.m. *Henry Wood Promenade Concerts*. See William C. Lynch, "Dennis Brain Recordings Discovered at Stanford University," *The Horn Call*, May 2005, p. 43. See also Sidney Harrison, "First Week of the Proms" in *Radio Times* 128, no. 1654 (July 24–30, 1955): 5. See also mention of this concert in article by C. B. Rees, "Impressions . . . Dennis Brain" in *London Musical Events*, no. 10, September 1955, p. 25. Pettitt (1989), 196–97; Marshall (1996), 26.
12. Archive collection: BLSA call no. 30B 5872-5874; Leech nos. 1209–1211; dubbing no. T11571WR. BBC radio program listing in *Radio Times* 93, no. 1205 (November 3–9, 1946): 16, November 5, Third Programme 6:45 p.m. Liverpool Philharmonic Orchestra. For the first performance, see Pettitt (1989), 44.
13. BBC radio program listing in *Radio Times* 130, no. 1688 (March 18–24, 1956): no page given, March 18, Home Service, 3 p.m. *Sunday Symphony Concert*. According to the P as B file, the duration of the concerto was 13'15".
14. Archives collections: Yleisradio Finland (Finnish Broadcasting Company), Studio Helsinki. Radio Sound Archives, Box 15, Fin-00024; BLSA call no. B5017/01. Marshall (1996), 27.
15. Pettitt (1987), 165; Discographical data collected by Michael Gray available from the CHARM Discography, *charm.rhul.ac.uk/discography* (accessed February 13, 2010).
16. Archives collections: BLSA call no.1CDR0004385 BD4; Leech nos. 30B 7045; 7046 (incomplete recording). WSA no. 1192. BBC radio program listing in *Radio Times* 110, no. 1421 (February 4–10, 1951): 23, LP, February 5, 12:45–1:45 p.m. Concert Hour. Pettitt (1989), 196–97; Marshall (1996), 27; Lynch (2005), 43.
17. The only recording of these extracts from the rehearsal as well as the complete performance during the rehearsal prior to the broadcast, was made for private use. A complete private recording from the broadcast that day also exists. BBC radio program listing in *Radio Times* 135, no. 1753 (June 16–22, 1957): 51, LP, *Light Programme Music Festival*, June 22, 8:45–10:00 p.m. *Radio Times* states (idem) that the "concert is also being relayed by Stateradiofonien, Copenhagen, Nordeutscher Rundfunk, Hamburg, and Yleisradio, Helsinki." Pettitt (1989), 196–97; Marshall (1996), 30. The score for Rhapsody and Rondo for Horn and Orchestra, in the composer's horn and piano reduction, is published by Mills Music, London.

18. The only recording is in private hands, whereabouts unknown. BBC radio program listing in *Radio Times* 132, no. 1707 (July 29–August 4, 1956): 31, August 1, Third Programme, 10:40–11:20 p.m. *Fricker and Hamilton*. Pettitt (1979), 179; Michael Meckna, *Twentieth-Century Brass Soloists*, Bio-Critical Sourcebooks on Musical Performance (Westport, CT: Greenwood Press, 1994), 142; Marshall (1996), 11. The P as B file states the date of transmission, August 1, 1956, and the time of transmission, 10:45 p.m., which differs by five minutes from the time as stated above (in advance of the broadcast) in *Radio Times*. Meckna (1994), 142, states "James's recording of Fricker's Sonata is more dramatic than that of Dennis Brain, for whom the work was originally written."
19. Discography data collected by Michael Gray, available from The CHARM Discography, website *charm.rhul.ac.uk/discography* (accessed February 13, 2010). Stephen Pettitt informed the authors, April 28, 2010, that a single matrix of part of the first movement is all that was recorded.
20. Discography data collected by Michael Gray, available from The CHARM Discography, *charm.rhul.ac.uk/discography* (accessed February 13, 2010). Stephen Pettitt informed the authors on April 28, 2010, that all matrices for this recording were destroyed in 1955. At present it has not been possible to verify if a test pressing or other copy of this complete recording has survived.
21. BBC radio program listing in *Radio Times* 127, no. 1649 (June 19–25, 1955): 15, June 22, Third Programme 8:15 p.m. Aldeburgh Festival Chamber Music. WAC. Pettitt (1989), 190–91; Marshall (1996), 8; Lynch (2005), 43.
22. Archives collections: BBC cat.no. MX30; LP 2383-2; BLSA call no. 1CD0276751 SEQ7. BBC radio program listing in *Radio Times* 136, no. 1762 (August 18–24, 1957): 48, August 24, Home Service 11:00–11:40 a.m. Pettitt (1989), 192–93; Marshall (1996), 11; BBC Sound Archives catalogs (Humanities 2 Reading Room, British Library) Supplement I, p. 87. The composer's handwritten parts, including an unpublished "alternative notation" version of the last movement, is now in possession of the authors. Published (without the alternative notation Finale) by Schott & Co., 1951, no. 5613a.
23. Archive collection: BLSA call no. 1SE0039285 1 Pye. Pettitt, "London Baroque Ensemble" ms., p. 12; Marshall (1996), 5. The authors thank Yukihiro Okitsu for providing the information about which of the eleven dances were recorded, and in which order they appear on this EMI CD.
24. Archive collection: BLSA call nos. 2LP0062233; 1LPO110425 2. Pettitt ms. "London Baroque Ensemble," 9; Marshall (1996), 10 and idem, Appendix C, p. 158.
25. BBC radio program listing in *Radio Times* 105, no. 1367 (December 25, 1949–January 1, 1950): 39, December 30, Third Programme 10:55–11:30 p.m. WAC Brain source file ref. 4(11). The source file quotes the P as B file's actual time of transmission: 10:56 p.m.
26. BBC radio program listing in *Radio Times* 111, no. 1430 (April 8–14, 1951): 25, April 11, Third Programme 6:00–6:35 p.m. WAC "P as B" ref. gives the following: 18:00-18:27 ½. Published by Enoch. Duration: 31'30". Repeat broadcast WAC P as B ref. Third Programme, August 19, 1951, transmission time, 23:27 ½ . Duration: 24'47". Recording of the broadcast, Third Programme, April 11, 1951. Recording reference no. SBS 2729. Movements are: 1st mvt. Doucement mouvementé; 2nd mvt. Modérément—Vivement; 3rd mvt. Allegrement, mais pas trop vif. The authors are grateful to Erin O'Neill, Archives Researcher at BBC Written Archives, for providing the P as B references.
27. BBC radio program listing in *Radio Times* 98, no. 1268 (February 1–7, 1948): 9, February 1, Third Programme, 6:30–7:10 p.m. Archive collections: BLSA call no. 1CD00298172 BD5-8.
28. Archive collections: BLSA "Sir Charles Mackerras Collection" call no. C961/97 BD1; M554W BD 1; WSA no. 1150. Joan Chissell, "Music Diary," *Radio Times* 133, no. 1727

(December 16–22, 1956): 4. BBC radio program listing in *Radio Times* 133, no. 1727 (December 16–22, 1956): 19, December 17, Third Programme 8:40–10:00 p.m. Pettitt (1989), 192–93; Marshall (1996), 14; Lynch (2005), 43. According to a Pdf file by Paul Scharfenberger dated February 5, 2010, the first performance in London was April 25, 1791. He does not mention the performers. */musicandhistory.com/pdf/1791-1800.pdf*

29. Pauline Del Mar, in a letter to Gamble, December 5, 2005, mentioned an attempt by Brain to record the four parts of Hindemith's Sonata. She recalled that he did not quite manage to complete all four parts. See also discography data collected by Michael Gray, available from The CHARM Discography website *charm.rhul.ac.uk/discography/search/search_simple* (accessed February 13, 2010).

30. Clough and Cuming (1958), 953; Pettitt (1989), 194–95. Pettitt gives no recording date. Marshall (1996), 18. (K.166), p. 20 (K.375 Minuet and Trio). Marshall gives no recording date. Smith (2002), 102.

31. Archive collection: BLSA call nos.T11744WR; 2CDR0000578 BD7 (1st mvt.); BD8 (2nd mvt.); BD9 (3rd mvt.); BD10 (part 1 of 4th mvt.); BD13 (part 2 of 4th mvt.). List nos. JD403 W3 (first, second, and third movements); 30B 6316 (fourth movement); cat. no. 30B 6313-6316; C738/786-789; Leech nos. 1454–57. Harold Rutland, "Music Diary," *Radio Times* 118, no. 1524 (January 25–31, 1953): 27. BBC radio program listing in *Radio Times,* ibid., p. 31, January 28, Third Programme, 8:20–9:00 p.m. *Richard Strauss.* Pettitt (1989), 196–97. The first concert performance information is from an original concert program, private collection.

32. All London Chamber Orchestra/ London Chamber Players recordings are conducted by Anthony Bernard.

33. Marshall (1996), 5, no recording date. The date is from Smith (2002), 172.

34. Archive collection: BLSA list no. 30B 4923; dubbing no. NP10682WR. Harold Rutland, "The Week's Music," *Radio Times* 110, no. 1421 (February 4–10): 11. BBC radio program listing in *Radio Times,* ibid., p. 21, February 4, Third Programme 9:15–10:00 p.m. (Part 1). Choral and Orchestral Concert. Not listed in the Brain source file. Rutland's article quoted with permission from Kathy Day, BBC Magazines Limited.

35. BBC radio program listing in *Radio Times* 102, no. 1318, p. 13, January 18, Third Programme, 10:10–11:10 p.m. *A Serenade.*

36. The authors are grateful to EMI North America for providing the recording date for this piece.

37. All London Mozart Players recordings are conducted by Harry Blech.

38. Marshall (1996), 14, no recording date. Smith (2002), 102, gives the recording date.

39. Mozart Symphony No. 40, recorded December 22, 1952. Marshall (1996), 20.

40. Marshall (1996), 29, lists the complete recording of June 8, 1944, reissued by Beulah on 1PD11. Smith (2002), 38.

41. Smith (2002), 38.

42. Marshall (1996), 30; Smith (2002), 45.

43. Marshall (1996), 32; Smith (2002), 51.

44. Marshall (1996), 34; Smith (2002), 53.

45. Pettitt (1987), 229; Pettitt (1989), 190–91; Marshall (1996), 3.

46. Pettitt (1987), 263; Pettitt (1989), 198–99; Marshall (1996), 4.

47. Pettitt (1987), 229; Marshall (1996), 5.

48. Pettitt (1987), 280; Marshall (1996), 5.

49. BBC radio program listing in *Radio Times* 136, no. 1763 (August 25–31, 1957): 51, August 30, Third Programme, Part 2: 9:05–9:45 p.m. Marshall (1996), 5.

50. Pettitt (1987), 243; Marshall (1996), 5.
51. Pettitt (1987), 261; Marshall (1996), 5.
52. Pettitt (1987), 278; Marshall (1996), 5.
53. C. B. Rees (1955), 25.
54. Pettitt (1987), 165; Marshall (1996), 6; John Hunt, *Makers of the Philharmonia* (London: John Hunt, 1996), 48.
55. Pettitt (1987), 150; Marshall (1996), 6; Michael Smith, Frank Andrews, and Ernie Bayly, Jr. *Columbia Gramophone Company Limited: Columbia "DX" and "YBX" 12 inch Series of 78 RPM Discs 1930–1959*. Matrix Publishing, 1997, p. 138.
56. Pettitt (1987), 235; Marshall (1996), 6; Smith (1997), 178.
57. Pettitt (1987), 184, gives 1948; Marshall (1996), 7, gives 1949; Hunt (1996), 116, gives 1948.
58. Trevor Harvey, "Analytical Notes and First Reviews: Orchestral," *Gramophone* 33, no. 385 (June 1955): 8. This lists the separate parts of the Suite that are not listed in Pettitt or Marshall. Pettitt (1987), 221; Marshall (1996), 7.
59. Pettitt (1987), 272; Marshall (1996), 7; Hunt (1996), 15.
60. Pettitt (1987), 172; Marshall (1996), 7; Hunt (1996), 100.
61. Pettitt (1987), 254; Marshall (1996), 7; Hunt (1996), 81.
62. Scott Goddard sleeve notes to EMI Concert Classics XLP 30010. Pettitt (1987), 280; Marshall (1996), 7; Hunt (1996), 100.
63. Pettitt (1987), 295; Marshall (1996), 7; Hunt (1996), 169.
64. All references to the two Brahms Toscanini concerts at the Royal Festival Hall, September 29 and October 1, 1952, see Pettitt (1987), 227, Pettitt (1989), 198–99; Marshall (1996), 7.
65. Pettitt (1987), 274; Marshall (1996), 7.
66. Pettitt (1987), 225; Marshall (1996), 7.
67. Pettitt (1987), 161; Marshall (1996), 7; Hunt (1996), 117.
68. Pettitt (1987), 220; Marshall (1996), 7.
69. Pettitt (1987), 242; Marshall (1996), 7.
70. Pettitt (1987), 299; Marshall (1996), 7.
71. Alan Civil letter to Martin Prowse, October 8, 1968.
72. Pettitt (1987), 278; Marshall (1996), 7.
73. Pettitt (1987), 264; Marshall (1996), 8; Hunt (1996), 132.
74. "Analytical Notes and First Reviews," *Gramophone* 23, no. 276 (May 1946): 142. Pettitt (1987), 151; Marshall (1996), 8.
75. Pettitt (1987), 257; Marshall (1996), 9; Hunt (1996), 206.
76. Pettitt (1987), 275; Marshall (1996), 10.
77. Alec Robertson, "Analytical Notes and First Reviews: Orchestral," *Gramophone* 28, no. 332 (January 1951): 172. Pettitt (1987), 193; Marshall (1996), 10.
78. Pettitt (1987), 187; Marshall (1996), 10.
79. Alec Robertson, "Analytical Notes and First Reviews," *Gramophone* 28, no. 332 (January 1951): 172–73.
80. Pettitt (1987), 259; Marshall (1996), 10.
81. BBC radio program listing in *Radio Times* 136, no. 1763 (August 25–31, 1957): 51, August 30, Third Programme, Part 1: 8:00–8:50. Marshall (1996), 10.
82. Pettitt (1987), 259; Marshall (1996), 10.
83. Pettitt (1987), 247; Marshall (1996), 10; Hunt (1996), 19.
84. Pettitt (1987), 287; Marshall (1996), 10; Hunt (1996), 100.
85. Pettitt (1987), 153; Marshall (1996), 11; Hunt (1996), 19; Smith (1997), 122.
86. Pettitt (1987), 210; Marshall (1996), 11.

87. Pettitt (1987), 258; Marshall (1996), 11.
88. Pettitt (1987), 162; Marshall (1996), 11; Smith (1997), 131.
89. Pettitt (1987), 179; Marshall (1996), 12; Hunt (1996), 102.
90. Pettitt (1987), 289; Marshall (1996), 12; Hunt (1996), 191.
91. Pettitt (1987), 228; Marshall (1996), 13.
92. Pettitt (1987), 300; Marshall (1996), 14.
93. Pettitt (1987), 243; Marshall (1996), 14. MS transcripts of Philharmonia booking sheets by Pettitt give a session on June 28 at Abbey Road.
94. Pettitt (1987), 231; Marshall (1996), 15.
95. Marshall (1996), 15.
96. Pettitt (1987), 229; Marshall (1996), 16; Hunt (1996), 174.
97. Pettitt (1989), 192–93; Pettitt (1987), 217; Marshall (1996), 17.
98. Pettitt (1987), 255; Marshall (1996), 17; Hunt (1996), 85.
99. Pettitt (1987), 273.
100. Pettitt (1989), 198–99; Pettitt (1987), 160.
101. Pettitt (1989), 198–99; Pettitt (1987), 260; Marshall (1996), 18.
102. Pettitt (1987), 279; Pettitt (1989), 194–95; Marshall (1996), 17; Pettitt, sleeve notes to EMI Classics 2 06010 2 (2008), pp. 9–13.
103. Pettitt (1987), 294; Marshall (1996), 20.
104. Pettitt (1987), 228; Marshall (1996), 23.
105. Pettitt (1987), 206; Marshall (1996), 24; Hunt (1996), 177.
106. Pettitt (1987), 233; Marshall (1996), 24; Hunt (1996), 32.
107. Pettitt (1987), 277; Marshall (1996), 26; Hunt (1996), 91.
108. Pettitt (1987), 210; Marshall (1996), 26.
109. Pettitt (1987), 246; Marshall (1996), 27; Hunt (1996), 162.
110. BBC radio program listing in *Radio Times* 107, no. 1388 (May 21–27, 1950,): 21, May 22, Third Programme, Part 1: 7:30–8:01; Part 2: 8:30–9:30 p.m. (not Strauss) Philharmonia Concert Society. Wagner and Strauss. "Philharmonia Orchestra: Strauss's Valediction," *The Times,* Late London Edition, May 23, 1950, p. 6, col. g. Pettitt (1987), 194; Pettitt (1989), 120, 198–99; Marshall (1989), 27.
111. BBC radio program listing in *Radio Times* 116, no. 1495 (July 6–12, 1952): 39, July 12, Third Programme, Part 1: 8:20–9:05 p.m.; Part 2: 9:25–10:10 p.m. Part 2 only for Strauss's *Vier Letzte Lieder*. Harold Rutland, "What a Good Orchestra Is Like," *Radio Times* 116, no. 1495 (July 6–12, 1952): 7.
112. Pettitt (1987), 246; Marshall (1996), 27; Hunt (1996), 162.
113. Alan Blyth: sleeve notes to CD: CDM 7 63655 2, p. 8. Neill Sanders, speaking to delegates of the International Horn Society, Dennis Brain Seminar, University of North Texas, May 17, 1991, private tape, quoted in Chapter 5.
114. Pettitt (1987), 301.
115. Alec Robertson, "Analytical Notes and First Reviews: Operatic," *Gramophone* 35, no. 415 (December 1957): 279–80.
116. "Opera and Concerts," *Monthly Musical Record* 77, no. 892 (December 1947): 269. BBC radio program listing in *Radio Times*, 97, no. 1253 (October 19–25, 1947): 4, October 19, Third Programme, Part 1: 7:00–7:40; Part 2: 7:55–8:40 p.m. Part 2 has *Sinfonia Domestica*. "Richard Strauss Festival: Domestic Symphony," *The Times,* Late London Edition, October 21, 1947, p. 6, column f. Pettitt (1987), 158 (concert advertisement).
117. Pettitt (1987), 210; Marshall (1996), 28.
118. Pettitt (1987), 175; Marshall (1996), 28; Hunt (1996), 68.

119. Pettitt (1987), 254; Marshall (1996), 28; Hunt (1996), 93.
120. Pettitt (1987), 220; Marshall (1996), 29.
121. Pettitt (1987), 228; Marshall (1996), 30.
122. Pettitt (1987), 221; Marshall (1996), 32.
123. Pettitt (1989), 104.
124. Ibid.
125. Pettitt (1987), 176; Marshall (1996), 32; Hunt (1996), 95.
126. Pettitt (1987), 208; Marshall (1996), 32.
127. Pettitt (1987), 286; Pettitt (1989), 140; Marshall (1996), 33. For *Les Patineurs Waltz* (Skater's Waltz) recorded by Karajan and Lambert, see Pettitt (1987), 191, 244; Marshall (1996), 33.
128. Pettitt (1987), 155; Marshall (1996), 33.
129. Alec Robertson, "Analytical Notes and First Reviews: Orchestral," *Gramophone* 24, no. 277 (June 1946): 5. See quote in Chapter 5. Pettitt (1987), 152; Marshall (1996), 34; Hunt (1996), 73; Smith (1997), 121.
130. All RAF Symphony Orchestra recordings conducted by Wing Commander R. P. O'Donnell.
131. The concert master of the Royal Opera Orchestra, Covent Garden, was Charles Taylor.
132. BBC radio program listing in *Radio Times* 123, no. 1547 (June 20–26, 1954): 43, June 25, Third Programme, 6:04–10:50 p.m. *Der Ring Des Niebelungen. Siegfried.*
133. Conducted by Sir Thomas Beecham, unless otherwise stated.
134. Michael Gray, *Beecham: A Centenary Discography* (London: Duckworth, 1979). See also revised edition published by Sir Thomas Beecham Society, 1997, pp. 93–94; Marshall (1996), 4.
135. Malcolm Macdonald, "Analytical Notes and First Reviews: Orchestral," *Gramophone* 31, no. 368 (January 1954): 282.
136. Marshall (1996), 5.
137. Gray (1979), 92–93.
138. Pettitt (1989), 91–92, 198–99, gives July 2, 1947. Marshall (1996), 6. BBC radio program listing in *Radio Times* 95, no. 1237 (June 29–July 5, 1947): 16, July 2, Third Programme, 6:35–9:50 p.m. Act 2 of *Les Troyens à Carthage*, 7:45–8:40 p.m.
139. Alec Robertson, "Analytical Notes and First Reviews: Choral and Song," *Gramophone* 31, no. 368 (January 1954): 297. Gray (1979), 95; Prowse (1969), 679.
140. Gray (1979), 62; Pettitt (1989), 90.
141. Gray (1979), 89.
142. Gray (1979), 91.
143. Gray (1979), 77; Marshall (1996), 9. Archive collections: BLSA call no. 2LP0070172 14.
144. Gray (1979), 95–96; Alec Robertson, "Analytical Notes and First Reviews: Operatic and Song," *Gramophone* 31, no. 366 (November 1953): 199.
145. Gray (1979), 83.
146. Gray (1979), 61–62; S. G., "Gramophone Notes," *Monthly Musical Record* 77, no. 892 (December 1947): 270–71.
147. Harold Rutland, "A Consummate Masterpiece," *Radio Times* 99, no. 1279 (April 18–24, 1948): 5. Idem, p. 19. Third Programme, April 23, 6:55–9:15 p.m. According to *Radio Times*, this was a studio performance. A commercial recording was made in May and July of 1948. See Gray (1979), 76–77.
148. Gray (1979), 65.
149. Gray (1979), 94; Marshall (1996), 12. Alan Civil, unpublished letter to Martin Prowse, October 8, 1968.
150. Gray (1979), 74–75.

151. Gray (1979), 85. Information about the recording dates for the Introduction and Fugue, Michael Gray to Stephen Gamble, April 6, 2010.
152. Gray (1979), 64.
153. P. J. Coveney, "Gramophone Records," *Music Survey* 2, no. 2 (Autumn 1949): 128. R. C., "Gramophone Notes," *Monthly Musical Record* 80, no. 915 (March–April 1950): 74. Gray (1979), 76.
154. Lyndon Jenkins, sleeve notes to Dutton's first double-CD issue: 2CDEA 5025-5026 (2000), p. 2.
155. Gray (1979), 97. The authors are grateful to Michael Gray for providing the Philips recording session dates that Peter Sermon gave to him. Letter from Alan Civil to Martin Prowse, October 8, 1968. Prowse (1969), 678. Prowse described the recording as "that delightful resurrection" showing the horn section "in full cry."
156. BBC radio program listing in *Radio Times* 95, no. 1227 (April 20–26, 1947): 20, April 26, Home Service, 3:30–5:00 p.m. S. G., "Opera and Concerts," *Monthly Musical Record* 77, no. 887 (June 1947): 130.
157. Alec Robertson, "Analytical Notes and First Reviews: Operatic and Songs," *Gramophone* 29, no. 341 (October 1951): 105; Pettitt (1989), 198–99. Pettitt gives a different recording date for the Testament CD issue: August 21, 1950. See also idem, p. 114, for Brain's part in Glyndebourne's July 1951 production of *Così fan tutte* with Busch. Paul Campion and Rosie Runciman, *Glyndebourne Recorded* (London: Julia MacRae Books, 1994), 49.
158. The authors are grateful to Yukihiro Okitsu for drawing our attention to this new CD release by Guild Historical (UK).
159. Gray (1979), 75; Pettitt (1989), 194–95; Marshall (1996), 18. Archive collections: BLSA call no. 1CD021136 BD3.
160. Gray (1979), 69.
161. Graham Melville-Mason, sleeve notes to CD: IMG Artists 7 24357 59382 (2003), p. 10.
162. Gray (1979), 68.
163. Gray (1979), 85; Prowse (1969), 679.
164. S. G., "Gramophone Notes," *Monthly Musical Record* 80, no. 913 (January 1950): 18. Gray (1979), 66, 72; Prowse (1969), 679. Prowse described Brain's eloquence "often combined with a brilliance of execution which distinguishes the Prelude to Act II of Strauss's *Le Bourgeois Gentilhomme.*"
165. S. G., "Gramophone Notes," *Monthly Musical Record* 78, no. 896 (May 1948): 102. Gray (1979), 73.
166. Gray (1979), 97; Marshall (1996), 29.
167. Gray (1979), 68; Marshall (1996), 29.
168. Letter from Alan Civil to Martin Prowse, October 8, 1968. Gray (1979), 97; Marshall (1996), 32.
169. Gray (1979), 97; Marshall (1996), 32.
170. Gray (1979), 70; Marshall (1996), 32.
171. Gray (1979), 65.
172. We have researched Brain's BBC recordings at the BBC Written Archives, Caversham, the Humanities 2 Reading Room, British Library, and through the British Library Sound Archive catalog. Pettitt (1989), 190–97, was consulted to confirm recording dates and other details. The recordings are also listed in Marshall (1996), 4–32.
173. BBC radio program listing in *Radio Times,* Home Service, August 24, 1957, p. 48, Home Service live from Edinburgh International Festival, 11:00–11:40 a.m. *Alphabetical Index to Recorded Programmes Permanent Library Catalogue Supplement 1,* p. 87. Hereafter cited as Supplement 1.

174. BBC radio program listing in *Radio Times* 134, no. 1736 (February 17–23, 1957): 35, February 18, Third Programme, 6:20–7:05 p.m. *Chamber Music. Alphabetical Index to BBC Sound Archives Catalogue Supplement 2: Complete Collated Edition 1970–71*, 360. Hereafter cited as Supplement 2.
175. Supplement 1, p. 87. BBC radio program listing in *Radio Times* 134, no. 1735 (February 10–16, 1957): 42, February 15, Home Service, 9:45–10:15 p.m.
176. Pettitt (1989), 190–91; Marshall (1996), 8; Supplement 1, p. 87.
177. BBC radio program listing in *Radio Times* 133, no. 1720 (October 28–November 3, 1956): 49, November 3, Third Programme 10:35–11:15 p.m. Supplement 2, p. 360.
178. BBC radio program listing in *Radio Times* 134, no. 1738 (March 3–9, 1957): 38, March 5, Home Service, 9:45–10:15 p.m. *Chamber Music*. Supplement 1, p. 87.
179. Supplement 1, p. 87.
180. BBC radio program listing in *Radio Times* 134, no. 1732 (January 20–26, 1957): 18, January 21, Home Service, 7 p.m. *Music to Remember*. Supplement 2, p. 360.
181. BBC radio program listing in *Radio Times* 118, no. 1524 (January 25–31, 1953): 31, January 28, Third Programme, 10:00–11:05 p.m. Supplement 2, p. 360.
182. BBC radio program listing in *Radio Times* 136, no. 1764 (September 1–7, 1957): 43, September 5, Third Programme 6:20–7:00 p.m. Supplement 1, p. 87.
183. Ibid.
184. BBC radio program listing in *Radio Times* 136, no. 1762 (August 18–24, 1957): 48, August 24, Home Service 11:00-11:40 a.m. Supplement 1, p. 87.
185. Ibid.
186. BBC radio program listing in *Radio Times* 136, no. 1764 (September 1–7, 1957): 43, September 5, Third Programme 6:20-7:00 p.m. Supplement 1, p. 87.
187. Supplement 2, p. 360.
188. BBC radio program listing in *Radio Times* 134, no. 1736 (February 17–23, 1957): 35, February 18, Third Programme 6:20-7:05 p.m. Pettitt (1989), 194–95.
189. BBC radio program listing in *Radio Times* 85, no. 1104 (November 26–December 2 1944): 8, November 27, Home Service 9:30–11:00 p.m. "The Bayeux Tapestry. A dramatic chronicle of the invasion of England by the Norman Duke William, and of the tragic end of Harold, last of the Saxon kings, as recorded in the famous tapestry. Written by Morna Stuart and produced by Josephine Plummer. Music chosen and arranged by Alec Robertson." *Alphabetical Index to Recorded Programmes Permanent Library Catalogue*, p. 298. *Radio Times* was checked for a broadcast date of September 26, 1944, and none was found. Supplement 2, p. 360.
190. BBC radio program listing in *Radio Times* 118, no. 1524 (January 25–31, 1953): 31, January 28, Third Programme, 10:00–11:05 p.m. Supplement 2, p. 360.
191. Supplement 2, p. 360. BBC radio program listing in *Radio Times* 134, no. 1734 (February 3–9, 1957): 31, February 6, Third Programme 10:10–11:10 p.m. *Mátyás Seiber*. The first of four programs of music by Seiber.
192. Supplement 1, p. 87. BBC radio program listing in *Radio Times* 135, no. 1753 (June 16–22, 1957): 26, June 16, Home Service 6:15–7:00 p.m. *At Home*.
193. All recordings are listed in Pettitt (1989), 191–97, and Marshall (1996), 4–25.
194. All recordings are listed in Pettitt (1989), 190–97, and Marshall (1996), 3–28. Most can be found listed at the British Library Sound Archive's online catalog by searching for "Dennis Brain." For London Baroque Ensemble recordings listed in this discography, a search of the catalog for "London Baroque Ensemble Karl Haas" yields 66 entries. Not all have Brain as the principal horn.

195. Pettitt (1989), 190–91; Marshall (1996), 3; Smith (2002), 611. Norman Del Mar letter to Gamble on September 4, 1990: "Yes, I too have the Decca Brandenburg I; the names of the players could not be given, as Dennis was under contract to Columbia at the time, but apart from the two of us, the solo violin was Fred Grinke, one of the oboes was Leonard Brain, and the 1st Oboe and 1st Bassoon Natalie and Cecil James, respectively . . ."
196. Smith (1997), 112; Pettitt (1989), 190–91.
197. Smith (2002), 173; Pettitt (1989), 190–91.
198. BBC radio program listing in *Radio Times* 120, no. 1550 (July 26–August 1, 1953): 33, July 30, Third Programme 7:30–8:45 p.m. Part 2: 9 p.m. Britten Serenade. Ernest Bradbury, "The Greatest of All Operas," *Radio Times,* July 26-August 1, 1953, p. 29. The article's title is misleading. Mozart's *Don Giovanni*, broadcast from Salzburg, is the main subject, but the article also reviews the forthcoming broadcast of the Britten Serenade. Pettitt (1989), 190–91; Marshall (1996), 8.
199. Pettitt (1989), 192–93; Marshall (1996), 11; Smith (2002), 41.
200. The authors are grateful to Norman Morrison for supplying the recording date for Brain's two contributions to this long-playing record. Information in a letter from Norman Morrison to Gamble, August 3, 1999.
201. BBC radio program listing in *Radio Times* 136, no. 1764 (September 1–7, 1957): 43, September 5, Third Programme 6:20–7:00 p.m. Pettitt (1989), 192–93; Dressler (1991), 49; Marshall (1996), 15; Tully Potter, "Brain plays Beethoven, Hindemith, Gordon Jacob and Gilbert Vinter" in sleeve notes to BBC Legends BBCL 4164-2 (2001), p. 7; Lynch (2005), 43.
202. Smith (1997), 110, who also gives which movements were recorded by Turner and by Sargent; Pettitt (1989), 194–95.
203. Smith (2002), 43; Pettitt (1989), 194–95.
204. Smith (1997), 176; Pettitt (1989), 196–97.
205. Smith (1997), 134; Pettitt (1989), 196–97.
206. Pettitt MS (n.d.), "London Baroque Ensemble," p. 7, which lists the personnel, dates, and venue. See also Pettitt (1989), 196–97; Marshall (1996), 28.
207. Pettitt MS (n.d.), "London Baroque Ensemble" p. 12, which lists the personnel, date, time, and venue of the recording. See also Pettitt (1989), 196–97; Marshall (1996), 28.
208. Kaminski Ballade, see Pettitt (1989), 192–93; Marshall (1996), 15. The score is published by Barenreiter-Ausgabe 2099 (no date). Copy in Heinrich Kaminski Gesellschaft e V.D-79761, Waldshut-Tiengen, Hauptstrasse 20, Germany. Information concerning this score, kindly sent to the authors by the Archivist, Herbert Müller-Lupp. The computerized database numbers are transcribed from a database listing of Dennis Brain's German archives sent to the authors by Jörg Wyrschowy, archivist at Siftung Deutsches Rundfunkarchiv, (DRA) Frankfurt. Information from the original index cards of the archives at Deutschlandradio Kultur was sent to the authors by Dr. Susanne Paulukat. For all the above former RIAS archive recordings, see also listed in Pettitt (1989), 190–97 and Marshall (1996), 4–25.
209. For the previously unlisted NDR recordings of Beethoven and Hindemith Sonatas with Hansen, and Dukas *Villanelle* with Alfred Westphal, as well as catalog data for the other recordings listed, the authors are grateful to Alexander Eisenreich of NDR Archives.
210. For NDR recordings, see Pettitt (1989), 194–97.
211. For SDR recordings, see op.cit., 190–95. The authors are grateful to Susanne Schiek-Ernau, of SWR archives (preserving all the SDR recordings listed) for providing full catalog details of Brain recordings.

212. For some of the SWR archives listed here, see Pettitt (1989), 194–95. The authors wish to thank the staff of SWR for providing full catalog details of their current Brain archives and for finding additional recordings not previously listed.
213. West Deutsches Rundfunk, Köln, confirmed from WDR Archives. See also Pettitt (1989), 194–95.
214. Pettitt (1989), 190–91 for Britten; pp. 190–91 for Dukas; pp. 194–95 for Schubert; pp. 196–97 for Schumann.
215. Pettitt (1989), 194–95.
216. Complete listing by William C. Lynch, "Dennis Brain Recordings Discovered at Stanford University," *The Horn Call* 35, no. 3 (May 2005): 42–44.
217. BBC radio program listing in *Radio Times* 128, no. 1653 (July 17–23, 1955): 49, July 23, Third Programme 6 p.m.; for the horn lecture, Pettitt (1989), 196–97.
218. BBC radio program listing in *Radio Times*, April 4–10, 1954, p. 25, April 6, Third Programme 8:00–9:05 p.m. Concert of Music by Franz Schubert. *Auf dem Strom* with Richard Lewis and Ernest Lush, was performed in Part 1. See also "Concerts: BBC Third Programme Presents" in *The Times*, London Royal Edition, March 27, 1954, p. 2, column b. Pettitt (1989), 194–95; Marshall (1996), 25. The Schubert *Auf dem Strom* from this broadcast appears to have been the only piece from this concert broadcast that was recorded.
219. British Pathé's website reference 1227_01_255 at britishpathe.com/results.php?search=Edinburgh+Festival&o=20. Scroll to: "Festival in Edinburgh" 1953 (incorrect—it should be a publication date of 1955 for the 1954 Festival). Click View. The catalog entry shows:

> Canister: DOCS Film ID: 1227.01
> Sort number: DOCS Tape: *PM1227*

Loan as a VHS archive copy at Scottish Screen Archives, Glasgow. Catalogue no. 1493 "Festival in Edinburgh" (1955). Address: Curator, Scottish Screen Archives, 1 Bowmont Gardens, Glasgow GL2 9LR. Edinburgh Festival. The film is in two parts. Brain features in Part 1 at 4:36 into the film.
220. Hans Keller, "Mátyás Seiber," *Musical Times* 96, no. 1353 (November 1955): 584. The Seiber Fantasy was published by Suvinizerboni.

Appendix A. Brain Ensemble Music Library

1. *WAC RCONT1, Artists File 2 Brain Dennis, 1950–1952*; letter from Brain to Stevens, November 3, 1951. See also transcribed by Stoneman (2007), 32.
2. WAC *RCONT1, Artists File 2 Brain Dennis, 1950–1952*; letter from Brain to Stevens, November 3, 1951.
3. Schilling was a pupil of Heinrich Kaminski, whose Ballade for horn and piano was performed by Brain for the Radio in the American Sector in Berlin, with Klaus Billing, in 1950. Discography, II *International Archives Collections*: 2.*Germany: Deutschlandradio Kultur*. The former RIAS archives are now in their possession. Stoneman (2007), 33.
4. WAC *RCONT1, Artists File 2 Brain, Dennis, 1950–1952*; letter from Brain to Denis Stevens, November 3, 1951.

Appendix B. The Early Horn

1. Dennis Brain, *The Early Horn*, transmitted Third Programme, July 23, 1955 6:00–6:55 p.m. Pre-recorded July 6 on TBS 15752. Speech, July 11 on TLO 82995. Rehearsal, 3:30, recorded 5:30–6:00 in Concert Hall, Broadcasting House. Edited July 19, 9:30–12:30 in H.1 Trial no.

TLO 83028. Producer, Roger Fiske. Microfilm talk scripts reference "T51 (BRAD-BRAI)." The private recordings used for reconstructing this broadcast include Harry Newstone's private recording sent to the authors and also a fragment, formerly in the Western Sound Archives and now preserved at Stanford Library of Recorded Sound. With permission from Mrs. Yvonne Brain, James Codd, Head of BBC Written Archives, and Vicky Mitchell, Copyright Executive, BBC Commercial Agency.

2. This was an anonymous seventeenth-century horn call, although Méhul had used it for his *Le Jeune Henri* Overture, a piece that Brain had recorded with the RPO, conducted by Sir Thomas Beecham, in December 1953. See Alan Civil's letter to Martin Prowse, quoted in Chapter 4, stating the horn personnel for RPO recordings.

3. The Bach cantata No. 208 was actually first performed in 1713, although during Brain's lifetime it was thought to be 1716.

4. Mozart's Concerto in D, K.412 was actually composed last, not first, as established in 1987 by Alan Tyson in "Mozart's D Major Horn Concerto: Questions of Date and Authenticity," *Mozart: Studies of the Autograph Scores* (Cambridge, MA: Harvard University, 1987), 246–61.

Appendix C. Talking About the Horn

1. WAC RCONT1, Artists File III, 1953–1956. Contract dated March 8, 1956, giving date, time, venue, rehearsal, and other information. Letter from Rosemary Jellis, Overseas Talks, to Miss Firth, Music Bookings, March 7, 1956. This document also gives the date, time, service, and repeat broadcast information. Reproduced with kind permission of Mrs. Yvonne Brain and of James Codd, Head of BBC Written Archives.

2. WAC. P as B file details of this broadcasts supplied to the authors by Archive Researcher Erin O'Neill. For the Dittersdorf Partita, see Discography II. International Collections. British Library Sound Archive.

Appendix D. Articles About the Horn

1. Reproduced with kind permission from Mrs. Yvonne Brain and Chris Helme, *The Conductor*, published by the National Association of Brass Band Conductors. Website: *www.nabbc.org.uk*

2. Reproduced with kind permission from Mrs. Yvonne Brain and Lyndon Chapman, Besson and Buffet Crampon.

3. Letter from Robert Northridge, a boarder at Portora Royal School (1955–1962) and a staff member from 1973 (Vice Principal in 2006) to Gamble on June 5, 2006.

Works Consulted

Books

Abegg, W. *Heinrich Kaminski.* Tutzing: Verlegt BEI Hans Schneider, 1986.
Brymer, Jack. *From Where I Sit.* London: Cassell, 1979.
Burton-Page, Piers. *Philharmonic Concerto: The Life and Music of Sir Malcolm Arnold.* London: Methuen, 1994.
Campion, Paul, and Rosie Runciman. *Glyndebourne Recorded.* London: Julia MacRae Books, 1994.
Carpenter, Humphrey. *Benjamin Britten: A Biography.* London: Faber and Faber, 1992.
Cole, Hugo. *Malcolm Arnold: An Introduction to His Music.* London: Faber and Faber, 1989.
Cousins, Farquharson. *On Playing the Horn.* 2nd ed.. Chapel-en-Frith, Derbyshire: Caron Publications, 1992.
Day, Timothy. *A Century of Recorded Music: Listening to Musical History.* New Haven, CT: Yale University Press, 2000.
Fako, Nancy Jordan. *Philip Farkas and His Horn: A Happy, Worthwhile Life.* Elmurst, IL: Crescent Park Music Publications, 1998.
Gray, Michael. *Beecham: A Centenary Discography.* London: Duckworth, 1979; rev, ed, by Sir Thomas Beecham Society, 1997.
Gregory, Robin. *The Horn.* London: Faber and Faber, 1961.
Hawkins, Frank V. *A Hundred Years of Chamber Music.* London: South Place Ethical Society, 1987.
Hess, Myra Dame, et al., *National Gallery Concerts 10th October 1939–10th October 1944.* London: Printed for the Trustees, 1944.
Heyworth, Peter. *Otto Klemperer: His Life and Times. Vol. 2: 1933–1973.* Cambridge: Cambridge University Press, 1996.
Hoffnung, Annetta. *Hoffnung: His Biography.* London: Gordon Fraser, 1988.
Hunt, John. *Makers of the Philharmonia.* London: John Hunt, 1996.
Ivry, Benjamin. *Francis Poulenc.* London: Phaidon Press, 1996.
Jackson, Gerald. *First Flute.* London: J. M. Dent & Sons, 1968.
Jefferson, Alan. *Sir Thomas Beecham: A Centenary Tribute.* London: Macdonald and Jane's, 1979.
Kennedy, Michael. *Britten.* rev. ed. London: J. M. Dent 1993.
Kok, Alexander. *A Voice in the Dark: The Philharmonia Years.* Ampleforth, North Yorkshire: Emerson Edition E 414, 2002.
Marshall, Robert L. *Dennis Brain on Record: A Comprehensive Discography of His Solo, Chamber, and Orchestral Recordings.* Newton Center, MA: Margun Music, 1996.

McBeth, Amy. *A Discography of 78 RPM Era Recordings of the Horn: Solo and Chamber Literature with Commentary*. Discographies, Number 74. Westport, CT: Greenwood Press, 1997.

Meckna, Michael. *Twentieth-Century Brass Soloists*. Bio-Critical Sourcebooks on Musical Performance. Westport, CT: Greenwood Press, 1994.

Mellers, Wilfrid. *Francis Poulenc*. Oxford: Oxford University Press, 1993.

Osborne, Richard. *Herbert von Karajan: A Life in Music*. London: Chatto & Windus, 1998.

Morley-Pegge, R. *Instruments of the Orchestra: The French Horn*. 2nd ed. London: Ernest Benn Limited, 1973.

Pettitt, Stephen. *Philharmonia Orchestra: A Record of Achievement 1945–1985*. London: Robert Hale, 1985.

________. *Philharmonia: A Complete Discography, 1945–1987*. London: John Hunt, 1987.

________. *Dennis Brain: A Biography*. London: Robert Hale, 1989.

Railton, Dame Ruth. *Daring to Excel: The Story of the National Youth Orchestra of Great Britain*. London: Secker & Warburg, 1992.

Rees, Jasper. *I Found My Horn* (US title: *A Devil to Play*). London: Wiedenfeld & Nicolson, 2008.

Sanders, Alan, comp. *Walter Legge: A Discography*. Westport, CT: Greenwood Press, 1984.

———. ed. *Walter Legge: Words and Music*. London, Duckworth, 1998.

Schwarzkopf, Elisabeth. *On and Off the Record: A Memoir of Walter Legge*. London: Faber, 1982, and New York, Scribner, 1982.

Smith, Michael, Frank Andrews, and Ernie Bayly, Jr. *Columbia Gramophone Company Limited: Columbia "DX" and "YBX" 12 inch Series of 78 RPM Discs 1930–1959*. NP: Matrix Publishing, 1997.

Smith, Michael. *The Decca Recording Company Limited: Decca 78 rpm Records 1929 to 1954. 10-inch prefixed A, M and Z series. 12 inch prefixes K, S, T and X series. A Discography.* London: City of London Phonograph and Gramophone Society, 2002.

Tschaikov, Basil. *The Music Goes Round and Around*. Peterborough: Fastprint Publishing, 2009.

Traber, Weingarten, ed. *Verdrängte Musik: Berliner Komponisten Im Exil* (*Suppressed Music: Berlin Composers in Exile*). Berlin: Argon, 1987.

Tucker, Norman. *Norman Tucker, Musician: An Autobiography*. London: J. Audrey Ellison, 1978.

Yancich, Milan. *An Orchestra Musician's Odyssey*. Rochester, NY: Wind Music Inc., 1995.

BBC Sound Archive Catalogs

Alphabetical Index to BBC Sound Archives Catalogue. Accessions 1973–April 1984. Vol. I, A-EVA, p. 318. Humanities 2 Reading Room, British Library, London.

Alphabetical Index to BBC Sound Archives Catalogue Supplement 2: Complete Collated Edition 1970–71, p. 360.

Alphabetical Index to Recorded Programmes Permanent Library Catalogue Supplement 1, p. 87.

BBC Sound Archives: A Chronological List of Sound Recordings from January to December 1955. HUS 025 348 209 42. Humanities 2 Reading Room, British Library, London.

Articles and Chapters

"Academy and College Notes." *Musical Times* 78, no. 1131 (May 1937): 455; 79, no. 1145 (July 1938): 531; 79, no. 1148 (October 1938): 779; 80, no. 1155 (May 1939): 380; 80, no. 1156 (June 1939): 462.

"Analytical Notes and First Reviews." *Gramophone* 23, no. 276 (May 1946): 142.

A. J. "London Concerts: Eugene Goossens." *Musical Times* 93, no. 1310 (April 1952): 180.

———. "London Concerts: Two Beecham Concerts." *Musical Times* 94, no. 1324 (June 1953): 276–77.

Anderson, W. R. "Analytical Notes and First Reviews: Orchestral." *Gramophone* 23, no. 276 (May 1946): 142; 24, no. 279 (August 1946): 32; 24, no. 280 (September 1946): 49; 25, no. 289 (June 1947): 4; 25, no. 298 (March 1948): 151.

———. "The Edinburgh Festival." *Musical Times* 93, no. 1316 (October 1952): 459.

———. "The Edinburgh Festival." *Musical Times* 95, no. 1340 (October 1954): 555–56.

Brain, Dennis. "French Horn Playing." *The Conductor* 3, no. 10 (October 1954): 3, 8.

———. "About the French Horn." *Brass Today*, London, Besson & Co., 1957, 60–63.

———. "The French Horn." *Brass Today*, 1961, London, Besson & Co., 19–20.

Britten, Benjamin. "Dennis Brain 1921–1957," *Tempo* 46 (Winter 1958): 5–6.

Brymer, Jack. "Royal Philharmonic." *Symphony*, no. 4 (November 1950): 5–6.

Catterick, Tony. "A Pupil of Dennis Brain." *The Horn Player* 2, no. 3 (December 2005): 35.

Chiba, Kaoru. Yukihiro Okitsu, trans. "My teacher, Dennis Brain." First published in Japanese by Ongaku-No-Tomo-Sha Corp November 1989, p. 152.

Clough, F. F., and G. J. Cuming. "Diskography." *Gramophone Record Review* 55 (October 1958): 953.

Cousins, Farquharson. "The Degenerate Horn." *Music and Letters* 31, no. 4 (October 1950): 378–380.

Coveney, P. J. "Gramophone Records." *Music Survey* 2, no. 2 (Autumn, 1949): 128.

Decker, James. "Dennis Brain—The American Perspective: James Decker on Hollywood Musicians." *The Horn Player* 4, no. 2,(August 2007): 28.

Del Mar, Norman. "Dennis Brain." *Dictionary of National Biography, 1951–1960*. Ed. E. T. Williams and Helen Palmer. London: Oxford University Press, 1971.

———. "The Great Interpreters, No. 18. Dennis Brain." *Gramophone Record Review* 55 (October 1958): 951–53.

Dressler, John C. "Dennis Brain: A Bibliography." *The Horn Call*, October 1991, 49–50.

Eger, Joseph. "Breaking the Endurance Barrier." *Woodwind World*, May 1958, 6.

Gamble, Stephen. "A Horn Virtuoso's Writings." *The Horn Player* 4, no. 3 (December 2007): 28–29.

H. F. "Analytical Notes and First Reviews: Orchestral." *Gramophone* 30, no. 357 (February 1953): 225.

———. "Analytical Notes and First Reviews: Orchestral." *Gramophone* 30, no. 358 (March 1953): 250.

Hamburger, Paul. "Gramophone Records." *Music Survey* 2, no. 3 (Winter 1950): 209.

Harris, Paul. "Lost and Found: The Remarkable Story of Malcolm Arnold's Wind Quintet." *The Horn Call*, October 2003, 80.

Harvey, Trevor. "Analytical Notes and First Reviews: Orchestral." *Gramophone* 32, no. 377 (October 1954): 193; 32, no. 377 (October 1954): 197; 32, no. 384 (May 1955): 522; 33, no. 385 (June 1955): 8; 33, no. 385 (June 1955): 12–13; 34, no. 408 (May 1957): 448; 35, no. 412 (September 1957): 135, 138.

Hussey, Dyneley. "The Musician's Gramophone." *Musical Times* 95, no. 1336 (June 1954): 314–16.

———. "Music in London: Britten's Canticles." *Musical Times* 96, no. 1348 (June 1955): 323–24.

———. "Musician's Gramophone." *Musical Times* 96, no. 1349 (July 1955): 367.

———. "Provincial Events: The Cheltenham Festival." *Musical Times* 98, no. 1375 (September 1957): 506.

I. C. "Analytical Notes and First Reviews: Orchestral." *Gramophone* 31, no. 364 (September 1953): 98.

———. "Analytical Notes and First Reviews: Orchestral." *Gramophone* 31, no. 370 (March 1954): 385.

Iwano, Yuichi. "Kaoru Chiba's 'Bachi's' Biography." *The Horn Call* October 2008, 36.

J. O. C. "Gordon Jacob's Horn Concerto." *Musical Times* 92, no. 1301 (July 1951): 324.

Jones, Leighton. "Alfred Brain: The Forgotten English Horn Virtuoso?" *The Horn Magazine* 10, no. 3 (April 2003): 18–27.

Keller, Hans. "Mysore Concerts." *Music Survey* 3, no. 3 (March 1951): 205.

———. "Matyas Seiber." *Musical Times* 96, no. 1353 (November 1955): 584.

Kolodin, Irving. *Saturday Review of Literature,* November 12, 1955.

Kuwahara, Satoshi, trans.Yukihiro Okitsu. "Profile of the Master." The "Seiron" Magazine, Tokyo, Japan (Sankei Simbun Co., 1-7-2 Otemachi, Chiyoda-ku) Aug. 1999.

"London Concerts." *Musical Times* 83, no. 1189 (March 1942): 95.

"London Concerts: Orchestral Concerts." *Musical Times* 84, no. 1201 (March 1943): 95.

"London Concerts: Some First Performances." *Musical Times* 96, no. 1345 (March 1955): 152–53.

Lynch, William C. "Dennis Brain Recordings Discovered at Stanford University." *The Horn Call,* May 2005, 42–44.

Macdonald, Malcolm. "Analytical Notes and First Reviews." *Gramophone* 31, no. 361 (June 1953): 12, 13–14.

———. "Analytical Notes and First Reviews: Orchestral." *Gramophone* 31, no. 361 (July 1953): 38–39; 31, no. 364 (September 1953): 96; 31, no. 367 (December 1953): 234; 31, no. 368 (January 1954): 282; 31, no. 371 (April 1954): 429; 32, no. 377 (October 1954): 197–98; 32, no. 380 (January 1955): 352; 36, no. 429 (February 1959): 402.

———. "Analytical Notes and First Reviews: Chamber Music." *Gramophone* 32, no. 381 (February 1955): 399.

Mann, W. S. "Analytical Notes and First Reviews." *Gramophone* 37, no. 439 (December 1959): 284–85.

Mason, Colin. "Britten, Benjamin, Canticle III 'Still Falls the Rain' (Edith Sitwell) for Tenor, Horn and Piano, Op. 55." *Music and Letters* 38, no. 1 (January 1957): 104–5.

Matsubara, Chiyoshige. "Memories of 'Bachi'—Kaoru Chiba (1928–2008)." *The Horn Call,* October 2008, 37.

McNaught, William. "New Music, Britten Serenade." *Musical Times* 85, no. 1219 (September 1944): 275–76.

———. "Gramophone Notes." *Musical Times* 86, no. 1231 (September 1945): 276.

———. "Gramophone Notes: Britten's Serenade." *Musical Times* 87, no. 1235 (January 1946): 16–17.

Meckna, Michael. "The Legacy of Dennis Brain." *The Horn Call* 71, no. 2 (April 1991): 55–56.

Mitchell, Donald. "Chelsea Symphony Orchestra, and Norman Del Mar, Chelsea Town Hall, 31st May 1949." *Music Survey* 2, no. 1 (1949): 58.

———. "London Concerts: Orchestral, Choral and Vocal." *Musical Times* 97, no. 1360 (June 1956): 316.

———. "London Concerts: Concerts." *Musical Times* 97, no. 1360 (June 1956): 318.

———. "Some First Performances: Instrumental." *Musical Times* 95, no. 1335 (May 1955): 266–67.

———. "Some First Performances." *Musical Times* 97, no. 1360 (June 1956): 316.

Morley-Pegge, R. "The Degenerate Horn." *Music and Letters* 32, no. 1 (October 1951): 94–96.

"Music in the Provinces: Cambridge." *Musical Times* 84, no. 1206 (August 1943): 255.

"Music in the Provinces: Cambridge." *Musical Times* 86, no. 1228 (June 1945): 189.

"Music in the Provinces: Liverpool." *Musical Times* 86, no. 1228 (June 1945): 189–90.

Nakagawa, Genri, trans.Yukihiro Okitsu. "Unpainted Great Masters Part 2," Interview, July 23, 1973. First published in Japan by Ongaku-No-Tomo-Sha Corp, 1975.

"National Gallery Concerts." *Musical Times* 83, no. 1188 (February 1942): 62.

Neumeyer, David. "University of Texas, Notes." *Bläserkonzert I from Paul Hindemith Samtliche Werk*. Bloomington, IN: November 1982.

Obituary of Dennis Brain. *The Strad* 68, no. 810 (October 1957): 197.

"Opera and Concerts." *Monthly Musical Record* 77, no. 891 (November 1947): 241–42.

"Opera and Concerts." *Monthly Musical Record* 77, no. 892 (December 1947): 269.

Parker, Maurice. "Sir Thomas Beecham 1946–1953; 1954–1960 Concert and Theatrical Calendar."*Grand Baton*, Sir Thomas Beecham Society, 1986. Microfiche.

Payne, Arthur C. "Stars of the Record World. Mr. Aubrey Brain." *Gramophone and Talking Machine News* 19, no. 443B (September 1927): 291.

Porter, Andrew. "Analytical Notes and First Reviews: Orchestral." *Gramophone* 29 no. 347 (April 1952): 251; 31, no. 361 (July 1953): 39; 31, no. 364 (September 1953): 99; 31, no. 368 (January 1954): 286; 31, no. 368 (January 1954): 290; 31, no. 369 (February 1954): 331–32; 32, no. 377 (October 1954): 194; 32, no. 380 (January 1955): 346–47; 35, no. 409 (June 1957): 11–12.

Potts, Joseph, E. "The Royal Philharmonic Orchestra 1946–67." *Grand Baton* 6 no. 1 (February 1969): 31, 34.

"Promenade Concerts." *Musical Times* 87, no. 1242, 253.

Prowse, Martin J. "The Unfamiliar Dennis Brain." *Audio-Record Review*, October 1969, 678–79

R. C. "Concerts and Opera." *Monthly Musical Record* 76, no. 881 (November 1946): 217–18; 77, no. 891 (November 1947): 243; 79, no. 908 (July–August 1949): 157; 81, no. 926 (May 1951): 101.

———. "Gramophone Notes." *Monthly Musical Record* 80, no. 915 (March–April 1950): 74.

R. H. "Analytical Notes and First Reviews: Orchestral." *Gramophone* 28, no. 325 (June 1950): 6.

R. W. "Analytical Notes and First Reviews: Orchestral." *Gramophone* 26, no. 301 (June 1948): 9.

Redlich, Hans. H. "In Memoriam Heinrich Kaminski." *Monthly Musical Record* 77, no. 889 (September 1947): 185–86.

Rees, C. B. "Impressions . . . Dennis Brain." *London Musical Events*, no. 10 (September 1955): 24–25.

Robertson, Alec. "Analytical Notes and First Reviews: Instrumental." *Gramophone* 21, no. 252 (May 1944): 180.

———. "Analytical Notes and First Reviews: Instrumental." *Gramophone* 23, no. 268 (September 1945): 43.

———. "The Great Tradition Henry Purcell 1658–Benjamin Britten 1913." *Gramophone* 23, no. 271 (December 1945): 78–79.

———. "Analytical Notes and First Reviews: Orchestral." *Gramophone* 24, no. 277 (June 1946): 5; 25, no. 293 (October 1947): 65; 28, no. 332 (January 1951): 172–73.

———. "Analytical Notes and First Reviews: Songs." *Gramophone* 24, no. 278 (July 1946): 21.

———. "Analytical Notes and First Reviews: Songs." *Gramophone* 24, no. 280 (September 1946): 50.

———. "Analytical Notes and First Reviews: Operatic and Song." *Gramophone* 24, no. 286 (March 1947): 150–51; 29, no. 341 (October 1951): 105; 30, no. 356 (January 1953): 203; 30, no. 359 (April 1953): 294; 31, no. 366 (November 1953): 199.

———. "Analytical Notes and First Reviews: Choral and Song." *Gramophone* 31, no. 368 (January 1954): 295, 297–99.

———. "Analytical Notes and First Reviews: Choral and Song." *Gramophone* 31, no. 369 (February 1954): 348.

———. "Analytical Notes and First Reviews: Operatic." *Gramophone* 32, no. 379 (December 1954): 317; 35, no. 415 (December 1957): 279–80.

———. "Dennis Brain." *Gramophone* 35, no. 413 (October 1957): 169.

Rosenthal, Irving. "The Edinburgh Festival." *Woodwind*, October 1952, 14.

Ruff, Willie. "Paul Hindemith and the Sound of the Horn." *The Horn Call* 27, no. 1 (October 1986): 52.

Rutland, Harold. "Notes and Comments, Dennis Brain." *Musical Times* 98, no. 1375 (September 1957): 548.

S. G. "Gramophone Notes." *Monthly Musical Record* 75, no. 871 (November 1945): 209; 76, no. 878 (July–August 1946): 138; 76, no. 879 (September 1946): 165–66; 77, no. 892 (December 1947): 270–71; 78, no. 896 (May 1948): 102; 80, no. 913 (January 1950): 18; 80, no. 914 (February 1950): 45.

———. "Opera and Concerts." *Monthly Musical Record* 77, no. 887 (June 1947): 130.

Sackville-West, Edward. "A Quarterly Retrospect October–December 1952." *Gramophone* 30, no. 357 (February 1953): 217.

Sadie, Stanley. "The Wind Music of J. C. Bach." *Music and Letters* 37, no. 2 (April 1956): 107–17.

Salter, Lionel. "Analytical Notes and First Reviews. Orchestral: Eighteenth Century Music." *Gramophone* 26, no. 311 (April 1949): 174.

———. "Analytical Notes and First Reviews: Orchestral." *Gramophone* 27, no. 314 (July 1949): 24; 27, no. 316 (September 1949): 58; 28, no. 325 (June 1950): 5; 29, no. 342 (November 1951): 129; 31, no. 363 (August 1953): 68; 31, no. 364 (September 1953): 100.

———. "Analytical Notes and First Reviews. Orchestral: Hindemith Concert Music for Brass and Strings and Concertino for Horn and Orchestra, Vienna Symphony Orchestra (Prof. Haefner), Franz Koch (horn). Nixa SPLP515." *Gramophone* 29, no. 346 (March 1952): 226.

———. "Analytical Notes and First Reviews. Orchestral: Strauss, R. Horn Concertos: No. 1 in E-flat major Op. 11, No. 2 in E-flat major. Dennis Brain (horn), Philharmonia Orchestra, conducted by Wolfgang Sawallisch. Columbia 33CX 1491." *Gramophone* 35, no. 414 (November 1957): 220.

Sawbridge, Paul. "CD Reviews: Dennis Brain—The Horn Player EMI Classics—Icon 2 06010 2." *Horn Player* 5, no. 2 (Autumn 2008): 40.

Schonberg, Gordon. "Sinclair Lott is Horn Soloist in D. Brain Memorial Concert." *Woodwind World* 2, no. 2 (March 1958): 4.

Schonberg, Harold C. "Letter From America." *Gramophone* 28, no. 331 (December 1950): 106.
Schuller, Gunther. "Horn Literature: Schoeck, Othmar, Concerto for Horn and String Orchestra 1952." *Woodwind*, March 1955, 10.
———. "Horn Literature: Five Pieces for Five Horns." *Woodwind*, March 1955, 10.
Schweikert, Norman, and Sally Schweikert. "Memories of Kaoru Chiba." *The Horn Call*, October 2008, 37–38.
Snedeker, Jeffrey. "A Letter from Dennis Brain." *The Horn Call*, August 2000, 77. See also the same letter reproduced in *The Horn Call*, May 1971, 48–49.
Stevens, Denis, "Analytical Notes and First Reviews: Orchestral." *Gramophone* 32, no. 378 (November 1954): 250–51.
Stoneman, Jonathan. "Dennis Brain and the BBC." *The Horn Player* 4, no. 2 (August 2007): 30–33.
Thompson, Michael. "Dennis Brain." *BBC Music Magazine* 9, no. 3 (November 2000): 65.
Thoresby, Christina. "Stravinsky at the Venice Festival." *Strad* 67, no. 799 (November 1956): 248.
T. K. D. "Music Society." *Portora School Magazine*, Easter Term, March 1956, p. 9.
Tyson, Alan. "Mozart's D Major Horn Concerto: Questions of Date and Authenticity." In *Mozart: Studies of the Autograph Scores*. Cambridge, MA: Harvard University, 1987, 246–61.
Wagstaff, Ian, and Gareth Morris. "Aubrey and Son." *The Horn Magazine* 1, no. 2 (Spring 1993): 13.
Wright, Anthony. "Anthony Lewis Concerto for Horn." *Music and Musicians* 4, June 1956.

Newspapers Consulted

The Guardian
Manchester Guardian
The Scotsman
Daily Telegraph
Northern Echo
The Times
Sunday Times
York Evening Press
The York Gazette and Herald
Canada
Toronto Daily Star
Japan
Sankei Shimbun
United States
Tour of the Royal Philharmonic Orchestra, 1950
Chicago Tribune
The Illini
Kentucky Kernel
New York Times
Rockford Morning Star
Times-Picayune
Tour of the Philharmonia, 1955
Boston Sunday Herald
Chicago Daily Tribune
Christian Science Monitor
Detroit Free Press
Grand Rapids Press
Hartford Times
Kalamazoo Gazette
Michigan Daily
New Haven Register
New York Herald Tribune
New York Nation
New York Times
Philadelphia Inquirer
Philadelphia Sunday Bulletin
Springfield (MA) Republic
Springfield (MA) Union
Washington Daily News
Washington Evening Star
Washington Evening Star
Washington Post

Music Scores

Arnold, Malcolm. *Horn Concerto No. 2, Op. 68*. London: Paterson's Publications, 1988. Order no. PAT62001.

Bowen, York. *Concerto Op. 150 for Horn and Strings (horn & piano)*. Ampleforth, York, North Yorkshire: Emerson Edition 440, 2006.

Britten, Benjamin. *Serenade for Tenor, Horn and Strings, op. 31*. United States: Winthrop Rogers, 1944; London: Hawkes & Son. No. H 15595a.

Fricker, Peter Racine. *Quintet for Flute, Oboe, Clarinet, Bassoon and Horn, Op. 5*. London: Schott and Co., 1951. No. S & Co. 5613a.

Jacob, Gordon. *Concerto for Horn and Strings Arranged for Horn and Piano by the Composer*. London: Stainer & Bell, 1951. No. 2627.

Kaminski, Heinrich. *Ballade für Waldhorn und Klavier*. Bärenreiter-Ausgabe 2099. Copy from Heinrich Kaminski Gesellschaft e.V., D-79761 Waldshut-Tiengen, Haupstrasses 20, Germany.

Lewis, Anthony. *Concerto for Horn and String Orchestra. Version For Horn and Piano*. London: Alfred Lengnick & Co., 1959.

Schoeck, Othmar. *Concerto for Horn and String Orchestra, op. 65*. London: Hawkes & Son, 1952. B&H. no. 17201.

Tomlinson, Ernest. *Rhapsody and Rondo for Horn and Orchestra. Piano Reduction and Solo Part Complete*. London: Mills Music, 1962. No. M.M. 883.

Biographical Index

D

E

F

G

H

N

O

P

R

S

T

V

W

Y

Z

General Index